Lecture Notes in Computer Science 2102

Edited by G. Goos, J. Hartmanis and J. van Leeuwen

Springer
Berlin
Heidelberg
New York
Barcelona
Hong Kong
London
Milan
Paris
Singapore
Tokyo

Gérard Berry   Hubert Comon
Alain Finkel (Eds.)

Computer Aided
Verification

13th International Conference, CAV 2001
Paris, France, July 18-22, 2001
Proceedings

 Springer

Series Editors

Gerhard Goos, Karlsruhe University, Germany
Juris Hartmanis, Cornell University, NY, USA
Jan van Leeuwen, Utrecht University, The Netherlands

Volume Editors

Gérard Berry
Esterel Technologies
885 av. Julien Lefebvre, 06270 Villeneuve-Loubet, France
E-mail: Gerard.Berry@esterel-technologies.com
Hubert Comon and Alain Finkel
LSV, CNRS UMR 8643, ENS de Cachan
61 av. du Président Wilson, 94235 Cachan Cedex, France
E-mail: {comon/finkel}@lsv.ens-cachan.fr

Cataloging-in-Publication Data applied for

Die Deutsche Bibliothek - CIP-Einheitsaufnahme

Computer aided verification : 13th international conference ; proceedings /
CAV 2001, Paris, France, July 18 - 22, 2001. Gérard Berry ... (ed.). -
Berlin ; Heidelberg ; New York ; Barcelona ; Hong Kong ; London ; Milan ;
Paris ; Singapore ; Tokyo : Springer, 2001
  (Lecture notes in computer science ; Vol. 2102)
  ISBN 3-540-42345-1

CR Subject Classification (1998): F.3, D.2.4, D.2.2, F.4.1, I.2.3, B.7.2., C.3

ISSN 0302-9743
ISBN 3-540-42345-1 Springer-Verlag Berlin Heidelberg New York

Springer-Verlag Berlin Heidelberg New York
a member of BertelsmannSpringer Science+Business Media GmbH

http://www.springer.de

© Springer-Verlag Berlin Heidelberg 2001
Printed in Germany

Typesetting: Camera-ready by author, data conversion by Christian Grosche, Hamburg
Printed on acid-free paper   SPIN: 10839493   06/3142   5 4 3 2 1 0

Preface

This volume contains the proceedings of the conference on *Computer-Aided Verification* (CAV 2001), held in Paris, Palais de la Mutualité, July 18–22, 2001. CAV 2001 was the 13th in a series of conferences dedicated to the advancement of the theory and practice of computer-assisted formal analysis methods for software and hardware systems. The CAV conference covers the spectrum from theoretical results to concrete applications, with an emphasis on practical verification tools and algorithms and techniques needed for their implementation.

Program Committee of CAV 2001

Rajeev Alur (Penn. & Bell labs)
Henrik Reif Andersen (Copenhagen)
Gérard Berry (Esterel T., co-chair)
Randy Bryant (CMU)
Jerry Burch (Cadence)
Ching-Tsun Chou (Intel)
Edmund Clarke (CMU)
Hubert Comon (LSV & Stanford, co-chair)
David Dill (Stanford)
E. Allen Emerson (Austin)
Alain Finkel (LSV, co-chair)
Patrice Godefroid (Bell labs)
Orna Grumberg (Technion)
Somesh Jha (Wisconsin)

Bengt Jonsson (Uppsala)
Robert Kurshan (Lucent Bell Labs)
Kim G. Larsen (Aalborg)
Ken Mc Millan (Cadence)
Kedar Namjoshi (Bell labs)
Christine Paulin-Mohring (Orsay)
Carl Pixley (Motorola)
Kavita Ravi (Cadence)
Natarajan Shankar (SRI)
Mary Sheeran (Chalmers & Prover T.)
Tom Shiple (Synopsys)
A. Prasad Sistla (Chicago)
Fabio Somenzi (Colorado)
Yaron Wolfsthal (IBM)

CAV Steering Committee

Edmund Clarke (CMU)
Robert Kurshan (Lucent Bell Labs)

Amir Pnueli (Technion)
Joseph Sifakis (IMAG Grenoble)

The program of CAV 2001 consisted of:

- 2 tutorials, respectively by David Basin on "Monadic Logics on Strings and Trees" and by Pascal Van Hentenryck on "Constraint Solving Techniques";

- 2 invited conference presentations by David Parnas on "Software Documentation and the Verification Process" and Xavier Leroy on "Java Bytecode Verification: An Overview";

- 33 regular paper presentations, which consitute the core of this volume. The accepted papers were selected from 106 regular paper submissions. Each submission received an average of 4 referee reviews.

- 13 tool presentations, whose descriptions can also be found in this volume. The tool presentations were selected among 27 submissions, and were reviewed in the same way as the regular papers. For each tool presentation, there was also a demo at the conference. The increasing number of tool submissions and presentations shows both the liveliness of the field and its applied flavor.

In addition, there were five satellite workshops on Inspection in Software Engineering, Logical Aspects of Cryptographic Protocol Verification, Runtime Verification, Software Model Checking, and Supervisory Control of Discrete Event Systems. The publication of these workshops proceedings was managed by their respective chair, independently of the present proceedings.

The CAV conference was colocated with the related *Static Analysis Symposium*, to enable participants to attend both.

We would like to thank here the numerous external reviewers who helped to set up a high quality program and whose names appear in the list below.

Referees

Parosh Abdulla	Craig Damon	Jim Grundy
Luca de Alfaro	Dennis Dams	Anubhav Gupta
Nina Amla	Satyaki Das	Gary Hachtel
Laurent Arditi	Giorgio Delzanno	John Harrison
Mohammad Awedh	Jurgen Dingel	John Havlicek
Ilan Beer	Xiaoqun Du	Nevin Heintze
Gerd Behrmann	Surrendra Dudani	Loïc Henry-Gérard
Wendy Belluomni	Jean Duprat	H. Hermanns
Shoham Ben-David	Bruno Dutertre	Yatin Hoskote
Sergey Berezin	Stephen Edwards	Jin Hou
Yves Bertot	Cindy Eisner	John Hughes
Mark Bickford	Kousha Etessami	Marten van Hulst
Michel Bidoit	Eitan Farchi	Hans Hüttel
Bruno Blanchet	Alan Fekete	Anna Ingólfsdóttir
Roderick Bloem	Jean-Christophe Filliâtre	S. Purushothaman Iyer
Ahmed Bouajjani	D. Fink	Jae-Young Jang
Amar Bouali	Bernd Finkbeiner	Bertrand Jeannet
Patricia Bouyer	Dana Fisman	Henrik Ejersbo Jensen
Glenn Bruns	Limor Fix	HoonSang Jin
Annette Bunker	Emmanuel Fleury	Robert Jones
Doron Bustan	Ranan Fraer	Yan Jurski
Gianpiero Cabodi	Laurent Fribourg	M. Kaltenbach
Franck Cassez	Pascale le Gall	Gila Kamhi
Pierre Casteran	Danny Geist	Sagi Katz
Pankaj Chauhan	Amit Goel	Sharon Keidar
Michael Colon	Ganesh Gopalakrishnan	Shinji Kimura
Laurent Cosserat	Jean Goubault-Larrecq	Nils Klarlund
Robert Damiano	Susanne Graf	Orna Kupferman

Shuvendu Lahiri
Yassine Lakhnech
Avner Landver
François Laroussinie
Salvatore La Torre
Jérôme Leroux
Cédric Lhoussaine
J. Liu
Monika Maidl
Oded Maler
P. Manolios
Will Marrero
In-Ho Moon
John Moondanos
Supratik Mukhopadhyay
Kuntal Nanshi
L. Nee
Brian Nielsen
John O'Leary
Avigail Orni
Sam Owre
George Pappas
Abelardo Pardo
SeungJoon Park

Doron Peled
Antoine Petit
Laure Petrucci
Claudine Picaronny
Laurence Pierre
Slawomir Pilarski
A. Pita
K.V.S. Prasad
Mukul Prasad
Frédéric Prost
Laurence Puel
Shaz Qadeer
Olivier Roux
Harald Ruess
Jun Sawada
Karsten Schmidt
Steve Schneider
Philippe Schnoebelen
Kenneth Scott
Roberto Segala
Sanjit Seshia
Ali Sezgin
Subash Shankar
Kanna Shimizu

Ofer Shtrichman
Joao-Marques Silva
Robert de Simone
Eli Singerman
Henny Sipma
Oleg Sokolsky
Maria Sorea
Gunnar Staalmarck
Aaron Stump
Grégoire Sutre
Armando Tacchella
Xavier Thirioux
Ferucio Laurentiu Tiplea
Ashish Tiwari
Richard Trefler
Helmut Veith
Michael G. Walker
Chao Wang
Dong Wang
Thomas Wilke
Karen Yorav
Sergio Yovine
Jun Yuan

We would like to thank the members of the organizing committee for their enormous amount of work in organizing CAV 2001. We appreciated their assistance in so many time-consuming tasks.

Organizing Committee

Sylviane Audet
Patricia Bouyer
Véronique Cortier
Marie Duflot
Alain Finkel

Emmanuel Fleury
Jean Goubault-Larrecq
Anne Labroue
Jérôme Leroux
Nicolas Markey

Laure Petrucci
Claudine Picaronny
Philippe Schnoebelen
Muriel Roger
Françoise Tort

Our special thanks are due to Patricia Bouyer, Nicolas Markey, and Philippe Schnoebelen who maintained the CAV 2001 web site and who installed the START software. We are also grateful to Laure Petrucci for her hard work in preparing the proceedings.

Sponsors

The conference was sponsored by several companies and academic institutions:

Avant!	Esterel Technologies	Microsoft
Cadence Design Systems	France Télécom	Motorola
CNRS	INRIA	Prover Technology
EATCS	Intel	Texas Instruments
EDF	LSV	Trusted Logic
ENS Cachan	Mairie de Paris	Universities Paris 6 & 7

July 2001   Gérard Berry, Hubert Comon, and Alain Finkel

Table of Contents

Invited Talk

Infinite State Systems

Temporal Logics and Verification

Tool Presentations: Model-Checking and Automata Techniques

Microprocessor Verification, Cache Coherence

SAT, BDDs, and Applications

Timed Automata

Software Documentation
and the Verification Process

David Lorge Parnas

Department of Computing and Software
Faculty of Engineering, McMaster University
Hamilton, Ontario, Canada L8S 4L7
parnas@qusunt.cas.mcmaster.ca

Abstract. In the verification community it is assumed that one has a specification of the program to be proven correct. In practice this is never true. Moreover, specifications for realistic software products are often unreadable when formalised. This talk will present and discuss more practical formal notation for software documentation and the role of such documentation in the verification process.

Certifying Model Checkers

Kedar S. Namjoshi

Bell Laboratories, Lucent Technologies
kedar@research.bell-labs.com
http://www.cs.bell-labs.com/who/kedar

Abstract. Model Checking is an algorithmic technique to determine whether a temporal property holds of a program. For linear time properties, a model checker produces a counterexample computation if the check fails. This computation acts as a "certificate" of failure, as it can be checked easily and independently of the model checker by simulating it on the program. On the other hand, no such certificate is produced if the check succeeds. In this paper, we show how this asymmetry can be eliminated with a *certifying* model checker. The key idea is that, with some extra bookkeeping, a model checker can produce a *deductive proof* on either success or failure. This proof acts as a certificate of the result, as it can be checked mechanically by simple, non-fixpoint methods that are independent of the model checker. We develop a deductive proof system for verifying branching time properties expressed in the mu-calculus, and show how to generate a proof in this system from a model checking run. Proofs for linear time properties form a special case. A model checker that generates proofs can be used for many interesting applications, such as better ways of exploring errors in a program, and a tight integration of model checking with automated theorem proving.

1 Introduction

Model Checking [CE81,QS82] is an algorithmic technique to determine whether a temporal property holds of a program. Perhaps the most useful property of the model checking algorithm is that it can generate a counterexample computation if a linear time property fails to hold of the program. This computation acts as a "certificate" of failure, as it can be checked easily and efficiently by a method independent of model checking – i.e., by simulating the program to determine whether it can generate the computation. On the other hand, if it is determined that a property holds, model checkers produce only the answer "yes"! This does not inspire the same confidence as a counterexample; one is forced to assume that the model checker implementation is correct. It is desirable, therefore, to provide a mechanism that generates certificates for either outcome of the model checking process. These certificates should be easily checkable by methods that are independent of model checking.

In this paper, we show how such a mechanism, which we call a *certifying model checker*, can be constructed. The key idea is that, with some extra bookkeeping, a model checker can produce a *deductive proof* on either success or

G. Berry, H. Comon, and A. Finkel (Eds.): CAV 2001, LNCS 2102, pp. 2–13, 2001.

failure. The proof acts as a certificate of the result, since it can be checked independently using simple, non-fixpoint methods. A certifying model checker thus provides a bridge from the "model-theoretic" to the "proof-theoretic" approach to verification [Eme90].

We develop a deductive proof system for verifying mu-calculus properties of programs, and show it to be sound and relatively complete. We then show how to construct a deductive proof from a model checking run. This is done by by storing and analyzing sets of states that are generated by the fixpoint computations performed during model checking. The proof system and the proof generation process draw upon results in [EJ91] and [EJS93], which relate model checking for the mu-calculus to winning parity games. A prototype implementation of a proof generator and proof checker for linear time properties has been developed for the COSPAN [HHK96] symbolic model checker.

The ability to generate proofs which justify the outcome of model checking makes possible several interesting applications. For instance,

- A certifying model checker produces a proof of property f on success, and a proof of $\neg f$ on failure. The proof of $\neg f$ is a compact representation of *all* possible counterexample computations. As is shown later, it can be exponentially more succinct than a single computation. Particular counterexample computations can be "unfolded" out of the proof by an interactive process which provides a better understanding of the flaws in the program than is possible with a single computation.
- Producing a deductive proof makes it possible to tightly integrate a certifying model checker into an automated theorem prover. For instance, the theorem prover can handle meta-reasoning necessary for applying compositional or abstraction methods, while checking subgoals with a certifying model checker. The proofs produced by the model checker can be composed with the other proofs to form a single, checkable, proof script.

The paper is organized as follows. Section 2 contains background information on model checking and parity games. Section 3 develops the deductive proof system for verifying mu-calculus properties, and Section 4 shows how such proofs can be generated by slightly modifying a mu-calculus model checker. Applications for certifying model checkers are discussed in detail in Section 5. Section 6 concludes the paper with a discussion of related work.

2 Preliminaries

In this section, we define the mu-calculus and alternating tree automata, and show how mu-calculus model checking can be reduced to determining winning strategies in parity games.

2.1 The Mu-Calculus

The mu-calculus [Koz82] is a branching time temporal logic that subsumes [EL86] commonly used logics such as LTL, ω-automata, CTL, and CTL*. The logic is parameterized with respect to two sets: Σ (state labels) and Γ (action labels). There is also a set of variable symbols, V. Formulas of the logic are defined using the following grammar, where l is in Σ, a is in Γ, Z is in V, and μ is the least fixpoint operator.

$$\Phi ::= l \mid Z \mid \langle a \rangle \Phi \mid \neg \Phi \mid \Phi \wedge \Phi \mid (\mu Z : \Phi)$$

To simplify notation, we assume that Σ and Γ are fixed in the rest of the paper. A formula must have each variable under the scope of an even number of negation symbols. A formula is *closed* iff every variable in it is under the scope of a μ operator. Formulas are evaluated over labeled transition systems (LTS's) [Kel76]. An LTS is a tuple (S, s_0, R, L), where S is a non-empty set of *states*, $s_0 \in S$ is the *initial state*, $R \subseteq S \times \Gamma \times S$ is the *transition relation*, and $L : S \to \Sigma$ is a *labeling function* on states. We assume that R is *total*; i.e., for any s and a, there exists t such that $(s, a, t) \in R$. The evaluation of a formula f, represented as $\|f\|_c$, is a subset of S, and is defined relative to a *context* c mapping variables to subsets of S. The evaluation rule is given below.

- $\|l\|_c = \{s | s \in S \wedge L(s) = l\}$, $\|Z\|_c = c(Z)$,
- $\|\langle a \rangle \Phi\|_c = \{s | (\exists t : R(s, a, t) \wedge t \in \|\Phi\|_c)\}$,
- $\|\neg \Phi\|_c = S \setminus \|\Phi\|_c$, $\|\Phi_1 \wedge \Phi_2\|_c = \|\Phi_1\|_c \cap \|\Phi_2\|_c$,
- $\|(\mu Z : \Phi)\|_c = \bigcap \{T : T \subseteq S \wedge \|\Phi\|_{c[Z \leftarrow T]} \subseteq T\}$, where $c[Z \leftarrow T]$ is the context c' where, for any X, $c'(X)$ is T if $X = Z$, and $c(X)$ otherwise.

A state s in the LTS *satisfies* a closed mu-calculus formula f iff $s \in \|f\|_\perp$, where $\perp$ maps every variable to the empty set. The LTS satisfies f iff s_0 satisfies f. Mu-calculus formulas can be converted to positive normal form by introducing the operators $\Phi_1 \vee \Phi_2 = \neg(\neg(\Phi_1) \wedge \neg(\Phi_2))$, $[a]\Phi = \neg \langle a \rangle (\neg \Phi)$ and $(\nu Z : \Phi) = \neg(\mu Z : \neg \Phi(\neg Z))$, and using de Morgan rules to push negations inwards. The result is a formula where negations are applied only to elements of Σ.

Mu-Calculus Signatures: Consider a closed mu-calculus formula f in positive normal form, where the μ-variables are numbered $Y_1, \ldots, Y_n$ in such a way that if (μY_i) occurs in the scope of (μY_j) then $j < i$. Streett and Emerson [SE84] show that, with every state s of an LTS M that satisfies f, one can associate a lexicographically minimum n-vector of ordinals called its *signature*, denoted by $sig(s, f)$. Informally, $sig(s, f)$ records the minimum number of unfoldings of least fixpoint operators that are necessary to show that s satisfies f. For example, for the CTL property $EF(p) = (\mu Y_1 : p \vee \langle \tau \rangle Y_1)$, $sig(s, EF(p))$ is the length of the shortest τ-path from s to a state satisfying p.

Formally, for an n-vector of ordinals v, let f^v be a formula with the semantics defined below. Then $sig(s, f)$ is the smallest n-vector v such that $s \in \|f^v\|_\perp$. First, define the new operator μ^k, for an ordinal k, with the semantics $\|(\mu^k Y : \Phi)\|_c = Y^k$, where $Y^0 = \emptyset$, $Y^{i+1} = \|\Phi\|_{c[Y \leftarrow Y^i]}$, and for a limit ordinal λ, $Y^\lambda = (\cup k : k < \lambda : Y^k)$.

- $\|l^v\|_c = \|l\|_c$, $\|(\neg l)^v\|_c = \|\neg l\|_c$, $\|Z^v\|_c = \|Z\|_c$,
- $\|(\langle a \rangle \Phi)^v\|_c = \|\langle a \rangle (\Phi^v)\|_c$, $\|([a]\Phi)^v\|_c = \|[a](\Phi^v)\|_c$,
- $\|(\Phi_1 \wedge \Phi_2)^v\|_c = \|\Phi_1^v \wedge \Phi_2^v\|_c$, $\|(\Phi_1 \vee \Phi_2)^v\|_c = \|\Phi_1^v \vee \Phi_2^v\|_c$
- $\|(\mu Y_j : \Phi)^v\|_c = \|\Phi^v\|_{c'}$, where $c' = c[Y_j \leftarrow \|(\mu^{v[j]} Y_j : \Phi)\|_c]$
- $\|(\nu Z : \Phi)^v\|_c = \|\Phi^v\|_{c'}$, where $c' = c[Z \leftarrow \|(\nu Z : \Phi)\|_c]$.

2.2 Alternating Automata and Parity Games

An alternating automaton is another way of specifying branching time temporal properties. For sets Σ and Γ of state and transition labels respectively, an alternating automaton is specified by a tuple (Q, q_0, δ, F), where Q is a non-empty set of states, $q_0 \in Q$ is the initial state, and δ is a transition function mapping a pair from $Q \times \Sigma$ to a positive boolean expression formed using the operators $\wedge$, $\vee$ applied to elements of the form $true, false, q, \langle a \rangle q$ and $[a]q$, where $a \in \Sigma$, and $q \in Q$. F is a *parity* acceptance condition, which is a non-empty list $(F_0, F_1, \ldots, F_n)$ of subsets of Q. An infinite sequence over Q satisfies F iff the smallest index i for which a state in F_i occurs infinitely often on the sequence is even. For simplicity, we assume that the transition relation of the automaton is in a normal form, where F is a partition of Q, and $\delta(q, l)$ has one of the following forms: $q_1 \wedge q_2, q_1 \vee q_2, \langle a \rangle q_1, [a]q_1, true, false$. Converting an arbitrary automaton to an equivalent automaton in normal form can be done with a linear blowup in the size.

A *tree* is a prefix-closed subset of $\mathbb{N}^*$, where λ, the empty sequence, is called the *root* of the tree. A labeled tree t is a tree together with two functions $N_t : t \to \Sigma$ and $E_t : edge(t) \to \Gamma$, where $edge(t) = \{(x, x.i)|x \in t \wedge x.i \in t\}$. We require the transition relation of such a tree to be total.

The acceptance of a labeled tree t by the automaton is defined in terms of a two-player infinite game. A *configuration* of the game is a pair (x, q), where x is a node of the tree and q is an automaton state. If $\delta(q, N_t(x))$ is *true*, player I wins, while player II wins if it is *false*. For the other cases, player I chooses one of q_1, q_2 if it is $q_1 \vee q_2$, and chooses an a-successor to x if it is $\langle a \rangle q_1$. Player II makes similar choices at the $\wedge$ and $[a]$ operators. The result is a new configuration (x', q'). A *play* of the game is a maximal sequence of configurations generated in this manner. A play is winning for player I iff either it is finite and ends in a configuration that is a win for I, or it is infinite and satisfies the automaton acceptance condition. The play is winning for player II otherwise. A *strategy* for player I (II) is a partial function that maps every finite sequence of configurations and intermediate choices to a choice at each player I (II) position. A *winning* strategy for player I is a strategy function where every play following that strategy is winning for I, regardless of the strategy for II. The automaton *accepts* the tree t iff player I has a winning strategy for the game starting at (λ, q_0). An LTS M *satisfies* the automaton iff the automaton accepts the computation tree of M.

Theorem 0. [EJ91,JW95] For any closed mu-calculus formula f, there is a linear-size alternating automaton A_f such for any LTS M, M satisfies f iff M satisfies A_f. The automaton is derived from the parse graph of the formula.

A strategy s is *history-free* iff the outcome of the function depends only on the last element of the argument sequence. By results in [EJ91], parity games are determined (one of the players has a winning strategy), and the winner has a history-free winning strategy. From these facts, winning in the parity game generated by an LTS $M = (S, s_0, R, L)$ and an automaton $A = (Q, q_0, \delta, F)$ can be cast as model checking on a product LTS, $M \times A$, of configurations

[EJS93]. The LTS $M \times A = (S', s_0', R', L')$ is defined over state labeling $\Sigma' = \{I, II, win_I, win_{II}\} \times \{f_0, \ldots, f_n\}$ and edge labeling $\Gamma' = \{\tau\}$, and has $S' = S \times Q$ and $s_0' = (s_0, q_0)$. The first component of $L'(s, q)$ is I if $\delta(q, L(s))$ has the form $q_1 \vee q_2$ or $\langle a \rangle$, II if it has the form $q_1 \wedge q_2$ or $[a]q_1$, win_I if it has the form $true$, and win_{II} if it has the form $false$. The second component is f_i iff $q \in F_i$. R' is defined as follows. For a state (s, q), if $\delta(q, L(s))$ is $true$ or $false$, then (s, q) has no successors; if $\delta(q, L(s))$ is $q_1 \vee q_2$ or $q_1 \wedge q_2$, then (s, q) has two successors (s, q_1) and (s, q_2); if $\delta(a, L(s))$ is $\langle a \rangle q_1$ or $[a]q_1$, then (s, q) has a successor (t, q_1) for every t such that $R(s, a, t)$ holds, and no other successors.

Let $\mathcal{W}_I = (\sigma_0 Z_0 \ldots \sigma_n Z_n : \Phi_I(Z_0, \ldots, Z_n))$, where σ_i is ν if i is even and μ otherwise, and $\Phi_I(Z_0, \ldots, Z_n) = win_I \vee (I \wedge (\wedge i : f_i \Rightarrow \langle \tau \rangle Z_i)) \vee (II \wedge (\wedge i : f_i \Rightarrow [\tau]Z_i))$. The formula $\mathcal{W}_I$ describes the set of configurations from which player I has a winning strategy. Similarly, player II has a winning strategy from the the complementary set $\mathcal{W}_{II}$, where $\mathcal{W}_{II} = (\delta_0 Z_0 \ldots \delta_n Z_n : \Phi_{II}(Z_0, \ldots, Z_n))$, where δ_i is μ if i is even, and ν otherwise, and $\Phi_{II}(Z_0, \ldots, Z_n) = win_{II} \vee (I \wedge (\wedge i : f_i \Rightarrow [\tau]Z_i)) \vee (II \wedge (\wedge i : f_i \Rightarrow \langle \tau \rangle Z_i))$.

Theorem 1. (cf. [EJS93]) For an LTS M and a normal form automaton A of the form above, M satisfies A iff $M \times A, (s_0, q_0) \models \mathcal{W}_I$.

3 The Proof System

Deductive proof systems for verifying sequential programs rely on the two key concepts of *invariance* (e.g., loop invariants) and *progress* (e.g., rank functions, variant functions) [Flo67,Hoa69]. These concepts reappear in deductive verification systems for linear temporal logic [MP83,MP87,CM88], and also form the basis for the proof system that is presented below.

Suppose that $M = (S, s_0, R, L)$ is an LTS, and $A = (Q, q_0, \delta, F)$ is a normal form automaton, where $F = (F_0, F_1, \ldots, F_{2n})$. To show that M satisfies A, one exhibits (i) for each automaton state q, a predicate (the invariant) ϕ_q over S, expressed in some *assertion language*, (ii) non-empty, well founded sets $W_1, \ldots, W_n$ with associated partial orders $\preceq_1, \ldots, \preceq_n$, and (iii) for each automaton state q, a partial rank function $\rho_q : S \to (W, \preceq)$, where $W = W_1 \times \ldots \times W_n$ and $\preceq$ is the lexicographic order defined on W using the $\{\preceq_i\}$ orders.

We extend the $\preceq$ order to apply to elements a, b in $W_1 \times \ldots \times W_k$, for some $k < n$ by $a \preceq b$ iff $(a_1, \ldots, a_k, 0, 0, \ldots, 0) \preceq (b_1, \ldots, b_k, 0, 0, \ldots, 0)$, where we assume, without loss of generality, that 0 is an element common to all the W_i's. For an automaton state q, define the relation $\lhd_q$ over $W \times W$ as follows. For any a, b, $a \lhd_q b$ holds iff for the (unique, since F is a partition) index k such that $q \in F_k$, either $k = 0$, or $k > 0, k = 2i$ and $(a_1, \ldots, a_i) \preceq (b_1, \ldots, b_i)$, or $k = 2i - 1$ and $(a_1, \ldots, a_i) \prec (b_1, \ldots, b_i)$. We use the label l to denote the predicate $l(s) \equiv (L(s) = l)$, and the notation $[f]$ to mean that the formula f is valid. Note that, in the following, $\langle a \rangle$ and $[a]$ are operators interpreted on M. The invariants and rank function must satisfy the following three local conditions. In these conditions, the variable k has type W.

- **Consistency:** For each $q \in Q$, $[\phi_q \Rightarrow (\exists k : (\rho_q = k))]$ (ρ_q is defined for every state in ϕ_q)

- *Initiality:* $\phi_{q_0}(s_0)$ (the initial state satisfies its invariant)
- *Invariance and Progress:* For each $q \in Q$, and $l \in \Sigma$, depending on the form of $\delta(q,l)$, check the following.
  - *true:* there is nothing to check.
  - *false:* $[\phi_q \Rightarrow \neg l]$ holds,
  - $q_1 \wedge q_2$: $[\phi_q \wedge l \wedge (\rho_q = k) \Rightarrow (\phi_{q_1} \wedge (\rho_{q_1} \lhd_q k)) \wedge (\phi_{q_2} \wedge (\rho_{q_2} \lhd_q k))]$
  - $q_1 \vee q_2$: $[\phi_q \wedge l \wedge (\rho_q = k) \Rightarrow (\phi_{q_1} \wedge (\rho_{q_1} \lhd_q k)) \vee (\phi_{q_2} \wedge (\rho_{q_2} \lhd_q k))]$
  - $\langle a \rangle q_1$: $[\phi_q \wedge l \wedge (\rho_q = k) \Rightarrow \langle a \rangle (\phi_{q_1} \wedge (\rho_{q_1} \lhd_q k))]$
  - $[a]q_1$: $[\phi_q \wedge l \wedge (\rho_q = k) \Rightarrow [a](\phi_{q_1} \wedge (\rho_{q_1} \lhd_q k))]$

Theorem 2. (Soundness) The proof system is sound.

Proof. Given a proof in the format above, we have to show that M satisfies A. We do so by exhibiting a winning strategy for player I in the parity game. For a configuration (s, q), let $\rho_q(s)$ be its associated rank. Inductively, assume that at any configuration (s, q) on a play, $\phi_q(s)$ is true. This holds at the start of the game by the Initiality requirement. Suppose that $L(s) = l$. Based on the form of $\delta(q, l)$, we have the following cases:

- *true:* the play terminates with a win for player I,
- *false:* this case cannot arise, as the inductive invariant contradicts the proof assertion $[\phi_q \Rightarrow \neg l]$.
- $q_1 \wedge q_2, [a]q_1$: Player II plays at this point, with the new configuration satisfying the inductive hypothesis by the proof.
- $q_1 \vee q_2$: Player I chooses the q_i for which the $\vee$ proof assertion holds. The new configuration (s, q_i) thus satisfies the inductive hypothesis.
- $\langle a \rangle q_1$: Player I chooses the a-successor t of s which is a witness for the $\langle a \rangle$ formula. Hence, $\phi_{q_1}(t)$ holds.

Thus, a finite play terminates with $\delta(q, l) = true$, which is a win for player I. In an infinite play, by the definition of $\lhd_q$, whenever the play goes through a configuration (s, q) with q in a odd-indexed set F_{2i-1}, the rank decreases strictly in the positions $1..i$, and the only way it can increase in these components is if the play later goes through a configuration (s', q') with q' in an even indexed set of smaller index. So, if an odd indexed set occurs infinitely often, some even indexed set with smaller index must also occur infinitely often, which implies that the smallest index that occurs infinitely often must be even. Thus, the defined strategy is winning for player I, so M satisfies A. □

Theorem 3. (Completeness) The proof system is relatively complete.

Proof. We show completeness relative to the expressibility of the winning sets, as is done for Hoare-style proof systems for sequential programs [Coo78]. Assume that M satisfies A. By Theorem 1, $M \times A, (s_0, q_0) \models \mathcal{W}_I$. The history-free winning strategy for player I corresponds to a sub-structure N of $M \times A$, which has a single outgoing edge at each player I state.

For each automaton state q, let $\phi_q(s) \equiv (M \times A, (s, q) \models \mathcal{W}_I)$. The rank function is constructed from the mu-calculus signatures of states satisfying the formula $\mathcal{W}_I$. For each automaton state q, let the function ρ_q have domain ϕ_q. For every state (s, q) satisfying $\mathcal{W}_I$, let $\rho_q(s)$ be the n-vector that is the signature of $\mathcal{W}_I$ at (s, q).

We now show that all the conditions of the proof rule are satisfied for these choices. Consistency holds by the definition of the ρ_q functions. Initiality holds by the definition of ϕ_q, since (s_0, q_0) satisfies $\mathcal{W}_I$. From the definition of signatures and the shape of the formula defining $\mathcal{W}_I$, it it not difficult to show that at each transition from a state in N, the signature for $\mathcal{W}_I$ decreases strictly in the first i components if the state is in F_{2i-1}, and is non-increasing in the first i components if the state is in F_{2i}. This corresponds directly to the progress conditions in the proof rule. For each state (s, q) in N, $\phi_q(s)$ is true, so the invariance conditions also hold. If $\delta(q, l)$ is *false*, then for any state s with $L(s) = l$, (s, q) represents a win for player II, so that $s \notin \mathcal{W}_I$, and $\phi_q \wedge l$ is unsatisfiable, as desired.   □

Proofs for Linear Time Properties: Manna and Pnueli [MP87] show that every ω-regular linear time property can be represented by a $\forall$-automaton, which accepts an ω-string iff *all* runs of the automaton on the string satisfy a co-Büchi acceptance condition. Model checking the linear time property h is equivalent to checking the branching time property $\mathsf{A}(h)$. By the $\forall$ nature of acceptance, the A quantifier can, informally, be distributed through h, resulting in a tree automaton where δ is defined using only $[a]$ and $\wedge$ operators. Specializing our proof system to such automata results in a proof system similar to that in [MP87].

Proofs for LTS's with Fairness: So far, we have only considered LTS's without fairness constraints. Fairness constraints, such as weak or strong fairness on actions, are sometimes required to rule out undesired computations. Manna and Pnueli [MP87] observe that there are two possible ways of handling fairness: one can either incorporate the fairness constraints into the property, or incorporate them into the proof system. They point out that these approaches are closely related. Indeed, the modified proof system corresponds to a particular way of proving the modified property using the original proof system. Therefore, we prefer to keep the simplicity of the proof system, and incorporate any fairness constraints into the property.

4   Proof Generation and Checking

The completeness proof in Theorem 3 shows how to generate a proof for a successful model checking attempt. Such proofs can be generated both by explicit-state and symbolic model checkers. For symbolic model checkers, the invariant assertions are represented by formulas (i.e., BDD's), and it is desirable also for the rank functions to be converted to predicates; i.e., to represent the terms $(\rho_q = k)$ and $(\rho_{q_1} \lhd_q k)$ as the predicates $\rho_=(q, k)$ and $\rho_\lhd(q_1, q, k)$, respectively. Individual proof steps become validity assertions in the assertion language which, for a finite-state model checker, is propositional logic. It is possible for the proof generator and the proof checker to use different symbolic representations and different validity checking methods. For instance, the model checker can be based on BDD methods, while the proof checker represents formulas with syntax trees and utilizes a SAT solver to check validity.

Since we use alternating automata to specify properties, the automaton that defines $\neg f$ can be obtained easily by dualizing A_f: exchanging *true* and *false*, $\wedge$ and $\vee$, and $\langle a \rangle$ and $[a]$ in the transition relation and replacing the parity condition F with its negation $(\emptyset, F_0, \ldots, F_{2n})$. A winning strategy for player I with the dual automaton is a winning strategy for player II with the original automaton. Thus, the set $\mathcal{W}_{II} = \neg \mathcal{W}_I$ can be used to construct a proof of $\neg f$ relative to the dual automaton. To avoid doing extra work to create a proof for $\neg f$ on failure, it is desirable to record approximations for both the μ and ν variables while evaluating $\mathcal{W}_I$: if f holds, the approximations for the μ variables are used to calculate the rank function; if not, a dual proof can be constructed for $\neg f$, using the negations of the approximations recorded for the ν variables of $\mathcal{W}_I$, which are the μ variables in $\mathcal{W}_{II}$. This strategy is followed in our prototype proof generator for COSPAN.

Example: To illustrate the proof generation process, consider the following program and property. All transitions of the program are labeled with τ.

Program $M(m : \mathbb{N})$ (* circular counter *)
var $c : (0..2^m - 1)$; initially $c = 0$; transition $c' = (c + 1) \bmod 2^m$

Property A (* AGF$(c = 0)$, i.e., on all paths, $c = 0$ holds infinitely often *)
states $= \{q_0, q_1\}$; initially q_0;
transition $\delta(q_0, true) = [\tau]q_1, \delta(q_1, c = 0) = q_0, \delta(q_1, c \neq 0) = [\tau]q_1$
parity condition (F_0, F_1), where $F_0 = \{q_0\}, F_1 = \{q_1\}$.

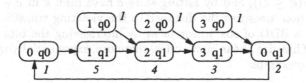

Fig. 1. The Graph of $M \times A$ for $m = 2$.

The $\mathcal{W}_I$ formula, as defined in Section 2.2, simplifies to the following, since every state of $M \times A$ is a II-state: $\mathcal{W}_I = (\nu Z_0 : (\mu Z_1 : \Phi_I(Z_0, Z_1)))$, where $\Phi_I(Z_0, Z_1) = ((q_0 \Rightarrow [\tau]Z_0) \wedge (q_1 \Rightarrow [\tau]Z_1))$. This formula evaluates to *true* on $M \times A$. Thus, ϕ_{q_0} and ϕ_{q_1}, as calculated in the proof of Theorem 3, are both *true* (i.e., $c \in \{0..2^m - 1\}$). The rank function is calculated by computing the signatures of states satisfying $\mathcal{W}_I$. As there is a single odd index in the parity condition, the signature is a singleton vector, which may be represented by a number. By the definition in Section 2.1, the signature of a state satisfying $\mathcal{W}_I$ is the smallest index i for which the state belongs to $(\mu^i Z_1 : \Phi_I(\mathcal{W}_I, Z_1))$. This formula simplifies to $(\mu^i Z_1 : (q_0 \vee [\tau]Z_1))$, which essentially calculates the distance to the q_0 state.

The italicized number next to each state in Figure 1 shows its rank. The rank functions are, therefore, $\rho_{q_0}(c) = 1$ and $\rho_{q_1}(c) = if\ (c = 0)\ then\ 2\ else\ (6 - c)$. By construction, the Consistency and Initiality properties of the proof are satisfied. Instantiating the general proof scheme of Section 3, the Invariance and Progress obligations reduce to the following, all of which can be seen to hold.

- $[\phi_{q_0}(c) \wedge \textit{true} \wedge (\rho_{q_0}(c) = k) \Rightarrow [\tau](\phi_{q_1}(c))]$
- $[\phi_{q_1}(c) \wedge (c = 0) \wedge (\rho_{q_1}(c) = k) \Rightarrow (\phi_{q_0}(c) \wedge (\rho_{q_0}(c) < k))]$, and
- $[\phi_{q_1}(c) \wedge (c \neq 0) \wedge (\rho_{q_1}(c) = k) \Rightarrow [\tau](\phi_{q_1}(c) \wedge (\rho_{q_1}(c) < k))]$

Proofs vs. Counterexamples: A natural question that arises concerns the relationship between a proof for $\neg f$ and a counterexample computation for f. This is elucidated in the theorem below.

Theorem 4. For a program M and a linear time, co-Büchi $\forall$-automaton A, if M does not satisfy A, and $M \times A$ has m bits and a counterexample of length n, it is possible to construct a proof for $\neg A$ that needs $2mn$ bits. On the other hand, a proof can be exponentially more succinct than any counterexample.

Proof. In general, a counterexample consists of a path to an accepting state, and a cycle passing through that state. Define the invariants ϕ_q so that they hold only of the states on the counterexample, and let the rank function measure the distance along the counterexample to an accepting state. This can be represented by BDD's of size $2mn$.

On the other hand, consider the program in Figure 1, and the property $G(c' > c)$. This is false only at $c = 2^m - 1$, so the shortest counterexample has length $2^m + 1$. We can, however, prove failure by defining the invariant to be $\textit{true}$ (really, $\mathsf{EF}(c' \leq c)$), and by letting state c have rank k iff $c + k = 2^m - 1$. This rank function measures the distance to the violating transition. It can be represented by a BDD of size linear in m by interleaving the bits for c and k. Thus, the proof has size linear in m and is, therefore, exponentially more succinct than the counterexample. □

5   Applications

The ability to generate proofs which justify the outcome of model checking makes possible several interesting applications for a certifying model checker.

1. Generating Proofs vs. Generating Counterexamples: We have shown how a certifying model checker can produce a proof of property f upon success and a proof for $\neg f$ on failure. Both types of proofs offer insight on *why* the property succeeds (or fails) to hold of the program. Inspecting success proofs closely may help uncover vacuous justifications or lack of appropriate coverage. The generated proof for $\neg f$ is a compact representation of *all* counterexample computations. This proof can be "unfolded" interactively along the lines of the strategy description in the soundness proof of Theorem 2. This process allows the exploration of various counterexamples *without* having to perform multiple model checking runs (cf. [SS98]).

2. Detecting Errors in a Model Checker: The proof produced by a certifying model checker stands by itself; i.e., it can be checked for correctness independently of the model checker. For instance, the model checker may use BDD's, but the proof can be checked using a SAT solver. It is possible, therefore, to detect errors in the model checker[1]. For instance, if the model checker declares success but produces an erroneous proof, this may be due to a mistake in the implementation which results in a part of the state space being overlooked during model checking.

3. Integrating Model Checking with Theorem Proving: Efforts to integrate model checking with theorem proving [JS93,RSS95] have added such a capability at a shallow level, where the result of model checking is accepted as an axiom by the theorem prover. This has been addressed in [YL97,Spr98], where tableau proofs generated using explicit state model checkers are imported into theorem provers. Our proof generation procedure allows symbolic proofs, which are more compact than explicit state proofs, to be used for the same purpose.

Theorem proving, in one form or another, has been used to design and verify abstractions of infinite state systems (cf. [MNS99]), to prove conditions for sound compositional reasoning (cf. [McM99]), and to prove parameterized systems correct (cf. [BBC+00]). In the first two cases, model checking is applied to small subgoals. Proofs generated by a certifying model checker for these subgoals can be composed with the other proofs to produce a single, mechanically checkable, proof script. In the last case, the model checker can be used to produce proofs about small instances of parameterized systems. The shape of the invariance and progress assertions in these proofs can often suggest the assertions needed for proving the general case, which is handled entirely with the theorem prover. This approach has been applied in [PRZ01,APR+01] to invariance properties.

4. Proof Carrying Code: A certifying model checker can produce proofs for arbitrary temporal properties. These proofs can be used with the "proof-carrying-code" paradigm introduced in [NL96] for mobile code: a code producer sends code together with a generated correctness proof, which is checked by the code consumer. The proof generator in [NL98] is tailored to checking memory and type safety. Using a certifying model checker, one can, in principle, generate proofs of arbitrary safety and liveness properties, which would be useful for mobile protocol code.

6   Conclusions and Related Work

There is prior work on automatically generating explicit state proofs for properties expressed in the mu-calculus and other logics, but the proof system and the algorithm of this paper appear to be the first to do so for symbolic representations. In [Kic,YL97], algorithms are given to create tableau proofs in the style of [SW89]. In parallel with our work, Peled and Zuck [PZ01] have developed an algorithm for automatically generating explicit state proofs for LTL properties. The game playing algorithm of [SS98] implicitly generates a kind of proof.

Explicit state proofs are of reasonable size only for programs with small state spaces. For larger programs, symbolic representations are to be preferred,

---

[1] So a certifying model checker can be used to "certify" itself!

as they result in proofs that are more compact. While the tableau proof system has been extended to symbolic representations in [BS92], the extension requires an external, global termination proof. In contrast, our proof system embeds the termination requirements as locally checkable assertions in the proof.

The proof system presented here is closely related to those of [MP87] (for ∀-automata) and [FG96] (for fair-CTL), but generalizes both systems. The proof system is specifically designed to be locally checkable, so that proofs can be checked easily and mechanically. For some applications, it will be necessary to add rules such as modus ponens to make the proofs more "human-friendly". As we have discussed, though, there are many possible applications for proofs that are generated and checked mechanically, which opens up new and interesting areas for the application of model checking techniques.

Acknowledgments

I would like to thank the members of the formal methods group at Bell Labs, and Hana Chockler, Dave Naumann and Richard Trefler for many interesting discussions on this topic.

References

[APR+01] T. Arons, A. Pnueli, S. Ruah, J. Xu, and L. Zuck. Parameterized verification with automatically computed inductive assertions. In *CAV*, 2001.

[BBC+00] N. Bjorner, A. Browne, M. Colón, B. Finkbeiner, Z. Manna, H. Sipma, and T. Uribe. Verifying temporal properties of reactive systems: A STeP tutorial. *Formal Methods in System Design*, 2000.

[BS92]   J. Bradfield and C. Stirling. Local model checking for infinite state spaces. *TCS*, 96, 1992.

[CE81]   E.M. Clarke and E. A. Emerson. Design and synthesis of synchronization skeletons using branching time temporal logic. In *Workshop on Logics of Programs*, volume 131 of *LNCS*, 1981.

[CM88]   K.M. Chandy and Jayadev Misra. *Parallel Program Design: A Foundation*. Addison-Wesley, 1988.

[Coo78]   S.A. Cook. Soundness and completeness of an axiom system for program verification. *SIAM J. Comput*, 1978.

[EJ91]   E.A. Emerson and C.S. Jutla. Tree automata, mu-calculus and determinacy (extended abstract). In *FOCS*, 1991.

[EJS93]   E. Allen Emerson, C.S. Jutla, and A.P. Sistla. On model-checking for fragments of μ-calculus. In *CAV*, 1993.

[EL86]   E.A. and C-L. Lei. Efficient model checking in fragments of the propositional mu-calculus (extended abstract). In *LICS*, 1986.

[Eme90]   E.A. Emerson. Temporal and modal logic. In J. van Leeuwen, editor, *Handbook of Theoretical Computer Science: Volume B, Formal Models and Semantics*. North-Holland Pub. Co./MIT Press, 1990.

[FG96]   L. Fix and O. Grumberg. Verification of temporal properties. *Journal of Logic and Computation*, 1996.

[Flo67]   R. Floyd. Assigning meaning to programs. In *Mathematical Aspects of Computer Science XIX*. American Mathemetical Society, 1967.

[HHK96] R.H. Hardin, Z. Har'el, and R.P. Kurshan. COSPAN. In *CAV*, volume 1102 of *LNCS*, 1996.

[Hoa69] C.A.R. Hoare. An axiomatic basis for computer programming. *Communications of the ACM*, 1969.

[JS93]   J.J. Joyce and C-J.H. Seger. The HOL-Voss system: Model-checking inside a general-purpose theorem-prover. In *HUG*, volume 780 of *LNCS*, 1993.

[JW95]   D. Janin and I. Walukiewicz. Automata for the modal mu-calulus and related results. In *MFCS*, 1995.

[Kel76] R.M. Keller. Formal verification of parallel programs. *CACM*, 1976.

[Kic]   A. Kick. Generation of witnesses for global mu-calculus model checking. available at http://liinwww.ira.uka.de/~kick.

[Koz82] D. Kozen. Results on the propositional mu-calculus. In *ICALP*, 1982.

[McM99] K.L. McMillan. Verification of infinite state systems by compositional model checking. In *CHARME*, 1999.

[MNS99] P. Manolios, K.S. Namjoshi, and R. Summers. Linking theorem proving and model-checking with well-founded bisimulation. In *CAV*, 1999.

[MP83]   Z. Manna and A. Pnueli. How to cook a temporal proof system for your pet language. In *POPL*, 1983.

[MP87]   Z. Manna and A. Pnueli. Specification and verification of concurrent programs by ∀-automata. In *POPL*, 1987.

[NL96]   G.C. Necula and P. Lee. Safe kernel extensions without run-time checking. In *OSDI*, 1996.

[NL98]   G.C. Necula and P. Lee. The design and implementation of a certifying compiler. In *PLDI*, 1998.

[PRZ01] A. Pnueli, S. Ruah, and L. Zuck. Automatic deductive verification with invisible invariants. In *TACAS*, volume 2031 of *LNCS*, 2001.

[PZ01]   D. Peled and L. Zuck. From model checking to a temporal proof. In *The 8th International SPIN Workshop on Model Checking of Software*, volume 2057 of *LNCS*, 2001.

[QS82]   J-P. Queille and J. Sifakis. Specification and verification of concurrent systems in CESAR. In *Proc. of the 5th International Symposium on Programming*, volume 137 of *LNCS*, 1982.

[RSS95] S. Rajan, N. Shankar, and M.K. Srivas. An integration of model checking with automated proof checking. In *CAV*, volume 939 of *LNCS*, 1995.

[SE84]   R.S. Streett and E.A. Emerson. The propositional mu-calculus is elementary. In *ICALP*, 1984. Full version in *Information and Computation* 81(3): 249-264, 1989.

[Spr98] C. Sprenger. A verified model checker for the modal μ-calculus in Coq. In *TACAS*, volume 1384 of *LNCS*, 1998.

[SS98]   P. Stevens and C. Stirling. Practical model-checking using games. In *TACAS*, 1998.

[SW89]   C. Stirling and D. Walker. Local model checking in the modal mu-calculus. In *TAPSOFT*, 1989. Full version in TCS vol.89, 1991.

[YL97]   S. Yu and Z. Luo. Implementing a model checker for LEGO. In *FME*, volume 1313 of *LNCS*, 1997.

Formalizing a JVML Verifier for Initialization in a Theorem Prover

Yves Bertot

INRIA Sophia Antipolis
2004 Route des Lucioles
06902 Sophia Antipolis Cedex, France
Yves.Bertot@inria.fr

1 Introduction

The byte-code verifier is advertised as a key component of the security and safety strategy for the Java language, making it possible to use and exchange Java programs without fearing too much damage due to erroneous programs or malignant program providers. As Java is likely to become one of the languages used to embed programs in all kinds of appliances or computer-based applications, it becomes important to verify that the claim of safety is justified.

We worked on a type system proposed in [7] to enforce a discipline for object initialization in the Java Virtual Machine Language and implemented it in the Coq [5] proof and specification language. We first produced mechanically checked proofs of the theorems in [7] and then we constructed a functional implementation of a byte-code verifier. We have a mechanical proof that this byte-code verifier only accepts programs that have a safe behavior with respect to initialization. Thanks to the extraction mechanism provided in Coq [17], we obtain a program in CAML that can be directly executed on sample programs.

A safe behavior with respect to initialization means that the fields of any object cannot be accessed before this object initialized. To represent this, the authors of [7] distinguish between uninitialized objects, created by a new instruction and initialized objects. Initialization is represented by an init instruction that replaces an uninitialized object with a new initialized object. Access to fields is represented abstractly by a use instruction, which operates only if the operand is an initialized object. Checking that initialization is properly respected means checking that use is never called with the main operand being an unitialized object.

There are two parts in this work. The first part simply consists in the mechanical verifications of the claims appearing in [7]. This relies on a comparison between operational semantics rules and typing rules. In terms of manpower involved, this only required around three weeks of work. This shows that proof tools are now powerful enough to be used to provide mechanical verifications of theoretical ideas in programming language semantics (especially when semantic descriptions are given as sets of inference rules).

The second part consists in producing a program, not described in [7], that satisfies the requirements described there. To develop this program, we have

G. Berry, H. Comon, and A. Finkel (Eds.): CAV 2001, LNCS 2102, pp. 14–24, 2001.

analyzed the various constraints that should be satisfied for each instruction and how these constraints could be implemented using a unification algorithm. In all, the experiments that the proof tool can also be used as a programming tool, with the advantage that logical reasoning can be performed on program units even before they are integrated in a completely functioning context.

This paper is a short abstract of a paper published as an INRIA research report under the title *A Coq formalization of a Type Checker for Object Initialization in the Java Virtual Machine* [2].

1.1 Related Work

Several teams around the world have been working on verifying formally that the properties of the Java language and its implementation suite make it a reasonably safe language. Some of the work done is based on pen-and-paper proofs that the principles of the language are correct, see for instance [22, 6, 14].

Closer to our concerns are the teams that use mechanical tools to verify the properties established about the formal descriptions of the language. A very active team in this field is the Bali team at University of Munich who is working on a comprehensive study of the Java language, its properties and its implementation [15, 13, 19] using the Isabelle proof system [18]. Other work has been done with the formal method B and the associated tools [3], at Kestrel Institute using Specware [8, 20], or in Nijmegen [9, 10] using both PVS [16] and Isabelle.

2 Formalizing the Language and Type System

2.1 Data-Types

The formalization we studied is based on a very abstract and simplified description of the Java Virtual Machine language. The various data-types manipulated in the programs are represented by abstract sets: ADDR for addresses in programs, VAR for variable names, integer for numeral values, T for classes.

The type of classes being left abstract, the way objects of a given class are constructed is also left abstract. We will actually rely on the minimal assumptions that there is a family of types representing the values in each class, such a family is represented by a function from T to the type of data-types, written in Coq as the following parameter to the specification.

```
Parameter object_value:T -> Set.
```

Since the objective of this study is initialization, there is a distinct family of sets for uninitialized object of a given class:

```
Parameter uninitialized_value: T -> Set.
```

We also assume the existence of test equality functions for uninitialized objects.

With all this, we express that the set of values manipulated by the abstract Java virtual machine is the disjoint sum of the set of integers, the set of object values and the set of uninitialized object values, with the following definition:

```
Inductive value: Set :=
    int_val: integer ->value
  | obj: (t:T) (object_value t) ->value
  | un: (t:T) (a:ADDR) (uninitialized_value t) ->value.
```

This inductive definition shows that a value can be in one of three cases, represented by three *constructors*. The first constructor, int_val expresses that a value can be an integer, the second constructor, obj expresses that a value can be an initialized object in some class T, the third constructor, un, expresses that a value can be an unitialized object for some class T, and that this value is also tagged with an address. Note that this definition uses a feature called *dependent types*: viewed as a function, the constructor obj takes a first argument t in T and a second argument whose type depends on the first one: this type must be object_value T.

The formal description of the Java Virtual Machine language as used in [7] boils down to a 10 constructor inductive type in the same manner. We named this type jvmli.

2.2   Operational Semantics

In [7], the operational semantics are given as a set of inference rules which describe the constraints that must hold between input and output data for each possible instruction. We handle judgments of the form

$$P \vdash \langle pc, f, s \rangle \rightarrow \langle pc', f', s' \rangle.$$

These judgments must be read as *for program P, one step of execution starting from the program counter pc, variable value description f, and stack s returns the new program counter pc', the new variable value description f', and stack s'.* Stacks are simply represented as finite lists of objects of type value. to represent memory, we use functions written f, f', from variable names (type VAR) to values (type value).

For instance, the language has an instruction load that fetches a value in memory and places it on the stack. This is expressed with this inference rule:

$$\frac{P[pc] = \texttt{load } x}{P \vdash \langle pc, f, s \rangle \rightarrow \langle pc+1, f, f[x] \cdot s \rangle}$$

Special attention must be paid to the way initialization works. Initializing an object means performing a side-effect on this object and all references to the object should view this side-effect. Thus, if several references of the same object have been copied in the memory then all these references should perceive the effect of initialization.

This is expressed with two rules. First the new instruction always creates an object that is different from all objects already present in memory (in this rule $\overline{A}^\sigma$ is a short notation for (uninitialized_value σ)) .

$$\frac{P[pc] = \texttt{new } \sigma \quad a \in \overline{A}^\sigma \quad Unused(a, f, s)}{P \vdash \langle pc, f, s \rangle \rightarrow \langle pc+1, f, a \cdot s \rangle}$$

Second, all occurrences (i.e., references) of an object in memory are modified when it is initialized (A^σ is a short notation for object_value σ, $[a'/a]f$ is the function that maps x to $f(x)$ if $f(x) \neq a$ and to a' if $f(x) = a'$, and $[a'/a]s$ is the same stack as s except that instances of a have been replaced with a').

$$\frac{P[pc] = \text{init } \sigma \quad a \in A^{\sigma,pc} \quad a' \in A^\sigma \quad Unused(a', f, s)}{P \vdash \langle pc, f, a \cdot s \rangle \to \langle pc + 1, [a'/a]f, [a'/a]s \rangle}$$

All these rules are easily expressed as constructors for inductive propositions, that are a common features in many modern proof tools.

2.3 Type System

In [7] the authors propose a set of typing rules for jvmli programs. This type system is based on the existence of a representation of all types for the stack and the variables at all lines in the program. It handles judgments of the form

$$F, S, i \vdash P$$

meaning *the type information for variables in F and for stacks in S is consistent with line i of program P*. The variable F actually represents a function over addresses, such that $F(i)$ is a function over variable names, associating variable names to types (we will write F_i instead of $F(i)$). Similarly S represents a function over addresses, where S_i is a stack of types. Consistency between type information with the program expresses that the relations between types of memory locations correspond to the actual instruction found at that address in the program. It also involves relations between types at line i at types at all lines where the control will be transfered after execution of this instruction.

For instance, the typing rule for load expresses that the type information at the line $i + 1$ must indicate that some data has been added on the stack when compared with the type information at line i.

$$\frac{P[i] = \text{load } x}{F_{i+1} = F_i}$$
$$S_{i+1} = F_i(x) \cdot S_i$$
$$i + 1 \in Dom(P)$$
$$\overline{F, S, i \vdash P}$$

For new and init there are a few details that change with respect to the operational semantics. While the operational semantics required that the object added on top of the stack by new should be unused in the memory, the type system also requires that the type corresponding to this data should be unused. For init, the operational semantics requires that the new initialized value should be unused but this premise has no counterpart in the typing rule. Still the typing rule for init requires that all instances of the uninitialized type found on top of the stack should be replaced by an initialized type. In these rules we use σ to denote the type of initialized objects and σ_i to denote the types of uninitialized objects created at address i.

$$\frac{\begin{array}{c} P[i] = \text{new } \sigma \\ F_{i+1} = F_i \\ S_{i+1} = \sigma_i \cdot S_i \\ \sigma_i \notin S_i \\ \forall x. F_i(x) \neq \sigma_i \end{array}}{F, S, i \vdash P} \qquad \frac{\begin{array}{c} P[i] = \text{init } \sigma \\ F_{i+1} = [\sigma/\sigma_j] F_i \\ S_i = \sigma_i \cdot \alpha \\ S_{i+1} = [\sigma/\sigma_j] \alpha \end{array}}{F, S, i \vdash P}$$

A singularity of this description is that all inference rules have the same conclusion, so that the proof procedures that usually handle these operational semantics descriptions [4] failed to be useful in this study.

3   Consistency of the Type System

The main theorem in [7] is a soundness theorem, saying that once we have proved that a program is well-typed this program will behave in a sound manner. Here this decomposes in a one-step soundness theorem: if a program P is well-typed at address i with respect to type information given by F and S, then executing this instruction from a state that is consistent with F and S at address i should return a new state that is also consistent with F and S at the address given by the new program counter.

This proof of soundness is pretty easy to perform, since the operational semantics rule and the typing rule are so close. However special attention must be paid to the problem of initialization because of the use of substitution. At the operational level, initialization works by substituting all instances of the uninitialized object with an initialized instance. At the type-system level, the same operation is performed, but how are we going to ensure that exactly the same location will be modified in both substitutions?

The solution to this problem is introduced in [7] under the form of a predicate ConsistentInit which basically expresses that whenever two locations have the same uninitialized type, then these locations contain the same value. In other terms, although there may be several values with the same uninitialized type, we can reason as if there was only one, because two different values will never occur at the same time in memory. This ensures that the substitutions in the operational rule for init and in the typing rule for init modify the memory in a consistent way.

The theorem of soundness is then expressed not only in terms of type consistency between the state and the type information at address i, but also in terms of the ConsistentInit property. We also have to prove that this ConsistentInit property is invariant through the execution of all instructions. Proving this invariant represents a large part of the extra work imposed by initialization. A more detailed presentation of the proof is given in the extended version of this paper [2]. We also proved a progress theorem that expresses that if the state is coherent with some type information and the instruction at address

i is not a halt instruction then execution can progress at address i. The two theorems can be used to express that program execution for well-typed programs progresses without errors until it reaches a halt statement.

4   Constructing an Effective Verifier

The type system does not correspond to an algorithm, since it assumes that the values F and S have been provided. An effective byte-code verifier has to construct this information. According to the approach advocated in [7], one should first produce this data, possibly using unsafe techniques, and then use the type verification described in the previous section to verify that the program is well-typed according to that information. The approach we study in this section is different: we attempt to construct F and S is such a way that the program is sure to be well-typed if the construction succeeds: it is no longer necessary to check the program after the construction.

In [12], T. Nipkow advocates the construction of the type information as the computation of a fix-point using Kildall's algorithm [11]. We have used a similar technique, based on traversing the control flow graph of the program and finding a least upper bound in a lattice. The lattice structure we have used is the lattice structure that underlies unification algorithms and we have, in fact, re-used a unification algorithm package that was already provided in the user libraries of the proof system [21]. However, the general approach of Nipkow was not followed faithfully, because the constraints we need to ensure are not completely stable with respect to the order used as a basis for unification. As a result, we still need to perform a verification pass after the data has been constructed.

4.1   Decomposing Typing Rules into Constraints

The typing constraints imposed for each instruction can be decomposed into more primitive constraints. We have isolated 8 such kinds of constraints. To explain the semantics of these constraints, we have a concept of *typing states*, with an order between typing states, $\preceq$. Typing states are usually denoted with variables of the form t, t'. We have a function add_constraint' to add constraints.

1. (tc_all_vars i j). This one expresses that the types of variables at lines i and j have to be the same.
2. (tc_stack i j). This one expresses that the types in stacks at lines i and j have to be the same.
3. (tc_top i τ). This one expresses that the type on top of the stack at line i has to be the type τ.
4. (tc_pop i j). This one expresses that the stack at line j has one less element than the stack at line i.
5. (tc_push i j x). This one expresses that the stack at line j is the same as the stack at line i where a type has been added, this type being the type of variable x at line i.

6. $(\texttt{tc\_push\_type}\ i\ j\ \tau)$. This one is like the previous one except that the type is given in the constraint.
7. $(\texttt{tc\_store}\ i\ x\ j)$. This one expresses that the variables at line j have the same type as at line i, except for the variable x, which receives at line j the type that is on top of the stack at line i, also the stack at line j is the same as the stack at line i with the top element removed.
8. $(\texttt{tc\_init}\ i\ j\ \sigma)$. This one expresses most of the specific constraints that are required for the instruction $\texttt{init}$. Its semantics is more complicated to describe and it is actually expressed with three properties. The first property expresses that the stack must have an uninitialized type on top:

$\texttt{tc\_init\_stack\_exists}$:
$\forall i, j, t, \sigma.$
$\quad (\texttt{add\_constraint}'\ (\texttt{tc\_init}\ i\ j\ \sigma)\ t) = (\texttt{Some}\ t) \Rightarrow$
$\quad (\texttt{stack\_defined}\ t\ i) \Rightarrow$
$\qquad \exists k, \alpha. \quad S_t(i) = \sigma_k \cdot \alpha$

The second property expresses that all variables that referred to that uninitialized type at line i must be updated with a new initialized type at line j (we define a function *subst* on functions from VAR to types to represent the substitution operation).

$\texttt{tc\_init\_frame}$:
$\forall i, j, k, t, \sigma, \alpha.$
$\quad (\texttt{add\_constraint}'\ (\texttt{tc\_init}\ i\ j\ \sigma)\ t) = (\texttt{Some}\ t) \Rightarrow$
$\quad S_t(i) = \sigma_k \cdot \alpha \Rightarrow$
$\qquad F_t(j) = (\textit{subst}\ F_t(i)\ \sigma_k\ \sigma)$

The third property expresses the same thing for stacks (we also have a function *subst_stk* to represent the substitution operation on stacks).

$\texttt{tc\_init\_stack}$:
$\forall i, j, k, t, \sigma, \alpha.$
$\quad (\texttt{add\_constraint}'\ (\texttt{tc\_init}\ i\ j\ \sigma)\ t) = (\texttt{Some}\ t) \Rightarrow$
$\quad S_t(i) = \sigma_k \cdot \alpha \Rightarrow$
$\qquad S_t(j) = (\textit{subst\_stk}\ \alpha\ \sigma_k\ \sigma)$

In these statements, the predicate $(\texttt{stack\_defined}\ t\ i)$ expresses that even though the state t may be incomplete, it is necessary that it already contains enough information to know the height of the stack at line i.

The constraints for each instruction are expressed by composing several primitive constraints. For instance, the constraints for $(\texttt{load}\ x)$ at line i are the following ones:

$$(\texttt{tc\_all\_vars}\ i\ (i+1)) \qquad (\texttt{tc\_push}\ i\ (i+1)\ x)$$

A special case is the instruction $(\texttt{new}\ \sigma)$, which creates an uninitialized value, i.e., a value of type σ_i if we are at address i. We associate to this instruction the following constraints:

$$(\texttt{tc\_all\_vars}\ i\ (i+1)) \qquad (\texttt{tc\_push\_type}\ i\ (i+1)\ \sigma_i)$$

These constraints do not express the requirement that the type of the uninitialized object, σ_i, must not already be present in the memory at line i (this was expressed by the predicate *Unused* in the typing rule).

We use an order $\preceq$ between typing information states, such that $t \preceq t'$ means that t' contains strictly more information about types than t. In fact, this order is simply the instantiation order as used in unification theory. All constraints, except the constraint tc_init are preserved through $\preceq$. The requirements for initialization and for creating a new unitialized object are not preserved, this explains why we have to depart from Kildall's algorithm.

4.2 Relying on Unification

We use unifiable terms to represent successive states of the verifier and unifiable terms to represent constraints. Applying a constraint c to a type state t is implemented as applying the most general unifier of c and t to t to obtain a new state t'. Let us call *cumulative constraints* constraints of the kinds 1 to 7 in the enumeration above. These are the constraints that are stable with respect to the order $\preceq$.

The fragments F and S of the typing state actually are bi-dimensional arrays. For F the lines of the arrays are indexed with addresses, while the columns correspond to variables. For S the lines are also indexed with addresses, and each line gives the type of the stack at the corresponding address. When representing these notions as unifiable terms, they can be encoded as lists of lists.

The unifiable terms are composed of variables and terms of the form

$$f_i(t_1, \ldots, t_k)$$

for a certain number of function operators f_i. These operators are as follows:

- fcons and fnil are the constructors for lists.
- fint is the operator for the type of integer values, (otype σ) is used for types of initialized objects of class σ, and (utype σ i) for types of unitialized objects created at address i.

The initial typing state is the pair of a variable, to express that nothing is known about F in the beginning and a term of the form fcons(fnil, X) to express that we know that the stack at line 0 is the empty stack and that we do not know anything about the stack on other lines yet.

The unifiable terms corresponding to cumulative constraints are easily expressed as iterations of the basic function operators. To make this practical we define a few functions to represent these iterations. For instance, we construct the term

$$\text{fcons}(X_{k+1}, \ldots \text{fcons}(X_{k+j-1}(\text{fcons}(t, X_{k+j})) \ldots)$$

by a calling a function (place_one_list t j ($k+1$)). The third argument, $k+1$, is used to shift the indices of the variables occurring at places 1, $\ldots$, $j-1$ in the list. This term represents a list where the jth element is constrained by t

and all other elements are left unconstrained (even the length of the list is not constrained much, it only needs to be greater than j).

Similarly, (mk_two_list t_1 t_2 *gap* i k) will construct the list whose length has to be greater than $i + gap$ and whose elements at ranks i and $i + gap$ are constrained by t_1 and t_2 respectively (here again the last argument, k is used to shift the indices of all the extra variables inserted in the list).

We do not describe the encoding of all constraints, but we can already express the encoding of the constraint (tc_push i j x) (when $j > i$):

$$\lceil (\text{tc\_push } i \; j \; x) \rceil =$$
$$(\text{place\_one\_list} \; (\text{place\_one\_list} \; X_k \; x \; k + 2) \; i \; (k + x + 2)),$$
$$(\text{mk\_two\_list} \; X_{k+1} \; (\text{fcons} \; X_k \; X_{k+1}) \; (j - i) \; i \; (k + x + i + 2))$$

Proving that the constraints are faithfully represented by the unifiable terms we associate to them requires that we show how functions like place_one_list behave with respect to some interpretation functions, mostly based on some form of nth function to return the nth element of a list. For instance, if F,S represent the typing state, knowing the type of variable x at line i simply requires that we compute the unifiable term given by (nth (nth F i) x).

4.3   A Two Pass Algorithm

The algorithm performs a first pass where all cumulative constraints are applied to the initial typing state to obtain preliminary information about all types of variables and stacks at all lines. The constraint tc_init for initializations is also applied, even though we know that it will be necessary to re-check that the constraint is still satisfied for the final state.

The second pass does not modify the typing state anymore. It simply verifies that the final typing state does satisfy the restrictive constraint imposed by instructions new and init. For (new σ) at line i, it means verifying that the type σ_i occurs nowhere in the variables or the stack at line i. For (init σ) it means checking again that the unifiable term $\lceil (\text{tc\_init } i \; (i + 1) \; \sigma) \rceil$ unifies with the final state.

5   Conclusion

The extraction mechanism of Coq makes it possible to derive from this proof development a program that will run on simple examples. This program is very likely to be unpractical: no attention has been paid to the inherent complexity of the verification mechanism. At every iteration we construct terms whose size is proportional to the line number being verified: in this sense the algorithm complexity is already sure to be more than quadratic.

Still, even if the exact representation of the typing state and constraints are likely to change to obtain a more usable verifier, we believe that the decomposition of its implementation and certification in the various phases presented in this paper is likely to remain relevant. These phases are:

1. Proving the soundness of a type system that uses data not in the program,
2. Proving that a program can build the missing data and ensure the typing constraints,
3. Setting aside the constraints that may not be preserved through the refinements occurring each time a line is processed,
4. Traverse the program according to its control flow graph,

With a broader perspective, this development of a certified byte-code verifier shows that very recent investigations into the semantics of programming languages can be completely mechanized using modern mechanical proof tools. The work presented here took only two months to mechanize completely and the part of this work that consisted in mechanizing the results found in [7] took between one and two weeks. This is also an example of using a type-theory based proof system as a programming language in the domain of program analysis tools, with all the benefits of the expressive type system to facilitate low-error programming and re-use of other programs and data-structures, as we did with the unification algorithm of [21]. Future development on this work will lead to more efficient, but still certified, implementations of this algorithm and and integration in a more complete implementation such as the one provided in [1].

References

1. G. Barthe, G. Dufay, L. Jakubiec, S. Melo de Sousa, and B. Serpette. A Formal Executable Semantics of the JavaCard Platform. In D. Sands, editor, *Proceedings of ESOP'01*, volume 2028 of *LNCS*, pages 302–319. Springer-Verlag, 2001.
2. Yves Bertot. A coq formalization of a type checker for object initialization in the java virtual machine. Research Report RR-4047, INRIA, 2000.
3. Ludovic Casset and Jean-Louis Lanet. How to formally specify the java byte code semantics using the b method. In *proceedings of the Workshop on Formal Techniques for Java Programs at ECOOP 99*, June 1999.
4. Christina Cornes and Delphine Terrasse. Automatizing inversion of inductive predicates in coq. In *Types for Proofs and Programs*, volume 1158 of *Lecture Notes in Computer Science*. Springer-Verlag, 1995.
5. Gilles Dowek, Amy Felty, Hugo Herbelin, Gérard Huet, Chet Murthy, Catherine Parent, Christine Paulin-Mohring, and Benjamin Werner. *The Coq Proof Assistant User's Guide*. INRIA, May 1993. Version 5.8.
6. Stephen N. Freund and John C. Mitchell. A Formal Framework for the Java Bytecode Language and Verifier. In *ACM Conference on Object-Oriented Programming: Systems, Languages and Applications*, November 1999.
7. Stephen N. Freund and John C. Mitchell. A Type System for Object Initialization in the Java Bytecode Language. *ACM Transactions on Programming Languages and Systems*, September 2000.
8. A. Goldberg. A specification of Java loading and bytecode verification. In *Proceedings of 5th ACM Conference on Computer and Communication Security*, 1998.
9. Ulrich Hensel, Marieke Huisman, Bart Jacobs, and Hendrik Tews. Reasoning about classes in object-oriented languages: Logical models and tools. In *Proceedings of European Symposium on Programming (ESOP '98)*, volume 1381 of *LNCS*, pages 105–121. Springer-Verlag, March 1998.

10. Marieke Huisman. *Java program verification in Higher-order logic with PVS and Isabelle*. PhD thesis, University of Nijmegen, 2001.
11. G. A. Kildall. A unified approach to global program optimization. In *Proceedings of the ACM Symposium on Principles of Programming Languages*, pages 194–206, 1973.
12. Tobias Nipkow. Verified bytecode verifiers. unpublished, available at URL http://www.in.tum.de/~nipkow/pubs/bcv2.html, 2000.
13. Tobias Nipkow, David von Oheimb, and Cornelia Pusch. μJava: Embedding a programming language in a theorem prover. In Friedrich L. Bauer and Ralf Steinbrüggen, editors, *Foundations of Secure Computation*, volume 175 of *NATO Science Series F: Computer and Systems Sciences*, pages 117–144. IOS Press, 2000.
14. R. O'Callahn. A simple, comprehensive type system for java bytecode subroutines. In *ACM Symposium on Principles of Programming Languages*, pages 70–78. ACM Press, 1999.
15. David von Oheimb and Tobias Nipkow. Machine checking the Java specification: Proving type-safety. In Jim Alves-Foss, editor, *Formal Syntax and Semantics of Java*, LNCS. Springer, 1998. To appear.
16. Sam Owre, John Rushby, Natarajan Shankar, and Friedrich von Henke. Formal verification for fault-tolerant architectures: Prolegomena to the design of PVS. *IEEE Transactions on Software Engineering*, 21(2):107–125, feb 1995.
17. Christine Paulin-Mohring and Benjamin Werner. Synthesis of ML programs in the system Coq. *Journal of Symbolic Computation*, 15:607–640, 1993.
18. Lawrence C. Paulson and Tobias Nipkow. *Isabelle : a generic theorem prover*, volume 828 of *Lecture Notes in Computer Science*. Springer-Verlag, 1994.
19. Cornelia Pusch. Proving the soundness of a Java bytecode verifier specification in Isabelle/HOL. In W. Rance Cleaveland, editor, *Tools and Algorithms for the Construction and Analysis of Systems (TACAS'99)*, volume 1579 of *LNCS*, pages p. 89–103. Springer-Verlag, 1999.
20. Z. Qian. A formal specification of Java Virtual machine instructions for objects, methods, and subroutines. In *Formal Syntax and Semantics of Java*, volume 1523 of *Lecture Notes in Computer Science*. Springer-Verlag, 1999.
21. Joseph Rouyer. Développement de l'algorithme d'unification dans le calcul des constructions avec types inductifs, September 1992. (In french), available at URL http://coq.inria.fr/contribs/unification.html.
22. Raymie Stata and Martín Abadi. A type system for Java bytecode subroutines. In *Proceedings of the 25th Annual ACM Symposium on Principles of Programming Languages*, pages 149–160. ACM Press, January 1998.

Automated Inductive Verification of Parameterized Protocols*

Abhik Roychoudhury[1] and I.V. Ramakrishnan[2]

[1] School of Computing, National University of Singapore
3 Science Drive 2, Singapore 117543
abhik@comp.nus.edu.sg
[2] Dept. of Computer Science, SUNY Stony Brook
Stony Brook, NY 11794, USA
ram@cs.sunysb.edu

Abstract. A parameterized concurrent system represents an infinite family (of finite state systems) parameterized by a recursively defined type such as chains, trees. It is therefore natural to verify parameterized systems by inducting over this type. We employ a program transformation based proof methodology to automate such induction proofs. Our proof technique is geared to automate nested induction proofs which do not involve strengthening of induction hypothesis. Based on this technique, we have designed and implemented a prover for parameterized protocols. The prover has been used to automatically verify safety properties of parameterized cache coherence protocols, including broadcast protocols and protocols with global conditions. Furthermore we also describe its successful use in verifying mutual exclusion in the Java Meta-Locking Algorithm, developed recently by Sun Microsystems for ensuring secure access of Java objects by an arbitrary number of Java threads.

1 Introduction

There is a growing interest in verification of *parameterized* concurrent systems since they occur widely in computing *e.g.* in distributed algorithms. Intuitively, a parameterized system is an infinite family of finite state systems parameterized by a recursively defined type *e.g.* chains, trees. Verification of distributed algorithms (with arbitrary number of constituent processes) can be naturally cast as verifying parameterized systems. For example, consider a distributed algorithm where n users share a resource and follow some protocol to ensure mutually exclusive access. Model checking [6, 21, 24] can verify mutual exclusion for only finite instances of the algorithm, *i.e.* for $n = 3$, $n = 4, \ldots$ but not for any n.

In general, automated verification of parameterized systems has been shown to be undecidable [2]. Thus, verification of parameterized networks is often accomplished via theorem proving [14, 17, 22], or by synthesizing network invariants

---

* This work was partially supported by NSF grants CCR-9711386, CCR-9876242 and EIA-9705998. The first author was a Ph.D. student at SUNY Stony Brook during part of this work.

G. Berry, H. Comon, and A. Finkel (Eds.): CAV 2001, LNCS 2102, pp. 25–37, 2001.

[7, 19, 28]. Alternatively, one can identify subclasses of parameterized systems for which verification is decidable [9, 10, 13, 15]. Another approach [8, 11, 12, 16, 18] finitely represents the state space of a parameterized system and applies (symbolic) model checking over this finite representation.

Since a parameterized system represents an infinite family parameterized by a recursively defined type, it is natural to prove properties of parameterized systems by inducting over this type. In a recent paper [25] we outlined a methodology for constructing such proofs by suitably extending the resolution based evaluation mechanism of logic programs. In our approach, the parameterized system and the property to be verified are encoded as a logic program. The verification problem is reduced to the problem of determining the equivalence of predicates in this program. The predicate equivalences are then established by *transforming* the predicates. The proof of semantic equivalence of two predicates proceeds automatically by a routine induction on the structure of their transformed definitions. One of our transformations (unfolding) represents resolution and performs on-the-fly model checking. The others (*e.g.* folding) represent deductive reasoning. The application of these transformations are arbitrarily interleaved in the verification proof of a parameterized system. This allows our framework to tightly integrate algorithmic and deductive verification.

Summary of Contributions. In this paper, we employ our logic program transformation based approach for inductive verification of real-life parameterized protocols. The specific contributions are:

1. We construct an automatic and programmable first order logic based prover with limited deductive capability. The prover can also exploit knowledge of network topology (chain, tree etc) to facilitate convergence of proofs.
2. Our program transformation based technique produces induction proofs. We clarify the connection between our transformations and inductive reasoning.
3. Our technique is not restricted to specific network topologies. We have verified chain, ring, tree, star and complete graph networks. Furthermore by enriching the underlying language to Constraint Logic Programming (CLP), the technique can be extended to verify infinite families of infinite state systems such as parameterized real-time systems.
4. Besides verifying parameterized cache coherence protocols such as Berkeley RISC and Illinois, we also report the verification of mutual exclusion in Java meta-locking algorithm. It is a real-life distributed algorithm recently developed by Sun Microsystems to ensure mutual exclusion in accessing Java objects by an arbitrary number of Java threads. Previously, the designers of the protocol gave an informal correctness argument [1], and model checking of instances of the protocol were done [4]. This is the first machine generated proof of the algorithm which is parameterized by the number of threads.

The rest of the paper is organized as follows. Section 2 presents an overview of our program transformation based proof technique for parameterized systems presented in [25]. Section 3 clarifies the connection between program transformations and inductive reasoning. Section 4 discusses the functioning of our automated prover for parameterized protocols. Section 5 presents the successful

```
nat(0).                         efp(S) :- p(S).
nat(s(X)) :- nat(X).            efp(S) :- trans(S, T), efp(T).
trans(s(X), X).                 thm(X) :- nat(X), efp(X).
p(0).
```
System Description   Property Description

Fig. 1. Proving Liveness in Infinite Chain.

use of our prover in verifying parameterized cache coherence protocols as well
as the Java meta-locking algorithm. Finally, Section 6 concludes the paper with
related work and possible directions for future research.

2   Overview

In this section, we recapitulate our core technique for inductive verification [25]
through a very simple example. Let us consider an unbounded length chain whose
states are numbered $n, n-1, \ldots, 0$. Further suppose that the start state is n, the
end state is 0 and a proposition p is true in state 0. Suppose we want to prove
the CTL property **EF** p for every state in the chain. Alternatively, we can view
this chain as an infinite family of finite chains of length $0,1,2,\ldots$ and the proof
obligation as proving **EF** p for every start state of the infinite family. Either
way, our proof obligation amounts to $\forall n \in \mathbb{N}\ n \models \mathbf{EF}$ p. Our proof technique
dispenses this obligation by an induction on n.

Encoding the Problem. In the above example, the states are captured by
natural numbers which we represent by a logic program predicate nat (refer
Figure 1; the term s(K) denotes the number K+1). The transition relation is
captured by a binary predicate trans s.t. trans(S, T) is true iff there exists
a transition from state S to state T. [1] The temporal property **EF** p is encoded
as a unary predicate efp s.t. for any state S, efp(S) $\Leftrightarrow$ S $\models$ **EF** p. The first
clause of efp succeeds for states in which proposition p holds. The second clause
of efp checks if a state satisfying p is reachable after a finite sequence of tran-
sitions. Thus $\forall n \in \mathbb{N}\ n \models \mathbf{EF}$p iff $\forall$X nat(X) $\Rightarrow$ efp(X). Moreover this holds if
$\forall$X thm(X) $\Leftrightarrow$ nat(X) in P_0.

Proof by Program Transformations. We perform inductive verification via
logic program transformations using the following steps. A detailed technical
presentation of this proof technique appears in [25].

1. Encode the system and property description as a logic program P_0.

---
[1] For realistic parameterized systems, the global transition relation is encoded recursively in terms of local transition relations of constituent processes; see section 4.

2. Convert the verification proof obligation to predicate equivalence proof obligation(s) of the form $P_0 \vdash \mathrm{p} \equiv \mathrm{q}$ (p, q are predicates)
3. Construct a transformation sequence $P_0, P_1, \ldots, P_k$ s.t.
   (a) Semantics of P_0 = Semantics of P_k
   (b) from the syntax of P_k we infer $P_k \vdash \mathrm{p} \equiv \mathrm{q}$

For our running example, the logic program encoding P_0 appears in Figure 1. We have reduced the verification proof obligation to showing the predicate equivalence $P_0 \vdash$ `thm` $\equiv$ `nat`. We then transform program P_0 to obtain a program P_k where `thm` and `nat` are defined as follows.

```
thm(0).                      nat(0).
thm(s(X)) :- thm(X).         nat(s(X)) :- nat(X).
```

Thus, since the transformed definitions of `thm` and `nat` are "isomorphic", their semantic equivalence can be inferred from syntax. In general, we have a sufficient condition called *syntactic equivalence* which is checkable in polynomial time w.r.t. program size (refer [25, 27] for a formal definition).

Note that inferring the semantic equivalence of `thm` and `nat` based on the syntax of their transformed definitions in program P_k proceeds by induction on the "structure" of their definitions in P_k (which in this example amounts to an induction on the length of the chain). The program transformations employed in constructing the sequence $P_0, P_1, \ldots, P_k$ correspond to different parts of this induction proof. In the next section, we will clarify this connection between program transformations and inductive reasoning.

3 Program Transformations for Inductive Verification

Unfold/Fold Program Transformations. We transform a logic program to another logic program by applying transformations that include unfolding and folding. A simple illustration of these transformations appears in Figure 2. Program P'_1 is obtained from P'_0 by unfolding the occurrence of `q(X)` in the definition of p. P'_2 is obtained by folding `q(X)` in the second clause of p in P'_1 using the definition of p in P'_0 (an earlier program). Intuitively, unfolding is a step of clause resolution whereas folding replaces instance of clause bodies (in some earlier program in the transformation sequence) with its head. A formal definition of the unfold/fold transformation rules, along with a proof of semantics preservation of any interleaved application of the rules, appears in [26].

```
                                 p(0).                                  p(0).
p(X) :- [q(X)].        Unf.      p(s(X)) :- [q(X)].       Fold          p(s(X)) :- p(X).
q(0).                  -->       q(0).                    -->           q(0).
q(s(X)) :- q(X).                 q(s(X)) :- q(X).                       q(s(X)) :- q(X).
```

Program P'_0 — Program P'_1 — Program P'_2

Fig. 2. Illustration of Unfold/Fold Transformations.

An Example of Inductive Verification. We now apply these transformations to the definition of thm in the program P_0 shown in Figure 1. First we unfold nat(X) in the definition clause of thm to obtain the following clauses. This unfolding step corresponds to uncovering the schema on which we induct, *i.e.* the schema of natural numbers.

```
thm(0) :- efp(0).
thm(s(X)) :- nat(X), efp(s(X)).
```

We now repeatedly unfold efp(0). These steps correspond to showing the base case of our induction proof. Note that showing the truth of efp(0) is a finite state verification problem, and the unfolding steps employed to establish this exactly correspond to on-the-fly model checking. We obtain:

```
thm(0).
thm(s(X)) :- nat(X), efp(s(X)).
```

We repeatedly unfold efp(s(X)) in the second clause of thm. These steps correspond to finite part of the induction step, *i.e.* the reasoning that allows us to infer $n + 1 \models \mathbf{EF}$ p provided the induction hypothesis $n \models \mathbf{EF}$ p holds. We get

```
thm(0).
thm(s(X)) :- nat(X), efp(X).
```

Finally, we fold the body of the second clause of thm above using the original definition of thm in P_0. Application of this folding step enables us to recognize the induction hypothesis (thm(X) in this case) in the induction proof.

```
thm(0).
thm(s(X)) :- thm(X).
```

The semantic equivalence of thm and nat can now be shown from their syntax (by a routine induction on the structure of their definitions). This completes the verification (by induction on nat).

What Kind of Induction? Since unfolding represents a resolution step, it can be used to prove the base case and the finite part of the induction step. However, folding recognizes the occurrence of clauses of a predicate p *in an earlier program* $P_j (j \leq i)$, within the current program P_i. Thus, folding is *not* the reverse of unfolding. It can be used to remember the induction hypothesis and recognize its occurrence. Application of unfold/fold transformations constructs induction proofs which proceed without strengthening of hypothesis. This is because the folding rule only recognizes instances of an earlier definition of a predicate, and does not apply any generalization. In the next section, we will discuss how our transformation based proof technique can support nested induction proofs.

4   An Automated Prover for Parameterized Protocols

The inductive reasoning accomplished by our transformation based proof technique has been exploited to build an automated prover for parameterized protocols. Note that our program transformation based technique for proving predicate equivalences can be readily extended to prove predicate implication proof obligations of the form $P_0 \vdash p \Rightarrow q$.[2]

Since our transformations operate on *definite logic programs* (logic programs without negation), we only verify temporal properties with either the least or the greatest fixed point operator. For the rest of the paper, we restrict our attention to only proof of *invariants*.

4.1   System and Property Specification

To use our prover, first the initial states and the transition relation of the parameterized system are specified as two logic program predicates gen and trans. The global states of the parameterized system are represented by unbounded terms, and gen, trans are predicates over these terms. The recursive structure of gen and trans depends on the topology of the parameterized network being verified. For example, consider a network of similar processes where any process may perform an autonomous action or communicate with any other process. We can model the global state of this parameterized network as an unbounded list of the local states of the individual processes. The transition relation trans can then be defined over these global states as follows:

```
trans([H|T], [H1|T1]) :- ltrans(H, in(Act), H1),
                         trans_rest(T, out(Act), T1).
trans([H|T], [H1|T1]) :- ltrans(H, out(Act), H1),
                         trans_rest(T, in(Act), T1).
trans([H|T], [H1|T]) :- ltrans(H, self(Act), H1).
trans([H|T], [H|T1]) :- trans(T, T1).

trans_rest([S|T], A, [S1|T]) :- ltrans(S, A, S1).
trans_rest([H|T], A, [H|T1]) :- trans_rest(T, A, T1).
```

Thus, each process can perform an autonomous action (denoted in the above as self(A)) or an input/output action (denoted as in(A)/out(A)) where matching input and output actions synchronize. The predicate ltrans encodes the local transition relation of each process. For the global transition relation trans, the last clause recursively searches the global state representation until one of the first three rules can be applied. The third clause allows any process to make an autonomous action. The first and second clauses correspond to the scenario where *any* two processes communicate with each other. In particular, the first (second) clause of trans allows a process to make an in(A) (out(A)) action and invokes trans_rest to recursively search for another process which makes the corresponding out(A) (in(A)) action.

A safety property, denoted in CTL as **AG** ¬bad can be verified by proving transition invariance. We prove that (1) a bad state is reachable only from a bad state, and (2) none of the initial states satisfying gen are bad. This is shown by

---

[2] The proof obligation $P_0 \vdash p \Rightarrow q$ formally means: for all ground substitutions θ we have $p(\overline{X})\theta \in M(P_0) \Rightarrow q(\overline{X})\theta \in M(P_0)$ where $M(P_0)$ is the set of ground atoms which are logical consequences of the first-order formulae represented by logic program P_0.

establishing (1) bad_dest ⇒ bad_src, and (2) bad_start ⇒ false where the predicates bad_dest, bad_src and bad_start are defined as:

```
bad_dest(S, T) :- trans(S, T), bad(T).
bad_src(S, T) :- trans(S, T), bad(S).
bad_start(S) :- gen(X), bad(X).
```

4.2   Controlling the Proof Search

A skeleton of the proof search conducted by our prover is given below. Given a predicate implication $P_0 \vdash p \Rightarrow q$ the prover proceeds as follows.

1. Repeatedly *unfold* the clauses of p and q according to an unfolding strategy which is is designed to guarantee termination.
2. Apply *folding* steps to the unfolded clauses of p, q.
3. (a) *Compare* the transformed definitions of p and q to compute a finite set $\{(p_1, q_1), \ldots, (p_k, q_k)\}$ s.t. proving $\bigwedge_{1 \leq 1 \leq k} P_0 \vdash p_1 \Rightarrow q_1$ completes the proof of $P_0 \vdash p \Rightarrow q$ (*i.e.* p ⇒ q can then be shown via our syntactic check).
   (b) Prove $P_0 \vdash p_1 \Rightarrow q_1, \ldots, P_0 \vdash p_k \Rightarrow q_k$ via program transformations.

Since the proof of each predicate implication proceeds by induction (on the structure of their definition), nesting of the proof obligations $P_0 \vdash p_1 \Rightarrow q_1, \ldots, P_0 \vdash p_k \Rightarrow q_k$ within the proof of $P_0 \vdash p \Rightarrow q$ corresponds to nesting of the corresponding induction proofs. Note that for the example in Figure 1, steps (1) and (2) were sufficient to complete the proof and therefore step (3) did not result in any nested proof obligations.

The above proof search skeleton forms the core of our automated prover which has been implemented on top of the XSB logic programming system [29]. Note that the proof search skeleton is nondeterministic *i.e.* several unfolds or several folds may be applicable at some step. For space considerations we omit a full discussion on how a transformation step is selected among all applicable transformations The interested reader is referred [27] (Chapter 6) for a detailed discussion, including a description of how the unfolding strategy guarantees termination. However, note that the prover allows the user to provide some problem-specific information at the *beginning* of the proof, namely *(i)* Network topology (linear, tree etc.) of the parameterized system, *(ii)* which predicates in the program encode the *safety property* being verified. This user guidance enables the prover to select the transformation steps in the proof attempt (which then proceeds without *any* user interaction). Below we illustrate illustrate how the user-provided information guides the prover's proof search.

Network Topology. The communication pattern between the different constituent processes of a parameterized network is called its network topology. To illustrate the role of network topology in our proof search let us suppose that we are proving bad_dest⇒ bad_src (refer Section 4.1). In the proof of bad_dest⇒ bad_src, we first unfold and fold the clauses of bad_dest and bad_src. The prover then compares these transformed clauses and detects new predicate implications to be proved. In this final step, the prover exploits the knowledge of the network topology to choose the new predicate implications. For example, suppose the parameterized family being verified is a binary tree network whose left and right subtrees do not communicate directly. Let the clauses of bad_dest and bad_src after unfolding and folding be:

```
bad_dest(f(root1,L1,R1), f(root2,L2,R2)) :- p(L1,L2), q(R1,R2).
bad_src(f(root1,L1,R1), f(root2,L2,R2)) :- p'(L1,L2), q'(R1,R2).
```

then by default $p \wedge q \Rightarrow p' \wedge q'$ needs to be proved to establish bad_dest $\Rightarrow$ bad_src. Instead, the prover recognizes that p, p' (q, q') are predicates defined over left (right) subtrees. Thus it partitions the proof obligation $p \wedge q \Rightarrow p' \wedge q'$ into two separate obligations defined over the left and right subtrees (whose transitions are independent of each other): $p \Rightarrow p'$ and $q \Rightarrow q'$. In other words, knowledge of transition system is exploited by the prover to choose nested proof obligations (as a heuristic for faster convergence of the proof attempt).

Predicates Encoding Temporal Property. By knowing which program predicates encode the safety property, the prover avoids unfolding steps which may disable deductive steps leading to a proof. To see how, note that the logic program encoding of a verification problem for parameterized systems inherently has a "*producer-consumer*" nature. For example to prove transition invariance, we need to show bad_dest $\Rightarrow$ bad_src (refer Section 4.1) where bad_dest(S, T) :- trans(S, T), bad(T). The system description predicate (trans) is the producer, since by unfolding it produces instantiations for variable T. Suppose by unfolding trans(S, T) we instantiate variable T to a term $\bar{t}$ representing global states of the parameterized family. Now, by unfolding bad($\bar{t}$) we intend to *test* whether bad holds in states represented by $\bar{t}$. In other words, the property description predicate is a consumer. Unfolding of bad($\bar{t}$) should consume the instantiation $\bar{t}$, rather than producing further instantiation via unification. Hence our prover incorporates heuristics to prevent unfoldings of property description predicates which result in instantiation of variables. Such unfolding steps can disable deductive steps converging to a proof e.g. folding of conjunction of trans and bad to bad_dest. The user-provided information tells us which predicates encode the safety property and enables us to identify these unfolding steps.

In general, to prove $P_0 \vdash p \Rightarrow q$, we first repeatedly unfold the clauses of p and q. Deductive steps like folding are applied subsequently. Therefore, it is possible to apply finite sequence of unfolding steps $P_0 \rightarrow \ldots \rightarrow P_i \rightarrow \ldots \rightarrow P_n$ s.t. a folding step applicable in program P_i which leads to a proof of $P_0 \vdash p \Rightarrow q$ is disabled in P_n. One way to prevent such disabling of deductive steps is to check for applicable deductive steps ahead of unfolding steps. However, this would add theorem proving overheads to model checking (model checking is accomplished by unfolding). Our goal is to perform zero-overhead theorem proving, where deductive steps are never applied if model checking alone can complete the verification task. The other solution is to incorporate heuristics for identifying unfolding steps which disable deductive steps. This approach is taken in our prover. The prover prevents any unfolding of a predicate encoding temporal property which generates variable instantiations.

5   Case Studies and Experimental Results

In this section, we first illustrate the use of our prover in proving mutual exclusion of the Java meta-locking algorithm [1]. Then, in section 5.2 we present the experimental results obtained on parameterized cache coherence protocols, including (a) single bus broadcast protocols e.g. Mesi, (b) single bus protocols with global conditions e.g. Illinois, and (b) multiple bus hierarchical protocols.

5.1   Mutual Exclusion of Java Meta-Lock

In recent years, Java has gained popularity as a concurrent object oriented language, and hence substantial research efforts have been directed to efficiently implementing the different language features. In Java language, any object can be synchronized upon by different threads via synchronized methods and synchronized statements. Mutual exclusion in the access of an object is ensured since a synchronized method first acquires a lock on the object, executes the method and then releases the lock. To ensure fairness and efficiency in accessing any object, each object maintains some *synchronization data*. Typically this synchronization data is a FIFO queue of the threads requesting the object. Note that to ensure mutually exclusive access of an object, it is necessary to observe a protocol while different threads access this synchronization data. The Java meta-locking algorithm [1] solves this problem. It is a distributed algorithm which is observed by each thread and any object for accessing the synchronization data of that object. It is a time and space efficient scheme to ensure mutually exclusive access of the synchronization data, thereby ensuring mutually exclusive access of any object. Model checking has previously been used to verify *instances* of the Java Meta-locking algorithm, obtained by fixing the number of threads [4].

The formal model of the algorithm consists of asynchronous parallel composition (in the sense of Milner's CCS) of an object process, a *hand-off* process and an arbitrary number of thread processes. To completely eliminate busy waiting by any thread, the algorithm performs a *race* between a thread acquiring the meta-lock and the thread releasing the meta-lock. The winner of this race is determined by the hand-off process, which serves as an arbiter.

We model the object process without the synchronization data since we are only interested in verifying mutually exclusive access of this data. Apart from the synchronization data, the meta-locking algorithm *implicitly* maintains another queue : the queue of threads currently contending for the meta-lock to access the synchronization data. However, for verifying mutual exclusion we only model the length of this queue. The local state of the object process therefore contains a natural number, the number of threads waiting for the meta-lock. This makes the object an infinite state system.

The thread and the hand-off processes are finite state systems. A thread synchronizes with the object to express its intention of acquiring/releasing the meta-lock. A thread that faces no contention from other threads while acquiring/releasing the meta-lock is said to execute the *fast path*. Otherwise, it executes the *slow path* where it gets access to the meta-lock in a FIFO discipline. When its turn comes, it is woken up by the hand-off process which receives acquisition/release requests from the acquiring/releasing threads.

We straightforwardly encoded the state representations and the transitions in the formal model of the protocol as a logic program. The modeling of the protocol took less than a week, with the help of a colleague who had previously modeled it in a CCS-like language for model checking. A global state in the logic program encoding is a 3-tuple (Th, Obj, H) where Th is an unbounded list of thread states, Obj is a state of the object process (containing an unbounded term representing a natural number) and H is a state of the hand-off process.

Our prover automatically proves transition invariance for a strengthening of the mutual exclusion invariant (the mutual exclusion invariant states that < 2 threads own the meta-lock). This strengthening was done manually, by reasoning about the local states of the hand-off and object processes. This is because the mutual exclusion invariant is not preserved by every transition (even though a state violating mutual exclusion is never reachable from the initial state of the algorithm). Thus, to prove mutual exclusion by transition invariance the invariant to be proved must be strengthened. Since our inductive prover cannot strengthen induction hypothesis in a proof, the strengthening was done manually. However, once the strengthened invariant is fed, the proof proceeds completely automatically. The timings and the number of proof steps are reported in Table 1 and further discussed in next section.

Recall from section 4.1 that for transition invariance we need to show two predicate implications bad_start ⇒ false and bad_src ⇒ bad_dest. Since our proof technique supports nested induction, our prover proves 39 predicate implications (including these two) in the mutual exclusion proof of Java meta-lock. The 37 other predicate implications are automatically discovered and proved by our prover. The nesting depth of the inductive mutual exclusion proof is 3.

Table 1. Summary of Protocol Verification Results.

Protocol	Invariant	Time(secs)	# Unfolding	#Deductive
Meta-Lock	#owner + #handout < 2	129.8	1981	311
Mesi	#m + #e < 2	3.2	325	69
	#m + #e = 0 ∨ #s = 0	2.9	308	63
Illinois	#dirty < 2	35.7	2501	137
Berkeley RISC	#dirty < 2	6.8	503	146
Tree-cache	#bus_with_data < 2	9.9	178	18

5.2 Experimental Results

Table 1 presents experimental results obtained using our prover: a summary of the invariants proved along with the time taken, the number of unfolding steps and the number of deductive steps (i.e. folding, and comparison of predicate definitions) performed in constructing the proof. The total time involves time taken by (a) unfolding steps (b) deductive steps, and (c) the time to invoke nested proof obligations. All experiments reported here were conducted on a Sun Ultra-Enterprise workstation with two 336 MHz CPUs and 2 GB of RAM. In the table, we have used the following notational shorthand: $\#s$ denotes the number of processes in local state s. *Mesi* and *Berkeley RISC* are single bus broadcast protocols [3, 11, 12]. *Illinois* is a single bus cache coherence protocol with global conditions which cannot be modeled as a broadcast protocol [8, 23]. *Tree-cache* is a binary tree network which simulates the interactions between the cache agents in a hierarchical cache coherence protocol [27].

The running times of our prover are slower than the times for verifying single bus cache coherence protocols reported in [8]. Unlike [8], our prover implements the proof search via meta-programming. It is feasible to implement our proof search at the level of the underlying abstract machine thereby improving efficiency. Moreover, note that the abstraction based technique of [8] is not suitable for verifying parameterized tree networks.

The number of deductive steps in our proofs is consistently small compared to the number of unfolding steps, since our proof search strategy applies deductive steps lazily. Due to its tree topology, the state representation of *Tree-cache* has a different term structure. This results in a larger running time with fewer transformation steps as compared to other cache coherence protocols. Finally, the proof of Java meta-locking algorithm involves nested induction over both control and data of the protocol. This increases the number of nested proof obligations, and hence the running time.

6   Related Work and Conclusions

Formal verification of parameterized systems has been researched widely in the last decade. Some of the well studied techniques include network invariants [7, 19, 20, 28] (where a finite state process invariant is synthesized), and use of general purpose theorem provers *e.g.* PVS [22], ACL2 [17], Coq [14]. In the recent past, a lot of activity has been directed towards developing automated techniques for verifying (classes of) parameterized systems. These include identification of classes for which parameterized system verification is decidable [9, 10, 13, 15], and application of model checking over rich languages [8, 12, 16, 18].

The rich language model checking approach finitely represents the state space and transition relation of a parameterized family via rich languages *e.g.* regular, tree-regular languages for linear, tree networks. Note that our approach achieves a *different* finite representation; we finitely represent infinite sets of states as recursively defined logic program predicates. In comparison to the rich language approach, our technique is not tied to specific classes of networks based on the choice of the rich language. Thus we have verified parameterized networks of various topologies *e.g.* chain, ring, tree, complete graph, star networks. Moreover, the rich language approach constructs proofs by state space traversal (uniform proofs) whereas our proofs are inductive.

Our prover is a lightweight automated inductive theorem prover for constructing nested induction proofs. Note that in our approach, the induction schema as well as the lemmas to be used in the inductive proof must be implicit in the logic program itself. This is a *limitation* of our method. Besides, our proof technique does not support strengthening of induction hypothesis in an inductive proof. However, if the schema and the lemmas are implicit in the logic program, our syntax based transformations uncover the induction schema and reason about its different cases by uncovering the requisite lemmas.

As future work, we plan to integrate automated invariant strengthening techniques [5] into our proof technique. This would involve developing a proof methodology containing both program analysis (to strengthen invariants) and program transformation (to inductively prove the invariants).

Acknowledgments

The authors would like to thank Samik Basu for his help in modeling the Java meta-locking algorithm.

References

1. O. Agesen et al. An efficient meta-lock for implementing ubiquitous synchronization. In *ACM SIGPLAN International Conference on Object-Oriented Programming Systems, Languages and Applications (OOPSLA)*, 1999. Technical report available from http://www.sun.com/research/techrep/1999/abstract-76.html.
2. K. Apt and D. Kozen. Limits for automatic verification of finite-state systems. *Information Processing Letters*, 15:307–309, 1986.
3. J. Archibald and J.-L. Baer. Cache coherence protocols: Evaluation using a multiprocessor simulation model. *ACM Transactions on Computer Systems*, 4, 1986.
4. S. Basu, S.A. Smolka, and O.R. Ward. Model checking the Java meta-locking algorithm. In *IEEE International Conference on the Engineering of Computer Based Systems*. IEEE Press, April 2000.
5. N. Bjorner, I.A. Browne, and Z. Manna. Automatic generation of invariants and intermediate assertions. *Theoretical Computer Science*, 173(1):49–87, 1997.
6. E.M. Clarke, E.A. Emerson, and A.P. Sistla. Automatic verification of finite-state concurrent systems using temporal logic specifications. *ACM Transactions on Programming Languages and Systems*, 8(2), 1986.
7. E.M. Clarke, O. Grumberg, and S. Jha. Verifying parameterized networks. *ACM Transactions on Programming Languages and Systems*, 19(5), 1997.
8. G. Delzanno. Automatic verification of parameterized cache coherence protocols. In *Computer Aided Verification (CAV)*, *LNCS 1855*, 2000.
9. E.A. Emerson and K.S. Namjoshi. Reasoning about rings. In *ACM SIGPLAN International Conference on Principles of Programming Languages (POPL)*, 1995.
10. E.A. Emerson and K.S. Namjoshi. Automated verification of parameterized synchronous systems. In *Computer Aided Verification (CAV)*, *LNCS 1102*, 1996.
11. E.A. Emerson and K.S. Namjoshi. On model checking for non-deterministic infinite state systems. In *IEEE Symposium on Logic in Computer Science (LICS)*, 1998.
12. J. Esparza, A. Finkel, and R. Mayr. On the verification of broadcast protocols. In *IEEE Symposium on Logic in Computer Science (LICS)*, 1999.
13. S. German and A. Sistla. Reasoning about systems with many processes. *Journal of the ACM*, 39:675–735, 1992.

14. INRIA Rocquencourt, URL http://pauillac.inria.fr/coq/doc/main.html, Paris, France. *The Coq Proof Assistant : Reference Manual*, 1999.
15. C. N. Ip and D. L. Dill. Verifying systems with replicated components in Murφ. *Formal Methods in System Design*, 14(3), May 1999.
16. B. Jonsson and M. Nilsson. Transitive closures of regular relations for verifying infinite-state systems. In *International Conference on Tools and Algorithms for Construction and Analysis of Systems (TACAS), LNCS 1785*, 2000.
17. M. Kaufmann, P. Manolis, and J.S. Moore. *Computer-Aided Reasoning: An approach*. Kluwer Academic, 2000.
18. Y. Kesten, O. Maler, M. Marcus, A. Pnueli, and E. Shahar. Symbolic model checking with rich assertional languages. In *Computer Aided Verification (CAV), LNCS 1254*, 1997.
19. R.P. Kurshan and K. Mcmillan. A structural induction theorem for processes. *Information and Computation*, 117:1–11, 1995.
20. D. Lesens, N. Halbwachs, and P. Raymond. Automatic verification of parameterized linear networks of processes. In *ACM SIGPLAN International Conference on Principles of Programming Languages (POPL)*, pages 346–357, 1997.
21. O. Lichtenstein and A. Pnueli. Checking that finite state concurrent programs satisfy their linear specification. In *ACM SIGPLAN International Conference on Principles of Programming Languages (POPL)*, 1985.
22. S. Owre, N. Shankar, and J. Rushby. PVS: A Prototype Verification System. In *International Conference on Automated Deduction (CADE)*, 1992.
23. F. Pong and M. Dubois. A new approach for the verification of cache coherence protocols. *IEEE Transacations on Parallel and Distributed Systems*, 6(8), 1995.
24. J.P. Queille and J. Sifakis. Specification and verification of concurrent programs in CESAR. In *International Symposium on Programming, LNCS 137*, 1982.
25. A. Roychoudhury, K. Narayan Kumar, C. R. Ramakrishnan, I.V. Ramakrishnan, and S. A. Smolka. Verification of parameterized systems using logic program transformations. In *International Conference on Tools and Algorithms for Construction and Analysis of Systems (TACAS), LNCS 1785*, pages 172–187, 2000.
26. A. Roychoudhury, K. Narayan Kumar, C.R. Ramakrishnan, and I.V. Ramakrishnan. A parameterized unfold/fold transformation framework for definite logic programs. In *International Conference on Principles and Practice of Declarative Programming (PPDP), LNCS 1702*, pages 396–413, 1999.
27. Abhik Roychoudhury. *Program Transformations for Verifying Parameterized Systems*. PhD thesis, State University of New York at Stony Brook, Available from http://www.cs.sunysb.edu/~abhik/papers, 2000.
28. P. Wolper and V. Lovinfosse. Verifying properties of large sets of processes with network invariants. In *LNCS 407*, 1989.
29. XSB. The XSB logic programming system v2.2, 2000. Available for downloading from http://xsb.sourceforge.net/.

Efficient Model Checking Via Büchi Tableau Automata*

Girish S. Bhat[1], Rance Cleaveland[2], and Alex Groce[3]

[1] Cosine Communications, Inc.
girish23@hotmail.com
[2] Department of Computer Science, SUNY at Stony Brook
rance@cs.sunysb.edu
[3] School of Computer Science, Carnegie-Mellon University
agroce+@cs.cmu.edu

Abstract. This paper describes an approach to engineering efficient model checkers that are generic with respect to the temporal logic in which system properties are given. The methodology is based on the "compilation" of temporal formulas into variants of alternating tree automata called *alternating Büchi tableau automata* (ABTAs). The paper gives an efficient on-the-fly model-checking procedure for ABTAs and illustrates how translations of temporal logics into ABTAs may be concisely specified using inference rules, which may be thus seen as high-level definitions of "model checkers" for the logic given. Heuristics for simplifying ABTAs are also given, as are experimental results in the CWB-NC verification tool suggesting that, despite the generic ABTA basis, our approach can perform better than model checkers targeted for specific logics. The ABTA-based approach we advocate simplifies the retargeting of model checkers to different logics, and it also allows the use of "compile-time" simplifications on ABTAs that improves model-checker performance.

1 Introduction

Temporal-logic model-checking algorithms determine whether or not a given system's behavior conforms to requirements formulated as properties in an appropriate temporal logic. Numerous algorithms for different logics and system modeling formalisms have been developed and implemented [2, 6, 8, 9, 14, 20, 24, 25, 27], and case studies have demonstrated the utility of the technology (see [10] for a survey).

Traditional model checkers work for one logic and one class of system models. For example, the algorithm in [9] checks whether systems given as Kripke structures obey properties expressed in CTL, while the automaton-based approach of [29] works on Kripke structures and properties given in linear-time temporal logic. Other algorithms have been developed in the context of labeled transition systems and the modal mu-calculus [14], Modecharts and real-time logics [32], and so on. This paradigm for model checking has yielded great research insights, but it has the disadvantage that changes to the modeling formalism (e.g. by changing the interpretation of state and transition labels) or the logic (e.g. by introducing domain-specific operators) necessitate a redesign

---

* Research supported by US Air Force Office of Scientific Research grant F49620-95-1-0508; US Army Research Office grants P-38682-MA, DAAD190110003, and DAAD190110019; and US National Science Foundation grants CCR-9257963, CCR-9505562, CCR-9996086, and CCR-9988489.

G. Berry, H. Comon, and A. Finkel (Eds.): CAV 2001, LNCS 2102, pp. 38–52, 2001.
© Springer-Verlag Berlin Heidelberg 2001

and reimplementation of the relevant model-checking algorithm. The amount of work needed to "retarget" a model checker can be an important factor hampering the uptake of the technology.

The goal of this paper is to demonstrate the utility of an alternative view of model checking that relies on translating temporal formulas into intermediate structures, *alternating Büchi tableau automata* (ABTA) [6], that a model checker then works on. ABTAs are variants of alternating tree automata [23] that support efficient model checking while enabling various "compile-time" optimizations to be performed. They also support the abstract definition, via "proof rules," of translation procedures for different temporal logics. By factoring out the formulation of model-checking questions from the routines that answer them, our framework simplifies retargeting model checkers to different system formalisms and temporal logics.

The remainder of this paper develops as follows. The next section presents the system models considered in this paper and defines ABTAs. Section 3 then develops an efficient on-the-fly model-checking algorithm for a large class of ABTAs, and the section following describes simplifications that may be performed on ABTAs. A method for translating temporal logics into ABTAs is given via an extended example in Section 5, and the section following describes an implementation and experimental results. Section 7 discusses related work, while the final section contains our conclusions and future work. An appendix contains full pseudo-code for the model-checking algorithm.

2 Transition Systems and Tableau Automata

This section defines our system models and introduces alternating Büchi tableau automata. In what follows we fix disjoint sets $(p, p', p_1, \ldots \in)\mathcal{A}$ and $(\theta, \theta', \theta_1, \ldots \in)\mathcal{A}_{\text{act}}$ of atomic *state* and *action* propositions, respectively.

2.1 Transition Systems

Transition systems encode the operational behavior of systems.

Definition 1. A transition system (TS) is a tuple $\langle S, A, \ell_S, \ell_A, \longrightarrow, s_I \rangle$ where S is a set of states; A is a set of actions; $\ell_S : S \longrightarrow 2^A$ is the *state labeling function*; $\ell_A : A \longrightarrow 2^{A_{\text{act}}}$ is the *action labeling function*; $\longrightarrow \subseteq S \times A \times S$ is the *transition relation*; and s_I is the *start state*. ∎

Intuitively, S contains the states a system may enter and A the atomic actions a system may perform. The labeling functions ℓ_S and ℓ_A indicate which atomic propositions hold of a given state or action, while $\longrightarrow$ encodes the execution steps the system may engage in and s_I the initial state of the system. We write $s \xrightarrow{\alpha} s'$ in lieu of $\langle s, \alpha, s' \rangle \in \longrightarrow$.

Definition 2. Let $\mathcal{T} = \langle S, A, \ell_S, \ell_A, \longrightarrow, s_I \rangle$ be a TS.

1. A *transition sequence* from $s_0 \in S$ is a sequence $\sigma = s_0 \xrightarrow{\alpha_1} s_1 \xrightarrow{\alpha_2} \cdots \xrightarrow{\alpha_k} s_k$, where $0 \leq k \leq \infty$. We define the *length* of σ, $|\sigma|$, to be k. If $|\sigma| = \infty$ we call σ *infinite*; otherwise, it is *finite*.
2. An *execution* from s_0 is a maximal transition sequence from s_0, that is, a sequence σ with the property that either $|\sigma| = \infty$, or $|\sigma| < \infty$ and $s_{|\sigma|} \not\xrightarrow{\alpha} s'$ for any $\alpha \in A$ and $s' \in S$.

If $s \in S$ then we use $\mathcal{E}_{\mathcal{T}}(s)$ to denote the set of executions in $\mathcal{T}$ from s. ∎

2.2 Alternating Büchi Tableau Automata

In this paper we use *alternating Büchi tableau automata* (ABTAs) as an intermediate representation for system properties. ABTAs are alternating tree automata, although they differ in subtle and noteworthy ways from the automata introduced in [23]; Section 7 gives details. To define ABTAs formally we first introduce the following syntactic sets. Let $\neg$ be a distinguished negation symbol; we define $\mathcal{L} = \mathcal{A} \cup \{\neg p \mid p \in \mathcal{A}\}$ to be the set of state literals and $\mathcal{L}_{act} = \mathcal{A}_{act} \cup \{\neg\theta \mid \theta \in \mathcal{A}_{act}\}$ to be the set of action literals. We also use $\Theta, \Theta', \ldots$ to range over subsets of $\mathcal{L}_{act}$. ABTAs may now be defined as follows.

Definition 3. An *alternating Büchi tableau automaton* (ABTA) is a tuple $\langle Q, \ell, \longrightarrow, q_I, \mathcal{F}\rangle$, where Q is a finite set of *states*; $\ell : Q \to \mathcal{L} \cup \{\neg, \wedge, \vee, [\Theta], \langle\Theta\rangle\}$ is the *state labeling*; $\longrightarrow \subseteq (Q \times Q)$, the *transition relation*, satisfies the condition below for all $q \in Q$; $q_I \in Q$ is the start state; and $\mathcal{F} \subseteq 2^S$ is the acceptance condition. The additional condition $\to$ must satisfy is:

$$|\{q' \mid q \to q'\}| \begin{cases} = 0 \text{ if } \ell(q) \in \mathcal{L} \\ \geq 1 \text{ if } \ell(q) \in \{\wedge, \vee\} \\ = 1 \text{ if } \ell(q) \in \{\neg, \langle\Theta\rangle, [\Theta]\} \end{cases}$$

As ABTAs are special node-labeled graphs we use typical graph-theoretic notions, including cycle, path, strongly-connected component, etc. We also write $q \to^* q'$ if there exists a path from q to q' in ABTA $\mathcal{B}$. We say that an ABTA is *well-formed* if, whenever $\ell(q) = \neg$, then q does not appear on a cycle of $\to$ edges. We only consider well-formed ABTAs in what follows.

Besides alternating tree automata, ABTAs may be viewed as abstract syntax for a fragment of the mu-calculus [6]. They may also be seen as defining system properties in terms of how the property in question is to be "proved", and we develop this intuition in presenting their semantics. More specifically, an ABTA defines a property of transition systems by encoding a "proof schema" for establishing that the property holds for a transition system. The states in the ABTA can be seen as goals, with the labels in the states defining the relationship that must hold between a state and its "subgoals". So if one wishes to show that a transition-system state s "satisfies" a state q in an ABTA, and the label of q is $\wedge$, then one must show that s satisfies each of q's children. The $[\Theta]$ and $\langle\Theta\rangle$ labels correspond to single-step modalities; for a transition-system state s to satisfy an ABTA state q whose label is $[\Theta]$, one must show that for each s' such that $s \xrightarrow{\alpha} s'$ for some α "satisfying" Θ, s' must satisfy the (unique) successor of q. Finally, the acceptance sets enable "proofs" to be infinite: an "infinite positive" proof is deemed valid if every "path" in the proof "touches" each set in F infinitely often, while an infinite "negative proof" is valid if it fails to "touch" at least one set in F infinitely often. (The first clause is the same as the generalized Büchi acceptance condition defined in [15]. It should also be noted that the second clause indicates that ABTAs have a "co-Büchi" component to their acceptance condition.) These intuitions may be formalized in terms of "runs" of an ABTA. To define these we first introduce the following terminology.

Definition 4. Let $\mathcal{T} = \langle S, A, \ell_S, \ell_A, \longrightarrow, s_I\rangle$ be a TS with $s \in S$.

1. Let $p \in \mathcal{A}$. Then $s \models_\mathcal{T} p$ if and only if $p \in \ell_S(s)$, and $s \models_\mathcal{T} \neg p$ if and only if $p \notin \ell_S(s)$.
2. Let $\theta \in \mathcal{A}_{\text{act}}$. Then $\alpha \models_\mathcal{T} \theta$ if and only if $\theta \in \ell_A(\alpha)$, and $\alpha \models_\mathcal{T} \neg\theta$ if and only if $\theta \notin \ell_A(\alpha)$.
3. Let $\Theta \subseteq \mathcal{L}_{\text{act}}$. Then $\alpha \models_\mathcal{T} \Theta$ if and only if $\alpha \models \theta$ for every $\theta \in \Theta$. We write $s \xrightarrow{\Theta} s'$ if and only if $s \xrightarrow{\alpha} s'$ for some $\alpha \in A$ such that $\alpha \models_\mathcal{T} \Theta$ and $s \not\xrightarrow{\Theta}$ if there is no s' such that $s \xrightarrow{\Theta} s'$.

∎

Definition 5. A *run* of an ABTA $\mathcal{B} = \langle Q, \ell, \rightarrow_B, q_I, \mathcal{F} \rangle$ on a TS $\mathcal{T} = \langle S, A, \ell_S, \ell_A, \rightarrow_\mathcal{T}, s_I \rangle$ is a maximal tree in which the nodes are classified as *positive* or *negative* and are labeled by elements of $Q \times S$ as follows.

- The root of the tree is a positive node and is labeled with $\langle q_I, s_I \rangle$.
- If σ is a positive (negative) node with label $\langle q, s \rangle$ such that $\ell(q) = \neg$ and $q \rightarrow_B q'$, then σ has one negative (positive) child labeled $\langle q', s \rangle$.
- Otherwise, for a positive node σ labeled with $\langle q, s \rangle$:
  - If $\ell(q) \in \mathcal{L}$ then σ is a leaf.
  - If $\ell(q) = \wedge$ and $\{ q' \mid q \rightarrow_B q' \} = \{q_1, .. q_m\}$, then σ has positive children $\sigma_1, .., \sigma_m$, with σ_i labeled by $\langle q_i, s \rangle$.
  - If $\ell(q) = \vee$ then σ has one positive child, σ', and σ' is labeled with $\langle q', s \rangle$ for some $q' \in \{ q' \mid q \rightarrow_B q' \}$.
  - If $\ell(q) = [\Theta]$, $q \rightarrow q'$, and $\{ s' \mid s \xrightarrow{\Theta}_\mathcal{T} s' \} = \{s_1, .., s_m\}$ then σ has positive children $\sigma_1, .., \sigma_m$, with σ_i is labeled by $\langle q', s_i \rangle$.
  - If $\ell(q) = \langle \Theta \rangle$ and $q \rightarrow q'$ then σ has one positive child σ', and σ' is labeled by $\langle q', s' \rangle$ for some s' such that $s \xrightarrow{\Theta}_\mathcal{T} s'$.
- Otherwise, for a negative node σ labeled with $\langle q, s \rangle$:
  - If $\ell(q) \in \mathcal{L}$ then σ is a leaf.
  - If $\ell(q) = \wedge$ then σ has one negative child labeled with $\langle q', s \rangle$ for some $q' \in \{ q' \mid q \rightarrow_B q' \}$.
  - If $\ell(q) = \vee$ and $\{ q' \mid q \rightarrow_B q' \} = \{q_1, .. q_m\}$, then σ has negative children $\sigma_1, .., \sigma_m$, with σ_i labeled by $\langle q_i, s \rangle$.
  - If $\ell(q) = [\Theta]$ and $q \rightarrow_B q'$ then σ has one negative child σ' labeled by $\langle q', s' \rangle$ for some s' such that $s \xrightarrow{\Theta}_\mathcal{T} s'$.
  - If $\ell(q) = \langle \Theta \rangle$, $q \rightarrow_B q'$, and $\{ s' \mid s \xrightarrow{\Theta}_\mathcal{T} s' \} = \{s_1, .., s_m\}$ then σ has negative children $\sigma_1, .., \sigma_m$, with σ_i is labeled by $\langle q', s_i \rangle$.

∎

In a well-formed ABTA, every infinite path has a suffix that contains either positive or negative nodes, but not both. Such a path is referred to as *positive* in the former case and *negative* in the latter. We now define the notion of *success* of a run.

Definition 6. Let R be a run of ABTA $\mathcal{B} = \langle Q, \ell, \rightarrow_B, q_I, \mathcal{F} \rangle$ on a TS $\tilde{\mathcal{T}} = \langle S, A, \ell_S, \ell_A, \rightarrow_\mathcal{T}, s_I \rangle$.

1. A *positive leaf* labeled $\langle q, s \rangle$ is *successful* if and only if $s \models_\mathcal{T} \ell(q)$ or $\ell(q) = [\Theta]$ and $s \not\xrightarrow{\Theta}_\mathcal{T}$.

2. A *negative leaf* is *successful* if and only if $s \not\models_T \ell(q)$ or $\ell(q) = \langle\Theta\rangle$ and $s \xrightarrow{\Theta}_T$.
3. A *positive path* is *successful* if and only if for each $F \in \mathcal{F}$ some $q \in F$ occurs infinitely often.
4. A *negative path* is *successful* if and only if for some $F \in \mathcal{F}$ there is no $q \in F$ that occurs infinitely often.

Run R is *successful* if and only if every leaf and every infinite path in R is successful. TS $\mathcal{T}$ *satisfies* $\mathcal{B}$ ($\mathcal{T} \models \mathcal{B}$) if and only if there exists a successful run of $\mathcal{B}$ on $\mathcal{T}$.   ∎

It is straightforward to establish the following, where if $\mathcal{B}$ is an ABTA with state q then $\mathcal{B}[q]$ is the ABTA $\mathcal{B}$ with the start state changed to q.

Lemma 1. *Let $\mathcal{T}$ be a TS, let $\mathcal{B} = \langle Q, \ell, \longrightarrow_B, q_I, \mathcal{F}\rangle$ be an ABTA, and let $q, q' \in Q$ be such that $q \longrightarrow_B q'$ and $\ell(q) = \neg$. Then $\mathcal{T} \models \mathcal{B}[q]$ if and only if $\mathcal{T} \not\models \mathcal{B}[q']$.*

Next we define the subset of *and-restricted* ABTAs.

Definition 7. ABTA $\langle Q, \ell, \rightarrow, q_I, \mathcal{F}\rangle$ is *and-restricted* if and only if every $q \in Q$ satisfies:

1. if $\ell(q) = \wedge$ then there is at most one q' such that $q \rightarrow q'$ and $q' \rightarrow^* q$; and
2. if $\ell(q) = [\Theta]$ and $q \rightarrow q'$ then $q' \not\rightarrow^* q$.   ∎

And-restriction plays an important role in our model-checking procedure, and we comment more on it here. In an and-restricted ABTA the strongly-connected component of a state labeled by $\wedge$ can contain at most one of the state's children; a state labeled by $[\Theta]$ on the other hand is guaranteed to belong to a different strongly-connected component that its child. And-restrictedness differs from the notion of *hesitation* introduced in [23]; an ABTA would be hesitant if, roughly speaking, every strongly-connected component of a node labeled by $\wedge$ or $[\Theta]$ would contain only nodes labeled by $\wedge$ or Θ. Nevertheless, and-restrictedness plays the same role in our theory that hesitation does in [23]: automata obeying these conditions give rise to more efficient model-checking routines while still providing sufficient expressiveness to encode logics such as CTL*.

3   ABTAs and Model Checking

Checking whether or not $\mathcal{T} \models \mathcal{B}$ for TS $\mathcal{T}$ and ABTA $\mathcal{B}$ reduces to searching for the existence of a successful run of $\mathcal{B}$ on $\mathcal{T}$. This section presents an efficient on-the-fly algorithm for this check in the setting of and-restricted ABTAs.

3.1   TSs, ABTAs, and Product Graphs

Our ABTA model-checking algorithm works by exploring the "product graph" of an ABTA and a TS. In what follows, fix ABTA $\mathcal{B} = \langle Q, \ell, \longrightarrow_B, q_I, \mathcal{F}\rangle$ and TS $\mathcal{T} = \langle S, A, \ell_S, \ell_A, \longrightarrow_T, s_I\rangle$, and assume that $\mathcal{F} = \{F_0, \ldots F_{n-1}\}$. The *product graph* of $\mathcal{B}$ and $\mathcal{T}$ has vertex set $V = Q \times S \times \{0, \ldots, n-1\}$ and edges $E \subseteq V \times V$ defined by $(\langle q, s, i\rangle, \langle q', s', i'\rangle) \in E$ if and only if:

- there exist nodes σ and σ' in some run of $\mathcal{B}$ on $\mathcal{T}$ labeled $\langle q, s\rangle$ and $\langle q', s'\rangle$ respectively and such that $\sigma \rightarrow \sigma'$; and
- either $q \notin F_i$ and $i' = i$, or $q \in F_i$ and $i' = (i + 1) \bmod n$.

$E_N \subseteq E$ consists of those edges $(\langle q, s, i \rangle, \langle q', s', i' \rangle)$ such that q and q' are in different strongly-connected components in $\mathcal{B}$, while $E_R = E - E_N$. We sometimes refer to E_N as the *nonrecursive* relation and to E_R as the *recursive* relation. A vertex $\langle q, s, i \rangle$ in the product graph is said to be *accepting* if and only if $q \in \mathcal{F}_0$ and $i = 0$.

3.2 Searching the Product Graph

We now present an algorithm for determining if the product graph mentioned above contains a successful run in the case that the ABTA $\mathcal{B}$ is and-restricted. The routine is based on the memory-efficient on-the-fly algorithm for emptiness-checking of Büchi word automata in [15]; as is the case in that algorithm our goal is to eliminate the storage penalty associated with the "strongly-connected component" algorithms [23]. The alterations are necessitated by the fact that ABTAs contain conjunctive as well as disjunctive states and are intended to accept TSs (i.e. trees) rather than words.

Like the algorithm in [15] ours employs two depth-first searches, DFS1 and DFS2, that attempt to mark nodes as either true or false. The purpose of the former is to search for true and false leaves in the product graph, and to "restart" the latter whenever an accepting node is found. The latter determines whether or not the node given to it is reachable from itself via nodes not previously traversed by DFS2. The success of DFS2 has implications for the existence of runs with successful paths. Pseudo-code for the these procedures may be found in the appendix.

When exploring $v = \langle q, s, i \rangle$, DFS1 uses the label of q in $\mathcal{B}$ and the transitions from s in $\mathcal{T}$ to guide its search. The non-recursive successors of v are processed first via recursive calls to DFS1; if the results do not immediately imply the truth or falsity of v, then DFS1 is called recursively on v's recursive children. (Note that this simplifies the treatment of negation: no explicit treatment of "infinite negative paths" is necessary in the algorithm. Also note that since ABTAs are and-restricted, all but one of the children of a node labeled by $\wedge$ can have their truth values determined by recursive calls to DFS1. This latter fact is crucial to the correctness of our algorithm.) If these results are inconclusive, and v is accepting, then DFS2 is called to determine if v is reachable from itself. If this is the case, then v is labeled as true. (DFS2 cycles involving FALSE states are, of course, not allowed).

A subtlety arises in our setting when a recursive child v' of v has been visited previously by DFS1 and v' has not been marked true or false. The node v' cannot necessarily be assumed to be false, as is implicitly done in [15], because there may be a successful cycle in the same strongly-connected component as it that was not detected until after DFS1 (v') terminated. To avoid needless recomputation in this case, we maintain a *dependency* set for each node; these sets contain nodes that should become true if the indicated node is found to be true. In the example above we would insert v into the dependency set of v'; if v' is later marked as true, then v would be as well.

Theorem 8. DFS1 $(\langle q_I, s_I, 0 \rangle)$ *returns "true" if and only if* $\mathcal{T} \models \mathcal{B}$.

Theorem 9. *Let* $\mathcal{B} = \langle Q, \ell, \longrightarrow_B, q_I, \mathcal{F} \rangle$ *be an ABTA and* $\mathcal{T} = \langle S, A, \ell_S, \ell_A, \longrightarrow_T , s_I \rangle$ *be a TS. Then* DFS1 $(q_I, s_I, 0)$ *runs in time linear in the size of the product graph of* $\mathcal{B}$ *and* $\mathcal{T}$, *whose vertex set is bounded in size by* $|Q| \cdot |S| \cdot |\mathcal{F}|$, *where* $|\mathcal{F}|$ *is the number of component sets in* $\mathcal{F}$.

4   Reducing ABTAs

The previous theorem indicates that the time needed to check whether or not $\mathcal{T} \models \mathcal{B}$ depends intimately on the number of states in $\mathcal{B}$. Consequently, any preprocessing that reduces the number of states in $\mathcal{B}$ can have a significant impact on model-checker performance. In this section we present several heuristics that may be used to eliminate states in ABTAs.

Büchi State Set Minimalization. The ABTA acceptance condition specifies that an infinite (positive) path in a run is successful if and only if that path contains an infinite number of states from each of the sets of accepting states. This can only occur when a cycle in the ABTA contains at least one state from each set of accepting states. Moreover, a state not part of any such cycle can safely be removed from all member sets in $\mathcal{F}$, since no infinite path going through that state can satisfy the Büchi condition.

To check for such states we perform a depth-first search for cycles that contain at least one member of each set of accepting states. If for a particular state such a cycle does not exist, that state is removed from all accepting sets that contain it. While not reducing the size of the ABTA directly, this transformation is important for two reasons.

1. *It improves the performance of other reductions.* Some of the other reductions may only be applied to states that are members of the same accepting sets. Eliminating states from accepting sets improves their performance.
2. *The size of the product automaton is reduced.* Each state in the product graph contains an index reflecting the member set of $\mathcal{F}$ "currently" being searched for. This search procedure is unnecessary for states not having the kind of cycle just described; by removing these states from acceptance sets, unnecessary vertices associated with this search can be avoided.

Constant Propagation. Some atomic state propositions are uniformly true or false of all TS states, and these values can be propagated upwards as far as possible.

Associative Joining. Because $\vee$ and $\wedge$ are associative we can also apply another reduction: for any $\wedge(\vee)$-labeled state q with a transition to another $\wedge(\vee)$-labeled state q', where q and q' are in the same sets of accepting states, remove the transition from q to q' and add outgoing transitions from q to every state to which q' had a transition. This is applied recursively (if q' has a transition to another $\wedge(\vee)$-labeled state q'' we also add its outgoing transitions to q, and so forth). This has two benefits: (1) the state q' may become unreachable and hence removable, thereby reducing ABTA size and (2) model checking avoids passing through q' (and q'', etc.) in the depth-first searches starting from q. Because q and q' must be in the same sets of accepting states, this simplification is much more effective performed after accepting-state set minimalization.

Quotienting via Bisimulation. The final simplification involves merging states with the same "structure." We do this using bisimulation [26]. Specifically, we alter the traditional definition of bisimulation to take account of state labels and acceptance set information, and we then quotient $\mathcal{B}$ by this equivalence. To ensure maximum reduction this should always be the last simplification applied.

5 Translating Temporal Formulas into ABTAs

A virtue of ABTA-based model checking is that translation procedures for temporal logics into ABTAs may be defined abstractly via "proof rules." This section illustrates this idea via an example, by giving the rules needed to translate a variant of CTL* into ABTAs. The logic, which we call *Generalized CTL** (GCTL*), extends CTL* by allowing formulas to constrain actions as well as states. While the logic itself is not very novel, it does contain "deviations" from CTL* that typically require alterations to a CTL* model checker. Our intention is to show that proof-rule-based translations, coupled with generic ABTA technology, can make it easier to define such "alterations".

The syntax for our logic is given below, where $p \in \mathcal{A}$ and $\theta \in \mathcal{A}_{\text{act}}$.

$$S ::= p \mid \neg p \mid S \wedge S \mid S \vee S \mid A\mathcal{P} \mid E\mathcal{P}$$
$$\mathcal{P} ::= \theta \mid \neg \theta \mid S \mid \mathcal{P} \wedge \mathcal{P} \mid \mathcal{P} \vee \mathcal{P} \mid X\mathcal{P} \mid \mathcal{P}U\mathcal{P} \mid \mathcal{P}V\mathcal{P}$$

The formulas generated by S are *state* formulas, while those generated by $\mathcal{P}$ are *path* formulas. The state formulas constitute the formulas of GCTL*. In what follows we use $\psi, \psi', \psi_1, \ldots$ to range over state formulas and $\phi, \phi', \phi_1, \ldots$ to range over path formulas.

Semantically, the logic departs from traditional CTL* in two respects. Firstly, the paths that path formulas are interpreted over have the form $s_0 \xrightarrow{\alpha_1} s_1 \xrightarrow{\alpha_2} \cdots$ and thus contain actions as well as states. Secondly, as TSs may contain deadlocked states some provision must be made for finite maximal paths as models. The GCTL* semantics follows a standard convention in temporal logic by allowing the last state in a finite maximal path to "loop" to itself; the action component of these implicit transitions is assumed to violate all atomic action propositions $\theta \in \mathcal{A}_{\text{act}}$.

Mathematically, a state satisfies $A\phi$ ($E\phi$) if every execution (some execution) emanating from the state satisfies ϕ. An execution satisfies a state formula if the initial state in the execution does, and it satisfies θ if the execution contains at least one transition and the label of the first transition on the path satisfies θ. A path satisfies $\neg\theta$ if either the first transition on the path is labeled by an action not satisfying θ or the path has no transitions. X represents the "next-time operator" and has the usual semantics when the path is not deadlocked. A deadlocked path of form s satisfies $X\Phi$ if s satisfies Φ. $\phi_1 U \phi_2$ holds of a path if ϕ_1 remains true until ϕ_2 becomes true. The constructor V may be thought of as a "release operator"; a path satisfies $\phi_1 V \phi_2$ if ϕ_2 remains true until ϕ_1 "releases" the path from the obligation. This operator is the dual of the until operator. The details of the semantics are standard and omitted.

In GCTL* X is self-dual. Thus, while the application of negation is restricted in this logic we nevertheless have the following.

Lemma 2. *Let ψ be a state formula in GCTL*. Then there exists a formula* neg(ψ) *such that any state in any TS satisfies* neg(ψ) *if and only if it does not satisfy ψ.*

Our approach to generating ABTAs from GCTL* formulas uses goal-directed rules to construct tableaux from formulas. These rules operate on "formulas" of the form $E\Phi$ and $A\Phi$, where Φ is a set of path formulas. Intuitively, these terms are short-hand for $E(\bigwedge_{\phi \in \Phi} \phi)$ and $A(\bigvee_{\phi \in \Phi} \phi)$, respectively. We also call a set Θ of action literals *positive* if it contains some $\theta \in \mathcal{A}_{\text{act}}$. Otherwise it is referred to as *negative*. We use $\Psi, \Psi_1, \ldots \ldots$ and $\Gamma, \Gamma_1, \ldots$ to denote positive sets and negative sets respectively.

$$R1 \ \wedge : \ \frac{\psi_1 \wedge \psi_2}{\psi_1 \ \ \psi_2} \qquad R2 \ \vee : \ \frac{\psi_1 \vee \psi_2}{\psi_1 \ \ \psi_2} \qquad R3 \ \vee : \ \frac{E(\psi)}{\psi}$$

$$R4 \ \neg : \ \frac{\neg\psi}{\psi} \qquad R5 \ \neg : \ \frac{A(\Phi)}{E(neg\ \Phi)}$$

$$R6 \ \wedge : \ \frac{E(\Phi, \psi)}{E(\Phi) \ \ E(\psi)} \qquad R7 \ \wedge : \ \frac{E(\Phi, \phi_1 \wedge \phi_2)}{E(\Phi, \phi_1, \phi_2)} \qquad R8 \ \vee : \ \frac{E(\Phi, \phi_1 \vee \phi_2)}{E(\Phi, \phi_1) \ \ E(\Phi, \phi_2)}$$

$$R9 \ \vee : \ \frac{E(\Phi, \phi_1 \vee \phi_2)}{E(\Phi, \phi_1, \phi_2) \ \ E(\Phi, \phi_2, X(\phi_1 \vee \phi_2))} \qquad R10 \ \vee : \ \frac{E(\Phi, \phi_1 \cup \phi_2)}{E(\Phi, \phi_2) \ \ E(\Phi, \phi_1, X(\phi_1 \cup \phi_2))}$$

$$R11 \ \langle \Psi \rangle : \ \frac{E(\Psi, X\phi_1, \ldots, X\phi_n)}{E(\phi_1, \ldots, \phi_n)} \qquad R12 \ \langle\langle \Gamma \rangle\rangle : \ \frac{E(\Gamma, X\phi_1, \ldots, X\phi_n)}{E(\phi_1, \ldots, \phi_n)}$$

Ψ is a positive set of action literals, while Γ is a negative set.

Fig. 1. Tableau Rules for GCTL*.

To construct an ABTA for state formula ψ one first generates the states and transitions. Intuitively states will correspond to state formulas, with the initial state being ψ itself. To generate new states from an existing state ψ', one applies the rules in Figure 1 to ψ' in the order specified. That is, one determines which of R1–12 is applicable to ψ', beginning with R1, by comparing the form of ψ' to the formula appearing in the "goal position" of each rule. The label of the rule then becomes the label of the state, and the subgoals of the rule are then added as states (if necessary), and transitions from ψ' to these states added. Leaves are labeled by the state literals they contain. This procedure is repeated until no new states are added; it is guaranteed to terminate [6].

For notational simplicity we have introduced a new label in Rule R12. Intuitively, if an ABTA state is labeled $\langle\langle \Gamma \rangle\rangle$ then it behaves like $\langle \Gamma \rangle$ for nondeadlocked TS states. For deadlocked states, the state is required to satisfy the single descendant. This operator can be encoded using the other ABTA constructs.

To define the acceptance condition $\mathcal{F}$, suppose $\phi \equiv \phi_1 \cup \phi_2 \in q$ and let $F_\phi = \{ q' \in Q \mid (\phi \notin q' \ and \ X\phi \notin q') \ or \ \phi_2 \in q' \}$. Then $\mathcal{F} = \{ F_\phi \mid \phi \equiv \phi_1 \cup \phi_2 \ and \ \exists q \in Q. \phi \in q \}$. We now have the following [6].

Theorem 10. *Let ψ be a GCTL* formula and let $\mathcal{B}_\psi$ be the BTA obtained by the translation procedure described above. Then the following hold.*

1. *$\mathcal{B}_\psi$ is and-restricted.*
2. *Let $\mathcal{T} \equiv \langle S, \rightarrow, L, s_0 \rangle$ be a TS. Then $s_0 \models_{\mathcal{T}} p$ if and only if $\mathcal{T}$ is accepted by $\mathcal{B}_p$.*

In general B_ψ will be exponential in the size of ψ. However, if ψ falls within the GCTL* fragment of GCTL*, then B_ψ is linear in the size of ψ.

We close this section with some comments on and-restrictedness. Our model-checking routine only works on and-restricted ABTAs, which means that the rule-based approach described above for producing model checkers only works if the rules generate and-restricted ABTAs. In practice this means that in rules labeled by $\wedge$, at most one subgoal can be "recursive", i.e. can include the formula identified in the goal. For temporal logics based on CTL* this restriction is not problematic, since the recursive characterizations of standard modalities only involve one "recursive call". For logics such as the mu-calculus in which arbitrary recursive properties may be specified the relevant rules would not satisfy this restriction, and the approach advocated in this paper would not be applicable. (It should be noted, however, that sublogics of the mu-calculus, such as the L2 fragment identified in [17], do fit into our framework.)

6 Implementation and Empirical Assessment

To assess our ideas in practice we implemented ABTAs in the CWB-NC verification tool [12]. The procedures we coded (in Standard ML) included: basic ABTA manipulation routines (819 lines); the ABTA model-checking routine given in Section 3 (631 lines); and ABTA simplification routines described in Section 4 (654 lines). The routines made heavy use of existing CWB-NC data structures for manipulating automata. This code is "generic" in the sense that it would be used by any ABTA-based model checker implemented in the CWB-NC.

We also implemented a front-end for GCTL* using the Process Algebra Compiler (PAC) [13], a parser- and semantic-routine generator for the CWB-NC. We used sets of actions as atomic action propositions and included only "true" and "false" as atomic state propositions, with with obvious interpretations. The code for the front-end included 214 lines of yacc and 605 lines of auxiliary code, with most of the latter being devoted to the calculation of acceptance-set information and the implementation of Rule 5 in Figure 1. It should be noted that of this code, approximately 15% is GCTL* specific; the rest could also be used defining e.g. a CTL* model checker.

To study the performance of our implementation we used two existing case studies included in the current distribution of the CWB-NC to compare our generic ABTA-based model checker for GCTL* with the model checker for the L2 fragment of the mu-calculus that is included in the CWB-NC release. The systems studied included a rendering of the SCSI-2 Bus Protocol [7] and a description of the Slow-Scan fault-tolerant communications protocol [11]. In both applications mu-calculus formulas encode key properties of the systems in question. We used the existing models but translated the formulas in question into GCTL*; we then ran our ABTA-based model checker for GCTL* in order to compare its efficiency with the CWB-NC's mu-calculus checker. We also performed a deadlock-freedom check in both logics as well.

The properties included several involving fairness constraints. Emblematic of these is Property 2 in [7], which asserts that any phase in the SCSI-2 protocol eventually ends, provided the initiator in the protocol does not repeatedly issue an ATN signal. This property may be encoded in GCTL* as follows

AG({@begin_Phase} ⇒ (F{@end_Phase}∨GF{@obs_setATN, @obsplace}))

This formula asserts that along all paths, whenever the action @begin_Phase occurs, then either the action @end_Phase is performed or at least one of the actions @obs_setATN and @obsplace occurs infinitely often. (The @obspace action is needed for reasons relating to the modeling.) The corresponding mu-calculus used in the case study is given below.

$$\neg(\mu X.(\texttt{@begin\_Phase})(\mu Y.\nu Z.(\texttt{@begin\_Phase})\texttt{tt} \vee (\texttt{@end\_Phase})X \vee$$
$$\langle -\{\texttt{@obsplace},\texttt{@obs\_setATN},\texttt{@end\_Phase}\}\rangle Z \vee$$
$$(\{\texttt{@obsplace},\texttt{@obs\_setATN}\})Y) \vee \langle -\{\texttt{@begin\_Phase}\}\rangle X)$$

Table 1. SCSI-2 Performance Data for ABTA Model Checker. All times are in seconds.

Reference # in [7]	Unsimplified ABTA size	Simplified ABTA size	ABTA Time	Mu-calculus Time
1	42	24	2739.670	3423.990
2	54	8	533.400	1022.430
3	12	8	676.220	542.180
4	12	8	401.300	483.470
5	42	20	410.540	943.560
6	57	8	509.420	984.600
NoDeadlock	7	5	593.240	704.850

Tables 1 and 2 give our experimental results. For each of the formulas we record: the size of the ABTA before and after simplication, and the running times of the ABTA-based GCTL* model checker and the CWB-NC model checker on the equivalent mu-calculus formula. Timing information was collected on a Sun Enterprise E450 with two 336 MHz processors and 2 GB of main memory. Some comments are in order.

- Some ABTA state-space reduction is due to our encoding of the constructs F and G in terms of U and V. These encodings use constants tt ("true") and ff ("false"), which constant-propagation then eliminates. Introducing explicit rules for these constructs would yield smaller initial ABTAs at the expense of a larger set of rules.
- The papers [7] and [11] describes several different models. In each case we used the largest: 62,000, and 12,000 states, respectively.
- The mu-calculus model-checker implements the on-the-fly algorithm given in [5, 17], which runs in $O(|M| \cdot |\phi| \cdot ad(\phi))$, where $|M|$ is the size of the system, $|\phi|$ the size of the formula, and $ad(\phi)$ the alternation depth of ϕ.
- In the SCSI-2 example, Formulas 2, 5 and 6 involve fairness constraints, with 2 and 6 having the same shape. Formulas 1, 3 and 4 are safety properties, with 3 and 4 having the same shape. Thus, the minimized automata for 2 and 6 have the same number of states, as do 3 and 4. That 2 and 3 have the same size is a coincidence.
- In the Slow-Scan example, only Formulas 1, 2, 8 and 9 involve fairness.
- Because the translation procedure in Figure 1 treats A by dualizing it (i.e. converting it into $\neg E \neg$), the ABTA for deadlock-freedom has more states than usual.

Based on the figures in the tables, we can draw the following conclusions.

1. *The ABTA checker dramatically outperforms the mu-calculus checker on formulas involving fairness.* The factor by which the time required by the latter exceeded that needed by the former ranged from 1.9 (SCSI-2 Property 6) to 5.3 (Slow-Scan Property 9), with the average being 3.1. This behavior is a result of the fact that due to the fairness constraints, the mu-calculus formulas all have alternation-depth 2, and the time-complexity of the mu-calculus routine is affected by alternation depth.

2. *The ABTA model checker also outperforms the mu-calculus checker for safety properties.* In all but two cases the ABTA routine outperforms the mu-calculus routine, with the over-all average improvement factor being 1.6.

Table 2. Slow-Scan Performance Data for ABTA Model Checker. All times are in seconds.

Name	Reference # in [11]	Unsimplified ABTA size	Simplified ABTA size	ABTA Time	Mu-calculus Time
failures-responded	1	52	13	2.890	13.600
failures-responded-again	2	59	16	144.720	471.780
can-tick	3	12	8	205.580	328.430
failures-possible	4	5	4	0.020	0.080
failures-possible-again	5	14	9	118.790	189.380
no-false-alarms	6	7	5	1.670	2.760
no-false-alarms-again	7	14	8	139.210	221.540
eventually-silent	8	92	14	159.710	409.190
react-on-repair	9	26	10	137.630	729.550
no-deadlock	-	7	5	205.930	200.220

7 Related Work

Alternating tree automata are studied extensively as a basis for branching-time model checking in [23]. However, ABTAs differ from the automata in [23] in ways that we believe ease their use in practice; we summarize these below.

Transition relation: In [23] the authors embed propositional constructs inside the transition relation. In ABTAs propositional constructs are used to label states. This offers advantages when ABTAs are simplified; for example, we may use the traditional notion of bisimulation equivalence to minimize ABTAs.

Negation: The automata in [23] do not use negation in the definition of transitions; ABTAs do allow the use of a negation operator to label states. This allows the acceptance component of an ABTA to be simpler ("Büchi-like") than the Rabin condition in [23] and also simplifies the model-checking algorithm.

Algorithm: Because of our Büchi-like condition and our consideration of and-restricted ABTAs, we are able to adapt the memory-efficient on-the-fly algorithm of [15], which is also time-efficient. The time-efficient algorithm of [23] relies on the construction of strongly-connected components, which our algorithm avoids.

We reiterate that and-restricted alternating automata differ markedly from hesitant alternating automata as introduced in [23]. In particular, and-restricted ABTAs require no definition of "levels of weakness" or classification of states as existential/universal. The price we must pay is that "recursion through ∧" is limited.

Another alternating-tree-automaton-based approach to model checking may be found in [30]. The algorithm relies on the use of games to avoid the construction of the strongly-connected components used in [23]. An implementation is described in [31].

Methods for simplifying Büchi word automata have been given in [19, 28]. The papers both present simulation-based techniques for reducing the number of states in such automata, and [28] shows how acceptance sets for generalized Büchi automata may be reduced. Neither paper considers alternating or tree automata.

The mu-calculus [22] has also been proposed as an intermediate language for translation-based model checking [3, 6, 16, 18]. Tool support for this translational-scheme remains problematic, however, owing in part to the complexity of the translation procedures for logics like CTL*. Our performance figures also suggest that the alternation-depth factor in mu-calculus model-checking algorithms has practical impacts: our ABTA model-checker significantly outperforms the mu-calculus checker on formulas with nontrivial alternation-depth.

8 Conclusions and Directions for Future Research

This paper presents a generic approach to building model-checkers that relies on the use of intermediate structures called alternating Büchi tableau automata. These automata support efficient model checking and simplification routines, and they also admit the definition of abstract proof-rule-based translation procedures for temporal formulas into ABTAs. This eases the task of retargeting a model-checker, since one need only specify the translation into ABTAs of the logic in question. We demonstrated the utility of our ideas by developing a translation-based model checker for a variant of CTL*.

As future work we would like to develop automated support for the generation of ABTA translators from proof rules and high-level specifications of acceptance conditions. We are also interested in an efficient model-checking algorithm for all AB-TAs, and we would like to investigate compositional techniques for ABTAs based on the partial-model-checking ideas of [4]. Finally, it would be interesting to adapt the simulation-based automaton simplifications presented in [19, 28] to ABTAs.

References

1. *LICS '86*, Cambridge, Massachusetts, June 1986. IEEE Computer Society Press.
2. R. Alur, C. Courcoubetis, and D. Dill. Model-checking for real-time systems. In *LICS '90*, pages 414–425, Philadelphia, Jun. 1990. IEEE Computer Society Press.
3. H.R. Andersen. Model checking and boolean graphs. *TCS*, 126(1):3–30, Apr. 1994.
4. H.R. Andersen. Partial model checking. In *LICS '95*, pages 398–407, San Diego, Jul. 1995. IEEE Computer Society Press.
5. G. Bhat and R. Cleaveland. Efficient local model checking for fragments of the modal μ-calculus. In T. Margaria and B. Steffen, eds., *TACAS '96*, *LNCS* 1055:107–126, Passau, Mar. 1996. Springer-Verlag.
6. G. Bhat and R. Cleaveland. Efficient model checking via the equational μ-calculus. In *LICS '96*, pages 304–312, New Brunswick, Jul. 1996. IEEE Computer Society Press.
7. G. Bhat, R. Cleaveland, and G. Luettgen. A practical approach to implementing real-time semantics. *Annals of Software Engineering*, 7:127–155, Oct. 1999.
8. J.R. Burch, E.M. Clarke, K.L. McMillan, D.L. Dill, and L.J. Hwang. Symbolic model checking: 10^{20} states and beyond. *Information and Computation*, 98(2):142–170, Jun. 1992.
9. E.M. Clarke, E.A. Emerson, and A.P. Sistla. Automatic verification of finite-state concurrent systems using temporal logic specifications. *ACM TOPLAS*, 8(2):244–263, Apr. 1986.
10. E.M. Clarke and J.M. Wing. Formal methods: state of the art and future directions. *ACM Computing Surveys*, 28(4):626–643, Dec. 1996.
11. R. Cleaveland, G. Luettgen, V. Natarajan, and S. Sims. Modeling and verifying distributed systems using priorities: A case study. *Software Concepts and Tools*, 17(2):50–62, 1996.

12. R. Cleaveland and S. Sims. The NCSU Concurrency Workbench. In R. Alur and T. Henzinger, eds., *CAV '96*, *LNCS* 1102:394–397, New Brunswick, Jul. 1996. Springer-Verlag.
13. R. Cleaveland and S. Sims. Generic tools for verifying concurrent systems. *Science of Computer Programming*, to appear.
14. R. Cleaveland and B. Steffen. A linear-time model-checking algorithm for the alternation-free modal mu-calculus. *Formal Methods in System Design*, 2:121–147, 1993.
15. C. Courcoubetis, M.Y. Vardi, P. Wolper, and M. Yannakakis. Memory efficient algorithms for verification of temporal properties. *Formal Methods in System Design*, 1:275–288, 1992.
16. M. Dam. CTL* and ECTL* as fragments of the modal mu-calculus. *TCS*, 126(1):77–96, Apr. 1994.
17. E.A. Emerson, C. Jutla, and A.P. Sistla. On model-checking for fragments of μ-calculus. In C. Courcoubetis, ed., *CAV '93*, *LNCS* 697:385–396, Elounda, Jul. 1993. Springer-Verlag.
18. E.A. Emerson and C.-L. Lei. Efficient model checking in fragments of the propositional mu-calculus. In [1], pages 267–278.
19. K. Etessami and G. Holzmann. Optimizing buechi automata. In C. Palamidessi, ed., *CON-CUR 2000*, *LNCS* 1877:153–169, State College, Aug. 2000. Springer-Verlag.
20. R. Gerth, D. Peled, M. Vardi, and P. Wolper. Simple on-the-fly automatic verification of linear temporal logic. In *PSTV '95*, pages 3–18, Warsaw, Jun. 1995. Chapman and Hall.
21. G.J. Holzmann. *Design and Validation of Computer Protocols*. Prentice-Hall, 1991.
22. D. Kozen. Results on the propositional μ-calculus. *TCS*, 27(3):333–354, Dec. 1983.
23. O. Kupferman, M.Y. Vardi, and P. Wolper. An automata-theoretic approach to branching-time model checking. *JACM*, 47(2):312–360, Mar. 2000.
24. K. Larsen, P. Pettersson, and W. Yi. UPPAAL in a nutshell. *Software Tools for Technology Transfer*, 1(1+2):134–152, Oct. 1997.
25. R. Mateescu and H. Garavel. XTL: A meta-language and tool for temporal logic model-checking. In T. Margaria and B. Steffen, eds., *STTT'98*, Aalborg, Jul. 1998.
26. R. Milner. *Communication and Concurrency*. Prentice-Hall, London, 1989.
27. J.P. Queille and J. Sifakis. Specification and verification of concurrent systems in CESAR. In M. Dezani-Ciancaglini and U. Montanari, eds., *Proc. Int. Symp. in Programming*, *LNCS* 137: 337–351, Turin, Apr. 1982. Springer-Verlag.
28. F. Somenzi and R. Bloem. Efficient Büchi automata from LTL formulae. In E.A. Emerson and A.P. Sistla, eds., *CAV 2000*, *LNCS* 1855:247–263, Chicago, Jul. 2000. Springer-Verlag.
29. M. Vardi and P. Wolper. An automata-theoretic approach to automatic program verification. In [1], pages 332–344.
30. W. Visser and H. Barringer. Practical CTL* model checking - should SPIN be extended? *Software Tools for Technology Transfer*, 2(4):350–365, Apr. 2000.
31. W. Visser, H. Barringer, D. Fellows, G. Gough, and A. Williams. Efficient CTL* model checking for analysis of rainbow designs. In H. Li and D. Probst, eds., *CHARME'97*, pages 128–145, Montréal, Oct. 1997. IFIP WG 10.5, Chapman and Hall.
32. J. Yang, A. Mok, and Farn Wang. Symbolic model checking for event-driven real-time systems. *ACM TOPLAS* 19(2):386–412, Mar. 1997.

A   Pseudo-Code for ABTA Model Checking

```
DFS2 (v = ⟨q, s, i⟩,  v' = ⟨q', s', i'⟩) : bool =
    mark v visited by DFS2.
    C_r := {v_r ∈ V | E_R(v, v_r)}.
    if v' ∈ C_r then return TRUE.
    foreach v_r ∈ C_r s.t. v_r not marked FALSE do
        if v_r not marked visited by DFS2 then
            if DFS2(v_r, v') then return TRUE.
    return FALSE.
```

```
markAndPropagate (v=⟨q,s,i⟩, val : bool) : bool =
  if not val then return FALSE.
  mark v TRUE.
  foreach v' ∈ Depend(v) do
    remove v' from Depend(v);
    markAndPropagate (v', TRUE).
  return TRUE.

DFS1 (v=⟨q,s,i⟩) : bool =
  if v marked TRUE then return TRUE.
  mark v visited by DFS1.
  cₙ := {v' ∈ Q | Eₙ(v,v')}.
  cᵣ := {v' ∈ Q | Eᵣ(v,v')}.
  case (ℓ(q)):
    p ∈ A:
        return (markAndPropagate (v, s ∈ ℓₛ(p)))).
    ¬:
        foreach vₙ ∈ cₙ do
          return (markAndPropagate (v, not DFS1(vₙ))).
    [Θ], ∧:
        foreach vₙ ∈ cₙ do
            if not DFS1(vₙ) then return FALSE.
        if cᵣ = ∅ then
            return (markAndPropagate (v, TRUE)).
        for the vᵣ ∈ cᵣ do
            if vᵣ marked visited by DFS1 then
                insert v in Depend(vᵣ).
            else
                if DFS1(vᵣ) then
                    return (markAndPropagate (v, TRUE)).
        if (accepting(v)) then
            return (markAndPropagate (v, DFS2(v,v))).
        return FALSE.
    ∨, ⟨Θ⟩:
        foreach vₙ ∈ cₙ do
          if DFS1(vₙ) then
              return (markAndPropagate (v, TRUE)).
        foreach vᵣ ∈ cᵣ do
          if vᵣ marked visited by DFS1 then
              insert v in Depend(vᵣ).
          else
              if DFS1(vᵣ) then
                  return (markAndPropagate (v, TRUE))
        if (accepting(v)) then
            return (markAndPropagate (v, DFS2(v,v))).
        return FALSE.
```

Fast LTL to Büchi Automata Translation

Paul Gastin and Denis Oddoux

LIAFA, Université Paris 7, Paris, France
{Paul.Gastin,Denis.Oddoux}@liafa.jussieu.fr

Abstract. We present an algorithm to generate Büchi automata from
LTL formulae. This algorithm generates a very weak alternating co-Büchi
automaton and then transforms it into a Büchi automaton, using a generalized Büchi automaton as an intermediate step. Each automaton is
simplified on-the-fly in order to save memory and time. As usual we
simplify the LTL formula before any treatment. We implemented this
algorithm and compared it with Spin: the experiments show that our
algorithm is much more efficient than Spin. The criteria of comparison
are the size of the resulting automaton, the time of the computation and
the memory used. Our implementation is available on the web at the
following address: http://verif.liafa.jussieu.fr/ltl2ba

1 Introduction

To prove that a program satisfies some property, a standard method is to use
Linear Time Logic (LTL) model checking. When the property is expressed with
an LTL formula, the model checker usually transforms the negation of this formula into a Büchi automaton, builds the product of that automaton with the
program, and checks this product for emptiness. In this paper we focus on the
generation of a Büchi automaton from an LTL formula, trying to improve the
time and space of the computation and the size of the resulting automaton.

Spin [4] is a very popular LTL model checker. However, the algorithm it
uses to generate a Büchi automaton from an LTL formula, presented in [3],
may be quite slow and may need a large amount of memory, even for some
usual LTL formulae. In particular, this algorithm has a very bad behavior on
formulae with fairness conditions: it is almost impossible to use Spin to generate
a Büchi automaton from a formula containing 5 or more fairness conditions,
both because of the computation time and of the memory needed. For example,
consider a simple response formula $G(q \rightarrow F r)$ with n fairness conditions:

$$\theta_n = \neg((G F p_1 \wedge \ldots \wedge G F p_n) \rightarrow G(q \rightarrow F r)) . \tag{1}$$

A formula of this type is very often encountered in LTL model checking. Moreover, the fairness conditions and the right-hand side property are usually more
complex. The value of n is very often greater than 5. Alas, in this case, Spin
fails to produce the Büchi automaton within a reasonable amount of time and
memory (see Table 1).

G. Berry, H. Comon, and A. Finkel (Eds.): CAV 2001, LNCS 2102, pp. 53–65, 2001.
© Springer-Verlag Berlin Heidelberg 2001

Table 1. Comparison on the Formulae θ_n for $1 \leq n \leq 10$. Time is in sec, space in kB. (N/A): no answer from the server within 24 h. ($\dagger$): the program died, giving no result.

	Spin		Wring		EQLTL	LTL2BA–		LTL2BA	
	time	space	time	space	time	time	space	time	space
θ_1	0.18	460	0.56	4,100	16	0.01	9	0.01	9
θ_2	4.6	4,200	2.6	4,100	16	0.01	19	0.01	11
θ_3	170	52,000	16	4,200	18	0.01	86	0.01	19
θ_4	9,600	970,000	110	4,700	25	0.07	336	0.06	38
θ_5			1,000	6,500	135	0.70	1,600	0.37	48
θ_6			8,400	13,000	N/A	12	8,300	4.0	88
θ_7			$72,000^\dagger$	$43,000^\dagger$		220	44,000	32	175
θ_8						4,200	260,000	360	250
θ_9						97,000	1,600,000	3,000	490
θ_{10}								36,000	970

Spin's algorithm was improved by [1] (LTL2AUT), [2] (EQLTL), [10] (Wring): these papers did not modify the basis of the algorithm, but improved it using the same core algorithm, rewriting LTL formulae, and simplifying the resulting Büchi automaton. These improvements are quite efficient but the actual transformation of the LTL formula to a Büchi automaton, which is similar to the tableau construction explained in [3], may still perform badly on some natural formulae such as θ_n. Some experiments are presented in Table 1. Note that Wring is written in Perl while Spin and LTL2BA are written in C and that EQLTL is used through a web server. Hence the figures are still relevant but should not be compared litterally. See Sect. 7 for more details.

In this paper, we present a new algorithm to generate a Büchi automaton from an LTL formula. Our algorithm is not based on the tableau construction presented in [3]. Instead, using the classical construction (see e.g. [12]), we first produce an alternating automaton from the LTL formula, with n states where n is less than the size of the formula. This alternating automaton turns out to be *very weak* as shown by Rohde [9]. Thanks to that property, instead of generating directly a Büchi automaton with $2^n \times 2^n$ states, we are able to build first a generalized Büchi automaton, that is a Büchi automaton with labels and accepting conditions on transitions instead of states, with at most 2^n states. Using a generalized Büchi automaton is one of the most important improvements of our algorithm. The best solution would be to design a model-checking algorithm using directly this generalized Büchi automaton, but in order to compare our work with other ones and to use existing model-checking algorithms, we transform this automaton into a classical Büchi automaton. The method we use is very classical, and we obtain a Büchi automaton with at most $n \times 2^n$ states.

The second main improvement stems from our simplifications of the automata. Since our construction goes in several steps, we are able to simplify the automata at each step, improving the efficiency of the following steps. The simplifications dramatically reduce the number of states and transitions of the automata, especially of the generalized Büchi automaton. Moreover, each simplification is performed on-the-fly during the construction of each automaton. This is a major improvement on a posteriori simplifications. The amount of memory used is about the size of the simplified automaton, instead of being the size of the unsimplified automaton which may be quite huge. The time needed is also reduced dramatically because we are exploring a much smaller part of the automaton during the construction.

Using our new algorithm, we built a tool which is available on the web at http://verif.liafa.jussieu.fr/ltl2ba. Our tool is much more efficient than any other tool we have tried, in computation time and especially in memory. The results of our algorithm on the formulae θ_n with on-the-fly simplifications (LTL2BA) and with a posteriori simplifications (LTL2BA−) are detailed in Table 1. More experimental results are presented in Sect. 7. There we also discuss the size of the generated automaton. From this point of view also our algorithm is usually better than Spin though occasionally it may produce a bigger automaton. Note that Spin, LTL2BA− and LTL2BA give exactly the same resulting automaton on the formulae θ_n. Wring and EQLTL give bigger automata.

The paper is organized as follows. Section 2 begins with some preliminaries defining linear temporal logic and its semantics. Sections 3 to 5 describe our algorithm and some proofs of its correctness. Section 6 presents our simplification methods and Sect. 7 describes some experimental results.

2   Preliminaries: Linear Temporal Logic (LTL)

LTL was introduced to specify the properties of the executions of a system. A finite set Prop contains all atomic properties of states. With the standard Boolean operators ($\neg$, $\wedge$, $\vee$) we can only express static properties. For dynamical properties, we use temporal operators such as X (next), U (until), R (release), F (eventually) and G (always).

Definition 1 (Syntax). *The set of LTL formulae on the set* Prop *is defined by the grammar* $\varphi ::= p \mid \neg\varphi \mid \varphi \vee \varphi \mid X\varphi \mid \varphi \, U \, \varphi$, *where* p *ranges over* Prop.

The semantics of LTL usually defines whether an execution σ of a given system satisfies a formula. Actually the semantics only depends on the atomic propositions that stand in each state of σ. Then for our purpose we consider only sequences of sets of atomic propositions.

Definition 2 (Semantics). *Let* $u = u_0 u_1 \dots$ *be a word in* Σ^ω *with* $\Sigma = 2^{\text{Prop}}$. *Let* φ *be an LTL formula. The relation* $u \models \varphi$ *(u models φ) is defined as follows:*

- $u \models p$ *if* $p \in u_0$,
- $u \models \neg\varphi_1$ *if* $u \not\models \varphi_1$,
- $u \models \varphi_1 \vee \varphi_2$ *if* $u \models \varphi_1$ *or* $u \models \varphi_2$,
- $u \models X\varphi_1$ *if* $u_1 u_2 \dots \models \varphi_1$,
- $u \models \varphi_1 \, U \, \varphi_2$ *if* $\exists k \geq 0,\ u_k u_{k+1} \dots \models \varphi_2$ *and* $\forall 0 \leq i < k,\ u_i u_{i+1} \dots \models \varphi_1$.

Only basic operators have been defined above. We will of course also use the derived operators defined by:

$$tt \stackrel{def}{=} p \vee \neg p \ , \ ff \stackrel{def}{=} \neg tt \ , \ \varphi_1 \wedge \varphi_2 \stackrel{def}{=} \neg(\neg \varphi_1 \vee \neg \varphi_2) \ , (2)$$

$$\varphi_1 \, R \, \varphi_2 \stackrel{def}{=} \neg(\neg \varphi_1 \, U \, \neg \varphi_2) \ , \ F \varphi \stackrel{def}{=} tt \, U \, \varphi \ \text{and} \ G \varphi \stackrel{def}{=} ff \, R \, \varphi = \neg F \neg \varphi \ . (3)$$

An LTL formula that is neither a disjunction ($\vee$) nor a conjunction ($\wedge$) is called a *temporal formula*.

An LTL formula can be written in *negative normal form*, using only the predicates in Prop, their negations, and the operators $\vee$, $\wedge$, X, U, and R. Notice that this operation does not change the number of temporal operators of the formula. From now on, we suppose that every LTL formula is in negative normal form.

Example 1. Let $\theta = \neg(G \, F \, p \rightarrow G(q \rightarrow F \, r))$ be our running example along the paper. The negative normal form of θ is $(ff \, R \, (tt \, U \, p)) \wedge (tt \, U \, (q \wedge (ff \, R \, \neg r)))$.

Before any construction our algorithm simplifies the formula, using a set of rewriting rules that reduce the number of temporal operators. This is relevant since the complexity of our algorithm is based on this number. Some of these rules are presented in [2],[10]. We will not discuss them in this paper.

3   LTL to Very Weak Alternating Automata (VWAA)

This section explains a classical construction: building a VWAA from an LTL formula. Alternating automata have been introduced by Muller and Schupp in [6],[7],[8]. Then in [9], Rohde defined VWAA as he needed them for a work on transfinite words. VWAA were also described in [5]. However, our definition is somewhat different from the classical one.

Definition 3. *A co-Büchi very weak alternating co-Büchi automaton is a five-tuple* $\mathcal{A} = (Q, \Sigma, \delta, I, F)$ *where:*

- *Q is the set of states,*
- *Let Q' be the set of conjunctions of elements of Q. The empty conjunction is denoted by tt. We identify Q' with 2^Q in the following,*
- *Σ is the alphabet, and we let $\Sigma' = 2^\Sigma$,*
- *$\delta : Q \rightarrow 2^{\Sigma' \times Q'}$ is the transition function,*
- *$I \subseteq Q'$ is the set of initial states,*
- *$F \subseteq Q$ is the set of final states (co-Büchi),*
- *there exists a partial order on Q such that $\forall q \in Q$, all the states appearing in $\delta(q)$ are lower or equal to q.*

The definition of a classical alternating automaton would be the same except for the last condition on the partial order.

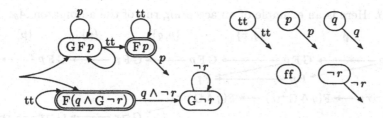

Fig. 1. Automaton $\mathcal{A}_\theta$. Some states (*right*) are unaccessible, they will be removed.

Remark 1. The transition function looks different from the usual definition (Δ : $Q \times \Sigma \rightarrow \mathcal{B}^+(Q)$). We made those changes for implementation reasons, in order to ease the manipulation of the data structures and to save time and space during the computation. The classical representation of our transition function is given by:

$$\Delta(q,a) = \bigvee_{\substack{(\alpha,e) \in \delta(q) \\ a \in \alpha}} e \ . \tag{4}$$

Conversely we may obtain our definition from the classical one, essentially by taking the disjunctive normal form. Hence the two definitions are equivalent.

Notice that in the transition function we use Σ' instead of Σ: so that transitions that differ only by the action can be gathered. In practice, this usually reduces a lot the number of transitions. However the automaton still reads words in Σ^ω.

Example 2. You can see the representation of a VWAA on Fig. 1. States in F are circled twice. Notice that arrows with the same origin represent one transition to a conjunction of states. In this example, we have:

- $I = \{\mathrm{G\,F}\,p \wedge \mathrm{F}(q \wedge \mathrm{G} \neg r)\}$,
- $\delta(p) = \{(\Sigma_p, \mathrm{tt})\}$ where $\Sigma_p = \{a \in \Sigma \mid p \in a\}$,
- $\delta(\mathrm{G\,F}\,p) = \{(\Sigma_p, \mathrm{G\,F}\,p), (\Sigma, \mathrm{G\,F}\,p \wedge \mathrm{F}\,p)\}$.

A *run* σ of $\mathcal{A}$ on a word $u_0 u_1 \ldots \in \Sigma^\omega$ is a labeled DAG (V, E, λ) such that :

- V is partitioned in $\bigcup_{i=0}^{\infty} V_i$ with $E \subseteq \bigcup_{i=0}^{\infty} V_i \times V_{i+1}$,
- $\lambda: V \rightarrow Q$ is the labeling function,
- $\lambda(V_0) \in I$ and $\forall x \in V_i, \exists (\alpha, e) \in \delta(\lambda(x)), u_i \in \alpha$ and $e = \lambda(E(x))$.

A run σ is *accepting* if any (infinite) branch in σ has only a finite number of nodes labeled in F (co-Büchi acceptance condition). $\mathcal{L}(\mathcal{A})$ is the set of words on which there exists an accepting run of $\mathcal{A}$. Note that, Büchi and co-Büchi acceptance conditions are equivalent for VWAA; one only has to replace F by $Q \setminus F$.

Example 3. Here is an example of an accepting run of the automaton $\mathcal{A}_\theta$:

$$
\begin{array}{ccccc}
\emptyset & \{q,r\} & \{p,q\} & \{p\} & \{p\}
\end{array}
$$

$$
\begin{array}{l}
\mathrm{G\,F}\,p \longrightarrow \mathrm{G\,F}\,p \longrightarrow \mathrm{G\,F}\,p \longrightarrow \mathrm{G\,F}\,p \longrightarrow \mathrm{G\,F}\,p \dashrightarrow \\
\qquad\qquad\quad \mathrm{F}\,p \longrightarrow \mathrm{F}\,p \\
\mathrm{F}(q \wedge \mathrm{G}\,\neg r) \longrightarrow \mathrm{F}(q \wedge \mathrm{G}\,\neg r) \longrightarrow \mathrm{F}(q \wedge \mathrm{G}\,\neg r) \\
\qquad\qquad\qquad\qquad\qquad\qquad\qquad\quad \mathrm{G}\,\neg r \longrightarrow \mathrm{G}\,\neg r \dashrightarrow
\end{array}
$$

In the definition of the VWAA associated with an LTL formula, we use two new operators. $\otimes$ helps treating conjunctions, and $\overline{\psi}$ gives roughly the DNF of ψ, allowing us to restrict the states of the automaton to the temporal subformulae of φ.

Definition 4. *For $J_1, J_2 \in 2^{\Sigma' \times Q'}$ we define*
$$J_1 \otimes J_2 = \{(\alpha_1 \cap \alpha_2, e_1 \wedge e_2) \mid (\alpha_1, e_1) \in J_1 \text{ and } (\alpha_2, e_2) \in J_2\},$$
For an LTL formula ψ we define $\overline{\psi}$ by: $\overline{\psi} = \{\psi\}$ if ψ is a temporal formula, $\overline{\psi_1 \wedge \psi_2} = \{e_1 \wedge e_2 \mid e_1 \in \overline{\psi_1} \text{ and } e_2 \in \overline{\psi_2}\}$ and $\overline{\psi_1 \vee \psi_2} = \overline{\psi_1} \cup \overline{\psi_2}$.

Here is the first step of our algorithm, building a VWAA from an LTL formula. Notice that the number of states of this automaton is at most the size of the formula.

Step 1. Let φ be an LTL formula on a set Prop. We define the VWAA $\mathcal{A}_\varphi$ by:

- Q is the set of temporal subformulae of φ,
- $\Sigma = 2^{\mathrm{Prop}}$,
- $I = \overline{\varphi}$,
- F is the set of until subformulae of φ, that is formulae of type $\psi_1 \mathrm{U} \psi_2$,
- δ is defined as follows (Δ extends δ to all subformulae of φ):

$$
\left\{
\begin{array}{rl}
\delta(\mathrm{tt}) =& \{(\Sigma, \mathrm{tt})\} \\
\delta(p) =& \{(\Sigma_p, \mathrm{tt})\} \text{ where } \Sigma_p = \{a \in \Sigma \mid p \in a\} \\
\delta(\neg p) =& \{(\Sigma_{\neg p}, \mathrm{tt})\} \text{ where } \Sigma_{\neg p} = \Sigma \backslash \Sigma_p \\
\delta(\mathrm{X}\,\psi) =& \{(\Sigma, e) \mid e \in \overline{\psi}\} \\
\delta(\psi_1 \mathrm{U} \psi_2) =& \Delta(\psi_2) \cup (\Delta(\psi_1) \otimes \{(\Sigma, \psi_1 \mathrm{U} \psi_2)\}) \\
\delta(\psi_1 \mathrm{R} \psi_2) =& \Delta(\psi_2) \otimes (\Delta(\psi_1) \cup \{(\Sigma, \psi_1 \mathrm{R} \psi_2)\})
\end{array}
\right.
$$

$$
\left\{
\begin{array}{rl}
\Delta(\psi) =& \delta(\psi) \text{ if } \psi \text{ is a temporal formula} \\
\Delta(\psi_1 \vee \psi_2) =& \Delta(\psi_1) \cup \Delta(\psi_2) \\
\Delta(\psi_1 \wedge \psi_2) =& \Delta(\psi_1) \otimes \Delta(\psi_2)
\end{array}
\right.
$$

Using the partial order "subformula of" it is easy to prove that $\mathcal{A}_\varphi$ is very weak.

Remark 2. One can notice that the elements of Σ' used in our definition are intersections of the sets Σ, Σ_p and $\Sigma_{\neg p}$. Hence, they can be denoted by conjunctions of literals, as in the following examples : $p \wedge q \wedge \neg r$ for $\Sigma_p \cap \Sigma_q \cap \Sigma_{\neg r}$, tt for Σ. Note that intersection and test for inclusion can be easily performed with this representation.

Example 4. Figure 1 shows the result of Step 1 on the formula θ defined in Ex. 1.

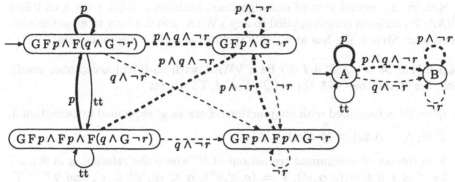

Fig. 2. Automaton $\mathcal{G}_{\mathcal{A}_\theta}$, before (*left*) and after (*right*) Simplification.

Theorem 1. $\mathcal{L}(\mathcal{A}_\varphi) = \{u \in \Sigma^\omega \mid u \models \varphi\}$.

Proof. The idea of the proof is to show recursively that for any subformula ψ of φ, the language accepted by $\mathcal{A}_\varphi$ with $I = \overline{\psi}$ is equal to $\{u \in \Sigma^\omega \mid u \models \psi\}$. The main difficulties are encountered for $\psi = \psi_1 \mathbin{U} \psi_2$ (this is where the acceptance condition comes into play) and $\psi = \psi_1 \mathbin{R} \psi_2$. □

4   VWAA to Generalized Büchi Automata (GBA)

At that point we have obtained a VWAA for our LTL formula φ. The problem is that the usual method to transform an alternating automaton into a Büchi automaton produces an automaton that is much too big. This is why we generate first a GBA, which is a Büchi automaton with *several* acceptance conditions on *transitions* instead of states.

Definition 5. *A generalized Büchi automaton is a five-tuple* $\mathcal{G} = (Q, \Sigma, \delta, I, \mathcal{T})$ *where :*

- *Q is the set of states,*
- *Σ is the alphabet, and we let $\Sigma' \subseteq 2^\Sigma$,*
- *$\delta : Q \to 2^{\Sigma' \times Q}$ is the transition function,*
- *$I \subseteq Q$ is the set of initial states,*
- *$\mathcal{T} = \{T_1, \dots, T_r\}$ where $T_j \subseteq Q \times \Sigma' \times Q$ are the accepting transitions.*

Example 5. The automata on Fig. 2 are examples of GBAs. In these examples, $r = 2$: dashed transitions are in T_1 and bold transitions are in T_2. An accepting run has to use infinitely many dashed transitions and infinitely many bold transitions.

A *run* σ of $\mathcal{G}$ on a word $u_0 u_1 \dots \in \Sigma^\omega$ is a sequence $q_0, q_1, \dots$ of elements of Q such that $q_0 \in I$ and $\forall i \geq 0$, $\exists \alpha_i \in \Sigma'$ such that $u_i \in \alpha_i$ and $(\alpha_i, q_{i+1}) \in \delta(q_i)$. A run σ is *accepting* if for each $1 \leq j \leq r$ it uses infinitely many transitions from T_j. $\mathcal{L}(\mathcal{G})$ is the set of words on which there exists an accepting run of $\mathcal{G}$.

Here is the second step of our algorithm, building a GBA from a co-Büchi VWAA. It can be of course applied to any VWAA, and not only to an automaton issued from Step 1. $\mathcal{G}_A$ has at most $2^{|Q|}$ states and $|F|$ acceptance sets.

Step 2. Let $\mathcal{A} = (Q, \Sigma, \delta, I, F)$ be a VWAA with co-Büchi acceptance conditions. We define the GBA $\mathcal{G}_A = (Q', \Sigma, \delta', I, \mathcal{T})$ where:

- $Q' = 2^Q$ is identified with conjunctions of states as explained in Definition 3,
- $\delta''(q_1 \wedge \ldots \wedge q_n) = \displaystyle\bigotimes_{i=1}^{n} \delta(q_i)$,
- δ' is the set of $\preccurlyeq$-minimal transitions of δ'' where the relation $\preccurlyeq$ is defined by $t' \preccurlyeq t$ if $t = (e, \alpha, e')$, $t' = (e, \alpha', e'')$, $\alpha \subseteq \alpha'$, $e'' \subseteq e'$, and $\forall T \in \mathcal{T}$, $t \in T \Rightarrow t' \in T$,
- $\mathcal{T} = \{T_f \mid f \in F\}$ where
  $T_f = \{(e, \alpha, e') \mid f \notin e'$ or $\exists(\beta, e'') \in \delta(f), \alpha \subseteq \beta$ and $f \notin e'' \subseteq e'\}$.

Remark 3. One may notice that using $f \notin e$ instead of $f \notin e'$ in the definition of T_f would have been more intuitive, since it corresponds to the case where in the run of $\mathcal{A}$ there is no edge with both ends labeled by f. But our definition is also correct. The proof of the following main theorem is more complicated with this definition but the experimental results are much better with it, especially regarding the simplifications.

Example 6. Figure 2 shows the result of Step 2 on the automaton $\mathcal{A}_\theta$ of Fig. 1.

Theorem 2. $\mathcal{L}(\mathcal{G}_A) = \mathcal{L}(\mathcal{A})$.

Remark 4. This is the point where we need the alternating automaton to be very weak (this theorem is false for classical alternating automata). Consider an infinite branch in a run of $\mathcal{A}$ on a given word : since $\mathcal{A}$ is very weak, the sequence of the labels on this branch is decreasing, and has to be ultimately constant since Q is finite. Then "having only a finite number of nodes labeled in F" is equivalent to "having an infinite number of nodes labeled in $Q\backslash F$". This is crucial in the proof.

Proof. Let $\sigma = (V, E, \lambda)$ be an accepting run of $\mathcal{A}$ on a word $u = u_0 u_1 \ldots$ $V = \bigcup_{i \geq 0} V_i$, $E = \bigcup_{i \geq 0} E_i$, with $E_i \subseteq V_i \times V_{i+1}$. We are first going to build a new run of $\mathcal{A}$ on u, redefining gradually the sets V_i and E_i to $V_i' \subseteq V_i$ and E_i', $\forall i \geq 0$.

Let $V_0' = V_0$. Now suppose that V_i' has been defined. By definition of a run, $\forall x \in V_i'$, $\exists \alpha_x$ such that $u_i \in \alpha_x$, and $(\alpha_x, e_x) \in \delta(\lambda(x))$ where $e_x = \lambda(E_i(x))$. Let $\alpha = \bigcap_{x \in V_i'} \alpha_x$ and $e = \bigcup_{x \in V_i'} e_x$.

By definition of δ'', $t = (\lambda(V_i'), \alpha, e)$ is in δ'': there exists a transition $t' = (\lambda(V_i'), \alpha', e')$ in δ' such that $t' \preccurlyeq t$ and t' is minimal. Note that t' is a transition of $\mathcal{G}_A$, and that $u_i \in \alpha \subseteq \alpha'$. Since $t' \in \delta' \subseteq \delta''$, $\forall x \in V_i'$, $\exists(\alpha_x', e_x') \in \delta(\lambda(x))$ such that $\alpha' = \bigcap_{x \in V_i'} \alpha_x'$ and $e_x' = \bigcup_{x \in V_i'} e'$.

Moreover $\forall x \in V_i'$ such that $\lambda(x) = f \in F$ and $t' \in T_f$, there exists $(\alpha_x'', e_x'') \in \delta(f)$ such that $f \notin e_x'' \subseteq e'$ and $\alpha' \subseteq \alpha_x''$. For all other elements x of V_i', let $e_x'' = e_x'$ and $\alpha_x'' = \alpha_x'$.

Let $V_{i+1}' = \{y \in V_{i+1} \mid \lambda(y) \in e'\}$ and $E_i' = \{(x,y) \in V_i' \times V_{i+1}' \mid \lambda(y) \in e_x''\}$. Note that $\lambda(E_i'(x)) = e_x''$ since $e_x'' \subseteq e' = \lambda(V_i')$ and that $E_i'(V_i')$ may be *strictly* contained in V_{i+1}'.

Claim. $\forall i \geq 0$, $\forall f \in F$, the following property holds:
if $\exists (x,y) \in E_i'$, $\lambda(x) = \lambda(y) = f$ then $\exists (x,y) \in E_i$, $\lambda(x) = \lambda(y) = f$.

Proof. If $\forall x \in V_i'$, $\lambda(x) \neq f$ then the claim is true. Otherwise $\exists x \in V_i' \subseteq V_i$, $\lambda(x) = f$. Assume that $\exists y \in E_i'(x)$ with $\lambda(y) = f$. Then we have $f \in e_x''$, and by definition of e_x'' we deduce that $t' \notin T_f$. Since $t' \preccurlyeq t$ we have $t \notin T_f$ and we deduce easily that $f \in e_x$, which proves the claim.

Let $V' = \bigcup_{i \geq 0} V_i'$, $E' = \bigcup_{i \geq 0} E_i'$ and λ' be the restriction of λ to V'. From the construction, one can easily see that $\sigma' = (V', E', \lambda')$ is a new run of $\mathcal{A}$ on u. We show first that σ' is an accepting run. Suppose that σ' is not accepting: since $\mathcal{A}$ is very weak, the labels on an infinite branch of a run are ultimately constant. Hence if σ' is not accepting, then there exists an infinite branch of σ' ultimately labeled by some $f \in F$. Using the claim, there exists in σ an infinite branch which is ultimately labeled by f. This is impossible since σ is accepting.

Let $e_i = \lambda(V_i')$, $\forall i \geq 0$. We have $e_0 = \lambda(V_0) \in I$ and from our construction we get $\forall i \geq 0$, $\exists \alpha_i$ such that $u_i \in \alpha_i$ and (e_i, α_i, e_{i+1}) is a transition of $\mathcal{G}_A$: $\sigma'' = e_0, e_1, \ldots$ is a run of $\mathcal{G}_A$ on u. Now let us prove that σ'' is accepting. Let $i \geq 0$ and $f \in F$. We intend to prove that at some depth $j \geq i$ the transition (e_j, α_j, e_{j+1}) is in T_f.

If $f \notin e_{i+1}$ then $j = i$ will do. Otherwise let $j > i$ be the smallest depth where $(f, f) \notin \lambda(E_j')$. Note that j exists, otherwise there would be an infinite branch in σ' ultimately labeled by f and σ' would not be accepting. Since we know that $f \in e_j$, let x be the node of V_j' labeled by f. From our construction we know that $\exists (e_x'', \alpha_x'') \in \delta(f)$, $f \notin e_x'' \subseteq e_{j+1}$ and $\alpha_j \subseteq \alpha_x''$. We can conclude that (e_j, α_j, e_{j+1}) is in T_f.

Therefore, from any accepting run σ of $\mathcal{A}$, we have built an accepting run σ'' of $\mathcal{G}_A$ on the same word and we get the first inclusion $\mathcal{L}(\mathcal{A}) \subseteq \mathcal{L}(\mathcal{G}_A)$.

Conversely let $\sigma' = e_0, e_1, \ldots$ be an accepting run of $\mathcal{G}_A$ on a word $u = u_0 u_1 \ldots$ Hence $e_0 \in I$ and $\forall i \geq 0$, $\exists \alpha_i$, $u_i \in \alpha_i$ and $(\alpha_i, e_{i+1}) \in \delta'(e_i)$. Let $V = \bigcup_{i \geq 0} V_i$ where $V_i = \{(p,i) \mid p \in e_i\}$ and let $\lambda(p,i) = p$ so that $\lambda(V_i) = e_i$.

By definition of δ', $\forall x \in V_i$, $\exists (\alpha_x, e_x) \in \delta(\lambda(x))$ such that $e_x \subseteq e_{i+1}$ and $\alpha_i \subseteq \alpha_x$. Moreover $\forall f \in F$, if $(e_i, \alpha_i, e_{i+1}) \in T_f$ then either $f \notin e_i$, or $\lambda(x) = f$ for some x in V_i and in that case we can choose α_x and e_x such that $f \notin e_x$. Let E be defined by $(x,y) \in E$ if $\exists i \geq 0$, $x \in V_i$, $y \in V_{i+1}$ and $\lambda(y) \in e_x$.

We can easily see that $\sigma = (V, E, \lambda)$ is a run of $\mathcal{A}$ on u. Now suppose that σ is not accepting: as we proved before, there would exist in σ an infinite branch with all nodes ultimately labeled by some $f \in F$. But σ' is accepting so it has

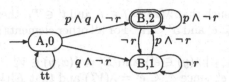

Fig. 3. Automaton $\mathcal{B}_{\mathcal{G}_{A_\theta}}$ after Simplification.

infinitely many transitions in T_f, and for each such transition there is no edge in E with both ends labeled by f at the corresponding depth. Hence this is impossible.

Therefore from any accepting run σ' of $\mathcal{G}_A$, we have built an accepting run σ of A on the same word, proving the converse inclusion $\mathcal{L}(\mathcal{G}_A) \subseteq \mathcal{L}(A)$.   □

5   GBA to Büchi Automata (BA)

At that point we have obtained a GBA for our LTL formula φ. We simply have to transform it into a BA to complete our algorithm. This construction is quite easy and well-known, but for the sake of completeness we explain it briefly. We will begin by defining a BA, using once more the same modifications concerning the alphabet and the transition function.

Definition 6. *A Büchi automaton is a five-tuple* $\mathcal{B} = (Q, \Sigma, \delta, I, F)$ *where:*

- *Q is the set of states,*
- *Σ is the alphabet, and we let $\Sigma' \subseteq 2^\Sigma$,*
- *$\delta : Q \to 2^{\Sigma' \times Q}$ is the transition function,*
- *$I \subseteq Q$ is the set of initial states,*
- *$F \subseteq Q$ is the set of repeated states (Büchi condition).*

A *run* σ of $\mathcal{B}$ on a word $u_0 u_1 \ldots \in \Sigma^\omega$ is a sequence $q_0, q_1, \ldots$ of elements of Q such that $q_0 \in I$ and $\forall i \geq 0$, $\exists \alpha_i \in \Sigma'$ such that $u_i \in \alpha_i$ and $(\alpha_i, q_{i+1}) \in \delta(q_i)$. A run σ is *accepting* if there exists infinitely many states in F. $\mathcal{L}(\mathcal{B})$ is the set of words on which there exists an accepting run of $\mathcal{B}$.

Here is the third step of our algorithm, building a BA from a GBA. If $\mathcal{B}$ has n states and r acceptance conditions, then $\mathcal{B}_\mathcal{G}$ has at most $(r+1) \times n$ states.

Step 3. Let $\mathcal{G} = (Q, \Sigma, \delta, I, \mathcal{T})$ be a GBA with $\mathcal{T} = \{T_1, \ldots, T_r\}$. We define the BA $\mathcal{B}_\mathcal{G} = (Q \times \{0, \ldots, r\}, \Sigma, \delta', I \times \{0\}, Q \times \{r\})$ where:

- $\delta'((q, j)) = \{(\alpha, (q', j')) \mid (\alpha, q') \in \delta(q) \text{ and } j' = next(j, (q, \alpha, q'))\}.$

with $next(j, t) = \begin{cases} \max\{j \leq i \leq r \mid \forall j < k \leq i, \ t \in T_k\} & \text{if } j \neq r \\ \max\{0 \leq i \leq r \mid \forall 0 < k \leq i, \ t \in T_k\} & \text{if } j = r \end{cases}$

Example 7. Figure 3 shows the result of Step 3 on the automaton $\mathcal{G}_{A_\theta}$ of Fig. 2.

Theorem 3. $\mathcal{L}(\mathcal{B}_\mathcal{G}) = \mathcal{L}(\mathcal{B})$.

Remark 5. There exist many similar algorithms transform a GBA into a BA. They often consist in building the synchronous product of the GBA with some automaton verifying that every acceptance condition is verified infinitely often. This automaton differs from one algorithm to another. We chose one that gives good results for the size of the resulting BA after simplification.

6 Simplification

Simplification is really important in our algorithm. Since each step produces a new automaton from the result of the previous step, the more we simplify each result, the faster our algorithm is and the least memory it uses.

After each step, we simplify the automaton obtained, using iteratively three rules until no more simplification occurs:

- A state that is not accessible can be removed,
- If a transition t_1 implies a transition t_2, then t_2 can be removed,

	$t_1 = (q, \alpha_1, q_1)$ implies $t_2 = (q, \alpha_2, q_2)$ if
In a VWAA,	$\alpha_2 \subseteq \alpha_1$ and $q_1 \subseteq q_2$
In a GBA,	$\alpha_2 \subseteq \alpha_1$, $q_1 = q_2$ and $\forall t \in \mathcal{T}, t_2 \in T \Rightarrow t_1 \in T$
In a BA,	$\alpha_2 \subseteq \alpha_1$ and $q_1 = q_2$

- If two states q_1 and q_2 are equivalent, then they can be merged.

	q_1 and q_2 are equivalent if
In a VWAA,	$\delta(q_1) = \delta(q_2)$ and $q_1 \in F \iff q_2 \in F$
In a GBA,	$\delta(q_1) = \delta(q_2)$ and $\forall(\alpha, q') \in \delta(q_1), \forall T \in \mathcal{T},$
	$(q_1, \alpha, q') \in T \iff (q_2, \alpha, q') \in T$
In a BA,	$\delta(q_1) = \delta(q_2)$ and $q_1 \in F \iff q_2 \in F$

Note that for a GBA issued from Step 2, the condition $(q_1, \alpha, q') \in T_j$ does not depend on q_1 so that the condition simply becomes $\delta(q_1) = \delta(q_2)$.

This simplification procedure is really efficient to reduce the size of the automata. But the strength of our algorithm is that the last two simplification rules are also used *on-the-fly*: after a transition has been created, it is compared with the other transitions already calculated from the same state, and the ones that become useless are immediately deleted; after all the transitions of a state have been created, that state is compared with the other states that have already been created, and is merged to one of those states if possible. This method is important since usually many states and transitions are to be simplified, and simplifying them on-the-fly saves a lot of time and space.

In Table 1, the results of the algorithm with or without on-the-fly simplification are compared (LTL2BA− is our algorithm with a posteriori simplification only). For the formula θ_n defined in (1), the unsimplified GBA has 2^{n+1} states, whereas the simplified GBA has only 2 states. Using on-the-fly simplification avoids the intermediary exponential automaton which explains the great improvement, even if the time and memory used by LTL2BA are still exponential.

7 Experimental Results

In this section we compare the results of some recent algorithms transforming an LTL formula into a BA.

Spin is a model-checker developed by Bell Labs since 1980. It contains an algorithm transforming an LTL formula into a BA, presented in [3]. The program is written in C, and we used version 3.4.1. (released Aug 2000).

Wring is an algorithm presented in [10]. The program is written in Perl, so the comparison with our work cannot be read literally, and the amount of memory used is just an approximation we made using the Unix command 'top'.

EQLTL is an algorithm presented in [2]. The program is not publicly available, but a demo is proposed on the web. All we could do was to measure the time needed by the web interface to start responding to our request. We do not even know what type of machine handles the request. Consequently the times we gave should be taken with caution.

LTL2BA is a program written in C as Spin, in order to make reliable comparison between the two programs. **LTL2BA−** is the same program, with a posteriori simplification only.

Tests were made on a Sun Ultra 10 station with 1 GB of RAM.

As explained in the introduction, we compared the tools on usual LTL formulae, taking the example of the formula θ_n defined in (1). The result of the comparison is detailed in Table 1.

Another type of usual LTL formulae, often encountered in model-checking, is formulae like: $\varphi_n = \neg(p_1 \mathbin{U} (p_2 \mathbin{U} (\ldots \mathbin{U} p_n) \ldots))$. We made the same tests on these fomulae in Table 2. Again our algorithm outperforms the other ones.

Table 2. Comparison on the Formulae φ_n for $2 \leq n \leq 8$. Time is in sec, Space in kB.

	Spin		Wring		EQLTL	LTL2BA	
	time	space	time	space	time	time	space
φ_2	0.01	8	0.07	4,100	8	0.01	3.2
φ_3	0.03	110	0.29	4,100	8	0.01	5.5
φ_4	0.75	1,700	1.34	4,200	9	0.01	11
φ_5	43	51,000	10	4,200	11	0.01	13
φ_6	1,200	920,000	92	4,500	15	0.15	25
φ_7			720	6,000	27	9.2	48
φ_8					92	1,200	93

We also compared the algorithms on random LTL formulae of a fixed size, using a tool presented in [11]. For compatibility reasons, the only comparison we could realize was between our algorithm and Spin's. Here the results are issued from a test on 200 random formulae of size 10, where both algorithms are compared on the *same* formulae. See Table 3 for details.

Table 3. Comparison on Random Formulae of a Fixed Size.

	Spin		LTL2BA	
	avg.	max.	avg.	max.
time of computation (seconds)	14.23	4521.65	0.01	0.04
number of states	5.74	56	4.51	39
number of transitions	14.73	223	9.67	112

References

1. M. Daniele, F. Giunchiglia, and M. Vardi. Improved automata generation for linear temporal logic. In *Proc. 11th International Computer Aided Verification Conference*, pages 249–260, 1999.
2. K. Etessami and G. Holzmann. Optimizing Büchi automata. In *Proceedings of 11th Int. Conf. on Concurrency Theory (CONCUR)*, 2000.
3. R. Gerth, D. Peled, M. Vardi, and P. Wolper. Simple on-the-fly automatic verification of linear temporal logic. In *Protocol Specification Testing and Verification*, pages 3–18, Warsaw, Poland, 1995. Chapman & Hall.
4. G. Holzmann. The model checker SPIN. *IEEE Transactions on Software Engineering*, 23(5):279–295, May 1997.
5. O. Kupferman and M. Vardi. Weak alternating automata are not that weak. In *Proc. 5th Israeli Symposium on Theory of Computing and Systems ISTCS'97*, pages 147–158. IEEE, 1997.
6. D. Muller and P. Schupp. Alternating automata on infinite objects: Determinacy and Rabin's theorem. In *Proceedings of the Ecole de Printemps d'Informatique Théoretique on Automata on Infinite Words*, volume 192 of *LNCS*, pages 100–107, Le Mont Dore, France, May 1984. Springer.
7. D. Muller and P. Schupp. Alternating automata on infinite trees. *Theoretical Computer Science*, 54(2-3):267–276, October 1987.
8. D. Muller and P. Schupp. Simulating alternating tree automata by nondeterministic automata: New results and new proofs of the theorems of Rabin, McNaughton and Safra. *Theoretical Computer Science*, 141(1–2):69–107, April 1995.
9. S. Rohde. Alternating automata and the temporal logic of ordinals. *PhD Thesis in Mathematics, University of Illinois at Urbana-Champaign*, 1997.
10. F. Somenzi and R. Bloem. Efficient Büchi automata from LTL formulae. In *CAV: International Conference on Computer Aided Verification*, 2000.
11. H. Tauriainen. A randomized testbench for algorithms translating linear temporal logic formulae into Büchi automata. In *Workshop Concurrency, Specifications and Programming*, pages 251–262, Warsaw, Poland, 1999.
12. M. Vardi. *An Automata-Theoretic Approach to Linear Temporal Logic*, volume 1043 of *Lecture Notes in Computer Science*, pages 238–266. Springer-Verlag Inc., New York, NY, USA, 1996.

A Practical Approach to Coverage in Model Checking

Hana Chockler[1], Orna Kupferman[1]*, Robert P. Kurshan[2], and Moshe Y. Vardi[3]**

[1] Hebrew University, School of Engineering and Computer Science
Jerusalem 91904, Israel
{hanac,orna}@cs.huji.ac.il
http://www.cs.huji.ac.il/~{hanac,orna}
[2] Bell Laboratories, 700 Mountain Avenue
Murray Hill, NJ 07974, U.S.A.
k@research.bell-labs.com
[3] Rice University, Department of Computer Science
Houston, TX 77251-1892, U.S.A.
vardi@cs.rice.edu
http://www.cs.rice.edu/~vardi

Abstract. In formal verification, we verify that a system is correct with respect to a specification. When verification succeeds and the system is proven to be correct, there is still a question of how complete the specification is, and whether it really covers all the behaviors of the system. In this paper we study coverage metrics for model checking from a practical point of view. Coverage metrics are based on modifications we apply to the system in order to check which parts of it were actually relevant for the verification process to succeed. We suggest several definitions of coverage, suitable for specifications given in linear temporal logic or by automata on infinite words. We describe two algorithms for computing the parts of the system that are not covered by the specification. The first algorithm is built on top of automata-based model-checking algorithms. The second algorithm reduces the coverage problem to the model-checking problem. Both algorithms can be implemented on top of existing model checking tools.

1 Introduction

In *model checking* [CE81,QS81,LP85], we verify the correctness of a finite-state system with respect to a desired behavior by checking whether a Kripke structure that models the system satisfies a specification of this behavior, expressed in terms of a temporal logic formula or a finite automaton [CGP99]. Beyond being fully-automatic, an additional attraction of model-checking tools is their ability to accompany a negative answer to the correctness query by a counterexample to the satisfaction of the specification in the system. Thus, together with a negative answer, the model checker returns some erroneous execution of the system. These counterexamples are very important and they can be essential in detecting subtle errors in complex designs [CGMZ95]. On the other

---

* Supported in part by BSF grant 9800096.
** Supported in part by NSF grant CCR-9700061, NSF grant CCR-9988322, BSF grant 9800096, and by a grant from the Intel Corporation.

G. Berry, H. Comon, and A. Finkel (Eds.): CAV 2001, LNCS 2102, pp. 66–78, 2001.
© Springer-Verlag Berlin Heidelberg 2001

hand, when the answer to the correctness query is positive, most model-checking tools terminate with no further information to the user. Since a positive answer means that the system is correct with respect to the specification, this at first seems like a reasonable policy. In the last few years, however, there has been growing awareness to the importance of suspecting the system of containing an error also in the case model checking succeeds. The main justification of such suspects are possible errors in the modeling of the system or of the behavior, and possible incompleteness in the specification.

There are various ways to look for possible errors in the modeling of the system or the behavior. One way is to detect *vacuous satisfaction* of the specification [BBER97,KV99], where cases like antecedent failure [BB94] make parts of the specification irrelevant to its satisfaction. For example, the specification $\varphi = G(req \to Fgrant)$ is vacuously satisfied in a system in which *req* is always **false**. A similar way is to check the validity of the specification. Clearly, a valid specification is satisfied trivially, and suggests some problem. A related approach is taken in the process of constraint validation in the verification tool FormalCheck [Kur98], where sanity checks include a search for enabling conditions that are never enabled, and a replacement of all or some of the constraints by **false**. FormalCheck also keeps track of variables and values of variables that were never used in the process of model checking.

It is less clear how to check completeness of the specification. Indeed, specifications are written manually, and their completeness depends on the competence of the person who writes them. The motivation for such a check is clear: an erroneous behavior of the system can escape the verification efforts if this behavior is not captured by the specification. In fact, it is likely that a behavior that is not captured by the specification also escapes the attention of the designer, who is often the one to provide the specification.

In simulation-based verification techniques, coverage metrics are used in order to reveal states that were not visited during the testing procedure (i.e, not "covered" by this procedure) [HMA95,HYHD95,DGK96,HH96,KN96,FDK98,MAH98,BH99,FAD99]. These metrics are a useful way of measuring progress of the verification process. However, the same intuition cannot be applied to model checking because the process of model checking visits all states. We can say that in testing, a state is "uncovered" if it is not essential to the success of the testing procedure. The similar idea can be applied to model checking, where the state is defined as "uncovered" if its labeling is not essential to the success of the model checking process. This approach was first suggested by Hoskote et al. [HKHZ99]. Low coverage can point to several problems. One possibility is that the specification is not complete enough to fully describe all the possible behaviors of the system. Then, the output of a coverage check is helpful in completing the specification. Another possibility is that the system contains redundancies. Then, the output of the coverage check is helpful in simplifying the system.

There are two different approaches to coverage in model checking. One approach, introduced by Katz et al. [KGG99], states that a well-covered system should closely resemble the tableau of its specification, thus the coverage criteria of [KGG99] are based on the analysis of the differences between the system and the tableau of its specification. We find the approach of [KGG99] too strict – we want specifications to be much more abstract than their implementations. In addition, the approach is restricted to universal safety specifications, whose tableaux have no fairness constraints, and it is computationally hard to compute the coverage criteria. Another approach, introduced in [HKHZ99], is to check the influence of small changes in the system on the satisfaction of the specification. Intuitively, if a part of the system can be changed without violating the specification, this part is *uncovered* by the specification. Formally, for a Kripke structure K, a state w in K, and an *observable signal* q, the *dual structure* $\tilde{K}_{w,q}$ is obtained from K by *flipping* the value of q in w (the signal q corresponds to a Boolean variable that is **true** if w is labeled with q and is **false** otherwise. When we say that we flip the value of q, we mean that we switch the value of this variable). For a specification φ, Hoskote et al. define the set q-$cover(K, \varphi)$ as a set of states w such that $\tilde{K}_{w,q}$ does not satisfy φ. A state is covered if it belongs to q-$cover(K, \varphi)$ for some observable signal q. Indeed, this indicates that the value of q in w is crucial for the satisfaction of φ in K. It is easy to see that for each observable signal, the set of covered states can be computed by a naive algorithm that performs model checking of φ in $\tilde{K}_{w,q}$ for each state w of K. The naive algorithm, however, is very expensive, and is useless for practical applications [1]. In [CKV01], we suggested two alternatives to the naive algorithm for specifications in the branching time temporal logic CTL. The first algorithm is symbolic and it computes the set of pairs $\langle w, w' \rangle$ such that flipping the value of q in w' falsifies φ in w. The second algorithm improves the naive algorithm by exploiting overlaps in the many dual structures that we need to check. The two algorithms are still not attractive: the symbolic algorithm doubles the number of BDD's variables, and the second algorithm requires the development of new procedures. Also, these algorithms cannot be extended to specifications in LTL, as they heavily use the fixed-point characterization of CTL, which is not applicable to LTL.

In this paper we study coverage metrics for model checking from a practical point of view. First, we consider specifications given as formulas in the linear temporal logic LTL or by automata on infinite words. These formalisms are used in many model-checking tools (e.g., [HHK96,Kur98]), and we suggest alternative definitions of coverage, which suit better the linear case. Second, we describe two algorithms for LTL specifications. Both algorithms can be relatively easily implemented on top of existing model checking tools.

Let us describe informally our alternative definitions. For a Kripke structure K, let $\mathcal{K}$ be the unwinding of K to an infinite tree. Recall that a dual structure $\tilde{K}_{w,q}$ is obtained in [HKHZ99,CKV01] by flipping the value of the signal q in the state w of K. A state w of K may correspond to many w-*nodes* in $\mathcal{K}$. The definition of coverage that refers to $\tilde{K}_{w,q}$ flips the value of q in all the w-nodes in $\mathcal{K}$. We call this *structure coverage*. Alternatively, we can examine also *node coverage*, where we flip the value of q in a single w-node in $\mathcal{K}$, and *tree coverage*, where we flip the value of q in some w-nodes. Each approach measures a different sensitivity of the satisfaction of the specification to

---

[1] Hoskote et al. describe an alternative algorithm that is symbolic and runs in linear time, but their algorithm handles specifications in a very restricted syntax (a fragment of the universal fragment ∀CTL of CTL) and it does not return the set q-$cover(K, \varphi)$, but a set that corresponds to a different definition of coverage, which is sometimes counter-intuitive. For example, the algorithm is syntax-dependent, thus, equivalent formulas may induce different coverage sets; in particular, the set of states q-covered by the tautology $q \rightarrow q$ is the set of states that satisfy q, rather than the empty set, which meets our intuition of coverage.

changes in the system. Intuitively, in structure coverage we check whether the value of q in all the occurrences of w has been crucial for the satisfaction of the specification. On the other hand, in node coverage we check whether the value of q in some occurrence of w has been crucial for the satisfaction of the specification[2].

The first algorithm we describe computes the set of node-covered states and is built on top of automata-based model-checking algorithms. In automata-based model checking, we translate an LTL specification φ to a nondeterministic Büchi automaton $A_{\neg\varphi}$ that accepts all words that do not satisfy φ [VW94]. Model checking of K with respect to φ can then be reduced to checking the emptiness of the product $K \times A_{\neg\varphi}$. When K satisfies φ, the product is empty. A state w is covered iff flipping the value of q in w makes the product nonempty. This observation enables us to compute the set of node covered states by a simple manipulation of the set of reachable states in the product $K \times A_{\neg\varphi}$, and the set of states in this product from which a fair path exists. Fortunately, these sets have already been calculated in the process of model checking. We describe an implementation of this algorithm in the tool COSPAN, which is the engine of FormalCheck [HHK96,Kur98]. We also describe the changes in the implementation that are required in order to adapt the algorithm to handle structure and tree coverage.

In the second algorithm we reduce the coverage problem to model checking. Given an LTL specification φ and an observable signal q, we construct an *indicator* formula $Ind_q(\varphi)$, such that for every structure K and state w in K, the state w is node q-covered by φ iff w satisfies $Ind_q(\varphi)$. The indicator formulas we construct are in μ-calculus with both past and future modalities, their length is, in the worst case, exponential in the size of the specification φ, they are of alternation depth two for general LTL specifications, and are alternation free for safety LTL specifications. We note that the exponential blow-up may not appear in practice. Also, tools that support symbolic model checking of μ-calculus with future modalities can be extended to handle past modalities with no additional cost [KP95]. In the full version of the paper we show that bisimilar states may not agree on their coverage, which is why the indicators we construct require both past and future modalities.

The two algorithms that we present in this paper are derived from the two possible approaches to linear-time model checking. The first approach is to analyze the product of the system with the automaton of the negation of the property. The second approach is to translate the property to a μ-calculus formula and then check the system with respect to this formula. Both approaches may involve exponential blow-up. In the first approach, the size of the automaton can be exponential in the size of the property, and in the second approach the size of the μ-calculus formula can be exponential in the size of the property.

2   Preliminaries

2.1   Structures and Trees

We model systems by Kripke structures. A *Kripke structure* $K = \langle AP, W, R, w_{in}, L \rangle$ consists of a set AP of atomic propositions, a set W of states, a total transition relation

---

[2] As we show in Section 2.2, this intuition is not quite precise, and node coverage does not imply structure coverage, which is why tree coverage is required.

$R \subseteq W \times W$, an initial state $w_{in} \in W$, and a labeling function $L : W \to 2^{AP}$. If $R(w, w')$, we say that w' is a successor of w. For a state $w \in W$, a w-path $\pi = w_0, w_1, \ldots$ in K is a sequence of states in K such that $w_0 = w$ and for all $i \geq 0$, we have $R(w_i, w_{i+1})$. If $w_0 = w_{in}$, the path π is called an *initialized path*. The labeling function L can be extended to paths in a straightforward way, thus $L(\pi) = L(w_0) \cdot L(w_1) \cdots$ is an infinite word over the alphabet 2^{AP}. A *fair Kripke structure* is a Kripke structure augmented with a fairness constraint. We consider here the Büchi fairness condition. There, $K = \langle AP, W, R, w_{in}, L, \alpha \rangle$, where $\alpha \subseteq W$ is a set of fair states. A path of K is *fair* if it visits states in α infinitely often. Formally, let $inf(\pi)$ denote the set of states repeated in π infinitely often. Thus, $w \in inf(\pi)$ iff $w_i = w$ for infinitely many i's. Then, π is fair iff $inf(\pi) \cap \alpha \neq \emptyset$. The *language* of K, denoted $\mathcal{L}(K)$ is the set of words $L(\pi)$ for the initialized fair paths π of K. Often, it is convenient to have several initial states in K. Our results hold also for this model.

For a finite set Υ, an Υ-tree T is a set $T \subseteq \Upsilon^*$ such that if $x \cdot v \in T$ where $x \in \Upsilon^*$ and $v \in \Upsilon$, then also $x \in T$. The elements of T are called *nodes* and the empty word ε is the *root* of T. For every $x \in T$, the nodes $x \cdot v \in T$ where $v \in \Upsilon$ are the *children* of x. Each node x of T has a *direction* in Υ. The direction of the root is some designated member of Υ, denoted by v_0. The direction of a node $x \cdot v$ is v. We denote by $dir(x)$ the direction of node x. A node x such that $dir(x) = v$ is called v-*node*. A *path* ρ of a tree T is a set $\rho \subseteq T$ such that $\varepsilon \in \rho$ and for every $x \in \rho$ there exists a unique $v \in \Upsilon$ such that $x \cdot v \in \rho$. For an alphabet Σ, a Σ-*labeled* Υ-tree is a pair $\langle T, V \rangle$, where $V : T \to \Sigma$ labels each node of T with a letter from Σ.

A Kripke structure K can be unwound into an infinite computation tree in a straightforward way. Formally, the tree that is obtained by unwinding K is denoted by $\mathcal{K}$ and is the 2^{AP}-labeled W-tree $\langle T^K, V^K \rangle$, where $\varepsilon \in T^K$ and $dir(\varepsilon) = w_{in}$, for all $x \in T^K$ and $v \in W$ with $R(dir(x), v)$, we have $x \cdot v \in T^K$, and for all $x \in T^K$, we have $V^K(x) = L(dir(x))$. That is, V^K maps a node that was reached by taking the direction w to $L(w)$.

2.2 Coverage

Given a system and a formula that is satisfied in this system, we check the influence of modifications in the system on the satisfaction of the formula. Intuitively, a state is *covered* if a modification in this state falsifies the formula in the initial state of the structure. We limit ourselves to modifications that flip the value of one atomic proposition (an observable signal) in one state of the structure[3]. Flipping can be performed in different ways. Through the execution of the system we can visit a state several times, each time in a different context. This gives rise to a distinction between "flipping always", "flipping once", and "flipping sometimes", which we formalize in the definitions of *structure coverage*, *node coverage*, and *tree coverage* below. We first need some notations.

For a domain Y, a function $V : Y \to 2^{AP}$, an observable signal $q \in AP$, and a set $X \subseteq Y$, the *dual function* $\tilde{V}_{X,q} : Y \to 2^{AP}$ is such that $\tilde{V}_{X,q}(x) = V(x)$ for all $x \notin X$,

---

[3] In [CKV01], we consider richer modifications (e.g., modifications that change both the labeling and the transitions), and show how the algorithms described there for the limited case can be extended to handle richer modifications. Extending the algorithms described in this paper to richer modifications is nontrivial.

$\tilde{V}_{X,q}(x) = V(x) \setminus \{q\}$ if $x \in X$ and $q \in V(x)$, and $\tilde{V}_{X,q}(x) = V(x) \cup \{q\}$ if $x \in X$ and $q \notin V(x)$. When $X = \{x\}$ is a singleton, we write $\tilde{V}_{x,q}$. For a Kripke structure $K = \langle AP, W, R, w_{in}, L \rangle$, an observable signal $q \in AP$, and a state $w \in W$, we denote by $\tilde{K}_{w,q}$ the structure obtained from K by flipping the value of q in w. Thus, $\tilde{K}_{w,q} = \langle AP, W, R, W_{in}, \tilde{L}_{w,q} \rangle$, where $\tilde{L}_{w,q}(v) = L(v)$ for $v \neq w$, $\tilde{L}_{w,q}(w) = L(w) \cup \{q\}$, in case $q \notin L(w)$, and $\tilde{L}_{w,q}(w) = L(w) \setminus \{q\}$, in case $q \in L(w)$. For $X \subseteq T^K$ we denote by $\tilde{K}_{X,q}$ the tree that is obtained by flipping the value of q in all the nodes in X. Thus, $\tilde{K}_{X,q} = \langle T^K, \tilde{V}_{X,q}^K \rangle$. When $X = \{x\}$ is a singleton, we write $\tilde{K}_{x,q}$.

Definition 1. *Consider a Kripke structure K, a formula φ satisfied in K, and an observable signal $q \in AP$.*

- *A state w of K is* structure q-covered *by φ iff the structure $\tilde{K}_{w,q}$ does not satisfy φ.*
- *A state w of K is* node q-covered *by φ iff there is a w-node x in T^K such that $\tilde{K}_{x,q}$ does not satisfy φ.*
- *A state w of K is* tree q-covered *by φ iff there is a set X of w-nodes in T^K such that $\tilde{K}_{X,q}$ does not satisfy φ.*

Note that, alternatively, a state is structure q-covered iff $\tilde{K}_{X,q}$ does not satisfy φ for the set X of all w-nodes in $\mathcal{K}$. In other words, a state w is structure q-covered if flipping the value of q in all the instances of w in $\mathcal{K}$ falsifies φ, it is node q-covered if a single flip of the value of q falsifies φ, and it is tree q-covered if some flips of the value of q falsifies φ.

For a Kripke structure $K = \langle AP, W, R, w_{in}, L \rangle$, an LTL formula φ, and an observable signal $q \in AP$, we use $SC(K, \varphi, q)$, $NC(K, \varphi, q)$, and $TC(K, \varphi, q)$, to denote the sets of states that are structure q-covered, node q-covered, and tree q-covered, respectively in K.

Membership of a given state w in each of the sets above can be decided by running an LTL model checking algorithm on modified structures. For $SC(K, \varphi, q)$, we have to model check $\tilde{K}_{w,q}$. For $NC(K, \varphi, q)$ and $TC(K, \varphi, q)$, things are a bit more complicated, as we have to model check several (possibly infinitely many) trees. Since, however, the set of computations in these trees is a modification of the language of K, it is possible to obtain these computations by modifying K as follows. For tree coverage, we model check the formula φ in the structure obtained from K by adding a copy w' of the state w in which q is flipped. Node coverage is similar, only that we have to ensure that the state w' is visited only once, which can be done by adding a copy of K to which we move after a visit in w'. It follows that the sets $SC(K, \varphi, q)$, $NC(K, \varphi, q)$, and $TC(K, \varphi, q)$ can be computed by a naive algorithm that runs the above checks $|W|$ times, one time for each state w. In Sections 3 and 4 we describe two alternatives to this naive algorithm.

We now study the relation between the three definitions. It is easy to see that structure and node coverage are special cases of tree coverage, thus $SC(K, \varphi, q) \subseteq TC(K, \varphi, q)$ and $NC(K, \varphi, q) \subseteq TC(K, \varphi, q)$ for all K, φ, and q. The relation between structure coverage and node coverage, however, is not so obvious. Intuitively, in structure coverage we check whether the value of q in all the occurrences of w has been crucial for the satisfaction of the specification. On the other hand, in node coverage we check whether the value of q in some occurrence of w has been crucial for the satisfaction of the specification. It may therefore seem that node coverage induces bigger covered sets. The following example shows that in that general case neither one of the covered sets $SC(K, \varphi, q)$ and $NC(K, \varphi, q)$ is a subset of the other. Let K be a Kripke structure with one state w, labeled q, with a self-loop. Let $\varphi_1 = Fq$. It is easy to see that $\tilde{K}_{w,q}$ does not satisfy φ_1. On the other hand, $\mathcal{K}$ is an infinite tree that is labeled with q everywhere, thus $\tilde{\mathcal{K}}_{x,q}$ satisfies φ_1 for every node x. So, w is structure q-covered, but not node q-covered. Now, let $\varphi_2 = Gq \vee G \neg q$. It is easy to see that $\tilde{K}_{w,q}$ satisfies φ_2. On the other hand, $\tilde{\mathcal{K}}_{x,q}$ is a tree that is labeled with q in all nodes $y \neq x$, thus $\tilde{\mathcal{K}}_{x,q}$ does not satisfy φ_2. So, w is tree q-covered, but it is not structure q-covered. As a corollary, we get the following theorem.

Theorem 1. *There is a Kripke structure K, LTL formulas φ_1 and φ_2, and an observable signal q such that $SC(K, \varphi_1, q) \not\subseteq NC(K, \varphi_1, q)$ and $NC(K, \varphi_2, q) \not\subseteq SC(K, \varphi_2, q)$.*

2.3 Automata

A *nondeterministic Büchi automaton* over infinite words is $\mathcal{A} = \langle \Sigma, S, \delta, S_0, \alpha \rangle$, where Σ is an alphabet, S is a set of states, $\delta : S \times \Sigma \to 2^S$ is a transition relation, $S_0 \subseteq S$ is a set of initial states, and $\alpha \subseteq S$ is the set of accepting states. Given an infinite word $\tau = \sigma_0 \cdot \sigma_1 \cdots$ in Σ^ω, a run r of $\mathcal{A}$ on τ is an infinite sequence of states $s_0, s_1, s_2 \ldots$ such that $s_0 \in S_0$ and for all $i \geq 0$, we have $s_{i+1} \in \delta(s_i, \sigma_i)$. The set $inf(r)$ is the set of states that appear in r infinitely often. Thus, $s \in inf(r)$ iff $s_i = s$ for infinitely many i's. The run r is *accepting* iff $inf(r) \cap \alpha \neq \emptyset$ [Büc62]. That is, a run is accepting iff it visits some accepting state infinitely often. The language of $\mathcal{A}$, denoted $\mathcal{L}(\mathcal{A})$, is the set of infinite words $\tau \in \Sigma^\omega$ such that there is an accepting run of $\mathcal{A}$ on τ. Finally, for $s \in S$, we define $\mathcal{A}^s = \langle \Sigma, S, \delta, \{s\}, \alpha \rangle$ as $\mathcal{A}$ with initial set $\{s\}$.

We assume that specifications are given either by LTL formulas or by nondeterministic Büchi automata. It is shown in [VW94] that given an LTL formula φ, we can construct a nondeterministic Büchi automaton $\mathcal{A}_\varphi$ over the alphabet 2^{AP} such that $\mathcal{A}_\varphi$ accepts exactly all the words that satisfy φ. Formally, $\mathcal{L}(\mathcal{A}_\varphi) = \{\tau \in (2^{AP})^\omega : \tau \models \varphi\}$.

3   An Automata-Based Algorithm for Computing Coverage

In this section we extend automata-based model-checking algorithms to find the set of covered states. In automata-based model checking, we translate an LTL specification φ to a nondeterministic Büchi automaton $\mathcal{A}_{\neg\varphi}$ that accepts all words that do not satisfy φ [VW94]. Model checking of K with respect to φ can then be reduced to checking the emptiness of the product $K \times \mathcal{A}_{\neg\varphi}$. Let $K = \langle AP, W, R, w_{in}, L \rangle$ be a Kripke structure that satisfies φ, and let $\mathcal{A}_{\neg\varphi} = \langle 2^{AP}, S, \delta, S_0, \alpha \rangle$ be the nondeterministic Büchi automaton for $\neg\varphi$. The product of K with $\mathcal{A}_{\neg\varphi}$ is the fair Kripke structure $K \times \mathcal{A}_{\neg\varphi} = \langle AP, W \times S, M, \{w_{in}\} \times S_0, L', W \times \alpha \rangle$, where $M(\langle w, s \rangle, \langle w', s' \rangle)$ iff $R(w, w')$ and $s' \in \delta(s, L(w))$, and $L'(\langle w, s \rangle) = L(w)$. Note that an infinite path π in $K \times \mathcal{A}_{\neg\varphi}$ is fair iff the projection of π on S satisfies the acceptance condition of $\mathcal{A}_{\neg\varphi}$.

Since K satisfies φ, we know that no initialized path of K is accepted by $\mathcal{A}_{\neg\varphi}$. Hence, $\mathcal{L}(K \times \mathcal{A}_{\neg\varphi})$ is empty.

Let $P \subseteq W \times S$ be the set of pairs $\langle w, s \rangle$ such that $\mathcal{A}_{\neg\varphi}$ can reach the state s as it reads the state w. That is, there exists a sequence $\langle w_0, s_0 \rangle, \ldots, \langle w_k, s_k \rangle$ such that $w_0 = w_{in}$, $s_0 \in S_0$, $w_k = w$, $s_k = s$, and for all $i \geq 0$ we have $R(w_i, w_{i+1})$ and $s_{i+1} \in \delta(s_i, L(w_i))$. Note that $\langle w, s \rangle \in P$ iff $\langle w, s \rangle$ is reachable in $K \times \mathcal{A}_{\neg\varphi}$. For an observable signal $q \in AP$ and $w \in W$, we define the set $P_{w,q} \subseteq W \times S$ as the set of pairs $\langle w', s' \rangle$ such that w' is a successor of w and $\mathcal{A}_{\neg\varphi}$ can reach the state s' as it reads the state w' in a run in which the last occurrence of w has q flipped. Formally, if we denote by $\tilde{L}_q : W \to 2^{AP}$ the labeling function with q flipped (that is, $\tilde{L}_q(w) = L(w) \cup \{q\}$ if $q \notin L(w)$, and $\tilde{L}_q(w) = L(w) \setminus \{q\}$ if $q \in L(w)$), then

$$P_{w,q} = \{\langle w', s' \rangle : \text{ there is } s \in S \text{ such that } \langle w, s \rangle \in P, R(w, w'), \text{ and } s' \in \delta(s, \tilde{L}_q(w))\}.$$

Recall that a state w is node q-covered in K iff there exists a a w-node x in T^K such that $\tilde{K}_{x,q}$ does not satisfy φ. We can characterize node q-covered states also as follows (see the full version for the proof).

Theorem 2. *Consider a Kripke structure K, an LTL formula φ, and an observable signal q. A state w is node q-covered in K by φ iff there is a successor w' of w and a state s' such that $\langle w', s' \rangle \in P_{w,q}$ and there is a fair $\langle w', s' \rangle$-path in $K \times \mathcal{A}_{\neg\varphi}$.*

Theorem 2 reduces the problem of checking whether a state w is node q-covered to computing the relation $P_{w,q}$ and checking for the existence of a fair path from a state in the product $K \times \mathcal{A}_{\neg\varphi}$. Model-checking tools compute the relation P and compute the set of states from which we have fair paths. Therefore, Theorem 2 suggests an easy implementation for the problem of computing the set of node-covered states. We describe a possible implementation in the tool COSPAN, which is the engine of FormalCheck [HHK96,Kur98]. We also show that the implementation can be modified in order to handle structure and tree coverage.

In COSPAN, the system is modeled by a set of modules, and the desired behavior is specified by an additional module $\mathcal{A}$. The language $\mathcal{L}(\mathcal{A})$ is exactly the set of wrong behaviors, thus the module $\mathcal{A}$ stands for the automaton $\mathcal{A}_{\neg\varphi}$ in cases the specification is given an LTL formula φ. In order to compute the set of node q-covered states, the system has to nondeterministically choose a step in the synchronous composition of the modules, in which the value of q is flipped in all modules that refer to q. Note that this is the same as to choose a step in which the module $\mathcal{A}$ behaves as if it reads the dual value of q. This can be done by introducing two new Boolean variables *flip* and *flag*, local to $\mathcal{A}$. The variable *flip* is nondeterministically assigned **true** or **false** in each step. The variable *flag* is initialized to **true** and is set to **false** one step after *flip* becomes **true**. Instead of reading q, the module $\mathcal{A}$ reads $q \oplus (\textit{flip} \wedge \textit{flag})$. Thus, when both *flip* and *flag* hold, which happens exactly once, the value of q is flipped ($\oplus$ stands for exclusive or). So, the synchronous composition of the modules is not empty iff the state that was visited when *flip* becomes **true** for the first time is node q-covered. The complexity of model checking is linear in the size of the state space of the model, which is bounded by $O(2^n)$, where n is the number of state variables. We increase the number of state variables by 2, thus the complexity of coverage computation is still $O(2^n)$.

With a small change in the implementation we can also check tree coverage. Since in tree coverage we can flip the value of q several times, the variable *flag* is no longer needed. Instead, we need $\log |W|$ variables $x_1, \ldots, x_{\log |W|}$ for encoding the state w that is now being checked for tree q-coverage. The state w is not known in advance and the variables $x_1, \ldots, x_{\log |W|}$ are initialized non-deterministically and then kept unchanged to maintain the encoding of some state of the system. The variable *flip* is nondeterministically assigned **true** or **false** in each step. Instead of reading q, the module $\mathcal{A}$ reads $q \oplus (flip \wedge at\_w)$, where at_w holds iff the encoding of the current state coincides with $x_1, \ldots, x_{\log |W|}$. Thus, when both *flip* and at_w hold, which may happen several times, yet only when the current state is w, the value of q is flipped. So, the synchronous composition of the modules is not empty iff the state that was visited when *flip* becomes **true** for the first time is tree q-covered. Finally, by nondeterministically choosing the values of $x_1, \ldots, x_{\log |W|}$ at the first step of the run and fixing *flip* to **true**, we can also check structure coverage.

The complexity of coverage computation for tree and structure coverage is a function of the size of the state space, which is at most exponential in the number of state variables. For both tree and structure coverage, we double the number of variables by introducing n new variables that encode the flipped state. Thus, the state-space size is $O(2^{2n})$ instead of $O(2^n)$. While symbolic algorithms may have the same worst-case complexity as enumerative algorithms, in practice they are typically superior for many classes of applications. We believe that there is an ordering of the BDD variables that would circumvent the worst-case complexity. On the other hand, the naive approach always require 2^n model-checking iterations. Thus, our algorithm is likely to perform better than the naive approach.

In our definitions of coverage we assumed that a change in the labeling of states does not affect the transitions of the system. This is why the transitions of the modules that model the behavior of the system remain unchanged when flipping happens. A different definition, which involves changes in the transition relation is required when we assume that the states are encoded by atomic propositions in AP and the transition relation is given as a relation between values of the atomic propositions in AP. Then, flipping q in a state w causes changes in the transitions to and from w [CKV01]. Thus, in this case it is not enough to change the module $\mathcal{A}$ in order to compute the covered sets and we also have to change the modules of the system. This can be achieved by defining the variables *flip* and *flag* globally, and referring to their value in all modules of the system. This involves a broader change in the source code of the model.

Note that our algorithm is independent of the fairness condition being Büchi, and it can handle any fairness condition for which the model-checking procedure supports the check for fair paths. Also, it is easy to see that the same algorithm can handle systems with multiple initial states.

4   Indicators for LTL Formulas

In this section we reduce the computation of node q-covered sets to model checking. Given an LTL formula φ and an observable signal q, we want to find an *indicator* formula for φ that distinguishes between the covered and uncovered states in all Kripke structures. Formally, we have the following.

Definition 2. *Given an LTL formula φ and an observable signal q, an indicator for φ and q is a formula $Ind_q(\varphi)$ such that for all Kripke structures K that satisfy φ, we have*

$$\{w \in W : w \models Ind_q(\varphi)\} = NC(K, \varphi, q).$$

The motivation of indicators is clear. Once $Ind_q(\varphi)$ is found, global model-checking procedures can return the set of node q-covered states.

We show that for LTL formulas, we can construct indicators in the full μ-calculus, where we allow both future and past modalities (see [Koz83] for a definition of μ-calculus with future modalities). Formally, the full μ-calculus for a set AP of atomic propositions and the set Var of variables includes the following formulas:

- **true, false,** p, for $p \in AP$, and y, for $y \in Var$.
- $\neg\varphi_1$, $\varphi_1 \vee \varphi_2$, and $\varphi_1 \wedge \varphi_2$ for full μ-calculus formulas φ_1 and φ_2.
- $AX\varphi$, $EX\varphi$, $AY\varphi$, and $EY\varphi$ for full μ-calculus formula φ.
- $\mu y.\varphi(y)$ and $\nu y.\varphi(y)$, where $y \in Var$ and φ is a full μ-calculus formula monotone in y.

A *sentence* is a formula that contains no free atomic proposition variables. The semantics of full μ-calculus sentences is defined with respect to Kripke structures. The semantics of the path quantifiers A ("for all paths") and E ("there exists a path"), and the temporal operators X ("next"), and Y ("yesterday") assumes that both future and past are branching [KP95]. That is, for a state w, we have $w \models AX\varphi$ iff for all v such that $R(w, v)$, we have $v \models \varphi$, and $w \models AY\psi$ iff for all u such that $R(u, w)$, we have $u \models \psi$. We assume that the initial states of the Kripke structure are labeled with a special atomic proposition $init$ ($w_0 \models AY\mathbf{false}$ and $init \not\models AY\mathbf{true}$).

The construction of $Ind_q(\varphi)$ proceeds as follows. We first construct a formula, denoted Ψ, that describes $A_{\neg\varphi}$. The formula Ψ is a disjunction of formulas ψ_s, for states s of $A_{\neg\varphi}$, and it describes states of $A_{\neg\varphi}$ that participate in an accepting run of $A_{\neg\varphi}$. For each state s, the formula ψ_s is the conjunction of two formulas, $Reach_s$ and Acc_s, defined as follows.

- The formula $Reach_s$ is satisfied in a state w of a Kripke structure K iff there exists a run of $A_{\neg\varphi}$ on an initialized path of K that visits the state s as it reads w.
- The formula Acc_s is satisfied in a state w of a Kripke structure K iff there exists an accepting run of $A_{\neg\varphi}^s$ on a w-path of K (recall that $A_{\neg\varphi}^s$ is defined as $A_{\neg\varphi}$ with initial set $\{s\}$).

Then, $\Psi = \bigvee_{s \in S} Reach_s \wedge Acc_s$. So, for every Kripke structure K, a state w in K satisfies Ψ iff there exists a state $s \in S$ such that there exists an accepting run of $A_{\neg\varphi}$ on an initialized path of K that visits the state s as it reads w. The formulas $Reach_s$ refer to the past and are constructed as in [HKQ98] using past modalities. The formulas Acc_s refer to the future and are constructed as in [EL86,BC96], using future modalities [4].

---

[4] The algorithms in [HKQ98,EL86,BC96] construct μ-systems of equational blocks, and not μ-calculus formulas. The translation from μ-formulas to μ-systems may involve an exponential

Note that $K \not\models \varphi$ iff there exists $w \in W$ such that $w \models \Psi$. Since K satisfies φ, there is no state $w \in W$ that satisfies Ψ. Our goal is to find the node q-covered states of K. These are the states that satisfy Ψ after a flip of the value of q in them [5]. In order to simulate such a flip, we have to separate between the part that describes present behavior, and the parts that describe past or future behavior in the formulas $Reach_s$ and Acc_s, respectively. For that, we first replace all μ-calculus formulas by equivalent *guarded* formulas. A μ-calculus formula is *guarded* if for all $y \in Var$, all the occurrences of y are in the scope of X or Y [BB87]. It is shown in [KVW00] that given a μ-calculus formula, we can construct an equivalent guarded formula in linear time. Then, in order to separate the part that describes present behavior, we replace each formula $\mu y . f(y)$ by the equivalent formula $f(\mu y . f(y))$. For example, the formula $\mu y . p \vee AXy$ is replaced by $p \vee AX\mu y . p \vee AXy$. In fact, when constructed as in [HKQ98], the formulas $Reach_s$ are already pure-past formulas, they do not refer to the present, and the above separation is required only for the formulas Acc_s.

We can now complete the construction of the indicators. We distinguish between two cases. In the first case, w is labeled q and we check whether changing the label to $\neg q$ creates an accepting run of $\mathcal{A}_{\neg \varphi}$. In the second case, w is labeled $\neg q$ and we check whether changing the label to q creates an accepting run of $\mathcal{A}_{\neg \varphi}$. Let $NC^+(K, \varphi, q)$ be the set of node q-covered states of K for φ and q that are labeled with q, that is, $NC^+(K, \varphi, q) = NC(K, \varphi, q) \cap \{w \in W : q \in L(w)\}$. Let Ψ_q^+ be the formula obtained from Ψ by replacing with q each occurrence of $\neg q$ that is not in the scope of a temporal operator. A state $w \in W$ satisfies Ψ_q^+ iff there exists a state $s \in S$ and an accepting run of $\mathcal{A}_{\neg \varphi}$ on an initialized path of K that visits the state s as it reads w with the value of q flipped. Thus, the set $NC^+(K, \varphi, q)$ is exactly the set $\{w \in W : w \models \Psi^+\}$. In the similar way we can define $NC^-(K, \varphi, q)$ as the set $NC(K, \varphi, q) \cap \{w \in W : q \notin L(w)\}$, and the formula Ψ_q^- that is obtained from Ψ by replacing with $\neg q$ each positive occurrence of q that is not in the scope of a temporal operator. The set $NC^-(K, \varphi, q)$ is exactly the set $\{w \in W : w \models \Psi^-\}$. Now, the indicator formula for φ is $Ind_q(\varphi) = \Psi_q^+ \vee \Psi_q^-$.

Theorem 3. *Given an LTL formula φ and an observable signal q, there exists a full μ-calculus formula $Ind_q(\varphi)$ of size exponential in φ such that for every Kripke structure K, the set of node-uncovered states of K with respect to φ and q is exactly the set of states of K that satisfy $Ind_q(\varphi)$.*

As discussed in [HKQ98,EL86,BC96], Ψ has alternation depth 2 (alternation is required in order to specify Büchi acceptance) and is alternation free if φ is a safety formula (then, $\mathcal{A}_{\neg \varphi}$ can be made an automaton with a looping acceptance condition [Sis94]). The size of the automaton $\mathcal{A}_{\neg \varphi}$ is exponential in the size of the formula φ [VW94], and the size of the formulas $Reach_s$ and Acc_s is linear in the size of $\mathcal{A}_{\neg \varphi}$. Hence, the size of indicator formula $Ind_q(\varphi)$ is exponential in the size of φ.

---

blow-up. While the our algorithm is described here in terms of μ-calculus formulas, we can work with μ-systems directly. The operators $\wedge$ and $\vee$ on μ-formulas are defined on the systems of equational blocks as well.

[5] This semantics naturally translates to node coverage. For structure and tree coverage other definitions are needed.

We note that the exponential blow-up may not appear in practice [KV98,BRS99]. Since the semantics of μ-calculus with past modalities refers to structure, rather than trees (that is, the past is branching), model checking algorithms for μ-calculus with only future modalities can be modified to handle past without increasing complexity [KP95]. Model-checking complexity $K \models \psi$ for a μ-calculus formula ψ with alternation depth 2 is quadratic in $|K| \cdot |\psi|$ [EL86]. For alternation-free μ-calculus, the complexity is linear [CS91]. So, the complexity of finding the covered set using our reduction is $(|K| \cdot 2^{O(|\varphi|)})^2$ for general LTL properties and is $O(|K| \cdot 2^{O(|\varphi|)})$ for safety properties.

Remark 1. Two-way bisimulation extends bisimulation by examining both successors and predecessors of a state [HKQ98]. Two states w and w' are two-way bisimilar iff they satisfy the same full μ-calculus formulas. Since indicators are full μ-calculus formula, it follows that if w and w' are two-way bisimilar, they agree on the value of the indicator formula, thus w is node q-covered iff w' is node q-covered. In other words, the *distinguishing power* of node coverage is not greater than that of two-way bisimulation. In the full version we show that node coverage can distinguish between one-way bisimilar states. Thus, the use of full μ-calculus is essential for the construction of indicators.

References

[BB87]   B. Banieqbal and H. Barringer. Temporal logic with fixed points. In *Temporal Logic in Specification, LNCS* 398, pp. 62–74, 1987.

[BB94]   D. Beaty and R. Bryant. Formally verifying a microprocessor using a simulation methodology. In *Proc. 31st DAC*, pp. 596–602. IEEE Computer Society, 1994.

[BBER97] I. Beer, S. Ben-David, C. Eisner, and Y. Rodeh. Efficient detection of vacuity in ACTL formulas. In *Proc. 9th CAV, LNCS* 1254, pp. 279–290, 1997.

[BC96]   G. Bhat and R. Cleaveland. Efficient local model-checking for fragments of the modal μ-calculus. In *Proc. TACAS, LNCS* 1055, 1996.

[BGS00]   R. Bloem, H.N. Gabow, and F. Somenzi. An algorithm for strongly connected component analysis in $n \log n$ symbolic steps. In *FMCAD, LNCS,*2000.

[BH99]   J.P. Bergmann and M.A. Horowitz. Improving coverage analysis and test generation for large designs. In *Proc 11th CAD*, pp. 580–584, November 1999.

[BRS99]   R. Bloem, K. Ravi, and F. Somenzi. Efficient decision procedures for model checking of linear time logic properties. In *Proc. 11th CAV, LNCS* 1633, pp. 222–235, 1999.

[Büc62]   J.R. Büchi. On a decision method in restricted second order arithmetic. In *Proc. Internat. Congr. Logic, Method. and Philos. Sci. 1960*, pp. 1–12, Stanford, 1962. Stanford University Press.

[CE81]   E.M. Clarke and E.A. Emerson. Design and synthesis of synchronization skeletons using branching time temporal logic. In *Proc. Workshop on Logic of Programs, LNCS* 131, pp. 52–71, 1981.

[CGMZ95] E.M. Clarke, O. Grumberg, K.L. McMillan, and X. Zhao. Efficient generation of counterexamples and witnesses in symbolic model checking. In *Proc. 32nd DAC*, pp. 427–432. IEEE Computer Society, 1995.

[CGP99]   E.M. Clarke, O. Grumberg, and D. Peled. *Model Checking*. MIT Press, 1999.

[CKV01]   H. Chockler, O. Kupferman, and M.Y. Vardi. Coverage metrics for temporal logic model checking. In *TACAS, LNCS* 2031, pp. 528 – 542, 2001.

[CS91]   R. Cleaveland and B. Steffen. A linear-time model-checking algorithm for the alternation-free modal μ-calculus. In *Proc. 3rd CAD, LNCS* 575, pp. 48–58, 1991.

[DGK96]   S. Devadas, A. Ghosh, and K. Keutzer. An observability-based code coverage metric for functional simulation. In *Proc. 8th CAD*, pp. 418–425, 1996.

[EL86]   E.A. Emerson and C.-L. Lei. Efficient model checking in fragments of the propositional μ-calculus. In *Proc. 1st LICS*, pp. 267–278, Cambridge, June 1986.

[FAD99]   F. Fallah, P. Ashar, and S. Devadas. Simulation vector generation from HDL descriptions for observability enhanced-statement coverage. In *Proc. of the 36th DAC*, pp. 666–671, June 1999.

[FDK98]   F. Fallah, S. Devadas, and K. Keutzer.   OCCOM: efficient computation of observability-based code coverage metrics for functional simulation. In *Proc. of the 35th DAC*, pp. 152–157, June 1998.

[HH96]   R.C. Ho and M.A. Horowitz. Validation coverage analysis for complex digital designs. In *Proc 8th CAD*, pp. 146–151, November 1996.

[HHK96]   R.H. Hardin, Z. Har'el, and R.P. Kurshan. COSPAN. In *Proc. 8th CAV LNCS* 1102, pp. 423–427, 1996.

[HKHZ99] Y. Hoskote, T. Kam, P.-H Ho, and X. Zhao. Coverage estimation for symbolic model checking. In *Proc. 36th DAC*, pp. 300–305, 1999.

[HKQ98]   T.A. Henzinger, O. Kupferman, and S. Qadeer.   From pre-historic to post-modern symbolic model checking. In *Proc 10th CAV, LNCS* 1427, 1998.

[HMA95]   Y. Hoskote, D. Moundanos, and J. Abraham.   Automatic extraction of the control flow machine and application to evaluating coverage of verification vectors. In *Proc. of ICDD*, pp. 532–537, October 1995.

[HYHD95] R. Ho, C. Yang, M. Horowitz, and D. Dill. Architecture validation for processors. In *Proc. of the 22nd Annual Symp. on Comp. Arch.*, pp. 404–413, June 1995.

[KGG99]   S. Katz, D. Geist, and O. Grumberg. "Have I written enough properties ?" a method of comparison between specification and implementation. In *10th CHARME, LNCS* 1703, pp. 280–297, 1999.

[KN96]   M. Kantrowitz and L. Noack. I'm done simulating: Now what? verification coverage analysis and correctness checking of the DEC chip 21164 alpha microprocessor. In *Proc. 33th DAC*, pp. 325–330, June 1996.

[Koz83]   D. Kozen. Results on the propositional μ-calculus. *Theoretical Computer Science*, 27:333–354, 1983.

[KP95]   O. Kupferman and A. Pnueli. Once and for all. In *Proc. 10th IEEE Symp. on Logic in Comp. Sci.*, pp. 25–35, San Diego, June 1995.

[Kur98]   R.P. Kurshan. *FormalCheck User's Manual*. Cadence Design, Inc., 1998.

[KV98]   O. Kupferman and M.Y. Vardi. Relating linear and branching model checking. In *IFIP Work. Conf. on Programming Concepts and Methods*, pp. 304 – 326, New York, June 1998. Chapman & Hall.

[KV99]   O. Kupferman and M.Y. Vardi. Vacuity detection in temporal model checking. In *10th CHARME, LNCS* 1703, pp. 82–96, 1999.

[KVW00]   O. Kupferman, M.Y. Vardi, and P. Wolper.   An automata-theoretic approach to branching-time model checking. *Journal of the ACM*, 47(2):312–360, March 2000.

[LP85]   O. Lichtenstein and A. Pnueli. Checking that finite state concurrent programs satisfy their linear specification. In *Proc. 12th POPL*, pp. 97–107, 1985.

[MAH98]   D. Moumdanos, J.A. Abraham, and Y.V. Hoskote. Abstraction techniques for validation coverage analysis and test generation. *IEEE Trans. on Computers*, 1998.

[QS81]   J.P. Queille and J. Sifakis. Specification and verification of concurrent systems in Cesar. In *Proc. 5th Int. Symp. on Programming, LNCS* 137, pp. 337–351, 1981.

[Sis94]   A.P. Sistla. Satefy, liveness and fairness in temporal logic. *Formal Aspects of Computing*, 6:495–511, 1994.

[VW94]   M.Y. Vardi and P. Wolper. Reasoning about infinite computations. *Information and Computation*, 115(1):1–37, November 1994.

A Fast Bisimulation Algorithm

Agostino Dovier[1], Carla Piazza[2], and Alberto Policriti[2]

[1] Dip. di Informatica, Univ. di Verona
Strada Le Grazie 15, 37134 Verona, Italy
dovier@sci.univr.it
[2] Dip. di Matematica e Informatica, Univ. di Udine
Via Le Scienze 206, 33100 Udine, Italy
{piazza,policriti}@dimi.uniud.it

Abstract. In this paper we propose an efficient algorithmic solution to the problem of determining a *Bisimulation* Relation on a finite structure. Starting from a set-theoretic point of view we propose an algorithm that optimizes the solution to the *Relational coarsest Partition problem* given by Paige and Tarjan in 1987 and its use in model-checking packages is briefly discussed and tested. Our algorithm reaches, in particular cases, a linear solution.
Keywords: Bisimulation, non well-founded sets, automata, verification.

1 Introduction

It is difficult to accurately list all the fields in which, in one form or another, the notion of *bisimulation* was introduced and now plays a central rôle. Among the most important ones are: Modal Logic, Concurrency Theory, Formal Verification, and Set Theory.

Several existing verification tools make use of bisimulation in order to minimize the state spaces of systems description. The reduction of the number of states is important both in compositional and in non-compositional model checking. Bisimulation serves also as a means of checking equivalence between transition systems. The verification environment XEVE [5] provides bisimulation tools which can be used for both minimization and equivalence test. In general, in the case of explicit-state representation, the underlying algorithm used is the one proposed by Kanellakis and Smolka [17], while Bouali and de Simone algorithm [6] is used in the case of symbolic representation. The Concurrency Factory project [8] tests bisimulation using techniques based on the Kanellakis and Smolka algorithm. As for the criticism on the use of bisimulation algorithms, Fisler and Vardi observe in [10] that "bisimulation minimization does not appear to be viable in the context of invariance verification", but in the context of compositional verification it "makes certain problems tractable that would not be so without minimization" [2,21].

The first significant result related to the algorithmic solution of the bisimulation problem is in [16], where Hopcroft presents an algorithm for the minimization of the number of states in a given finite state automaton. The problem is equivalent to that of determining the coarsest partition of a set *stable* with

G. Berry, H. Comon, and A. Finkel (Eds.): CAV 2001, LNCS 2102, pp. 79–90, 2001.

respect to a finite set of functions. A variant of this problem is studied in [20], where it is shown how to solve it in linear time in case of a single function. Finally, in [19] Paige and Tarjan solved the problem for the general case (i.e., bisimulation) in which the stability requirement is relative to a relation E (on a set N) with an algorithm whose complexity is $O(|E| \log |N|)$.

The main feature of the linear solution to the single function coarsest partition problem (cf. [20]), is the use of a *positive* strategy in the search for the coarsest partition: the starting partition is the partition with singleton classes and the output is built via a sequence of steps in which two or more classes are merged. Instead, Hopcroft's solution to the (more difficult) many functions coarsest partition problem is based on a (somehow more natural) *negative* strategy: the starting partition is the input partition and each step consists of the split of all those classes for which the stability constraint is not satisfied. The interesting feature of Hopcroft's algorithm lies in its use of a clever ordering (the so-called "process the smallest half" ordering) for processing classes that must be used in a split step. Starting from an adaptation of Hopcroft's idea to the relational coarsest partition problem, Paige and Tarjan succeeded in obtaining their fast solution [19]. The algorithm presented in [4] is based on the naïve negative strategy, but on each iteration it stabilizes only reachable blocks with respect to all blocks. This is improved in [18], where only reachable blocks are stabilized with respect to reachable blocks only.

In this paper we present a procedure that integrates positive and negative strategies to obtain the algorithmic solution to the bisimulation problem and hence to the relational coarsest partition problem. The strategy we develop is driven by the set-theoretic notion of *rank* of a set. The algorithm we propose uses [20] and [19] as subroutines and terminates in linear time in many cases, for example when the input problem corresponds to a bisimulation problem on acyclic graphs (well-founded sets). It operates in linear time in other cases as well and, in any case, it runs at a complexity less than or equal to that of the algorithm by Paige and Tarjan [19]. Moreover, the partition imposed by the rank allows to process the input without storing the entire structure in memory at the same time.

The paper is organized as follows: in the next section we introduce the set-theoretic formulation of the bisimulation problem. The subsequent Section 3 contains the algorithm for the well-founded case. Section 4 presents the basic idea of our proposed algorithm and its optimizations are explained in the following section. In Section 6 we show how our results and methods can be adapted to the *multi-relational* coarsest partition problem (i.e., bisimualtion on labeled graphs) and in Section 7 we discuss some testing results. Some conclusions are drawn in Section 8. Detailed proofs of all the statements in this paper can be found in [9].

2 The Problem: A Set-Theoretic Perspective

One of the main features of intuitive (naïve) Set Theory is the well-foundedness of membership. As a consequence, standard axiomatic set theories include the *foundation* axiom that forces the membership relation to form no cycles or infinite descending chains. In the 80's the necessity to consider theories that do not assume this strong constraint (re-)emerged in many communities; hence various proposals for (axiomatic) non well-founded set theories (and universes) were developed (see [11, 1, 3]).

Sets can be seen as nothing but *accessible pointed graphs* (cf. Definition 1). Edges represent membership, $m \rightarrow n$ means that m has n as an element, and the nodes in the graph denote all the sets which contribute in the construction of the represented set.

Definition 1. *An* accessible pointed graph (apg) $\langle G, n \rangle$ *is a directed graph* $G = \langle N, E \rangle$ *together with a distinguished node* $n \in N$ *such that all the nodes in* N *are reachable from* n.

The resulting set-theoretic semantics for apg's, introduced and developed in [1], is based on the natural notion of *picture* of an apg. The extensionality axiom—saying that two objects are equal if and only if they contain exactly the same elements—is the standard criterion for establishing equality between sets. If extensionality is assumed it is immediate to see that, for example, different acyclic graphs can represent the same set. However, extensionality leads to a cyclic argument (no wonder!) whenever one tries to apply it as a test to establish whether two cyclic graphs represent the same non well-founded set (*hyperset*). To this end a condition (*bisimulation*) on apg's can be stated in accordance with extensionality: two apg's are bisimilar if and only if they are representations of the same set.

Definition 2. *Given two graphs* $G_1 = \langle N_1, E_1 \rangle$ *and* $G_2 = \langle N_2, E_2 \rangle$, *a bisimulation between* G_1 *and* G_2 *is a relation* $b \subseteq N_1 \times N_2$ *such that:*

1. $u_1 \, b \, u_2 \land \langle u_1, v_1 \rangle \in E_1 \Rightarrow \exists v_2 \in N_2(v_1 \, b \, v_2 \land \langle u_2, v_2 \rangle \in E_2)$
2. $u_1 \, b \, u_2 \land \langle u_2, v_2 \rangle \in E_2 \Rightarrow \exists v_1 \in N_1(v_1 \, b \, v_2 \land \langle u_1, v_1 \rangle \in E_1)$.

Two apg's $\langle G_1, n_1 \rangle$ *and* $\langle G_2, n_2 \rangle$ *are bisimilar if and only if there exists a bisimulation* b *between* G_1 *and* G_2 *such that* $n_1 \, b \, n_2$.

We can now say that two hypersets are equal if their representations are bisimilar. For example the apg $\langle \langle \{n\}, \emptyset, \rangle, n \rangle$ represents the empty set $\emptyset$. The hyperset Ω, i.e. the unique hyperset which satisfies the equation $x = \{x\}$ (see [1]), can be represented using the apg $\langle \langle \{n\}, \{\langle n, n \rangle\} \rangle, n \rangle$. Any graph such that each node has at least one outgoing edge can be shown to be a representation of Ω. It is clear that for each set there exists a collection of apg's which are all its representations. It is always the notion of bisimulation which allows us to find a *minimum* representation (there are no two nodes representing the same hyperset). Given an apg $\langle G, n \rangle$ that represents a set S, to find the minimum representation for S it is sufficient to consider the maximum bisimulation $\equiv$ between G and G. Such a bisimulation $\equiv$ always exists and is an equivalence relation over the set of nodes of G. The minimum representation of S is the apg $\langle G/\equiv, [n] \rangle$ (see [1]) which is usually called *bisimulation contraction of* G.

An equivalent way to present the problem is to define the concept of bisimulation as follows.

Definition 3. *Given a graph $G = \langle N, E \rangle$, a bisimulation on G is a relation $b \subseteq N \times N$ such that:*

1. $u_1 \, b \, u_2 \land \langle u_1, v_1 \rangle \in E \Rightarrow \exists v_2 (v_1 \, b \, v_2 \land \langle u_2, v_2 \rangle \in E)$
2. $u_1 \, b \, u_2 \land \langle u_2, v_2 \rangle \in E \Rightarrow \exists v_1 (v_1 \, b \, v_2 \land \langle u_1, v_1 \rangle \in E).$

A bisimulation on G is nothing but a bisimulation between G and G. The problem of recognizing if two graphs are bisimilar and the problem of determining the maximum bisimulation on a graph are equivalent. Two disjoint apg's $\langle \langle N_1, E_1 \rangle, \nu_1 \rangle$ and $\langle \langle N_2, E_2 \rangle, \nu_2 \rangle$ are bisimilar if and only if $\nu_1 \equiv \nu_2$, where $\equiv$ is the maximal bisimulation on $\langle \langle N_1 \cup N_2 \cup \{\mu\}, E_1 \cup E_2 \cup \{\langle \mu, \nu_1 \rangle, \langle \mu, \nu_2 \rangle\} \rangle, \mu \rangle$, with μ a new node. We consider the problem of finding the minimum graph bisimilar to a given graph, that is, the *bisimulation contraction* of a graph.

The notion of bisimulation can be connected to the notion of *stability*:

Definition 4. *Let E be a relation on the set N, E^{-1} its inverse relation, and P a partition of N. P is said to be* stable *with respect to E iff for each pair B_1, B_2 of blocks of P, either $B_1 \subseteq E^{-1}(B_2)$ or $B_1 \cap E^{-1}(B_2) = \emptyset$.*

Given a set N, k relations $E_1, \ldots, E_k$ on N, and a partition P of N, the *multirelational coarsest partition* problem consists of finding the coarsest refinement of P which is stable with respect to $E_1, \ldots, E_k$. As noted in [17], the algorithm of [19] that determines the coarsest partition of a set N stable with respect to k relations solves exactly the problem of *testing if two states of an observable Finite States Process (FSP)* are strongly equivalent. Our bisimulation problem is a particular case of *observable FSPs strong equivalence* problem ($k = 1$). In Section 6 we show how the case of bisimulation over a labeled graph (*multirelational* case) can be linearly reduced to our bisimulation problem. This means that the problem of finding the bisimulation contraction of a graph is equivalent to the multi-relational coarsest partition problem.

3   The Well-Founded Case

We start by considering the case of acyclic graphs (well-founded sets). Similarly to what is done in the minimization of Deterministic Finite Automata, it is possible to to determine the coarsest partition P stable w.r.t. E through the computation of a greatest fixpoint. A "negative" (and blind with respect to the relation) strategy is applicable: start with the coarsest partition $P = \{N\}$, choose a class B (the splitter) and split all the classes using B whenever P is *not* stable. The complexity of the algorithm, based on a negative strategy, presented in [19] for this problem is $O(|E| \log |N|)$.

We will take advantage of the set-theoretic point of view of the problem in order to develop a selection strategy for the splitters depending on the relation E. Making use of the ordering induced by the notion of *rank* we will start from a partition which is a refinement of the coarsest one; then we will choose the splitters using the ordering induced by the rank. These two ingredients allow to obtain a linear-time algorithm.

Definition 5. *Let* $G = \langle N, E \rangle$ *be a directed acyclic graph. The* rank *of a node* n *is recursively defined as follows:*

$$\begin{cases} rank(n) = 0 & \text{if } n \text{ is a leaf} \\ rank(n) = 1 + \max\{rank(m) : \langle n, m \rangle \in E\} & \text{otherwise} \end{cases}$$

The notion of *rank* determines a partition which is coarser than the maximum bisimulation.

Proposition 1. *Let* m *and* n *be nodes of an acyclic graph* G. *If* $m \equiv n$, *then* $rank(m) = rank(n)$.

The converse, of course, is not true. Let P be a partition of N such that for each block B in P it holds that $m, n \in B$ implies $rank(m) = rank(n)$; then every refinement of P fulfills the same property. Hence, we can assign to a block B the rank of its elements.

Algorithm 1 (Well-Founded Case).

1. **for** $n \in N$ **do compute** $rank(n)$; — compute the ranks
2. $\rho := \max\{rank(n) : n \in N\}$;
3. **for** $i = 0, \ldots, \rho$ **do** $B_i := \{n \in N : rank(n) = i\}$;
4. $P := \{B_i : i = 0, \ldots, \rho\}$; — P is the partition to be refined initialized with the B_i's
5. **for** $i = 0, \ldots, \rho$ **do**
   (a) $D_i := \{X \in P : X \subseteq B_i\}$; — determine the blocks currently at rank i
   (b) **for** $X \in D_i$ **do**
       $G := \mathbf{collapse}(G, X)$; — collapse nodes at rank i
   (c) **for** $n \in N \cap B_i$ **do** — refine blocks at higher ranks
       for $C \in P$ **and** $C \subseteq B_{i+1} \cup \ldots \cup B_\rho$ **do**
         $P := (P \setminus \{C\}) \cup \{\{m \in C : \langle m, n \rangle \in E\}, \{m \in C : \langle m, n \rangle \notin E\}\}$;

Step 1 can be performed in time $O(|N| + |E|)$ by a depth-first visit of the graph. Collapsing nodes $a_1, \ldots, a_k$, as in step 5(b), consists in eliminating all nodes but a_1 and replacing all edges incident to $a_2, \ldots, a_k$ by edges incident to a_1. Despite the nesting of **for**-loops the following holds.

Proposition 2. *The algorithm for the well-founded case correctly computes the bisimulation contraction of its input acyclic graph* $G = \langle N, E \rangle$ *and can be implemented so as to run in linear time* $O(|N| + |E|)$.

An example of computation of the above algorithm can be seen in Figure 1. In

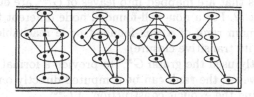

Fig. 1. Minimization Process.

all the examples we present, the computation steps proceed from left to right.

Those who are familiar with OBDDs ([7]) or with k-layered DFA's ([15]) can read our algorithm for the well-founded case as a generalization of the minimization algorithm for k-layered DFA. In the well-founded case we admit that a node at the i-th layer may reach a node at the j-th layer with $j > i$.

4   Basic Idea for the General Case

The presence of cycles causes the usual notion of rank (cf. Definition 5) to be not adequate: an extension of such a notion must be defined.

Definition 6. *Given a graph* $G = \langle N, E \rangle$, *let* $G^{scc} = \langle N^{scc}, E^{scc} \rangle$ *be the graph obtained as follows:*

$$N^{scc} = \{c : c \text{ is a strongly connected component in } G\}$$
$$E^{scc} = \{\langle c_1, c_2 \rangle : c_1 \neq c_2 \text{ and } \exists n_1 \in c_1, n_2 \in c_2(\langle n_1, n_2 \rangle \in E)\}$$

Given a node $n \in N$, *we refer to the node of* G^{scc} *associated to the strongly connected component of* n *as* $c(n)$.

Observe that G^{scc} is acyclic and if G is acyclic then G^{scc} is G itself.

We need to distinguish between the well-founded part and the non-well-founded part of a graph G.

Definition 7. *Let* $G = \langle N, E \rangle$ *and* $n \in N$. $G(n) = \langle N(n), E \upharpoonright N(n) \rangle$ *is the subgraph of* G *of the nodes reachable from* n. $WF(G)$, *the well-founded part of* G, *is* $WF(G) = \{n \in N : G(n) \text{ is acyclic}\}$.

Observe that $\langle G(n), n \rangle$ is an apg; if $n \in WF(G)$ then it denotes a well-founded set.

Definition 8. *Let* $G = \langle N, E \rangle$. *The* rank *of a node* n *of* G *is defined as:*

$$\begin{cases} rank\,(n) = 0 & \textit{if } n \textit{ is a leaf in } G \\ rank\,(n) = -\infty & \textit{if } c(n) \textit{ is a leaf in } G^{scc} \textit{ and } n \textit{ is not a leaf in } G \\ rank\,(n) = \max(\{1 + rank\,(m) : \langle c(n), c(m) \rangle \in E^{scc}, m \in WF(G)\} \cup \\ \qquad\qquad\quad \{rank\,(m) : \langle c(n), c(m) \rangle \in E^{scc}, m \notin WF(G)\}) & \textit{otherwise} \end{cases}$$

Since G^{scc} is always acyclic, the definition is correctly given. If G is acyclic then $G = G^{scc}$ and the above definition reduces to the one given in the well-founded case (Def. 5). Nodes that are mapped into leaves of G^{scc} are either bisimilar to $\emptyset$ or to the hyperset Ω. For a non-well-founded node different from Ω the rank is 1 plus the maximum rank of a well-founded node reachable from it (i.e., a well-founded set in its transitive closure).

We have explicitly used the graph G^{scc} to provide a formal definition of the notion of rank. However, the rank can be computed directly on G by two visits of the graph, avoiding the explicit construction of G^{scc}.

Proposition 3. *Let m and n be nodes of a graph G:*

1. *$m \equiv \Omega$ if and only if $rank(m) = -\infty$;*
2. *$m \equiv n$ implies $rank(m) = rank(n)$.*

The converse of Proposition 3.2 is not true. Moreover, the rank of $c(n)$ in G^{scc} (that can be computed using Def. 5) is not necessarily equal to the rank of n in G.

Given a graph $G = \langle N, E \rangle$ with $\rho = \max\{rank(n) : n \in N\}$, we call the sets of nodes $B_{-\infty}, B_0, \ldots, B_\rho$, where $B_i = \{n \in N : rank(n) = i\}$, the *rank components* of G.

Since we proved in the previous section that the bisimulation contraction can be computed in linear time on well-founded graphs, it is easy to see that we can use the algorithm for the well-founded case in order to process the nodes in $WF(G)$ for the general case. Hence, we can assume that the input graph for the general case does not contain two different bisimilar well-founded nodes.

Algorithm 2 (General Case).

1. **for** $n \in N$ **do** compute $rank(n)$; — compute the ranks
2. $\rho := \max\{rank(n) : n \in N\}$;
3. **for** $i = -\infty, 0, \ldots, \rho$ **do** $B_i := \{n \in N : rank(n) = i\}$;
4. $P := \{B_i : i = -\infty, 0, \ldots, \rho\}$; — P partition to be refined initialized with the B_i's
5. $G := \mathbf{collapse}(G, B_{-\infty})$; — collapse all the nodes of rank $-\infty$
6. **for** $n \in N \cap B_{-\infty}$ **do** — refine blocks at higher ranks
       for $C \in P$ and $C \neq B_{-\infty}$ **do**
           $P := (P \setminus \{C\}) \cup \{\{m \in C : \langle m, n \rangle \in E\}, \{m \in C : \langle m, n \rangle \notin E\}\}$;
7. **for** $i = 0, \ldots, \rho$ **do**
       (a) $D_i := \{X \in P : X \subseteq B_i\}$; — determine the blocks currently at rank i
           $G_i := \langle B_i, E \restriction B_i \rangle$; — isolate the subgraph of rank i
           $D_i := \mathbf{Paige\text{-}Tarjan}(G_i, D_i)$; — process rank i
       (b) **for** $X \in D_i$ **do**
           $G := \mathbf{collapse}(G, X)$; — collapse nodes at rank i
       (c) **for** $n \in N \cap B_i$ **do** — refine blocks at higher ranks
           for $C \in P$ and $C \subseteq B_{i+1} \cup \ldots \cup B_\rho$ **do**
               $P := (P \setminus \{C\}) \cup \{\{m \in C : \langle m, n \rangle \in E\}, \{m \in C : \langle m, n \rangle \notin E\}\}$;

In steps 1–4 we determine the ranks and we initialize a variable P representing the computed partition using the ranks. The collapse operation (steps 5 and 7(b)) is as in the well-founded case. Splits of higher rank blocks is instead done in steps 6 and 7(c). Step 7 is the core of the algorithm, where optimizations will take place. For each rank i we call the procedure of [19] on $G_i = \langle B_i, E \restriction B_i \rangle$, with a cost $O(|E \restriction B_i| \log |B_i|)$ and we update the partition P on nodes of rank greater than i. From these observations:

Proposition 4. *If $G = \langle N, E \rangle$ is a graph, then the worst case complexity of the above algorithm is $O(|E| \log |N|)$. The algorithm for the general case on input G correctly computes the bisimulation contraction of G.*

Proof. (Sketch) The global cost is no worse than (for some $c_1, c_2 \in \mathbb{N}$):

$$c_1(|N| + |E|) + \sum_{i=1}^{\rho} c_2(|E \upharpoonright B_i| \log |B_i|) = O(|E| \log |N|). \qquad (1)$$

The complexity of the method sketched above is asymptotically equivalent to that of Paige and Tarjan. However, as for the well-founded Algorithm 1, we take advantage of a refined initial partition and of a selection strategy of the blocks to be setected for splitting blocks of higher ranks. In a single rank, the negative strategy of the Paige-Tarjan algorithm is applied to the rank components which, in general, are much smaller than the global graph. In particular, for families of graphs such that ρ is $\Theta(|N|)$ and the size of the each rank component is bounded by a constant c the global cost becomes linear (cf. formula (1)).

5   Optimizations in the General Case

We present here two situations in which we are able to optimize our algorithm. In some cases, a linear running time is reached. Other possible optimizations are presented in [9].

First Optimization. This optimization makes use of the **Paige-Tarjan-Bonic** procedure [20]. Such a procedure can be used in some cases to solve the coarsest partition problem in linear time adopting a "positive" strategy. Its integration in our algorithm produces a global strategy that can therefore be considered as a mixing of positive and negative strategies.

Definition 9. *A node n belonging to a rank component $B_i \subseteq N$ is said to be a multiple node if $|\{m \in B_i : \langle n, m \rangle \in E\}| > 1$.*

Whenever B_i has no multiple nodes, we can replace the call to **Paige-Tarjan** in step $7(a)$ with a call to **Paige-Tarjan-Bonic**. This allows us to obtain a *linear time* performance at rank i (in the formula (1) the term $c_2(|E \upharpoonright B_i| \log |B_i|)$ can be replaced by $c_3(|E \upharpoonright B_i| + |B_i|)$ for some $c_3 \in \mathbb{N}$).

Proposition 5. *The optimized algorithm for the general case on input G correctly computes the bisimulation contraction of G. If $G = \langle N, E \rangle$ is a graph with no multiple nodes, then its worst case complexity is $O(|N| + |E|)$.*

In Figure 2 we show an example of a graph on which the above optimization can be performed and the overall algorithm turns out to be linear.

Second Optimization. The crucial consideration behind the second optimization we propose is the following: the outgoing edges of a node u allow one to establish to which other nodes of the same rank component it is bisimilar. If we have some means to know that u is not bisimilar to any other nodes of its rank component, we can simply delete all edges outgoing from u. The deletion of a set of edges splits a rank component (i.e., we can recalculate the rank) and makes it possible

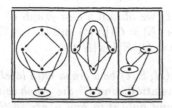

Fig. 2. Example of the First Kind of Optimization.

to recursively apply our algorithm on a simpler case. The typical case in which the above idea can be applied occurs when, at a given iteration i, there exists a block X in the set D_i of the blocks of rank i which is a singleton set $\{n\}$: then all the outgoing edges from the node n can be safely deleted. In next section we show the usefulness of this optimization in cases coming from formal verification.

6   Labeled Graphs

In several applications (e.g., Concurrency, Databases, Verification) graphs to be tested for bisimilarity have labels on edges (typically, denoting *actions*) and, sometimes, labels on nodes (typically, stating a *property* that must hold in a state). If only edges are labeled, we are in the context of the multi-relation coarsest partition problem. The definition of bisimulation has to be refined in order to take into consideration the labels on nodes and the labels on edges.

Definition 10. *Let L be a finite set of labels and A be a finite set of actions. Given a labeled graph $G = \langle N, E, \ell \rangle$, with $E \subseteq N \times A \times N$ (we use $u \overset{a}{\rightarrow} v \in E$ for $\langle u, a, v \rangle \in E$) and $\ell : N \longrightarrow L$, a labeled bisimulation on G is a symmetric relation $b \subseteq N \times N$ such that:*

- *if $u_1 \, b \, u_2$, then $\ell(u_1) = \ell(u_2)$;*
- *if $u_1 \, b \, u_2$ and $u_1 \overset{a}{\rightarrow} v_1 \in E$, then there is an edge $u_2 \overset{a}{\rightarrow} v_2 \in E$ and $v_1 \, b \, v_2$.*

Let us analyze how our algorithm can solve the extended problem. To start, assume that only nodes are labeled. The only change is in the initialization phase: the partition suggested by the *rank* function must be refined so as to leave in the same block only nodes with the same label. Then the algorithm can be employed without further changes. Assume now that edges can be labeled.

$$m \overset{a}{\longrightarrow} n \quad \Rightarrow \quad m \longrightarrow \mu \longrightarrow n$$
$$\boxed{\ell(m)} \quad \boxed{\ell(n)} \qquad \boxed{\ell(m)} \quad \boxed{\ell(\mu) = \langle m, a \rangle} \quad \boxed{\ell(n)}$$

Fig. 3. Removing Edges Labels.

We suggest the following encoding: for each pair of nodes m, n and for each label a such that there is an edge $m \overset{a}{\rightarrow} n \in E$ (see also Fig. 3):

- remove the edge $m \overset{a}{\rightarrow} n$;
- add a new node μ, labeled by the pair $\langle m, a \rangle$;
- add the two (unlabeled) new edges $m \rightarrow \mu, \mu \rightarrow n$.

Starting from $G = \langle N, E, \ell \rangle$ we obtain a new graph $G' = \langle N', E', \ell \rangle$, with $E' \subseteq N \times N$, where $|N'| = |N| + |E| = O(|N|^2)$ and $|E'| = 2|E|$. Thus, our algorithm can run in $O(|E'| \log |N'|) = O(|E| \log |N|)$.

Proposition 6. *Let $G = \langle N, E, \ell \rangle$ be a graph with labeled edges and nodes, $\equiv$ be its maximum labeled bisimulation, and G' the graph with labeled nodes obtained from G. Then, $m \equiv n$ if and only if m and n are in the same class at the end of the execution of Algorithm 2 on G' with the initial partition (Step 4) further split using node labels.*

7 Testing

To the best of our knowledge there is no "official" set of benchmarks for testing an algorithm such as the one we propose in our paper. We decided to test our implementation in the context of formal verification using model checkers and considering the transition graphs they generate from a given program. In particular, we have considered the transition systems generated by the examples in the SPIN package [14]: built using ideas from [13], their aim is to check that the implementation of a protocol verifies a formal specification. Usually, the graphs generated consist of a unique strongly connected component and the set of possible labels is huge. When we rewrite them into unlabeled graphs, we usually obtain graphs on which we can perform the second optimization proposed in Section 5. Such an optimization allows us to delete edges in the graphs, obtaining graphs on which the algorithm runs in linear time. In Figure 4 we show the graph obtained for the process Cp0 of the Snooping Cache protocol. From left to right are depicted: the labeled graph generated, its corresponding unlabeled graph, the graph after our optimization, and, finally, its bisimulation contraction that can be computed in linear time.

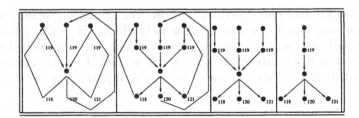

Fig. 4. Bisimulation Contraction of Cp0 from Snoopy.

These considerations about the "topology" of verification graphs suggested us some examples on which compare the performances of our algorithm with that of Paige and Tarjan. Details about the implementation (both in C and in Pascal), the machine used for the tests together with the code and the results of further tests are available at http://www.sci.univr.it/~dovier/BISIM. The graphs for Test 1 (cf. Figure 5) we present here are transitive closures of binary trees. The graphs for Test 2 are obtained by linking with cycles nodes at the

	Test1				Test2			
Nodes	8191	16383	32767	65535	8204	16397	32782	65551
Edges	90114	196610	425896	917506	102411	221196	475149	1015822
PT	.22	.49	1.09	2.91	.49	1.10	2.47	5.77
Alg	.06	.12	.33	.71	.23	.55	1.25	2.86

Fig. 5. Two Tests (Time in Seconds).

same level of the graphs of the first test. Then the "even" nodes of these cycles are connected by an edge to a node of an acyclic linear graph.

8 Conclusion and Further Developments

We proposed algorithms to determine the minimum, bisimulation equivalent, representation of a directed graph or, equivalently, to test bisimilarity between two directed graphs. The algorithms are built making use of algorithmic solution to the relational and single function coarsest partition problem as subroutines. In the acyclic case the performance of the sketched algorithm is linear while, in the cyclic case turns out to be linear when there are no multiple nodes. In general its performance is no worse than that of the best known solution for the relational coarsest partition problem.

In [10], Fisler and Vardi compare three minimization algorithms with an invariance checking algorithm (which does not use minimization) and argue that the last is more efficient. The minimization algorithms they consider are those of Paige and Tarjan [19], of Bouajjani, Fernandez and Halbwachs [4], and of Lee and Yannakakis [18]. An important conclusion they draw is that even if the last two algorithms are tailored to verification contexts, while the Paige and Tarjan one is not, the latter performs better. This suggests that "minimization algorithms tailored to verification settings should pay attention to choosing splitters carefully". We have presented here an algorithm, which is not specifically tailored to verification, but whose main difference w.r.t. the Paige and Tarjan's one is that it performs better choices of the splitters and of the initial partition thanks to the use of the notion of rank. In some cases we obtain linear time runs, moreover the initial partition we use allows to process the input without storing the entire structure in memory at the same time.

Our next task will be the integration of this algorithm with the symbolic model-checking techniques. Further studies relative to the applicability of the circle of ideas presented here to the problem of determining *simulations* (cf. [12]) are also under investigation.

Acknowledgements

We thank Nadia Ugel for her C implementation and the anonymous referees for useful suggestions. The work is partially supported by MURST project: *Certificazione automatica di programmi mediante interpretazione astratta*.

References

1. P. Aczel. *Non-well-founded sets*, volume 14 of *Lecture Notes, Center for the Study of Language and Information*. Stanford, 1988.
2. A. Aziz, V. Singhal, G. Swamy, and R. Brayton. Minimizing interacting finite state machines: a compositional approach to language containment. In *Proc. Int'l Conference on Computer Design*, 1994.
3. J. Barwise and L. Moss. *Vicious Circles. On the Mathematics of non-well-founded phenomena*. Lecture Notes, Center for the Study of Language and Information. Stanford, 1996.
4. A. Bouajjani, J.C. Fernandez, and N. Halbwachs. Minimal model generation. In E. Clarke and R. Kurshan, editors, *Proc. Int'l Conference on Computer-Aided Verification CAV'90*, volume 531 of *LNCS*, pages 197–203. Springer, 1990.
5. A. Bouali. XEVE, an ESTEREL verification environment. In A. J. Hu and M. Y. Vardi, editors, *Proc. Int'l Conference on Computer-Aided Verification CAV'98*, LNCS, pages 500–504. Springer, 1998.
6. A. Bouali and R. de Simone. Symbolic bisimulation minimization. In *Proc. Int'l Conference on Computer-Aided Verification CAV'92*, volume 663 of *LNCS*, pages 96–108. Springer, 1992.
7. R.E. Bryant. Graph based algorithms for Boolean function manipulation. *IEEE Transaction on Computers*, C-35(8):677–691, 1986.
8. R. Cleaveland, J. Parrow, and B. Steffen. The concurrency workbench: A semantics-based tool for the verification of concurrent systems. *ACM Transactions on Programming Languages and Systems (TOPLAS)*, 15(1):36–72, 1993.
9. A. Dovier, C. Piazza, and A. Policriti. A fast bisimulation algorithm. TR UDMI/14/00/RR, Dip. di Matematica e Informatica, Univ. di Udine, 2000. http://www.dimi.uniud.it/~piazza/bisim.ps.gz.
10. K. Fisler and M.Y. Vardi. Bisimulation and model checking. In *Proc. Correct Hardware Design and Verification Methods*, volume 1703 of *LNCS*, pages 338–341. Springer, 1999.
11. M. Forti and F. Honsell. Set theory with free construction principles. *Annali Scuola Normale Superiore di Pisa, Cl. Sc.*, IV(10):493–522, 1983.
12. M.R. Henzinger, T.A. Henzinger, and P.W. Kopke. Computing simulations on finite and infinite graphs. In *Proc. 36th IEEE Symp. on Foundations of Computer Science, FOCS 1995*, pages 453–462, 1995.
13. G.J. Holzmann. *Design and Validation of Computer Protocols*. Prentice Hall, 1991.
14. G.J. Holzmann. The model checker SPIN. *IEEE Transactions on Software Engineering*, 23(5), 1997.
15. G.J. Holzmann and A. Puri. A minimized automaton representation of reachable states. *Software Tools for Technology Transfer*, 2(3):270–278, November 1999.
16. J.E. Hopcroft. An n log n algorithm for minimizing states in a finite automaton. In *Theory of Machines and Computations, Ed. by Zvi Kohavi and Azaria Paz*, pages 189–196. Academic Press, 1971.
17. P.C. Kanellakis and S.A. Smolka. CCS expressions, finite state processes, and three problems of equivalence. *Information and Computation*, 86(1):43–68, 1990.
18. D. Lee and M. Yannakakis. Online minimization of transition systems. In *Proc. 24th ACM Symposium on Theory of Computing*, pages 264–274, May 1992.
19. R. Paige and R.E. Tarjan. Three partition refinement algorithms. *SIAM Journal on Computing*, 16(6):973–989, 1987.
20. R. Paige, R.E. Tarjan, and R. Bonic. A linear time solution to the single function coarsest partition problem. *Theoretical Computer Science*, 40(1):67–84, 1985.
21. F. Rahim. Property-dependent modular model checking application to VHDL with computational results. In *Proc. Int'l Workshop HLDVT*, 1998.

Symmetry and Reduced Symmetry in Model Checking*

A. Prasad Sistla[1] and Patrice Godefroid[2]

[1] University of Illinois at Chicago
Department of Electrical Engineering and Computer Science
Chicago, IL 60607, USA
[2] Bell Laboratories, Lucent Technologies, Naperville, IL 50566, USA

Abstract. Symmetry reduction methods exploit symmetry in a system in order to efficiently verify its temporal properties. Two problems may prevent the use of symmetry reduction in practice: (1) the property to be checked may distinguish symmetric states and hence not be preserved by the symmetry, and (2) the system may exhibit little or no symmetry. In this paper, we present a general framework that addresses both of these problems. We introduce "Guarded Annotated Quotient Structures" for compactly representing the state space of systems even when those are asymmetric. We then present algorithms for checking any temporal property on such representations, including non-symmetric properties.

1 Introduction

In the last few years there has been much interest in symmetry-based reduction methods for model checking concurrent systems [10, 2, 4, 5, 8, 12]. These methods exploit automorphisms, of the global state graph of the system to be verified, induced by permutations on process indices and variables. Existing symmetry-reduction methods, for verification of a correctness property given by a temporal formula ϕ, can be broadly classified into two categories: the first class of methods [2, 4, 10, 12] consider only those automorphisms that preserve the atomic predicates appearing in ϕ, construct a *Quotient Structure* (*QS*) and check the formula ϕ on the *QS* using traditional model-checking algorithms; the second class of methods [5] consider all automorphisms, induced by process/variable permutations, and construct an *Annotated Quotient Structure* (*AQS*), and unwind it to verify the formula ϕ.

In this paper, we generalize symmetry-based reduction in several ways. First, the mathematical framework, used to formalize symmetry reduction, supports *any* automorphism on the system's state graph; for example, automorphisms induced by permutations on variable-value pairs can be considered in addition to those induced by permutations on process indices and variables. Thus, this framework allows for more automorphisms and hence greater reduction.

* Sistla's work is supported in part by the NSF grant CCR-9988884 and was partly done while visiting Bell Laboratories.

G. Berry, H. Comon, and A. Finkel (Eds.): CAV 2001, LNCS 2102, pp. 91–103, 2001.

Second, we introduce the notion of *Guarded Annotated Quotient Structure* (*GQS*) to represent, in a very compact way, the state graph of systems with little or even no symmetry. In a nutshell, a *GQS* is an *AQS* whose edges are also associated with a guard representing the condition under which the corresponding original program transition is executable. Given a program P and its reachability graph G, by adding edges to G (via a transformation of P), we obtain another graph H that has more symmetry than G, and hence can be represented more compactly. A *GQS* for G can be viewed as an *AQS* for H whose edges are labeled with guards in such a way that the original edges of G can be recovered from the representation of H. To verify a temporal formula ϕ, the *GQS* is unwound as needed, by tracking the values of the atomic predicates in ϕ and the guards of the *GQS*, so that only edges in G are considered. The *GQS* of G can be much smaller than its *QS* because it is defined from a larger set of automorphisms: a *GQS* is derived by considering all the automorphisms of H, which exhibits more symmetry than G, including those automorphisms that do not preserve the atomic predicates in ϕ. We show that unwinding *GQS* on-demand, in order to verify a property ϕ, can be done without ever generating a structure larger than *QS*.

Third, we present two new techniques for further optimizing the model-checking procedure using *GQS*s. These techniques minimize the amount of unwinding necessary to check a formula ϕ and may yield an exponential improvement in performance. The first technique, called *formula decomposition*, consists of decomposing ϕ into groups of top-level sub-formulas so that atomic predicates with in a group are correlated; the satisfaction of ϕ can then be checked by checking each group of sub-formulas separately, which in turn can be done by successively unwinding the *GQS* with respect to only the predicates appearing in each group separately; therefore, unwinding *GQS* with respect to all the atomic predicates appearing in ϕ simultaneously can be avoided. The second technique, called *sub-formula tracking*, consists of identifying a maximal set of "independent" sub-formulas of ϕ and unwinding the *GQS* by tracking these sub-formulas only. These two complementary techniques can be applied recursively.

The paper is organized as follows. Section 2 introduces the background information and notation. Section 3 introduces *GQS* and the model-checking method employing it. Section 4 presents the techniques based on formula decomposition and sub-formula tracking. Section 5 presents preliminary experimental results. Section 6 contains concluding remarks and related work. Proofs of theorems are omitted due to space limitations.

2   Background

A Kripke structure K is a tuple $(S, E, \mathcal{P}, L)$ where S is a set of elements, called states, $E \subseteq S \times S$ is a set of edges, $\mathcal{P}$ is a set of atomic propositions and $L : S \to 2^{\mathcal{P}}$ is a function that associates a subset of $\mathcal{P}$ with each state in S. CTL^* is a logic for specifying temporal properties of concurrent programs (e.g., see [3]). It includes the temporal operators U (until), X (nexttime) and the existential path quantifier E. Two types of CTL^* formulas are defined inductively: path formulas and state formulas. Every atomic proposition is a state formula as well as a path formula. If p and q are state formulas (resp., path formulas) then $p \land q$ and $\neg p$ are also state formulas (resp., path formulas). If p and q are path formulas then pUq, Xp are path formulas and $E(p)$ is a state formula. Every state formula is also a path formula. We use the abbreviation $EF(p)$ for $E(TrueUp)$ and $AG(p)$ for $\neg(EF\neg p)$. A CTL^* formula is a state formula. CTL is the fragment of CTL^* where all path formulas are of the form pUq or of the form Xp where p, q are state formulas. CTL^* formulas are interpreted over Kripke structures (e.g, see [3] for a detailed presentation of the semantics of CTL^*).

Let $K = (S, R, \mathcal{P}, L)$ and $K' = (S', R', \mathcal{P}, L')$ be two Kripke structures with the same set of atomic propositions. A bisimulation between K and K' is a binary relation $U \subseteq S \times S'$ such that, for every $(s, s') \in U$, the following conditions are all satisfied: (1) $L(s) = L'(s')$; (2) for every t such that $(s, t) \in R$, there exists $t' \in S'$ such that $(t, t') \in U$ and $(s', t') \in R'$; and (3) for every t' such that $(s', t') \in R'$, there exists $t \in S$ such that $(t, t') \in U$ and $(s, t) \in R$. We say that a state $s \in S$ is bisimilar to a state $s' \in S'$, if there exists a bisimulation U between K and K' such that $(s, s') \in U$. It is well-known that bisimilar states satisfy the same CTL^* formulas.

We define a predicate over a set S as a subset of S. Let ϕ be a bijection on S, i.e., a one-to-one mapping from S to S. Let C be a predicate over S. Let $f(C)$ denote the set $\{f(x) : x \in C\}$. Let f^{-1} denote the inverse of the bijection ϕ. If f, g are two bijections then we let fg denote their composition in that order; note that in this case, fg is also a bijection. Throughout the paper we use the following identity relating the inverse and composition operators: $(fg)^{-1} = g^{-1}f^{-1}$.

Let $G = (S, E)$ be the reachability graph of a concurrent program where S denotes a set of nodes/states and $E \subseteq S \times S$. An automorphism of G is a bijection on S such that, for all $s, t \in S$, $(s, t) \in E$ iff $(f(s), f(t)) \in E$. We say that an automorphism respects a predicate C over S if $f(C) = C$. The set of all automorphisms of a graph forms a group $Aut(G)$. Given a set $P_1, ..., P_k$ of predicates over S, the set of automorphisms of G that respect $P_1, ..., P_k$ form a subgroup of $Aut(G)$.

Let $\mathcal{G}$ be a group of automorphisms of G. We say that states $s, t \in S$ are equivalent, denoted by $s \equiv_{\mathcal{G}} t$, if there exists some $f \in \mathcal{G}$ such that $t = f(s)$. As observed in [2, 4, 10], $\equiv_{\mathcal{G}}$ is an equivalence relation. A *quotient structure* of G with respect to $\mathcal{G}$ is a graph $(\bar{S}, \bar{E})$ where $\bar{S}$ contains exactly one node in each equivalence class of $\equiv_{\mathcal{G}}$ and $(\bar{s}, \bar{t}) \in \bar{E}$ iff there exists some t such that $t \equiv_{\mathcal{G}} \bar{t}$ and $(\bar{s}, t) \in E$. Each state $\bar{s} \in \bar{S}$ represents all states in S that belong to its equivalence class. Different quotient structures can be defined by choosing different representatives for each equivalence class. However, all these structures are isomorphic. We denote by $rep(s, \mathcal{G})$ the representative element of the equivalence class to which s belongs. In what follows, $QS(G, \mathcal{G})$ denotes the quotient structure obtained by choosing a unique representative for each equivalence class.

A predicate P on the edges of G is a subset of $S \times S$. We say that an edge (s, t) in E, satisfies P if $(s, t) \in P$. Let $True$ denote the set $S \times S$. For an edge predicate P and automorphism ϕ on states, let $f(P) = \{(f(s), f(t)) : (s, t) \in P\}$. Given a group $\mathcal{G}$ of automorphisms on G, we can extend the equivalence relation $\equiv_{\mathcal{G}}$ from states in S to edges in E as follows: two edges $e = (s, t)$ and $e' = (s', t')$ are equivalent (written as $e \equiv_{\mathcal{G}} e'$) if there exists some $g \in \mathcal{G}$ such that $s' = g(s)$ and $t' = g(t)$. It is easy to see that $\equiv_{\mathcal{G}}$ on E is an equivalence relation [9].

3   Model Checking Using Guarded Annotated Quotient Structures

In this section, we introduce Guarded Annotated Quotient Structures (GQS) as extensions of Annotated Quotient Structures considered in [4, 5]. These structures can be defined with respect to arbitrary automorphisms and can compactly represent the state space of systems that contain little symmetry. For example, consider a resource allocation system composed of a resource controller and three identical user processes, named a, b and c. When multiple user processes request the resource at the same time, the controller process allocates it to one of the requesting users according to the following priority scheme: user a is given highest priority while users b and c have the same lower priority. This system exhibits some symmetry since users b and c are "interchangeable". Now consider a similar system but where the three user processes are given equal priority. This system exhibits more symmetry since all three users are now "interchangeable". Thus, the system without priorities has more symmetry than the system with priorities. A guarded annotated quotient structure allows us to verify systems with reduced symmetry (e.g., a system with priorities) by treating these as if they had more symmetry (e.g., a system without priorities) and without compromising the accuracy of the verification results. For instance, in the state graph G, of the above resource allocation system with priorities, a state s where all three users have requested the resource has only one outgoing edge (granting the resource to user a). By adding two other edges from s (granting the resource to the two other user processes), the state graph H of the system without priorities can be defined. Since H exhibits more symmetry than G, it can be verified more efficiently. Thus, by viewing G as H extended with guards so that G can be re-generated if needed, model checking can be done more efficiently.

Formally, let $H = (S, F)$ be a graph such that $F \supseteq E$ and $Aut(G) \subseteq Aut(H)$, i.e., H is obtained by adding edges to $G = (S, E)$ such that every automorphism of G is also an automorphism of H.[1] Let $\mathcal{H}, \mathcal{G}$ be groups of automorphisms of H and G, respectively, such that $\mathcal{H} \supseteq \mathcal{G}$. As indicated earlier, $\equiv_{\mathcal{H}}$ defines equivalence relations on the nodes and edges of H. For any edge $e \in F$, let $Class(e, \mathcal{H})$ denote the set of edges in the equivalence class of e defined by $\equiv_{\mathcal{H}}$. Let $\mathcal{Q} = \{Q_1, ..., Q_l\}$ be a set of predicates on S such that each automorphism in

---

[1] Our results can easily be extended to allow the addition of nodes as well as edges. Note that adding edges/nodes to a graph may sometimes reduce symmetry.

$\mathcal{G}$ also respects all the predicates in $\mathcal{Q}$. Let $QS(G,\mathcal{G}) = (\bar{U}, \bar{E})$ be the quotient structure of G with respect to $\mathcal{G}$ as defined earlier.

A *Guarded Annotated Quotient Structure* of $H = (S, F)$ with respect to $\mathcal{H}$, denoted by $GQS(H, \mathcal{H})$, is a triple $(\bar{V}, \bar{F}, C)$ where $\bar{V} \subseteq S$ is a set of states that contains one representative for each equivalence class of states defined by $\equiv_{\mathcal{H}}$ on S, $\bar{F} \subseteq \bar{V} \times \bar{V} \times \mathcal{H}$ is a set of labeled edges such that, for every $\bar{s} \in \bar{V}$ and $t \in S$ such that $(\bar{s}, t) \in F$, there exists an element $(\bar{s}, \bar{t}, f) \in \bar{F}$ such that $f(\bar{t}) = t$, and C is a function that associates a predicate $C(e)$ with each labeled edge $e \in \bar{F}$ such that (1) $C(e) \cap Class(e, \mathcal{H}) = E \cap Class(e, \mathcal{H})$ (i.e., $C(e)$ denotes all edges in $Class(e, \mathcal{H})$ that are edges in the original graph G) and (2), for all $g \in \mathcal{G}$, $g(C(e)) = C(e)$ (i.e., g respects the edge predicate C).

Given a labeled edge $e = (\bar{s}, \bar{t}, f) \in \bar{F}$, $f \in \mathcal{H}$ is called the label of e and denotes an automorphism that can be used to obtain the corresponding original edge in F; the edge predicate $C(e)$ can in turn be used to determine whether this edge is also an edge of G. Labels of edges in $\bar{F}$ and the edge predicate C are used to unwind $GQS(H, \mathcal{H})$ when necessary during model checking, as described later. Note that edge predicates C that satisfy the above conditions always exist: for instance, taking $C(e) = E$ always satisfies the definition. In practice, a compact representation of an edge predicate C satisfying the conditions above can be obtained directly from the description of the concurrent program. For example, in the case of the resource allocation system, the edge predicate $C(e)$ is defined as follows: if the labeled edges e denotes the allocation of the resource to a user, then $C(e)$ asserts that if there is a request from user a then a is allocated the resource; for all other labeled edges, $C(e)$ is the predicate *True*. Similarly, the automorphisms labeling edges in $\bar{F}$ can also have succinct implicit representations. For example, any automorphism induced by permutations of n process indices as considered in [4, 5, 8] can be represented by an array of n variables ranging over n. Tools like SMC [14] and Murphi [10] includes optimized algorithms for representing and manipulating such sets of permutations.

Given a set $\mathcal{Q}$ of predicates over S that are all respected by the automorphisms in $\mathcal{G}$, we define three Kripke structures $K\_Stru(G, \mathcal{Q})$, $QS\_Stru(G, \mathcal{G}, \mathcal{Q})$ and $GQS\_Stru(H, \mathcal{H}, \mathcal{Q})$ derived from $G = (S, F)$, $QS(G, \mathcal{G}) = (\bar{U}, \bar{E})$ and $GQS(H, \mathcal{H}) = (\bar{V}, \bar{F}, C)$, respectively. We show that *these three Kripke structures are pairwise bisimilar, and hence can all be used for CTL^* model checking.* Since $\mathcal{G}$ is a subgroup of $\mathcal{H}$, each equivalence class of $\equiv_{\mathcal{H}}$ is a union of smaller equivalences classes defined by $\equiv_{\mathcal{G}}$. Thus, the number of equivalence classes of $\equiv_{\mathcal{H}}$ is smaller than those of $\equiv_{\mathcal{G}}$, and $GQS(H, \mathcal{H})$ contains (possibly exponentially) fewer nodes than $QS(G, \mathcal{G})$. $QS(G, \mathcal{G})$ itself can be much smaller than G.

For each predicate Q_j $(1 \le j \le l)$ in $\mathcal{Q}$, we introduce an atomic proposition denoted q_j. Let $\mathcal{X} = \{q_i : 1 \le i \le l\}$. Let $K\_Stru(G, \mathcal{Q})$ denote the Kripke structure $(S, E, \mathcal{X}, L)$ where for any $s \in S$, $L(s) = \{q_j : s \in Q_j\}$. The Kripke structure $QS\_Stru(G, \mathcal{G}, \mathcal{Q})$ is given by $(\bar{U}, \bar{E}, \mathcal{X}, M)$ where $M(\bar{s}) = \{q_j : \bar{s} \in Q_j\}$. The following theorem has been proven in [4, 2, 10].

Theorem 1. *There exists a bisimulation between the structures $K\_Stru(G, Q)$ and $QS\_Stru(G, \mathcal{G}, Q)$ such that every state $s \in S$ is bisimilar to its representative in $\bar{U}$.*

Therefore, any CTL^* formula over atomic propositions in $\mathcal{X}$ is satisfied at a state s in $K\_Stru(G, Q)$ iff it is satisfied at its representative $rep(s, \mathcal{G})$ in $QS\_Stru(G, \mathcal{G}, Q)$.

If the edge predicate C is implicitly represented by a collection of edge predicates $\Theta_1, ..., \Theta_r$, the Kripke structure $GQS\_Stru(H, \mathcal{H}, Q)$ is obtained from $GQS(H, \mathcal{H})$ by partially unwinding it and by tracking the node predicates in Q (i.e., the predicates $Q_1, ..., Q_l$) and the edge predicates $\Theta_1, ..., \Theta_r$ during this unwinding process. In other words, the unwinding is performed with respect to the predicates $Q_1, ..., Q_l$ and $\Theta_1, ..., \Theta_r$, not with respect to the states of G, in order to limit the unwinding as much as possible. This partial unwinding can be viewed as a particular form of "predicate abstraction", and is a generalization of the unwinding process described in [4, 5]. Precisely, the Kripke structure $GQS\_Stru(H, \mathcal{H}, Q)$ is the tuple $(W, T, \mathcal{X}, N)$ where W, T and N are defined as follows:

- For all $\bar{s} \in \bar{V}$, $(\bar{s}, Q_1, ..., Q_l, \Theta_1, ..., \Theta_r) \in W$.
- Let $u = (\bar{s}, X_1, ..., X_l, \Phi_1, ..., \Phi_r)$ be any node in W, $e = (\bar{s}, \bar{t}, f)$ be a labeled edge in $\bar{F}$ and j be an integer such that Θ_j is the edge predicate $C(e)$. Further, assume that the edge $(\bar{s}, f(\bar{t}))$ satisfies the predicate Φ_j. For all such u and e, the node $v = (\bar{t}, f^{-1}(X_1), ..., f^{-1}(X_l), f^{-1}(\Phi_1), ..., f^{-1}(\Phi_r))$ is in W and the edge (u, v) is in T.
- For all $u = (\bar{s}, X_1, ..., X_l, \Phi_1, ..., \Phi_r) \in W$, $N(u) = \{q_i : \bar{s} \in X_i\}$.

The following theorem states that $QS\_Stru(G, \mathcal{G}, Q)$ and $GQS\_Stru(H, \mathcal{H}, Q)$ are bisimilar.

Theorem 2. *Given $QS\_Stru(G, \mathcal{G}, Q)$ and $GQS\_Stru(H, \mathcal{H}, Q)$ as previously defined, let $Z \subseteq \bar{U} \times W$ be a binary relation defined such that $(s, u) \in Z$ iff there exists an automorphism $f \in \mathcal{H}$ such that $f(t) = s$ and $u = (t, f^{-1}(Q_1), ..., f^{-1}(Q_l), f^{-1}(\Theta_1), ..., f^{-1}(\Theta_r))$. Then, the following properties hold:*

1. *Z is a bisimulation between $QS\_Stru(G, \mathcal{G}, Q)$ and $GQS\_Stru(H, \mathcal{H}, Q)$.*
2. *For all $u \in W$, there exists a node $s \in \bar{U}$ such that $(s, u) \in Z$.*
3. *Two nodes $u = (t, X_1, ..., X_l, \Phi_1, ..., \Phi_r)$ and $u' = (t', Y_1, ..., Y_l, \Delta_1, ..., \Delta_r)$ of $GQS\_Stru(H, \mathcal{H}, Q)$ are related to a single node s of $QS\_Stru(G, \mathcal{G}, Q)$ through Z iff $t = t'$ and there exists some h in $\mathcal{H}$ such that $h(t) = t$ and $X_i = h(Y_i)$ for all $i = 1, ..., l$, and $\Phi_j = h(\Delta_j)$ for all $j = 1, ..., r$.*

From the previous theorem, we see that multiple nodes in $GQS\_Stru(H, \mathcal{H}, Q)$ can be related through Z to a single node in $QS\_Stru(G, \mathcal{G}, Q)$. Hence, in principle, $GQS\_Stru(H, \mathcal{H}, Q)$ can sometimes have more nodes than $QS\_Stru(G, \mathcal{G}, Q)$. The following construction can be used to further reduce the number of nodes in $GQS\_Stru(H, \mathcal{H}, Q)$ so that the reduced structure has no more nodes than $QS\_Stru(G, \mathcal{G}, Q)$. First, observe that all the nodes in $GQS\_Stru(H, \mathcal{H}, Q)$ that are related through Z to a single node s in $QS\_Stru(G, \mathcal{G}, \mathcal{Q})$ can be represented by a single node since they are all bisimilar to each other. The algorithm for generating $GQS\_Stru(H, \mathcal{H}, \mathcal{Q})$ can be modified to apply this reduction to construct a smaller Kripke structure $Greduced\_Stru(H, \mathcal{H}, \mathcal{Q})$. Nodes in $GQS\_Stru(H, \mathcal{H}, \mathcal{Q})$ that are related to a single node in $QS\_Stru(G, \mathcal{G}, \mathcal{Q})$ can be detected by evaluating the condition stated in Part 3 of Theorem 2. It can be shown that, if $\mathcal{G}$ is the maximal subgroup of $\mathcal{H}$ consisting of all automorphisms of G that respect $Q_1, ..., Q_l$, then $Greduced\_Stru(H, \mathcal{H}, \mathcal{Q})$ has the same number of nodes as $QS\_Stru(G, \mathcal{G}, \mathcal{Q})$ and Z defines an isomorphism between the two structures; otherwise, $Greduced\_Stru(H, \mathcal{H}, \mathcal{Q})$ has fewer nodes than $QS\_Stru(G, \mathcal{G}, \mathcal{Q})$.

In summary, the procedure for incrementally constructing the reachable part of $Greduced\_Stru(H, \mathcal{H}, \mathcal{Q})$ from $GQS(G, \mathcal{H})$ is the following. We maintain a set $To\_explore$ of nodes that have yet to be treated. Initially, $To\_explore$ contains nodes of the form $(s_0, Q_1, ..., Q_l, \Theta_1, ..., \Theta_r)$ where s is the representative of an equivalence class containing an initial state. We iterate the following procedure until $To\_explore$ is empty. We remove a node $u = (t, X_1, ..., X_l, \Phi_1, ..., \Phi_r)$ from $To\_explore$. For each labeled edge $e = (t, t', f)$ in $GQS(G, \mathcal{H})$, we check if the edge $(t, f(t'))$ satisfies the edge predicate Φ_j, where j is the index such that Θ_j is the edge predicate $C(e)$. If this condition is satisfied we do as follows. We construct the node $v = (t', Y_1, ..., Y_l, \Delta_1, ..., \Delta_r)$ where $Y_i = f^{-1}(X_i)$ for $1 \leq i \leq l$ and $\Delta_j = f^{-1}(\Phi_j)$ for $1 \leq j \leq r$. Then, we check if there exists a node $w = (t', Z_1, ..., Z_l, \Psi_1, ..., \Psi_r)$ in the partially constructed $Greduced\_Stru(H, \mathcal{H}, \mathcal{Q})$ and a $h \in \mathcal{H}$ such that $t' = h(t')$ and $Z_i = h(Y_i)$ for all $i = 1, ..., l$, and $\Psi_j = h(\Delta_j)$ for all $j = 1, ..., r$ (i.e., the condition of Part 3 of Theorem 2 is checked). If this condition is satisfied, we add an edge from u to w; otherwise, we add v as a new node, include it in $To\_explore$ and add an edge from u to v.

Consider a CTL^* formula ϕ defined over a set $prop(\phi)$ of atomic propositions that each corresponds to a predicate in $\mathcal{Q}$. Let $pred(\phi) \subseteq \mathcal{Q}$ denote the set of predicates corresponding to $prop(\phi)$. From Theorem 2, it is easy to see that the formula ϕ is satisfied at node s in $K\_Stru(G, \mathcal{Q})$ iff it is satisfied at the node $u = (rep(s, \mathcal{H}), f^{-1}(R_1), ..., f^{-1}(R_m), f^{-1}(\Theta_1), ..., f^{-1}(\Theta_r))$ in the structure $GQS\_Stru(H, \mathcal{H}, \mathcal{R})$ where f is the automorphism such that $s = f(rep(s, \mathcal{H}))$. Thus, model checking the CTL^* formula ϕ can be done on the Kripke structures $GQS\_Stru(H, \mathcal{H}, pred(\phi))$ or $Greduced\_Stru(H, \mathcal{H}, pred(\phi))$ obtained by unwinding $GQS(H, \mathcal{H})$ with respect to the set $pred(\phi)$ of predicates only. Let us call this the *direct approach*.

4 Formula Decomposition and Sub-formula Tracking

In this section, we discuss two complementary techniques that can improve the direct approach of the previous section.

4.1   Formula Decomposition

Any CTL^* state formula ϕ can be rewritten as a boolean combination of atomic propositions and existential sub-formulas of the form $\mathsf{E}\phi'$. Let $Eform(\phi)$ denote the set of existential sub-formulas of ϕ that are not sub-formulas of any other existential sub-formula of ϕ (i.e., they are the top-level existential sub-formulas of ϕ). Checking whether a state s satisfies a state formula ϕ can be done by checking whether s satisfies each sub-formula in $Eform(\phi)$ separately, and then combining the results.

For each $\phi' \in Eform(\phi)$, we can determine whether s satisfies ϕ' in the structure $K\_Stru(G, \mathcal{Q})$ by unwinding $GQS(H, \mathcal{H})$, with respect to the predicates in $pred(\phi')$ only, to obtain the Kripke structure $GQS\_Stru(H, \mathcal{H}, pred(\phi'))$ and by checking if the corresponding node satisfies ϕ' in this structure. Formulas in $Eform(\phi)$ that have the same set of atomic propositions can be grouped and their satisfaction can be checked at the same time using the same unwinding. Obviously, unwinding with respect to smaller sets of predicates can yield dramatic performance improvements.

Correlations between predicates can also be used to limit the number of unwindings necessary for model checking. Two predicates Q_i and Q_j in $\mathcal{Q}$ are *correlated* if, for all $f \in \mathcal{H}$, $f(Q_i) = Q_i$ iff $f(Q_j) = Q_j$. It is easy to see that the relation "correlated" is an equivalence relation. We say that two atomic propositions are correlated if their corresponding predicates are correlated. Correlations between predicates can sometimes be detected very easily. For instance, with the framework of [4, 5] where automorphisms induced by process permutations are considered, two predicates referring to variables of a same process are correlated: the predicates $x[1] = 5$ and $y[1] = 10$ are correlated if $x[1]$ and $y[1]$ refer to the local variables x and y of process 1, respectively.

If two predicates Q_i and Q_j are correlated, the following property can be proven: if C is a subset of $\mathcal{Q}$ containing Q_i and $C' = C \cup \{Q_j\}$, then the Kripke structures obtained by unwinding with respect to either C or C' will be isomorphic. The above property allows us to combine unwindings corresponding to different formulas in $Eform(\phi)$ whose atomic propositions are correlated. First, we define an equivalence relation among formulas in $Eform(\phi)$: two formulas x and y in $Eform(\phi)$ are equivalent if every atomic proposition in x is correlated to some atomic proposition in y, and vice versa. This equivalence relation partitions $Eform(\phi)$ into disjoint groups $G_1, ..., G_w$. Let $pred(G_i) = \{\cup pred(\phi') : \phi' \in G_i\}$. Now for each group G_i, we can unwind $GQS(H, \mathcal{H})$ with respect to $pred(G_i)$ and check whether each formula in G_i is satisfied at $rep(s, \mathcal{H})$.

The number of unwindings can be further reduced by ordering the groups $G_1, ..., G_w$ as follows. We say that G_i *is above* G_j if every predicate in $pred(G_j)$ is correlated to some predicate in $pred(G_i)$. The relation "above" is a partial order. We call G_i a *top-group* if there is no group above it. Observe that, if G_i is above G_j, we can combine their unwindings. Hence, if $H_1, .., H_v$ denote the top-groups defined by the groups $G_1, ..., G_w$ ($v \le w$), we can unwind $GQS(H, \mathcal{H})$ with respect to the predicates in $pred(H_i)$ for each group H_i separately, and check the satisfaction in state s of each formula in H_i and in all the groups G_i "below" it using this unwinding.

Note that using the formula decomposition technique can sometimes be less efficient than the direct approach of the previous section. This can be the case when there is a lot of overlap between the sets $pred(H_i)$ of predicates corresponding to the groups H_i obtained after partitioning $Eform(\phi)$.

4.2 Sub-formula Tracking

A CTL^* formula sometimes exhibits itself some internal symmetry. Exploiting formula symmetry was already proposed in [4]. Here, we generalize these ideas by presenting a unified unwinding process where decomposition and symmetry in a formula can be both exploited simultaneously.

Let ϕ be a CTL^* formula. Consider two state sub-formulas ϕ' and ϕ'' of ϕ. We say that ϕ' *dominates* ϕ'' in ϕ if ϕ'' is a sub-formula of ϕ' and every occurrence of ϕ'' in ϕ is inside an occurrence of ϕ'. We say that ϕ' and ϕ'' are *independent* in ϕ if neither of them dominates the other in ϕ. Thus, formulas that are not sub-formulas of each other are independent. Note that even if a formula is a sub-formula of another formula, it is possible for them to be independent: for instance, in the formula q given by $E(EGq_1 \cup E(q_1 \cup q_2))$, the state sub-formulas q_1 and $E(q_1 \cup q_2)$ are independent since there is an occurrence of q_1 which does not appear in the context of $E(q_1 \cup q_2)$. Let $Sform(\phi)$ be the set of all sub-formulas of ϕ that are state formulas. Let $\mathcal{R}$ be a subset of $Sform(\phi)$. We say that $\mathcal{R}$ is a *maximal independent set* if it is a maximal subset of $Sform(\phi)$ such that the state formulas in $\mathcal{R}$ are all pairwise independent. There can be many such maximal independent subsets of $Sform(\phi)$. For instance, the set of all atomic propositions appearing in ϕ is obviously a maximal independent set. For the formula q given above, the set consisting of EGq_1 and $E(q_1 \cup q_2)$ is a maximal independent set.

In what follows, we are interested in exploiting "good" maximal independent sets, i.e., sets $\mathcal{R}$ whose elements are symmetric or partially symmetric. A formula q is *symmetric* if, for every automorphism f in $\mathcal{G}$, $f(q) = q$; it is *partially symmetric* when this property holds for almost all f in $\mathcal{G}$. In general, detecting whether a sub-formula is symmetric is computationally hard. However, when syntactically symmetric constructs (similar to those in $ICTL^*$ [5]) are used, it is then easy to determine whether a sub-formula is symmetric. For instance, when only process permutations are used as automorphisms (as in [4,5]), the sub-formula $\bigwedge_{i \in I} h(i)$ is symmetric when I is the set of all process indices and $h(i)$ is a formula that only refers to the local variables of process i; the same sub-formula is partially symmetric when I contains most process indices.

Let $\mathcal{R} = \{R_1, ..., R_m\}$ be a (preferably good) maximal independent set of sub-formulas of ϕ. We also view each element R_i of $\mathcal{R}$ as a predicate, i.e., as the set of states that satisfy the CTL^* formula R_i. Consider the Kripke structure $GQS\_Stru(H, \mathcal{H}, \mathcal{R})$ obtained by unwinding $GQS(H, \mathcal{H})$ with respect to $\mathcal{R}$. In a similar way, we can define $Greduced\_Stru(H, \mathcal{H}, \mathcal{R})$ following the procedure of Section 3.

Let ψ denote the formula obtained from ϕ by replacing every occurrence of the sub-formula R_i by a fresh atomic proposition r_i, for all $i = 1, ..., m$. The following theorem relates the satisfaction of ϕ and ψ.

Theorem 3. *Let s be a state in S and f be an automorphism in $\mathcal{H}$ such that $s = f(rep(s, \mathcal{H}))$. Then, the formula ϕ is satisfied at state s in the structure $K\_Stru(G, \mathcal{Q})$ iff ψ is satisfied at the node $u = (rep(s, \mathcal{H}), f^{-1}(R_1), ..., f^{-1}(R_m), f^{-1}(\Theta_1), ..., f^{-1}(\Theta_r))$ in the structure $GQS\_Stru(H, \mathcal{H}, \mathcal{R})$ iff ψ is satisfied at node u in the structure $Greduced\_Stru(H, \mathcal{H}, \mathcal{R})$.*

Thus, the previous theorem makes it possible to check a formula ϕ "hierarchically", by recursively checking sub-formulas R_i and then combining the results via the unwinding of $GQS(H, \mathcal{H})$ with respect to $\mathcal{R}$ only.

We now discuss the construction of the structures $GQS\_Stru(H, \mathcal{H}, \mathcal{R})$ and $Greduced\_Stru(H, \mathcal{H}, \mathcal{R})$. The states of both of these structures are of the form $(\bar{s}, X_1, ..., X_m, \Phi_1, ..., \Phi_r)$, where each X_i is a CTL^* state formula obtained by applying some automorphism to R_i during the unwinding process. Remember that, during the construction process, we need to be able to check whether a newly generated node $v = (\bar{t}, Y_1, ..., Y_m, \Delta_1, ..., \Delta_r)$ is the same as some previously generated node $u = (\bar{s}, X_1, ..., X_m, \Phi_1, ..., \Phi_r)$, i.e., whether $\bar{s} = \bar{t}$, $Y_i = X_i$ for all $i = 1, ..., m$, and $\Delta_j = \Phi_j$ for all $j = 1, ..., r$. Checking whether $\bar{s} = \bar{t}$ and $\Delta_j = \Phi_j$ for all $j = 1, ..., r$ can usually be done efficiently as previously discussed. However, checking whether $Y_i = X_i$ can be hard since each of these can now be any CTL^* state formulas, and checking equivalence of such formulas is computationally hard in general. Note that, if the CTL^* formula ϕ uses syntactically symmetric constructs such as those in $ICTL^*$ [4], then this check can always be done efficiently.

Another important aspect in the construction of $GQS\_Stru(H, \mathcal{H}, \mathcal{R})$ is the generation of $N(\bar{s})$ for each state $\bar{s}$. For a node $u = (\bar{s}, X_1, ..., X_m, \Phi_1, ..., \Phi_r)$, $r_i \in N(u)$ iff $\bar{s} \in X_i$. Since X_i can now be any CTL^* state formula, this means that $\bar{s} \in X_i$ iff $\bar{s}$ satisfies the formula X_i in the Kripke structure $K\_Stru(G, \mathcal{Q})$. Since X_i is obtained by applying a sequence of automorphisms in $\mathcal{H}$ to the state sub-formula R_i of ϕ, we know that $X_i = f(R_i)$ for some $f \in \mathcal{H}$. This automorphism f can be made available at the time of generation of u by maintaining automorphisms with states in the set $To\_explore$ used in the algorithm for generating $Greduced\_Stru(H, \mathcal{H}, \mathcal{Q})$ given in Section 3. Thus, checking whether $\bar{s} \in X_i$ reduces to checking whether $\bar{s}$ satisfies the sub-formula $f(R_i)$ in $K\_Stru(G, \mathcal{Q})$, which itself holds iff $f^{-1}(\bar{s})$ satisfies R_i in $K\_Stru(G, \mathcal{Q})$. The latter can be checked by recursively applying the above procedure to R_i instead of ϕ.

We thus obtain a complete recursive procedure which constructs different structures corresponding to the different sub-formulas R_i of ϕ. Note that the formula decomposition technique of Section 4.1 can be used to decompose sub-formulas R_i. Thus, formula decomposition and sub-formula tracking are complementary and can be both applied recursively. It is to be noted that if no good maximal independent set $\mathcal{R}$ can be found then the procedure of Subsection 4.1 should be applied directly.

Example

We illustrate the method by a brief example. Assume that we are using automorphisms induced by process permutations, as in [4, 5]. Consider a concurrent system of n processes. Consider the problem of model-checking with respect to the formula ϕ given by $E(q_1 U \wedge_{i \in I} Eh(i))$ where $h(i)$ is a path formula with no further path quantifiers and it only refers to the local propositions of process i, I is the set of all process indices excepting process 1, q_1 is the local proposition of process 1. Let ϕ' denote the sub-formula $\wedge_{i \in I} Eh(i)$. This is a partially symmetric sub-formula. We take $\mathcal{R}$ to be the set $\{q_1, \phi'\}$, since it is a "good" maximal independent set.

We construct $GQS\_Stru(H, \mathcal{H}, \mathcal{R})$. Let M be the total number of nodes in $GQS(H, \mathcal{H})$. M can be exponentially smaller than the number of nodes in the full reachability graph, i.e., the number of nodes in $K\_Stru(G, \mathcal{Q})$. It is not difficult to show that the number of nodes in $GQS\_Stru(H, \mathcal{H}, \mathcal{R})$ is at most nM. During the construction of $GQS\_Stru(H, \mathcal{H}, \mathcal{R})$, we need to determine which of its nodes satisfy the sub-formula ϕ'. To determine this, we invoke the procedure of subsection 4.1 only once. During this procedure, for each $i \in I$, we determine the nodes that satisfy the sub-formula $Eh(i)$. This is done by unwinding $GQS(H, \mathcal{H})$. The resulting structure is also of size at most nM. Thus the over all complexity of this procedure is $O(n^2 M)$.

However, if we use the direct approach and unwind $GQS(H, \mathcal{H})$ (or if we use $QS\_Stru(G, \mathcal{G}, pred(\phi))$) then we will get the full reachability graph. Thus we see that the above example is a case for which the method of this section is exponentially better than the direct approach; (an example program is the resource controller with n identical user processes). On other hand, one can give examples where the direct method is better than the method of this section. As observed, this occurs for cases when the formula has no symmetric (or partially symmetric) sub-formulas. It is to be noted that the formula ϕ, given above, is not an $ICTL^*$ formula and hence the methods of [4, 5] can't be applied.

5   Experimental Results

In this section, we report some preliminary experimental results evaluating the techniques proposed in this paper. Experiments were performed in conjunction with the SMC tool [14]. A first example is the simple resource allocation system described at the beginning of Section 3. We considered a variant of the system with priorities where user 1 is given higher priority than all other users. We checked the following property for various values of i: is it possible to reach a global state where one of the first i users is holding the resource and the resource is still available?

We used two approaches to check the above property. Both approaches give correct answer. The first approach employs the structure $QS\_Stru(G, \mathcal{G}, \mathcal{Q})$; here $\mathcal{G}$ is the set of automorphisms induced by process permutations that fix each of the first i processes and arbitrarily permute the other user processes. The

Table 1. Comparison of the Two Approaches.

Value of i	First Approach i.e., employing QS_Stru	Second approach,i.e., using formula decomposition
2	14/2676	14/1863
3	19/3260	16/1864
4	39/4270	18/1865
5	130/6505	20/1866
6	575/11404	22/1867

second approach uses formula decomposition of Section 4.1. The decomposed sub-formulas are checked by unwinding $GQS(H, \mathcal{H})$ with respect to the atomic predicates of the sub-formulas independently; here $\mathcal{H}$ is the of automorphisms, induced by process permuations, that arbitrarily permute all the user processes. Formula decomposition was performed manually and SMC was used to check the sub-cases.

Table 1 compares the run-time and memory usage of the two approaches, for the resource allocation system described above with a total number of 80 user processes. Each entry in the table has the form x/y where x is the run-time in seconds and y is the memory usage in Kbytes. Clearly, the second approach, i.e. the approach with formula decomposition, performs better than the first approach; the difference in their performances becomes more pronounced for larger values of i.

We also performed experiments using the Fire-wire protocol (with administrator module) considered in [14], using a configuration with three stations. We checked whether it is possible for either stations 1 or 2 not to receive an acknowledgment after a message is sent. Again, we compared the above two approaches. The first approach took 80 seconds and used 24 Mbytes of memory to complete the verification, while the second approach (i.e. the direct approach with formula decomposition) took 58 seconds and used 12.8 Mbytes of memory.

6   Conclusion and Related Work

We have presented new algorithmic techniques for exploiting symmetry in model checking. We have generalized symmetry reduction to a larger class of automorphisms, so that systems with little or no symmetry can be verified more efficiently using symmetry reduction. We also presented novel techniques based on formula decomposition and sub-formula tracking. Preliminary experimental results are encouraging. Full implementation, and further evaluation with respect to real world examples, needs to be carried out as part of future work.

As mentioned earlier, symmetry reduction in model checking has been extensively studied in [10, 2, 4, 5, 8, 12, 13, 6, 7]. The problem of verifying properties of systems with little or no symmetry was first considered in [6, 7]. The work presented in [7] considered also considers general automorphisms. There, only the verification of symmetric properties was discussed. In contrast, our algorithms can be used to verify any property specified in CTL^*, even if the property is not symmetric. [5] presents a verification method for $ICTL^*$ formulas. Our sub-formula tracking technique can also be used to efficiently verify properties specified in $ICTL^*$, in addition to being applicable to any CTL^* formula. Formula symmetry was explicitly considered in [4] where quotient structures are constructed with respect to automorphisms representing symmetries of the program as well as of the formula. Our sub-formula tracking technique indirectly uses formula symmetry dynamically as the GQS is unwound.

References

1. Aggarwal S., Kurshan R. P., Sabnani K. K.: *A Calculus for Protocol Specification and Validation*. in Protocol Specification, Testing and Verification III, H. Ruden, C. West (ed's), pp19–34, North-Holland, 1983.
2. Clarke, E. M., Filkorn, T., Jha, S.: *Exploiting Symmetry in Temporal Logic Model Checking*. CAV93, LNCS **697** Springer-Verlag, 1993.
3. Emerson, E. A.: *Temporal and modal logic*. In J. van Leeuwen, editor, *Handbook of Theoretical Computer Science*. Elsevier/MIT Press, Amsterdam/Cambridge, 1990.
4. Emerson, E. A., Sistla, A. P.: *Symmetry and Model Checking*. CAV93, LNCS **697** Springer-Verlag, 1993; journal version appeared in Formal Methods in System Design, 9(1/2),1996, pp 105-130.
5. Emerson, E. A., Sistla, A. P.: *Utilizing Symmetry when Model Checking under Fairness Assumptions: An Automata-theoretic Approach*. CAV95, LNCS **939** Springer-Verlag, 1995.
6. Emerson E. A., Treffler R., *From Symmetry to Asymmetry: New techniques for Symmetry Reduction in Model-checking*, Proc. of CHARME 1999.
7. Emerson E. A., Havlicek J. W., *Virtual Symmetry Reductions*, Proc. of LICS 2000.
8. Gyuris, V., Sistla, A. P.: *On-the-Fly Model Checking under Fairness that Exploits Symmetry*. CAV97, LNCS **1254** Springer-Verlag, 1997; To appear in Formal Methods in System Design.
9. Godefroid, P.: *Exploiting Symmetry when Model-Checking Software*, Proceedings of FORTE/PSTV'99, Beijing, 1999.
10. Ip, C. N., Dill, D. L.: *Better Verification through Symmetry*. Formal Methods in System Design **9** 1/2, pp41–75, 1996.
11. Jensen, K.: *Colored Petri Nets: Basic Concepts, Analysis Methods, and Practical Use, Vol2*. Analysis Methods, EATCS Monographs, Springer-Verlag, 1994.
12. Jha, S.: *Symmetry and Induction in Model Checking*, Ph. D. Thesis, Computer Science Department, Carnegie-Mellon University, 1996.
13. Kurshan, R. P.: *Computer Aided Verification of Coordinated Processes: The Automata Theoretic Approach*, Princeton University Press, Princeton NJ, 1994.
14. Sistla A. P., Gyuris V., Emerson E. A., *SMC: A Symmetry based Model Checker for Verification of Safety and Liveness Properties*, ACM Transactions on Software Engineering Methodologies, Vol 9, No 2, pp 133-166, April 2000.

Transformation-Based Verification
Using Generalized Retiming

Andreas Kuehlmann[1] and Jason Baumgartner[2]

[1] Cadence Berkeley Labs, Berkeley, CA 94704
[2] IBM Enterprise Systems Group, Austin, TX 78758

Abstract. In this paper we present the application of generalized retiming for temporal property checking. Retiming is a structural transformation that relocates registers in a circuit-based design representation without changing its actual input-output behavior. We discuss the application of retiming to minimize the number of registers with the goal of increasing the capacity of symbolic state traversal. In particular, we demonstrate that the classical definition of retiming can be generalized for verification by relaxing the notion of design equivalence and physical implementability. This includes (1) omitting the need for equivalent reset states by using an initialization stump, (2) supporting negative registers, handled by a general functional relation to future time frames, and (3) eliminating peripheral registers by converting them into simple temporal offsets. The presented results demonstrate that the application of retiming in verification can significantly increase the capacity of symbolic state traversal. Our experiments also demonstrate that the repeated use of retiming interleaved with other structural simplifications can yield reductions beyond those possible with single applications of the individual approaches. This result suggests that a tool architecture based on re-entrant transformation engines can potentially decompose and solve verification problems that otherwise would be infeasible.

1 Introduction

The main bottleneck of temporal property checking is the potentially exorbitant computational resources necessary for state traversal. In general, there is no clear dependency between the structure or size of the analyzed circuit and the resource requirements to perform reachability analysis. However, a smaller number of state bits, i.e., registers, generally correlates with a lower memory and runtime consumption for performing state traversal. In particular, for BDD-based techniques [1, 2] fewer registers result in fewer BDD variables which typically decreases the size of the BDDs representing the set of states and transitions among them. Similarly, in SAT-based state enumeration [3], the complexity of the state recording device directly depends on the number of registers. A second motivation for our work comes from the observation that a reduced number of registers often decreases the functional correlation between them. Intuitively, this produces a less scattered state encoding which results in a more compact BDD or cube structure for BDD or SAT-based reachability analysis, respectively.

In this paper we discuss the application of retiming to reduce the number of registers with the goal of improving symbolic reachability analysis. Retiming is commonly referred to as a structural transformation of a circuit-based design description

G. Berry, H. Comon, and A. Finkel (Eds.): CAV 2001, LNCS 2102, pp. 104–117, 2001.

that changes the positions of the state holding elements without modifying the input-output behavior [4]. Traditionally, the use of retiming is focused on design synthesis with two constraints that fundamentally limit the solution space: the circuit must be physically implementable and it must preserve its original input-output behavior. In property verification these restrictions can be lifted, which results in significantly more freedom for register minimization. There are three extensions of classical retiming for a generalized application in verification. First, a temporally partitioned state traversal eliminates the restriction on the retimed circuit of having an equivalent reset state. Second, a generalized symbolic state traversal algorithm can handle "negative registers." This significantly increases the solution space for legal retimings by removing the non-negative register count constraints from the problem formulation. Third, state bits which are exclusively driven by primary inputs or drive only primary outputs represent a mere temporal shift of peripheral values, and can be suppressed for state space traversal.

In this paper we describe the application of retiming for verification using these three generalizations. This work provides a specific approach in a more general scheme for property checking which uses a set of targeted circuit transformations. In an engine-based architecture, a retiming engine is applied as one step in a series of transformations which gradually simplify the verification problem until it can be solved by a terminal engine (e.g., BDD- or SAT-based). Note that such a modular, transformation-based approach was key in making automatic logic synthesis practical [5].

2   Illustrating Example

Figure 1a shows a circuit example with six registers $R_1, \ldots, R_6$, two inputs a and b, and one output p. Using a notation introduced in Section 4, the initial states of the six registers are assumed to be $I = (I_{21}^1, I_{24}^1, I_{24}^2, I_{36}^1, I_{54}^1, I_{6p}^1) = (1, 0, 0, 1, 0, 1)$. The subscript and superscript denote the circuit arc and the register position along this arc, respectively. Further, let $p \equiv 1$ be a predicate to be checked for all reachable states.

Retiming moves registers forward and backward across gates with the goal of minimizing their count. The corresponding optimization problem can be formulated as an Integer Linear Program (ILP) using a directed graph model of the circuit [4]. The graph vertices and arcs represent gates and interconnection (i.e., wires), respectively. A special *host* vertex is introduced which is connected to all inputs and outputs. Figure 1b shows the retiming graph for the given example. The arc labels denote the number of registers at the corresponding nets. The ILP determines a *lag* for each vertex which represents the number of registers moved backward through it [4].

The original definition of retiming for synthesis requires preserving input-output behavior. With this restriction, the circuit of Figure 1a cannot be retimed since registers R_1 and R_2 have incompatible initial states and cannot be merged by a backward move. To show this, if both registers were shared with a joint initial state of 1, the sequence $(a, b) = ((0, 0), (1, 0), (0, 0))$ would produce $p = (1, 1, 1)$ and $p = (1, 1, 0)$ in the original and retimed circuit, respectively. Similarly, for a joint initial state of 0 the sequence $(a, b) = ((1, 0), (0, 0), (1, 0), (0, 0))$ would distinguish the behavior of the circuits.

In verification, we need not to preserve input-output equivalence of the retimed circuit as long as we can preserve the truth of the given properties. The requirement for

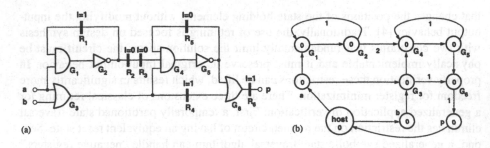

Fig. 1: Retiming Example: (a) Original Circuit, (b) Retiming Graph.

equivalent reset states can be relaxed by unrolling the circuit for multiple cycles until the set of retimed initial states is uniquely determined. This corresponds to a temporal decomposition of the verification task into two parts: (1) checking a bounded acyclic initialization structure, further referred to as the *retiming stump*, and (2) checking the retimed circuit, further referred to as the *retimed recurrence structure*. The first part involves a SAT check to prove the correctness of the properties for the time frames that are included in the retiming stump. The second part involves model checking the retimed circuit, which effectively provides an inductive correctness proof for all remaining time frames. The initialization state of the retimed circuit can be computed by symbolically simulating the retiming stump up to the retimed recurrence structure.

Registers at the inputs and outputs are mere temporal signal offsets and do not impact the state reachability of the circuit core [6]. Thus, they can be ignored during reachability analysis. For failing properties, the offsets are restored by temporal shifts in the counter-example trace. Adopting the terminology from Malik et al. [7] we will refer to this method as *peripheral retiming*. For peripheral retiming the host vertex is removed from the retiming graph, causing the ILP to pull as many registers as possible out of the circuit. Figure 2a shows the graph for a maximal peripheral retiming of the example ignoring initial state equivalence. The arc labels represent the register counts of the original and retimed circuit. The vertex labels denote their lag, i.e., the number of registers that have been pushed backward through them. As shown, by merging R_1 and R_2 and removing R_6, the register count could be reduced from six to four.

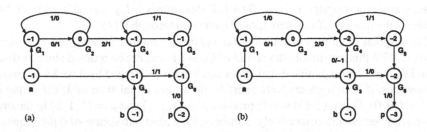

Fig. 2: Graphs for relaxed retimings for the example of Fig. 1: (a) peripheral retiming ignoring reset state equivalence, (b) retiming with negative registers permitted.

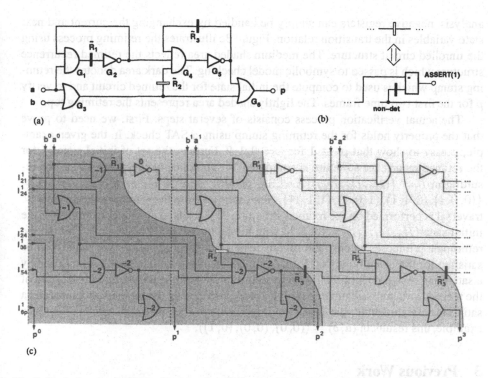

Fig. 3: Retiming result of Fig. 2b: (a) retimed circuit, (b) intuitive interpretation of negative registers, (c) interpretation of the unrolled circuit structure (dark: retiming stump, medium shaded: retiming recurrence structure, lightly shaded: retiming top).

A third relaxation of retiming is achieved by enabling negative register counts at the arcs. This approach is motivated by the fact that registers merely denote functional relations between different time frames. In logic synthesis, clocked or unclocked delay elements are used to physically implement these relations. Such delays can only realize backward constraints, each consisting of a combinational expression in the present and a variable in a future time frame. In symbolic verification, this limitation can be lifted and arbitrary relations can be handled. This includes forward constraints between variables in the current time frame and expressions in future time frames, represented by negative registers. In contrast to the common case of symbolic forward traversal, constraints imposed by negative registers delay the decision about the actual reachability of a state until all referred future time frames are processed. This results in a third component for the above described temporal verification decomposition, reflected by the *retiming top*.

To enable negative registers, the non-negativity constraints on the arc labels are removed from the ILP. Figure 2b shows the resulting retiming graph for the example. By using one negative register, the total register count is reduced to three. Figure 3a shows the resulting circuit. Note that these three registers reflect the actual temporal relations present in the loops and reconverging paths of the original circuit. Figure 3b gives an intuitive interpretation of negative registers in a circuit context. In symbolic reachability analysis, negative registers can simply be handled by exchanging the current and next state variables in the transition relation. Figure 3c illustrates the retiming process using the unrolled circuit structure. The medium shaded area reflects the retimed recurrence structure which is passed to symbolic model checking. The dark area denotes the retiming stump which is used to compute the initial state for the retimed circuit and to verify p for the first two time frames. The lightly shaded area represents the retiming top.

The actual verification process consists of several steps. First, we need to prove that the property holds for the retiming stump using a SAT check. In the given example, it easy to show that $p^i \equiv 1$ for $i = 0, 1, 2$. Further, the set of initial states $\tilde{I}$ for the retimed recurrence structure is computed by symbolically executing the stump, resulting in $\tilde{I} = \{(\tilde{I}^1_{12}, \tilde{I}^1_{34}, \tilde{I}^1_{54}) \mid \exists a^0.\exists b^0.\exists v.(\tilde{I}^1_{12} \equiv a^0 \wedge \tilde{I}^1_{34} \equiv v \wedge \tilde{I}^1_{54} \equiv 1)\} = \{(0, 0, 1), (0, 1, 1), (1, 0, 1), (1, 1, 1)\}$. Next, starting from these initial states, symbolic traversal is performed on the retimed structure. This leads to a counter example for the initial state $(\tilde{I}^1_{12}, \tilde{I}^1_{34}, \tilde{I}^1_{54}) = (0, 1, 1)$ with the inputs $a^1 = 0$ and $b^1 = 0$. Further, the retiming top imposes a constraint on the negative register $\tilde{I}^1_{34} \equiv a_2 \vee b_2$ which can be satisfied for the given failing state. A complete counter-example trace is composed by a satisfying assignment of the retiming stump for generating the required reset state of the retimed structure, a counter-example trace generated by the retimed structure, and a satisfying assignment for the constraint imposed by the negative registers. For the given example, this results in $(a, b) = ((0, 0), (0, 0), (0, 1))$.

3   Previous Work

The application of structural circuit transformations in sequential verification is a relatively new research area. Hasteer et al. [8] proposed the concepts of retiming and state space folding for sequential equivalence checking. Their state-folding technique works for circuits in which the number of latches contained in loops and reconverging paths is constant modulo n. In this case n succeeding state transitions can be concatenated for symbolic state traversal. Baumgartner et al. [9] extend the state-folding concept to handle arbitrary registers and general CTL property checking. The idea of state space folding is orthogonal to the retiming approach described in this paper, and the combination of both techniques is a promising subject of our future research.

For logic optimization, Leiserson and Saxe [10] describe the application of structural retiming and propose an ILP [4] formulation using a graph model. Malik et al. [7] were the first to introduce peripheral retiming with the objective of moving a maximum number of registers to the circuit boundaries. This makes the combinational circuit core as large as possible for providing maximum freedom for conventional combinational optimizations. They also introduced the concept of negative registers as a method of temporarily "borrowing" registers from inputs and outputs. After finishing the combinational optimization, these registers are "legalized" by retiming them back to positive registers. In contrast, our paper describes the direct application of negative registers for verification and gives formal algorithms to fully handle them.

The problem of generating valid initial states for the retimed circuit has been addressed in several publications. Touati and Brayton [11] proposed a method for adding reset circuitry which forces an equivalent initial state. Even et al. [12] described a modified retiming algorithm that favors forward retiming, allowing a simple computation of the initial states. All previous work on reset state computation assumes input-output equivalence. In this paper we propose a method of eliminating that limitation for verification and describe how a more generalized reset state can be obtained.

Gupta et al. [6] were first to propose the application of maximal peripheral retiming in the context of simulation-based verification. They showed that peripheral registers can be omitted during test generation without compromising the coverage of the resulting transition tour. Still, their approach is focused on test generation and does not consider full reachability. Further, the paper does not address the initialization problem and does not use the concept of negative registers. The work of Cabodi et al. [13], which uses retiming to enhance symbolic reachability analysis, is the closest to ours. However, they use an original synthesis retiming algorithm with the above mentioned limitations regarding enforced reset state equivalence and non-negative registers. Further, the applied retiming grid is based on next-state functions which significantly reduces the optimization freedom. Consequently, the reported results show mostly modest improvements over existing techniques.

4 Generalized Retiming for Verification

Let $C = (G, E)$ denote a circuit where G represents a set of combinational gates, primary inputs, and primary outputs, and $E \subseteq G \times G$ is a set of arcs connecting the gates. Each arc $(u, v) \in E$ is associated with a non-negative weight $w(u, v)$ representing the number of registers at this arc. Clearly, for all hardware designs we can assume that the initial register count of all arcs is non-negative: i.e., $w(u, v) \geq 0$. Further, without loss of generality, we assume that the circuit does not contain combinational loops.

Let $I_{uv}^i, 1 \leq i \leq w(u, v)$ denote the initial value of register i along arc (u, v) and $g_u(f_{ju}, \ldots, f_{ku})$ be the function of gate u using the functions $f_{ju}, \ldots, f_{ku}$ of arcs $(j, u), \ldots, (k, u)$ at its inputs. If u represents a primary input, g_u denotes the sampled input value at a given time. The state of C at time $t \geq 0$ is computed recursively as:

$$f_{uv}^t = \begin{cases} I_{uv}^{w(u,v)-t} & \text{if } t < w(u, v), \\ g_u^{t-w(u,v)} & \text{otherwise,} \end{cases}$$

$$g_u^t = g_u(f_{ju}^t, \ldots, f_{ku}^t). \tag{1}$$

This definition of f can be used to express the function of any internal net of the design modeled by C. For example, the value at time t of the net connecting the output of register i with the input of register $i + 1$ of arc (u, v) is $f_{uv}^{t+w(u,v)-i}$.

A retiming of C is defined as a gate labeling $r : G \rightarrow \mathbb{Z}$, where $r(u)$ is the *lag* of gate u denoting the number of registers that are moved backward through it. The new arc weights $\tilde{w}$ of the retimed circuit $\tilde{C}$ are computed as follows:

$$\tilde{w}(u, v) = w(u, v) + r(v) - r(u). \tag{2}$$

In this context we are interested in minimizing the total number of registers of $\tilde{C}$:

$$\sum_{\forall (u,v) \in E} |\tilde{w}(u, v)| \rightarrow \min. \tag{3}$$

Note that due to the missing host vertex, the formulation aims at maximal peripheral retiming which removes registers from the primary inputs and outputs. The given modeling does not take into account that the registers of the outgoing arcs from a gate can be shared and must be counted only once in the objective function. A correct ILP modeling of "register sharing" can be achieved by a slightly modified problem formulation for which the details are presented in [4]. In contrast to retiming for synthesis, we do not impose a non-negative constraint on $\tilde{w}$. Therefore, the new circuit may have negative arc weights, representing negative registers.

Equation (2) imposes an equivalence relation on the set of retimings. Two retimings r_1 and r_2 result in identical circuits and are said to be equivalent if and only if $r_1 = r_2 + c$, where c denotes an integer constant. We define a normalized retiming r' as:

$$r' = r - \max_{\forall u} r(u). \tag{4}$$

In the following we will use the term retiming to denote normalized retimings. Similar to formula (1), for a given retiming r the state of $\tilde{C}$ at time t can be computed as:

$$\tilde{f}_{uv}^t = \begin{cases} \tilde{I}_{uv}^{\tilde{w}(u,v)-t} & \text{if } t < \tilde{w}(u,v), \\ \tilde{g}_u^{t-\tilde{w}(u,v)} & \text{otherwise,} \end{cases}$$

$$\tilde{g}_u^t = g_u(\tilde{f}_{ju}^t, \ldots, \tilde{f}_{ku}^t), \tag{5}$$

where the $\tilde{I}_{uv}^i$ represent the initial states of $\tilde{C}$. In contrast to formula (1), it is not obvious that this formula is well formed, because the $\tilde{w}(u,v)$ can assume negative values.

Theorem 1. *Let C be a circuit containing a finite number of gates, arcs, and non-negative registers without combinational loops, and r be a retiming resulting in circuit $\tilde{C}$. The evaluation of formula (5) for computing the state of $\tilde{C}$ at time t will terminate for any finite $t \geq 0$.*

Proof. First, it is obvious that t remains non-negative during the evaluation of (5). Second, since C and therefore $\tilde{C}$ contain a finite number of gates, any non-terminating evaluation of formula (5) must involve an infinite recursion on at least one gate. Let u be one of those gates and $p = u \xrightarrow{(u,u_1)} u_1 \xrightarrow{(u_1,u_2)} \ldots \xrightarrow{(u_n,u)} u$ be the circular path in $\tilde{C}$ corresponding to the recursion. The difference between t and t' of two suceeding recursions is then $t - t' = \tilde{w}(u,u_1) + \tilde{w}(u_1,u_2) + \ldots + \tilde{w}(u_n,u)$. A substitution using (2) leads to $t - t' = w(u,u_1) + w(u_1,u_2) + \ldots + w(u_n,u)$. All registers are positive ($w(u_i,u_j) \geq 0$), and there are no combinational loops ($\exists(u_i,u_j) \in p \text{ with } w(u_i,u_j) > 0$). Therefore t strictly decreases after each recursion which causes the evaluation to terminate once $t < \tilde{w}(u_i,v_j)$ for some arc $(u_i,u_j) \in p$. $\square$

The retiming stump of a retiming r is a partial unrolling of C and is defined as:

$$S = \{s_{uv}^t \mid s_{uv}^t = f_{uv}^t \land (u,v) \in E \land 0 \leq t < \tilde{w}(u,v) - r(v)\}. \tag{6}$$

The new verification structure is composed of S and $\tilde{C}$, where S provides the arc functions for the first cycles and the initial states for the positive registers of $\tilde{C}$ as follows:

$$\tilde{I}_{uv}^i = s_{uv}^{\tilde{w}(u,v)-i-r(v)}, \quad 0 < i \leq \tilde{w}(u,v). \tag{7}$$

Note that this formula is well formed for normalized retimings because $r(v) \leq 0$.

Theorem 2. *Let C be a circuit containing a finite number of gates, arcs, and non-negative registers without combinational loops and r be a retiming resulting in circuit $\tilde{C}$ and the retiming stump S. The following relations provide a bijective mapping between each arc function of $\{\tilde{C}, S\}$ to the corresponding arc function of C and vise versa:*

$$f_{uv}^t = \begin{cases} s_{uv}^t & \text{if } t < \tilde{w}(u,v) - r(v), \\ \tilde{f}_{uv}^{t+r(v)} & \text{otherwise,} \end{cases} \tag{8}$$

$$s_{uv}^t = f_{uv}^t \quad \text{if } t < \tilde{w}(u,v) - r(v),$$
$$\tilde{f}_{uv}^t = f_{uv}^{t-r(v)}. \tag{9}$$

Proof. First we show that function (8) correcly maps $\{\tilde{C}, S\}$ to C: For $t < \tilde{w}(u,v) - r(v)$, (8) reflects the definition of s given in (6). For $t \geq \tilde{w}_{uv} - r(v)$, after substitution using (5), we must show that $f_{uv}^t = g_u(\tilde{f}_{iu}^{t+r(v)-\tilde{w}(u,v)}, \ldots, \tilde{f}_{ju}^{t+r(v)-\tilde{w}(u,v)})$ which is done by inductively proving for the arguments of g_u that $\tilde{f}_{iu}^{t+r(v)-\tilde{w}(u,v)} = f_{iu}^{t-w(u,v)}$. *Base case* $(t + r(v) - \tilde{w}(u,v) < \tilde{w}(i,u))$: Using (5) and (7) we get $\tilde{f}_{iu}^{t+r(v)-\tilde{w}(u,v)} = \tilde{I}_{iu}^{\tilde{w}(i,u)-t-r(v)+\tilde{w}(u,v)} = f_{iu}^{t+r(v)-\tilde{w}(u,v)-r(u)}$ which, after applying (2), shows the required equality. *Inductive step* $(t + r(v) - \tilde{w}(u,v) \geq \tilde{w}(i,u))$: A substitution using (5) results in $\tilde{f}_{iu}^{t+r(v)-\tilde{w}(u,v)} = g_i(\tilde{f}_{hi}^{t+r(v)-\tilde{w}(u,v)-\tilde{w}(i,u)}, \ldots, \tilde{f}_{ki}^{t+r(v)-\tilde{w}(u,v)-\tilde{w}(i,u)})$. If $\tilde{w}(i,u) > 0$ we can immediately reduce the arguments of g_i by induction which results in $g_i(f_{hi}^{t-w(u,v)-w(i,u)}, \ldots, \tilde{f}_{ki}^{t+w(u,v)-w(i,u)}) = f_{iu}^{t-w(u,v)}$ and show equivalence. If $\tilde{w}(i,u) \leq 0$, then the right hand side needs to be further expanded until an inductive reduction can be performed. A termination analysis similar to the proof of theorem 1 can be applied showing the superscript value of f will eventually decrease and therefore the expansion will terminate after a finite number of steps. Next, showing that (9) correctly maps $\{\tilde{C}, S\}$ to C is straight forward by using the definition for s for the first part and an inductive proof identical to the one used in the first theorem for the second part. □

Corollary 1. *Let $\tilde{C}$ be derived from C by retiming and c be a Boolean constant, then*

$$\forall t.(f_{uv}^t \equiv c) \Leftrightarrow \forall t.[(0 \leq t < \tilde{w}(u,v) - r(v)) \Rightarrow (s_{uv}^t \equiv c)] \wedge \forall t'.(\tilde{f}_{uv}^{t'} \equiv c). \tag{10}$$

In other words, generalized retiming provides a circuit transformation that is sound and complete for verifying properties of the form $AG(p)$, where the primary circuit inputs are non-deterministic and p is a predicate on any net of the circuit. Its application for more complex safety properties requires that the property formula be expressed as a circuit which is composed with the actual design before retiming can be applied. Similarly, in order to handle constrained circuit inputs, the verification environment must be composed with the circuit before retiming can be applied.

Corollary 2. *Let $\tilde{C}$ be a circuit derived from C by retiming and S be the corresponding retiming stump. Further, let $AG(p)$ be a property that fails for $\tilde{C}$ for an initial state $\tilde{I}$*

resulting in a counter-example trace $\tilde{T}$. *The counter example* T *for the original circuit* C *can be obtained by applying formula (8) on* $\tilde{T}$ *and* S.

In essence, formula (8) provides the mechanism for trace lifting that back-translates any counter example from the retimed circuit to the original circuit.

5   Transformation-Based Verification

We implemented the retiming transformation as a re-entrant reduction engine with a "push" interface similar to a BDD package. The engine consumes a circuit from a higher-level engine, performs retiming, and then passes the resulting circuit down to a lower-level engine. For debugging of failing properties, the engine implements a back-translation mechanism that passes counter-example traces from the lower-level engine back to the higher-level. This setting allows an iterative usage of retiming and other reduction algorithms until the circuit can be passed to a "terminal" decision engine.

As an internal data structure we use a two-input AND/INVERTER graph similar to the one presented in [14] except that registers are modeled as edge attributes. This representation allows the application of several on-the-fly reduction algorithms, including inverter "dragging" and forward retiming of latches, both enabling a generalized identification of functionally identical structures by hashing. As an ILP solver we utilized the primal network simplex algorithm from IBM's Optimization Solutions Library (OSL) [15] to solve the register minimization problem.

As a second simplification engine, we implemented an algorithm for combinational redundancy removal which was adopted from an equivalence checking application [14]. This engine uses BDD sweeping and a SAT procedure to identify and eliminate functionally equivalent circuit structures, including the removal of redundant registers. As a terminal reachability engine we adapted VIS [16] version 1.4 (beta) for our experiments. In addition to the partitioned transition relation algorithm, VIS 1.4 incorporates a robust hybrid image computation approach.

6   Experimental Results

We performed a number of experiments to evaluate the impact of retiming on symbolic reachability analysis, using 31 sequential circuits from the ISCAS89 benchmarks and 27 circuits randomly selected from IBM's Gigahertz Processor (GP) design. All experiments were done on an IBM RS/6000 Model 260, with a 256 MBytes memory limit.

In the first set of experiments we assessed the potential of generalized retiming for reducing register count. In particular, we evaluated an iterative scheme where the retiming engine (RET) and the combinational reduction engine (COM) are called in an interleaved manner. The results for the ISCAS and GP circuits are given in Table 1. For the ISCAS benchmarks, we list only the circuits with more than 16 registers since smaller designs are of less interest for these experiments. Columns 2, 3, and 4 report the number of registers of the original circuit, after applying COM only, and RET only, respectively. The following columns give the register counts after performing various numbers of iterations of COM followed by RET. The number of negative registers, if non-zero, is given in parentheses. For brevity, we report only up to three iterations;

Table 1: Retiming results for ISCAS circuits (upper part) and GP circuits (lower part).

Design	Number of Registers (negative)						Relative Reduction (Best)	Max. Lag	Time (s) / Memory (MB) (Best)	Results of [6]/ [13] (Registers)
	Original	COM Only	RET Only	COM-RET 1 Iteration	COM-RET 2 Iterations	COM-RET 3 Iterations				
PROLOG	136	81	45 (1)	45 (1)	45 (3)	44 (2)	67.6%	2	1.4 / 22.4	- / -
S1196	18	16	16	14	14	14	22.2%	1	0.6 / 10.7	16 / -
S1238	18	17	16	15	14	14	22.2%	1	0.9 / 21.1	17 / -
S1269	37	37	36	36	36	36	2.7%	1	0.4 / 6.2	- / -
S13207_1	638	513	390	343	292 (1)	289	54.7%	11	3.8 / 34.7	- / -
S1423	74	74	72	72	72	72	2.7%	1	0.5 / 6.2	72 / 74
S1512	57	57	57	57	57	57	0.0%	1	0.5 / 6.2	- / 57
S15850_1	534	518	498	488	485	485	9.2%	6	5.3 / 31.8	- / -
S3271	116	116	110	110	110	110	5.2%	5	0.7 / 7.0	- / 116
S3330	132	81	44 (2)	44 (3)	44 (2)	44 (2)	66.7%	3	0.7 / 7.0	- / -
S3384	183	183	72	72	72	72	60.7%	6	0.7 / 7.1	- / 147
S35932	1728	1728	1728	1728	1728	1728	0.0%	1	7.2 / 38.0	- / -
S382	21	21	15	15	15	15	28.6%	1	0.3 / 5.9	15 / -
S38584_1	1426	1415	1375	1375	1374	1374	3.6%	5	29.4 / 127.4	- / -
S400	21	21	15	15	15	15	28.6%	0	0.3 / 5.9	15 / -
S444	21	21	15	15	15	15	28.6%	1	0.3 / 5.9	15 / -
S4863	104	88	37	37	37	37	64.4%	4	0.9 / 7.3	- / 96
S499	22	22	22	22	20	20	9.1%	1	0.6 / 15.1	- / -
S526N	21	21	21	21	21	21	0.0%	2	0.4 / 5.9	- / -
S5378	179	164	112 (6)	112 (6)	111 (6)	111 (6)	38.0%	5	1.6 / 18.4	- / 144
S635	32	32	32	32	32	32	0.0%	1	0.4 / 5.9	- / -
S641	19	17	15	15	15	15	21.1%	2	0.4 / 5.9	18 / -
S6669	239	231	92	75	75	75	68.6%	5	1.6 / 14.1	- / -
S713	19	17	15	15	15	15	21.1%	2	0.4 / 5.9	- / -
S838_1	32	32	32	32	32	32	0.0%	0	0.5 / 6.1	- / -
S9234_1	211	193	172	172	165	131	37.9%	3	2.5 / 26.2	- / -
S938	32	32	32	32	32	32	0.0%	0	0.4 / 6.1	- / -
S953	29	29	6	6	6	6	79.3%	0	0.4 / 6.1	- / -
S967	29	29	6	6	6	6	79.3%	0	0.4 / 6.1	- / -
S991	19	19	19	19	19	19	0.0%	2	0.4 / 6.0	- / -
C_RAS	431	431	378	370	348	348	19.3%	3	6.0 / 22.6	- / -
D_DASA	115	115	100	100	100	100	13.0%	2	0.9 / 7.1	- / -
D_DCLA	1137	1137	771	750	750	750	34.0%	1	35.4 / 36.2	- / -
D_DUDD	129	129	100	100	100	100	22.5%	3	0.9 / 7.0	- / -
L_IBBC	195	195	40	40	38	36	81.5%	2	1.6 / 21.6	- / -
L_IFAR	413	413	142	139	136	136	67.1%	4	3.1 / 19.5	- / -
L_IFEC	182	182	45	45	45	45	75.3%	6	0.7 / 7.0	- / -
L_IFPF	1546	1356	673 (4)	661 (4)	449 (2)	442 (2)	71.4%	10	46.5 / 127.9	- / -
L_EMQ	220	220	87	88	74	74	66.4%	4	3.4 / 18.5	- / -
L_EXEC	535	535	163	137	135	134	75.0%	6	9.8 / 28.1	- / -
L_FLUSH	159	159	1	1	1	1	99.4%	3	0.8 / 7.0	- / -
L_LMQ	1876	1831	1190	1185	433 (3)	425 (3)	77.3%	3	50.7 / 139.1	- / -
L_LRU	237	237	94	94	94	94	60.3%	2	1.1 / 7.1	- / -
L_PNTR	541	541	245	245	245	245	54.7%	3	1.8 / 8.8	- / -
L_TBWK	307	307	124	124	40	40	87.0%	3	2.7 / 18.0	- / -
M_CIU	777	686	415	415	411	387 (1)	50.2%	15	26.3 / 76.6	- / -
S_SCU1	373	373	204	200	192	192	48.5%	3	9.0 / 20.6	- / -
S_SCU2	1368	1368	566	565	426	423	69.1%	5	102.2 / 67.4	- / -
V_CACH	173	155	104 (2)	96 (3)	96 (2)	95 (1)	45.1%	9	1.1 / 24.0	- / -
V_DIR	178	151	87	83	43	42 (1)	76.4%	5	0.9 / 22.3	- / -
V_L2FB	75	75	26	26	26	26	65.3%	2	0.5 / 5.9	- / -
V_SCR1	150	128	52	48 (1)	48 (1)	48	68.0%	4	0.7 / 10.9	- / -
V_SCR2	551	551	86	82	82	82	85.1%	4	4.4 / 15.0	- / -
V_SNPC	93	93	21	21	21	21	77.4%	4	0.5 / 6.8	- / -
V_SNPM	1421	1216	233 (7)	233 (7)	231 (11)	227 (8)	84.0%	15	14.7 / 65.2	- / -
W_GAR	242	232	91 (1)	90	90	79 (1)	67.4%	2	3.2 / 25.4	- / -
W_SFA	64	64	42	42	41	41	35.9%	1	1.0 / 16.0	- / -

Table 2: Effect of retiming on reachability analysis (C = completed within the time limit of four hours, H = hybrid image computation, I = IWLS95 image computation).

Design	Original Circuit			Reduced Circuit				Relative Improvement
	Number of Registers	Reachability Steps, Algo	Time (sec) / Memory(MB)	Number of Registers	Reachability Steps, Algo	BDD$_{init}$ Nodes	Time (sec) / Memory(MB)	Time / Memory
PROLOG	136	17 C I	2285 / 134.5	45	16 C H	611	81.6 / 27.5	96.4% / 79.6%
S1196	18	4 C I	1.1 / 6.5	14	2 C I	122	0.5 / 6.3	54.5% / 3.1%
S1238	18	4 C I	1.2 / 6.5	14	2 C I	159	0.1 / 6.3	91.7% / 3.1%
S1269	37	11 C H	13194 / 185.5	36	11 C H	901	13395 / 187.5	-1.5% / -1.1%
S3330	132	17 C H	668.0 / 35.3	45	16 C I	194	35.8 / 15.6	94.6% / 55.8%
S382	21	13 C I	< 0.1 / 6.2	15	11 C I	17	< 0.1 / 6.1	0.0% / 1.6%
S400	21	10 C I	< 0.1 / 6.2	15	10 C H	16	< 0.1 / 6.1	0.0% / 1.6%
S444	21	4 C I	< 0.1 / 6.1	15	3 C H	27	< 0.1 / 6.1	0.0% / 0.0%
S4863	104	3 I	14400 / 174.2	37	4 C I	199	14.8 / 16.6	99.9% / 90.5%
S499	22	1 C H	0.2 / 6.2	20	1 C H	21	< 0.1 / 6.2	100% / 0.0%
S641	19	6 C I	0.8 / 6.4	15	5 C I	15	1.0 / 6.4	-25.0% / 0.0%
S713	19	6 C I	0.9 / 6.3	15	5 C I	15	0.6 / 6.4	33.3% / -1.6%
S953	29	6 C I	0.8 / 6.4	6	5 C H	7	< 0.1 / 6.1	100% / 4.7%
S967	29	4 C I	1.1 / 6.3	6	3 C H	7	< 0.1 / 6.1	100% / 3.2%
C_RAS	431	1028 C I	724.3 / 57.2	370	1026 C I	415	424.0 / 51.8	41.5% / 9.4%
D_DASA	115	6 C I	19.7 / 7.8	100	5 C I	200	33.0 / 11.6	-67.5% / -48.7%
D_DUDD	129	13 C I	953.3 / 112.8	100	11 C H	2568	359.1 / 33.7	62.3% / 70.1%
L_IBBC	195	5 C H	145.3 / 11.4	40	3 C H	41	4.4 / 6.4	97.0% / 43.9%
L_IFAR	413	5 I	14400 / 87.0	139	22 C I	719	2302 / 102.0	84.0% / -17.2%
L_IFEC	182	6 C I	66.3 / 8.4	45	2 C H	151	28.0 / 6.9	57.8% / 17.9%
L_EMQ	220	8 C H	323.7 / 17.0	88	5 C H	5519	205.6 / 33.0	36.5% / -94.1%
L_EXEC	535	5 H	14400 / 63.2	137	9 C I	1856	593.6 / 103.2	95.9% / -63.3%
L_FLUSH	159	4 C I	37.4 / 7.7	1	2 C H	2	< 0.1 / 6.2	100% / 19.5%
L_PNTR	541	6 C I	6687 / 138.5	245	3 C I	242	2423 / 51.2	63.8% / 63.0%
L_TBWK	307	6 C H	184.1 / 9.1	124	4 C H	123	74.0 / 7.4	59.8% / 18.7%
S_SCU1	373	14 C H	8934 / 165.8	200	12 C H	755	1195 / 118.1	86.6% / 28.8%
V_CACH	173	11 C H	92.1 / 17.2	97	8 C I	910	20.0 / 8.9	78.3% / 48.3%
V_DIR	178	8 C H	57.9 / 8.3	83	2 C I	95	11.1 / 7.0	80.8% / 15.7%
V_L2FB	75	4 C I	2.9 / 6.3	26	2 C H	27	< 0.1 / 6.1	100% / 3.2%
V_SCR1	150	20 C H	250.0 / 17.7	48	17 C I	90	5.0 / 15.5	98.0% / 12.4%
V_SCR2	551	22 C I	1201 / 105.0	82	20 C I	220	260.0 / 36.7	78.4% / 65.0%
V_SNPC	93	4 C H	4.9 / 6.6	21	1 C H	17	< 0.1 / 6.2	100% / 6.1%
W_GAR	242	11 C I	109.8 / 25.0	90	9 C H	191	82.5 / 13.0	24.9% / 48.0%
W_SFA	64	7 C I	3.7 / 6.8	42	6 C I	14	3.6 / 6.9	2.7% / -1.5%

more iterations provided only marginal improvements. The reported maximum lag in column 9 gives an indication of the size of the retiming stump.

Overall, the results indicate that generalized retiming has a significant potential for reducing the number of registers for verification. For the ISCAS benchmarks we obtained a maximum register reduction of 79% with an average of 27%. For the processor circuits we achieved an average reduction of 62%.

The number of negative registers generated by retiming is surprisingly small. This can be explained by the two-input AND/INVERTER data structure used as circuit representation. One can show that within each strongly connected component (SCC) of such circuits, there exists an optimal retiming with only positive registers. Only paths between the SCCs may require negative registers for an optimal solution.

Table 2 gives the performance results for symbolic reachability analysis. We report results for all circuits of Table 1 for which retiming resulted in a register reduction and reachability analysis could be completed. We ran each experiment with two options for the VIS image computation: the IWLS95 partitioned transition relation method and the

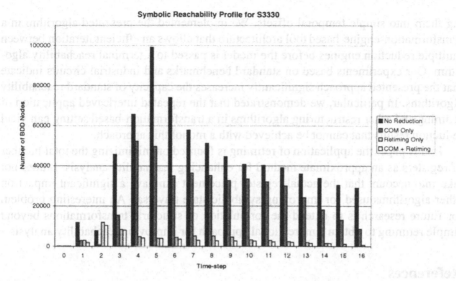

Fig. 4: BDD size profile for traversing S3330 with method IWLS95 after various transformations.

hybrid approach. The best of the two results on a per-example basis are then reported. Although after reduction we can complete traversal for only three additional circuits, the results clearly show that retiming significantly improves the overall performance. The CPU time is decreased by an average of 53.1% for ISCAS and 64.0% for GP circuits, respectively. The corresponding memory reductions are 17.2% and 12.3%, respectively. The cumulative run time speedup is 55.7% for the ISCAS benchmarks and 83.5% for the GP circuits. To illustrate the complexity of the retiming stump, we report the BDD sizes for the initial states in column 7. As shown, these BDDs remain fairly small and do not impact the complexity of the reachability analysis.

Figure 4 shows the profile of the BDD size while traversing benchmark S3330 for the original circuit and after applying various reduction steps. This example demonstrates how retiming typically benefits the performance of the traversal. To further illustrate the effect of retiming on the correlation of the state encoding, we analyzed the traversal of circuit S4863. Reachability timed out during the third traversal step of the original circuit. Using retiming, the correlation between the remaining registers was completely removed resulting in full reachability of all 2^{37} states. While such a profound result is likely atypical, this is strong evidence of the power of both structural simplification and retiming to reduce register correlation.

7   Conclusions and Future Work

We presented the application of generalized retiming for enhancing symbolic reachability analysis. We discussed three extensions of the classical retiming approach which include: (1) eliminating the need for equivalent reset states by introducing the concept of an initialization stump, (2) supporting negative registers, handled as general functional relations to future time frames, and (3) removing peripheral registers by converting them into simple temporal offsets. We implemented the presented algorithm in a transformation-engine-based tool architecture that allows an efficient iteration between multiple reduction engines before the model is passed to a terminal reachability algorithm. Our experiments based on standard benchmarks and industrial circuits indicate that the presented approach significantly increases the capacity of standard reachability algorithms. In particular, we demonstrated that the repeated interleaved application of retiming and other restructuring algorithms in a transformation-based setting can yield reduction results that cannot be achieved with a monolithic approach.

In this paper the application of retiming is focused on minimizing the total number of registers as an approximate method for enhancing reachability analysis. It does not take into account that the actual register placement can have a significant impact on other algorithms used for improving symbolic state traversal. An interesting problem for future research is to extend the formulation of structural transformations beyond simple retiming to obtain a more global approach for improving reachability analysis.

References

1. O. Coudert, C. Berthet, and J. C. Madre, "Verification of synchronous sequential machines based on symbolic execution," in *International Workshop on Automatic Verification Methods for Finite State Systems*, Springer-Verlag, June 1989.
2. J. R. Burch, E. M. Clarke, K. L. McMillan, D. L. Dill, and L. J. Hwang, "Symbolic model checking: 10^{20} states and beyond," in *IEEE Symposium on Logic in Computer Science*, pp. 428–439, IEEE, June 1990.
3. T. Niermann and J. H. Patel, "HITEC: A test generation package for sequential circuits," in *The European Conference on Design Automation*, pp. 214–218, IEEE, February 1991.
4. C. Leiserson and J. Saxe, "Retiming synchronous circuitry," *Algorithmica*, vol. 6, pp. 5–35, 1991.
5. J. A. Darringer, D. Brand, J. V. Gerbi, W. H. Joyner, and L. H. Trevillyan, "Logic synthesis through local transformations," *IBM Journal on Research and Development*, vol. 25, pp. 272–280, July 1981.
6. A. Gupta, P. Ashar, and S. Malik, "Exploiting retiming in a guided simulation based validation methodology," in *Correct Hardware Design and Verification Methods (CHARME'99)*, pp. 350–353, September 1999.
7. S. Malik, E. M. Sentovich, R. K. Brayton, and A. Sangiovanni-Vincentelli, "Retiming and resynthesis: Optimizing sequential networks with combinational techniques," *IEEE Transactions on Computer-Aided Design*, vol. 10, pp. 74–84, January 1991.
8. G. Hasteer, A. Mathur, and P. Banerjee, "Efficient equivalance checking of multi-phase designs using retiming," in *IEEE International Conference on Computer-Aided Design*, pp. 557–561, November 1998.
9. J. Baumgartner, A. Tripp, A. Aziz, V. Singhal, and F. Andersen, "An abtraction algorithm for the verification of generalized C-slow designs," in *Conference on Computer Aided Verification (CAV'00)*, pp. 5–19, July 2000.
10. C. Leiserson and J. Saxe, "Optimizing synchronous systems," *Journal of VLSI and Computer Systems*, vol. 1, pp. 41–67, January 1983.
11. H. J. Touati and R. K. Brayton, "Computing the initial states of retimed circuits," *IEEE Transactions on Computer-Aided Design*, vol. 12, pp. 157–162, January 1993.
12. G. Even, I. Y. Spillinger, and L. Stok, "Retiming revisited and reversed," *IEEE Transactions on Computer-Aided Design*, vol. 15, pp. 348–357, March 1996.

13. G. Cabodi, S. Quer, and F. Somenzi, "Optimizing sequential verification by retiming trans-formations," in *37th ACM/IEEE Design Automation Conference*, pp. 601–606, June 2000.
14. A. Kuehlmann, M. K. Ganai, and V. Paruthi, "Circuit-based Boolean reasoning," in *Proceedings of the 38th ACM/IEEE Design Automation Conference*, ACM/IEEE, June 2001.
15. M. S. Hung, W. O. Rom, and A. Waren, *Optimization with IBM OSL*. Scientific Press, 1993.
16. The VIS Group, "VIS: A system for verification and synthesis," in *Conference on Computer Aided Verification (CAV'96)*, pp. 428–432, Springer-Verlag, July 1996.

Meta-BDDs: A Decomposed Representation for Layered Symbolic Manipulation of Boolean Functions

Gianpiero Cabodi

Dip. di Automatica e Informatica
Politecnico di Torino, Turin, Italy
cabodi@polito.it
http://www.polito.it/~cabodi

Abstract. We propose a BDD based representation for Boolean functions, which extends conjunctive/disjunctive decompositions. The model introduced (Meta-BDD) can be considered as a symbolic representation of $k-$Layer automata describing Boolean functions. A layer is the set of BDD nodes labeled by a given variable, and its characteristic function is represented using BDDs. Meta-BDDs are implemented upon a standard BDD library and they support layered (decomposed) processing of Boolean operations used in formal verification problems. Besides targeting reduced BDD size, the theoretical advantage of this form over other decompositions is being closed under complementation, which makes Meta-BDDs applicable to a broader range of problems.

1   Introduction

Binary Decision Diagrams [1] (BDDs) are a core technique for several applications in the field of Formal Verification and Synthesis. They provide compact implicit forms for functions depending on tens to hundreds of Boolean variables.

Many variants of the original BDD type [1] have been proposed to explore possible optimizations and extensions (see for example a survey in [2]). Dynamic variable ordering techniques (sifting [3]) have played a key role to push forward the applicability of BDDs and to face the ordering dependent memory explosion problem. Partitioned [4] and decomposed [5] forms have also been followed as a divide–and–conquer attempt to scale down the complexity of symbolic operations.

This paper follows the latter trend. We propose a decomposed representation for Boolean functions, which extends conjunctive/disjunctive decompositions. One of the limitations of conjunctive (disjunctive) decompositions is that they are biased to the zeroes (ones) of a Boolean function. Let us consides for instance a conjunctive form $f = \bigwedge_i f_i$, each one of the f_i components describes a subset of the zeroes (the OFF–set) of f. Dually for disjunctive forms. Both forms are not closed under negation: the negation of a conjunctive form is disjunctive (and vice–versa), so the application requires both forms, and practical/heuristic simplification rules, unless all formulas can be put in positive normal form.

---

[1] Reduced Ordered BDDs (ROBDDs), or simply BDDs whenever no ambiguity arises

G. Berry, H. Comon, and A. Finkel (Eds.): CAV 2001, LNCS 2102, pp. 118–130, 2001.
© Springer-Verlag Berlin Heidelberg 2001

Our work proposes a decomposed form evenly oriented to represent both the zeroes and the ones of a Boolean function. Besides looking at a compact format, we look for efficient symbolic manipulation in the decomposed form. Our solution can be canonical, it is closed under negation, and it supports standard Boolean operations and quantifiers, so it may be applied to BDD based combinational and sequential verification problems. To find the most suitable way of describing this new decomposed form, we adopt an automaton model, which has recently been proposed to describe Boolean functions within an explicit reachability framework [6]. We see a BDD (and the related Boolean function) as an automaton, and we describe it through a set of BDDs. We thus use the term *Meta-BDD* for the decomposed form.

In the sequel, we will briefly overview some preliminary concepts and related works, then we will introduce Meta-BDDs and the related symbolic manipulations. We will finally present some experimental results attained with a prototype implementation.

2   Preliminaries and Related Works

Binary Decision Diagrams (BDDs) [1, 2] are directed acyclic graphs providing a canonical representation of Boolean functions. Starting from a non reduced Ordered BDD (OBDD), the Reduced OBDD (ROBDD [1]) for a given Boolean function is obtained by repeatedly applying two well known reduction rules: (1) *Merging rule* (two isomorphic subgraphs are merged), and (2) *Deletion rule* (a BDD node whose two branches point to the same successor is deleted).

Simple graph algorithms, working *depth-first* on BDDs, implement many operators: APPLY, ITE (if-then-else), and existential/universal quantifiers are well-known examples. BDDs have been widely used in verification problems to represent functions as well as sets, by means of their characteristic functions. Operations on sets are efficiently implemented by Boolean operations on their characteristic functions. The notation χ_A is usually adopted for the *characteristic function* of a set A. For instance, let A, B be two sets, and χ_A, χ_B their characteristic functions, we write:

$$\chi_{A \cup B} = \chi_A \vee \chi_B, \chi_{A \cap B} = \chi_A \wedge \chi_B, \chi_{A-B} = \chi_A \wedge \neg \chi_B$$

For sake of simplicity, we make a little abuse of notation in the rest of this paper, and we make no distinction between the BDD representing a set, the characteristic function of the set and the set itself.

2.1   State Sets Represented by k−Layer DFAs

A given Boolean function $f(x) : \{0,1\}^k \rightarrow \{0,1\}$ is represented by Holzmann and Puri [6] as a Deterministic Finite Automaton (DFA). They introduce k−Layer *DFAs* to describe sets of states within a verification framework based on explicit reachability. An automaton accepts input strings of length k. In the Boolean case, $\{0,1\}$ is the input alphabet, the automaton accepts a set $S \subseteq \{0,1\}^k$ of k−tuples, and each layer in the automaton corresponds to an input bit of the function describing a state set.

A k−Layer DFA has one initial and two terminal states, the accepting terminal state 1, and the rejecting terminal state 0. The automaton is minimized

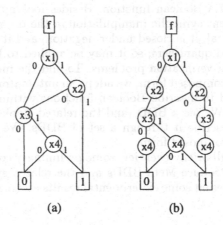

(a)   (b)

Fig. 1. *A BDD (a) and a k—Layer DFA (b) for the same Boolean function. The deletion rule is not applied to the k—Layer DFA.*

if states which have exactly the same successors are merged together. The automaton describing a Boolean function has a close relationship with the BDD representing it, with a variable ordering corresponding to the input string ordering. A k—Layer DFA is minimized by only using the merging rule, whereas the deletion rule is avoided, to keep input strings of length k.

As an example, Figure 1 shows the BDD (a) and the DFA (b) for the same Boolean function. Given a BDD variable ordering corresponding to the layers, the two representations have similar shapes, but no implicit variables are present in the k—Layer DFA.

2.2 McMillan's Conjunctive Decomposition

McMillan's canonical conjunctive decomposition [5] is another relevant starting point for this work. The automaton representation is proposed by McMillan, too. He sees a BDD representing a set of states as a *"finite state automaton that reads the values of the state variables in some fixed order, and finally accepts or rejects the given valuation"*.

A function $f(x_1, ..., x_n)$ is decomposed as $f = \bigwedge_{i=1}^{n} f_i$, the i-th conjunctive component being defined as $f_i = f^{(i)} \downarrow f^{(i-1)}$. The $f^{(i)}$ functions are the projections of f onto growing sets of variables $f^{(i)}(x_1, ..., x_i) = \exists(x_{i+1}, ..., x_n).f(x)$ and $\downarrow$ is the generalized cofactor "constrain" operator [7,8]. Conjunctive components have growing support ($f_i = f_i(x_1, ..., x_i)$), and the representation is canonical given a variable order for projections (which is not necessarily the same as the BDD variable order). Cofactoring is a major source of BDD size reduction for this representation, due to the BDD simplification properties of the generalized cofactor operator: the BDD representing $g \downarrow f$ is often (not always [2] !) smaller

---

[2] Since "constrain" may introduce new variables (and BDD nodes) in the cofactored term, simplification is not always achieved. Other variants of generalized cofactor have been introduced to expecially address simplification tasks. An example is the

than the BDD of g, and the decomposition $f^{(i)} = f^{(i-1)} \wedge (f^{(i)} \downarrow f^{(i-1)})$ exploits this fact, expecially in cases of factors with *disjoint supports* or supports including *conditionally independent variables*.

Conjunction, disjunction and projection (existential quantification) algorithms are also proposed in [5], in order to use the decomposition in symbolic model checking problems that can be put in positive normal form (with negation only allowed on literals). They can be summarized as follows.

Conjunction. is the simplest operation. The result of a conjunction fg is computed in two steps. An intermediate result t is first evaluated by conjoining the couples of corresponding components f_i and g_i bottom-up (with decreasing i), and applying a "reduction" [3] process:

$$t_n = f_n g_n$$
$$t_{i-1} = f_{i-1} g_{i-1} \exists x_i . t_i$$

The intermediate result is then "normalized" top-down (by increasing i) for canonicity (and BDD simplification): $h_i = t_i \downarrow h_1 \downarrow ... \downarrow h_{i-1}$. The decomposed conjunction thus results in a linear number of conjunction and projection operations, and a quadratic number of cofactor operations.

Disjunction. is a less natural operation for conjunctive decompositions. The i-th component of $h = f \vee g$ should be evaluated by taking into account all components of the operands from 1 to i:

$$t_i = \bigwedge_{j=1}^{i} f_j \vee \bigwedge_{j=1}^{i} g_j$$
$$h_i = t_i \downarrow h_1 \downarrow ... \downarrow h_{i-1}$$

This is not efficient, because of the explicit computation of conjunctions and delayed normalization. So a more efficient computation, with interleaved normalization, is proposed:

$$h_i = \bigwedge_{j=1}^{i} (f_j \downarrow h_1 \downarrow ... \downarrow h_{i-1}) \vee \bigwedge_{j=1}^{i} (g_j \downarrow h_1 \downarrow ... \downarrow h_{i-1})$$

resulting in a quadratic number of conjunction and cofactor, and a linear number of disjunction operations (which is more complex than the previous conjunction case).

Projection (Existential Quantification $h = \exists S.f.$) has the same problems as disjunction, and it is computed in a similar way: $h_i = \exists S.(\bigwedge_{j=1}^{i} (f_j \downarrow h_1 \downarrow ... \downarrow h_{i-1}))$ Again a quadratic number of conjunction and cofactor operations (and a linear number of quantifications) is required.

"restrict" cofactor [9], which locally abstracts from f variables not found in g. But some nice properties of "constrain" are lost, and canonicity of conjunctive decomposition is not guaranteed.

[3] Reduction is a term we bring from breadth-first BDD manipulation (indicating a postponed application of merging and deletion rules) [10]. It was not used in [5]

2.3   Incompletely Specified Boolean Functions

An incompletely specified Boolean function is a function defined over a subset of $\{0, 1\}^n$. The domain points where the function is not defined are called *don't care* set, whereas the points where the function is defined as true or false are called *ON-set* and *OFF-set*, respectively (the union of ON-set and OFF-set is called *care* set).

Given an incompletely specified function f, we will use the notation $f.on$ for the ON-set, $f.off$ for the OFF-set, and $f.dc$ for the don't care set. Two of them are enough to completely characterize f, since they have null mutual intersections and their union is the domain space. So f might be represented by the couple $f = (f.on, f.off)$, being $f.dc = \neg(f.on \vee f.off)$. Another way to represent f is the interval of completely specified functions $f = [f.on, \neg f.off]$.

3   Meta-BDDs. Describing a BDD by a Layered Set of BDDs

This section defines Meta-BDDs. They are **not** a new type of Decision Diagram for Boolean functions. We introduce them as a layered set of BDDs used to describe a Boolean function. We view a BDD as a DFA, and we use other BDDs to describe it by layers of variables, and to symbolically encode breadth–first computations of BDD operators.

We can also view Meta-BDDs as an extension of McMillan's canonical conjunctive decomposition [5]. Our representation is more general, since it includes conjunctive as well as disjunctive decompositions, and it is closed under Boolean negation. It is canonical under proper conditions.

Let us define the i-th layer as the set of nodes labeled by the x_i variable. We characterize the layer with the BDD paths reaching terminals (either 1 or 0) from x_i nodes. In the automaton view of BDDs, this means that the accepting or rejecting final state is decided when testing the x_i variable. In the case of Figure 1, there is no path to terminal nodes from the x_1 layer, there is one path to terminal 1 from the x_2 layer ($x_1 x_2 = 11$), 3 paths to 0 at the x_3 layer ($x_1 x_2 x_3 = \{000, 010, 100\}$), 3 paths to 1 ($x_1 x_2 x_3 x_4 = \{0011, 0111, 1011\}$) and 3 paths to 0 ($x_1 x_2 x_3 x_4 = \{0010, 0110, 1010\}$) from the x_4 layer.

We describe a layer of a given function f by means of a function capturing the zeroes (paths to 0) and ones (paths to 1) of f at that layer. More specifically, we encode the i-th layer of f with an incompletely specified function f_i, such that the ON-set ($f_i.on$) is the set of ones of f at the i-th layer, and the OFF-set ($f_i.off$) is the set of zeroes of f at the i-th layer. As a consequence, the don't care set ($f_i.dc$) is the set of ones/zeroes reached by f at other layers.

We informally introduce the *Meta* representation of f (Meta-BDD if symbolically encoded by BDDs), as the set of f_i layers that completely characterize f. For each layer we represent the two sets of paths leading to the 1 and 0 terminals at that layer. In the case represented in Figure 1, this leads to the Meta form of Figure 2(a).

A more accurate and formal definition of Meta-BDDs is obtained by introducing the Meta operator $<>^{\mathcal{M}}$, working on incompletely specified Boolean functions.

$$f_1 = (0,0) \qquad\qquad\qquad\qquad f_1 = (0,0)$$
$$f_2 = (x_1x_2, 0) \qquad\qquad\qquad f_2 = (x_1x_2, 0)$$
$$f_3 = (0, \neg(x_1x_2)\neg x_3) \qquad\qquad f_3 = (0, \neg x_3)$$
$$f_4 = (\neg(x_1x_2)x_3x_4, \neg(x_1x_2)x_3\neg x_4) \qquad f_4 = (x_4, \neg x_4)$$

(a)   (b)

Fig. 2. *Layered Meta representations of f. Each $f_i = (f_i.on, f_i.off)$ is exactly defined only for the ones and zeroes of f at the corresponding layer (a). Upper layers are used to simplify lower f_is by means of cofactoring (b).*

Definition 1. *Given two incompletely specified Boolean functions f and g, $h = <f, g>^{\mathcal{M}}$ is an incompletely specified function, such that the ON-set (OFF-set) of h is the ON-set (OFF-set) of f augmented with the portion of the ON-set (OFF-set) of g not covered by the care set of f:*

$$< f, g >^{\mathcal{M}} \stackrel{def}{=} \text{ITE}(\neg f.dc, f, g) \tag{1}$$

The above definition can be rewritten as

$$< f, g >^{\mathcal{M}} = h \text{ such that } \begin{cases} h.on = f.on \vee g.on \wedge \neg f.off \\ h.off = f.off \vee g.off \wedge \neg f.on \\ h.dc = f.dc \wedge g.dc \end{cases}$$

The operator returns the argument in the unary case $(< f >^{\mathcal{M}} = f)$ and it is associative

$$<< f, g >^{\mathcal{M}}, h >^{\mathcal{M}} = < f, < g, h >^{\mathcal{M}} >^{\mathcal{M}} = < f, g, h >^{\mathcal{M}}$$

We are now ready to formally define the Meta decomposition of f in n components.

Definition 2. *The Meta decomposition of a Boolean function f is an ordered set of components that produces f if given as argument to the $<>^{\mathcal{M}}$ operator:*

$$f_{[1,n]}^{\mathcal{M}} \stackrel{def}{=} < f_1, f_2, ..., f_n >^{\mathcal{M}} = f$$

A Meta-BDD is a BDD representation of a Meta decomposition.

We adopt $[i, j]$ subscripts to indicate intervals of components, and we optionally omit them if clear from the context (we use $f^{\mathcal{M}}$ instead of $f_{[1,n]}^{\mathcal{M}}$).

Applying equation (1) and associativity, a Meta decomposition can be recursively written as

$$f_{[i,j]}^{\mathcal{M}} = \text{ITE}(\neg f_i.dc, f_i, f_{[i+1,j]}^{\mathcal{M}})$$

which leads to the following expanded expression for f:

$$f = \text{ITE}(\neg f_1.dc, f_1, \text{ITE}(\neg f_2.dc, f_2, \text{ITE}(...\text{ITE}(\neg f_{n-1}.dc, f_{n-1}, f_n))))$$

The inspiring idea of this decomposition is that each component contributes a new piece to the ON-set and the OFF-set of f. In other words, f is progressively approximated and finally reached by a sequence of incompletely specified functions $f_{[1,1]}^{\mathcal{M}} \preceq f_{[1,2]}^{\mathcal{M}} \preceq \cdots \preceq f_{[1,n]}^{\mathcal{M}} = f$ ordered by the precedence relation

$$f_{[1,i]}^{\mathcal{M}} \preceq f_{[1,j]}^{\mathcal{M}} \iff (f_{[1,i]}^{\mathcal{M}}.on \subseteq f_{[1,j]}^{\mathcal{M}}.on) \wedge (f_{[1,i]}^{\mathcal{M}}.off \subseteq f_{[1,j]}^{\mathcal{M}}.off)$$

The functions have non decreasing ON-set and OFF-set, and the last one coincides with f.

We have a degree of freedom in selecting the sequence of functions converging to f. Starting from canonical conjunctive decomposition, we adopt the idea of projecting f onto growing sets of variables, so that $f_{[1,i]}^{\mathcal{M}}$ captures the ones and zeroes of f at the upper i layers (i.e. the BDD paths reaching 0 or 1 *forall* variables at the lower levels $(x > x_i)$). We thus choose $f_{[1,i]}^{\mathcal{M}}(x_1, ..., x_i)$ such that

$$f_{[1,i]}^{\mathcal{M}}(x_1, ..., x_i).on = \forall(x > x_i).f$$
$$f_{[1,i]}^{\mathcal{M}}(x_1, ..., x_i).off = \forall(x > x_i).\neg f$$

The $f_{[1,i]}^{\mathcal{M}}$ function is represented by the first i terms of the Meta decomposition $f_1, ..., f_i$. The definition does not provide a rule to uniquely compute the f_i components, given f. In fact, we have here another degree of freedom, as the f_i term is partially "covered" by the previous ones $(< i)$. So we might leave it partially unspecified, or better exploit this fact (as in [5]) and simplify the lower layers by cofactoring them with the don't care set of the upper ones: $f_i = f_{[1,i]}^{\mathcal{M}} \downarrow f_{[1,i-1]}^{\mathcal{M}}.dc$.

Since the don't care set of $f_{[1,i-1]}^{\mathcal{M}}$ is the intersection of the don't care sets of the first $i - 1$ components $(f_{[1,i-1]}^{\mathcal{M}}.dc = \bigwedge_{j=1}^{i-1} f_j.dc,$)we avoid computing it and we apply to f_i a chain of cofactors: $f_i = f_{[1,i]}^{\mathcal{M}} \downarrow f_1.dc \downarrow f_2.dc \downarrow ... \downarrow f_{i-1}.dc$. This would simplify the representation of Figure 2(a) to the form (b), which is obviously simpler.

Meta-BDDs and Conjunctive Decompositions. Meta decompositions include McMillan's conjunctive decomposition as the particular case with $f_{[1,i]}^{\mathcal{M}}.on = 0$ for all $i < n$ and $f_{[1,i]}^{\mathcal{M}}.off = \forall(x > x_i).\neg f = \neg\exists(x > x_i).f$. Given the above assumptions, the i-th component of $f^{\mathcal{M}}$ is $f_i = (0, \neg\exists(x > x_i).f \downarrow \exists(x > x_{i-1}).f)$, where the OFF-set is the complement of McMillan's generic conjunctive term.

Variable Ordering and Grouping. The ordering applied to the definition of a Meta-BDD is not required to be the same as the BDD ordering. Moreover, layers can be extended to groups of variables, i.e. each x_i in the previous definitions is a set of variables instead of a single variable. This has the advantage of reducing the number of layers in the decomposition, where each layer includes a set of variables (and the corresponding edges to terminals).

In our implementation, we observed best performance when using the same order for variables and layers, and grouping variables. For the cases we addressed (100 to 200 state variables), reasonable group sizes are 10 to 30 variables. Dynamic variable ordering is supported, provided that variable layers are rebuild each time a new variable order is produced. The overhead we experienced for this transformation is low compared to sifting time, and to the overall cost of image computations, since rebuilding variable groups is a linear operation and transforming a Meta-BDD from old layers to new ones is a variant of the BDD to Meta-BDD transformation (described in the next section).

Meta-BDDs and Canonicity. Meta-BDDs are canonical under conditions similar to McMillan's decomposition, i.e. that layer simplifications are done through constrain cofactor. Canonicity guarantees constant time equality check, but our experience in sequential reachability shows that we may give it up whenever non canonical representations produce memory reduction.

This is often the case for Meta-BDDs, where a **conditional** application of **reduction and constrain simplification** may filter out the decompositions producing benefits and abort the bad ones. This is a major point for the efficiency in our implementation where reductions and cofactorings are controlled by BDD size based heuristic decisions.

We also experienced the "restrict" cofactor [9], with worse results on the average, compared with controlled application of constrain. A possible reason for this fact is that restrict guarantees good local optimizations of individual functions, but operations involving restricted functions may blow up when combining terms with different restrict optimizations.

4 Symbolic Operations on Meta-BDDs

We describe in this section how basic Boolean operators can be applied to Meta-BDD decompositions. In particular, we will concentrate on the operations required by sequential verification tasks: standard logic operators and quantifiers. Our procedures are here proposed for the canonical case, and we omit for simplicity heuristic decision points for conditional application of reductions and cofactor simplifications.

First of all, Meta BDDs provide a constant time **Not** operation whose result is again a Meta-BDD. In fact, since Boolean negation swaps zeroes with ones, $\neg f^{\mathcal{M}}$ is computed by simply swapping the $(f_i.on, f_i.off)$ couples.

Going to BDD/Meta-BDD conversions and **Apply**-like operations, we operate them through a layered process, which is inspired by [10], where BDD operations are performed through a breadth–first two phase (**Apply-Reduce**) technique. But our method is implicit, we operate breadth–first through layer–by–layer iterations on the T-ROBDD implicit structure, represented by BDDs.

Figure 3 shows how we convert a BDD to a Meta-BDD. We initially assign all terminal edges to the bottom layer, i.e. we initialize all Meta-BDD components to 0, except the last one. Then we perform reduction and constrain simplification.

Reduction and constrain simplification are shown in Figure 4. METAREDUCE is a bottom–up process which finds BDD nodes with both cofactors pointing to the same terminal. The merged edges are moved to the upper layers. METACONSTRAIN (Figure 4(b)) operates the cofactor based simplification. The reduction and constrain operations are here represented by dedicated procedures, as post–processing steps of Meta-BDD operations. For best performance, they can be integrated within breadth–first manipulations, and operated by layers as soon as possible.

$$
\boxed{
\begin{array}{l}
\textsc{BDD2Meta } (f) \\
\quad \text{for } i = 1 \text{ to } n - 1 \\
\qquad f_i \leftarrow (0, 0) \\
\quad f_n \leftarrow (f, \neg f) \\
\quad f^{\mathcal{M}} \leftarrow (f_1, ..., f_n) \\
\quad \textsc{MetaReduce}(f^{\mathcal{M}}) \\
\quad \textsc{MetaConstrain}(f^{\mathcal{M}}) \\
\quad \text{return } f^{\mathcal{M}}
\end{array}
}
$$

Fig. 3. *Converting a BDD to Meta-BDD. All terminal edges are initially assigned to the bottom $(n-th)$ layer. They are moved to the proper upper layers by the reduction procedure. constrain simplification is finally operated*

$$
\boxed{
\begin{array}{ll}
\textsc{MetaReduce } (f^{\mathcal{M}}) & \textsc{MetaConstrain } (f^{\mathcal{M}}) \\
\quad \text{for } i = n - 1 \text{ downto } 1 & \quad \text{for } i = 1 \text{ to } n - 1 \\
\quad f_i.on \leftarrow f_i.on \vee \forall (x > x_i).f_{i+1}.on & \quad \text{for } j = i + 1 \text{ to } n \\
\quad f_i.off \leftarrow f_i.off \vee \forall (x > x_i).f_{i+1}.off & \qquad f_j \leftarrow f_j \downarrow f_i.dc \\
\quad f_{i+1} \leftarrow f_{i+1} \downarrow f_i.dc & \\
\\
\qquad\qquad (a) & \qquad\qquad\qquad (b)
\end{array}
}
$$

Fig. 4. *Reduction (a). Terminal edges are moved upward by a bottom-up iterative process. Move is achieved by adding the reduced part to f_i, then deleting it from f_{i+1} using cofactor. Constrain based simplification (b). A double iteration is operated to avoid explicit computation of $f_i^{\mathcal{M}}.dc$.*

As an example of APPLY operation, we show the conjunction (METAAND) procedure. Disjunction is obtained for free in terms of complementation and conjunction. The proposed algorithm is based on the following theorem

Theorem 1. *Let $f_{[j,i]}^{\mathcal{M}}$ and $g_{[j,i]}^{\mathcal{M}}$ be Meta decompositions, then*

$$
f_{[j,i]}^{\mathcal{M}} \wedge g_{[j,i]}^{\mathcal{M}} = < f_{[j,i-1]}^{\mathcal{M}} \wedge g_{[j,i-1]}^{\mathcal{M}}, r_i >^{\mathcal{M}}
$$

with r_i computed as:

$$
r_i.on = \bigvee_{l=1}^{i} f_l.on \wedge \bigvee_{l=1}^{i} g_l.on
$$
$$
r_i.off = f_i.off \wedge \neg \bigvee_{l=1}^{i-1} g_l.on \vee g_i.off \wedge \neg \bigvee_{l=1}^{i-1} f_l.on
$$

Proof Sketch. Let us consider conjunction as a symbolic breadth–first visit of the product automaton of f and g. The set of paths reaching 0 at the i–th layer is given by the paths where either f or g are 0 at the i–th layer, and they are not 1 at the upper ones $(< i)$ [4]. The set of paths to 1 is given by the paths where both automata (f and g) reach 1 at one of the first i layers.

Figure 5(a) shows our algorithm for conjunction. f' and g' are used to collect the overall ON-sets of the upper components ($\bigvee_l f_l.on$ and $\bigvee_l g_l.on$ in Theorem 1). Explicit computation of the above terms would be in contrast with

---

[4] Due to the cofactor based simplification, $f_i.off$ ($g_i.off$) could intersect the onset of upper components

$$
\begin{array}{l}
\text{META AND } (f^{\mathcal{M}}, g^{\mathcal{M}}) \\
\quad f' \leftarrow 1, g' \leftarrow 1, dc \leftarrow 1 \\
\quad \text{for } i = 1 \text{ to } n \\
\qquad f' \leftarrow f' \downarrow dc \\
\qquad g' \leftarrow g' \downarrow dc \\
\qquad r_i.off \leftarrow f_i.off \downarrow dc \wedge \neg f' \vee \\
\qquad\qquad g_i.off \downarrow dc \wedge \neg g' \\
\qquad f' \leftarrow f' \wedge f_i.on \downarrow dc \\
\qquad g' \leftarrow g' \wedge g_i.on \downarrow dc \\
\qquad r_i.on \leftarrow f' \vee g' \\
\qquad dc \leftarrow \neg (r_i.on \vee r_i.off) \\
\quad r^{\mathcal{M}} \leftarrow (r_1, ..., r_n) \\
\quad \text{META REDUCE}(r^{\mathcal{M}}) \\
\quad \text{META CONSTRAIN}(r^{\mathcal{M}}) \\
\quad \text{return } r^{\mathcal{M}}
\end{array}
$$

$$
\begin{array}{l}
\text{META EXIST } (f^{\mathcal{M}}, S) \\
\quad f' \leftarrow 1, dc \leftarrow 1 \\
\quad r^{\mathcal{M}} \leftarrow f^{\mathcal{M}} \\
\quad \text{for } i = 1 \text{ to } n \\
\qquad f' \leftarrow f' \downarrow dc \\
\qquad r_i \leftarrow r_i \downarrow dc \\
\qquad r_i.on \leftarrow \exists S. \bigwedge (f', r_i.on) \\
\qquad f' \leftarrow \bigwedge (f', \neg f_i.off) \\
\qquad r_i.off \leftarrow \neg \exists S.f' \\
\qquad dc \leftarrow \neg r_i.on \vee r_i.off \\
\quad \text{META REDUCE}(r^{\mathcal{M}}) \\
\quad \text{META CONSTRAIN}(r^{\mathcal{M}}) \\
\quad \text{return } r^{\mathcal{M}}
\end{array}
$$

(a)   (b)

Fig. 5. *Breadth–first computation of Boolean And (a) and existential quantification (b). The layers of the result are computed through top–down layered visits of the operands*

the purposes of the decomposed representation. We thus interleave the layer computations with cofactoring based simplifications, which allow us iteratively projecting f' and g' on decreasing subsets of the domain space. Cofactoring is done both to keep BDD sizes under control, and to achieve a preliminary reduction. Full bottom-up reduction and final constrain simplification are explicitly called as last steps.

Existential quantification (META EXIST procedure) is shown in Figure 5(b). Computation is again top-down, and based on the following theorem

Theorem 2. *Let $f_{[i,j]}^{\mathcal{M}}$ be a Meta decomposition, then*

$$
\exists S.f_{[i,j]}^{\mathcal{M}} = < \exists S.f_i, \exists S.(\neg f_i.off \wedge f_{[i+1,j]}^{\mathcal{M}}) >^{\mathcal{M}}
$$

Proof Sketch. Let us again concentrate on the layered automaton view of $\exists S.f_{[i,j]}^{\mathcal{M}}$. The existential quantification [5] of the first component ($\exists S.f_i$) captures all ones and zeroes reached at the i-th layer of the non reduced result (other ones/zeroes might be hoisted up when reducing lower levels). The ones and zeroes at lower layers ($> i$) are computed working with $f_{[i+1,n]}^{\mathcal{M}}$ (lower layers of the operand). But spurious ones introduced by cofactor transformations could produce wrong (overestimated) ones, so we need to force 0 within the OFF-set of the i-th component.

The algorithm of Figure 5(b) uses f' to accumulate the filtering function (conjunction of complemented OFF-sets). We do not represent f' as a mono-

---

[5] We compute the existential quantification of an incompletely specified function as $\exists s.f = (\exists S.f.on, \forall S.\neg f.off)$

lithic BDD, since this would again be a violation of our primary goal (decomposition). We thus use "clustered" BDDs (partitioned conjunctions performed under threshold control), and we also interleave layer computations with cofactor simplifications (as in METAAND).

Existential quantification is by far the most important (and expensive) operation in symbolic reachability analysis. Due to its combined usage with conjunction within image/preimage computations, BDD packages provide the so called "relational product" or "and-exist" operator, a recursive procedure specifically concieved to avoid the explicit intermediate BDD generated as a result of conjunction before existential quantification. We did the same with Meta-BDDs, and we implemented a METAANDEXIST procedure (not shown here) which properly integrates the previously shown METAAND and METAEXIST algorithms.

5   Experimental Results

The presented technique has been implemented and tested within a home-made reachability analysis tool, built on top of the Colorado University Decision Diagram (CUDD) package [11]. The experiments shown here are limited to reachability analysis of Finite State Machines, as a first and general framework, unrelated from the verification of specific properties. Our main goal is to prove that the sequential behavior of the circuits presented can be analyzed with relevant improvements by using Meta-BDDs. Combinational verification as well as BDD based SAT checks are other possible applications of Meta-BDDs.

We present data for a few ISCAS'89-addendum [12] benchmarks and some other circuits [13,15]. They have different sizes, within the range of circuits manageable by state-of-the-art reachability analysis techniques. We only report here data for the circuits we could traverse with some gain. The benchmark circuits we tried without any significant result are: s1269, s1423, s1512, s5378. We argue this is mainly due to the fact that no relevant cases of independent or conditionally independent variables are present in the state sets of those circuits. Table 1 collects statistics on the circuit used, and the results obtained. For

Table 1. *Comparing BDDs and Meta-BDDs in reachability analysis. 266 MHz Pentium II, memory limit 400 MB, time limit 36000 s.*

Circuit	FF	D	States	BDDs			Meta-BDDs			$\frac{|R|}{|R^M|}$
				BDD_{pk}	Mem	Time (Sift)	BDD_{pk}	Mem	Time (Sift)	
				[Knodes]	[MB]	[s]	[Knodes]	[MB]	[s]	
s3271	116	16	$1.31 \cdot 10^{31}$	-	-	Time-out	782	214	7973 (1190)	7.7
s3330	132	16	$7.27 \cdot 10^{17}$	-	Mem-out	-	4534	356	22345 (17532)	4.2
FIFOs	142	63	$5.01 \cdot 10^{21}$	1169	45	3691(3232)	183	24	3215 (170)	13
queue	82	45	$3.43 \cdot 10^{11}$	387	27	1873(1750)	132	21	921 (350)	19
Rotator$_{16}$	32	2	$1.00 \cdot 2^{32}$	65	14	25 (23)	12	5	1 (0)	1
Rotator$_{32}$	64	2	$1.00 \cdot 2^{64}$	-	Mem-out	-	390	17	831 (602)	1
Spinner$_{16}$	33	2	$1.00 \cdot 2^{33}$	30	5	7 (4)	7	4	2(1)	1
Spinner$_{32}$	65	2	$1.00 \cdot 2^{65}$	-	Mem-out	-	244	20	417 (331)	1

each circuit it first shows some common statistics: the number of latches (FF), the sequential depth (D), and the number of reached states (States). We then compare traversals based on the same image heuristic (IWLS95 by Ranjan et al. [14]), with standard BDDs and Meta-BDDs. Since conjunctively partitioned transition relations are not critical in terms of BDD size, we use Meta-BDDs only for state sets (and intermediate product of image computations). For both techniques we show peak live BDD nodes (BDD_{pk}), maximum memory usage (Mem) and CPU time (Time) with explicit indication of sifting time. We finally show the ratio BDD vs. Meta-BDD size for reachable state sets ($|R|/|R^M|$).

s3271 and s3330 are known to be hard to traverse circuits, both for time and memory costs. FIFO is a freely modified version of the example used in [5], whereas queue is a queue model from the NuSMV [15] distribution. Rotator [13] has two stages. An input register (subscript 16/32 is register size) is fed by primary inputs. An output register stores a rotated copy of the inputs register. The number of rotated bits is determined by a five bits control input. All states are reachable, but image computation is exponentially complex since the early quantification scheme pays the dependence of the output (input) register bits from all input register (primary input) bits. Spinner [13] is a similar circuit, where the input register can be loaded with the output register, too. These are both cases in which conditional independence can be efficently factored out by Meta-BDDs, in order to achieve relevant gains in intermediate image steps (even though no gains are shown in reachable states).

In all cases Meta-BDDs were able to "compress" reachable state sets and to produce overall improvements. The first two circuits could not be completed with standard BDDs in the adopted experimental setup.

Memory gains are clearly visible from peak BDD nodes, memory usage, and reachable state sets size ratio [6]. The overhead introduced to work with the decomposed form is visible in the reduced ratio sifting time vs. total time (except for the larger example, s3330 where sifting still dominates) and time reductions are mainly due to the smaller BDDs involved in computations.

6   Conclusions and Future Work

We propose a BDD based decomposition for Boolean functions, which extends conjunctive/disjunctive decompositions and may factor out variable indepen-dances and/or conditional independances with gains not achievable by standard BDDs.

Our work includes and extends [5], by proposing a representation closed under negation and applicable to a wider range of BDD based problems, and by exploring non-canonicity in terms of heuristically controlled decomposition and simplification steps. Experimental results on benchmark and home made circuits show relevant gains agaist standard BDDs in symbolic FSM traversals. Future works will investigate heuristics, and application to real verification tasks.

Acknowledgement

The author thanks Fabio Somenzi for the FIFOs, Rotator and Spinner source descriptions.

---

[6] The ratio $|R|/|R^M|$ is 1 in the case of Rotator and Spinner because the reachable state set is the entire state space (a constant function both with BDDs and MEta-BDDs). The BDD gains in those circuits are related to intermediate image BDDs.

References

1. R. E. Bryant. Graph–Based Algorithms for Boolean Function Manipulation. *IEEE Transactions on Computers*, C–35(8):677–691, August 1986.
2. R. E. Bryant. Symbolic Boolean Manipulation with Ordered Binary–Decision Diagrams. *ACM Computing Surveys*, 24(3):293–318, September 1992.
3. R. Rudell. Dynamic Variable Ordering for Ordered Binary Decision Diagrams. In *Proc. IEEE/ACM ICCAD'93*, pages 42–47, San Jose, California, November 1993.
4. J. Jain, J. Bitner, J. A. Abraham, and D. S. Fussel. Functional Partitioning for Verification and Related Problems. In *Brown/MIT VLSI Conference*, pages 210–226, March 1992.
5. K. L. McMillan. A conjunctively decomposed boolean representation for symbolic model checking . *Proc. CAV'96, Lecture Notes in Computer Science 1102, Springer Verlag*, pages 13–25, August 1996.
6. G.J. Holzmann and A. Puri. A minimized automaton representation of reachable states. *Software Tools for Technology Transfer,Springer Verlag*, 3(1), 1999.
7. O. Coudert, C. Berthet, and J. C. Madre. Verification of Sequential Machines Based on Symbolic Execution. In *Lecture Notes in Computer Science 407, Springer Verlag*, pages 365–373, Berlin, Germany, 1989.
8. H. Touati, H. Savoj, B. Lin, R. K. Brayton, and A. Sangiovanni-Vincentelli. Implicit Enumeration of Finite State Machines Using BDDs. In *Proc. IEEE ICCAD'90*, pages 130–133, San Jose, California, November 1990.
9. O. Coudert and J. C. Madre. A Unified Framework for the Formal Verification of Sequential Circuits. In *Proc. IEEE ICCAD'90*, pages 126–129, San Jose, California, November 1990.
10. R.K. Brayton R.K. Ranjan, J.V. Sanghavi and A. Sangiovanni-Vincentelli. High performance bdd package based on exploiting memory hierarchy. *Proc. ACM/IEEE DAC'96*, pages 635–640, June 1996.
11. F. Somenzi. CUDD: CU Decision Diagram Package – Release 2.3.0. Technical report, Dept. of Electrical and Computer Engineering, University of Colorado, Boulder, Colorado, October 1998.
12. MCNC Private Communication.
13. K. Ravi and F. Somenzi. Hints to Accelerate Symbolic Traversal. In *Correct Hardware Design and Verification Methods (CHARME'99)*, pages 250–264, Berlin, September 1999. Springer-Verlag. LNCS 1703.
14. R. K. Ranjan, A. Aziz, R. K. Brayton, B. Plessier, and C. Pixley. Efficient BDD Algorithms for FSM Synthesis and Verification. In *IWLS'95: IEEE International Workshop on Logic Synthesis*, Lake Tahoe, California, May 1995.
15. A. Cimatti, E.M. Clarke, F. Giunchiglia, and M. Roveri. NuSMV: a new Symbolic Model Verifyer. In *Proc. CAV'99, Lecture Notes in Computer Science 1633, Springer Verlag*, pages 495–499, July 1999.

CLEVER: Divide and Conquer Combinational Logic Equivalence VERification with False Negative Elimination

John Moondanos[1], Carl H. Seger[2], Ziyad Hanna[3], and Daher Kaiss[4]

[1] Logic Validation Technologies, Intel Corporation
john.moondanos@intel.com
[2] Strategic CAD Labs, Intel Corporation
carl.seger@intel.com
[3] Logic Validation Technologies, Intel Corporation
ziyad.hanna@intel.com
[4] Logic Validation Technologies, Intel Corporation
daher.kaiss@intel.com

Abstract. Formal equivalence verifiers for combinational circuits rely heavily on BDD algorithms. However, building monolithic BDDs is often not feasible for today's complex circuits. Thus, to increase the effectiveness of BDD-based comparisons, divide-and-conquer strategies based on cut-points are applied. Unfortunately, these algorithms may produce false negatives. Significant effort must then be spent for determining whether the failures are indeed real. In particular, if the design is actually incorrect, many cut-point based algorithms perform very poorly. In this paper we present a new algorithm that completely removes the problem of false negatives by introducing *normalized functions* instead of free variables at cut points. In addition, this approach handles the propagation of input assumptions to cut-points, is significantly more accurate in finding cut-points, and leads to more efficient counter-example generation for incorrect circuits. Although, naively, our algorithm [1] would appear to be more expensive than traditional cut-point techniques, the empirical data on more than 900 complex signals from a recent microprocessor design, shows rather the opposite.

1 Introduction

The design process of complex VLSI systems can be thought of as a series of system-model transformations, leading to the final model that is implemented in silicon. In this paper, we concentrate on formal verification techniques establishing logic functionality equivalence between circuit models at the RTL and schematic levels of abstraction. Traditionally, such techniques operate under the assumption that there is a 1-1 correspondence between the state nodes of the two circuit models, in effect transforming the problem of sequential circuit verification into one of combinational verification. Therefore, they are able to exploit

---

[1] US Patents are pending for this algorithm.

G. Berry, H. Comon, and A. Finkel (Eds.): CAV 2001, LNCS 2102, pp. 131–143, 2001.
© Springer-Verlag Berlin Heidelberg 2001

the power of Reduced Ordered Binary Decision Diagrams [1] (from now on called simply BDDs). Although BDDs are very useful in this domain, they still suffer from exponential memory requirements on many of today's complicated circuits.

To overcome this, many researchers have investigated alternative solutions based on a divide-and-conquer approach. They attempt to partition the specification and implementation circuits along **frontiers** of equivalent signal pairs called **cut-points**. The goal of the overall equivalence verification is now transformed into one of verifying the resulting sub-circuits. This situation is depicted in Fig. 1.

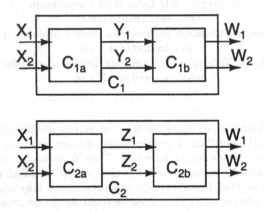

Fig. 1. Circuit Partitioning across Cut-Points.

The two circuits C_1 and C_2 compute their outputs (W_1, W_2) from their inputs (X_1, X_2). If the BDDs for the outputs as functions of the primary inputs grow exponentially in size, one could hope to reduce the complexity of the problem by exploiting the fact that internal nodes Y_1 and Y_2 of C_1 are equivalent to Z_1 and Z_2 of C_2, respectively. If this were the case, one could prove the equivalence of C_1 and C_2, by first establishing the equivalence of C_{1a} and C_{2a} and then the equivalence of C_{1b} and C_{2b}. It would be expected that potentially the sizes of the BDDs that correspond to the sub-circuits C_{1a}, C_{1b}, C_{2a} and C_{2b} are considerably smaller than the intractable sizes of C_1 and C_2, so that the verification of the original circuits could complete. The motivation behind such cut-point based techniques is the desire to exploit the potentially large numbers of similarities between the two circuit models.

Unfortunately, CP-based techniques suffer from some serious limitations. More specifically, when we perform the verification of C_{1b} against C_{2b} in Fig. 1, we consider Y_1, Y_2, Z_1, and Z_2 to be free variables (i.e., they can assume arbitrary boolean values, with $Y_1 = Z_1$ and $Y_2 = Z_2$). This can lead to problems in the verification of C_{1b} and C_{2b}. For example, consider the circuits in Fig. 2.

Let us assume that we could prove the equivalence of Y_1 and Y_2 to Z_1 and Z_2 respectively. Then if we introduced the same free variable A for (Y_1, Z_1) and

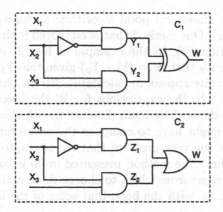

Fig. 2. False negative as a result of the free variables at the cut-points variables (Y_1, Z_1) and (Y_2, Z_2).

B for (Y_2, Z_2), we would compute that C_1 calculates $W = A \oplus B$, while C_2 calculates $W = A + B$. This does not allow us to conclude that the two circuits are equivalent. However, this is actually a false negative. The reason is that, due to the nature of the logic that generates them, Y_1 and Y_2 cannot be both 1 at the same time, i.e., they are **mutually exclusive**. The same is true for Z_1 and Z_2. As a result, the two circuits actually produce the same W functions, because for mutually exclusive input signals, XOR and OR gates produce the same results.

Given this problem, cut-point based verification algorithms usually perform the following operations:

1. Discover as many cut-points as possible, hoping to produce the smallest possible sub-circuits whose functions will be computed and compared with BDDs (**cp-identification**).
2. Choose out of these cut-points the ones that (based on various criteria) simplify the task of sub-circuit verification (**cp-selection**).
3. Perform the actual verification of the resulting sub-circuits (**eq-check**), and
4. Attempt to determine whether the corresponding circuit outputs that appear as inequivalent, are truly different or the algorithm produced false negatives (**fnr, false negative reduction**).

A comprehensive review of the existing cut-point based algorithms appears in [8]. For *cp-identification* traditionally **random simulation**, automatic test pattern generation (**ATPG**) or **BDD-based** techniques are employed. Out of the cut-points so identified, some are rejected in the cp-selection stage, according to various criteria that are outside the scope of this paper. The remaining are used to form the boundaries of the sub-circuits to be verified. Then the resulting sub-circuits are verified independently, most frequently with the use of BDDs. If all these sub-circuits are verified equal, then the original circuits are equal. Nevertheless, as we have showed in Fig. 2, the cut-point based algorithms can indicate that the circuits are different as a result of false negatives.

Thus, the presently known cut-point algorithms perform a final stage of false negative reduction (fnr). One method that is employed is that of re-substitution of the cut-point functions [9]. In the example of Fig. 2, we have for C_1 that $W = (Y_1 \oplus Y_2)$ and for C_2 that $W = (Y_1 + Y_2)$ given that $Y_1 = Z_1$ and $Y_2 = Z_2$. Although, the two circuits appear to calculate different outputs based on cut-points, if we compose into the expressions for W the functions of Y_1 and Y_2, we prove circuit equivalence. The main difficulties with this technique are that in the worst case we might have to compute the entire function of a circuit's output, which may be the very problem that we attempted to avoid by using the cut-points algorithm. The method presented in [8] is based on maintaining multiple cut-point frontiers from which to choose the functions to be composed into the output functions, with the hope that some of the frontiers will lead to the desired results.

Other false negative reduction techniques [4] are based on the idea of maintaining the set of values that the cut-points are allowed to assume. Again for the case of the circuit of Fig. 2, we can see that the cut-point variables (Y_1, Y_2) or (Z_1, Z_2) can belong only to the set $\{(0,0), (0,1), (1,0)\}$ since they are mutually exclusive. Such sets are encoded by BDDs and are used to restrict the comparisons of circuit node functions within the regions of allowed cut-point values. Unfortunately, maintaining and propagating these sets are often very difficult and computationally expensive. One other approach to the problem of false negative reduction is based on Automatic Test Pattern Generation techniques (ATPG) as in [5]. There, for each value combination of the cut-points that causes the circuit outputs to mismatch, they attempt to find (using an ATPG tool) the input pattern that can generate the cut-point value combination in question. The drawback of this algorithm is that one must call the ATPG tool for each cut-point value combination that causes a mismatch, until one determines whether the mismatch is a false negative or a real design problem. This can be time-consuming for a large number of cut-point value combinations.

The fundamental limitation of these approaches is that they fail to identify the cause of the false negatives. In this paper we identify the cause and we design an algorithm that allows us to eliminate false negatives early during the cp-identification stage of the algorithm. As the careful reader will realize this leads to a simpler algorithm, since we do not perform a final false negative reduction stage with potentially very expensive BDD operations.

2 Cut-Point Algorithm in CLEVER

2.1 Avoiding False-Negative Generation

Through the example we presented in the previous section, one can understand that the key reason for false negatives is the fact that not all value combinations can appear at the nodes of a cut-point frontier. In this section we restate the following observation from [6] which forms the basis for the development of our false negative elimination approach.

Proposition 1. *In a minimized circuit without re-convergent fanout, verification algorithms based on cut-point frontiers cannot produce false negative results.*

Proof. (*Sketch only*) *Intuitively, if there are no re-convergent fanouts then each cut-point can be completely controlled by its fanin cone. Additionally if the circuit is minimized it cannot have constant nodes. As a consequence all possible value combinations can appear at the signals of any cut-frontier, and therefore false negatives cannot happen.* □

Proposition 1 identifies the reason for the false negative result. Clearly, the reconvergent fanout of node X_2 makes Y_1 and Y_2 to be correlated. As a result not all possible value combinations can appear on Y_1 and Y_2, as implied by the introduction of free variables by some cut-point based techniques. A more sophisticated algorithm should not assign free variables on Y_1 and Y_2, since this will not allow the W signals in the two circuits to be identified as equal. Here we present an alternative approach, where instead of assigning a free variable to a cut-point, we assign a function that captures the correlation between cut-points. To make the BDD representation of this function as small as possible, we attempt to exclude from it the effect of the non-reconverging signals in the support of the cut-point, based on Proposition 1.

Let V be a cut-point that will be used to calculate additional cut-point frontiers. The logic gates from the previous cut-point frontier that generate V, implement a logic function $g(r, n)$. The variables r and n correspond to cut-points from the previous frontier. However, here, we have partitioned all these variables into two groups. The r variables correspond to cut-points with reconvergent fanout that leads outside of the cone of the signal V. On the other hand, the n variables correspond to cut-points that do not have fanout re-converging outside the cone of V. The goal here is to capture the effect of the re-converging signals on V, so that the r variables and the free variable we introduce for V do not assume incompatible values. We hope that by doing this, we can avoid introducing false negatives in the process of calculating the cut-points belonging to the next frontier.

Now, to capture the relationship between the r variables and signal V, we examine the situations where they force V to assume a specific value, either 1 or 0. The r signal values that can force V to be 1 are the ones for which, for every value combination of the n variables , V becomes 1. These values of r are captured by universally quantifying out the n variables from $g(r, n)$ as in the following function F_g :

$$F_g = F_g(r) = \forall n.g(r, n)$$

Subsequently, we call this function the **forced term** to be intuitively reminded of its meaning in the context of cut-points algorithms (although other naming conventions exist in the literature). Now, let us examine when the V signal equals 0. This happens for all those r values that make $g(r, n) = 0$ regardless of the values of the n signals. So V should be 0 whenever the following function P_g is 0:

$$P_g = P_g(r) = \exists n.g(r, n)$$

This function is the result of existentially quantifying out the n variables from $g(r, n)$ and will subsequently be called the **possible term**. Thus, if for a given value combination of the r variables, all the possible combinations of the n variables make $g(r, n) = 0$, then the free variable assigned to V in CP-based algorithms must obtain only the 0 value. Otherwise, we will have to cope with the potential appearance of false negatives. On the other hand, if some of the combinations of the n variables make $g(r, n) = 0$ and some others make it $g(r, n) = 1$ for a specific r variable value combination, then V can assume either 0 or 1 independently from the r variables.

From this discussion it becomes apparent that a more appropriate assignment to the V signal for the calculation of the cut-points in the next frontier and the avoidance of false negatives is:

$$vP_g + F_g = v.(\exists n.g(r, n)) + (\forall n.g(r, n)) \tag{1}$$

We call expression (1) the **normalized function** for the signal V, as opposed to the free variable that is assigned to it in other implementations of cut-point based algorithms. We also call the variable v that we introduce for the signal V the **eigenvariable** of V. To illustrate the use of *normalized functions* we consider the circuit of Fig. 2. X_2 has reconvergent fanout that affects both Y_1 and Y_2. The possible term for Y_1 is X_2', while the forced term is 0. Therefore, the normalized function for Y_1 is $v_1.X_2' + 0 = v_1.X_2'$. Similarly, for Y_2 the possible term is X_2, while the forced term is 0. So, Y_2 gets a normalized function of: $v_2.X_2 + 0 = v_2.X_2$. Now, signals Z_1 and Z_2 of C_2 get the same normalized functions as Y_1 and Y_2 respectively, since they implement the same functions in C_2 as their counterparts in C_1. So, the function for W in C_1 becomes $v_1.X_2' \oplus v_2.X_2$, while in C_2 we have that W implements $v_1.X_2' + v_2.X_2$. These two expressions are clearly equal since the two terms comprising them cannot be 1 at the same time. One can prove that the use of normalized functions solves the problem of false negatives in the general case as well. This is based on the fact that the range of a vector of Boolean functions is identical to the range of the corresponding vector of normalized functions. A rigorous proof of this claim appears in Appendix A.

2.2 Cut-Point Algorithm Implementation

For the comparison of the functions implemented by nodes n_s and n_i of the specification (spec) and the implementation (imp) models, we set the cut-point frontier to be initially the primary inputs of the cones that are driving the two signals. Then repeatedly we attempt to identify more cut-points lying ahead of the current cut-point frontier closer to n_s and n_i with the hope that eventually we will build the BDDs for these two nodes, so that we can compare them for equivalence. These BDDs are built not by assigning free variables for the cut-points on the present frontier but by assigning to every cut-point its corresponding normalized function.

As we see, our CLEVER cut-point based algorithm departs from the classical approach by **combining** the *cp-identification* and *false negative* reduction phases. The main benefit with respect to pre-existing algorithms is that

CLEVER correctly identifies the root cause of false negatives and tries to avoid creating them, so that it does not perform expensive operations to correct them. Furthermore, employing normalized functions allows us to correctly identify all internal signals of equal functionality that exist within the cones of the signals being compared. False negative elimination is usually not done for internal cut-points, and previous algorithms fail to identify every pair of sub-circuits with identical functionality. Thus, the algorithm presented here has the opportunity to work on smaller verification sub-problems, since it identifies all possible cut-points. In addition we do not have to perform any circuit transformations to increase the similarity of the circuit graphs.

One additional area where the presented approach with the use of normalized functions is fundamentally different from previous techniques is the generation of counter examples and the debugging of faulty circuits. In methods like the ones in [4], [5], [8], [9], when the outputs are not proven equal based on the last frontier, one does not know whether this is due to a false negative or a real circuit bug. Here, we do not have to perform a false negative elimination step, since we know that the difference of the outputs must always be due to the presence of a bug. In contrast to other algorithms that require the resubstitution of the cut-point variables by their driving functions, when we employ normalized functions there exists an efficient and simple algorithm that does not require large amounts of memory.

The validity of this algorithm is based again on the theory of Appendix A, where we show that the range of a function is identical to the range of its normalized version. Intuitively, the counter-example that we can produce for the outputs based on the signals of the last frontier will be in terms of values of eigenvariables and reconverging primary inputs. The goal is to use these values of eigenvariables and reconverging inputs to compute the corresponding values of the non-reconverging primary inputs. These must be computed to be compatible with the internal signal values implied by the cut-point assignment that was selected to expose the difference of the outputs.

Finally, one additional area where our cut-point based techniques can be contrasted with pre-existing approaches is the area of **input assumption** handling. This topic is not usually treated in publications of cut-point based algorithms. However, in our experience logic models of modern designs contain many assumptions on input signal behavior, without which the task of formal equivalence verification is impossible. In the case of our cut-point based algorithms we employ *parametric representations* to encode input assumptions as described in [10]. Normalized functions are ideally suited to capture the effect of boolean constraints on the inputs. This is the case because the validity of our algorithm still holds if it is invoked on *parametric variables* encoding the inputs of a circuit rather than the actual inputs themselves. One could even argue that the normalized functions are a parametric representation of the function driving a cut-point in terms of its eigenvariable and its reconverging input signals.

3 Results

The algorithms that are presented in this paper were developed to enable the equivalence verification of a set of difficult to verify signals from a next-generation microprocessor design. The results of the application of CLEVER on these complex circuit cones appear in Table 1. Note that this table lists results for the RTL to schematic netlist comparison. In Table 1 the numbers of the problematic signals for each circuit appear in the **Prb** column. The term problematic here refers to signals whose comparison was not possible by means of monolithic BDDs even though all possible ordering heuristics were exhausted (static and dynamic ordering). The column **IPs** lists the average number of inputs per signal cone. The next six columns of the table are partitioned into two sections, one for the SPEC model (the RTL) and one for the IMP (the transistor netlist). The **Comp** column refers to the average size in composite gates of the cones of the problematic signals. The **CP%** column lists the percentage of nodes in a model that are found by the classic cut-point algorithm to have nodes of identical functionality in the other model. Similarly, the **NCP%** column lists the percentage of nodes in a model that are found by the cut-point algorithm with normalized functions to have corresponding nodes of identical functionality in the other model. Finally, the **CP** and **NCP** columns list how many signal comparisons were completed by the classic cut-point algorithm with resubstitution and the cut-point algorithm with normalized functions, respectively.

Table 1. Statistics about the logic cones driving various problematic signals.

Ckt	Prb	IPs	SPEC (RTL)			IMP (Netlist)			CP	NCP
			Comp	CP%	NCP%	Comp	CP%	NCP%		
C_1	388	343	579	60%	74%	378	27%	61%	272	388
C_2	400	226	365	57%	66%	221	26%	56%	352	400
C_3	8	212	980	25%	69%	570	24%	39%	0	8
C_4	96	130	1040	72%	84%	410	48%	51%	76	96
C_5	15	260	810	20%	60%	650	25%	45%	0	15

One important detail becomes immediately evident from Table 1. The use of normalized functions in our cut-points techniques helps us identify a higher number of cut-points than the classic algorithm. This is the case because our cut-point based techniques do not produce false negatives. Clearly we identify more cut-points in the RTL model, but the difference becomes much more dramatic in the case of the logic model for the transistor netlist. This is to be expected because the logic model for the transistor netlist is more compact, since it is coming from the minimized model for the circuit implementation and as a result has many nodes with reconverging fanout. These nodes cause the classic cut-point algorithm to produce many false-negatives and fail to correctly identify many cut-points. As a result, the cut-point algorithm with normalized functions manages to complete the verification of approximately 200 more signals out of 900. In addition the C_4 netlist contained 14 output signals which initially were not equivalent with their specification models. These signals were debugged using Algorithm 2, since the classic algorithm with BDD resubstitution could not handle them.

The plot in Fig. 3 indicates the time requirements (in cpu sec) for the signal comparisons on HP Unix workstations with 512MB of RAM. The horizontal axis corresponds to the time it takes the classic cut-point algorithm (CP) for the comparisons of the signals in Table 1. The vertical axis corresponds to the time it takes the cut-points algorithm with normalized functions (NCP) for the same comparisons. The 200 signal comparisons for which the CP algorithm timed out are arbitrarily placed at the bottom right of the plot only to indicate the time it took the NCP algorithm to finish them. The diagonal line partitions the plot into two areas indicating which algorithm performed better.

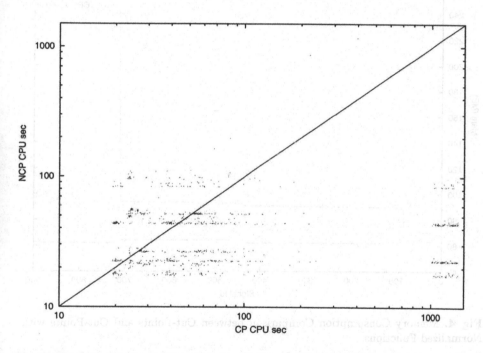

Fig. 3. Time Comparison of Cut-Points with Resubstitution and Cut-Points with Normalized Functions.

Figure 4 shows the memory requirements (in MB) for the signal comparisons from Table 1. The dashed lines correspond to the classic cut-points algorithm and the dots to the one with normalized functions. Signals are sorted according to increasing verification time and we can identify the point where memory requirements become exponential for the classic cut-points algorithm. The key observation here is that cut-point techniques with normalized functions require constant amounts of memory for a larger number of signals. This happens because normalized functions detect every possible cut-point, thus resulting in smaller verification problems and more controlled memory requirements. The second observation is that the classic cut-point algorithm with BDD resubstitution requires more memory. This is happening for two reasons. First, it may not produce a cut-point frontier close to the output because of failing to identify cut-points due to false negatives. So it would create bigger BDDs for the circuit output. The second reason is that if the outputs could not be proven equal, the classic cut-point algorithm needs to perform BDD resubstitution. This is necessary to determine whether the signal in-equivalence is real or a false negative. As a result the memory requirements for the BDDs that get created are increased.

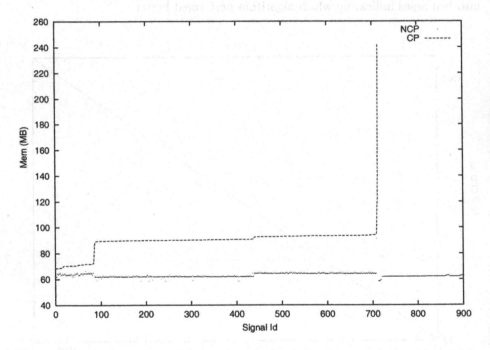

Fig. 4. Memory Consumption Comparison between Cut-Points and Cut-Points with Normalized Functions.

4   Summary

CLEVER is a tool for the formal equivalence verification of next generation microprocessor designs and employs a number of different engines for the verification of combinational circuits. Among them, one is based on BDD technology using the state of the art algorithms for monolithic BDDs. As it is well known monolithic BDDs suffer from certain limitations. For this reason CLEVER employs circuit divide and conquer techniques based on BDDs. In this paper, we have presented the main idea behind the divide and conquer algorithm in CLEVER. This algorithm is based on the concept of function normalization to provide an efficient means for avoiding the "false negatives problem" that appears in other combinational verification techniques based on circuit partitioning. In addition function normalization readily lends itself to simple counter-example generation and comprehensive handling of input assumptions. As a result, we are able to apply divide and conquer techniques for the comparison of complicated combinational signals, even in cases where the degree of similarity between the circuit models is limited between 20% to 30%.

References

1. R.E. Bryant: *Graph-based algorithms for boolean function manipulation*, IEEE Transactions on CAD, 1986
2. M. Fujita, H. Fujisawa, and N. Kawato: *Evaluation and Improvements of Boolean Comparison Method Based on Binary Decision Diagrams*, ICCAD 1988
3. R. Rudell: *Dynamic variable ordering for ordered binary decision diagrams*, ICCAD 1993, pp. 2-5
4. Y. Matsunaga: *An efficient equivalence checker for combinatorial circuits*, DAC 1996, pp. 629-634
5. S.M. Reddy, W. Kunz, and D.K. Pradhan: *Novel verification framework combining structural and OBDD methods in a synthesis environment*, DAC 1995, pp. 414-419
6. M. Abramovici , M.A. Breuer, and A.D. Friedman: *Digital Systems Testing and Testable Design*, Computer Science Press, 1990
7. T. Nakaoka, S. Wakabayashi, T. Koide, and N. Yoshida: *A Verification Algorithm for Logic Circuits with Internal Variables*, ISCAS 1995, pp. 1920-1923
8. A. Kuhlmann and F. Krohm: *Equivalence Checking using Cuts and Heaps*, DAC 1997
9. Pixley, et al. *Method for determining functional equivalence between design models* United States Patent 5754454, May 19, 1998
10. M.D. Aagaard, R.B. Jones, C.H. Seger: *Formal Verification Using Parametric Representations of Boolean Constraints*, DAC 1999, pp. 402-407.

Appendix A: Proofs

Let $B = \{0,1\}$ and R be a subset of B^k. Now R contains vectors of the form $s =< s_1, s_2, \ldots, s_k >$. Traditionally, such a set is represented by its characteristic function $\Re(s) = \Re(s_1, s_2, \ldots, s_k)$ which becomes 1 iff $s \in R$. If we consider the variables s_i to model signal values of a logic circuit model, we can view any set $\Re(s) = \Re(s_1, s_2, \ldots, s_k)$ as a signal relation. If there is actually no relation between the signals, then $\Re(s) \equiv 1$. Also, let $G(s) =< g_1(s), g_2(s), \ldots, g_k(s) >$ be a Vector Boolean Function, where $s =< s_1, s_2, \ldots, s_m >$ are the function inputs. Each $g_i(s)$ can be written as $g_i(r_i, n_i)$, where:

- r_i are the variables on which some other $g_j, j \neq i$ depends. These will be called the re-converging variables.
- n_i are the variables on which no other $g_j, j \neq i$ depends. These will be called the non-reconverging variables.

Now let us re-introduce the concepts of Forced and Possible Terms of Boolean Vector Functions. Let $\{x\}$ stand for all possible value combinations of $x = <x_1, x_2, \ldots, x_m>$ in $B^m = \{0, 1\}^m$. There are 2^m such combinations.

For $g_i(r_i, n_i)$ we define its Possible Term P_{g_i} as:

$$P_{g_i} = P_{g_i}(r_i) = \exists n_i.g_i(r_i, n_i) \tag{2}$$

and its Forced Term F_{g_i} as:

$$F_{g_i} = F_{g_i}(r_i) = \forall n_i.g_i(r_i, n_i) \tag{3}$$

The following lemmas follow directly from the properties of existential and universal quantification.

Lemma 1.

$$P_{g_i}(r_i) = 0 \Rightarrow F_{g_i}(r_i) = 0$$

Lemma 2.

$$F_{g_i}(r_i) = 1 \Rightarrow P_{g_i}(r_i) = 1$$

Also, let $\partial G = < \partial g_1, \partial g_2, \ldots, \partial g_k >$ stand for the Normalized Function of G, where G is a boolean vector function. More specifically, let us define ∂G as

$$< \partial g_1(r_i, n_i), \partial g_2(r_i, n_i), \ldots, \partial g_k(r_i, n_i) >$$

where

$$\partial g_i(r_i, n_i) = v_i.P_{g_i}(r_i) + F_{g_i}(r_i)$$

The variable v_i is a free Boolean variable, and is called the eigenvariable of g_i.

Also, let $[G]$ stand for the Range of the vector Boolean Function $G(s) = < g_1(s), g_2(s), \ldots, g_k(s) >$. Then $[G]$ is defined as:

$$[G] = \{b \in B^k | \exists s : b = < g_1(s), g_2(s), \ldots, g_k(s) > \}$$

where $s = < s_1, s_2, \ldots, s_m > \in B^m$, and $b = < b_1, b_2, \ldots, b_k > \in B^k$.

The main result of our algorithm is captured in the following theorem.

Theorem 1. *The Range of a function $G(s)$ is identical to the range of its normalized function $\partial G(s)$,*

$$[G(s)] \equiv [\partial G(s)]$$

We repeat that ∂g_i is a function of the eigenvariable v_i of g_i and its reconverging variables r_i, i.e. $\partial g_i = \partial g_i(v_i, r_i)$.

Similarly, we can say $\partial G = \partial G(v, r)$ where $v = < v_1, v_2, \ldots, v_k >$ the eigenvariables of $g_1, g_2, \ldots, g_k$, and

$r = < r_1, r_2, \ldots, r_k >$ are the reconverging variables of $g_1, g_2, \ldots, g_k$, respectively.

Keep in mind G has k functions of at most m variables each.

We will attempt now to prove Theorem 1.

Proof: Initially we will prove that $[G] \subseteq [\partial G]$.

Let $b = < b_1, b_2, \ldots, b_k > \in [G]$, where $b_i \in \{0, 1\}$.

$\Rightarrow \exists s' = (s'_1, s'_2, \ldots, s'_m) : b_i = g_i(s'_1, s'_2, \ldots, s'_m), i = 1, \ldots, k$

$\Rightarrow \exists r'_i, n'_i$ derived from $s' : b_i = g_i(r'_i, n'_i), i = 1, \ldots, k$.

Now, if $b_i = 1 \Rightarrow g_i(r'_i, n'_i) = 1 \Rightarrow P_{g_i}(r'_i) = 1$ according to formula 2. If we select the eigenvariable value $v'_i = 1$ we get that $\partial g_i(v'_i, r'_i) = v'_i.P_{g_i}(r'_i) + F_{g_i}(r'_i) = 1.1 + F_{g_i}(r'_i) = 1 = b_i$

On the other hand, if $b_i = 0 \Rightarrow g_i(r'_i, n'_i) = 0 \Rightarrow F_{g_i}(r'_i) = 0$ according to formula 3. If we select the eigenvariable value $v'_i = 0$ we get that $\partial g_i(v'_i, r'_i) = v'_i.P_{g_i}(r'_i) + F_{g_i}(r'_i) = 0.P_{g_i}(r'_i) + 0 = 0 = b_i$

So, for the bit pattern $b = < b_1, b_2, \ldots, b_k > \in [G]$, we have created a pattern $< \partial g_i(v'_1, r'_1) >, \ldots, \partial g_i(v'_k, r'_k) > \in [\partial G]$, which is identical to b. So, $b \in [\partial G]$ and $[G] \subseteq [\partial G]$.

To complete the proof of Theorem 1, we also need to prove: $[\partial G] \subseteq [G]$

To prove this, let $b = < b_1, b_2, \ldots, b_k > \in [\partial G]$.

$\Rightarrow \exists(v', r') : b = \partial G(v', r')$

$\Rightarrow \exists v'_i, r'_i : b_i = \partial g_i(v'_i, r'_i) = v'_i.P_{g_i}(r'_i) + F_{g_i}(r'_i), i = 1, \ldots, k$.

Now, in case $b_i = 0$. Then $b_i = \partial g_i(v'_i, r'_i) = 0 \Rightarrow F_{g_i}(r'_i) = 0$

$\Rightarrow \forall n_i.g_i(r'_i, n_i) = 0 \Rightarrow \exists n'_i : g_i(r'_i, n'_i) = 0$

$\Rightarrow \exists n'_i : g_i(r'_i, n'_i) = 0 = b_i$

On the other hand, if $b_i = 1 \Rightarrow P_{g_i}(r'_i) = 1$. Otherwise, if $P_{g_i}(r_i) = 0 \Rightarrow F_{g_i}(r_i) = 0$ according to the lemmas presented previously. This would make $v_i.P_{g_i} + F_{g_i} \equiv 0$ while we assumed it's a 1.

But, if $P_{g_i}(r'_i) = 1 \Rightarrow \exists n_i.g_i(r'_i, n'_i) = 1 \Rightarrow \exists n'_i : g_i(r'_i, n'_i) = 1 = b_i$.

So, for $b = < b_1, b_2, \ldots, b_k > \in [\partial G]$, we can construct another bit pattern $< g_i(r'_1, n'_1), \ldots, g_i(r'_k, n'_k) > \equiv < b_1, b_2, \ldots, b_k >$, which $\in [G]$. Therefore, $[\partial G] \subseteq [G]$, which completes our proof. $\square$

To establish the false-negative elimination claim, consider now the function G that is computed by forming the exclusive-OR of every pair of outputs from the two circuits to be compared. Since the range of ∂G is equal to the range of G, our claim follows trivially.

Finite Instantiations in Equivalence Logic with Uninterpreted Functions

Yoav Rodeh and Ofer Shtrichman

Weizmann Institute of Science, Rehovot, Israel
IBM Haifa Research Laboratory
{yrodeh,ofers}@wisdom.weizmann.ac.il

Abstract. We introduce a decision procedure for satisfiability of equivalence logic formulas with uninterpreted functions and predicates. In a previous work ([PRSS99]) we presented a decision procedure for this problem which started by reducing the formula into a formula in equality logic. As a second step, the formula structure was analyzed in order to derive a small range of values for each variable that is sufficient for preserving the formula's satisfiability. Then, a standard BDD based tool was used in order to check the formula under the new small domain. In this paper we change the reduction method and perform a more careful analysis of the formula, which results in significantly smaller domains. Both theoretical and experimental results show that the new method is superior to the previous one and to the method suggested in [BGV99].

1 Introduction

Deciding equivalence between formulas with uninterpreted functions is of major importance due to the broad use of uninterpreted functions in abstraction. Such abstraction can be used, for example, when checking a control property of a microprocessor, and it is sufficient to specify that the operations which the ALU performs are functions, rather than specifying what these operations are. Thus, by representing the ALU as an uninterpreted function, the verification process avoids the complexity of the ALU. This is the approach taken, for example, in [BD94], where a formula with uninterpreted functions is generated, such that its validity implies the equivalence between the CPU checked and another version of it, without a pipeline. Another example is given in [PSS98], where formulas with uninterpreted functions are used for *translation validation*, a process in which the correct translation of a compiler is verified by proving the equivalence between the source and target codes after each run.

In the past few years several different BDD-based procedures for checking satisfiability of such formulas have been suggested (in contrast to earlier decision procedures that are based on computing congruence closure [BDL96] in combination with case splitting). Typically the first step of these procedures is the reduction of the original formula φ to an equality formula (a propositional formula plus the equality sign) ψ such that ψ is satisfiable iff φ is. As a second step, different procedures can be used for checking ψ.

G. Berry, H. Comon, and A. Finkel (Eds.): CAV 2001, LNCS 2102, pp. 144–154, 2001.
© Springer-Verlag Berlin Heidelberg 2001

Goel et al. suggest in [GSZAS98] to replace all comparisons in ψ with new Boolean variables, and thus create a new Boolean formula ψ'. The BDD of ψ' is calculated ignoring the transitivity constraints of comparisons. They then traverse the BDD, searching for a satisfying assignment that will also satisfy these constraints. Bryant et al. at [BV00] suggested to avoid this potentially exponential traversing algorithm by explicitly computing a small set of constraints that are sufficient for preserving the transitivity constraints of equality. By checking ψ' conjoined with these constraints using a regular BDD package they were able to verify larger designs.

In [PRSS99] we suggested a method in which the Ackermann reduction scheme [Ack54] is used to derive ψ, and then ψ's satisfiability is decided by assigning a small domain for each variable, such that ψ is satisfiable if and only if it is satisfiable under this small domain. To find this domain, the equalities in the formula are represented as a graph, where the nodes are the variables and the edges are the equalities and disequalities (*disequality* standing for $\neq$) in ψ. Given this graph, a heuristic called *range allocation* is used in order to compute a small set of values for each variable. To complete the process, a standard BDD based tool is used to check satisfiability of the formula under the computed domain.

While both [PRSS99] and [GSZAS98] methods can be applied to any equality formula, Bryant et al. suggest in [BGV99] to examine the structure of the original formula φ. They prove that if the original formula φ uses comparisons between variables and functions only in a certain syntactically restricted way (denoted *positive equality*), the domain of the reduced formula can be restricted to a unique single constant for each variable. This result can also be applied for only subsets of variables (and functions) in the formula that satisfy this condition. However, this result cannot be obtained using Ackermann's reduction. Rather they use the reduction proposed in [BV98].

The method which we propose in this paper roughly uses the framework we suggested in [PRSS99]. We will use the reduction scheme suggested in [BV98] (rather than Ackermann's scheme) in order to generalize their result in the case of positive equality formulas. We also show how this shift, together with a more careful analysis of the formula structure, allows for a construction of a different graph, which results in a provably smaller domain. The smaller implied state space is crucial, as our experiments have shown, for reducing the verification time of these formulas.

2   Preliminaries and Definitions

We define the logic of equality with uninterpreted functions formally. The syntax of this logic is defined as follows:

$$
\begin{aligned}
\langle Formula \rangle \longleftarrow\ &\langle Boolean\text{-}Variable \rangle\ | \\
&\langle Predicate\text{-}Symbol \rangle(\langle Term \rangle, \ldots, \langle Term \rangle)\ | \\
&\langle Term \rangle = \langle Term \rangle\ |\ \neg\langle Formula \rangle\ |\ \langle Formula \rangle \vee \langle Formula \rangle \\
\langle Term \rangle \longleftarrow\ &\langle Term\text{-}Variable \rangle\ | \\
&\langle Function\text{-}Symbol \rangle(\langle Term \rangle, \ldots, \langle Term \rangle)\ | \\
&\mathbf{ITE}(\langle Formula \rangle, \langle Term \rangle, \langle Term \rangle)
\end{aligned}
$$

We refer to formulas in this logic as UF-formulas. We say that a UF-formula φ is satisfiable iff there is some interpretation M of the variables, functions and predicates of φ, such that $M \models \varphi$.

An equivalence logic formula (denoted E-formula) is a UF-formula that does not contain any function and predicate symbols. Throughout the paper we use φ and ψ to denote UF-formulas and E-formulas, respectively.

We allow our formulas to contain *let* constructs of the form *let* $X = \psi$ in $\varphi(X)$, which allows *term sharing* or the representation of circuits.

For simplicity of presentation, we will treat UF-formulas with no Boolean variables and predicates. Also, we will assume there are no **ITE** terms, and every uninterpreted function has just one argument. All these extensions, including the full proofs and examples, are handled in the full version of the paper [PRS01].

3 Deciding Satisfiability of E-Formulas

We wish to check the satisfiability of an E-formula ψ with variables V. In theory this implies that we need to check whether there exist some instantiation of V that satisfies ψ. Since ψ only queries equalities on the variables in V, it enjoys the *small model property*, which means that it is satisfiable iff it is satisfiable over a finite domain. It is not hard to see that the finite domain implied by letting each variable in V the range over $\{1 \ldots |V|\}$ is sufficient. However, this approach is not very practical, since it leads to a state space of $|V|^{|V|}$.

In [PRSS99] we suggested a more refined analysis, where rather than considering only $|V|$, we examine the actual structure of ψ, i.e. the equalities and disequalities in ψ. This analysis enables the derivation of a state space which is empirically much smaller than $|V|^{|V|}$. In this section we repeat the essential definitions from this work, except for several changes which are necessary for the new techniques that will be presented in later sections.

Definition 1. (E-Graphs): *An E-graph G is a triplet $G = \langle V, EQ, DQ \rangle$, where V is the set of vertices, and EQ (Equality edges) and DQ (Disequality edges) are sets of unordered pairs of vertices.*

Given an E-graph $G = \langle V, EQ, DQ \rangle$, we let $V(G) = V$, $DQ(G) = DQ$ and $EQ(G) = EQ$. We use $\leq$ to denote the sub-graph relation: $H \leq G$ iff $V(H) = V(G)$, $EQ(H) \subseteq EQ(G)$ and $DQ(H) \subseteq DQ(G)$. We will use E-graphs to represent partial information derived from the structure of a given E-formula; they can be viewed as a conservative abstraction of E-formulas.

We say that an assignment α (assigning values to the variables in V) satisfies edge (a, b) if (a, b) is an equality edge and $\alpha(a) = \alpha(b)$, or if (a, b) is a disequality edge and $\alpha(a) \neq \alpha(b)$. We write $\alpha \models G$ if α satisfies all edges of G. G is said to be satisfiable if there exists some α such that $\alpha \models G$.

Construction of E-Graph $G(\psi)$: For an E-formula ψ we construct the E-graph $G(\psi)$ (this is a construction suggested in [PRSS99]) by placing a node in $G(\psi)$ for each variable of ψ, and a (dis)equality edge for each (dis)equality term of ψ — by "equality" term we mean that the equality term appears under an even number of negations, and by "disequality", under an odd number.

Example 1. The E-formula $\psi_1 = (a = b) \wedge (\neg(c = b) \vee (a = c))$, results in the E-graph:

$$\mathcal{G}(\psi_1) = \langle\{a, b, c\}, \{(a, b), (a, c)\}, \{(c, b)\}\rangle$$

Notice that every proper subgraph of $\mathcal{G}(\psi_1)$ is satisfiable.

The important property of $\mathcal{G}(\psi)$ is that any two assignments α_1 and α_2 that satisfy exactly the same edges of $\mathcal{G}(\psi)$, will give the same result for ψ; i.e., $\alpha_1 \models \psi$ iff $\alpha_2 \models \psi$. This means that if ψ is satisfiable, then there is some satisfiable $\mathcal{H} \leq \mathcal{G}(\psi)$ such that every assignment that satisfies all edges of $\mathcal{H}$ will satisfy ψ (this $\mathcal{H}$ consists of all the edges of $\mathcal{G}(\psi)$ that are satisfied by ψ's satisfying assignment). We wish to generalize this property of $\mathcal{G}(\psi)$.

Definition 2. (Adequacy of E-Graphs to E-Formulas): *An E-graph $\mathcal{G}$ is adequate for E-formula ψ, if either ψ is not satisfiable, or there exists a satisfiable $\mathcal{H} \leq \mathcal{G}$ such that for every assignment α such that $\alpha \models \mathcal{H}$, $\alpha \models \psi$.*

For example, $\mathcal{G}(\psi)$ is adequate for ψ. We use the fact that an E-graph is adequate for ψ for finding a small set of assignments that will be sufficient for checking ψ:

Definition 3. (Adequacy of Assignment Sets to E-Graphs): *Given an E-graph $\mathcal{G}$, and R, a set of assignments to $V(\mathcal{G})$, we say that R is adequate for $\mathcal{G}$ if for every satisfiable $\mathcal{H} \leq \mathcal{G}$, there is an assignment $\alpha \in R$ such that $\alpha \models \mathcal{H}$.*

Proposition 1. *If E-graph $\mathcal{G}$ is adequate for ψ, and assignment set R is adequate for $\mathcal{G}$, then ψ is satisfiable iff there is $\alpha \in R$ such that $\alpha \models \psi$.*

Example 2. For our E-formula ψ_1 of Example 1, the following set is adequate for $\mathcal{G}(\psi_1)$:

$$R = \{(a \leftarrow 0, b \leftarrow 0, c \leftarrow 0), (a \leftarrow 0, b \leftarrow 0, c \leftarrow 1), (a \leftarrow 0, b \leftarrow 1, c \leftarrow 0)\}$$

Indeed, the assignment $(a \leftarrow 0, b \leftarrow 0, c \leftarrow 0) \in R$, satisfies ψ_1.

The range allocation procedure of [PRSS99] calculates an adequate assignment set R for a given input E-graph $\mathcal{G}$. In that procedure, the resulting R has an extra property: every $\alpha \in R$ is *diverse* w.r.t. $\mathcal{G}$. By this we mean that for every $u, v \in V(\mathcal{G})$, if u and v are not connected via equality edges in $\mathcal{G}$, then $\alpha(u) \neq \alpha(v)$. In [PRS01] we show how to alter any range allocator so that its output assignment set will be diverse w.r.t. the input E-graph (while retaining adequacy), without increasing the assignment set size. In light of this, we alter Definition 2 and Definition 3, by considering only assignments that are diverse w.r.t. to $\mathcal{G}$ (replace "assignment" by "assignment that is diverse w.r.t. $\mathcal{G}$" in both these definitions). This leaves Proposition 1 true, does not cause an increase in the size of the possible adequate assignment sets (as we just commented), and makes it easier for us to find an adequate E-graph for a given E-formula.

We will now rephrase the decision procedure for the satisfiability of UF-formulas as suggested in [PRSS99] according to the above definitions:

1. Reduce UF-formula φ to E-formula ψ using Ackermann's reduction.
2. Calculate the E-graph $\mathcal{G}(\psi)$.
3. Calculate an adequate set of assignments R for $\mathcal{G}(\psi)$.
4. Check if any of the assignments in R satisfies ψ. (This step is done symbolically, not by exhaustive search of R).

In this paper we alter Steps 1 and 2 of this procedure by replacing the reduction scheme, and by calculating a different adequate E-graph for ψ. We will later show that these changes guarantee smaller state spaces and thus a more efficient procedure.

4   Bryant et al. Reduction Method

We will denote this type of reduction of a UF-formula φ to an E-formula ψ by $T^{BV}(\varphi)$. The main property of $T^{BV}(\varphi)$ is that it is satisfiable iff φ is satisfiable. The formula $T^{BV}(\varphi)$ is given by replacing for all i, the function application F_i in φ by a new term $F_i^\star$. We explain the reduction using an example (see [PRS01] or [BV98] for details):

Example 3. Consider the following formula:

$$\varphi_1 := [F(F(F(y))) \neq F(F(y))] \wedge [F(F(y)) \neq F(x)] \wedge [x = F(y)]$$

We number the function applications such that applications with syntactically equivalent arguments are given the same index number:

$$\varphi_1 := [F_4(F_3(F_1(y))) \neq F_3(F_1(y))] \wedge [F_3(F_1(y)) \neq F_2(x)] \wedge [x = F_1(y)]$$

$T^{BV}(\varphi_1)$ is given by:

$$T^{BV}(\varphi_1) := (F_4^\star \neq F_3^\star) \wedge (F_3^\star \neq F_2^\star) \wedge (x = F_1^\star)$$

$$F_1^\star := f_1 \qquad\qquad F_2^\star := \begin{cases} f_1 & x = y; \\ f_2 & \text{Otherwise}; \end{cases}$$

$$F_4^\star := \begin{cases} f_1 & F_3^\star = y; \\ f_2 & F_3^\star = x; \\ f_3 & F_3^\star = F_1^\star; \\ f_4 & \text{Otherwise}; \end{cases} \qquad F_3^\star := \begin{cases} f_1 & F_1^\star = y; \\ f_2 & F_1^\star = x; \\ f_3 & \text{Otherwise}; \end{cases}$$

The general idea is that for every function application F_j of φ we define a new variable f_j which is the "basic" value of F_j. This means that $F_j^\star = f_j$ if no smaller (index wise) function application "overrides" f_j. This can happen, when there is some $i < j$ such that the argument of F_i and F_j are equal. In this case, for the minimal such i, we have $F_j^\star = f_i$.

In comparison, Ackermann's reduction for φ_1 is given by $T^A(\varphi_1)$:

$$\begin{bmatrix} (y = x \rightarrow f_1 = f_2) \wedge (y = f_1 \rightarrow f_1 = f_3) \wedge \\ (y = f_3 \rightarrow f_1 = f_4) \wedge (x = f_1 \rightarrow f_2 = f_3) \wedge \\ (x = f_3 \rightarrow f_2 = f_4) \wedge (f_1 = f_3 \rightarrow f_3 = f_4) \end{bmatrix} \wedge (f_4 \neq f_3) \wedge (f_3 \neq f_2) \wedge (x = f_1)$$

A hint to why Bryant's reduction is better for our purposes is the following claim:

Claim. For every UF-formula φ, if $\alpha \models T^A(\varphi)$ then $\alpha \models T^{BV}(\varphi)$.

While the converse does not hold. Thus, $T^{BV}(\varphi)$ has more satisfying assignments and therefore it should be easier to satisfy.

5   New E-Graph Construction

Given a UF-formula φ, we wish to construct a minimal E-graph that will be adequate for $T^{BV}(\varphi)$. We will first try to disregard all function arguments. Denote by $simp(\varphi)$ the E-formula received by replacing every function application F_i by its corresponding variable f_i. For example, for φ_1 of Section 4, $simp(\varphi_1) = ((f_4 \neq f_3) \wedge (f_3 \neq f_2) \wedge (x = f_1))$. Our initial E-graph will therefore be $\mathcal{G}(simp(\varphi))$.

If we take for example $\varphi_2 = F_1(x) \neq F_2(y)$, then $simp(\varphi_2) = f_1 \neq f_2$. $\mathcal{G}(simp(\varphi_2))$ then contains just one disequality edge between f_1 and f_2. An adequate assignment set for $\mathcal{G}(simp(\varphi_2))$, must contain an assignment α that assigns a different value for every variable in the E-graph, since α should be diverse w.r.t. to $\mathcal{G}(simp(\varphi_2))$. For example: $\alpha(f_1) = 0, \alpha(f_2) = 1, \alpha(x) = 2, \alpha(y) = 3$. Since $T^{BV}(\varphi_2) = f_1 \neq \mathbf{ITE}(x = y, f_1, f_2)$, we get that $\alpha \models T^{BV}(\varphi_2)$. And so we found an assignment that satisfies the formula.

Assume however, that our formula is slightly different: $\varphi_3 = F_1(x) \neq F_2(y) \wedge ((x = y) \vee True)$[1]. In this case $simp(\varphi_3) = f_1 \neq f_2 \wedge ((x = y) \vee True)$. Now, $\mathcal{G}(simp(\varphi_3))$ will also contain an equality edge between x and y. In this case, a possible adequate assignment set for this E-graph contains just one assignment α: $\alpha(f_1) = 0, \alpha(f_2) = 1, \alpha(x) = \alpha(y) = 2$. In this case however, $\alpha \not\models T^{BV}(\varphi_3)$. This is because the equality edge we added, indirectly caused the disequality edge between f_1 and f_2 to be disregarded. We will therefore add a rule to augment our E-graph with more edges in this case:

Tentative Rule 1. *If there is a disequality edge between f_i and f_j, add a disequality edge between their corresponding arguments.*

But this rule is not enough. We consider the following formula:

$$\varphi_4 = (F_1(x) = z) \wedge (F_2(y) \neq z) \wedge ((x = y) \vee True)$$

$\mathcal{G}(simp(\varphi_4))$ appears in Figure 1 as $\mathcal{G}_1$. In this case, the above Tentative Rule 1 does not apply, and we are left with the same problem, since a possible adequate assignment set for this E-graph contains just one assignment α: $\alpha(f_1) = \alpha(z) = 0, \alpha(f_2) = 1, \alpha(x) = \alpha(y) = 2$, and α does not satisfy $T^{BV}(\varphi_4)$. This is because a disequality edge between f_1 and f_2 is only implied in this E-graph, and so we wish to change Tentative Rule 1 so that it identifies implied disequality requirements.

We write $u \asymp_{\mathcal{G}} v$ if there exists a simple path between u and v in $\mathcal{G}$ consisting of equality edges except for exactly one disequality edge. This is what we mean by "implied" disequality edge. What this means is that an assignment where u and v differ may be needed to satisfy the formula. We alter Tentative Rule 1:

---

[1] Of course, any decent procedure will remove the right clause, but this *True* can be hidden as a more complex valid formula.

Rule 1. *If for f_i and f_j, $f_i \succeq_G f_j$ then add a disequality edge between their corresponding arguments.*

We now consider a similar UF-formula:

$$\varphi_5 = (True \vee (F_1(x) = z)) \wedge (F_2(y) \neq z) \wedge (x = y)$$

$\mathcal{G}(simp(\varphi_5))$ is exactly the same as before, and Rule 1 adds the disequality edge (x, y) to give $\mathcal{G}_2$ in Figure 1. The problem here is that a satisfying assignment α must satisfy $\alpha(x) = \alpha(y)$, and therefore $\alpha(F_2^\star) = \alpha(f_1)$. Since we also must have $\alpha(F_2^\star) \neq \alpha(z)$ to satisfy the formula, it implies $\alpha(f_1) \neq \alpha(z)$. This may not necessarily happen in any assignment given by the range allocator for our E-graph. This is because in our E-graph there is no representation for the fact that f_1 may "override" f_2. If we add an equality edge between f_1 and f_2 it will solve the problem. $\mathcal{G}_3$ of Figure 1 is the result of adding this edge.

We denote by $u \approx_G v$ the case where there is an equality path between u and v in $\mathcal{G}$.

Tentative Rule 2. *For f_i and f_j, with x_i and x_j their corresponding arguments, if $x_i \approx_G x_j$ then add the equality edge (f_i, f_j).*

This indeed solves our problem, but is not the best we can do. We have added an equality edge between f_1 and f_2 in our example, but it was not really necessary. We could have instead copied all edges involving f_2 to f_1. This is because there is no need for f_1 to be equal to f_2 if their arguments are equal. All that is needed is that the value f_1 gets respects all the requirements of f_2. Notice that this case is asymmetric: since f_1 may override f_2, only f_1 is required to answer to f_2's requirements.

We change Tentative Rule 2 to the following rule:

Rule 2. *For f_i and f_j, where $i < j$, with x_i and x_j their corresponding arguments, if $x_i \approx_G x_j$ then do one of the following:*

1. *add equality edge (f_i, f_j), or*
2. *for every (dis)equality edge (f_j, w) add a (dis)equality edge (f_i, w).*

And so, in our example, instead of adding an equality edge (f_1, f_2), we add a disequality edge (f_1, z) — see $\mathcal{G}_4$ of Figure 1.

The general idea of our new construction is therefore to start with $\mathcal{G}(simp(\varphi))$, and then apply Rule 1 and Rule 2 until no new edges are added. There are some missing details, specifically, the second option of Rule 2 needs to be postponed until the whole E-graph is constructed. We show the exact E-graph construction in the next section. Notice that this construction has a cone-of-influence flavor, since in $simp(\varphi)$ the arguments of uninterpreted functions disappear, and then only edges emanating from edges already in the E-graph are added.

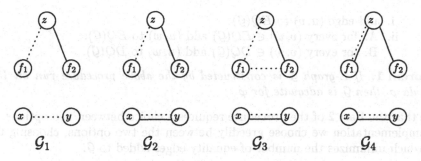

Fig. 1. The Iterative E-Graph Construction Process. Dashed lines represent equality edges, solid lines represent disequality edges.

6   Formal Description of E-Graph Construction

We define an A-graph (marked by $\mathfrak{G}$) to be an E-graph with the addition of *assignment edges*, which are directed. For an A-graph $\mathfrak{G}$ denote by $flat(\mathfrak{G})$ the E-graph resulting from replacing every assignment edge of $\mathfrak{G}$ by an equality edge.

For function application F_i of φ, define $arg(F_i)$ to be the variable of $T^{BV}(\varphi)$ corresponding to the argument of F_i. This means that if the argument of F_i is a variable v, then $arg(F_i) = v$, and if it is a function application G_j, then $arg(F_i) = g_j$.

The E-graph construction procedure is divided to two parts:

1. **A-graph construction:** Given a UF-formula φ we construct an A-graph $\mathfrak{G}$:
   (a) Let the vertices of $\mathfrak{G}$ be the variables of $T^{BV}(\varphi)$.
   (b) Add all edges of $\mathcal{G}(simp(\varphi))$ to $\mathfrak{G}$.
   (c) For every F_i and F_j such that $i < j$ and $arg(F_i) \approx_{flat(\mathfrak{G})} arg(F_j)$, add the following edges:
       i. Add assignment edge (f_i, f_j) to $\mathfrak{G}$.
       ii. If $f_i \asymp_{flat(\mathfrak{G})} f_j$ then add disequality edge $(arg(f_i), arg(f_j))$ to $\mathfrak{G}$.
   (d) Repeat step 1c until a no new edges are added.

   Example 4. For the UF-formula φ_1 of Example 3, the algorithm constructs the A-graph $\mathfrak{G}$ of Figure 2, while $\mathcal{G}$ is the E-graph constructed by the procedure suggested in [PRSS99].

2. **Transforming the A-graph to an E-graph:** The second step of the procedure is to transform the A-graph $\mathfrak{G}$ to an E-graph $\mathcal{G}$. For two vertices u and v, we denote $v \sqsubseteq_{\mathcal{G}} u$, if:
   (a) for every $(v, w) \in EQ(\mathcal{G})$, $(u, w) \in EQ(\mathcal{G})$.
   (b) for every $(v, w) \in DQ(\mathcal{G})$, $(u, w) \in DQ(\mathcal{G})$.
   We proceed:
   (a) Initially, $\mathcal{G} = \langle V(\mathfrak{G}), EQ(\mathfrak{G}), DQ(\mathfrak{G}) \rangle$
   (b) While there are vertices u, v, such that (u, v) is an assignment edge of $\mathfrak{G}$, and either $(u, v) \notin EQ(\mathcal{G})$ or $v \sqsubseteq_{\mathcal{G}} u$, choose one of the following options:

i. add edge (u,v) to $EQ(\mathcal{G})$.
ii. A. for every $(v,w) \in EQ(\mathcal{G})$ add (u,w) to $EQ(\mathcal{G})$.
    B. for every $(v,w) \in DQ(\mathcal{G})$ add (u,w) to $DQ(\mathcal{G})$.

Theorem 1. *If E-graph $\mathcal{G}$ is constructed by the above procedure run on UF-formula φ, then $\mathcal{G}$ is adequate for φ.*

Note that the Part 2 of the procedure requires a choice between two options. In our implementation we choose greedily between the two options, choosing the one which minimizes the number of equality edges added to $\mathcal{G}$.

Example 5. $\mathcal{G}_1$ and $\mathcal{G}_2$ in Figure 2 are the two possible E-graphs resulting from applying this Part 2 to $\mathfrak{G}$. As we can see both $\mathcal{G}_1$ and $\mathcal{G}_2$ are much smaller than $\mathcal{G}$ (the E-graph constructed by [PRSS99]). In fact, we can show that any adequate assignment set for $\mathcal{G}$ is of size at least 16, and on the other hand, there is an assignment set of size 4 for $\mathcal{G}_1$, and of size 2 for $\mathcal{G}_2$.

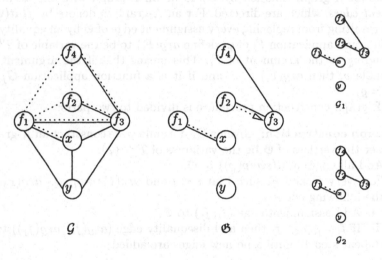

Fig. 2. Dashed lines represent equality edges, solid lines represent disequality edges, and dashed directed lines represent assignment edges.

7   Comparison with Previous Methods

If we examine the E-graph construction of [PRSS99], we see that it is basically the same as this new construction, except there is no conditioning on when to add new edges, instead, they are always added. In other words, remove all conditions of Step 1c in Part 1 of the procedure, and for every F_i and F_j add a disequality edge between their arguments, and an equality edge between f_i and f_j. Therefore, our E-graph will always be smaller than in [PRSS99], resulting in a smaller state space.

In [BGV99], it is proved that for a UF-formula φ in *positive equality*, every variable of $T^{BV}(\varphi)$ can be instantiated to a single constant. A UF-formula φ is said to be of *positive equality* if no equality terms of φ are in the input cone of a function application, and all equality terms of φ appear under an odd number of negations — they are in negative polarity[2]. It is easy to see that our A-graph construction for such formulas will result in an A-graph with no equality edges. Then, if we use our greedy heuristic for the Part 2 of the procedure, it will result in an E-graph consisting of only disequality edges. An adequate range for such an E-graph contains just one assignment, assigning each variable a distinct constant. We therefore achieve this optimal result for the positive equality segment of the formula, while improving on the other variables (since they give a range of $1 \ldots i$ to the i-th variable, resulting in a state space of $n!$, which we will always improve upon — see [PRSS99]).

8   Experimental Results and Conclusions

We implemented our new graph construction procedure, and then used the range allocator of [PRSS99] to construct a new procedure for checking satisfiability of UF-formulas. We compared our decision procedure with that of [PRSS99] on many example formulas that were generated by a tool for compiler translation validation [PSS98]. The results appear in Table 1, where the prefix *New* denotes the results of this paper, and the prefix *Old* the results of [PRSS99]. *space* denotes the resulting assignment set size. Since in all cases encountered the verification procedure either proved that the formula valid in less than 1 sec, or ran out of memory, we do not write the exact running time. Instead we write $\sqrt{}$ if the run completed, and $\times$ if it didn't. *Num. vars* denotes the number of variables in the example. There were many examples were both methods resulted in a very small state space (and running time), and therefore we mention only those were there was a significant difference between the two methods.

Table 1. New vs. Old E-graph Construction.

Example	New-finished	Old-finished	New-space	Old-space	Num. vars
15	$\sqrt{}$	$\times$	121	121	13
22	$\sqrt{}$	$\times$	2	$9.8 \cdot 10^{46}$	114
25	$\sqrt{}$	$\times$	1	$5.9 \cdot 10^{47}$	114
27	$\sqrt{}$	$\sqrt{}$	2	11520	26
43	$\sqrt{}$	$\times$	4	$3.4 \cdot 10^{108}$	160
44	$\sqrt{}$	$\sqrt{}$	4	$2.5 \cdot 10^{11}$	46
46	$\sqrt{}$	$\sqrt{}$	2	$1.6 \cdot 10^{22}$	67
47	$\sqrt{}$	$\sqrt{}$	1	$4.9 \cdot 10^{9}$	52

---

[2] The confusion between 'positive' equality and 'negative' polarity is due to the fact that in [BGV99], where this term was introduced, the analysis referred to validity checking, rather than satisfiability as in this paper.

As can be seen from the table, the new graph construction has an extreme effect on the state space size. Indeed, by using the new graph construction we were able to verify formulas which we could not with the previous method.

To conclude, we showed that the combination of Bryant et al. reduction method, Pnueli et al. range allocation, and a more careful analysis of the formula structure are very effective for verifying equality formulas with uninterpreted functions.

References

[Ack54]   W. Ackermann, "Solvable Cases of the Decision Problem", Studies in logic and the foundations of mathematics, North-Holland, Amsterdam, 1954.

[BD94]   J.R. Burch and D.L. Dill, "Automatic Verification of Microprocessor Control", In *Computer-Aided Verification CAV '94* .

[BDL96]   Clark W. Barrett, David L. Dill and Jeremy R. Levitt, "Validity Checking for Combinations of Theories with Equality", In *Formal Methods in Computer Aided Design FMCAD '96* .

[GSZAS98]   A. Goel, K. Sajid, H. Zhou, A. Aziz and V. Singhal, "BDD Based Procedures for a Theory of Equality with Uninterpreted Functions", In *Computer-Aided Verification CAV '98* .

[HIKB96]   R. Hojati, A. Isles, D. Kirkpatrick and R. K. Brayton, "Verification Using Finite Instantiations and Uninterpreted Functions", In *Formal Methods in Computer Aided Design FMCAD '96* .

[PRSS99]   A. Pnueli, Y. Rodeh, M. Siegel and O. Shtrichman, "Deciding Equality Formulas by Small Domain Instantiations", In *Computer-Aided Verification CAV '99* .

[PSS98]   A. Pnueli, M. Siegel and O. Shtrichman, "Translation Validation for Synchronous Languages", In *International Colloquium on Automata, Languages and Programming ICALP '98* .

[PRS01]   A. Pnueli, Y. Rodeh and O. Shtrichman, "Finite Instantiations in Equivalence Logic with Uninterpreted Functions", Technical report, Weizmann Institute of Science, 2001. http://www.wisdom.weizmann.ac.il/~verify/publication/2001/yrodeh_tr2001.ps.gz

[BV98]   R.E. Bryant and M. Velev, "Bit-level Abstraction in the Verification of Pipelined Microprocessors by Correspondence Checking", In *Formal Methods in Computer Aided Design FMCAD '98* .

[BGV99]   R.E. Bryant, S. German and M.N. Velev, "Exploiting Positive Equality in a Logic of Equality with Uninterpreted Functions", In *Computer-Aided Verification CAV '99* .

[BV00]   R.E. Bryant and M. N. Velev, "Boolean satisfiability with transitivity constraints", In *Computer-Aided Verification CAV 2000* .

Model Checking with Formula-Dependent Abstract Models

Alexander Asteroth, Christel Baier, Ulrich Aßmann

Universität Bonn, Römerstr. 164, 53117 Bonn, Germany
{aster,assmann,baier}@cs.uni-bonn.de

Abstract. We present a model checking algorithm for ∀CTL (and full CTL) which uses an iterative abstraction refinement strategy.
It terminates at least for all transition systems $\mathcal{M}$ that have a finite simulation or bisimulation quotient. In contrast to other abstraction refinement algorithms, we always work with abstract models whose sizes depend only on the length of the formula Φ (but not on the size of the system, which might be infinite).

1 Introduction

The state explosion problem is still the major problem for applying model checking to systems of industrial size. Several techniques have been suggested to overcome this limitation of model checking; including symbolic methods with BDDs [6, 33] or SAT-solvers [4], partial order reduction [35, 22, 40], compositional reasoning [29, 21] and abstraction [11, 26, 13, 27, 29, 16, 19]. See [14] for an overview.

In this paper, we concentrate on abstraction in a temporal logical setting. Let $\mathcal{M}$ be the concrete model that we want to verify against a temporal logical formula Φ. The rough idea of the (exact) abstraction approach is to replace $\mathcal{M}$ by a much smaller abstract model $\mathcal{A}_\alpha$ with the *strong preservation* property stating that $\mathcal{A}_\alpha \models \Phi$ iff $\mathcal{M} \models \Phi$. The subscript α stands for an abstraction function that describes the relation between concrete and abstract states. In the simplest case, α is just a function from the concrete state space S to the abstract state space. (the state space of the abstract model $\mathcal{A}_\alpha$). For instance, dealing with the abstraction function α that assigns to each concrete state s its (bi-)simulation equivalence class, we get the (bi-)simulation quotient system $\mathcal{M}_{bis}$ or $\mathcal{M}_{sim}$, for which strong preservation holds if Φ is a CTL^* resp. $\forall CTL^*$ formula [5, 13].

Algorithm 1 Schema of the Abstraction Refinement Approach.

construct an initial abstract model $\mathcal{A}_0$; $i := 0$;
REPEAT
    Model_Check($\mathcal{A}_i, \Phi$);
    IF $\mathcal{A}_i \not\models \Phi$ **THEN** $\mathcal{A}_{i+1} :=$ Refinement($\mathcal{A}_i, \Phi$) **FI**;
    $i := i + 1$;
UNTIL $\mathcal{A}_{i-1} \models \Phi$ or $\mathcal{A}_i = \mathcal{A}_{i-1}$;
IF $\mathcal{A}_{i-1} \models \Phi$ **THEN** return "yes" **ELSE** return "no" **FI**.

G. Berry, H. Comon, and A. Finkel (Eds.): CAV 2001, LNCS 2102, pp. 155–168, 2001.

If Φ is fixed these are unnecessarily large. In general, *conservative* abstractions that rely on the *weak preservation* property, stating that $\mathcal{A}_\alpha \models \Phi$ implies $\mathcal{M} \models \Phi$, yield much smaller abstract models. Such models can be used in the abstraction refinement schema shown in Algorithm 1 (e.g. [10, 18, 26, 23, 12]). Here, Model_Check(...) denotes any standard model checking algorithm and Refinement(...) an operator that adds further information about the original system $\mathcal{M}$ to $\mathcal{A}_i$ to obtain an abstract slightly more "concrete" model. A necessary property that ensures partial correctness of the above abstraction refinement technique is the strong preservation property for the final abstract model which might be obtained when no further refinement steps are possible.

The major difficulty is the design of a refinement procedure which on one hand should add enough information to the abstract model such that the "chances" to prove or disprove the property Φ in the next iteration increase in a reasonable measure while on the other hand the resulting new abstract model $\mathcal{A}_{i+1}$ should be reasonable small. The first goal can be achieved by specification-dependent refinement steps such as counterexample guided strategies [10, 26, 12] where the current abstract model $\mathcal{A}_i$ is refined according to an error trace that the model checker has returned for $\mathcal{A}_i$ or by strategies, that work with under- and/or overapproximations for the satisfaction relation $\models_\mathcal{M}$ of the concrete model, e.g. [18, 28, 31, 36]. To keep the abstract models reasonable small two general approaches can be distinguished. One approach focusses on small symbolic BDD representations of the abstract models (e.g. [10, 25, 31, 36, 15]), while other approaches attempt to minimize the number of abstract states (e.g. [11, 13, 27, 19]). While most of the fully automatic methods are designed for very large but finite concrete systems, most abstraction refinement techniques for infinite systems are semi-automatic and use a theorem prover to perform the refinement step or to provide the initial model $\mathcal{A}_0$ [17, 23, 9, 1, 38]. An entirely automatic abstraction technique that can treat infinite systems is presented in [34].

Our Contribution: In this paper, we present an abstraction refinement algorithm that works with abstract models with a *fixed* state space that just depends on the specification (temporal logical formula) but not on the concrete system. In our approach, the concrete system $\mathcal{M}$ to be verified is an ordinary (very large or infinite) transition system. We use the general abstraction framework suggested in [19] and deal with abstract models $\mathcal{A}_i$ with two transition relations. Although our ideas work for full *CTL*, we provide the explanations for the sublogic $\forall CTL$ for which the formalisms are simpler.

The rough idea of our algorithm is the use of abstract models $\mathcal{A}_i$ that are approximations of $\mathcal{A}_\Phi$, the abstract model that results from the original model $\mathcal{M}$ when we collapse all states that satisfy the same subformulas of Φ. (Here, Φ is the formula we want to check for $\mathcal{M}$.) Of course, the computation of the abstract model $\mathcal{A}_\Phi$ would be at least as hard as model checking the original system $\mathcal{M}$. Anyway, we can use the state space of $\mathcal{A}_\Phi$ (which consists of sets of subformulas of Φ or their negations) for the abstract models $\mathcal{A}_i$. Thus, the size of any of the abstract models $\mathcal{A}_i$ is at most exponential in the length $|\Phi|$ of the formula; independent on the size of the concrete system which might be infinite. Any abstract model $\mathcal{A}_i$ is equipped with an abstraction function α_i which stands for *partial knowledge* about the satisfaction relation $\models_\mathcal{M}$ in the concrete system $\mathcal{M}$. The abstraction function α_i maps any concrete state s to the abstract state $\sigma = \alpha_i(s)$ in $\mathcal{A}_i$ consisting of those subformulas Ψ of Φ where we already know that $s \models_\mathcal{M} \Psi$ for all

$\Psi \in \sigma$ and all those negated subformulas $\neg\Psi$ where $s \not\models_{\mathcal{M}} \Psi$ is already shown. Refining $\mathcal{A}_i$ means adding more information about the concrete satisfaction relation $\models_{\mathcal{M}}$; resulting in an abstract model $\mathcal{A}_{i+1}$ where $\alpha_{i+1}(s)$ is a superset of $\alpha_i(s)$. Partial correctness of our algorithm is guaranteed for (concrete) transition systems of arbitrary size. Our algorithm terminates at least if the concrete system has a finite simulation or bisimulation quotient. The only theoretical requirement for an entirely automatic implementation is the effectiveness of the dual predecessor predicate in the concrete system.

Related Work: Our methodology borrows ideas from many other abstraction refinement algorithms. We work with *under-* and *overapproximations* for the concrete satisfaction relation $\models_{\mathcal{M}}$ that we derive from the abstraction function α_i. Although such "sandwich" techniques are used by several other authors, e.g. [3,28,31], we are not aware any other method that is designed for general (possibly infinite) transition systems and works with abstract models of a fixed size. Our methodology is also close to the framework of [18] where an abstraction refinement algorithm for $\forall CTL$ and finite concrete transition systems is presented. [18] only needs underapproximations for the concrete satisfaction relation. The major difference to our algorithm is the treatment of formulas with a least or greatest fixed point semantics (such as $\forall\Diamond\Psi$ and $\forall\Box\Psi$) in the refinement step.[1] Abstraction techniques with under- and/or overapproximations that focus on abstract models with small BDD representations are presented in [31,36,15]. We also use ideas of stable partitioning algorithms for computing the quotient space with respect to simulation or bisimulation like equivalences [37,7,32,24,8]. However, instead of splitting blocks (sets of concrete states that are identified in the current abstract model) into new subblocks (and thus, creating new abstract states), our approach refines the abstract model by *moving subblocks* from one abstract state to another abstract state (which presents more knowledge about the satisfaction relation $\models_{\mathcal{M}}$).

The method is also loosely related to tableau based methods as presented in [30,39].

Outline: In Section 2, we explain our notation concerning transition systems, *CTL* and briefly recall the basic results on abstract interpretations which our algorithm relies on. The type of abstract models used in our algorithm is introduced in Section 3. Section 4 presents our abstraction refinement algorithm for $\forall CTL$ and sketches the ideas to handle full *CTL*. Section 5 concludes the paper.

2 Preliminaries

We expect some background knowledge on transition systems, temporal logic, model checking, abstraction and only explain the notations used throughout this paper. For further details see, e.g. [14].

Transition Systems : A transition system is a tuple $\mathcal{M} = (S, \rightarrow, I, AP, L)$ where S is a set of states, $I \subseteq S$ the set of initial states, AP a finite set of atomic propositions and $L : S \rightarrow 2^{AP}$ a labeling function which assigns to any state $s \in S$ the set $L(s)$ of atomic

---

[1] Our refinement operator works with a "one-step-lookahead" while [18] treats paths that might have length > 1. In fact, this explains why underapproximations are sufficient in the framework of [18] while we need both under- and overapproximations to mimic the standard least or greatest fixed point computation. The fact that we just refine according to single transitions (paths of length 1) makes it possible to treat infinite systems.

propositions that hold in s. $\to \subseteq S \times S$ denotes the transition relation. Let $Post(s) = \{s' \in S : s \to s'\}$, $\widetilde{Pre}(B) = \{s \in S : Post(s) \subseteq B\}$. A path in a transition system is a maximal sequence $\pi = s_0 \to s_1 \to \ldots$ of states such that $s_i \in Post(s_{i-1})$, $i = 1, 2, \ldots$. Here, maximality means that either π is infinite or ends in a terminal state (i.e., a state without successors).

Computation Tree Logic (CTL) : *CTL* (state) formulas in positive normal form are built from the following grammar.

$$\Phi ::= true \mid a \mid \neg a \mid \Phi_1 \wedge \Phi_2 \mid \Phi_1 \vee \Phi_2 \mid \forall \varphi \mid \exists \varphi \qquad \varphi ::= X\Phi \mid \Phi_1 U \Phi_2 \mid \Phi_1 \tilde{U} \Phi_2$$

with $a \in AP$. Here, X and U are the standard temporal modalities "Next step" and "Until" while $\tilde{U}$ denotes "weak until" (also often called "unless").[2] Operators for modelling "eventually" or "always" are derived as usual, e.g. $\forall \Diamond \Phi = \forall true U \Phi$ and $\forall \Box \Phi = \forall \Phi \tilde{U} false$. The universal fragment of *CTL* (where the application of "$\exists$" is not allowed) is denoted by $\forall CTL$. Similarly, $\exists CTL$ denotes the existential fragment of *CTL*. The satisfaction relation $\models_{\mathcal{M}}$ for *CTL* formulas and transition systems $\mathcal{M}$ is defined in the standard way. The satisfaction set for Φ in $\mathcal{M}$ is given by $Sat_{\mathcal{M}}(\Phi) = \{s \in S : s \models_{\mathcal{M}} \Phi\}$. We write $\mathcal{M} \models \Phi$ iff Φ holds for any initial state, i.e., iff $I \subseteq Sat_{\mathcal{M}}(\Phi)$. Although negation is only allowed on the level of atomic propositions, we shall use expressions of the type $\neg \Psi$ (with the intended meaning $s \models_{\mathcal{M}} \neg \Psi$ iff $s \not\models_{\mathcal{M}} \Psi$).

Abstract Interpretations : Let $\mathcal{M} = (S, \to, I, AP, L)$ be a transition system that models the "concrete system" (that we want to verify). Let S_A be an arbitrary set of "abstract states". In what follows, we use the Latin letter s for concrete states (i.e., states $s \in S$) and the greek letter σ for abstract states (i.e., states $\sigma \in S_A$). An *abstraction function* for $\mathcal{M}$ (with range S_A) is a function $\alpha : S \to S_A$ such that $\alpha(s) = \alpha(s')$ implies $L(s) = L(s')$. The induced *concretization function* $\gamma : S_A \to 2^S$ is just the inverse image function $\gamma = \alpha^{-1}$ (that is, $\gamma(\sigma) = \{s \in S : \alpha(s) = \sigma\}$). We use the results of [19] and associate with α two transition relations $\to_\alpha$ (which we shall use to get underapproximations for the satisfaction sets $Sat_{\mathcal{M}}(\cdot)$) and $\leadsto_\alpha$ (yielding overapproximations). They are given by

$$\sigma \to_\alpha \sigma' \text{ iff } \exists s \in \gamma(\sigma) \ \exists s' \in \gamma(\sigma') \text{ s.t. } s \to s'$$
$$\sigma \leadsto_\alpha \sigma' \text{ iff } \forall s \in \gamma(\sigma) \ \exists s' \in \gamma(\sigma') \text{ s.t. } s \to s'.$$

For any (abstract) path $\sigma_0 \leadsto_\alpha \sigma_1 \leadsto_\alpha \ldots$ and concrete state $s_0 \in \gamma(\sigma_0)$, there is a (concrete) path $s_0 \to s_1 \to \ldots$ in $\mathcal{M}$ such that $\alpha(s_i) = \sigma_i$, $i = 0, 1, \ldots$ while the corresponding statement for $\to_\alpha$ may be wrong. Vice versa, any (concrete) path $s_0 \to s_1 \to \ldots$ in $\mathcal{M}$ can be lifted to a path $\sigma_0 \to_\alpha \sigma_1 \to_\alpha \ldots$ where $\sigma_i = \alpha(s_i)$.

Let $\mathcal{U} = (S_A, \to_\alpha, I_\alpha, AP, L_\alpha)$ and $O = (S_A, \leadsto_\alpha, I_\alpha, AP, L_\alpha)$ be the transition system with state space S_A where the set of abstract initial states is $I_\alpha = \alpha(I) = \{\alpha(s) : s \in I\}$. The abstract labeling function $L_\alpha : A \to 2^{AP}$ is given by $L_\alpha(\sigma) = \alpha(s)$ for some/all concrete states $s \in \gamma(\sigma)$. Then, we have weak preservation of the following type.

---

[2] Any ordinary *CTL* formula (where also negation is allowed in the state formulas) can be transformed into positive normal form. Note that the dual to the until operator (often called the "release operator") can be obtained by $\neg(\neg \Phi_1 U \neg \Phi_2) = (\neg \Phi_1 \wedge \Phi_2) \tilde{U} (\Phi_1 \wedge \Phi_2)$.

Lemma 1. *(cf.* [13, 27, 19]*) Let s be a concrete state.*

(1) If Ψ is a $\forall CTL$ formula and $\alpha(s) \models_{\mathcal{U}} \Psi$ then $s \models_{\mathcal{M}} \Psi$.
(2) If Ψ is a $\exists CTL$ formula and $\alpha(s) \models_{O} \Psi$ then $s \models_{\mathcal{M}} \Psi$.

3 Abstract Φ-Models

Throughout this paper, we assume a fixed concrete transition system $\mathcal{M} = (S, \rightarrow, I, AP, L)$ without terminal states and a $\forall CTL$ formula Φ. When we refer to a subformula then we mean a formula which is not a constant *true* or *false*. $sub(\Phi)$ denotes the set of all subformulas of Φ. We may assume that, $AP \subseteq sub(\Phi)$. We refer to any subformula of Φ of the form $\Psi = \forall \varphi$ as a $\forall$subformula of Φ.

The Abstract State Space S_{Φ} : Let $cl(\Phi)$ denote the set of all subformulas Ψ of Φ and their negation $\neg \Psi$ (where we identify $\neg\neg a$ and a). I.e., $cl(\Phi) = sub(\Phi) \cup \{\neg \Psi : \Psi \in sub(\Phi)\}$. We define the set $S_{\Phi} \subseteq 2^{cl(\Phi)}$ as follows. S_{Φ} denotes the set of $\sigma \subseteq cl(\Phi)$ such that the following conditions (i) and (ii) hold. (i) for any atomic proposition $a \in AP$ and $\sigma \in S_{\Phi}$, either $a \in \sigma$ or $\neg a \in \sigma$. (ii) asserts the consistency of σ with respect to propositional logic and local consistency with respect to "until" and "weak until". We just mention the axioms for "until".[3]

1. If $\Psi_2 \in \sigma$ and $\forall \Psi_1 U \Psi_2 \in sub(\Phi)$ then $\forall \Psi_1 U \Psi_2 \in \sigma$.
2. If $\Psi_2 \notin \sigma$ and $\forall \Psi_1 U \Psi_2 \in \sigma$ then $\Psi_1 \in \sigma$ (provided that $\Psi_1 \notin \{true, false\}$).
3. If $\neg \Psi_1, \neg \Psi_2 \in \sigma$ and $\forall \Psi_1 U \Psi_2 \in sub(\Phi)$ then $\neg \forall \Psi_1 U \Psi_2 \in \sigma$.
4. If $\neg \forall \Psi_1 U \Psi_2 \in \sigma$ then $\neg \Psi_2 \in \sigma$.

The abstract models $\mathcal{U}_{\Phi}$ and O_{Φ} yield precise abstractions. Let $\alpha_{\Phi} : S \rightarrow S_{\Phi}$ be given by $\alpha_{\Phi}(s) = \{\Psi \in sub(\Phi) : s \models_{\mathcal{M}} \Psi\} \cup \{\neg \Psi : \Psi \in sub(\Phi), s \not\models_{\mathcal{M}} \Psi\}$. It is well-known [20] that for the abstract model that we get with the abstraction function α_{Φ} we just can establish the weak preservation property but do not have strong preservation. However, when we add a new atomic proposition a_{Ψ} for any $\forall$subformula Ψ of Φ then we get an abstract model for which a slight variant of the strong preservation property holds. Let

$$AP_{\Phi} = AP \cup \{a_{\Psi} : \Psi \text{ is a } \forall\text{subformula of } \Phi\}.$$

We put $a_{\Psi} = a$ if $\Psi = a$ is an atomic proposition. Let $L_{\mathcal{U}}, L_O : S_{\Phi} \rightarrow AP_{\Phi}$ be given by

$$L_{\mathcal{U}}(\sigma) = \{a_{\Psi} \in AP_{\Phi} : \Psi \in \sigma\}, \quad L_O(\sigma) = \{a_{\Psi} \in AP_{\Phi} : \neg \Psi \notin \sigma\}.$$

When dealing with underapproximations, we use the labeling function $L_{\mathcal{U}}$ while L_O will serve for the overapproximations. We define $\mathcal{U}_{\Phi} = (S_{\Phi}, \rightarrow_{\alpha_{\Phi}}, I_{\alpha_{\Phi}}, AP_{\Phi}, L_{\mathcal{U}})$ and $O_{\Phi} = (S_{\Phi}, \rightsquigarrow_{\alpha_{\Phi}}, I_{\alpha_{\Phi}}, AP_{\Phi}, L_O)$.

---

[3] For "weak until" we have essentially the same axioms as for "until". The propositional logical axioms are obvious; e.g. we require that "$\Psi \in \sigma$ implies $\neg \Psi \notin \sigma$" and the symmetric axiom "$\neg \Psi \in \sigma$ implies $\Psi \notin \sigma$". One of the axioms for conjunction is "$\Psi_1 \wedge \Psi_2 \in \sigma$ iff $\Psi_1 \in \sigma$ and $\Psi_2 \in \sigma$." Note that we do not require maximality; i.e., $\Psi, \neg \Psi \notin \sigma$ is possible if $\Psi \notin AP$.

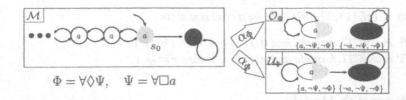

$$\Phi = \forall\Diamond\Psi, \quad \Psi = \forall\Box a$$

Intuitively, the labelings $L_{\mathcal{U}}$ and L_O with the auxiliary atomic propositions a_Ψ shall encode the information about the satisfaction set $Sat_{\mathcal{M}}(\Psi)$ that might got lost with the abstract transition relations $\rightarrow_\alpha$ and $\rightsquigarrow_\alpha$.

Example: For the concrete system $\mathcal{M}$ shown in the picture above and the formula $\Phi = \forall\Diamond\forall\Box a$, $\mathcal{M} \not\models \Phi$ while $O_\Phi \models \Phi$. In our examples we depict concrete states by circles, abstract states by ellipses. Their names are written below while the corresponding labels are written inside the states.□

The Formulas $\overline{\Psi}$ and $\widetilde{\Psi}$: For each subformula Ψ of Φ we define new $\forall CTL$ formulas $\overline{\Psi}$ and $\widetilde{\Psi}$ by structural induction. If Ψ is *true, false* or a literal then $\overline{\Psi} = \widetilde{\Psi} = \Psi$. If $\Psi = \Psi_1 \vee \Psi_2$ then $\overline{\Psi} = \overline{\Psi_1} \vee \overline{\Psi_2}$ and $\widetilde{\Psi} = \widetilde{\Psi_1} \vee \widetilde{\Psi_2}$. Conjunction is treated in a similar way. The transformations for "next step", "until" and "weak until" make use of the new atomic propositions. For $\Psi = \forall X\Psi_0$ we put $\overline{\Psi} = (\forall X\overline{\Psi_0}) \vee a_\Psi$ and $\widetilde{\Psi} = (\forall X\widetilde{\Psi_0}) \wedge a_\Psi$. If $\Psi = \forall\Psi_1 U\Psi_2$ then we put $\overline{\Psi} = \forall\overline{\Psi_1}U(\overline{\Psi_2} \vee a_\Psi)$ and $\widetilde{\Psi} = (\forall\widetilde{\Psi_1}U\widetilde{\Psi_2}) \wedge a_\Psi$. Similarly, we treat weak until. It is easy to see that for any concrete state s and $\Psi \in cl(\Phi)$:

$$\alpha_\Phi(s) \models_{\mathcal{U}_\Phi} \overline{\Psi} \quad \text{iff} \quad \alpha_\Phi(s) \models_{O_\Phi} \widetilde{\Psi} \quad \text{iff} \quad s \models_{\mathcal{M}} \Psi.$$

In the example above, we get $\widetilde{\Phi} = (\forall\Diamond\widetilde{\Psi}) \wedge a_\Phi$ where $\widetilde{\Psi} = (\forall\Box a) \wedge a_\Psi$ and the desired property $O_\Phi \not\models \widetilde{\Phi}$.

Abstract Φ-Models : $\mathcal{U}_\Phi$ and O_Φ contain all information that we need to model check the original system $\mathcal{M}$ against the formula Φ. In our abstraction refinement algorithm we make use of abstract models which can be viewed as approximations of $\mathcal{U}_\Phi$ and O_Φ.

Definition 1. *An* abstract Φ-model *for $\mathcal{M}$ is a tuple $\mathcal{A} = (\alpha, \gamma, \mathcal{U}, O)$ consisting of an abstraction function $\alpha : S \rightarrow S_\Phi$ with $\alpha(s) \subseteq \alpha_\Phi(s)$ for any concrete state $s \in S$, the concretization function $\gamma = \alpha^{-1} : S_\Phi \rightarrow S$ and the two transition systems $\mathcal{U} = (S_\Phi, \rightarrow_\alpha, I_\alpha, AP_\Phi, L_{\mathcal{U}})$ and $O = (S_\Phi, \rightsquigarrow_\alpha, I_\alpha, AP_\Phi, L_O)$ where $I_\alpha, \rightarrow_\alpha, \rightsquigarrow_\alpha$ are as in Section 2.* □

Intuitively, the sets $\alpha(s)$ consist of all subformulas Ψ of Φ where $s \models_{\mathcal{M}} \Psi$ has already been verified and all formulas $\neg\Psi$ where $s \not\models_{\mathcal{M}} \Psi$ has already been shown. However, there might be formulas $\Psi \in sub(\Phi)$ such that neither $\Psi \in \alpha(s)$ nor $\neg\Psi \in \alpha(s)$. For such formulas Ψ, we do not yet know whether $s \models_{\mathcal{M}} \Psi$.

Let $\mathcal{A} = (\alpha, \gamma, \mathcal{U}, O)$ be an abstract Φ-model. We associate with $\mathcal{A}$ two satisfaction relations. $\models_{\mathcal{U}}$ denotes the standard satisfaction relation for CTL and the transition system $\mathcal{U}$. As we assume that the concrete transition system $\mathcal{M}$ has no terminal states, all paths in $\mathcal{M}$ and $\mathcal{U}$ are infinite. However, the abstract transition system O might have terminal states. For O, we slightly depart from the standard semantics of CTL. For the finite paths in O, the satisfaction relation $\models_O$ treats weak until and until in the same way. Let $\pi = \sigma_0 \rightsquigarrow_\alpha \sigma_1 \rightsquigarrow_\alpha \ldots \rightsquigarrow_\alpha \sigma_n$ be a finite path. Then, $\pi \models_O \Psi_1 U \Psi_2$ iff $\pi \models_O \Psi_1 \tilde{U} \Psi_2$ iff either $\sigma_0, \sigma_1, \ldots, \sigma_n \models_O \Psi_1$ or there is some $k \in \{0, 1, \ldots, n\}$ with $\sigma_0, \sigma_1, \ldots, \sigma_{k-1} \models_O \Psi_1$ and $\sigma_k \models_O \Psi_2$.[4] The reason why we need this modification is that we "reverse" the result established by [19] stating that $\alpha(s) \models_O \Psi$ implies $s \models_M \Psi$ for any $\exists CTL$ formula Ψ (compare Lemma 1, part (2), and Lemma 2, part (b)) For infinite paths and any type of path formulas, we deal with the usual CTL semantics in O. Also for the next step and weak until operator and finite paths in O, we work with the usual semantics. (Thus, $\sigma \models_O \forall X \Psi$ holds for all terminal states σ in O.)

Lemma 2. *For any concrete state $s \in S$ and $\Psi \in sub(\Phi)$:*

(a) If $\alpha(s) \models_{\mathcal{U}} \overline{\Psi}$ then $s \models_M \Psi$.
(b) If $\alpha(s) \not\models_O \tilde{\Psi}$ then $s \not\models_M \Psi$.
(c) If $\Psi \in \alpha(s)$ then $\alpha(s) \models_{\mathcal{U}} \overline{\Psi}$.
(d) If $\neg\Psi \in \alpha(s)$ then $\alpha(s) \not\models_O \tilde{\Psi}$.

Any abstract Φ-model $\mathcal{A} = (\alpha, \gamma, \mathcal{U}, O)$ induces under- and overapproximations for the sets $Sat_M(\Psi) = \{s \in S : s \models_M \Psi\}$, $\Psi \in sub(\Phi)$.

Definition 2. *Let $Sat_{\mathcal{A}}^+(\Psi) = \{s \in S : \neg\Psi \notin \alpha(s)\}$, $Sat_{\mathcal{A}}^-(\Psi) = \{s \in S : \Psi \in \alpha(s)\}$.* □

Lemma 3. *$Sat_{\mathcal{A}}^-(\Psi) \subseteq Sat_M(\Psi) \subseteq Sat_{\mathcal{A}}^+(\Psi)$ for any $\Psi \in sub(\Phi)$.* □

Lemma 3 follows by $\alpha(s) \subseteq \alpha_\Phi(s)$. Clearly, given α or γ, the abstract Φ-model $\mathcal{A}$ is uniquely determined. Vice versa, given over- and underapproximations $Sat^+(\Psi)$ and $Sat^-(\Psi)$ for $Sat_M(\Psi)$ there exists a unique abstract Φ-model $\mathcal{A}$ with $Sat^+(\Psi) = Sat_{\mathcal{A}}^+(\Psi)$ and $Sat^-(\Psi) = Sat_{\mathcal{A}}^-(\Psi)$.[5]

Definition 3. *$\mathcal{A} \models \Phi$ iff $\Phi \in \sigma$ for all abstract initial states σ and $\mathcal{A} \models \neg\Phi$ iff there is an abstract initial state σ with $\neg\Phi \in \sigma$.*[6] □

Clearly, $\mathcal{A} \models \Phi$ iff $I \subseteq Sat_{\mathcal{A}}^-(\Phi)$ iff $\Phi \in \alpha(s)$ for any concrete initial state s. Similarly, $\mathcal{A} \not\models \Phi$ iff there is a concrete initial state s such that $\neg\Phi \in \alpha(s)$. By Lemma 2(c,d):

Lemma 4. *If $\mathcal{A} \models \Phi$ then $\mathcal{M} \models \Phi$. If $\mathcal{A} \models \neg\Phi$ then $\mathcal{M} \not\models \Phi$.* □

Blocks and the Partition $\Pi_{\mathcal{A}}$: We refer to the sets $B = \gamma(\sigma)$, $\sigma \in S_\Phi$, as *blocks* in $\mathcal{M}$ with respect to $\mathcal{A}$. Clearly, the collection $\Pi_{\mathcal{A}}$ of all blocks in $\mathcal{M}_{\mathcal{A}}$ is a partition of the concrete state space S. It should be noticed that for any block $B \in \Pi_{\mathcal{A}}$ either $B \subseteq Sat_{\mathcal{A}}^-(\Psi)$ or $B \cap Sat_{\mathcal{A}}^-(\Psi) = \emptyset$. The same holds for $Sat_{\mathcal{A}}^+(\Psi)$.

4   An Abstraction Refinement Model Checking Algorithm

Our algorithm (sketched in Algorithm 2) uses the abstraction refinement schema of Algorithm 1. We start with an abstract Φ-model $\mathcal{A}_0$ and will successively refine the model $\mathcal{A}_i$ until $\mathcal{A}_i \models \Phi$ or $\mathcal{A}_i \models \neg\Phi$. The output of our algorithm (sketched in Algorithm 2) is clear from Lemma 4.

---

[4] Alternatively, when we interpret a path formula $\Phi = \forall\varphi$ over O then we may use the standard semantics for CTL but switch from $\forall\Psi_1 U \Psi_2$ to the formula $\forall\Psi_1 U(\Psi_2 \vee (\Psi_1 \wedge \forall X false))$.

[5] Consider the model $\mathcal{A}$ induced by the abstraction function $\alpha(s) = \{\Psi : s \in Sat^-(\Psi)\} \cup \{\neg\Psi : s \notin Sat^+(\Psi)\}$.

[6] The reader should notice that $\mathcal{A} \not\models \Phi$ is *not* the same as $\mathcal{A} \models \neg\Phi$. $\mathcal{A} \not\models \Phi$ and $\mathcal{A} \not\models \neg\Phi$ is possible.

The initial abstract Φ-model is the abstract Φ-model $\mathcal{A}_0 = \mathcal{A}_{AP}$ that we get with the abstraction functions $\alpha_0 = \alpha_{AP} : S \to S_\Phi$ where $\alpha_{AP}(s) = \lceil L(s) \cup \{\neg a : a \in AP \setminus L(s)\} \rceil$. Here and in the following, $\lceil \sigma \rceil$ denotes the smallest element of S_Φ containing σ.[7]

The use of α_{AP} reflects the knowledge that all concrete states labeled with an atomic proposition a satisfy a while $\neg a$ holds for s if a is an atomic proposition not in $L(s)$. The status of more complex subformulas in Φ (whose truth value cannot be derived from the axioms for S_Φ) is still open. For the concrete system $\mathcal{M}$ and formula Φ depicted in the previous figure (Section 3), the initial abstract model $\mathcal{A}_0$ is as shown on below.

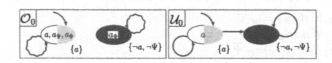

Algorithm 2 Main Procedure of the Abstraction Refinement Algorithm.

$\mathcal{A}_0 := \mathcal{A}_{AP}; \quad i := 0;$
REPEAT
    $\mathcal{A} :=$ Model_Check$(\mathcal{A}_i, \Phi)$;
    IF $\mathcal{A}_i \not\models \Phi$ and $\mathcal{A}_i \not\models \neg\Phi$ **THEN**
        FOR ALL $\forall$subformulas Ψ of Φ **DO**
            IF $Sat_{\mathcal{A}}^+(\Psi) \neq Sat_{\mathcal{A}}^-(\Psi)$ **THEN**
                $\mathcal{A} :=$ Refine$(\mathcal{A}, \Psi)$;
            ELSE
                replace Ψ by the atomic proposition a_Ψ
            FI
        OD
    FI
    $i := i + 1; \quad \mathcal{A}_i := \mathcal{A};$
UNTIL $\mathcal{A}_i \models \Phi$ or $\mathcal{A}_i \models \neg\Phi$;
IF $\mathcal{A}_i \models \Phi$ **THEN** return "yes" **ELSE** return "no" **FI**.

Model Checking the Abstract Φ-Model: Let $\mathcal{A}_i = (\alpha, \gamma, \mathcal{U}, O)$ be the current abstract Φ-model. In any iteration, we apply a standard model checker that successively treats any $\forall$subformulas Ψ of Φ for both transition systems $\mathcal{U}$ and O.

Let Ψ be a $\forall$subformula of Φ. First, we apply a standard model checking routine for $\mathcal{U}$ and the formula $\overline{\Psi}$ to calculate the satisfaction set $Sat_{\mathcal{U}}(\overline{\Psi}) = \{\sigma \in S_\Phi : \sigma \models_{\mathcal{U}} \overline{\Psi}\}$. We derive the set $NewSat(\Psi) = \{\sigma \in S_\Phi : \Psi \notin \sigma, \sigma \models_{\mathcal{U}} \overline{\Psi}\}$ of all abstract states σ where $\overline{\Psi}$ now holds while $\overline{\Psi}$ did not hold in the previous iteration. By Lemma 2, part (a), we know that Ψ holds for all concrete states $s \in \bigcup\{\gamma(\sigma) : \sigma \in NewSat(\Psi)\}$. Thus, we can improve the underapproximation $Sat_{\mathcal{A}_i}^-(\Psi)$ of $Sat_{\mathcal{M}}(\Psi)$ by adding all blocks $\gamma(\sigma)$ where $\sigma \in NewSat(\Psi)$ to $Sat_{\mathcal{A}_i}^-(\Psi)$.

---

[7] If $\sigma \subseteq 2^{cl(\Phi)}$ meets all axioms concerning propositional consistencies then σ can be extended (according to the axioms that we require for S_Φ) to a least superset $\lceil \sigma \rceil \in S_\Phi$ that contains σ. E.g. for $\Phi = \forall a \mathcal{U} b$, $\lceil \{b\} \rceil = \{b, \Phi\}$.

Second, we call a standard model checker for O and $\widetilde{\Psi}$ to obtain the set $NewSat(\neg\Psi)$ $= \{\sigma \in S_\Phi : \neg\Psi \notin \sigma,\ \sigma \not\models_O \widetilde{\Psi}\}$ of all abstract states σ where $\widetilde{\Psi}$ is not satisfied while $\widetilde{\Psi}$ did hold for σ in the previous iteration. Lemma 2, part (b), yields that none of the concrete states $s \in \bigcup\{\gamma(\sigma) : \sigma \in NewSat(\neg\Psi)\}$ satisfies Ψ. Hence, we may remove the blocks $\gamma(\sigma)$ where $\sigma \in NewSat(\neg\Psi)$ from $Sat^+_{\mathcal{A}_i}(\Psi)$ (i.e., we improve the overapproximation).

Algorithm 3 The Model-Checking-Routine Model_Check$(\mathcal{A}, \Phi)$.

Let γ be the concretization function of $\mathcal{A}$.
FOR ALL $\forall$subformulas Ψ of Φ **DO**
  calculate the set $NewSat(\Psi) = \{\,\sigma \in S_\Phi\ \sigma \models_\mathcal{U} \widetilde{\Psi}\ \text{and}\ \Psi \notin \sigma\}$;
  FOR ALL $\sigma \in NewSat(\Psi)$ **DO** $\gamma(\lceil\,\sigma \cup \{\Psi\}\,\rceil) := \gamma(\sigma) \cup \gamma(\lceil\,\sigma \cup \{\Psi\}\,\rceil)$;
  $\gamma(\sigma) := \emptyset$ **OD**;
  calculate the set $NewSat(\neg\Psi) = \{\,\sigma \in S_\Phi\ \sigma \not\models_O \widetilde{\Psi}\ \text{and}\ \neg\Psi \notin \sigma\}$;
  FOR ALL $\sigma \in NewSat(\neg\Psi)$ **DO** $\gamma(\lceil\,\sigma \cup \{\neg\Psi\}\,\rceil) := \gamma(\sigma) \cup \gamma(\lceil\,\sigma \cup \{\neg\Psi\}\,\rceil)$;
  $\gamma(\sigma) := \emptyset$ **OD**;
OD
return the abstract Φ-model induced by γ.

Algorithm 3 combines the two model checking fragments and returns a new abstract Φ-model $\mathcal{A}' = \text{Model\_Check}(\mathcal{A}_i, \Phi)$ with the abstraction function α' where $\alpha'(s)$ arises from $\alpha(s)$ by adding Ψ if $\alpha(s) \in NewSat(\Psi)$ and adding $\neg\Psi$ if $\alpha(s) \in NewSat(\neg\Psi)$.[8]

Example : For the initial model $\mathcal{A}_0$ in the running example, $NewSat(\Psi) = NewSat(\Phi) = NewSat(\neg\Psi) = \emptyset$ while $NewSat(\neg\Phi)$ consists of the black abstract state $\sigma = \{\neg a, \neg\Psi\}$. Therefore, we move $\gamma(\sigma)$ to $\sigma' = \{\neg a, \neg\Psi, \neg\Phi\}$ and obtain a model $\mathcal{A}$ with the following components $\mathcal{U}$ and O.

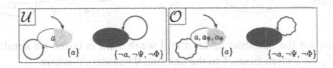

The refinement operator takes as input the abstract Φ-model $\mathcal{A}$ that the model checker returns and replaces $\mathcal{A}$ by another abstract Φ-model $\mathcal{A}_{i+1}$ where again the under- and overapproximations are improved. $\mathcal{A}_{i+1}$ is obtained by a sequence of refinement steps that successively treat any of the $\forall$subformulas of Φ. As usual, the subformulas should be considered in an order consistent with the subformula relation. Let us assume that $\mathcal{A}$ is the current abstract Φ-model to be refined according to a $\forall$subformula Ψ of Φ. If the over- and underapproximations for Ψ agree in $\mathcal{A}$, i.e., if $Sat^+_{\mathcal{A}}(\Psi) = Sat^-_{\mathcal{A}}(\Psi)$, then

---

[8] Any movement of blocks might change (improve) the current abstract Φ-model $\mathcal{A}$. Thus, any FOR-loop of Model_Check$(\mathcal{A},\Phi)$ is started with a model that might be even better than the original model $\mathcal{A}$.

we may conclude that $Sat_{\mathcal{A}}^{+}(\Psi) = Sat_{\mathcal{M}}(\Psi) = Sat_{\mathcal{A}}^{-}(\Psi)$. As the precise satisfaction set for Ψ is known there is no need for further treatment of Ψ. From this point on, Ψ (and its subformulas) can be ignored. Thus, we just replace Ψ by the atomic proposition a_{Ψ}. E.g. if $\Phi = \forall X(\forall \Diamond a \wedge b)$ and $\Psi = \forall \Diamond a$ then we replace Φ by $\forall X(a_{\Psi} \wedge b)$. Otherwise, i.e., if $Sat_{\mathcal{A}}^{-}(\Psi)$ is a proper subset of $Sat_{\mathcal{A}}^{+}(\Psi)$, we calculate $\mathcal{A}' = \text{Refine}(\mathcal{A}, \Psi)$ by:

> **CASE** Ψ **IS** $\forall X\Psi_0$ **THEN** return Refine_Forall_Next($\mathcal{A}$,Ψ);
>
> $\forall \Psi_1 U\Psi_2$ **THEN** return Refine_Forall_Until($\mathcal{A}$,Ψ);
>
> $\forall \Psi_1 \tilde{U}\Psi_2$ **THEN** return Refine_Forall_WeakUntil($\mathcal{A}$,Ψ);
>
> **ENDCASE**

First, we briefly sketch the next step operator. Let $\Psi = \forall X\Psi_0$. Clearly, all concrete states s where $Post(s) \subseteq Sat_{\mathcal{A}'}^{-}(\Psi_0)$ satisfy Ψ. Similarly, only those concrete states s where $Post(s) \subseteq Sat_{\mathcal{A}}^{+}(\Psi_0)$ are candidates to fulfill Ψ. Thus, we may replace $\mathcal{A}$ by the abstract Φ-model $\mathcal{A}'$ with

$$Sat_{\mathcal{A}'}^{+}(\Psi) = \widetilde{Pre}\left(Sat_{\mathcal{A}}^{+}(\Psi_0)\right), \quad Sat_{\mathcal{A}'}^{-}(\Psi) = \widetilde{Pre}\left(Sat_{\mathcal{A}}^{-}(\Psi_0)\right)$$

while the over- and underapproximations for $Sat_{\mathcal{M}}(\Psi')$ (where $\Psi' \neq \Psi$) do not change.
This change of $\mathcal{A}$ corresponds to a *splitting* of the blocks $B \in \Pi_{\mathcal{A}}$ into the subblocks $B \cap \tilde{P}$ and $B \setminus \tilde{P}$ where $\tilde{P} = \widetilde{Pre}(\ldots)$. The splitting is performed twice: first for $\tilde{P} = \widetilde{Pre}(Sat_{\mathcal{A}}^{-}(\Psi_0))$ which yields an "inter-

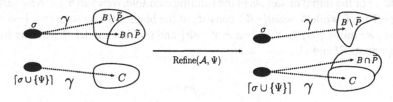

mediate" abstract Φ-model $\mathcal{A}''$; second we split the blocks in $\mathcal{A}''$ with the set $\tilde{P} = \widetilde{Pre}(Sat_{\mathcal{A}}^{+}(\Psi_0))$ In our algorithm the splitting operation does not create new abstract states. Let $B = \gamma(\sigma)$ where $\Psi, \neg\Psi \notin \sigma$ and $\tilde{P} = \widetilde{Pre}(Sat_{\mathcal{A}}^{-}(\Psi))$. We realize the splitting of B by *moving* the subblock $B \cap \tilde{P}$ from the abstract state σ to the abstract state $\lceil \sigma \cup \{\Psi\} \rceil$. Similarly, we treat the splitting according to the overapproximations.

The procedure for the handling of until and weak until is based on similar ideas. For $\Psi = \forall\Psi_1 U\Psi_2$ we switch from $\mathcal{A}$ to the abstract Φ-model $\mathcal{A}'$ where

$$Sat_{\mathcal{A}'}^{-}(\Psi) = Sat_{\mathcal{A}}^{-}(\Psi_2) \cup \left(Sat_{\mathcal{A}}^{-}(\Psi_1) \cap \widetilde{Pre}\left(Sat_{\mathcal{A}}^{-}(\Psi)\right)\right).$$

Then, we check whether the least fixed point computation of $Sat_{\mathcal{M}}(\Psi)$ via the under-approximations is finished. For this, we just need the information whether $\mathcal{A}' = \mathcal{A}$, i.e., whether at least one of the blocks has been split into proper subblocks (i.e., γ changed). If so and if Ψ_1 and Ψ_2 are propositional formulas (for which the precise satisfaction sets are already computed) then we may conclude that $Sat_{\mathcal{A}}^{-}(\Psi)$ agrees with $Sat_{\mathcal{M}}(\Psi)$. In this case, we switch from $\mathcal{A}$ to $\mathcal{A}''$ where $Sat_{\mathcal{A}''}^{+}(\Psi) = Sat_{\mathcal{A}}^{-}(\Psi)$ and replace Ψ by the atomic proposition a_{Ψ}. If the computation of $Sat_{\mathcal{M}}(\Psi)$ is not yet finished then we improve the upper bound. These ideas are presented in Algorithm 4. The treatment of weak until in the refinement step is almost the same as for until; the only difference being – as we have to calculate a greatest fixed point via overapproximations – that the roles of under- and overapproximations have to be exchanged.

Example : Let us revisit the running example. Let $\mathcal{A} = (\alpha, \gamma, \mathcal{U}, O)$ be the current abstract Φ-model the model checker has returned in the first iteration (see the picture above). Refinement starts with $\Psi = \forall\Box a$. We get $\widetilde{Pre}(Sat_{\mathcal{A}}^+(\Psi)) = \widetilde{Pre}(\gamma(\{a\})) = \gamma(\{a\}) \setminus \{s_0\}$. Thus, the grey concrete initial state s_0 is moved to $\{a, \neg\Psi\}$. All other refinement steps leave the model unchanged. Refine$(\mathcal{A}, \Phi)$ returns the model with components $\mathcal{U}_1, O_1$ as shown below.

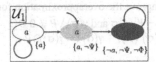 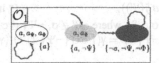

In the following model checking phase, $NewSat(\Psi) = NewSat(\Phi) = NewSat(\neg\Psi) = \emptyset$. $NewSat(\neg\Phi)$ consists of the grey abstract state $\sigma = \{a, \neg\Psi\}$. Therefore, we move $\gamma(\sigma) = \{s_0\}$ to the abstract state $\sigma' = \{a, \neg\Psi, \neg\Phi\}$. We obtain an abstract Φ-model $\mathcal{A}_2$ where the abstract interpretation of the concrete initial state s_0 is $\alpha_2(s_0) = \sigma'$. As σ' contains $\neg\Phi$, the condition $\mathcal{A}_2 \models \neg\Phi$ in the repeat-loop of Algorithm 2 holds (see Def. 3). Hence, Algorithm 2 terminates with the correct answer "no". $\Box$

Remark : There is no need for an explicit treatment of the *boolean connectives* $\vee$ and $\wedge$ in the model checking or refinement step. For instance, if $\Psi = \Psi_1 \vee \Psi_2$ is a subformula of Φ then improving the approximations for the sets $Sat_{\mathcal{M}}(\Psi_1)$ automatically yields an improvement for the underapproximation for $Sat_{\mathcal{M}}(\Psi)$. "Moving" a block B from an abstract state σ to the abstract state $\sigma' = \lceil \sigma \cup \{\Psi_1\} \rceil$ has the side effect that B is added to both $Sat_{\mathcal{A}}^-(\Psi_1)$ and $Sat_{\mathcal{A}}^-(\Psi)$. This is due to the axioms, we require for the elements in S_Φ. The corresponding observation holds for the overapproximations $Sat_{\mathcal{A}}^+(\cdot)$. $\Box$

Remark: The *atomic propositions* a_Ψ play a crucial role in both the model checking and the refinement procedure. The labelings $L_{\mathcal{U}}$ and L_O cover the information that might got lost due to the transition relations $\to_\alpha$ and $\leadsto_\alpha$. In the refinement phase, they are necessary to detect when the computation of a least or greatest fixed point is finished. $\Box$

Theorem 1. [Partial Correctness] *If Algorithm 2 terminates with the answer "yes" then $\mathcal{M} \models \Phi$. If Algorithm 2 terminates with the answer "no" then $\mathcal{M} \not\models \Phi$.* $\Box$

Because of the similarities with stable partitioning algorithms for calculating the (bi-) simulation equivalence classes [37, 7, 32, 24] it is not surprising that our algorithm terminates provided that the (bi-)simulation quotient space of $\mathcal{M}$ is finite.

Theorem 2. [Termination] *If the concrete model $\mathcal{M}$ has a finite simulation or bisimulation quotient then Algorithm 2 terminates.*

Algorithm 4 Refine_Forall_Until($\mathcal{A}, \Psi$) where $\Psi = \forall \Psi_1 U \Psi_2$.

Let γ be the concretization function of $\mathcal{A}$.

$\tilde{P} := \widetilde{Pre}(Sat_{\mathcal{A}}^-(\Psi))$; changed:= false;   (* improve the underapproximation for $Sat_{\mathcal{M}}(\Psi)$ *)

FOR ALL $\sigma \in S_\Phi$ where $\Psi \not\in \sigma$, $\Psi_1 \in \sigma$ and $\gamma(\sigma) \cap \tilde{P} \neq \emptyset$ **DO**

   $\gamma(\lceil \sigma \cup \{\Psi\} \rceil) := (\gamma(\sigma) \cap \tilde{P}) \cup \gamma(\lceil \sigma \cup \{\Psi\} \rceil)$; $\gamma(\sigma) := \gamma(\sigma) \setminus \tilde{P}$;   changed:= true;

OD;

IF not changed and Ψ_1, Ψ_2 are propositional formulas **THEN**

                     (* the least fixed point computation is finished; put $Sat_{\mathcal{A}}^+(\Psi) := Sat_{\mathcal{A}}^-(\Psi)$ *)

   replace Ψ by the atomic proposition a_Ψ;

   FOR ALL $\sigma \in S_\Phi$ with $\Psi \not\in \sigma$ and $\neg\Psi \not\in \sigma$ **DO**

      $\gamma(\lceil \sigma \cup \{\neg\Psi\} \rceil) := \gamma(\lceil \sigma \cup \{\neg\Psi\} \rceil) \cup \gamma(\sigma)$; $\gamma(\sigma) := \emptyset$;

   OD

ELSE

   $\tilde{P} := \widetilde{Pre}(Sat_{\mathcal{A}}^+(\Psi))$;   (* improve the overapproximation for $Sat_{\mathcal{M}}(\Psi)$ *)

   FOR ALL $\sigma \in S_\Phi$ where $\neg\Psi \not\in \sigma$, $\neg\Psi_1 \not\in \sigma$, $\neg\Psi_2 \in \sigma$ and $\gamma(\sigma) \setminus \tilde{P} \neq \emptyset$ **DO**

      $\gamma(\lceil \sigma \cup \{\neg\Psi\} \rceil) := \gamma(\lceil \sigma \cup \{\neg\Psi\} \rceil) \cup (\gamma(\sigma) \setminus \tilde{P})$; $\gamma(\sigma) := \gamma(\sigma) \cap \tilde{P}$

   OD

FI

Return the abstract Φ-model with concretization function γ.

Full *CTL*: Our algorithm can be extended to treat full *CTL*. The major difference is the handling of existential quantification which requires the use of the transition relation $\rightsquigarrow_\alpha$ when calculating the underapproximations while for the overapproximations we use the transition relation $\rightarrow_\alpha$. Given an abstract Φ-model $\mathcal{A} = (\alpha, \gamma, \mathcal{U}, O)$, we work (as before) with two satisfaction relations $\models_{\mathcal{U}}$ and $\models_O$. E.g. $\sigma \models_{\mathcal{U}} \exists \varphi$ iff there exists a path π in O (i.e., a path built from transitions w.r.t. $\rightsquigarrow_\alpha$) that starts in σ and $\pi \models_{\mathcal{U}} \varphi$. In the refinement phase, we use the predecessor predicate $Pre(\cdot)$ rather than $\widetilde{Pre}(\cdot)$. For instance, to improve the underapproximation for a subformula $\Psi = \exists \Diamond \Psi_0$ we split any block $B = \gamma(\sigma)$ (where $\Psi \not\in \sigma$) into $B \cap Pre(Sat_{\mathcal{A}}^-(\Psi))$ and $B \setminus Pre(Sat_{\mathcal{A}}^-(\Psi))$. Again, the partial correctness relies on the results of [19]. Termination can be guaranteed for any concrete system with a finite bisimulation quotient.

5 Concluding Remarks

We have presented a general abstraction refinement algorithm for model checking large or infinite transition systems against $\forall CTL$ (or *CTL*) formulas. Partial correctness can be established for any concrete transition system $\mathcal{M}$ which (if it is finite) could be represented by a BDD or might be a program with variables of an infinite type. Termination can be guaranteed for all concrete systems with a finite bisimulation quotient. For $\forall CTL$, our algorithm terminates also if only the simulation quotient is finite.

Clearly, the feasability of our algorithm crucially depends on the representation of the concrete system for which we have to extract the $\widetilde{Pre}$-information. In principle, our methodology can be combined with several fully or semi-automatic techniques that provide an abstract model. For large but finite concrete systems, we suggest a symbolic representation of the transition relation in $\mathcal{M}$ and the blocks in $\Pi_{\mathcal{A}}$ with BDDs. We just started to implement our method with a BDD representation for the concrete model $\mathcal{M}$ but, unfortunately, cannot yet report on experimental results. It might be interesting to see whether (and how) the abstraction techniques for BDDs (e.g. [15,31]) can be combined with our algorithm. To reason about infinite systems, the fully automatic approach of [34] seems to fit nicely in our framework as it works with a Pre-operator similar to the one that we use.

One of the further directions we intend to investigate is the study of real time systems or other types of transition systems that are known to have finite (bi-)simulation quotients [2, 24]. In principle, our technique should be applicable to establish qualitative properties of timed automata (expressed in CTL). It would be interesting to see whether our method can be modified to handle quantitative properties (e.g. specified in $TCTL$).

References

[1] P. Abdulla, A. Annichini, S. Bensalem, A. Boujjani, P. Habermehl, Y. Lakhnech. Verification of infinite state systems by combining abstraction and reachability analysis. In Proc. CAV'99, LNCS 1633, 1999.

[2] R. Alur, D. Dill. A theory of timed automata. *Theoretical Computer Science*, 126:183–235, 1994.

[3] A. Aziz, T. R. Shiple, V. Singhal, A. L. Sangiovanni-Vincentelli. Formula-dependent equivalence for compositional CTL model checking. Proc. CAV'94, LNCS 818, pp. 324–337, 1994.

[4] A. Biere, A. Cimatti, E. Clarke, M. Fujita, Y. Zhu. Symbolic model checking using SAT procedures instead of BDDs. In *Design Automation Conference*, pp.317–320, 1999.

[5] M. Browne, E. Clarke, O. Grumberg. Characterizing finite Kripke structures in Propositional Temporal Logic. *Theoretical Computer Science*, 59(1-2):115–131, July 1988.

[6] J. Burch, E. Clarke, K. McMillan, D. Dill, L. Hwang. Symbolic model checking 10^{20} states and beyond. *Information and Computation*, 1992.

[7] A. Bouajjani, Jean-Claude Fernandez, N. Halbwachs. Minimal model generation. Proc. CAV'90, LNCS 531, pp. 197–203, 1990.

[8] D. Bustan, O. Grumberg. Simulation based minimization. Computing Science Reports CS-2000-04, Computer Science Department, Technion, Haifa 32000, Israel, 2000.

[9] S. Bensalem, Y. Lakhnech, S. Owre. Computing abstractions of infinite state systems compositionally and automatically. LNCS 1427, Proc. CAV'98, pp. 319–331, 1998.

[10] F. Balarin, A. Sangiovanni-Vincentelli. An iterative approach to language containment. Proc. CAV'93, LNCS 697, pp. 29-40, 1993.

[11] P. Cousot, R. Cousot. Abstract interpretation a unified lattice model for static analysis of programs by construction or approximation of fixpoints. In Proc. POPL'77, pp. 238-252, 1977.

[12] E. Clarke, O. Grumberg, S. Jha, Y. Lu, H. Veith. Counterexample–guided abstraction refinement. LNCS 1855, Proc. CAV'00, pp. 154-169, 2000.

[13] E. Clarke, O. Grumberg, D. Long. Model checking and abstraction. *ACM Transactions on Programming Languages and Systems*, 16(5):1512–1542, September 1994.

[14] E. Clarke, O. Grumberg, D. Peled. *Model Checking*. MIT Press, 2000.

[15] E. Clarke, S. Jha, Y. Lu, D. Wang. Abstract BDDs: a technique for using abstraction in model checking. In Proc. Correct Hardware Design and Verification Methods, LNCS 1703, pp. 172–186, 1999.

[16] D. Dams. *Abstract Interpretation and Partition Refinement for Model Checking*. PhD thesis, Technische Universiteit Einhoven, 1996.

[17] J. Dingel, T. Filkorn. Model checking for infinite state systems using data abstraction, assumption commitment style reasoning and theorem proving. In Proc. CAV'95, LNCS 939, pp. 54–69, 1995.

[18] D. Dams, R. Gerth, O. Grumberg. Generation of reduced models for checking fragments of CTL. In Proc. CAV'93, LNCS 697, pp. 479–490, 1993.

[19] D. Dams, R. Gerth, O. Grumberg. Abstract interpretation of reactive systems. *ACM Transactions on Programming Languages and Systems*, 19(2):253–291, March 1997.

[20] E. A. Emerson. Temporal and modal logic. In Jan van Leeuwen, editor, *Handbook of Theoretical Computer Science, Volume B: Formal Models and Semantics*, pp. 995–1072. Elsevier Science Publishers, Amsterdam, The Netherlands, 1990.

[21] O. Grumberg, D. Long. Model checking and modular verification. *ACM Transactions on Programming Languages and Systems*, 16(3):843–871, 1994.

[22] P. Godefroid. Partial order methods for the verification of concurrent systems: An approach to the state explosion problem (Ph.D.Thesis, University of Liege) LNCS 1032, 1996.

[23] S. Graf, H. Saidi. Construction of abstract state graphs with PVS. In Proc. CAV'97, LNCS 1254, pp 72–83, 1997.

[24] M. Henzinger, T. Henzinger, P. Kopke. Computing simulations on finite and infinite graphs. In Proc. FOCS'95, pp. 453–462, IEEE Computer Society Press. 1995.

[25] P. Kelb, D. Dams, R. Gerth. Efficient symbolic model checking of the full μ-calculus using compositional abstractions. Computing Science Reports 95/31, Eindhoven University of Technology, 1995.

[26] R. Kurshan. *Computer-aided Verification of Coordinating Processes: The Automata-Theoretic Approach*. Princeton University Press, 1994.

[27] C. Loiseaux, S. Graf, J. Sifakis, A. Bouajjani, S. Bensalem. Property preserving abstractions for the verification of concurrent systems. *Formal Methods in System Design*, 6(1):11–44, January 1995.

[28] J. Lind-Nielsen, H. Andersen. Stepwise CTL model checking of State/Event systems. In Proc. CAV'99, LNCS 1633, pp. 316–327, 1999.

[29] D. Long. *Model Checking, Abstraction and Compositional Verification*. PhD thesis, Carnegie Mellon University, 1993.

[30] O. Lichtenstein and A. Pnueli. Checking that finite state concurrent programs satisfy their linear specification. In *Proceedings of the Twelfth Annual ACM Symposium on Principles of Programming Languages*, pages 97–107, New York, January 1985. ACM.

[31] W. Lee, A. Pardo, J.-Y. Jang, G. Hachtel, F. Somenzi. Tearing based automatic abstraction for ctl model checking. In *Proc. ICCAD'96*, pp. 76–81, 1996.

[32] D. Lee, M. Yannakakis. Online minimization of transition systems. In Proc. STOC'92, pp. 264–274, 1992. ACM Press.

[33] K. McMillan. *Symbolic Model Checking*. Kluwer Academic Publishers, 1993.

[34] K. Namjoshi, R. Kurshan. Syntactic program transformation for automatic abstraction. In Proc. CAV'2000, LNCS 1855, pp. 435–449, 2000.

[35] D. Peled. All from one, one from all: on model checking using representatives. In Proc. CAV'93, LNCS 697, pp. 409–423, 1993.

[36] A. Pardo, G. Hachtel. Automatic abstraction techniques for propositional μ-calculus model checking. In Proc. CAV'97, LNCS 1254, pp. 12–23, 1997.

[37] R. Paige, R. Tarjan. Three partition refinement algorithms. *SIAM Journal on Computing*, 16(6):973–989, 1987.

[38] H. Saidi, N. Shankar. Abstract and model check while you prove. In Proc. CAV'99, LNCS 1633, pp 443–454, 1999.

[39] H. B. Sipma, T. E. Uribe, Z Manna. Deductive Model Checking. In Proc. CAV'96, LNCS 1102, pp. 208–219, 1996

[40] A. Valmari. State of the art report: Stubborn sets. *Petri-Net Newsletters*, 46:6–14, 1994.

Verifying Network Protocol Implementations by Symbolic Refinement Checking

Rajeev Alur and Bow-Yaw Wang

Department of Computer and Information Science
University of Pennsylvania
{alur,bywang}@cis.upenn.edu
http://www.cis.upenn.edu/~{alur,bywang}

Abstract. We consider the problem of establishing consistency of code implementing a network protocol with respect to the documentation as a standard RFC. The problem is formulated as a refinement checking between two models, the implementation extracted from code and the specification extracted from RFC. After simplifications based on assume-guarantee reasoning, and automatic construction of witness modules to deal with the hidden specification state, the refinement checking problem reduces to checking transition invariants. The methodology is illustrated on two case-studies involving popular network protocols, namely, PPP (point-to-point protocol for establishing connections remotely) and DHCP (dynamic-host-configuration-protocol for configuration management in mobile networks). We also present a symbolic implementation of a reduction scheme based on compressing internal transitions in a hierarchical manner, and demonstrate the resulting savings for refinement checking in terms of memory size.

1 Introduction

Network protocols have been a popular domain of application for model checkers for over a decade (see, for instance, [15, 10]). A typical application involves checking temporal requirements, such as absence of deadlocks and eventual transmission, of a model of a network protocol, such as TCP, extracted from a textbook description or a standard documentation such as a network RFC (Request for Comments) document. While this approach is effective in detecting logical errors in a protocol design, there is still a need to formally analyze the actual implementation of the protocol standard to reveal implementation errors. While analyzing the code implementing a protocol, the standard specification, typically available as a network RFC, can be viewed as the abstract model. Since the standard provides implementation guidelines for different vendors on different platforms, analysis tools to detect inconsistencies with respect to the standard can greatly enhance the benefits of standardization.

The problem of verifying a protocol implementation with respect to its standardized documentation can naturally be formulated as *refinement checking*. The implementation model I is extracted from the code and the specification

G. Berry, H. Comon, and A. Finkel (Eds.): CAV 2001, LNCS 2102, pp. 169–181, 2001.
© Springer-Verlag Berlin Heidelberg 2001

model S is extracted from the RFC document. We wish to verify that $I \preceq S$ holds, where the notion $\preceq$ of refinement is based on language inclusion. A recent promising approach to *automated* refinement checking combines assume-guarantee reasoning with search algorithms [19, 14, 4], and has been successfully applied to synchronous hardware designs such as pipelined processors [20] and a VGI chip [13].

To establish the refinement, we employ the following three-step methodology (advocated, for instance in [4]). First, the refinement obligation is used to generate simpler subgoals by applying *assume guarantee reasoning* [23, 2, 5, 12, 19]. This reduces the verification of a composition of implementation components to individual components, but verifies an individual component only in the context of the specifications of the other components. Second concerns verification of a subgoal $I \preceq S$, when S has private variables. The classical approach is to require the user to provide a definition of the private variables of the specification in terms of the implementation variables (this basic idea is needed even for manual proofs, and comes in various disguises such as refinement maps [1], homomorphisms [17], forward-simulation maps [18], and witness modules [14, 19]). Consequently, the refinement check $I \preceq S$ reduces to $I \| W \preceq S$, where W is the user-supplied witness for private variables of S. As a heuristic for choosing W automatically, we had proposed a simple construction that transforms S to $Eager(S)$, which is like S, but takes a stuttering step only when all other choices are disabled [4]. Once a proper witness is chosen, the third and final step requires establishing that every reachable transition of the implementation has a matching transition of the specification, and can be done by an algorithmic state-space analysis for checking transition invariants.

For performing the reachability analysis required for verifying transition invariants efficiently, we propose an optimization of the symbolic search. The proposed algorithm is an adaptation of a corresponding enumerative scheme based on compressing unobservable transitions in a hierarchical manner [6]. The basic idea is to describe the implementation I in a hierarchical manner so that I is a tree whose leaves are atomic processes, and internal nodes compose their children and hide as many variables as possible. This suggests a natural optimization: while computing the successors of a state corresponding to the execution of a process, apply the transition relation repeatedly until a shared variable is accessed. A more effective strategy is to apply the reduction in a recursive manner exploiting the hierarchical structure. In this paper, we show how this hierarchical scheme can be implemented symbolically, and establish significant reductions in space and time requirements.

Our methodology for refinement checking is implemented in the model checker MOCHA [3]. Our first case study involves verifying part of the RFC specification of Point-to-Point Protocol (PPP) widely used to transmit multi-protocol datagrams [22]. The implementation ppp version 2.4.0 is an open-source package included in various Linux distributions. We extract the model ppp of the specification and the model pppd of the implementation manually. To establish the refinement, we need to assume that the communication partner behaves like the specification model, thus, employ assume-guarantee reasoning. The specification has many private variables, and we use the "eager witness" construction to reduce the problem to transition invariant check. Our analysis reveals an inconsistency between the C-code and the RFC document. The second case study concerns the Dynamic Host Configuration Protocol (DHCP) that provides a standard mechanism to obtain configuration parameters. We analyze the dhcp package version 2.0 patch level 5, the standard implementation distributed by Internet Software Consortium, with respect to its specification RFC 2131 [11].

2 Refinement Checking

In this section, we summarize the definition of processes, refinement relation over processes, and the methodology for refinement checking. The details can be found in [4].

The process model is a special class of *reactive modules* [5] that corresponds to asynchronous processes communicating via read-shared write-exclusive variables. A process is defined by the set of its variables, along with the constraints for initializing and updating variables. The variables of a process P are partitioned into three classes: *private* variables that cannot be read nor written by other processes, *interface* variables that are written only by P, but can be read by other processes, and *external* variables that can only be read by P, and written by other processes. Thus, interface and external variables are used for communication, and are called *observable* variables. The process controls its private and interface variables, and the environment controls the external variables. The separation between private and observable variables is essential to applying our optimization algorithm based on compressing internal transitions. The state space of the process is the set of possible valuations to all its variables. A state is also partitioned into different components as the variables are, for instance, controlled state and external state. The initial predicate specifies initial controlled states, and the transition predicate specifies how the controlled state is changed according to the current state.

In the following discussion, we write $B[X]$ for the set of predicates over variables in X. For the set of variables X, we write X' for the corresponding variables denoting updated values after executing a transition. Furthermore, for sets of variables $X = \{x_i\}$ and $Y = \{y_i\}$ with the same cardinality, $X = Y$ denotes $\wedge_i x_i = y_i$. For any subset Z of variables X and $P \in B[X]$, $\exists Z.P$ and $\forall Z.P$ stand for the existential and universal quantification over the variables in Z.

Definition 1. *A process P is a tuple (X, I, T) where*

- $X = (X_p, X_i, X_e)$ *is the (typed) variable declaration. X_p, X_i, X_e represent the sets of private variables, interface variables and external variables respectively. We define $X_c = X_p \cup X_i$ to be the controlled variables, and $X_o = X_i \cup X_e$ to be the observable variables;*
- *Given a set X of typed variables, a state over X is an assignment of variables to their values. We define Q_c to be the set of controlled states over X_c, Q_e*

to be the set of external states *over* X_e, $Q = Q_c \times Q_e$ *to be the set of states, and* Q_o *to be the set of* observable states *over* X_o;
- $I \in \mathcal{B}[X_c]$ *is the* initial predicate;
- $T \in \mathcal{B}[X, X_c']$ *is the* transition predicate *with the property (called* asynchronous property) *that* $(X_c' = X_c) \Rightarrow T$.

∎

The asynchronous property says that a process may idle at any step, and thus, the speeds of the process and its environment are independent. In order to support structured descriptions, we would like to build complex processes from simple ones. Three constructs, hide H in P, $P\|P'$ and $P[X := Y]$ for building new processes are defined. The hiding operator makes interface variables inaccessible to other processes, and its judicious use allows more transitions to be considered internal. The parallel composition operator allows to combine two processes into a single one. The composition is defined only when the controlled variables of the two processes are disjoint. The transition predicate of $P\|Q$ is thus the conjunction of transition predicates of P and Q. The renaming operator $P[X := Y]$ substitutes variables X in P by Y.

For a process P, the sets of its executions and observable traces are defined in the standard way. Given two processes P and Q, we say P *refines* Q, written $P \preceq Q$, if each observable trace of P is an observable trace of Q. Checking refinement relation is computationally hard, and we simplify the problem in two ways. First, our notion of refinement supports an *assume guarantee* principle which asserts that it suffices to establish separately $P_1\|Q_2 \preceq Q_1$ and $Q_1\|P_2 \preceq Q_2$ in order to prove $P_1\|P_2 \preceq Q_1\|Q_2$. This principle, similar in spirit to many previous proposals [23, 2, 5, 12, 19], is used to reduce the verification of a composition of implementation components to individual components, but verifies an individual component only in the context of the specifications of the other components. The second technique reduces checking language inclusion to verifying transition invariants. If the specification has no private variables, an observable implementation state corresponds to at most one state in the specification. The refinement check then corresponds to verifying that every initial state of P has a corresponding initial state of Q, and every reachable transition of P has a corresponding transition in Q. When Q has private variables, then the correspondence between implementation states and specification states should be provided by the user in order to make the checking feasible. The user needs to provide a witness W that assigns suitable values to the private variables of the specification in terms of implementation variables. It can be shown that $P \preceq Q$ follows from establishing $P\|W \preceq Q$. In our setting of asynchronous processes, it turns out that the witness W itself should not be asynchronous (that is, for asynchronous W, $P\|W \preceq Q$ typically does not hold). This implies that the standard trick of choosing the witness to be the subprocess Q^p of Q that updates its private variables, used in many of the case studies reported in [20, 13], does not work in the asynchronous setting. As a heuristic for choosing W automatically, we have proposed a construction that transforms Q^p to $Eager(Q^p)$, which is similar to the subprocess Q^p, but takes a stuttering step only when all other choices are disabled [4]. This construction is syntactically simple, and as our case studies demonstrate, turns out to be an effective way of automating witness construction. The complexity of the resulting check is proportional to the product of P and Q^p.

3   Symbolic Search with Hierarchical Reduction

In this section, we consider the problem of verifying $P \preceq Q$ when Q does not have any private variables. In this case, if one can check that all reachable P transitions have corresponding transitions in Q, then $P \preceq Q$ holds. Since all variables of Q appear in P, the corresponding transitions can be obtained by projection, and the problem can be solved by an appropriately modified reachability analysis. The core routine is $Next$: given a process P and a set R of its states, $Next(P, R)$ returns the set T of transitions of P starting in R along with the set S of successors of R. There is, however, a practical problem if one intends to implement the successor function $Next$ with existing BDD packages. Since $Next$ needs to return the set of transitions, early quantification, an essential technique for image computation, is less effective. In [6], we have reported a heuristic to improve the enumerative search algorithm. In this section, we propose a symbolic algorithm to implement it.

We use NEXT P represent the process obtained by merging "invisible" transitions of P where invisibility is defined to be both write-invisible (not writing to interface variables) and read-invisible (not reading from external variables). Let $T \in \mathcal{B}[X_p, X_i, X_o, X_p', X_i']$ be a transition predicate (the primed variables denote the updated values). The write-invisible transitions are captured by the predicate $T \wedge (X_i = X_i')$ (the second clause says that the interface variables stay unchanged) and read-invisible transitions correspond to $\forall X_e.T$ (the quantification ensures that the transition is not dependent on external variables). Thus, the *invisible* component T_i of T is $T \wedge (X_i = X_i') \wedge \forall X_e.T$, and the visible component T_v is $T \wedge \neg T_i$. Define the concatenation $T_1 \bowtie T_2$ of two transition predicates $T_1, T_2 \in \mathcal{B}[X, X']$ to be $\exists Z.T_1[X' \leftarrow Z] \wedge T_2[X \leftarrow Z]$.

Definition 2. *Let* $P = ((X_p, X_i, X_o), I, T)$ *be a process. Define* NEXT $P = ((X_p, X_i, X_o), I, T')$ *with* $T' = (X_c = X_c') \vee (\mu S.T_v \vee (T_i \bowtie S))$. ∎

The transition predicate of NEXT P is equivalent to $(X = X') \vee T_v^P \vee (T_i^P \bowtie T_v^P) \vee (T_i^P \bowtie T_i^P \bowtie T_v^P) \vee \cdots$. In other words, a transition in NEXT P is either a stuttering transition, or zero or more invisible transitions followed by a visible transition of P.

It can be shown that NEXT P and P are equivalent (modulo stuttering). Furthermore, the NEXT operator is congruent [4]. This allows us to apply the NEXT operator to every subprocess of a process constructed by parallel composition, hiding and instantiation. We proceed to describe a symbolic algorithm for state-space analysis of a process expression with nested applications of NEXT, without precomputing the transition relations of the subprocesses (such a precomputation would require an expensive transitive closure computation).

$\underline{\text{funct}}\ Next(M, R) \equiv$
$\quad \underline{\text{if}}\ M \equiv P$
$\quad \underline{\text{then}}\ helper := \lambda Q.\underline{\text{let}}\ Q_c := Q[X_c^P]$
$\qquad\qquad\qquad\qquad T_c := T_P \wedge Q_c$
$\qquad\qquad\qquad\qquad R' := (\exists X_c^P.T_P \wedge Q)[X_c'^P \leftarrow X_c^P]$
$\qquad\qquad\qquad\qquad R'' := R' \setminus cache$
$\qquad\qquad\qquad\qquad cache := cache \vee R'$
$\qquad\qquad\qquad\quad \underline{\text{in}}\ (T_c, R'')$
$\qquad\qquad \underline{\text{return}}\ NextAuc(P, helper, R)$
$\quad \underline{\text{elsif}}\ M \equiv M_1 \| M_2$
$\qquad \underline{\text{then}}\ (T_1, N_1) := Next(M_1, R)$
$\qquad\qquad\quad (T_2, N_2) := Next(M_2, R)$
$\qquad\qquad\quad S_1 = (\exists X_c^{M_2}.R) \wedge (X_c'^{M_1} = X_c^{M_1})$
$\qquad\qquad\quad S_2 = (\exists X_c^{M_1}.R) \wedge (X_c'^{M_2} = X_c^{M_2})$
$\qquad\qquad\quad T := (T_1 \wedge S_2) \vee (T_2 \wedge S_1) \vee (T_1 \wedge T_2)$
$\qquad\qquad\quad N' := (\exists X_c^M.R \wedge T_1 \wedge T_2)[X_c'^M \leftarrow X_c^M]$
$\qquad\qquad\quad N := N_1 \vee N_2 \vee N'$
$\qquad\qquad \underline{\text{return}}\ (T, N)$
$\quad \underline{\text{elsif}}\ M \equiv hideY inM_1$
$\qquad \underline{\text{then}}\ helper := \lambda Q.Next(M_1, Q)$
$\qquad\qquad \underline{\text{return}}\ NextAuc(M, helper, R)$
$\quad \underline{\text{fi}}$

Fig. 1. Algorithm *Next*.

The algorithm *Next* (figure 1) computes the visible transitions of a process M from the current states R by proceeding according to the structure of M. For each case, a tuple of transitions and a set of new states is returned. Each atomic process takes its turn to update its controlled variables as the algorithm traverses the expression. Whenever a state is reached by the current exploration, we check if it has been visited. If not, the state is put in the newly reached states. The transition compression of subprocesses is performed by applying NEXT implicitly in cases of atomic processes and hiding. This is achieved by invoking the function *NextAuc* to merge invisible transitions in these two cases. For parallel composition $M_1 \| M_2$, it is not necessary to do so since variable visibility remains the same. Therefore, the algorithm simply invokes itself recursively to obtain transitions T_1 and T_2 corresponding to subprocesses M_1 and M_2 respectively, and computes the composed transitions for the following three cases: (1) M_1 takes a transition in T_1 and M_2 stutters; (2) M_2 takes a transition in T_2 and M_1 stutters; and (3) both M_1 and M_2 take transitions in T_1 and T_2 respectively.

For atomic processes and the case of hiding, the *helper* function is given to *NextAuc* as a parameter. It returns transitions and new states of the subprocess before NEXT is applied. For hiding, the *helper* function simply returns the transitions and new states of M_1, and the algorithm *Next* lets *NextAuc* do the transition compression. For an atomic process, the *helper* function computes

comment: *helper* returns a tuple of lower-level transitions
comment: and newly reached states from the given set of states.
funct $NextAuc(M, helper, R) \equiv$
$\quad N := false$
$\quad T := false$
$\quad I := true$
$\quad Q := R$
$\quad$ do
$\quad\quad (T', N') := helper(Q)$
$\quad\quad T_i' := (T' \wedge (X_c'^M = X_c^M)) \wedge (\forall X_e^M . T')$
$\quad\quad T := (I \bowtie T') \vee T$
$\quad\quad I := I \bowtie T_i'$
$\quad\quad Q' := (\exists X_c^M . Q \wedge T_i')[X_c'^M \leftarrow X_c^M]$
$\quad\quad Q := N' \wedge Q'$
$\quad\quad N := N \vee (N' \setminus Q)$
$\quad$ while $Q \neq \emptyset$
$\quad$ return (T, N)

Fig. 2. Algorithm *NextAuc*.

transitions T_c and new states R''. It then returns the transitions and newly reached states after updating cache.

Figure 2 shows the *NextAuc* algorithm for invisible transition compression. The naive fixed-point computation hinted in definition 2 is expensive and unnecessary. Rather than computing fixed points, our algorithm generates the transition predicate of NEXT P on the fly by considering only the current states. The idea is to compute $T_i \bowtie \cdots \bowtie T_i \bowtie T_v$ incrementally until all visible transitions reachable from the current states are generated. Several variables are kept by the algorithm to perform the task. N accumulates newly reached states in each iteration, T consists of compressed transitions, I is the concatenation of consecutive invisible transitions and Q is the states reached by invisible transitions in the current iteration.

The algorithm *NextAuc* first computes the invisible component T_i' in T'. The new transitions T' are added to T after concatenated with previous invisible transitions. The concatenated invisible transition I is updated by appending T_i'. To compute states for the next iteration, the set Q' of all reached states by current invisible transitions is generated. The new states Q reached by invisible transitions are the intersection of the newly reached states N' and invisible states Q'. Finally, the visible states of N' are put into the new visible states N. The main correctness argument about the algorithm is summarized by:

Theorem 1. *Let M be a process, $R \in \mathcal{B}[X^M]$ and suppose $Next(M, R)$ returns (T, N). Then the predicate $T \wedge R$ captures the transitions of NEXT M starting in R, and N contains all successor states of R that are not previously visited.* ∎

Implementation. The symbolic algorithm for refinement checking is implemented in the model checker MOCHA [3]. The implementation is in Java using

Event	Action
Up : lower layer is Up	tlu : This-Layer-Up
Down : lower layer is Down	tld : This-Layer-Down
Open : administrative Open	tls : This-Layer-Started
Close : administrative Close	tlf : This-Layer-Finished
TO⁺ : Timeout with counter > 0	irc : Initialize-Restart-Count
TO⁻ : Timeout with counter expired	zrc = Zero-Restart-Count
RCR⁺ : Receive-Configure-Request (Good)	scr : Send-Configure-Request
RCR⁻ : Receive-Configure-Request (Bad)	
RCA : Receive-Configure-Ack	sca = Send-Configure-Ack
RCN : Receive-Configure-Nak/Rej	scn = Send-Configure-Nak/Rej
RTR : Receive-Terminate-Request	str = Send-Terminate-Request
RTA : Receive-Terminate-Ack	sta = Send-Terminate-Ack

TO^+ : Timeout with counter > 0, TO^- : Timeout with counter expired, RCR^+, RCR^-.

	0	1	2	3	4	5	6	7	8	9
	Initial	Starting	Closed	Stopped	Closing	Stopping	Req-Sent	Ack-Rcvd	Ack-Sent	Opened
Up	2	irc,scr/6								
Down			0	tls/1	0	1	1	1	1	tld/1
Open	tls/1	1	irc,scr/6	3	5	5	6	7	8	9
Close	0	tlf/0	2	2	4	4	irc,str/4	irc,str/4	irc,str/4	tld,irc,str/4
TO⁺					str/4	str/5	scr/6	scr/6	scr/8	
TO⁻					tlf/2	tlf/3	tlf/3	tlf/3	tlf/3	
RCR⁺			sta/2	irc,scr,sca/8	4	5	sca/8	sca,tlu/9	sca/8	tld,scr,sca/8
RCR⁻			sta/2	irc,scr,scn/6	4	5	scn/6	scn/7	scn/6	tld,scr,scn/6
RCA			sta/2	sta/3	4	5	irc/7	scr/6	irc,tlu/9	tld,scr/6
RCN			sta/2	sta/3	4	5	irc,scr/6	scr/6	irc,scr/8	tld,scr/6
RTR			sta/2	sta/3	sta/4	sta/5	sta/6	sta/6	sta/6	tld,zrc,sta/5
RTA			2	3	tlf/2	tlf/3	6	6	8	tld,scr/6

Fig. 3. The PPP Option Negotiation Automaton.

the BDD-packages from VIS [7]. The transition predicate is maintained in a conjunctive form. The details are omitted here due to lack of space.

4   Verification of Network Protocols

4.1   Point-to-Point Protocol

Point-to-Point Protocol (PPP) is designed to transmit multi-protocol datagrams for point-to-point communications [22]. To establish the connection, each end sends Link-layer Control Protocol (LCP) packets to configure and test the data link. The authentication may be followed after the link is established. Then PPP sends Network Control Protocol packets to choose and configure network-layer protocols. The link will be disconnected if explicit LCP or NCP packets close it, or certain external events occur (for instance, modem is turned off). In this case study, we focus on checking an implementation of the option negotiation automaton (section 4 in [22]) for link establishment.

Protocol RFC Specification. Figure 3 reproduces the transition table of the automaton as shown in section 4.1 of the specification. As one can see from the table, events and actions are denoted by symbols. For each entry in the table, it shows the actions and the new state of the automaton. If there are multiple actions to be performed in a state, they are executed in an arbitrary order.

```
        static void
        fsm_rtermack(f)
            fsm *f;
    {
        switch (f->state) {
        /* other cases here */
        case OPENED:
            if (f->callbacks->down)
                (*f->callbacks->down)(f);    /* Inform upper layers */
            fsm_sconfreq(f, 0);
            break;
        }
    }
```

Fig. 4. Code-style in fsm.c.

When initiating a PPP connection, the host first sends a configuration request packet (scr) to its peer and waits for the acknowledgment (RCA or RCN). The peer responds by checking the options sent in the request. If the options are acceptable, the peer sends a positive acknowledgment (sca). Otherwise, a negative acknowledgment (scn) is sent to the host. In any case, the peer also sends its configuration request packet to the host. They try to negotiate options acceptable to both of them. After they agree on the options, both move to the Opened state and start authentication phrase (or data transmission, if authentication is not required). The communication can be terminated by Close event explicitly or Down event (perhaps due to hardware failure). A termination request (str) is sent if the link is closed explicitly. A restart counter is used to monitor the responses to request actions (scr and str). If the host has not received the acknowledgment from the peer when the timer expires. It sends another request if the counter is greater than zero. Otherwise, it stops the connection locally.

Implementation. The implementation ppp version 2.4.0[1] is an open-source package included in various Linux distributions and widely used by Linux users. The package contains several tools for monitoring and maintaining PPP connections as well. The daemon pppd implements the protocol and is of our concern here. The file main.c uses the subroutines defined in fsm.c to maintain the finite state machine. Events and actions have their corresponding subroutines in fsm.c. In this work, we assume events and actions are handled correctly. Therefore we leave them as symbols as in the specification. Figure 4 shows how the program behaves on event RTA (receive terminate acknowledgment). For each state that can handle the RTA event, a case statement is put in the subroutine. For instance, if RTA is received when the state is Opened, it will inform the upper layers, send a configuration request (fsm_sconfreq) and returns. There are 2,589 lines in files main.c and fsm.c.

Modeling. Once we have defined the constants for events and actions. It is easy to construct a process for the automaton. The following guarded command

---

[1] Available at ftp://ftp.linuxcare.com.au/pub/ppp/ppp-2.4.0.tar.gz.

(written in the language of MOCHA [3]) models the behavior when the state is Opened and the event RTA occurs (figure 3).

```
[] state = Opened & in_p = in_v & evt = RTA & out_p ~= out_v ->
    act' := scr; out_p' := out_v; counter' := dec counter by 1;
    state' := Req_Sent; in_v' := ~in_p
```

The variable state denotes the current state, evt the event, and act the action. The variable counter represents the restart counter. It is decremented by one if the action scr is performed. The variables in_p and in_v model the input channel: the channel is empty if and only if they are equal. Similarly, out_p and out_v are for the output channel.

For the corresponding implementation (figure 4), more variables are needed to help us for modeling and recovering traces faithfully. We use the variable addr to record which subroutine is modeled by the current transition. The boolean variable timer is used to model the timeout event: if timer is true and the program is in the main loop, it may go to timeout handler. Other variables share the same meaning as those in the specification model.

```
[] addr = rtermack & state = Opened & out_p ~= out_v ->
    act' := scr; out_p' := out_v; timer' := true; counter' := 2;
    in_v' := ~in_p; addr' := input
```

Another process Link is used to model the network channel. It accepts an action from one automaton, translates it to an event, and forwards the event to the other automaton. We manually translate the C program to reactive modules. Since the program is well-organized (as seen in figure 4), it may be possible to translate it automatically. The resulting description in MOCHA contains 442 lines of code (182 lines for pppd and 260 lines for the specification).

Verification. Having built the models of the specification and implementation, we wish to apply the refinement check. However, certain aspects of the specification are not explicitly present in the implementation. For instance, the automaton is able to send a couple of packets in any order if it is in the state Stopped on event RCR^+ or RCR^-. Two variables are introduced to record which packets have been sent. These variables do not appear in the C program but only in the specification model. As discussed earlier, we need a witness to define these specification variables in terms of the implementation variables. We use the heuristic suggested in [4] to use the eager witness E, and check if $pppd \| E \preceq ppp$ where $pppd$ and ppp are the formal models of implementation and specification respectively. However, this refinement relation does not hold. It fails because $pppd$ is built with the assumption that it communicates with another PPP automaton. Consequently, we try to establish $pppd0 \| link \| pppd1 \preceq ppp0$, where $pppd0$, $ppp1$ are instances of the implementation model $pppd$, and $link$ is the model of the network channel. Using assume-guarantee reasoning, in conjunction with the witness module, this verification goal can be simplified to

$$pppd0 \| link \| ppp1 \| E \preceq ppp0.$$

This amounts to establishing that the implementation *pppd* refines the specification *ppp* assuming the communication partner satisfies the specification and using E as a witness for the private variables of the specification.

Analysis Result. To check the refinement obligation, we use a prototype built on top of the model checker MOCHA [3]. It produces a trace which describes an erroneous behavior of the implementation. The bug can be seen in the code segment shown in figure 4. On receiving RTA at state Opened, the automaton should bring down the link (tld), send a configuration request (scr) and go to state Req-Sent. However, the implementation does not update the state after it brings down the link and sends the request. In almost all circumstances, the bug is not significant. It can only be observed if the user tries to open the link instantaneously after the disconnection. Our translation lets us trace the bug in the C program easily. After we fix the bug, the refinement relation can be established.

In terms of computational requirements of the refinement check, in comparison to the IWLS image package available in VIS [7], our algorithm requires less memory: while the maximum MDD size with IWLS package is 265,389 nodes, our optimized algorithm the corresponding size is 188,544 nodes, a saving of about 30%. It takes IWLS package 5294.95s to finish while ours for 2318.87s, a saving of 56%.

4.2 Dynamic Host Configuration Protocol

The Dynamic Host Configuration Protocol (DHCP) provides a standard mechanism to obtain configuration parameters. It is widely used in mobile environment, especially for network address allocation. The protocol is designed based on the client-server model. Hosts which provide network parameters are called servers. They are configured by network administrators with consistent information. Clients, on the other hand, communicate with servers and obtain proper parameters to be a host in the network. In a typical scenario, a laptop obtains its network address after it is plugged in any network recognizing DHCP. The user can then access to the network without filling network parameters manually.

The DHCP specification [11] only describes the state machine informally. The state-transition diagram found in section 4.4 [11] gives a global view of the protocol. The details are written in English and scattered around the document. The dhcp package version 2.0 patch level 5[2] is the standard implementation distributed by Internet Software Consortium. We are interested in knowing whether the client (dhclient.c) is implemented correctly. The implementation does not appear to follow the specification strictly. For instance, it lacks two of the states shown in the state diagram. As a result, it is much more challenging to write down formal models for the specification and implementation in this case than for PPP. We adopt the same style and build four processes: the client specification *client*, the client implementation *dhclient*, the server *server* and the communication channel *link*. Since the implementation performs transitions in

---

[2] Available at http://www.isc.org/products/DHCP/dhcp-v2.html.

several stages, an eager module is introduced to resolve the timing difference. To make the model more realistic, we make the channel *link* lossy. We do not find any inconsistency during the check $dhclient\|link\|server\|E \preceq client$.

In terms of computational requirements of the refinement check, while the maximum MDD size with IWLS package is 13,692 nodes, our optimized algorithm the corresponding size is 29,192 nodes. However, IWLS package takes 350.84s in comparison to 82.70s in our algorithm. It takes 76% less in time in the presence of 53% more in space. We speculate the dynamic ordering algorithm causes this abnormality; further investigation is surely needed.

5 Conclusions

The main contribution of this paper is establishing applicability of refinement checking methodology to verification of implementations of network protocols with respect to RFC documentations. The relevance of the various steps in the methodology is supported by two case studies involving popular protocols, with an inconsistency discovered in one case. We have also proposed a symbolic search algorithm for compressing internal transitions in a hierarchical manner, and established the resulting savings in memory requirements.

In both case studies, the model extraction was done manually. This is unavoidable for extracting specification models since RFC documents typically describe the protocols in a tabular, but informal, format. As far as automating the generation of implementation models from C-code, the emerging technology for model extraction [8, 16, 9, 21] can be useful.

Acknowledgments. We thank Michael Greenwald for many details about PPP and DHCP protocols. This work is partially supported by NSF CAREER award CCR97-34115, by SRC contract 99-TJ-688, by Bell Laboratories, Lucent Technologies, and by Sloan Faculty Fellowship.

References

1. M. Abadi and L. Lamport. The existence of refinement mappings. *Theoretical Computer Science*, 82(2):253–284, 1991.
2. M. Abadi and L. Lamport. Composing specifications. *ACM TOPLAS*, 15(1):73–132, 1993.
3. R. Alur, L. de Alfaro, R. Grosu, T. Henzinger, M. Kang, R. Majumdar, F. Mang, C. Kirsch, and B. Wang. MOCHA: A model checking tool that exploits design structure. In *Proceedings of 23rd Intl. Conference on Software Engineering*, 2001.
4. R. Alur, R. Grosu, and B.-Y. Wang. Automated refinement checking for asynchronous processes. In *Proc. Third Intl. Workshop on Formal Methods in Computer-Aided Design*. Springer, 2000.
5. R. Alur and T. Henzinger. Reactive modules. *Formal Methods in System Design*, 15(1):7–48, 1999.
6. R. Alur and B.-Y. Wang. "Next" heuristic for on-the-fly model checking. In *CONCUR'99: Concurrency Theory, Tenth Intl. Conference*, LNCS 1664, pages 98–113. Springer, 1999.

7. R. Brayton, G. Hachtel, A. Sangiovanni-Vincentelli, F. Somenzi, A. Aziz, S. Cheng, S. Edwards, S. Khatri, Y. Kukimoto, A. Pardo, S. Qadeer, R. Ranjan, S. Sarwary, T. Shiple, G. Swamy, and T. Villa. VIS: A system for verification and synthesis. In *Proc. Eighth Intl. Conference on Computer Aided Verification*, LNCS 1102, pages 428–432. Springer-Verlag, 1996.

8. J. Corbett, M. Dwyer, J. Hatcliff, S. Laubach, C. Pasareanu, Robby, and H. Zheng. Bandera: Extracting finite-state models from Java source code. In *Proceedings of 22nd Intl. Conference on Software Engineering*, pages 439–448. 2000.

9. S. Das, D. Dill, and S. Park. Experience with predicate abstraction. In *Computer Aided Verification, 11th Intl. Conference*, LNCS 1633, pages 160–171. Springer, 1999.

10. J. Fernandez, H. Garavel, A. Kerbrat, R. Mateescu, L. Mounier, and M. Sighire-anu. CADP: A protocol validation and verification toolbox. In *Proc. Eighth Intl. Conference on Computer-Aided Verification*, LNCS 1102. Springer-Verlag, 1996.

11. R. Droms. *Dynamic Host Configuration Protocol*, March 1997. RFC 2131.

12. O. Grümberg and D. Long. Model checking and modular verification. *ACM Transactions on Programming Languages and Systems*, 16(3):843–871, 1994.

13. T. Henzinger, X. Liu, S. Qadeer, and S. Rajamani. Formal specification and verification of a dataflow processor array. In *Proc. Intl. Conference on Computer-aided Design*, pages 494–499, 1999.

14. T. Henzinger, S. Qadeer, and S. Rajamani. You assume, we guarantee: Methodology and case studies. In *CAV 98: Computer-aided Verification*, LNCS 1427, pages 521–525, 1998.

15. G. Holzmann. The model checker SPIN. *IEEE Trans. on Software Engineering*, 23(5):279–295, 1997.

16. G. Holzmann and M. H. Smith. Software model checking - extracting verification models from source code. In *Formal Methods for Protocol Engineering and Distributed Systems*, pages 481–497, Kluwer Academic Publ., 1999.

17. R. Kurshan. *Computer-aided Verification of Coordinating Processes: the automata-theoretic approach*. Princeton University Press, 1994.

18. N. Lynch and M. Tuttle. Hierarchical correctness proofs for distributed algorithms. In *Proc. Seventh ACM Symposium on Principles of Distributed Computing*, pages 137–151, 1987.

19. K. McMillan. A compositional rule for hardware design refinement. In *CAV 97: Computer-Aided Verification*, LNCS 1254, pages 24–35, 1997.

20. K. McMillan. Verification of an implementation of tomasulo's algorithm by compositional model checking. In *CAV 98: Computer-Aided Verification*, LNCS 1427, pages 110–121, 1998.

21. K. Namjoshi and R. Kurshan. Syntactic program transformations for automatic abstraction. In *Computer Aided Verification, 12th Intl. Conference*, LNCS 1855, pages 435–449. Springer, 2000.

22. W. Simpson. *The Point-to-Point Protocol*. Computer Systems Consulting Services, July 1994. STD 51, RFC 1661.

23. E. Stark. A proof technique for rely-guarantee properties. In *Found. of Software Technology and Theoretical Computer Science*, LNCS 206, pages 369–391, 1985.

Automatic Abstraction for Verification of Timed Circuits and Systems*

Hao Zheng, Eric Mercer, and Chris Myers

University of Utah, Salt Lake City UT 84112, USA
{hao,eemercer,myers}@vlsigroup.elen.utah.edu
http://async.elen.utah.edu

Abstract. This paper presents a new approach for verification of asynchronous circuits by using automatic abstraction. It attacks the state explosion problem by avoiding the generation of a flat state space for the whole design. Instead, it breaks the design into blocks and conducts verification on each of them. Using this approach, the speed of verification improves dramatically.

1 Introduction

In order to continue to produce circuits of increasing speed, designers are considering aggressive circuit design styles such as self-resetting or delayed-reset domino circuits. These design styles can achieve a significant improvement in circuit speed as demonstrated by their use in a gigahertz research microprocessor (guTS) at IBM [11]. Designers are also considering asynchronous circuits due to their potential for higher performance and lower power as demonstrated by the RAPPID instruction length decoder designed at Intel [22]. This design was 3 times faster while using only half the power of the synchronous design. The correctness of these new *timed circuit* styles is highly dependent upon their timing, so extensive timing verification is necessary during the design process. Unfortunately, these new circuit styles cannot be efficiently and accurately verified using traditional static timing analysis methods. This lack of efficient analysis tools is one of the reasons for the lack of mainstream acceptance of these design styles.

The formal verification of timed circuits often requires state space exploration which can explode even for modest size examples. To reduce the complexity incurred by state exploration, abstraction is necessary. In [2,21], safe approximations of internal signal behavior are found to reduce the size of the state space, but these methods are still exponential in the number of memory elements. In VIS [6], non-determinism is used to abstract the behavior of some circuit signals, but it is often too conservative and can introduce unreachable states which may exhibit hazards. In [20], a model checker is proposed based on hierarchical reactive machines. By taking advantage of the hierarchy information, it only tracks active variables so that the state space is reduced and verification time is improved, but this approach is best suited for software which has a more sequential nature. In [16], an abstraction technique is proposed for validation coverage

---

* This research is supported by NSF CAREER award MIP-9625014, SRC contract 97-DJ-487 and 99-TJ-694, and a grant from Intel Corporation.

G. Berry, H. Comon, and A. Finkel (Eds.): CAV 2001, LNCS 2102, pp. 182–193, 2001.

analysis and automatic test generation. It removes all datapath elements which do not affect the control flow and groups the equivalent transitions together resulting in a dramatic reduction in the state space. It is difficult, however, to distinguish the control from the datapath without help from the designers. In [13], an abstraction approach for the design of speed-independent asynchronous circuits from change diagrams is described. In this approach, each subcircuit is designed individually, and they are then recombined to produce the final circuit. This approach, however, does not address timing issues. In [10], a divide-and-conquer method is presented for the synthesis of asynchronous circuits. This method breaks up the state graph into a number of simpler subgraphs for each output, and each subgraph is solved individually. The results are then integrated together to construct the final solution. This method, however, requires a complete state graph to start with. An *assume-guarantee reasoning* strategy is shown [25]. In such cases, when verifying a component in a system, assumptions need to be made about the behavior of other components, and these assumptions are discharged when the correctness of other components is established. while our approach is similar to assume-guarantee reasoning, our approach does not require assumptions about the other components because their behavior is derived from the specifications using semantics-preserving abstraction. In [3], Belluomini describes the verification of domino circuits using ATACS. She shows that verifying flat circuits even of a moderate size can be very difficult, while the verification can be completed quickly using hand abstractions. However, these hand abstractions require an expert user and methods must be developed to check that the abstractions are a reliable model of the underlying behavior. This is the major motivation of this work.

Our approach begins with a high-level language, such as VHDL, that models a system hierarchically. The method then compiles each individual component into a timed Petri-net for verification. This paper proposes an abstraction technique applied to *timed Petri-nets*. This approach partitions the design into small blocks using specified structural information, and each block is verified separately. We have proven that under certain constraints if each block is verified to be correct, then the complete system is also correct. Our results show that taking advantage of the hierarchical information results in a substantial savings in verification time.

2   Timed Petri-Nets and Basic Trace Theory

Timed Petri-nets (TPNs) [19] are the graphical model to which our high-level specification is compiled. A one-safe TPN is modeled by the tuple $\langle P, T, F, M_0, \Delta \rangle$ where P is the set of places, T is the set of transitions, and $F \subseteq (P \times T) \cup (T \times P)$ is the flow relation, $M_0 \subseteq P$ is the initial marking, and Δ is an assignment of timing constraints to places. There are three kinds of transitions: $s+$ changes signal s from 0 to 1, $s-$ changes s from 1 to 0, and $\$$ which is a *sequencing transition*. A *marking* is a subset of places. For a place $p \in P$, the *preset* of p (denoted $\bullet p$) is the set of transitions connected to p (i.e., $\bullet p = \{t \in T \mid (t, p) \in F\}$), and the *postset* of p (denoted $p\bullet$) is the set of transitions to which p is connected (i.e., $p\bullet = \{t \in T \mid (p, t) \in F\}$). Presets and postsets for transitions are similarly

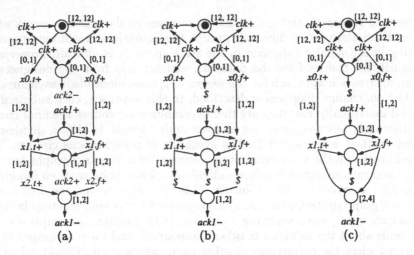

Fig. 1. Portion of the TPN for a STARI Circuit Composed of two FIFO Stages.

defined. A timing constraint consisting of a lower and upper bound is associated with each place in the TPN (i.e., $\Delta(p_i) = \langle l_i, u_i \rangle$). The lower bound is a non-negative integer while the upper bound is an integer greater than or equal to the lower bound or ∞. A benchmark for timed circuit design is the STARI communication circuit [9] which is used to communicate between two synchronous systems that are operating at the same clock frequency, but are out-of-phase due to clock skew. The STARI circuit is essentially a FIFO connecting the two systems. A portion of the TPN for a STARI circuit with 2 FIFO stages is shown in Figure 1(a). To simplify the diagram, places between transitions have been removed. A token indicates that the place is initially marked.

A transition t is enabled in a marking M if $\bullet t \subseteq M$. A timer is associated with each place $p \in M$. For each $p \in P$, $\texttt{timer}(p)$ is initialized to zero when p is put into the marking. All timers in a marking increase uniformly. Let $\texttt{lower}(p)$ and $\texttt{upper}(p)$ be the lower and upper bounds of the timing constraints of $p \in P$. For a $p \in M$, $\texttt{timer}(p)$ is *satisfied* if $\texttt{timer}(p) \geq \texttt{lower}(p)$; $\texttt{timer}(p)$ is *expired* if $\texttt{timer}(p) \geq \texttt{upper}(p)$. A transition t cannot occur until it is enabled in a marking and $\texttt{timer}(p)$ is satisfied for all $p \in \bullet t$. A transition t must fire before $\texttt{timer}(p)$ is expired for all $p \in \bullet t$. Firing a transition t changes the current marking M to a new marking $M' = (M - \bullet t) \cup t\bullet$, where $\texttt{timer}(p) = 0$ for all $p \in t\bullet$. The net is 1-safe if $(M - \bullet t) \cap t\bullet = \emptyset$.

The timing properties of a system are specified using a set of *constraint places*. Constraint places never actually enable a transition to fire. Instead, the constraint places are checked each time a transition fires in a marking. Failures caused by constraint places arise due to three conditions:

1. There exists a constraint place $p \in \bullet t$ such that $p \notin M$ when firing t.
2. $\texttt{timer}(p)$ is not satisfied for any constraint place $p \in \bullet t$ when firing t.
3. $\texttt{timer}(p)$ is expired for any constraint place $p \in \bullet t$ before firing t.

The dynamic behavior of a Petri net can be studied using reachability analysis. A marking M_n is said to be reachable from a marking M_0 if there exists a sequence of firings that changes M_0 to M_n. A *firing sequence* or *run* from a marking M_0 is defined as $\rho = M_0 \overset{t_1}{\rightarrow} M_1 \overset{t_2}{\rightarrow} M_2 \overset{t_3}{\rightarrow} \ldots \overset{t_n}{\rightarrow} M_n$. A sequence of transitions generated by a firing sequence ρ is called a trace. In the above example, M_n is reachable from M_0 through a trace $t_1 t_2 \ldots t_n$. Let X be the set of all possible traces produced by a Petri net N. X is *prefix-closed* and always includes the empty trace ϵ.

The same concept can be extended to TPNs. A state S of a TPN is a pair $(M, \texttt{timer})$, where M is a marking and $\texttt{timer}$ is a function $p \to \mathbf{Q}^+$ for all $p \in M$. The initial state S_0 is $(M_0, \texttt{timer}_0)$, where $\texttt{timer}_0(p) = 0$ for all $p \in M_0$. In a state $S = (M, \texttt{timer})$, a transition t can fire if t is enabled in M and $\texttt{timer}(p)$ is satisfied for all $p \in \bullet t$. The new state $S' = (M', \texttt{timer}')$ is obtained from S by firing t. $M' = (M - \bullet t) \cup t\bullet$ and $\texttt{timer}'(p) = 0$ for all $p \in t\bullet$. A *timed firing sequence* or *timed run* in a TPN is defined as $\rho = S_0 \overset{t_1}{\rightarrow} S_1 \overset{t_2}{\rightarrow} S_2 \overset{t_3}{\rightarrow} \ldots \overset{t_n}{\rightarrow} S_n$, where S_0 is the initial state. S_{i+1} is obtained from S_i by passing some time until all rules in $\bullet t_{i+1}$ are satisfied and then firing t_{i+1}. Let $\texttt{time}_i(\rho)$ be the sum of time that has passed for the system to reach the state S_i from the initial state S_0 through the firing sequence ρ. It is true that $\texttt{time}_0(\rho) = 0$ and $\texttt{time}_{i+1}(\rho) = \texttt{time}_i(\rho) + \tau$ where $l \leq \tau \leq u$, $l = max(\{\texttt{lower}(r)|r \in M_i \text{ for } r \in \bullet t_{i+1}\})$, and $u = max(\{\texttt{upper}(r)|r \in M_i \text{ for } r \in \bullet t_{i+1}\})$. Thus, a run ρ produces a timed trace $(t_1, \texttt{time}_1(\rho))(t_2, \texttt{time}_2(\rho)) \cdots$. Let X be the set of all possible timed traces produced by a timed Petri net N. X is also *prefix-closed*.

Since the reachability analysis of a TPN can be uniquely determined by all its possible timed traces, the system behavior can also be described using *trace theory*. Trace theory has been applied to the verification of both speed-independent [8] and timed circuits [7, 27]. A *timed trace*, x, is a sequence of events (i.e., $x = e_0 e_1 \ldots$). In trace theory, it is not necessary to distinguish the rising and falling transitions on the same signal, the signal name is used to represent both transitions on the same signal. Therefore, each *timed event* is of the form $e_i = (w_i, t_i)$ where w is a signal name in the TPN. t is a rational number indicating when a transition on a signal wire happens. A timed trace must satisfy the following two properties:

- *Monotonicity*: $t_i \leq t_{i+1}$ for all $i \geq 0$, and
- *Progress*: if x is infinite then for any time t there exists an i such that $t_i > t$.

The delete function, $\mathbf{del}(D)(x)$, removes all events of a trace $x = e_1 e_2 \ldots$ whose wire names are in a set D. More formally,

$$\mathbf{del}(D)(x) = \begin{cases} e_1 y & \text{if } w_1 \notin D \\ y & \text{if } w_1 \in D \end{cases} \tag{1}$$

where $y = \mathbf{del}(D)(e_2 e_3 \ldots)$ and $e_1 = (w_1, t_1)$. It is extended naturally to sets of traces. The inverse delete function, $\mathbf{del}^{-1}(D)(X)$, takes a set of wires, D, and a set of traces, X, and returns the set of traces which would be in X if all events with wire names in D are deleted (i.e., $\mathbf{del}^{-1}(D)(X) = \{x' \mid \mathbf{del}(D)(x') \in X\}$). Intuitively, if x is a trace not containing symbols from D, $\mathbf{del}^{-1}(D)(x)$ is the set of all traces that can be generated by inserting events in D at any time into x. Some useful properties of these two functions are below:

$$\mathbf{del}(D)(X) = \emptyset \Leftrightarrow X = \emptyset \qquad (2)$$

$$\mathbf{del}(D)(\mathbf{del}^{-1}(D')(X)) = \mathbf{del}^{-1}(D')(\mathbf{del}(D)(X)) \text{ when } D \cap D' = \emptyset \qquad (3)$$

$$\mathbf{del}(D)(\mathbf{del}^{-1}(D)(X)) = X \qquad (4)$$

$$\mathbf{del}(D)(X \cap X') \subseteq \mathbf{del}(D)(X) \cap \mathbf{del}(D)(X') \qquad (5)$$

A *prefix-closed trace structure* T is a three-tuple $\langle I, O, P \rangle$. I is a set of input wires, and O is a set of output wires where $I \cap O = \emptyset$. $A = I \cup O$ is the *alphabet* of the structure. $P = S \cup F$ is the set of all possible traces of a system where S and F are the *success set* and the *failure set* of T, respectively. The trace structure T of a TPN N can be derived using state space exploration on N. A function $\mathbf{trace}(N)$ is defined to return a trace structure which has the same inputs and outputs as N. P of $\mathbf{trace}(N)$ is the set of all possible timed traces produced by N. The function $\mathbf{fail}(X)$ is defined to return the set of all traces in P that cause safety violations or timing constraint violations. Therefore, $F = \mathbf{fail}(P)$. For hierarchical verification to succeed, the definition of $\mathbf{fail}(X)$ must satisfy the following requirement:

$$\mathbf{fail}(X) \subseteq \mathbf{fail}(X') \quad \text{if } X \subseteq X' \qquad (6)$$

where X and X' are two sets of traces. This requirement states that for two sets of traces, correctness checking does not affect the relation of the two sets. S contains all successful traces of a system, and $S = P - F$. A trace structure must be *receptive*, meaning that $PI \subseteq P$. Intuitively, this means a circuit cannot prevent the environment from sending an input.

Composition ($\|$) combines two circuits into a single circuit. Composition of two trace structures $T = \langle I, O, S, F \rangle$ and $T' = \langle I', O', S', F' \rangle$ is defined when $O \cap O' = \emptyset$. To compose two trace structures, the alphabets of both trace structures must first be made the same by adding new inputs as necessary to each structure. Inverse delete is extended to trace structures for this step as follows:

$$\mathbf{del}^{-1}(D)(T) = \langle I \cup D, O, \mathbf{del}^{-1}(D)(S), \mathbf{del}^{-1}(D)(F) \rangle \qquad (7)$$

This is defined only when $D \cap A = \emptyset$. After the two alphabets of the two structures are made to match, we need to find the traces that are consistent with the two structures. The intersection of these two trace structures is defined as follows:

$$T \cap T' = \langle I \cap I', O \cup O', S \cap S', (F \cap P') \cup (P \cap F') \rangle \qquad (8)$$

This is defined only when $A = A'$ and $O \cap O' = \emptyset$. A success trace in the composite must be a success trace in both components. A failure trace in the composite is a possible trace that is a failure trace in either component. The possible traces for the composite is $P \cap P'$. Composition can now be defined:

$$T \| T' = \mathbf{del}^{-1}(A' - A)(T) \cap \mathbf{del}^{-1}(A - A')(T') \qquad (9)$$

Another useful operation is **hide** which is used to make a set of wires, D, *internal* to the circuit. Given a trace structure T, $\mathbf{hide}(D)(T)$ is defined as follow:

$$\mathbf{hide}(D)(T) = \langle I, O - D, \mathbf{del}(D)(S), \mathbf{del}(D)(F) \rangle \qquad (10)$$

A trace structure is *failure-free* if its failure set is empty. Given two trace structures, T and T', we say T *conforms* to T' (denoted $T \preceq T'$) if $I = I', O = O'$, and for *all* environments E, if $E \parallel T'$ is failure-free, so is $E \parallel T$. Intuitively, if a system using T' cannot fail, neither can a system using T.

Lemma 1 below gives a simple sufficient condition to determine conformance between two trace structures. The condition $F \subseteq F'$ assures that if the environment does not cause a failure in T', it does not cause a failure in T. The condition $P \subseteq P'$ assures that if T' does not cause a failure in the environment, T does not cause one. Lemma 2 shows that if T conforms to T', this conformance is maintained in any environment. Proofs of these lemmas can be found in [8].

Lemma 1. $T \preceq T'$ if $I = I', O = O', F \subseteq F'$, and $P \subseteq P'$.

Lemma 2. If $T \preceq T'$ and T'' is any trace structure, then $T \parallel T'' \preceq T' \parallel T''$.

3 Automatic Abstraction and Safe Transformations

Formal verification of timed systems is typically based on a complete exploration of the state space. The state space grows exponentially in the complexity of the design. This limits verification to small designs. In general, a large and complex design is organized as a number of components, each of which has a well-defined interface. To verify a timed system, an environment must be provided. The environment has two functions during verification. First, it defines and supplies the input behavior which the system must be able to process for correct operation. Second, the outputs of the system must not cause the environment to fail. Each component either connects to other components, the environment, or both. Since the complexity of each component is often much less than the whole system, it is desirable to verify each component individually, and integrate the results for all components when available to form the solution for the whole system. If a component is chosen for verification, the rest of the components and the system environment together form the environment in which the component operates. To verify a component, only the interface behavior of the environment is important to the component. Therefore, if the internal behavior of the environment is abstracted away while preserving its interface behavior, the environment can be simplified reducing the complexity of verification.

To apply abstraction to TPNs, first, all internal signals relative to a chosen component are identified and all transitions on them converted to sequencing transitions; second, these sequencing transitions and the related places are removed safely from the TPNs, when possible. Consider the TPN shown in Figure 1(a). If we are synthesizing only the first stage of the two stage FIFO, then the signals $ack2$, $x2.t$, and $x2.f$ should be abstracted away. Transitions on these signals are changed to sequencing transitions as shown in Figure 1(b).

Next, transformations are applied to remove these sequencing transitions. Suzuhi and Murata [23,24] present a method of stepwise refinement of transitions and places into subnets. They show a sufficient condition that such subnets must satisfy which is dependent on the structure and initial marking of the net. The resulting net has the same liveness and safety properties as that of the original net. This refinement process, however, has to be repeated every

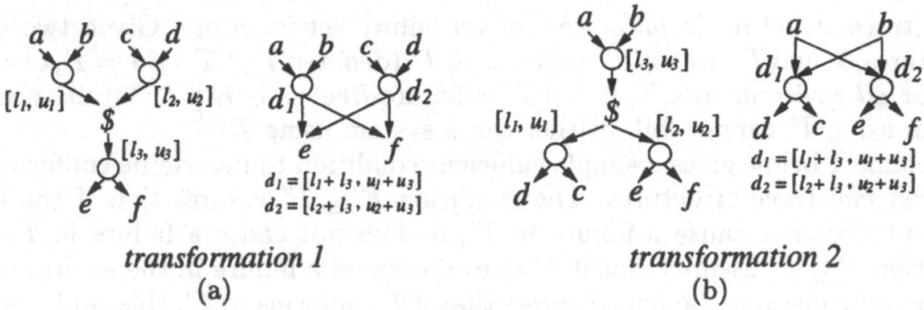

transformation 1
(a)

transformation 2
(b)

Fig. 2. Safe Transformation 1 and 2.

time the initial marking is changed. This makes automating the refinement difficult. Berthelot [5] presented several transformations that depend only on the structure of the net. In [18, 12, 17], several transformations for marked graphs are presented. These transformations reduce places and transitions in the graph while preserving liveness and safety. All these transformations, however, are only applied to untimed Petri nets.

We have developed several safe transformations for timed Petri nets. Safe transformations must obey two conditions. First, removal of a signal should never change the untimed semantics of the environment. Second, the timing information of the signal transitions produced by the environment must be preserved in a conservative fashion. To explain these two conditions more precisely, we use trace theory. Suppose N_E is the TPN describing the behavior of the environment, and T_E is its corresponding trace structure. The interface behavior of T_E is described by $\mathbf{del}(D)(P_E)$, where D is the set of signals internal to the environment, and P_E is the set of possible traces. The environment after abstraction and safe transformations is called the *abstracted environment*. In the abstracted environment, the internal signals, D, are removed from N_E to obtain the trace structure $T_A = \mathbf{trace}(\mathbf{abs}(D)(N_E))$. Function $\mathbf{abs}(D)(N_E)$ returns a TPN N_E' where the signals in D are abstracted away from N_E using safe transformations. Let X_1 and X_2 be the untimed trace sets produced by $\mathbf{abs}(D)(N_E)$ and N_E, respectively. To preserve the interface behavior, a safe transformation must satisfy that $X_1 = \mathbf{del}(D)(X_2)$ and $\mathbf{del}(D)(P_E) \subseteq P_A$, where D contains the internal signals of the environment to be removed and P_A is the possible trace set of T_A. Intuitively, this means a safe transformation should never remove any specified behavior, but it may add new behavior. In other words, the verification result might be a *false negative*, but never a *false positive*.

Figure 2 shows two simple transformations. Transformation 1 is used when a sequencing transition has a single or multiple places in its preset, and a single place in its postset. In transformation 2, the sequencing transition has a single place in its preset, and two or more places in its postset. While transformation 1 adds no extra behaviors, transformation 2 may create extra interleavings between b and c not seen before the transformation. For example, after the transformation, the system could generate a trace $(a, t_a)(c, t_a + l_1 + l_3)(e, t_a + u_2 + u_3)$, where t_a is when a fires. This trace is impossible in the system before the transformation.

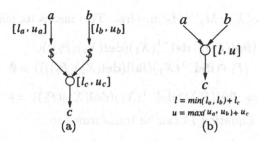

Fig. 3. Safe Transformation 3.

The third transformation which involves a merge place is depicted in Figure 3. This transformation like the last one may add additional timing behavior. However, if $l_a = l_b$ and $u_a = u_b$ then it is an exact transformation. This transformation is applied to the TPN in Figure 1(b) to obtain the reduced one shown in Figure 1(c). Numerous other safe transformations have been developed and proven to be correct. Due to space limitations, these transformations and all proofs are omitted here, but can be found in [29].

In order to perform verification using TPNs, the possible traces P can be found using a timed state space exploration procedure such as the one described in [4]. After safe transformations, it is true that $\mathbf{del}(D)(P_E) \subseteq P_A$ where $T_A = \mathbf{trace}(\mathbf{abs}(D)(N_E))$ and D contains the internal signals to be removed. This indicates that the interface behavior of the environment after transformations is a superset of that before transformations. From Equation 6, we get the following:

$$\mathbf{fail}(\mathbf{del}(D)(P_E)) \subseteq \mathbf{fail}(P_A) \tag{11}$$

This means that the failure set of the abstracted environment is a superset of the failure set of the unabstracted environment with internal signals hidden. Based on the above discussion and Lemma 1, the following lemma can be proved easily.

Lemma 3. *Given a system described by a TPN, N_E, with a trace structure T_E, where D is the set of internal signals of the system. If the function $\mathbf{abs}(D)(N_E)$ uses only safe transformations, then $\mathbf{hide}(D)(T_E) \preceq \mathbf{trace}(\mathbf{abs}(D)(N_E))$.*

Hierarchical verification verifies each block in a system individually. If each block is verified to be failure-free with its abstracted environment, then we can prove that the entire system is failure-free. This idea is formalized in the following theorems. Given two modules $M_1 = \langle I_1, O_1, P_1 \rangle$ and $M_2 = \langle I_2, O_2, P_2 \rangle$, we would like to verify that their composition, $M_1 \parallel M_2$, is failure-free. In the following theorem, X_1 and X_2 are the internal signal sets of M_1 and M_2, respectively (i.e., $X_1 = O_1 - I_2$, $X_2 = O_2 - I_1$, and $X_1 \cap X_2 = \emptyset$).

Theorem 1. *Let X_1 and X_2 be the internal signal sets of M_1 and M_2, respectively. If $M_1 \parallel \mathbf{hide}(X_2)(M_2)$ is failure-free, and $\mathbf{hide}(X_1)(M_1) \parallel M_2$ is failure-free, then $M = M_1 \parallel M_2$ is failure-free.*

Proof: First, the failure set of $M_1 \parallel M_2$ is

$$(\mathbf{del}^{-1}(X_2)(\mathbf{fail}(P_1)) \cap \mathbf{del}^{-1}(X_1)(P_2)) \cup$$
$$(\mathbf{del}^{-1}(X_1)(\mathbf{fail}(P_2)) \cap \mathbf{del}^{-1}(X_2)(P_1)) \tag{12}$$

Suppose $M_1 \parallel \mathbf{hide}(X_2)(M_2)$ is failure-free. This means its failure set is empty.

$$(\mathbf{fail}(P_1) \cap \mathbf{del}^{-1}(X_1)(\mathbf{del}(X_2)(P_2))) \cup$$
$$(P_1 \cap \mathbf{del}^{-1}(X_1)(\mathbf{fail}(\mathbf{del}(X_2)(P_2)))) = \emptyset \qquad (13)$$

$$\Rightarrow \mathbf{fail}(P_1) \cap \mathbf{del}^{-1}(X_1)(\mathbf{del}(X_2)(P_2)) = \emptyset \qquad (14)$$

Using Equation 4, Equation 14 can be transformed to:

$$\mathbf{del}(X_2)(\mathbf{del}^{-1}(X_2)(\mathbf{fail}(P_1))) \cap \mathbf{del}^{-1}(X_1)(\mathbf{del}(X_2)(P_2)) = \emptyset \qquad (15)$$

Using Equation 3, Equation 15 becomes:

$$\mathbf{del}(X_2)(\mathbf{del}^{-1}(X_2)(\mathbf{fail}(P_1))) \cap \mathbf{del}(X_2)(\mathbf{del}^{-1}(X_1)(P_2)) = \emptyset \qquad (16)$$

From Equation 5, Equation 16 can be transformed to:

$$\mathbf{del}(X_2)(\mathbf{del}^{-1}(X_2)(\mathbf{fail}(P_1)) \cap \mathbf{del}^{-1}(X_1)(P_2)) = \emptyset \qquad (17)$$

Finally, from Equation 2, we get the following result:

$$\mathbf{del}^{-1}(X_2)(\mathbf{fail}(P_1)) \cap \mathbf{del}^{-1}(X_1)(P_2) = \emptyset \qquad (18)$$

Now, suppose $M_2 \parallel \mathbf{hide}(X_1)(M_1)$ is failure-free. In a similar manner, we derive:

$$\mathbf{del}^{-1}(X_1)(\mathbf{fail}(P_2)) \cap \mathbf{del}^{-1}(X_2)(P_1) = \emptyset \qquad (19)$$

The union of Equation 18 and 19 is the failure set of $M_1 \parallel M_2$. Since both Equation 18 and 19 are empty, the failure set of $M_1 \parallel M_2$ is empty. ∎

Calculation of P is an exponential problem. Lemma 3 shows that $\mathbf{hide}(D)(T_E)$ $\preceq \mathbf{trace}(\mathbf{abs}(D)(N_E))$. Therefore, from Lemma 2, $M_1 \parallel \mathbf{hide}(X_2)(M_2) \preceq M_1 \parallel$ $\mathbf{trace}(\mathbf{abs}(X_2)(N_{M_2}))$ and $\mathbf{hide}(X_1)(M_1) \parallel M_2 \preceq \mathbf{trace}(\mathbf{abs}(X_1)(N_{M_1})) \parallel M_2$. Using the above conclusions, we show another very important theorem.

Theorem 2. *Let X_1 and X_2 be internal signal sets of M_1 and M_2, respectively. If $M_1 \parallel \mathbf{trace}(\mathbf{abs}(X_2)(M_2))$ is failure-free and $\mathbf{trace}(\mathbf{abs}(X_1)(M_1)) \parallel M_2$ is failure-free, then $M = M_1 \parallel M_2$ is failure-free.*

4   Results and Conclusions

We have incorporated our abstraction technique into our VHDL and HSE compiler [28] frontend to the ATACS tool. The charts in Figure 4 show the comparative runtimes for verification using POSET timing [4] with and without abstraction on two different FIFO circuits. Only the first few stages are shown as larger FIFO's cannot be verified without abstraction for the first FIFO. ATACS completes 7 stages on the flat design; but with abstraction, it completes 100 stages in about 6.5 minutes. The second example is a multiple stage controller for a self-timed FIFO that is very timing dependent [15]. Without abstraction, only 4 stages can be analyzed. With abstraction, we can analyze 100 stages in 23 minutes.

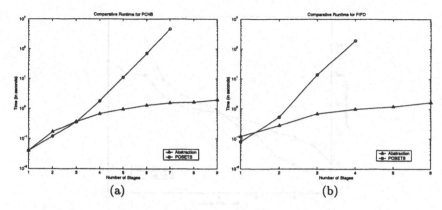

Fig. 4. Runtimes for PCHB and FIFO Example.

The last example is the STARI communication circuit described in detail in [9]. The STARI circuit is used to communicate between two synchronous systems that are operating at the same clock frequency, but are out-of-phase due to clock skew. The STARI circuit is composed of a number of FIFO stages built from 2 C-elements and 1 NOR-gate per stage. There are two properties that need to be verified: (1) each data value output by the transmitter must be inserted into the FIFO before the next one is output and (2) a new data value must be output by the FIFO before each acknowledgment from the receiver [26]. To guarantee the second property, it is necessary to initialize the FIFO to be approximately half-full [9]. In [26], the authors state that COSPAN which uses a region technique for timing verification [1] ran out of memory attempting to verify a 3 stage gate-level version of STARI on a machine with 1 GB of memory. This paper goes on to describe an abstract model developed by hand for STARI for which they could verify 8 stages in 92.4 MB of memory and 1.67 hours. A flat gate-level design for 10 stages can be verified in 124 MB and 20 minutes using POSET timing [4]. Our automated abstraction method verifies a 14 stage STARI with a maximum memory usage of 23 MB of memory for a single stage in about 5 minutes. Figure 5 shows the comparative runtimes for verification with and without abstraction on STARI using Bap, an enhanced version of the POSET timing analysis algorithm [14]. As shown in the chart, Bap can verify STARI for up to 12 stages with a memory usage of 277 MB. In the first few stages, the runtime for verification with abstraction is larger because abstraction itself takes time. When the complexity of the design grows, the runtime for flat verification grows much faster.

Since abstraction runtime grows polynomially in the size of the specification, the total runtime with abstraction grows in an approximately polynomial manner. This is substantially better than the exponential growth in the analysis of flat designs. We have also found that verification with abstraction is not only several orders of magnitude faster than that for flat designs, but also successful on several orders of magnitude more complex designs.

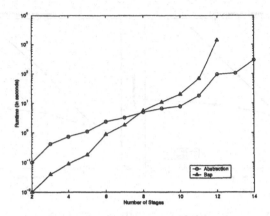

Fig. 5. Runtimes for Stari.

Acknowledgments

We would like to thank Wendy Belluomini of IBM and Tomohiro Yoneda of the Tokoyo Institute of Technology, Japan for their helpful comments.

References

1. R. Alur and R. P. Kurshan. Timing analysis in cospan. In *Hybrid Systems III*. Springer-Verlag, 1996.
2. Peter A. Beerel, Teresa H.-Y. Meng, and Jerry Burch. Efficient verification of determinate speed-independent circuits. In *Proc. International Conf. Computer-Aided Design (ICCAD)*, pages 261–267. IEEE Computer Society Press, November 1993.
3. W. Belluomini, C. J. Myers, and H. P. Hofstee. Verification of delayed-reset domino circuits using ATACS. In *Proc. International Symposium on Advanced Research in Asynchronous Circuits and Systems*, pages 3–12, April 1999.
4. W. Belluomini and C.J. Myers. Verification of timed systems using posets. In *International Conference on Computer Aided Verification.* Springer-Verlag, 1998.
5. G. Berthelot. Checking properties of nets using transformations. In *Lecture Notes in Computer Science, 222*, pages 19–40, 1986.
6. R. K. Brayton. Vis: A system for verification and synthesis. In *Proc. International Conf. Computer-Aided Design (ICCAD)*, pages 428–432, 1996.
7. J. R. Burch. *Trace Algebra for Automatic Verification of Real-Time Concurrent Systems*. PhD thesis, Carnegie Mellon University, 1992.
8. David L. Dill. *Trace Theory for Automatic Hierarchical Verification of Speed-Independent Circuits*. ACM Distinguished Dissertations. MIT Press, 1989.
9. M. R. Greenstreet. Stari: Skew tolerant communication. unpublished manuscript, 1997.
10. J. Gu and R. Puri. Asynchronous circuit synthesis with boolean satisfiability. In *IEEE Trans. CAD, Vol. 14, No. 8*, pages 961–973, 1995.
11. H. P. Hofstee, S. H. Dhong, D. Meltzer, K. J. Nowka, J. A. Silberman, J. L. Burns, S. D. Posluszny, and O. Takahashi. Designing for a gigahertz. *IEEE MICRO*, May-June 1998.

12. R. Johnsonbaugh and T. Murata. Additional methods for reduction and expansion of marked graphs. In *IEEE TCAS, vol. CAS-28, no. 1*, pages 1009–1014, 1981.
13. Michael Kishinevsky, Alex Kondratyev, Alexander Taubin, and Victor Varshavsky. *Concurrent Hardware: The Theory and Practice of Self-Timed Design*. Series in Parallel Computing. John Wiley & Sons, 1994.
14. E. Mercer, C. Myers, and Tomohiro Yoneda. Improved poset timing analysis in timed petri nets. Technical report, University of Utah, 2001. http://www.async.utah.edu.
15. Charles E. Molnar, Ian W. Jones, Bill Coates, and Jon Lexau. A FIFO ring oscillator performance experiment. In *Proc. International Symposium on Advanced Research in Asynchronous Circuits and Systems*, pages 279–289. IEEE Computer Society Press, April 1997.
16. D. Moundanos, J. Abraham, and Y. Hoskote. Abstraction techniques for validation coverage analysis and test generation. *IEEE TC*, 47(1):2–14, 1998.
17. T. Murata. Petri nets: Properties, analysis, and applications. In *Proceedings of the IEEE 77(4)*, pages 541–580, 1989.
18. T. Murata and J. Y. Koh. Reduction and expansion of lived and safe marked graphs. In *IEEE TCAS, vol. CAS-27, no. 10*, pages 68–70, 1980.
19. C. Ramchandani. *Analysis of Asynchronous Concurrent Systems by Timed Petri Nets*. PhD thesis, MIT, Feb. 1974.
20. R. Alur R.Grosu and M. McDougall. Efficient reachability analysis of hierarchical reactive machines. In *12th International Conference on Computer-Aided Verification, LNCS 1855*, pages 280–295, 2000.
21. Oriol Roig. *Formal Verification and Testing of Asynchronous Circuits*. PhD thesis, Univsitat Politècnia de Catalunya, May 1997.
22. Shai Rotem, Ken Stevens, Ran Ginosar, Peter Beerel, Chris Myers, Kenneth Yun, Rakefet Kol, Charles Dike, Marly Roncken, and Boris Agapiev. RAPPID: An asynchronous instruction length decoder. In *Proc. International Symposium on Advanced Research in Asynchronous Circuits and Systems*, pages 60–70, April 1999.
23. I. Suzuki and T. Murata. *Stepwise refinements for transitions and places*. New York: Springer-Verlag, 1982.
24. I. Suzuki and T. Murata. A method for stepwise refinements and abstractions of petri nets. In *Journal Of Computer System Science, 27(1)*, pages 51–76, 1983.
25. S. Tasiran, R. Alur, R. Kurshan, and R. Brayton. Verifying abstractions of timed systems. In *LNCS*, volume 1119, pages 546–562. Springer-Verlag, 1996.
26. S. Tasiran and R. K. Brayton. Stari: A case study in compositional and heirarchical timing verification. In *Proc. International Conference on Computer Aided Verification*, 1997.
27. Tomohiro Yoneda and Hiroshi Ryu. Timed trace theoretic verification using partial order reduction. In *Proc. International Symposium on Advanced Research in Asynchronous Circuits and Systems*, pages 108–121, April 1999.
28. Hao Zheng. Specification and compilation of timed systems. Master's thesis, University of Utah, 1998.
29. Hao Zheng. *Automatic Abstraction for Synthesis and Verification of Timed Systems*. PhD thesis, University of Utah, 2001.

Automated Verification of a Randomized Distributed Consensus Protocol Using Cadence SMV and PRISM[*]

Marta Kwiatkowska[1], Gethin Norman[1], and Roberto Segala[2]

[1] School of Computer Science, University of Birmingham, Birmingham B15 2TT, UK
{M.Z.Kwiatkowska,G.Norman}@cs.bham.ac.uk
[2] Dipartimento di Scienze dell'Informazione, Università di Bologna
Mura Anteo Zamboni 7, 40127 Bologna, Italy
segala@cs.unibo.it

Abstract. We consider the *randomized consensus* protocol of Aspnes and Herlihy for achieving agreement among N asynchronous processes that communicate via read/write shared registers. The algorithm guarantees termination in the presence of stopping failures within polynomial expected time. Processes proceed through possibly *unboundedly many* rounds; at each round, they read the status of all other processes and attempt to agree. Each attempt involves a *distributed random walk*: when processes disagree, a shared coin-flipping protocol is used to decide their next preferred value. Achieving polynomial expected time depends on the probability that all processes draw the same value being above an appropriate bound. For the non-probabilistic part of the algorithm, we use the proof assistant Cadence SMV to prove validity and agreement *for all N* and *for all rounds*. The coin-flipping protocol is verified using the probabilistic model checker PRISM. For a finite number of processes (up to 10) we automatically calculate the minimum probability of the processes drawing the same value. The correctness of the full protocol follows from the separately proved properties. This is the first time a complex randomized distributed algorithm has been mechanically verified.

1 Introduction

Randomization in the form of coin-flipping is a tool increasingly often used as a symmetry breaker in distributed algorithms, for example, to solve leader election or consensus problems. Such algorithms are inevitably difficult to analyse, and hence appropriate methods of automating their correctness proofs are called for. Furthermore, the use of random choices means that certain properties become probabilistic, and thus cannot be handled by conventional model checking tools.

We consider the *randomized consensus* protocol due to Aspnes and Herlihy [1] for achieving agreement among N asynchronous processes that communicate via read/write shared registers, which guarantees termination in the presence of

---

[*] Supported in part by EPSRC grants GR/M04617 and GR/M13046.

G. Berry, H. Comon, and A. Finkel (Eds.): CAV 2001, LNCS 2102, pp. 194–206, 2001.
© Springer-Verlag Berlin Heidelberg 2001

stopping failures in polynomial expected time. Processes proceed through possibly *unboundedly many* rounds; at each round, they read the status of all other processes and attempt to agree. Each agreement attempt involves a *distributed random walk* (a Markov decision process, i.e. a combination of nondeterministic and probabilistic choices): when processes disagree, a shared coin-flipping protocol is used to decide their next preferred value. Achieving polynomial expected time depends in an essential way on ensuring that the *probability* that all non-failed processes draw the same value being above an appropriate bound.

One possible approach to analyse this algorithm is to verify it using a probabilistic model checker such as PRISM [6]. However, there are a number of problems with this approach. Firstly, the model is infinite. Secondly, even when we restrict to a finite model by fixing the number of processes and rounds, the resulting models are very large: 9×10^6 states for the simpler (exponential expected time) protocol with 3 processes and 4 rounds. Thirdly, many of the requirements are non-probabilistic, and can be discharged with a conventional model checker. Therefore, we adopt a different approach, introduced by Pogosyants, Segala and Lynch [15]: we separate the algorithm into two communicating components, one non-probabilistic (an asynchronous parallel composition of processes which periodically request the outcome of a coin protocol) and the other probabilistic (a coin-flipping protocol shared by the processes). For the non-probabilistic part we use the proof assistant Cadence SMV[1], which enables us to verify the non-probabilistic requirements *for all N* and *for all rounds* by applying the reasoning introduced in [14]. The shared coin-flipping protocol is verified using the probabilistic model checker PRISM. For a finite number of processes (up to 10) we are able to mechanically calculate the minimum probability of the processes drawing the same value, as opposed to a lower bound established analytically in [1] using random walk theory. The correctness of the full protocol (for the finite configurations mentioned above) follows from the separately proved properties.

This is the first time a complex randomized distributed algorithm has been mechanically verified. Our proof structure is similar to the non-mechanical proof of [15], but the proof techniques differ substantially. Although we did not find any errors, the techniques introduced here are applicable more generally, for example, to analyse leader election [10] and Byzantine agreement [5].

Related Work: The protocol discussed in this paper was originally proposed in [1], then further analysed in [15]. Distributed algorithms verified with Cadence SMV for any number of processes include the bakery algorithm [14]. We know of two other probabilistic model checkers, ProbVerus [2] and E⊢MC^2 [9] (neither of which supports nondeterminism that is essential here).

2   The Protocol

Consensus problems arise in many distributed applications, for example, when it is necessary to agree whether to commit or abort a transaction in a distributed

---
[1] http://www-cad.eecs.berkeley.edu/~kenmcmil/smv

database. A *distributed consensus protocol* is an algorithm for ensuring that a collection of distributed processes, which start with some initial value supplied by their environment, eventually terminate agreeing on the same value. Typical requirements for such a protocol are:

Validity: If a process decides on a value, then it is the initial value of a process.
Agreement: Any two processes that decide must decide on the same value.
Termination: All processes eventually decide.

A number of solutions to the consensus problem exist (see [11] for overview). There are several complications, due to the type of model (synchronous or asynchronous) and the type of failure tolerated by the algorithm. If the processes can exhibit *stopping failures* then the **Termination** requirement is too strong and must be replaced by **wait-free termination:** All initialized and non-failed processes eventually decide. Unfortunately, the fundamental impossibility result of [7] demonstrates that there is *no deterministic* algorithm for achieving wait-free agreement in the asynchronous distributed model with communication via shared read/write variables even in the presence of one stopping failure[2]. One solution is to use randomization, which necessitates a weaker termination guarantee:
Probabilistic Wait-Free Termination: *With probability 1,* all initialized and non-failed processes eventually decide.

The algorithm we consider is due to Aspnes & Herlihy [1]. It is a complex algorithm using a sophisticated shared coin-flipping protocol. In addition to **Validity** and **Agreement**, it guarantees **Probabilistic wait-free termination** with polynomial expected time for the asynchronous distributed model with communication via shared read/write variables in the presence of stopping failures.

The algorithm proceeds in rounds. Each process maintains two multiple-read single-write variables, recording its preferred *value* 1 or 2 (initially unknown, represented as 0), and its current *round*. The contents of the array *start* determines the initial preferences. Additional storage is needed to record copies of the preferred value and round of all other processes as observed by a given process; we use arrays *values* and *rounds* for this purpose. Note that the round number is unbounded, and due to asynchrony the processes may be in different rounds at any point in time. In Cadence SMV we have the following variable declarations:

```
#define N 10 /* number of processes (can be changed without affecting the proof) */
ordset PROC 1..N; /* set of process identifiers */
ordset NUM 0..; /* round numbers */
typedef PC {INITIAL, READ, CHECK, DECIDE, FAIL}; /* process phases */
act : PROC; /* the scheduler's choice of process */
start : array PROC of 1..2; /* start[i], initial preference of i */
pc : array PROC of PC; /* pc[i], the phase of process i */
value : array PROC of 0..2; /* value[i], current preference of i */
round : array PROC of NUM; /* round[i], current round number of i */
values : array PROC of array PROC of 0..2;
```

---

[2] See [11] for solutions based on read/modify/write variables, such as test-and-set.

/* values[i][j], j's preference when last read by i */
rounds : **array** PROC **of array** PROC **of** NUM;
/* rounds[i][j], j's round number when last read by i */
count : **array** PROC **of** PROC; /* auxiliary counter for the reading loop */

The processes begin with the INITIALisation phase, where the unknown value is replaced with the preferred value from the array *start* and the round number is set to 1. Then each process repeatedly executes the READing then CHECKing phase until agreement. READing consists of reading the preferred value and round of all processes into the arrays *values* and *rounds*. Process i terminates in the CHECKing phase if it is a *leader* (i.e. its round is greater than or equal to that of any process) and if all processes whose round trails i's by at most 1 (i.e. are presumed not to have failed) agree. Otherwise, if all leaders agree, i updates its value to this preference, increments its round and returns to READing. In the remaining case, if i has a definite preference it "warns" that it may change by resetting it to 0 and returns to READing *without* changing its round number; if its preference is already 0, then i invokes a coin-flipping protocol to select a new value from {1, 2} *at random*, increments its round number and returns to READing.

In Cadence SMV a simplified protocol (we have removed the possibility of FAILure for clarity) can be described as follows, where the random choice of preference from {1, 2} has been replaced by a *nondeterministic assignment*:

```
switch (pc[act]) {
  INITIAL : {
    next(value[act]) := start[act];
    next(round[act]) := round[act] + 1;
    next(pc[act]) := READ; }
  READ : {
    next(pc[act]) := (count[act] = N) ? CHECK : READ;
    next(rounds[act][count[act]]) := round[count[act]];
    next(values[act][count[act]]) := value[count[act]];
    next(count[act]) := (count[act] = N) ? count[act] : count[act] + 1; }
  CHECK : {
    if (decide[act]) { /* all who disagree trail by two and I am a leader */
      next(pc[act]) := DECIDE;
    else if (agree[act][1] | agree[act][2]) { /* all leaders agree */
      next(pc[act]) := READ;
      next(count[act]) := 1;
      next(value[act]) := agree[act][1] ? 1 : 2; /* set value to leaders' preference */
      next(round[act]) := round[act] + 1; }
    else {
      next(pc[act]) := READ;
      next(count[act]) := 1;
      next(value[act]) := (value[act] > 0) ? 0 : {1, 2}; /* warn others or flip coin */
      next(round[act]) := (value[act] > 0) ? round[act] : round[act] + 1; } }
}
```

where the missing formulas *decide* and *agree* are defined below, assuming that $j \in obs_i$ (process i has observed j) if either $j < count[i]$ or $pc[i] = CHECK$:

$agree[i][v]$ is true if, according to i, all leaders whose values have been read by process i agree on value v, where v is either 1 or 2; formally:

$$agree[i][v] \stackrel{\text{def}}{=} \bigwedge_j array\_agree[i][v][j]$$
$$array\_agree[i][v][j] \stackrel{\text{def}}{=} j \in obs_i \to (rounds[i][j] \geq maxr[i] \to values[i][j] = v)$$
$$maxr[i] \stackrel{\text{def}}{=} \max_{j \in obs_i} rounds[i][j]$$

$decide[i]$ is true if, according to i, all that disagree trail by 2 or more rounds and i is a leader; formally:

$$decide[i] \stackrel{\text{def}}{=} maxr[i] = round[i] \wedge (m1\_agree[i][1] \vee m1\_agree[i][2])$$
$$m1\_agree[i][v] \stackrel{\text{def}}{=} \bigwedge_j array\_m1\_agree[i][v][j]$$
$$array\_m1\_agree[i][v][j] \stackrel{\text{def}}{=} j \in obs_i \to (rounds[i][j] \geq maxr[i] - 1 \to values[i][j] = v)$$

The above necessitates a variable, $maxr$, to store the maximum round number. The full protocol can be found at www.cs.bham.ac.uk/~dxp/prism/consensus.

It remains to provide a coin-flipping protocol which returns a preference 1 or 2, with a certain probability, whenever requested by a process in an execution. This could simply be a collection of N independent coins, one for each process, which deliver 1 or 2 with probability $\frac{1}{2}$ (independent of the current round). In [1] it is shown that such an approach yields *exponential* expected time to termination. The *polynomial expected time* is guaranteed by a *shared coin* protocol, which implements a collective random walk parameterised by the number of processes N and a constant $K > 1$ (independent of N). A new copy of this protocol is started *for each round*. The processes access a global shared counter, initially 0. On entering the protocol, a process flips a coin, and, depending on the outcome, increments or decrements the shared counter. Since we are working in a distributed scenario, several processes may simultaneously want to flip a coin, which is modelled as a *nondeterministic* choice between *probability distributions*, one for each coin flip. Note that several processes may be executing the protocol at the same time. Having flipped the coin, the process then reads the counter, say observing c. If $c \geq KN$ it chooses 1 as its preferred value, and if $c \leq -KN$ it chooses 2. Otherwise, the process flips the coin again, and continues doing so until it observes that the counter *has passed one of the barriers*. The barriers ensure that the scheduler cannot influence the outcome of the protocol by suspending processes that are about to move the counter in a given direction.

We denote by CF such a coin-flipping protocol and CF_r the collection of protocols, one for each round number r. Model checking of the shared coin protocol is described in Section 5.

3   The Proof Structure

Recall that to verify this protocol correct we need to establish the properties of **Validity**, **Agreement** and **Probabilistic wait-free termination**. The first two are independent of the actual values of probabilities. Therefore, we can verify these properties by *conventional model checking methods*, replacing the probabilistic choices with nondeterministic ones. In Section 4 we describe how we verify **Validity** and **Agreement** using the methods introduced in [12–14] for Cadence SMV.

We are left to consider **Probabilistic wait-free termination**. This property depends on the probability values with which either 1 or 2 is drawn, and, in particular, on the probabilistic properties of the coin-flipping protocol. However, there are several **probabilistic progress** properties which do *not* depend on any probabilistic assumptions. Similarly to the approach of [15] we analyse such properties in the non-probabilistic variant of the model, except we use Cadence SMV, thus *confining the probabilistic arguments* to a limited section of the analysis.

We now describe the outline of the proof based on [15]. First, we identify subsets of states of the protocol as follows: $\mathcal{D}$, the set of states in which all processes have decided; and $\mathcal{F}_v$, for $v \in \{1, 2\}$, the set of states where there exists $r \in \mathrm{N}$ and unique process i such that i's preferred *value* is v, i has just entered round r, and i is the only leader.

Non-probabilistic Arguments: There are a number of non-probabilistic arguments, see [15]. We state the two needed to explain the main idea of the proof:

Invariant 1 From any state, the maximum round does not increase by more than 1 without reaching a state in $\mathcal{F}_0 \cup \mathcal{F}_1 \cup \mathcal{D}$.

Invariant 2 From any state of $\mathcal{F}_v$ with maximum round r, if in round r all processes leave the protocol CF_r agreeing on the value v, then the maximum round does not increase by more than 2 without reaching a state in $\mathcal{D}$.

These properties are independent of the probabilities of the coin-flipping protocol. So we can replace the random choices of CF with nondeterministic ones, except in round r where CF_r must return value v for all processes.

Probabilistic Arguments: There are two probabilistic properties, listed below.

C1 For each fair execution of CF_r that starts with a reachable state of CF_r, *with probability 1* all processes that enter CF_r will eventually leave.

C2 For each fair execution of CF_r, and each value $v \in \{1, 2\}$, the probability that all processes that enter CF_r will eventually leave agreeing on the value v is at least p, where $0 < p \leq 1$.

Putting the Arguments Together: By **Invariant 1** and **C1** (since the coin-flipping protocol must return a value in order to continue), from *any* reachable state of the combined protocol, under any scheduling of nondeterminism, *with probability 1* one can always reach a state either in $\mathcal{D}$, $\mathcal{F}_1$ or $\mathcal{F}_2$ such that the maximum round number increases by *at most* 1. Next by **Invariant 2**, **C1** and **C2**, from a state in $\mathcal{F}_v$, under any scheduling of nondeterminism, *with probability at least p* one can always reach a state in $\mathcal{D}$ with the maximum round number increasing by *at most* 2. Therefore, from these two properties, starting from *any* reachable state of the combined protocol, under any scheduling of nondeterminism, *with probability at least* p one can always reach a state in $\mathcal{D}$ (all processes have decided) with the maximum round number increasing by *at most* $3(=1+2)$.

It then follows that the expected number of rounds until $\mathcal{D}$ is reached is $O(\frac{1}{p})$. Thus, using independent coins where $p = \frac{1}{2^N}$ the expected number of rounds is $O(2^N)$. For the shared coin protocol, since $p = \frac{K-1}{2K}$, it is $O(1)$ (i.e. constant). This is because the round number does not increase while the processes perform the shared coin protocol. However, we must take account of the number of steps performed within the shared coin protocol; by random walk theory this yields expected time of $(K + 1)^2 N^2 = O(N^2)$ [1], which is indeed polynomial.

In the sequel we show how to use Cadence SMV and PRISM to mechanically verify the non-probabilistic and probabilistic arguments respectively. These have to be carried out at a low level, and therefore constitute the most tedious and error-prone part of the analysis. The remaining part of the proof, in which the separately verified arguments are put together, is not proved mechanically. It is sufficiently high level that it can be easily checked by hand. We believe that a fully mechanical analysis can be achieved with the help of a theorem prover.

4   The Cadence SMV Proof

Cadence SMV is a proof assistant which supports several *compositional methods* [12–14]. These methods permit the verification of large, complex, systems by reducing the verification problem to small problems that can be solved automatically by model checking. Cadence SMV provides a variety of such techniques including *induction, circular compositional reasoning, temporal case splitting* and *data type reduction*. For example, data type reduction is used to reduce large or *infinite* types to small finite types, and temporal case splitting breaks the proof into *cases* based on the value of a given variable. Combining data type reduction and temporal case splitting can reduce a complex proof to checking only a small number of simple subcases, thus achieving significant space savings.

There are two main challenges posed by the algorithm we consider: the round numbers are *unbounded*, leading to an *infinite* data type *NUM*, and we wish to prove the correctness for *any* number of processes, or, in other words, for *all* values of N. We achieve this by suitably combining data type reduction (ordset) with induction, circular compositional reasoning and temporal case splitting.

We briefly explain the ordset data type reduction implemented in Cadence SMV [14] with the help of the type *NUM*. For a given value r this reduction constructs an abstraction of this type shown in Figure 1, where the only constant is 0. The only operations permitted on this type are: equality/inequality testing (between abstract values), equality/inequality test against a constant, and increment/decrement the value by 1. For example, the following are allowed: comparisons $r > 0$ and $r = 0$ (but not $r = 1$) and next$(r) := r + 1$. With these restrictions on the operations, the abstract representations as shown in Figure 1 are *isomorphic* for all $r \in NUM$. Therefore, it suffices to check a property for a *single* value of r. The reduction of the data type *PROC* is similar, except that there are two constants, 1 and N; see [14] for more detail.

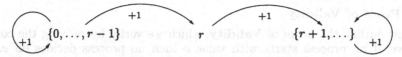

Fig. 1. Abstraction of *NUM*.

We now illustrate the `ordset` reduction with a simple property, concerning the *global maximum round*, that is, the maximum round number over all processes. In Cadence SMV we can define this as follows:

$\quad$ `next`$(gmaxr) :=$ `next`$(round[act]) > gmaxr$? `next`$(round[act])$: $gmaxr$;

However, since *act* ranges over *PROC*, the value of *gmaxr* depends on *all* instances *round*[*i*] for $i \in N$. We therefore introduce a *history* variable which records the value of *round*[*act*] and replaces the implicit dependence on N with a dependence on a single variable. We redefine *gmaxr* as follows:

$\quad$ `next`$(hist) :=$ `next`$(round[act])$;
$\quad$ `next`$(gmaxr) :=$ `next`$(hist) > gmaxr$? `next`$(hist)$: $gmaxr$;

We can now state that *gmaxr* is indeed the global maximum round number:

$\quad$ `forall` (i in *PROC*) $max[i]$: `assert` G ($round[i] \leq gmaxr$);

To prove this holds, we *case split* on the value of *round*[*i*] and suppose that $max[i]$ holds at time $t - 1$. Furthermore, by setting the variables that do not affect the satisfaction of $max[i]$ to be *free* (allowing these variables to range over *all* the possible values of their types), we can improve the efficiency of model checking by a factor of 10. Though perhaps not important for this simple property, such improvements are crucial for more complex properties, as without freeing certain variables model checking quickly becomes infeasible. The proof is:

```
forall (r in NUM) {
    subcase max[i][r] of max[i] for round[i] = r; /* case split on round[i] */
    using (max[i]), /* assume max[i] holds at time t − 1 */
    agree//free, decide//free, start//free, value//free, /* free variables */
    prove max[i] };
```

Through the `ordset` data type reduction SMV reduces this proof to checking $max[i][r]$ for a single value of i (=2) and a single value of r (=1).

The full proof of **Validity**, **Agreement** and **Non-probabilistic progress** is available at `www.cs.bham.ac.uk/~dxp/prism/consensus`. The proof consists of approximately 50 lemmas, requiring at most 270 MB of memory[3]. Judicious choice of data reduction/freeing is important, as otherwise SMV may return false, but SMV allows one to inspect the cone of influence to identify the variables that are used in the proofs.

---

[3] The version of Cadence SMV we have used is not fully compatible with the release of 08.08.00.

4.1   Proof of Validity

We now outline the proof of **Validity**, which we verify by proving the contra-positive: if no process starts with value v then no process decides on v. For simplicity suppose $v = 2$. The hypothesis is that no process starts with value 2:

forall (i in $PROC$) $valid\_assump[i]$: assert G $\neg$($start[i] = 2$);

which is assumed throughout the proof, and the conclusion is:

forall (i in $PROC$) $validity[i]$: assert G($pc[i] = DECIDE \rightarrow \neg(value[i] = 2)$);

The important step in proving $validity$ is seeing that if all processes start with preference 1, then any process i past its INITIAL phase, i.e. whose round number is positive, has preferred value 1 and the predicate $agree[i][1]$ holds. To prove $validity$ we therefore first prove the stronger properties:

forall (i in $PROC$) {
    $valid1[i]$: assert G ($round[i] > 0 \rightarrow value[i] = 1$);
    $valid2[i]$: assert G ($round[i] > 0 \rightarrow agree[i][1]$); }

We prove $valid1[i]$ by case splitting on $round[i]$ and assuming $valid2[i]$ holds at time $t - 1$. Also, since $round[i] = 0$ is a special case, we must add 0 to the abstraction of NUM (otherwise Cadence SMV returns false), i.e. NUM is abstracted to $0, \{1, \ldots, r-1\}, r, \{r+1, \ldots\}$. The proof in Cadence SMV has the following form:

forall (r in NUM) {
    subcase $valid1[i][r]$ of $valid1[i]$ for $round[i] = r$;
    using $valid\_assump[i]$, ($valid2[i]$), $NUM \rightarrow \{0, r\}, \ldots$, prove $valid1[i][r]$; }

To prove $valid2[i]$, we have the additional complication of $agree[i][1]$ being de-fined as the conjunction of an array ($array\_agree[i][1][j]$ for $j \in PROC$), which again contains an implicit dependency on all values of the set $PROC$. Instead, we consider each element of the array separately. In particular, we first prove the auxiliary property $valid3[i]$ elementwise, assuming $valid1$ holds, and again add 0 to the abstraction of NUM:

forall (i in $PROC$) forall (j in $PROC$) {
    $valid3[i][j]$: assert G ($round[i] > 0 \rightarrow array\_agree[i][1][j]$);
    forall (r in NUM) {
        subcase $valid3[i][j][r]$ of $valid3[i][j]$ for $maxr[i] = r$;
        using $valid\_assump[j]$, $valid1[j]$, $NUM \rightarrow \{0, r\}, \ldots$, prove $valid3[i][j][r]$; }}

Next we use $valid3[i][j]$ to prove $valid2[i]$ through a proof by *contradiction*: first consider the processes j such that $array\_agree[i][1][j]$ is false:

forall (i in $PROC$) $y[i] := \{ j : j$ in $PROC$, $\neg array\_agree[i][1][j] \}$;

Then we consider a particular $j \in y[i]$ when proving $valid2[i]$ while using the fact that $valid3[i][j]$ holds:

forall (j in $PROC$) {
    subcase $valid2[i][j]$ of $valid2[i]$ for $y[i] = j$;
    using $valid3[i][j], \ldots$, prove $valid2[i][j]$; }

The contradiction then arises since, by $valid3[i][j]$, $array\_agree[i][1][y[i]]$ must be true. The apparent circularity between these properties is broken since $valid1$ assumes $valid2$ at time $t - 1$.

4.2   Proof of Agreement

We now outline the proof of Invariant 6.3 of [15] which is used to prove **Agreement**, the most difficult of the requirements. First we define new predicates $fill\_maxr[i]$, $array\_fill\_agree[i][v][j]$ and $fill\_agree[i][v]$ to be the same as the corresponding predicates $maxr[i]$, $array\_agree[i][v][j]$ $agree[i][v]$, except an incomplete observation of a process is "filled in" with the actual values of the unobserved processes. More formally:

$$fill\_rounds[i][j] \overset{\text{def}}{=} \text{if } j \in obs_i \text{ then } rounds[i][j] \text{ else } round[j]$$
$$fill\_values[i][j] \overset{\text{def}}{=} \text{if } j \in obs_i \text{ then } values[i][j] \text{ else } value[j].$$

Invariant 6.3 of [15]. *Let i be a process. Given a reachable state, let $v = value[i]$. If $fill\_maxr[i] = round[i]$, $m1\_agree[i][v]$ and $fill\_agree[i][v]$, then*

a. $\forall_j$ $agree[j][v]$
b. $\forall_j$ $round[j] \geq round[i] \rightarrow value[j] = v$
c. $\forall_{j \in obs_i}$ $(round[j] = round[i] - 1 \land value[j] \neq v) \rightarrow fill\_maxr[j] \leq round[i]$.

We now describe our approach to proving Invariant 6.3. For simplicity, we have restricted our attention to when $v = 1$. To ease the notation we let:

$$C[i] \overset{\text{def}}{=} (fill\_maxr[i] = round[i]) \land m1\_agree[i][1] \land fill\_agree[i][1] \land (value[i] = 1).$$

We first split Invariant 6.3 into separate parts corresponding to the conditions a, b and c. The main reason for this is that the validity of the different cases depends on different variables of the protocol. We are therefore able to "free" more variables when proving the cases separately, and hence improve the efficiency of the model checking. Formally, conditions a and b of Invariant 6.3 are given by:

```
forall (i in PROC) forall (j in PROC)
    inv63a[i][j] : assert G ( C[i] → agree[j][1] );
    inv63b[i][j] : assert G ( C[i] → (round[j] ≥ round[i] → value[j] = 1) );
```

Note that, when proving $inv63a[i][j]$, $agree[j][1]$ is the conjunction of an array. We therefore use the same proof technique as outlined for $valid2[i]$ in Section 4.1, that is, we first prove:

```
forall (i in PROC) forall (j in PROC) forall (k in PROC)
    inv63ak[i][j][k] : assert G ( C[i] → array_agree[j][1][k] );
```

We encounter a similar problem with the precondition, $C[i]$, since $m1\_agree[i][1]$ and $fill\_agree[i][1]$ are conjunctions of arrays. In this case, we use a version of Lemma 6.12 of [15]. Informally, this lemma states: if $C[i]$ holds in the *next state* and the transition to reach this state does *not* involve process i changing the value of $round[i]$ or $value[i]$, then $C[i]$ holds in the *current state*. More precisely, we have the following properties:

```
forall (i in PROC) {
    lem612a[i] : assert G ( (¬(act = i) ∧ X (C[i])) → (C[i]) );
    lem612b[i] : assert G ( (act = i ∧ (pc[i] = READ) ∧ X (C[i])) → (C[i]) );
    lem612c[i] : assert G ( (act = i ∧ X ((pc[i] = DECIDE) ∧ C[i])) → (C[i]) ); }
```

When proving $inv63ak[i][j][k]$ we case split on $round[i]$ and assume $inv63ak$ $[i][j][k]$ and $inv63b[i][k]$ hold at time $t-1$ (Invariant 6.3c is not needed). Additional assumptions include those of Lemma 6.12 given above. Also, since $m1\_agree[i]$ involves $r-1$ where r is of type NUM, we abstract NUM to $\{0, \ldots, r-2\}, r-1, r, \{r+1, \ldots\}$. The actual proof in Cadence SMV has the following form:

```
forall (r in NUM) {
    subcase inv63ak[i][j][k][r] of inv63ak[i][j][k] for round[i] = r;
    using (inv63ak[i][j][k]), (inv63b[i][k]), lem612a[i], lem612b[i], lem612c[i],
    NUM → {r − 1 .. r}, ..., prove inv63ak[i][j][k][r]; }
```

5 Verification with PRISM

PRISM, a Probabilistic Symbolic Model Checker, is an experimental tool described in [6], see www.cs.bham.ac.uk/~dxp/prism. It is built in Java/C++ using the CUDD [16] package which supports MTBDDs. The system description language of the tool is a probabilistic variant of Reactive Modules. The specifications are given as formulas of the probabilistic temporal logic PCTL [8, 4]. PRISM builds a symbolic representation of the model as an MTBDD and performs the analysis implementing the algorithms of [3, 4]. It supports a symbolic engine based on MTBDDs as well as a sparse matrix engine.

A summary of experimental results obtained from the shared coin-flipping protocol modelled and analysed using the MTBDD engine is included in the table below. Further details, including the description of the coin-flipping protocol, can be found at www.cs.bham.ac.uk/~dxp/prism/consensus. Both properties C1 and C2 are expressible in PCTL. C1 is a probability 1 property, and therefore admits efficient *qualitative* [17] probabilistic analysis such as the probability-1 precomputation step [6], whereas C2, on the other hand, is *quantitative*, and requires calculating the minimum probability that, starting from the *initial state* of the coin-flipping protocol, *all* processes leave the protocol agreeing on a given value. Our analysis is mechanical, and demonstrates that the analytical lower bound $\frac{K-1}{2K}$ obtained in [1] is reasonably tight (the discrepancy is greater for smaller values of K, not included).

N	K	#states	construction time (s):	C1 time (s):	C2		
					time (s):	probability:	bound $(K-1)/2K$:
2	64	8,208	1.108	0.666	3689	0.493846	0.4921875
4	32	329,856	2.796	6.497	212784	0.494916	0.484375
8	16	437,194,752	54.881	59.668	1085300	0.47927	0.46875
10	8	10,017,067,008	26.719	139.535	986424	0.4463	0.4375

Fig. 2. Model Checking of the Coin-Flipping Protocol.

6 Conclusion

In this paper we have for the first time mechanically verified a complex randomized distributed algorithm, thus replacing tedious proofs by hand of a large numbers of lemmas with manageable, re-usable, and efficient proofs with Cadence SMV and an automatic check of the probabilistic properties with PRISM. The verification of the protocol is fully mechanised at the low level, while some simple high-level arguments are carried out manually. A fully automated proof can be achieved by involving a theorem prover for the manual part of the analysis. We believe that the techniques introduced here are applicable more generally, for example, to analyse [10, 5].

Acknowledgements

We are grateful to Ken McMillan for supplying a recent version of Cadence SMV and suggesting appropriate proof methods.

References

1. J. Aspnes and M. Herlihy. Fast randomized consensus using shared memory. *Journal of Algorithms*, 11(3):441–460, 1990.
2. C. Baier, E. Clarke, and V. Hartonas-Garmhausen. On the semantic foundations of Probabilistic VERUS. In C. Baier, M. Huth, M. Kwiatkowska, and M. Ryan, editors, *Proc. PROBMIV'98*, volume 22 of *ENTCS*, 1998.
3. C. Baier and M. Kwiatkowska. Model checking for a probabilistic branching time logic with fairness. *Distributed Computing*, 11:125–155, 1998.
4. A. Bianco and L. de Alfaro. Model checking of probabilistic and nondeterministic systems. In P. Thiagarajan, editor, *Proc. FST & TCS*, volume 1026 of *LNCS*, pages 499–513, 1995.
5. C. Cachin, K. Kursawe, and V. Shoup. Random oracles in Constantinople: Practical asynchronous byzantine agreement using cryptography. In *Proc. PODC'00*, pages 123–132, 2000.
6. L. de Alfaro, M. Kwiatkowska, G. Norman, D. Parker, and R. Segala. Symbolic model checking of concurrent probabilistic systems using MTBDDs and the Kronecker representation. In S. Graf and M. Schwartzbach, editors, *Proc. TACAS'2000*, volume 1785 of *LNCS*, pages 395–410, 2000.
7. M. Fischer, N. Lynch, and M.Paterson. Impossibility of distributed commit with one faulty process. *Journal of the ACM*, 32(5):374–382, 1985.
8. H. Hansson and B. Jonsson. A logic for reasoning about time and reliability. *Formal Aspects of Computing*, 6(4):512–535, 1994.
9. H. Hermanns, J.-P. Katoen, J. Meyer-Kayser, and M. Siegle. A Markov Chain Model Checker. In S. Graf and M. Schwartzbach, editors, *Proc. TACAS 2000*, volume 1785 of *LNCS*, pages 347–362, 2000.
10. A. Itai and M. Rodeh. The lord of the ring or probabilistic methods for breaking symmetry in distributed networks. Technical Report RJ 3110, IBM, 1981.
11. N. Lynch. *Distributed Algorithms*. Morgan Kaufmann, 1996.

12. K. McMillan. Verfication of an implementation of Tomasulo's algorithm by compositional model checking. In A. Hu and M. Vardi, editors, *Proc. CAV'98*, volume 1427 of *LNCS*, pages 110–121, 1998.
13. K. McMillan. Verification of infinite state systems by compositional model checking. In L. Pierre and T. Kropf, editors, *Proc. CHARME'99*, volume 1703 of *LNCS*, pages 219–233, 1999.
14. K. McMillan, S. Qadeer, and J. Saxe. Induction and compositional model checking. In E. Emerson and A. P. Sistla, editors, *Proc. CAV 2000*, volume 1855 of *LNCS*, pages 312–327, 2000.
15. A. Pogosyants, R. Segala, and N. Lynch. Verification of the randomized consensus algorithm of Aspnes and Herlihy: a case study. *Distributed Computing*, 13(3):155–186, 2000.
16. F. Somenzi. CUDD: CU decision diagram package. Public software, Colorado University, Boulder, 1997.
17. M. Vardi. Automatic verification of probabilistic concurrent finite state programs. In *Proc. FOCS'85*, pages 327–338, 1985.

Analysis of Recursive State Machines

Rajeev Alur[1,2], Kousha Etessami[1], and Mihalis Yannakakis[1]

[1] Bell Labs, Murray Hill, NJ
[2] Dept. of Comp. and Inf. Science, U. of Pennsylvania
{alur,kousha,mihalis}@research.bell-labs.com

Abstract. Recursive state machines (RSMs) enhance the power of ordinary state machines by allowing vertices to correspond either to ordinary states or to potentially recursive invocations of other state machines. RSMs can model the control flow in sequential imperative programs containing recursive procedure calls. They can be viewed as a visual notation extending Statecharts-like hierarchical state machines, where concurrency is disallowed but recursion is allowed. They are also related to various models of pushdown systems studied in the verification and program analysis communities.

After introducing RSMs, we focus on whether state-space analysis can be performed efficiently for RSMs. We consider the two central problems for algorithmic analysis and model checking, namely, reachability (is a target state reachable from initial states) and cycle detection (is there a reachable cycle containing an accepting state). We show that both these problems can be solved in time $O(n\theta^2)$ and space $O(n\theta)$, where n is the size of the recursive machine and θ is the maximum, over all component state machines, of the minimum of the number of entries and the number of exits of each component. We also study the precise relationship between RSMs and closely related models.

1 Introduction

In traditional model checking, the model is a finite state machine whose vertices correspond to system states and whose edges correspond to system transitions. In this paper we consider the analysis of *recursive state machines* (RSMs), in which vertices can either be ordinary states or can correspond to invocations of other state machines in a potentially recursive manner. RSMs can model control flow in typical sequential imperative programming languages with recursive procedure calls. Alternatively, RSMs can be viewed as a variant of visual notations for hierarchical state machines, such as Statecharts [10] and UML [5], where concurrency is disallowed but recursion is allowed.

More precisely, a recursive state machine consists of a set of component machines. Each component has a set of *nodes* (atomic states) and *boxes* (each of which is mapped to a component), a well-defined interface consisting of *entry* and *exit* nodes, and edges connecting nodes/boxes. An edge entering a box models the invocation of the component associated with the box, and an edge leaving a box corresponds to a return from that component. Due to recursion, the underlying

G. Berry, H. Comon, and A. Finkel (Eds.): CAV 2001, LNCS 2102, pp. 207–220, 2001.

global state-space is infinite and behaves like a *pushdown* system. While RSMs are closely related to pushdown systems, which are studied in verification and program analysis in many disguises [12, 6], RSMs appear to be the appropriate definition for visual modeling and allow tigher analysis.

We study the two most fundamental questions for model checking of safety and liveness properties, respectively: (1) *reachability*: given sets of initial and target nodes, is some target node reachable from an initial one, and (2) *cycle detection*: given sets of initial and target nodes, is there a cycle containing a target node reachable from an initial node. For cycle detection, there are two natural variants depending on whether or not one requires the recursion depth to be bounded in infinite computations. We show that all these problems can be solved in time $O(n\theta^2)$, where n is the size of the RSM, and θ is a parameter depending only on the number of entries and exits in each component. The number of entry points correspond to the parameters passed to a component, while the number of exit points correspond to the values returned. More precisely, for each component A_i, let d_i be the minimum of the number of entries and the number of exits of that component. Then $\theta = \max_i(d_i)$. Thus, if every component has either a "small" number of entry points, or a "small" number of exit points, then θ will be "small". The space complexity of the algorithms is $O(n\theta)$.

The first, and key, computational step in the analysis of RSMs involves determining reachability relationships among entry and exit points of each component. We show how the information required for this computation can be encoded as recursive Datalog-like rules of a special form. To enable efficient analysis, our rules will capture *forward* reachability from entry points for components with a small number of entries, and *backward* reachability from exit points for the other components. The solution to the rules can then be reduced to alternating reachability for AND-OR (game) graphs. In the second step of our algorithm, we reduce the problems of reachability and cycle detection with bounded/unbounded recursion depth to traditional graph-theoretic analysis on appropriately constructed graphs based on the information computed in the first step. Our algorithms for cycle detection lead immediately to algorithms for model checking for linear-time requirements expressed as LTL formulas or Büchi automata, via a product construction for Büchi automata with RSMs.

Related Work. Our definition of recursive state machines naturally generalizes the definition of hierarchical state machines of [1]. For hierarchical state machines, the underlying state-space is guaranteed to be finite, but can be exponential in the size of the original machine. Algorithms for analysis of hierarchical state machines [1] are adaptations of traditional search algorithms to avoid searching the same component repeatedly, and have the same time complexity as the algorithms of this paper. However, the "bottom-up" algorithms used in [1] for hierarchical machines can not be applied to RSMs.

RSMs are closely related to *pushdown systems*. Model checking of pushdown systems has been studied extensively for both linear- and branching-time requirements [6, 7, 9, 8]. These algorithms are based on an automata-theoretic approach.

Each configuration is viewed as a string over stack symbols, and the reachable configurations are shown to be a regular set that can be computed by a fixpoint computation. Esparza et al [8] do a careful analysis of the time and space requirements for various problems including reachability and cycle detection. The resulting worst case complexity is cubic, and thus, matches our worst case when $\theta = O(n)$. Their approach also leads, under more refined analysis, to the bound $O(nk^2)$ [8], where n is the size of the pushdown system and k is its number of *control states*. We will see that the number of control states of a pushdown system is related to the number of exit nodes in RSMs, but that by working with RSMs directly we can achieve better bounds in terms of θ.

Ball and Rajamani consider the model of Boolean programs, which can be viewed as RSMs extended with boolean variables [3]. They have implemented a BDD-based symbolic model checker that solves the reachability problem for Boolean programs. The main technique is to compute the *summary* of the input-output relation of a procedure. This in turn is based on algorithms for interprocedural dataflow analysis [12], which are generally cubic. As described in Section 5, when translating Boolean programs to RSMs, one must pay the standard exponential price to account for different combinations of values of the variables, but the price of analysis need not be cubic in the expanded state-space by making a careful distinction between local, read-global, and write-global variables.

In the context of this rich history of research, the current paper has four main contributions. First, while equivalent to pushdown systems and Boolean programs in theory, recursive state machines are a more direct, visual, state-based model of recursive control flow. Second, we give algorithms with time and space bounds of $O(n\theta^2)$ and $O(n\theta)$, respectively, and thus our solution for analysis is more efficient than the generally cubic algorithms for related models, even when these were geared specifically to solve flow problems in control graphs of sequential programs. Third, our algorithmic technique for both reachability analysis and cycle detection, which combines a mutually dependent forward and backward reachability analyses using a natural Datalog formulation and AND-OR graph accessibility, along with the analysis of an augmented ordinary graph, is new and potentially useful for solving related problems in program analysis to mitigate similar cubic bottlenecks. We also anticipate that it is more suitable for on-the-fly model checking and early error detection than the prior automata-theoretic solutions for analysis of pushdown systems. Finally, using our RSM model one is able to, at no extra cost in complexity, distinguish between infinite accepting executions that require a "bounded call stack" or "unbounded call stack". This distinction had not been considered in all previous papers.

Note: Results similar to ours have been obtained independently, and submitted concurrently, by [4] on a model identical to RSMs.

2 Recursive State Machines

Syntax. A *recursive state machine (RSM)* A over a finite alphabet Σ is given by a tuple $\langle A_1, \ldots, A_k \rangle$, where each *component state machine* $A_i = (N_i \cup B_i, Y_i, En_i, Ex_i, \delta_i)$ consists of the following pieces:

- A set N_i of *nodes* and a (disjoint) set B_i of *boxes*.
- A labeling $Y_i : B_i \mapsto \{1, \ldots, k\}$ that assigns to every box an index of one of the component machines, $A_1, \ldots, A_k$.
- A set of *entry* nodes $En_i \subseteq N_i$, and a set of *exit* nodes $Ex_i \subseteq N_i$.
- A transition relation δ_i, where transitions are of the form (u, σ, v) where (1) the source u is either a node of N_i, or a pair (b, x), where b is a box in B_i and x is an exit node in Ex_j for $j = Y_i(b)$; (2) the label σ is either ε, a silent transition, or in Σ; and (3) the destination v is either a node in N_i or a pair (b, e), where b is a box in B_i and e is an entry node in En_j for $j = Y_i(b)$.

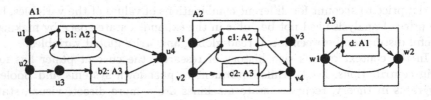

Fig. 1. A Sample Recursive State Machine.

We will use the term *ports* to refer collectively to the entry and exit nodes of a machine A_i, and will use the term *vertices* of A_i to refer to its nodes and the ports of its boxes that participate in some transition. That is, the transition relation δ_i is a set of labelled directed edges on the set V_i of vertices of the machine A_i. We let E_i be the set of underlying edges of δ_i, ignoring labels. Figure 1 illustrates the definition. The sample RSM has three components. The component A_1 has 4 nodes, of which $u1$ and $u2$ are entry nodes and $u4$ is the exit node, and two boxes, of which $b1$ is mapped to component A_2 and $b2$ is mapped to A_3. The entry and exit nodes are the control interface of a component by which it can communicate with the other components. Intuitively, think of component state machines as procedures, and an edge entering a box at a given entry as invoking the procedure associated with the box with given argument values. Entry-nodes are analogous to arguments while exit-nodes model values returned.

Semantics. To define the executions of RSMs, we first define the global states and transitions associated with an RSM. A (global) *state* of an RSM $A = \langle A_1, \ldots A_k \rangle$ is a tuple $\langle b_1, \ldots, b_r, u \rangle$ where $b_1, \ldots, b_r$ are boxes and u is a node. Equivalently, a state can be viewed as a string, and the set Q of global states of A is B^*N, where $B = \cup_i B_i$ and $N = \cup_i N_i$. Consider a state $\langle b_1, \ldots, b_r, u \rangle$ such that $b_i \in B_{j_i}$ for $1 \le i \le r$ and $u \in N_j$. Such a state is *well-formed* if $Y_{j_i}(b_i) = j_{i+1}$ for $1 \le i < r$ and $Y_{j_r}(b_r) = j$. A well-formed state of this form corresponds to the case when the control is inside the component A_j, which was entered via box b_r of component A_{j_r} (the box b_{r-1} gives the context in which A_{j_r} was entered, and so on). Henceforth, we assume states to be well-formed.

We define a (global) transition relation δ. Let $s = \langle b_1, \ldots, b_r, u \rangle$ be a state with $u \in N_j$ and $b_r \in B_m$. Then, $(s, \sigma, s') \in \delta$ iff one of the following holds:

1. $(u, \sigma, u') \in \delta_j$ for a node u' of A_j, and $s' = \langle b_1, \ldots, b_r, u' \rangle$.
2. $(u, \sigma, (b', e)) \in \delta_j$ for a box b' of A_j, and $s' = \langle b_1, \ldots, b_r, b', e \rangle$.
3. u is an exit-node of A_j, $((b_r, u), \sigma, u') \in \delta_m$ for a node u' of A_m, and $s' = \langle b_1, \ldots, b_{r-1}, u' \rangle$.
4. u is an exit-node of A_j, $((b_r, u), \sigma, (b', e)) \in \delta_m$ for a box b' of A_m, and $s' = \langle b_1, \ldots, b_{r-1}, b', e \rangle$.

Case 1 is when the control stays within the component A_j, case 2 is when a new component is entered via a box of A_j, case 3 is when the control exits A_j and returns back to A_m, and case 4 is when the control exits A_j and enters a new component via a box of A_m. The global states Q along with the transition relation δ define an ordinary transition system, denoted T_A.

We wish to consider recursive automata as generators of ω-languages. For this, we augment RSMs with a designated set of initial nodes, and with Büchi acceptance conditions. A *recursive Büchi automaton* (RBA) over an alphabet Σ consists of an RSM A over Σ, together with a set $Init \subseteq \cup_{i=1}^k En_i$ of initial nodes and a set $F \subseteq \cup_{i=1}^k N_i$ of *repeating* (accepting) nodes. (If F is not given, by default we assume $F = \cup_{i=1}^k N_i$ to associate a language $L(A)$ with RSM A and its $Init$ set). Given an RBA, $(A, Init, F)$, we obtain an (infinite) global Büchi automaton $B_A = (T_A, Init^*, F^*)$, where the initial states $Init^*$ are states $\langle e \rangle$ where $e \in Init$, and where a state $\langle b_1, \ldots b_r, v \rangle$ is in F^* if v is in F. For an infinite word $w = w_0 w_1 \ldots$ over Σ, a *run* π of B_A over w is a sequence $s_0 \xrightarrow{\sigma_0} s_1 \xrightarrow{\sigma_1} s_2 \cdots$ of states s_i and symbols $\sigma_i \in \Sigma \cup \{\varepsilon\}$ such that (1) $s_0 \in Init^*$, (2) $(s_i, \sigma_i, s_{i+1}) \in \delta$ for all i, and (3) the word w equals $\sigma_0 \sigma_1 \sigma_2 \cdots$ with all the ε symbols removed. A run π is *accepting* if for infinitely many i, $s_i \in F^*$.

We call a run π *bounded* if there is an integer m such that for all i, the length of the tuple s_i is bounded by m. It is *unbounded* otherwise. In other words, in a bounded (infinite) run the stack-length (number of boxes in context) always stays bounded. A word $w \in \Sigma^\omega$ is *(boundedly/unboundedly) accepted* by the RBA A if there is an accepting (bounded/unbounded) run of B_A on w. Note, w is boundedly accepted iff for some $s \in F^*$ there is a run π on w for which $s_i = s$ infinitely often. This is not so for unbounded accepting runs.

We let $L(A)$, $L_b(A)$ and $L_u(A)$ denote the set of words accepted, boundedly accepted, and unboundedly accepted by A, respectively. Clearly, $L_b(A) \cup L_u(A) = L(A)$, but $L_b(A)$ and $L_u(A)$ need not be disjoint. Given RBA A, we will be interested in two central algorithmic problems:

1. *Reachability:* Given A, for nodes u and v of A, let $u \Rightarrow v$ denote that some global state $\langle b_1, \ldots b_r, v \rangle$, whose node is v, is reachable from the global state

$\langle u \rangle$ in the global transition system T_A. Extending the notation, let $Init \Rightarrow v$ denote that for some $u \in Init$, $u \Rightarrow v$. Our goal in simple reachability analysis is to compute the set $\{v \mid Init \Rightarrow v\}$ of reachable vertices.

2. *Language emptiness:* We want to determine if $L(A)$, $L_b(A)$ and $L_u(A)$ are empty or not. We obtain thereby algorithms for model checking RSMs.

Notation. We use the following notation. Let v_i be the number of vertices and e_i the number of transitions (edges) of each component A_i, and let $v = \Sigma_i v_i$, $e = \Sigma_i e_i$ be the total number of vertices and edges. The *size* $|A|$ of a RSM A is the space needed to write down its components. Assuming, w.l.o.g., that each node and each box of each component is involved in at least one transition, $v \leq 2e$ and the size of A is proportional to its number of edges e. The other parameter that enters in the complexity is θ, a bound on the number of entries or exits of the components. Let $en_i = |En_i|$ and $ex_i = |Ex_i|$, be the number of entries and exits in the i'th component, A_i. Then $\theta = \max_{i \in \{1, \ldots, k\}} \min(en_i, ex_i)$. That is, every component has either no more than θ entries or no more than θ exits. There may be some components of each kind; we call components of the first kind *entry-bound* and the others *exit-bound*.

3 Algorithms for State-Space Analysis

Given a recursive automaton, A, in this section we show how problems such as reachability and language emptiness can be solved in time $O(|A|\theta^2)$; more precisely, in time $O(e\theta + v\theta^2)$ and space $O(e + v\theta)$. For notational convenience, we will assume without loss of generality that all entry nodes of the machines have no incoming edges and all exit nodes have no outgoing edges.

3.1 Reachability

Given A, we wish to compute the set $\{v \mid Init \Rightarrow v\}$. For clarity, we present our algorithm in two stages. First, we define a set of Datalog rules and construct an associated AND-OR graph G_A, which can be used to compute information about reachability within each component automaton. Next, we use this information to obtain an ordinary graph H_A, such that we can compute the set $\{v \mid Init \Rightarrow v\}$ by simple reachability analysis on H_A.

Step 1: The Rules and the AND-OR Graph Construction. As a first step we will compute, for each component A_i, a predicate (relation) $R_i(x, y)$. If A_i is entry-bound, then the variable x ranges over all entry nodes of A_i and y ranges over all vertices of A_i. If A_i is exit-bound, then x ranges over all vertices of A_i and y ranges over all exit nodes of A_i. The meaning of the predicate is defined as follows: $R_i(x, y)$ holds iff there is a path in T_A from $\langle x \rangle$ to $\langle y \rangle$.

The predicates $R_i(x, y)$ are determined by a series of simple recursive relationships which we will write in the style of Datalog rules [13]. Recall some terminology. An *atom* is a term $P(\tau)$ where P is a predicate (relation) symbol and τ is a tuple of appropriate arity consisting of variables and constants from appropriate domains. A *ground* atom has only constants. A Datalog rule has the form *head* ← *body*, where *head* is an atom and *body* is a conjunction of atoms. The meaning of a rule is that if for some instantiation σ, mapping variables of a rule to constants, all the (instantiated) conjuncts in the body of the rule $\sigma(body)$ are true, then the instantiated head $\sigma(head)$ must also be true. For readability, we deviate slightly from this notation and write the rules as "*head* ← *body*, under constraint C", where *body* includes only recursive predicates, and nonrecursive constraints are in C. We now list the rules for the predicates R_i. We distinguish two cases depending on whether the component A_i has more entries or exits. Suppose first that A_i is entry-bound. Then, we have the following three rules. (Technically, there is one instance of rule 3 for each box b of A_i.)

1. $R_i(x, x)$, $x \in En_i$
2. $R_i(x, w)$ ← $R_i(x, u)$, $x \in En_i$, $(u, w) \in E_i$
3. $R_i(x, (b, w))$ ← $R_i(x, (b, u)) \land R_j(u, w)$, $x \in En_i, b \in B_i, Y_i(b) = j$,
$$u \in En_j, w \in Ex_j.$$

Rule 1 says every entry node x can reach itself. Rule 2 says if an entry x can reach vertex u which has an edge to vertex w, then x can reach w. Rule 3 says if entry x of A_i can reach an entry port (b, u) of a box b, mapped say to the j'th component A_j, and the entry u of A_j can reach its exit w, then x can reach the exit port (b, w) of box b; we further restrict the domain to only apply this rule for ports of b that are vertices (i.e., $(b, u), (b, w)$ are incident to some edges of A_i). Rules for exit-bound component machines A_i are similar.

1. $R_i(x, x)$, $x \in Ex_i$
2. $R_i(u, x)$ ← $R_i(w, x)$, $x \in Ex_i$, $(u, w) \in E_i$
3. $R_i((b, u), x)$ ← $R_i((b, w), x) \land R_j(u, w)$, $x \in Ex_i, b \in B_i, Y_i(b) = j$,
$$u \in En_j, w \in Ex_j.$$

The Datalog program can be evaluated incrementally by initializing the relations with all ground atoms corresponding to instantiations of heads of rules with empty body (i.e., the atoms $R_i(x, x)$ for all entries/exits x of A_i), and then using the rules repeatedly to derive new ground atoms that are heads of instantiations of rules whose bodies contain only atoms that have been already derived. As we'll see below, if implemented properly, the time complexity is bounded by the number of possible instantiated rules and the space is bounded by the number of possible ground atoms. The number of possible ground atoms of the form $R_i(x, y)$ is at most $v_i\theta$, and thus the total number of ground atoms is at most $v\theta$. The number of instantiated rules of type 1 is bounded by the number of nodes, and the number of rules of type 2 is at most $e\theta$. The number of instantiated rules of type 3 is at most $v\theta^2$.

The evaluation of the Datalog program can be seen equivalently as the evaluation (reachability analysis) of a corresponding AND-OR graph $G_A = (V, E, Start)$. Recall that an AND-OR graph is a directed graph (V, E) whose vertices $V = V_\lor \cup V_\land$ consist of a disjoint union of _and_ vertices, $V_\land$, and _or_ vertices, V_V, and a subset of vertices *Start* is given as the initial set. Reachability is defined inductively: a vertex p is *reachable* if: **(a)** $p \in Start$, or **(b)** p is a V-vertex and $\exists p'$ such that $(p', p) \in E$ and such that p' is reachable, or **(c)** p is a $\wedge$-vertex and for $\forall p'$ such that $(p', p) \in E$, p' is reachable. It is well-known that reachability in AND-OR graphs can be computed in linear time (see, e.g., [2]).

We can define from the rules an AND-OR graph G_A with one V-vertex for each ground atom $R_i(x, y)$ and one $\wedge$-vertex for each instantiated body of a rule with two conjuncts, i.e., rule of type 3. The set *Start* of initial vertices is the set of ground atoms resulting from the instantiations of rules 1 that have empty bodies. Each instantiated rule of type 2 and 3 introduces the following edges: For a rule of type 2 (one conjunct in the body) we have an edge from the (V-vertex corresponding to the ground) atom in the body of the rule to the atom in the head. For an instantiated rule of type 3, we have edges from the V-vertices corresponding to the ground atoms in the body to the $\wedge$-vertex corresponding to the body, and from the $\wedge$-vertex to the V-vertex corresponding to the head. It can be shown that the reachable V-vertices in the AND-OR graph correspond precisely to the ground atoms that are derived by the Datalog program.

The AND-OR graph has $O(v\theta)$ V-vertices, $O(v\theta^2)$ $\wedge$-vertices and $O(e\theta + v\theta^2)$ edges and can be constructed in a straightforward way and evaluated in this amount of time. However, it is not necessary to construct the graph explicitly. Note that the $\wedge$-vertices have only one outgoing edge, so there is no reason to store them: once a $\wedge$-vertex is reached, it can be used to reach the successor V-vertex and there is no need to remember it any more. Indeed, evaluation methods for Datalog programs maintain only the relations of the program recording the tuples (ground atoms) that are derived. We describe now how to evaluate the program within the stated time and space bounds.

Process the edges of the components A_i to compute the set of vertices and record the following information: If A_i is entry-bound (respectively, exit-bound) create the successor list (resp. predecessor list) for each vertex. For each box, create a list of its entries and exits that are vertices, i.e., have some incident edges. For each component A_i and each of its ports u create a list of all boxes b in all the machines of the RSM A that are mapped to A_i in which the port u of b has an incident edge (is a vertex). The reason for the last two data structures is that it is possible that many of the ports of the boxes have no incident edges, and we do not want to waste time looking at them, since our claimed complexity bounds charge only for ports that have incident edges. It is straightforward to compute the above information from a linear scan of the edges of the RSM A.

Each predicate (relation) R_i can be stored using either a dense or a sparse representation. For example, a dense representation is a bit-array indexed by the domain (possible tuples) of the relation, i.e., $En_i \times V_i$ or $V_i \times Ex_i$. Initially all the bits are 0, and they are turned to 1 as new tuples (ground atoms) are derived. We maintain a list S of tuples that have been derived but not processed. The processing order (e.g., FIFO or LIFO or any other) is not important. Initially, we insert into S (and set their corresponding bits) all the ground atoms from rule 1, i.e., atoms of the form $R_i(x, x)$ for all entries x of entry-bound machines

A_i and exits of exit-bound machines A_i. In the iterative step, as long as S is not empty, we remove an atom $R_i(x, y)$ from S and process it. Suppose that A_i is entry-bound (the exit-bound case is similar). Then we do the following. For every edge $(y, z) \in E_i$ out of y, we check if $R_i(x, z)$ has been already derived (its bit is 1) and if not, then we set its bit to 1 and insert $R_i(x, z)$ into S. If y is an entry node of a box b, i.e. $y = (b, u)$, where say b is mapped to A_j, then for every exit vertex (b, w) of b we check if $R_j(u, w)$ holds; if it does and if $R_i(x, (b, w))$ has not been derived, we set its bit and insert $R_i(x, (b, w))$ into S. If y is an exit of R_i, then for every box b that is mapped to A_i and in which the corresponding port (b, y) is a vertex we do the following. Let A_k be the machine that contains the box b. If (b, x) is not a vertex of A_k nothing needs to be done. Otherwise, if A_k is entry-bound (respectively, exit-bound), we check for every entry (respectively, exit) z of A_k whether the corresponding rule 3 can be fired, that is, whether $R_k(z, (b, x))$ holds but $R_k(z, (b, y))$ does not (respectively, $R_k((b, y), z)$ holds but $R_k((b, x), z)$ does not). If so, we set the bit of $R_k(z, (b, y))$ (resp., $R_k((b, x), z)$) and insert the atom into S. Correctness follows from the following lemma.

Lemma 1. *A tuple (x, y) is added to the predicate R_i iff $R_i(x, y)$ is true in the given RSM A, i.e., $\langle x \rangle$ can reach $\langle y \rangle$ in the transition system T_A.*

Theorem 1. *Given RSM A, all predicates R_i can be computed in time $O(|A|\theta^2)$ and space $O(|A|\theta)$. (More precisely, time $O(e\theta + v\theta^2)$ and space $O(e + v\theta)$.)*

Step 2: The Augmented Graph H_A. Having computed the predicates R_i, for each component, we know the reachability among its entry and exit nodes. We need to determine the set of nodes reachable from the initial set *Init* in a global manner. For this, we build an ordinary graph H_A as follows. The set of vertices of H_A is $V = \cup V_i$, the set of vertices of all the components. The set of edges of H_A consists of all the edges of the components, and the following additional edges. For every box b of A_i, say b is mapped to A_j, include edges from the entry vertices (b, u) of b to the exit vertices (b, w) such that $R_j(u, w)$ holds. Lastly, add an edge from each entry vertex (b, u) of a box to the corresponding entry node u of the component A_j to which b is mapped. The main claim about H_A is:

Lemma 2. *$u \Rightarrow v$ in RSM A iff v is reachable from u in H_A.*

Thus, to compute $\{v \mid Init \Rightarrow v\}$, all we need to do is a linear-time depth first search in H_A. Clearly, H_A has v vertices and $e + v\theta$ edges. Thus we have:

Theorem 2. *Given an RSM A, the set $\{v \mid Init \Rightarrow v\}$ of reachable nodes can be computed in time $O(|A|\theta^2)$ and space $O(|A|\theta)$.*

In invariant verification we are given RSM A, and a set T of target nodes, and want to determine if $Init \Rightarrow v$ for some $v \in T$. This problem can be solved as above in the given complexity. Note that, unlike reachability in FSMs, this problem is PTIME-complete even for single-entry, non-recursive, RSMs [1].

For conceptual clarity, we have presented the reachability algorithm as a two-stage process. However, the two stages can be combined and carried out simultaneously, and this is what one would do in practice. In fact, we can do this *on-the-fly*, and have the reachability process drive the computation and trigger the rules; that is, we only derive tuples involving vertices only when they are reached by the search procedure. This is especially important if the RSM A is not given explicitly but has to be generated from an implicit description dynamically on-the-fly. We defer further elaboration to the full paper.

3.2 Checking Language Emptiness

Given an RBA $A = (\langle A_1, \ldots, A_k \rangle, Init, F)$, we wish to determine whether $L(A)$, $L_b(A)$, and $L_u(A)$ are empty. Since $L_b(A) \cup L_u(A) = L(A)$, it suffices to determine emptiness for $L_b(A)$ and $L_u(A)$. We need to check whether there are any bounded or unbounded accepting runs in $B_A = (T_A, Init^*, F^*)$. Our algorithm below for emptiness testing treats edges labeled by ε no differently than ordinary edges. This makes the algorithm report that $L(A)$ is non-empty even when the only infinite accepting runs in A include an infinite suffix of ε-labeled edges. We show in the next section how to overcome this. Our algorithm proceeds in the same two stage fashion as our algorithm for reachability. Instead of computing predicates $R_i(x, y)$, we compute a different predicate $Z_i(x, y)$ with the same domain $En_i \times V_i$ or $V_i \times Ex_i$, depending on whether A_i is entry- or exit-bound. Z_i is defined as follows: $Z_i(x, y)$ holds iff there is a path in B_A from $\langle x \rangle$ to $\langle y \rangle$ which passes through an accept state in F^*. We can compute Z_i's by rules analogous to those for R_i's. In fact, having previously computed the R_i's, we can use that information to greatly simplify the rules governing Z_i's, so that the corresponding rules are linear and can be evaluated by doing reachability in an ordinary graph (instead of an AND-OR graph). The rules for an entry-bound machine A_i are as follows.

1. $Z_i(x, y)$, if $R_i(x, y)$, and x or $y \in F^*$, $x \in En_i, y \in V_i$
2. $Z_i(x, w) \quad \leftarrow Z_i(x, u)$, for $x \in En_i$, $(u, w) \in E_i$
3a. $Z_i(x, (b, w)) \leftarrow Z_i(x, (b, u))$, if $R_j(u, w)$, $x \in En_i, b \in B_i, Y_i(b) = j$,
        $u \in En_j, w \in Ex_j$
3b. $Z_i(x, (b, w)) \leftarrow Z_j(u, w))$, if $R_i(x, (b, u))$, $x \in En_i, b \in B_i, Y_i(b) = j$,
        $u \in En_j, w \in Ex_j$

The rules for exit-bound components A_i are similar. Let G'_A be an ordinary graph whose vertices are the possible ground atoms $Z_i(x, y)$ and with edges (t_1, t_2) for each instantiated rule $t_2 \leftarrow t_1$. The set *Start* of initial vertices is the ground atoms from rule 1. Then the reachable vertices are precisely the set of true ground atoms $Z_i(x, y)$. G'_A has $O(v\theta)$ vertices and $O(e\theta + v\theta^2)$ edges. Again we do not need to construct it explicitly, but can store only its vertices and generate its edges as needed from the rules.

Lemma 3. *All predicates Z_i can be computed in time $O(|A|\theta^2)$ and space $O(|A|\theta)$.*

Having computed Z_i's, we can analyze the graph H_A for cycle detection. Let F_a be the set of edges of H_A of the form $((b, x), (b, y))$, connecting an entry vertex to an exit vertex of a box b, mapped say to A_j, and for which $Z_j(x, y)$ holds. Let F_u be the set of edges of the form $((b, x), x)$ where (b, x) is a vertex and x is an entry of the component to which box b is mapped (i.e., the edges that correspond to recursive invocations).

Lemma 4. *The language $L_u(A)$ is nonempty iff there is a cycle in H_A reachable from some vertex in $Init$, such that the cycle contains both: (1) an edge in F_a or a vertex in F, and (2) an edge in F_u.*

We need a modified version H'_A of H_A in order to determine emptiness of $L_b(A)$ efficiently. The graph H'_A is the same as H_A except the invocation edges in F_u are removed. Also, the set of initial vertices need to be modified: let En' denote the vertices en of H_A, where en is an entry node of some component in A, and en is reachable from some vertex in $Init$ in H_A.

Lemma 5. *$L_b(A)$ is nonempty iff there is a cycle in H'_A reachable from some vertex in En', such that the cycle contains an edge in F_a or a vertex in F.*

Both H_A and H'_A have v vertices and $O(e + v\theta)$ edges. We can check the conditions in the two lemmas in linear time in the graph size, using standard cycle detection algorithms.

Theorem 3. *Given RBA A, we can check emptiness of $L(A)$, $L_b(A)$ and $L_u(A)$ in time $O(|A|\theta^2)$ and space $O(|A|\theta)$.*

3.3 Model Checking with Büchi Automata

The input to the *automata-based model checking* problem consists of a RSM A over Σ and an ordinary Büchi automaton B over Σ. The model checking problem is to determine, whether the intersection $L(A) \cap L(B)$ is empty, or whether $L_b(A) \cap L(B)$ ($L_u(A) \cap L(B)$) is empty if we wish to restrict to bounded (unbounded) runs. Having given algorithms for determining emptiness of $L(A)$, $L_b(A)$, and $L_u(A)$ for RBAs, what model checking requires is a product construction, which given a Büchi automaton B and RSM A, constructs an RBA that accepts the intersection of the languages of the two. Also, in the last section we ignored ε's, now we show how to disallow an infinite suffix of ε's in an accepting run. We modify the given Büchi automaton B to obtain $B' = \langle Q'_B, \delta'_B, I_B, F_B \rangle$ as follows. For every state q, we add an extra state q'. We add a transition from q to q' labeled with ε, from q' to itself labeled with ε, and for every transition (q, σ, q'') of B, add a transition (q', σ, q''). B' accepts exactly the same words as B, except it allows a finite number of ε's to be interspersed between consecutive characters in a word from $L(B)$.

The product RBA $A' = A \otimes B$ of A and B is defined as follows. A' has the same number of components as A. For every component A_i of A, the entry-nodes En'_i of A'_i are $En_i \times Q_B$, and the exit-nodes Ex'_i of A'_i are $Ex_i \times Q_B$. The nodes N'_i of A'_i are $N_i \times Q_B$ while the boxes B'_i are the same as B_i with the same label (that is, a box mapped to A_j is mapped to A'_j). Transitions δ'_i within each

A_i' are defined as follows. Consider a transition (v, σ, v') in δ_i. Suppose $v \in N_i$. Then for every transition (q, σ, q') of B', A_i' has a transition $((v, q), \sigma, (v', q'))$ if v' is a node, and a transition $((v, q), \sigma, (b, (e, q')))$ if $v' = (b, e)$. The case when $v = (b, x)$ is handled similarly. Repeating nodes of A' are nodes of the form (v, q) with $q \in F_B$. The construction guarantees that $L(A \otimes B) = L(A) \cap L(B)$ (and $L_b(A \otimes B) = L_b(A) \cap L(B)$ and $L_u(A \otimes B) = L_u(A) \cap L(B)$). Analyzing the cost of the product, we get the following theorem:

Theorem 4. *Let A be an RSM of size n with θ as the maximum of minimum of entry-nodes and exit-nodes per component, and let B be a Büchi automaton of size m with a states. Then, checking emptiness of $L(A) \cap L(B)$ and of $L_{b,u}(A) \cap L(B)$, can be solved in time $O(n \cdot m \cdot a^2 \cdot \theta^2)$ and space $O(n \cdot m \cdot a \cdot \theta)$.*

4   Relation to Pushdown Systems

The relation between recursive automata and pushdown automata is fairly tight. Consider a *pushdown system* (PDS) given by $P = (Q_P, \Gamma, \Delta)$ over an alphabet Σ consisting of a set of control states Q_P, a stack alphabet Γ, and a transition relation $\Delta \subseteq (Q_P \times \Gamma) \times \Sigma \times (Q_P \times \{push(\Gamma), swap(\Gamma), pop\})$. That is, based on the control state and the symbol on top of the stack, the machine can update the control state, and either push a new symbol, swap the top-of-the-stack with a new symbol, or pop the stack. When P is augmented with a Büchi acceptance condition, the ω-language of the pushdown machine, $L(P)$, can then be defined in a natural way. Given a PDS P (or RBA A), we can build a recursive automaton A (PDS P, respectively) such that $L(P) = L(A)$, and $|A| \in O(|P|)$ ($|P| \in O(|A|)$), respectively). Translating from P to A, A has one component with number of exits (and hence θ) bounded by $|Q_P|$. Translating from A to P, the number of control states of P is bounded by the maximum number of exit points in A, not by θ. Both translations preserve boundedness. We have to omit details. For the detailed construction, please see the full paper.

5   Discussion

Efficiency and Context-Free Reachability: Given a recursive automaton of size n with θ maximum entry/exit-nodes per component, our reachability algorithm takes time $O(n \cdot \theta^2)$ and space $O(n\theta)$. It is unlikely that our complexity can be substantially improved. Consider the standard parsing problem of testing CFL-membership: for a fixed context-free grammar G, and given a string w of length n, we wish to determine if G can generate w. The classic C-K-Y algorithm for this problem requires $O(n^3)$ time. Using fast matrix multiplication, Valiant [14] was able to slightly improve the asymptotic bound, but his algorithm is highly impractical. A related problem is CFL-reachability ([15], 11]), where for a fixed grammar G, we are given a directed, edge-labeled, graph H, having size n, with designated source and target nodes s and t, and we wish to determine whether s can reach t in H via a path labeled by a string in $L(G)$.

CFL-membership is the special case of this problem where H is just a simple path labeled by w. Unlike CFL-membership, CFL-reachability is P-complete, and the best known algorithms require $\Omega(n^3)$ time ([15]). Using the close correspondence between recursive automata and context-free grammars, a grammar G can be translated to a recursive automaton A_G. To test CFL-reachability, we can take the product of A_G with H, and check for reachability. The product has size $O(n)$, with $O(n)$ entry-nodes per component, and $O(n)$ exit-nodes per component. Thus, since our reachability algorithm runs in time $O(n^3)$ in this case, better bounds on reachability for recursive automata would lead to better than cubic bounds for parsing a string and for CFL-reachability.

Extended Recursive Automata: In presence of variables, our algorithms can be adopted in a natural way by augmenting nodes with the values of the variables. Suppose we have an extended recursive automaton A with boolean variables (similar observations apply to more general finite domains), and the edges have guards and assignments that read/write these variables. Suppose each component refers to at most k variables (local or global), and that it has at most either d input variables or d output variables (i.e., global variables that it reads or writes, or parameters passed to and from it). Then, we can construct a recursive automaton of size at most $2^k \cdot |A|$ with the same number of components. The derived automaton has $\theta = 2^d$. Thus, reachability problems for such an extended recursive automaton can be solved in time $O(2^{k+2d} \cdot |A|)$. Note that such extended recursive automata are basically the same as the boolean programs of [3].

Concurrency: We have considered only sequential recursive automata. Recursive automata define context-free languages. Consequently, it is easy to establish that typical reachability analysis problems for a system of communicating recursive automata are undecidable. Our algorithms can however be used in the case when only one of the processes is a recursive automaton and the rest are ordinary state machines. To analyze a system with two recursive processes M_1 and M_2, one can possibly use abstraction and assume-guarantee reasoning: the user constructs finite-state abstractions P_1 and P_2 of M_1 and M_2, respectively, and we algorithmically verify that (1) the system with P_1 and P_2 satisfies the correctness requirement, (2) the system with M_1 and P_2 is a refinement of P_1, and (3) the system with P_1 and M_2 is a refinement of P_2.

Acknowledgements

We thank Tom Ball, Javier Esparza, and Sriram Rajamani for useful discussions. Research partially supported by NSF Grants CCR97-34115, CCR99-70925, SRC award 99-TJ-688, and a Sloan Faculty Fellowship.

References

1. R. Alur and M. Yannakakis. Model checking of hierarchical state machines. In *Proc. 6th ACM Symp. on Found. of Software Engineering*, pages 175–188, 1998.
2. H. Andersen. Model checking and boolean graphs. *TCS*, 126(1):3–30, 1994.
3. T. Ball and S. Rajamani. Bebop: A symbolic model checker for boolean programs. In *SPIN'2000*, volume 1885 of *LNCS*, pages 113–130, 2000.
4. M. Benedikt, P. Godefroid, and T. Reps. Model checking of unrestricted hierarchical state machines. To appear in ICALP'2001.
5. G. Booch, I. Jacobson, and J. Rumbaugh. *The Unified Modeling Language User Guide*. Addison Wesley, 1997.
6. A. Boujjani, J. Esparza, and O. Maler. Reachability analysis of pushdown automata: Applications to model checking. In *CONCUR'97*, pages 135–150, 1997.
7. O. Burkart and B. Steffen. Model checking the full modal mu-calculus for infinite sequential processes. *Theoretical Computer Science*, 221:251–270, 1999.
8. J. Esparza, D. Hansel, P. Rossmanith, and S. Schwoon. Efficient algorithms for model checking pushdown systems. In *Computer Aided Verification, 12th Int. Conference*, volume 1855 of *LNCS*, pages 232–247. Springer, 2000.
9. A. Finkel, B. Willems, and P. Wolper. A direct symbolic approach to model checking pushdown systems. In *Infinity'97 Workshop*, volume 9 of *Electronic Notes in Theoretical Computer Science*, 1997.
10. D. Harel. Statecharts: a visual formalism for complex systems. *Science of Computer Programming*, 8:231–274, 1987.
11. T. Reps. Program analysis via graph reachability. *Information and Software Technology*, 40(11-12):701–726, 1998.
12. T. Reps, S. Horwitz, and S. Sagiv. Precise interprocedural dataflow analysis via graph reachability. In *POPL*, pages 49–61, 1995.
13. J. D. Ullman. *Principles of Database and Knowledge-base systems*. Computer Science Press, 1988.
14. L. G. Valiant. General context-free recognition in less than cubic time. *J. of Computer and System Sc.*, 10:308–315, 1975.
15. M. Yannakakis. Graph-theoretic methods in database theory. In *Proc. 9th ACM Symp. on Principles of Database Systems*, pages 230–242, 1990.

Parameterized Verification with Automatically Computed Inductive Assertions*

Tamarah Arons[1], Amir Pnueli[1], Sitvanit Ruah[1], Ying Xu[2], and Lenore Zuck[2]

[1] Weizmann Institute of Science, Rehovot, Israel
{tamarah,amir,sitvanit}@wisdom.weizmann.ac.il
[2] New York University, New York
zuck@cs.nyu.edu

Abstract. The paper presents a method, called the method of *verification by invisible invariants*, for the automatic verification of a large class of parameterized systems. The method is based on the automatic calculation of candidate inductive assertions and checking for their inductiveness, using symbolic model-checking techniques for both tasks. First, we show how to use model-checking techniques over finite (and small) instances of the parameterized system in order to derive candidates for invariant assertions. Next, we show that the premises of the standard deductive INV rule for proving invariance properties can be automatically resolved by finite-state (BDD-based) methods with no need for interactive theorem proving. Combining the automatic computation of invariants with the automatic resolution of the VCs (verification conditions) yields a (necessarily) incomplete but fully automatic sound method for verifying large classes of parameterized systems. The generated invariants can be transferred to the VC-validation phase without ever been examined by the user, which explains why we refer to them as "invisible". The efficacy of the method is demonstrated by automatic verification of diverse parameterized systems in a fully automatic and efficient manner.

1   Introduction

The problem of *uniform verification of parameterized systems* is one of the most challenging problems in verification today. Given a parameterized system $S(N) : P[1]\| \cdots \|P[N]$ and a property p, uniform verification attempts to verify $S(N) \models p$ for every $N > 1$. Model checking is an excellent tool for *debugging* parameterized systems because, if the system fails to satisfy p, this failure can be observed for a specific (and usually small) value of N. However, once all the observable bugs have been removed, there remains the question whether the system is correct for all $N > 1$.

One method which can always be applied to verify parameterized systems is *deductive verification*. To verify that a parameterized system satisfies the invariance property $\Box p$, we may use rule INV presented in Fig. 1 [MP95a]. The

---

* This research was supported in part by the Minerva Center for Verification of Reactive Systems, a gift from Intel, a grant from the German - Israel Foundation for Scientific Research and Development, and ONR grant N00014-99-1-0131.

G. Berry, H. Comon, and A. Finkel (Eds.): CAV 2001, LNCS 2102, pp. 221–234, 2001.

system to be verified is assumed to a transition system, with an assertion Θ describing the initial states, and a state transition relation ρ relating the values of (unprimed) variables in a state to the (primed) values of the variables in its successor. Premise I1 claims that the initial state of the system satisfies φ. Premise

$$
\begin{array}{l}
\text{I1. } \Theta \; \rightarrow \; \varphi \\
\text{I2. } \varphi \wedge \rho \; \rightarrow \; \varphi' \\
\text{I3. } \varphi \; \rightarrow \; p \\
\hline
\qquad \Box p
\end{array}
$$

Fig. 1. The Invariance Rule INV.

I2 claims that φ remains invariant under ρ. An assertion φ satisfying premises I1 and I2 is called *inductive*. Excluding the rare cases in which the property p is already inductive, the deductive verifier has to perform the following tasks:

1. Divine (invent) the auxiliary assertion φ.
2. Establish the validity of premises I1–I3.

Performing interactive first-order verification of implications such as the premises of rule INV for any non-trivial system is never an easy task. Neither is it a one-time task, since the process of developing the auxiliary invariants requires iterative verification trials, where failed efforts lead to correction of the previous candidate assertion into a new candidate.

In this paper we show that, for a wide class of parameterized systems, both of these tasks can be automated and performed directly by an appropriately enhanced model checker. The proposed method, called *verification by invisible invariants*, is based on the following idea: We start by computing the set of all reachable states of $S(N)$ for a sufficiently large N. We then project this set of states on one of the processes, say $P[1]$. Under the assumption that the system is sufficiently symmetric, we conclude that whatever is true of $P[1]$ will be true of all other processes. Thus, we abstract the characterization of all reachable states of process $P[1]$, denoted $\psi(1)$, into a generic $\psi(j)$ and propose the assertion $\varphi = \forall j : \psi(j)$ as a candidate for the inductive assertion which can be used within rule INV. To check that the candidate assertion φ is inductive and also implies the property p, we establish a small-model property which enables checking the premises of rule INV over $S(N_0)$ for a specific N_0 determined by the size of the local state space of a process in the system. The two tasks of calculating the candidate assertion φ and checking that it satisfies the premises of rule INV are performed automatically with no user interaction. This leads to the fact that the user never sees, or has to understand, the automatically produced inductive assertion. This explains the name of *verification by invisible invariants*.

The method of invisible invariants was first presented in [PRZ01], where it was used to verify a non-trivial cache protocol proposed by Steve German [Ger00]. The presentation in [PRZ01] allowed the method to be used only for a very restricted class of systems. The main limitations were that the only predicates allowed in this class were equality comparisons between parameterized types, and the only arrays were of type $[1..N] \mapsto$ **bool**. In this paper, we extend the applicability of the method in several dimensions as follows:

- Allowing inequality comparisons of the form $u < v$ between parameterized types and operations such as $u + 1$ and $u \oplus 1$ (incrementation modulo N).
- Allowing several parameterized types and arrays that map one parameterized type to another.

These extensions significantly broaden the scope of applicability of the method, allowing us to deal with diverse examples such as various cache protocols, a 3-stage pipeline, Szymanski's algorithm for mutual exclusion, a token-ring algorithm, a restricted form of the Bakery algorithm, and an N-process version of Peterson's algorithm for mutual exclusion, all in a fully automatic and efficient manner.

Related Work. The problem of uniform verification of parameterized systems is, in general, undecidable [AK86]. There are two possible remedies to this situation: either we should look for restricted families of parameterized systems for which the problem becomes decidable, or devise methods which are sound but, necessarily incomplete, and hope that the system of interest will yield to one of these methods.

Among the representatives of the first approach we can count the work of German and Sistla [GS92] which assumes a parameterized system where processes communicate synchronously, and shows how to verify single-index properties. Similarly, Emerson and Namjoshi provided a decision procedure for proving a restricted set of properties on ring algortihms [EN95], and proved a PSPACE complete algorithm for verification of synchronously communicating processes [EN96]. Many of these methods fail when we move to asynchronous systems where processes communicate by shared variables. Perhaps the most advanced of this approach is the paper [EK00] which considers a general parameterized system allowing several different classes of processes. However, this work provides separate algorithms for the cases that the guards are either all disjunctive or all conjunctive. A protocol such as the cache example we consider in [PRZ01] which contains some disjunctive and some conjunctive guards, cannot be handled by the methods of [EK00].

The sound but incomplete methods include methods based on explicit induction ([EN95]) network invariants, which can be viewed as implicit induction ([KM95], [WL89], [HLR92], [LHR97]), methods that can be viewed as abstraction and approximation of network invariants ([BCG86], [SG89], [CGJ95], [KP00]), and other methods that can be viewed as based on abstraction ([ID96]). The papers in [CR99a,CR99b,CR00] use structural induction based on the notion of a network invariant but significantly enhance its range of applicability by using a generalization of the data-independence approach which provides a powerful abstraction capability, allowing it to handle network with parameterized topologies. Most of these methods require the user to provide auxiliary constructs, such as a network invariant or an abstraction mapping. Other attempts to verify parameterized protocols such as Burn's protocol [JL98] and Szymanski's algorithm [GZ98,MAB+94] relied on abstraction functions or lemmas provided by the user. The work in [LS97] deals with the verification of safety properties of parameterized networks by abstracting the behavior of the system. PVS ([SOR93]) is used to discharge the generated VCs.

Among the automatic incomplete approaches, we should mention the methods relying on "regular model-checking" [KMM+97,ABJN99,JN00,PS00], where a class of systems which include our bounded-data systems as a special case is analyzed representing linear configurations of processes as a word in a regular language. Unfortunately, many of the systems analyzed by this method cause the analysis procedure to diverge and special *acceleration* procedures have to be applied which, again, requires user ingenuity and intervention.

The works in [ES96,ES97,CEFJ96,GS97] study symmetry reduction in order to deal with state explosion. The work in [ID96] detects symmetries by inspection of the system description. Closer in spirit to our work is the work of McMillan on compositional model-checking (e.g. [McM98b]), which combines automatic abstraction with finite-instantiation due to symmetry.

2   The Systems We Consider

Let $\mathbf{type}_0$ denote the set of boolean and fixed (unparameterized) finite-range basic types which, for simplicity, we often denote as **bool**. Let $\mathbf{type}_1, \ldots, \mathbf{type}_m$ be a set of basic parameterized types, where each $\mathbf{type}_i$ includes integers in the range $[1..N_i]$ for some $N_i \in \mathbb{N}^+$. The systems we study include variables that are either $\mathbf{type}_i$ variables, for some $i \in \{0, \ldots, m\}$, or arrays of the type $\mathbf{type}_i \mapsto \mathbf{type}_j$ for $i > 0, j \geq 0$. For a system that includes types $\mathbf{type}_1, \ldots, \mathbf{type}_k$, we refer to $N_1, \ldots, N_k$ as the *system's parameters*. Systems are distinguished by their *signatures*, which determine the types of variables allowed, as well as the assertions allowed in the transition relation and the initial condition. Whenever the signature of a system includes the type $\mathbf{type}_i \mapsto \mathbf{type}_j$, we assume by default that it also includes the types $\mathbf{type}_i$ and $\mathbf{type}_j$.

Atomic formulae may compare two expressions of the same type, where the only allowed expressions are a variable y or an array reference $z[y]$. Thus, if y and $\tilde{y}$ are $\mathbf{type}_i$ variables, then $y \leq \tilde{y}$ is an atomic formula, and so are $z[y] \leq z[\tilde{y}]$, $x \leq z[y]$, and $z[y] \leq x$ for an array $z : \mathbf{type}_i \mapsto \mathbf{type}_j$ and $x : \mathbf{type}_j$.

Formulae, used in the transition relation and the initial condition, are obtained from the atomic formulae by closing them under negation, disjunction, and existential quantifiers, for appropriately typed quantifiers.

A *bounded-data discrete system* (BDS) $S = \langle V, \Theta, \rho \rangle$ consists of

- V–A set of *system variables*, as described above. A *state* of the system S provides a type-consistent interpretation of the system variables V. For a state s and a system variable $v \in V$, we denote by $s[v]$ the value assigned to v by the state s. Let Σ denote the set of states over V.
- $\Theta(V)$–The *initial condition*: A formula characterizing the initial states.

- $\rho(V, V')$–The *transition relation*: A formula, relating the values V of the variables in state $s \in \Sigma$ to the values V' in an S-successor state $s' \in \Sigma$.

For all the systems we consider here, we assume that the transition relation can be written as

$$\exists \underbrace{h_1^1, \ldots, h_{H_1}^1}_{\textbf{type}_1}, \ldots, \underbrace{h_1^k, \ldots, h_{H_k}^k}_{\textbf{type}_k} \forall \underbrace{t_1^1, \ldots, t_{T_1}^1}_{\textbf{type}_1}, \ldots, \underbrace{t_1^k, \ldots, t_{T_k}^k}_{\textbf{type}_k} : R(\vec{h}, \vec{t})) \qquad (1)$$

where $R(\vec{h}, \vec{t})$ is a well-typed quantifier-free formula. It follows that every BDS is associated with $H_1, \ldots, H_K$ and $T_1, \ldots, T_K$.

Note that Θ and ρ are restricted to "formulae" defined in the previous section. Since in this paper we only consider the verification of invariance properties, we omitted from the definition of a BDS the components that relate to fairness. When we will work on the extension of these methods to liveness, we will add the relevant fairness components.

A computation of the BDS $S = \langle V, \Theta, \rho \rangle$ is an infinite sequence of states $\sigma : s_0, s_1, s_2, \ldots$, satisfying the requirements:

- *Initiality* — s_0 is initial, i.e., $s_0 \models \Theta$.
- *Consecution* — For each $\ell = 0, 1, \ldots$, the state $s_{\ell+1}$ is a S-successor of s_ℓ. That is, $\langle s_\ell, s_{\ell+1} \rangle \models \rho(V, V')$ where, for each $v \in V$, we interpret v as $s_\ell[v]$ and v' as $s_{\ell+1}[v]$.

Mainly, we consider systems with signature $\langle \textbf{type}_1 \mapsto \textbf{type}_0, \textbf{type}_1 \mapsto \textbf{type}_2 \rangle$. This signature admits arrays which are subscripted by $\textbf{type}_1$-elements and range over either $\textbf{type}_0$ or $\textbf{type}_2$. We name the variables in such a system as follows: $x_1, \ldots, x_a$ are $\textbf{type}_0$ variables, $y_1, \ldots, y_b$ are $\textbf{type}_1$ variables, $z_1, \ldots, z_c$ are arrays of type $\textbf{type}_1 \mapsto \textbf{type}_0$, $u_1, \ldots, u_d$ are $\textbf{type}_2$ variables, and $w_1, \ldots, w_e$ are arrays of type $\textbf{type}_1 \mapsto \textbf{type}_2$.

We keep these naming convention for systems with simpler signatures. Thus, a system with no $\textbf{type}_2$ variables will have only x-, y-, or z-variables. We assume that the description of each system contains a z-variable π that includes the location of each process.

3 The Method of Invisible Invariants

Our goal is to provide an automated procedure to generate proofs according to INV. While in general the problem is undecidable [AK86], we offer a heuristic that had proven successful in many cases for the systems we study, where the strengthening assertions are of the form $\forall i_1, \ldots, i_r : \psi(\vec{i})$ where $i_1, \ldots, i_r$ are all mutually distinct typed variables, and $\psi(\vec{i})$ is a quantifier-free formula. We elaborate the method for the case of systems with signature $\langle \textbf{type}_1 \mapsto \textbf{type}_0, \textbf{type}_1 \mapsto \textbf{type}_2 \rangle$ as defined in Section 2. Thus, we are seeking an assertion of the type $\forall i_1^1, \ldots, i_{I_1}^1, i_1^2, \ldots, i_{I_2}^2 : \psi(\vec{i^1}, \vec{i^2})$ where for $i_1^\ell, \ldots, i_{I_\ell}^\ell$ are all mutually distinct $\textbf{type}_\ell$ variables for $\ell = 1, 2$, and $\psi(\vec{i^1}, \vec{i^2})$ is a quantifier-free formula. In the next sections we obtain (small) bounds for the parameters of this family of systems, such that it suffices to prove the premises of INV on systems whose parameters are bounded by those bounds. This offers a decision procedure for the premises of rule INV, which greatly simplifies the process of deductive verification. Yet, it still leaves open the task of inventing the strengthening assertion φ, which may become quite complex for all but the simplest systems. In this section we propose a heuristic for an algorithmic construction of an inductive assertion for a given BDS. In particular, we provide an algorithm to construct an inductive assertion of the form we are seeking for a two-parameter systems $S(N_1^0, N_2^0)$, where N_1^0 and N_2^0 are the bounds computed for the system.

1. Let *reach* be the assertion characterizing all the reachable states of system $S(N_1^0, N_2^0)$. Since $S(N_1^0, N_2^0)$ is finite-state, *reach* can be computed by standard model-checking techniques.
2. Let ψ_{I_1,I_2} be the assertion obtained from *reach* by projecting away all the references to **type**$_1$ values other than $1, \ldots, I_1$, and **type**$_2$ values other than $1, \ldots, I_2$.
3. Let $\psi(i^{\vec{1}}, i^{\vec{2}})$ be the assertion obtained from ψ_{I_1,I_2} by *abstraction*, which involves the following transformations: For every $j = 1, \ldots, I_1$ and and $k = 1, \ldots, I_2$, replace any reference to $z_r[j]$ by a reference to $z_r[i_j^1]$, any reference to $w_r[j] = k$ (resp. $w_r[j] \neq k$) by a reference to $w_r[i_j^1] = i_k^2$ (resp. $w_r[i_j^1] \neq i_k^2$), any sub-formula of the form $y_r = j$, $j \leq I_1$ by the formula $y_r = i_j^1$, any sub-formula of the form $y_r = v$ for $v > I_1$ by the formula $\bigwedge_{j=1}^{I_1} y_r \neq i_j^1$, any sub-formula of the form $u_r = k$, $k \leq I_2$, by the formula $u_r = i_k^2$, and any sub-formula of the form $u_r = v$ for $v > I_2$ by the formula $\bigwedge_{k=1}^{I_2} u_r \neq i_k^2$.
4. Let $\varphi := \bigwedge_{1 \leq i_1^1 < \ldots < i_{I_1}^1 \leq N_1^0, 1 \leq i_1^2 < \ldots < i_{I_2}^2 \leq N_2^0} \psi(i^{\vec{1}}, i^{\vec{2}})$.
5. Check that φ is inductive over $S(N_1^0, N_2^0)$.
6. Check that $\varphi \to p$ is valid.

If tests (5) and (6) both yield a positive result, then the property p has been verified. The procedure described here is a generalization of a similar procedure in [PRZ01].

4   Obtaining the Bounds

In this section we obtain (small) bounds for the parameters of various systems according to their signatures, and show that it suffices to prove the premises of INV on systems whose parameters are within these bounds. We first present our main claim, which establishes the bounds for the most general system.

Consider a BDS $S(N_1, N_2)$ with signature $\langle$**type**$_1 \mapsto$ **bool**, **type**$_1 \mapsto$ **type**$_2\rangle$ to which we wish to apply proof rule INV with the assertions φ and p having each the form $\forall i_1^1, \ldots, i_{I_1}^1, i_1^2, \ldots, i_{I_2}^2 : \psi(i^{\vec{1}}, i^{\vec{2}})$, where every i_j^1 (resp. i_r^2) is a **type**$_1$ (resp. **type**$_2$) variable, and $\psi(i^{\vec{1}}, i^{\vec{2}})$ is a quantifier free formula. The transition relation of the system is described by equation (1) with $k = 2$.

Consider a state s of the system $S(N_1, N_2)$. The *size* of s is (N_1, N_2). We say that (N_1, N_2) is smaller than (N_1', N_2'), and denote it by $(N_1, N_2) \preceq (N_1', N_2')$ if $N_1 \leq N_1'$ and $N_2 \leq N_2'$.

Lemma 1. *The premises of rule* INV *are valid over* $S(N_1, N_2)$ *for all* $(N_1, N_2) \succeq$ $(2, 2)$ *iff they are valid over* $S(N_1, N_2)$ *for all* $(N_1, N_2) \preceq (N_1^0, N_2^0)$ *where* $N_1^0 =$ $b + I_1 + H_1$ *and* $N_2^0 = d + I_2 + H_2 + e(b + I_1 + H_1)$.

Proof. The most complex verification condition in rule INV is premise (I2) which can be written as: $(\forall \vec{j} : \psi(\vec{j})) \wedge (\exists \vec{h} \forall \vec{t} : R(\vec{h}, \vec{t})) \to \forall \vec{i} : \psi'(\vec{i})$ To prove the claim, it suffices to show that if the formula

$$(\forall \vec{j} : \psi(\vec{j})) \wedge (\forall \vec{t} : R(\vec{h}, \vec{t})) \wedge \neg \psi'(\vec{i}) \tag{2}$$

is satisfiable over a state of size $(N_1, N_2) \succeq (2, 2)$, it is also satisfiable over a state of size $(\alpha_1, \alpha_2) \preceq (N_1^0, N_2^0)$.

Let s be a state of size $(N_1, N_2) \succeq (2, 2)$ which satisfies assertion (2). Let $Val_1 \subseteq [1..N_1]$ be the set of (pairwise) distinct values the state s assigns to the variables $V_{aug}^1 = \{h_1^1, \ldots, h_{H_1}^1, i_1^1, \ldots, i_{I_1}^1, y_1, \ldots, y_b\}$. Let $\alpha_1 = |Val_1|$; obviously, $\alpha_1 \leq H_1 + I_1 + b = N_1^0$ and $\alpha_1 \leq N_1$. Similarly, let $Val_2 \subseteq [1..N_2]$ be the set of (pairwise) distinct values the state s assigns to the variables $V_{aug}^2 = \{h_1^2, \ldots, h_{H_2}^2, i_1^2, \ldots, i_{I_2}^2, u_1, \ldots, u_d\} \cup \{w_\ell[k] : \ell = 1, \ldots, e, \ k \in Val_1\}$ Let $\alpha_2 = |Val_2|$; obviously, $\alpha_2 \leq H_2 + I_2 + d + e(H_1 + I_1 + b) = N_2^0$ and $\alpha_2 \leq N_2$.

For every $\ell = 1, 2$, assume the distinct $\textbf{type}_\ell$ values are sorted $v_1^\ell < v_2^\ell < \cdots < v_{\alpha_\ell}^\ell$. Let Π_ℓ be a permutation on $[1..N_\ell]$ such that for every $j = 1, \ldots, \alpha_\ell$, $\Pi_\ell^{-1}(v_j^\ell) = j$. The two permutations, Π_1, and Π_2, help construct a new state where the range of values assigned to the variables in V_{aug}^1 (resp. V_{aug}^2) is reduced from $[1..N_1]$ (resp. $[1..N_2]$) to $[1..\alpha_1]$ (resp. $[1..\alpha_2]$).

Consider now a state $\tilde{s}$ of size (α_1, α_2), where: $\tilde{x}_r = x_r$ for every $r \in [1..a]$, $\tilde{y}_r = \Pi_1^{-1}(y_r)$ for every $r \in [1..b]$, $\tilde{z}_r[h] = z_r[\Pi_1(k)]$ for every $r \in [1..c]$ and $k \in [1..\alpha_1]$, $\tilde{u}_r = \Pi_2^{-1}(u_r)$ for every $r \in [1..d]$, and $\tilde{w}_r[k] = \Pi_2^{-1}(w_r[\Pi_1(k)])$ for every $r \in [1..e]$ and $k \in [1..\alpha_1]$.

It is easy to establish, by induction on the structure of the quantifier-free formulae ψ and R, that the evaluation of formula (2) over $\tilde{s}$ yields the same truth values as the evaluation of formula (2) over s. Consequently, $\tilde{s}$ is a state of size (α_1, α_2) that satisfies formula (2). $\square$

The Class $\langle \textbf{type}_1 \mapsto \textbf{bool} \rangle$. This is the class of systems which have boolean and other finite-domain parameterized arrays. The algorithms belonging to this class are MUX-SEM (mutual exclusion by semaphores), a 3-stages pipeline [BD94], [McM98a], Steve German's cache [Ger00,PRZ01], and the Illinois' Cache Algorithm [PP84,Del00], all studied in [PRZ01]. In addition, it includes Szymanski's mutual exclusion algorithm [Szy88] and token ring algorithms.

This class extends the class of systems considered in [PRZ01], which only allowed comparison for equality between two y_r variables, by allowing tests for inequalities. Since there are no $\textbf{type}_2$ variables in the system, an immediate consequence of Lemma 1 is:

Corollary 1. *Let* $S(N)$ *be a parameterized system of signature* $\langle \textbf{type}_1 \mapsto \textbf{bool} \rangle$ *to which we wish to apply proof rule* INV *with the assertions* φ *and* p *having each the form* $\forall i_1, \ldots, i_r : \psi(i_1, \ldots, i_r)$. *Then, the premises of rule* INV *are valid over* $S(N)$ *for all* $N > 1$ *iff they are valid over* $S(N)$ *for all* N, $1 < N \leq N_0$, *where* $N_0 = b + I + H$.

In Fig. 2, we present a mutual exclusion algorithm due to B. Szymanski [Szy88], which uses inequality comparisons between process indices. In the system, $b = 0$ and $H = 2$. To apply this claim for system SZYMANSKI, where the property

$$
\begin{array}{l}
\textbf{in} \quad N: \qquad \textbf{integer where } N > 1 \\
\textbf{local } zw, zs : \textbf{array } [1..N] \textbf{ of boolean where } zw = zs = 0 \\
\prod_{i=1}^{N} P[i] :: \begin{bmatrix} \textbf{loop forever do} \\ \begin{bmatrix} \ell_0 : \textbf{NonCritical} \\ \ell_1 : \textbf{await } \forall j : \neg zs[j] \\ \ell_2 : (zw[i], zs[i]) := (1, 1) \\ \ell_3 : \textbf{If } \exists j : at\_\ell_{1,2}[j] \\ \qquad \textbf{then } zs[i] := 0; \textbf{ go-to } \ell_4 \\ \qquad \textbf{else } zw[i] := 0; \textbf{ go-to } \ell_5 \\ \ell_4 : \textbf{await } \exists j : zs[j] \wedge \neg zw[j] \textbf{ then } (zw[i], zs[i]) := (0, 1) \\ \ell_5 : \textbf{await } \forall j : \neg zw[j] \\ \ell_6 : \textbf{await } \forall j : j < i : \neg zs[j] \wedge \neg zw[j] \\ \ell_7 : \textbf{Critical} \\ \ell_8 : zs[i] := 0 \end{bmatrix} \end{bmatrix}
\end{array}
$$

Fig. 2. Parameterized Mutual Exclusion Algorithm SZYMANSKI.

to be verified is mutual exclusion, which can be specified by $p : \quad \forall i \neq j : \neg(at\_\ell_7[i] \wedge at\_\ell_7[j])$, we set $I = 2$, which led to a cutoff value of $N_0 = 4$.

Transition Relations with "+1" or "$\oplus 1$" Constrains: Some of the parameterized systems which we wish to verify have atomic sub-formulae of the forms $h_2 = h_1 + 1$ or $h_2 = h_1 \oplus 1$ (which stands for $h_2 = (h_1 \bmod N) + 1$) within their transition relations. We resolve this difficulty by observing that

$$\exists h_1, h_2 : h_2 = h_1 + 1 \wedge \forall \vec{t} : R(h_1, h_2, \vec{t}) \leftrightarrow$$
$$\exists h_1, h_2 : h_1 < h_2 \wedge (\forall t : t \leq h_1 \vee h_2 \leq t) \wedge \forall \vec{t} : R(h_1, h_2, \vec{t})$$
$$\exists h_1, h_2 : h_2 = h_1 \oplus 1 \wedge \forall \vec{t} : R(h_1, h_2, \vec{t}) \leftrightarrow \exists h_1, h_2 : \Big((h_1 < h_2 \wedge \forall t : t \leq h_1 \vee$$
$$h_2 \leq t) \vee (h_2 < h_1 \wedge \forall t : h_2 \leq t \leq h_1) \Big) \wedge \forall \vec{t} : R(h_1, h_2, \vec{t})$$

In the first translation, we ensure that $h_2 = h_1 + 1$ by requiring that h_1 be smaller than h_2 and that, for every other index t, either t is smaller or equal to h_1 or it is greater or equal to h_2. In the second translation, expected to capture the constraint $h_2 = h_1 \oplus 1$, we repeat the characterization of $h_2 = h_1 + 1$ but also allow the option that $h_1 = N$ and $h_2 = 1$. This is ensured by $h_2 < h_1 \wedge \forall t : h_2 \leq t \leq h_1$. Since $(\forall t : P(t) \vee \forall t : Q(t)) \leftrightarrow \forall t_1, t_2 : (P(t_1) \vee Q(t_2))$, the formulae above can be easily expressed in the form required for transition relation. Thus, the cutoff value established in Corollary 1 is still valid for both these cases.

In Fig. 3, we present a program which coordinates mutual exclusion by passing a token around a ring. The signature of the system is $\langle \textbf{type}_1 \mapsto \textbf{bool} \rangle$. The transition relation for this program includes the atomic formula $h_2 = h_1 \oplus 1$. The program consists of N client processes $C[1], \ldots, C[N]$ which can enter their critical section only when they have the token. Process $C[i]$ has the token when the token variable *token* equals i. In addition, there are N *transmission* processes such that process $T[i]$ is responsible for moving the token from client $C[i]$ to client $C[i \oplus 1]$ whenever process $C[i]$ is in its non-critical section. For this program we

$$
\prod_{i=1}^{N} C[i] ::
\begin{array}{l}
\textbf{in} \quad N: \quad \textbf{integer where } N > 1 \\
\textbf{local } token : [1..N] \\
\left[
\begin{array}{l}
\textbf{loop forever do} \\
\left[
\begin{array}{l}
\ell_0 : \text{NonCritical} \\
\ell_1 : \textbf{await } i = token \\
\ell_2 : \text{Critical}
\end{array}
\right]
\end{array}
\right]
\end{array}
\quad \| \quad
\prod_{i=1}^{N} T[i] ::
\left[
\begin{array}{l}
\textbf{loop forever do} \\
\left[
\begin{array}{l}
m_0 : \textbf{when } at\_\ell_0[i] \wedge \\
\quad token = i \\
\quad token := i \oplus 1
\end{array}
\right]
\end{array}
\right]
$$

Fig. 3. Parameterized Mutual Exclusion Algorithm TOKEN-RING.

have the parameters $b = 1$ (a single $[1..N]$-variable: *token*), and $H = 2$. According to Corollary 1, to establish an inductive assertion of the form $\forall i_1, i_2 : \psi(i_1, i_2)$ for program TOKEN-RING, it suffices to take a cutoff value of $N_0 = 5$.

The Class $\langle \text{type}_1 \mapsto \textbf{bool}, \text{type}_1 \mapsto \text{type}_2 \rangle$. In Fig. 4, we present a program which implements a restricted version of the Bakery Algorithm by Lamport.

$$
\prod_{i=1}^{N_1} C[i] ::
\begin{array}{l}
\textbf{in} \quad N_1, N_2 : \textbf{integer where } N_1 > 1, N_2 > 1 \\
\textbf{local} \quad w \quad : \textbf{array } [1..N_1] \textbf{ of } [1..N_2] \textbf{ where } w = N_1 \\
\qquad\quad\; z \quad : \textbf{array } [1..N_1] \textbf{ of boolean where } z = 0 \\
\left[
\begin{array}{l}
\textbf{loop forever do} \\
\left[
\begin{array}{l}
\ell_0 : \text{NonCritical} \\
\ell_1 : \bigvee\limits_{u=1}^{N_2} \textbf{when } \forall j : (\neg z[j] \vee u > w[j]) \textbf{ do } (z[i], w[i]) := (1, u) \\
\ell_2 : \textbf{await } \forall j : (\neg z[j] \vee w[i] < w[j]) \\
\ell_3 : \text{Critical} \\
\ell_4 : z[i] := 0
\end{array}
\right]
\end{array}
\right]
\end{array}
$$

$$
\|
$$

$$
\prod_{i=1}^{N_1} R[i] ::
\left[
\begin{array}{l}
\textbf{loop forever do} \\
m_0 : \bigvee\limits_{u=1}^{N_2}
\left[
\begin{array}{l}
\textbf{when } z[i] \wedge \forall j : (\neg z[j] \vee w[j] < u \vee w[j] \geq w[i]) \textbf{ do} \\
w[i] := u
\end{array}
\right]
\end{array}
\right]
$$

Fig. 4. Parameterized Mutual Exclusion Algorithm BAKERY.

In the standard Bakery algorithm the variables $w[i]$ are unbounded natural numbers. Here we bound them by N_2. To make sure that they do not get stuck at N_2 and prevent any new values to be drawn at statement ℓ_1, we have the *reducing process* $R[i]$ which attempts to identify a *gap* just below the current value of $w[i]$. Such a gap is a positive natural number u smaller than $w[i]$ and which is not currently occupied by any $w[j]$ for an active $C[j]$, and such that all active $w[j]$ are either below u or above $w[i]$. Client $C[j]$ is considered active if $z[j] = 1$. On identifying such a gap u, process $R[i]$ *reduces* $w[i]$ to u. The disjunction $\bigvee_{u=1}^{N_2}$ occurring at statements ℓ_1 and m_0 denotes a non-deterministic choice over all possible values of u in the range $[1..N_2]$, provided the chosen value of u satisfies the condition appearing in the enclosed **when** statement.

The property of mutual exclusion, it can be written as $p : \forall i \neq j : \neg(at\_\ell_3[i] \wedge at\_\ell_3[j])$. Since both i and j are of type type_1, this leads to a choice of $I_1 = 2$

and $I_2 = 0$. From the program we can conclude that $b = 0$, $d = 0$, and $e = 1$ (corresponding to the single $[1..N_1] \mapsto [1..N_2]$ array w). The transition relation can be written in the form $\exists i, u : \forall \vec{t} : R$, leading to $H_1 = 1$ (the auxiliary variable i) and $H_2 = 1$ (the auxiliary variable $u : \text{type}_2$). Using these numbers, we obtain a cutoff value pair $(N_1^0, N_2^0) = (3, 4)$.

Arbitrary Stratified Systems. Lemma 1 can be generalized to systems with arbitrary array types, as long as the type structure is *stratified*, i.e., $i < j$ for each type $\text{type}_i \mapsto \text{type}_j$. Consider a stratified BDS with k parameterized types $\text{type}_1, \ldots, \text{type}_k$. Let b_i be the number of type_i vairables in the system, and let e_{ij} be the number of $\text{type}_i \mapsto \text{type}_j$ arrays in the system.

Corollary 2. *Let S be a k-parameter BDS with $k \geq 1$ stratified types to which we wish to apply proof rule* INV *with the assertions φ and p having each the form $\forall i_1^1, \ldots, i_{I_1}^1, \ldots, i_1^k, \ldots, i_{I_k}^k : \psi(\vec{i})$. Then, the premises of rule* INV *are valid over $S(N_1, \ldots, N_k)$ for all $N_1, \ldots, N_k > 1$ iff they are valid over $S(N_1^0, \ldots, N_k^0)$ where $N_1^0 = b_1 + H_1 + I_1$, and for every $i = 2, \ldots, k$, $N_i^0 = (b_i + H_i + I_i) + \sum_{j=1}^{i-1}(e_{ji} \cdot N_j^0)$.*

5   Systems with Unstratified Array Structure

There are many interesting systems for which the restriction of stratification does not apply. For example, consider program PETERSON presented in Fig. 5, which implements a mutual exclusion algorithm due to Peterson. Obviously, this system has an unstratified array structure.

```
            in      N   : integer where N > 1
            type  Pr_id : [1..N]
                  Level : [0..N]
            local   y   : array Pr_id of Level where y = 0
                    s   : array Level of Pr_id
                 ┌ loop forever do                                              ┐
                 │  ┌ ℓ₀ : NonCritical                                        ┐ │
    N            │  │ ℓ₁ : (y[i], s[1]) := (1, i)                             │ │
    ‖   P[i] ::  │  │ ℓ₂ : while y[i] < N do                                  │ │
   i=1           │  │    ┌ ℓ₃ : await s[y[i]] ≠ i ∨ ∀j ≠ i : y[j] < y[i] ┐  │ │
                 │  │    └ ℓ₄ : (y[i], s[y[i]+1]) := (y[i]+1, i)          ┘  │ │
                 │  │ ℓ₅ : Critical                                          │ │
                 │  └ ℓ₆ : y[i] := 0                                         ┘ │
                 └                                                              ┘
```

Fig. 5. Parameterized Mutual Exclusion Algorithm PETERSON.

When the system has an unstratified array structure, we lose the capability of reducing any counter-model which violates $(\forall \vec{j} : \psi(\vec{j})) \wedge (\exists \vec{h} \forall \vec{t} : R(\vec{h}, \vec{t})) \rightarrow \forall \vec{i} : \psi'(\vec{i})$ to a model of size not exceeding N_0. But this does not imply that we cannot resolve this verification condition algorithmically. The first step in any deductive proof of a formula such as the above formula is that of *skolemization* which removes all existential quantifications on the left-hand side and all universal quantifications on the right-hand side of the implication, leading to

$$(\forall \vec{j} : \psi(\vec{j})) \;\wedge\; (\forall \vec{t} : R(\vec{h}, \vec{t})) \;\;\rightarrow\;\; \psi'(\vec{i}) \tag{3}$$

In subsequent steps, the deductive proof instantiates the remaining universal quantifications for $\vec{j}$ and $\vec{t}$ by concrete terms. Most often these concrete terms are taken from the (now) free variables of (3), namely, $\vec{h}$ and $\vec{i}$. Inspired by this standard process pursued in deductive verification, we suggest to replace Formula (3) by

$$(\bigwedge_{\vec{j} \in \{\vec{h},\vec{i}\}} \psi(\vec{j})) \;\wedge\; (\bigwedge_{\vec{t} \in \{\vec{h},\vec{i}\}} R(\vec{h}, \vec{t})) \;\;\rightarrow\;\; \psi'(\vec{i}), \tag{4}$$

which is obtained by replacing the universal quantification over $\vec{j}$ and $\vec{t}$ by a conjunction in which each conjunct is obtained by instantiating the relevant variables ($\vec{j}$ or $\vec{t}$) by a subset (allowing replication) of the free variables $\vec{h}$ and $\vec{i}$. The conjunction should be taken over all such possible instantiations. The resulting quantifier-free formula is not equivalent to the original formula (3) but the validity of (4) implies the validity of (3). For a quantifier-free formula such as (4), we have again the property of model reduction, which we utilize for formulating the appropriate decision procedure for unstratified systems.

Consider an unstratified system $S(N)$ with b variables of type $[1..N]$ and e arrays of type $[1..N] \mapsto [1..N]$. As before, let H denote the number of existentially quantified variables in the definition of ρ and let I denote the number of universally quantified variables in the definition of φ. Furthermore, assume that the transition relation or candidate assertion do not contain nested arrays references. For example, we will replace the formula $s[y[i]] \neq i$ by $y[i] = h \wedge s[h] \neq i$, where h is a fresh auxiliary variable. Let $\text{INV}^\wedge$ denote a version of rule INV in which all premises have been skolemized first and then, the remaining universal quantifications replaced by conjunctions over all instantiations by the free variables in each formula.

Claim. Let $S(N)$ be a parameterized system as described above. Then if $S(N_0)$ satisfies the premises of rule INV applied to property p for $N_0 = (e+1)(b+I+H)$, we can conclude that p is an invariant of $S(N)$ for every $N > 1$.

For strongly typed systems, such as PETERSON, where comparisons and assignments are only allowed between elements of the same type, we can provide more precise bounds. Assume that the system has two types and that each of the bounds can be split into two components. Then the bound on N_0 can be refined into $N_0 = \max(b_1 + I_1 + H_1 + e_{21}(b_2 + I_2 + H_2), b_2 + I_2 + H_2 + e_{12}(b_1 + I_1 + H_1))$, where e_{21} and e_{12} denote the number of $\text{type}_1 \mapsto \text{type}_2$ and $\text{type}_2 \mapsto \text{type}_1$-arrays. For the case of PETERSON, we have $b_1 = b_2 = 0$, $I_1 = I_2 = 2$, $H_1 = 1$, $H_2 = 2$, and $e_{12} = e_{21} = 1$, which leads to $N_0 = 7$.

6 The Proof of the Pudding

According to a common saying "the proof of the pudding is in the eating". In this section, we present the experimental results obtained by applying the method of *invisible invariants* to various systems. Table 1 summarizes these results.

The second column of the table specifies the number of processes used in the verification process. In some cases, we took a value higher than the required minimum. The τ_1 column specifies the time (in seconds) it took to compute the reachable states. Column τ_2 specifies the time it took to compute the candidate inductive assertion. Finally, column τ_3 specifies the time it took to check the premises of rule INV.

The systems on the left are each a single-type system which only employs equality comparison in their transition relations and candidate assertions. SZYMANSKI employs inequalities, and TOKEN-RING needs the relation $h_2 = h_1 \oplus 1$ in its transition relation. BAKERY is a stratified two-type system employing inequality comparisons, and PETERSON is an unstratified two-type system. To obtain inductiveness in the Illinois' cache protocol we had to add an auxiliary variable called *last_dirty* which records the index of the last process which made its cache entry dirty.

Table 1. Summary of Experimental Results.

System	N_0	τ_1	τ_2	τ_3
MUX-SEM	5	.01	.01	.01
S. German's Cache	4	10.21	10.72	133.04
Illinois's Cache	4	1.47	.04	.58
3-stages Pipeline	6	20.66	.27	29.59

System	N_0	τ_1	τ_2	τ_3
SZYMANSKI	4	< .01	.06	.06
TOKEN-RING	5	< .01	< .01	< .01
BAKERY	5		.41	.16	.25
PETERSON	(6,7)		79	1211	240

7   Conclusion and Future Work

The paper studies the problem of uniform verification of parameterized systems. We have introduced the method of verification by invisible invariants–a heuristic that has proven successful for fully automatic verification of safety properties for many parameterized systems.

We are currently working on extending the method so that it also encompasses liveness properties. To prove liveness properties, one has to come up with a well-founded domain and a ranking function from states into the well-founded domain. The ranking function has to be such that no state leads into a higher ranked state, and, because of fairness, every state eventually must lead into a lower ranked state. Thus, we need to extend the method of invisible invariants to generate well founded domains and ranking, as well as to have the counter-part of Lemma 1 to produce cutoff values for the case of liveness properties.

Acknowledgment

We wish to express our deep gratitude to Elad Shahar who, not only constructed the TLV programmable model-checker which we used to implement all the verification tasks described in this work, but also modified and extended it as we went along, graciously responding to any new needs and requests raised during the research.

References

[ABJN99] P.A. Abdulla, A. Bouajjani, B. Jonsson, and M. Nilsson. Handling global conditions in parametrized system verification. In *CAV'99, LNCS 1633*, pp. 134–145, 1999.

[AK86]   K. R. Apt and D. Kozen. Limits for automatic program verification of finite-state concurrent systems. *Information Processing Letters*, 22(6), 1986.

[BCG86]   M.C. Browne, E.M. Clarke, and O. Grumberg. Reasoning about networks with many finite state processes. In *PODC'86*, pp. 240–248, 1986.

[BD94]   J. R. Burch and D. L. Dill. Automatic verification of pipelined microprocessor control. In *CAV'94, LNCS 818*, pp. 68–80, 1994.

[CEFJ96] E.M. Clarke, R. Enders, T. Filkorn, and S. Jha. Exploiting symmetry in temporal logic model checking. *Formal Methods in System Design*, 9(1/2), 1996.

[CGJ95]   E.M. Clarke, O. Grumberg, and S. Jha. Verifying parametrized networks using abstraction and regular languages. In *CONCUR'95*, pp. 395–407.

[CR99a]   S.J. Creese and A.W. Roscoe. Formal verification of arbitrary network topologies. In *Proc. of the Int. Conf. on Parallel and Distributed Processing Techniques and Applications (PDPTA'99)*. CSREA Press, 1999.

[CR99b]   S.J. Creese and A.W. Roscoe. Verifying an infinite family of inductions simultaneously using data independence and fdr. In *FORTE/PSTV'99*.

[CR00]   S.J. Creese and A.W. Roscoe. Data independent induction over structured networks. In *Proc. of the Int. Conf. on Parallel and Distributed Processing Techniques and Applications (PDPTA'00)*. CSREA Press, 2000.

[Del00]   G. Delzanno. Automatic verification of parametrized cache coherence protocols. In *CAV'00, LNCS 1855*, pp. 53–68, 2000.

[EK00]   E.A. Emerson and V. Kahlon. Reducing model checking of the many to the few. In *CADE'00*, pp. 236–255, 2000.

[EN95]   E. A. Emerson and K. S. Namjoshi. Reasoning about rings. In *POPL'95*.

[EN96]   E.A. Emerson and K.S. Namjoshi. Automatic verification of parameterized synchronous systems. In *CAV'96, LNCS 1102*, 1996.

[ES96]   E. A. Emerson and A. P. Sistla. Symmetry and model checking. *Formal Methods in System Design*, 9(1/2), 1996.

[ES97]   E. A. Emerson and A. P. Sistla. Utilizing symmetry when model checking under fairness assumptions. *TOPLAS*, 19(4), 1997.

[Ger00]   S. German. Personal Communication, 2000.

[GS92]   S.M. German and A.P. Sistla. Reasoning about systems with many processes. *JACM*, 39:675–735, 1992.

[GS97]   V. Gyuris and A. P. Sistla. On-the-fly model checking under fairness that exploits symmetry. In *CAV'97, LNCS 1254*, 1997.

[GZ98]   E.P. Gribomont and G. Zenner. Automated verification of szymanski's algorithm. In *TACAS'98, LNCS 1384*, pp. 424–438, 1998.

[HLR92]   N. Halbwachs, F. Lagnier, and C. Ratel. An experience in proving regular networks of processes by modular model checking. *Acta Informatica*, 29(6/7):523–543, 1992.

[ID96]   C.N. Ip and D. Dill. Verifying systems with replicated components in Murφ. In *CAV'96, LNCS 1102*, 1996.

[JL98]   E. Jensen and N.A. Lynch. A proof of burn's n-process mutual exclusion algorithm using abstraction. In *TACAS'98, LNCS 1384*, pp. 409–423, 1998.

[JN00]   B. Jonsson and M. Nilsson. Transitive closures of regular relations for verifying infinite-state systems. In *TACAS'00, LNCS 1785*, 2000.

[KM95]   R.P. Kurshan and K.L. McMillan. A structural induction theorem for processes. *Inf. and Comp.*, 117:1–11, 1995.

[KMM⁺97] Y. Kesten, O. Maler, M. Marcus, A. Pnueli, and E. Shahar. Symbolic model checking with rich assertional languages. In *CAV'97, LNCS 1254*, pp. 424–435, 1997.

[KP00]   Y. Kesten and A. Pnueli. Control and data abstractions: The cornerstones of practical formal verification. *STTT*, 4(2):328–342, 2000.

[LHR97]   D. Lesens, N. Halbwachs, and P. Raymond. Automatic verification of parameterized linear networks of processes. In *POPL'97*, 1997.

[LS97]   D. Lesens and H. Saidi. Automatic verification of parameterized networks of processes by abstraction. In *INFINITY'97*, 1997.

[MAB⁺94] Z. Manna, A. Anuchitanukul, N. Bjørner, A. Browne, E. Chang, M. Colón, L. De Alfaro, H. Devarajan, H. Sipma, and T.E. Uribe. STeP: The Stanford Temporal Prover. Technical Report STAN-CS-TR-94-1518, Stanford University, 1994.

[McM98a] K.L McMillan. Getting started with smv. Technical report, Cadence Berkeley Labs, 1998.

[McM98b] K.L. McMillan. Verification of an implementation of Tomasulo's algorithm by compositional model checking. In *CAV'98, LNCS 1427*, pp. 110–121.

[MP95a]   Z. Manna and A. Pnueli. *Temporal Verification of Reactive Systems: Safety.* Springer-Verlag, New York, 1995.

[PP84]   M.S. Papamarcos and J.H. Patel. A low-overhead coherence solution for multiprocessors with private cache memories. In *Proc. Int. Symp. on Shared Memory Multiprocesors (ISCA'84)*, pp. 348–354, 1984.

[PRZ01]   A. Pnueli, S. Ruah, and L. Zuck. Automatic deductive verification with invisible invariants. In *TACAS'01, LNCS*, pp. 82–97, 2001.

[PS00]   A. Pnueli and E. Shahar. Liveness and acceleration in parameterized verification. In *CAV'00, LNCS 1855*, pp. 328–343, 2000.

[SG89]   Z. Shtadler and O. Grumberg. Network grammars, communication behaviors and automatic verification. In *Automatic Verification Methods for Finite State Systems*, volume 407 of *LNCS*, pp. 151–165, 1989.

[SOR93]   N. Shankar, S. Owre, and J.M. Rushby. The PVS proof checker: A reference manual (draft). Technical report, Comp. Sci.,Laboratory, SRI International, 1993.

[Szy88]   B. K. Szymanski. A simple solution to Lamport's concurrent programming problem with linear wait. In *Proc. 1988 International Conference on Supercomputing Systems*, pp. 621–626, 1988.

[WL89]   P. Wolper and V. Lovinfosse. Verifying properties of large sets of processes with network invariants. In *Automatic Verification Methods for Finite State Systems*, volume 407 of *LNCS*, pp. 68–80, 1989.

EVC: A Validity Checker for the Logic of Equality with Uninterpreted Functions and Memories, Exploiting Positive Equality, and Conservative Transformations*

Miroslav N. Velev[1] and Randal E. Bryant[1,2]

[1] Department of Electrical and Computer Engineering
mvelev@ece.cmu.edu
[2] School of Computer Science
Carnegie Mellon University, Pittsburgh, PA 15213, U.S.A.
http://www.cs.cmu.edu/~{bryant,mvelev}
mvelev@ece.cmu.edu

Abstract. The property of Positive Equality [2] dramatically speeds up validity checking of formulas in the logic of Equality with Uninterpreted Functions and Memories (EUFM) [4]. The logic expresses correctness of high-level microprocessors. We present EVC (Equality Validity Checker)—a tool that exploits Positive Equality and other optimizations when translating a formula in EUFM to a propositional formula, which can then be evaluated by any Boolean satisfiability (SAT) procedure. EVC has been used for the automatic formal verification of pipelined, superscalar, and VLIW microprocessors.

1 Introduction

Formal verification of microprocessors has historically required extensive manual intervention. Burch and Dill [4] raised the degree of automation by using flushing—feeding the implementation processor with bubbles in order to complete partially executed instructions—to compute a mapping from implementation to specification states. The correctness criterion is that one step of the implementation should be equivalent to 0, or 1, or up to *k* (for an implementation that can fetch up to *k* instructions per cycle) steps of a specification single-cycle processor when starting from equivalent states, where equivalency is determined via flushing. However, the verification efficiency has still depended on manually provided case-splitting expressions [4][5] when using the specialized decision procedure SVC [16]. In order to apply the method to complex superscalar processors, Hosabettu [9] and Sawada [15] required months of manual work, using the theorem provers PVS [13] and ACL2 [10], respectively. We present EVC, a validity checker for the logic of EUFM, as an alternative highly efficient tool.

2 Hardware Description Language

In order to be verified with EVC, a high-level implementation processor and its specification must be defined in our Hardware Description Language (HDL). That

---

* This research was supported by the SRC under contract 00-DC-684.

G. Berry, H. Comon, and A. Finkel (Eds.): CAV 2001, LNCS 2102, pp. 235 - 240, 2001.

HDL is similar to a subset of Verilog [17], except that word-level values do not have dimensions but are represented with a single term-level expression, according to the syntax of EUFM [4]. Hence, nets are required to be declared of type term or type bit. Additionally, a net can be declared as input, e.g., the phase clocks that determine the updating of state or the signals that control the flushing. The HDL has constructs for the definition of memories and latches (see Fig. 2 for the description of two stages of the processor in Fig. 1). Memories and latches can have multiple input and/or output ports—of type inport and outport, respectively. Latch ports have an enable signal and a list of data signals. Memory ports additionally have an address signal after the enable. Logic gates—and, or, not, = (term-level equality comparator), and mux (multiplexor, i.e., ITE operator)—are used for the description of the control path of a processor. Uninterpreted functions and uninterpreted predicates—such as ALU in   Fig. 2—are used to abstract blocks of combinational logic—the ALU in Fig. 1—as black boxes. Uninterpreted functions and uninterpreted predicates with no arguments are considered as term variables and Boolean variables, respectively, and can be used to abstract constant values that have special semantic meaning, e.g., the data value 0.

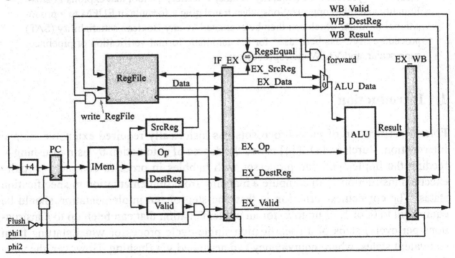

Fig. 1. Block Diagram of a 3-Stage Pipelined Processor.

In order to fully exploit the efficiency of Positive Equality, the designer of high-level microprocessors must follow some simple restrictions. Data operands must not be compared by equality comparators, e.g., in order to determine a branch-on-equal condition. Instead, the equality comparison must be abstracted with the same uninterpreted predicate in both the implementation and the specification processor. Also, a flush signal must be included in the implementation processor, as shown in Fig. 1, in order to turn newly fetched instructions into bubbles during flushing. That extra input will be optimized away by setting it to 0 (the value during normal operation) when translating the high-level processor description to a gate-level synthesizable HDL.

we improve the upper bound. These ideas are presented in Algorithm 4. The treatment of weak until in the refinement step is almost the same as for until; the only difference being – as we have to calculate a greatest fixed point via overapproximations – that the roles of under- and overapproximations have to be exchanged.

Example : Let us revisit the running example. Let $\mathcal{A} = (\alpha, \gamma, \mathcal{U}, O)$ be the current abstract Φ-model the model checker has returned in the first iteration (see the picture above). Refinement starts with $\Psi = \forall \Box a$. We get $\widetilde{Pre}(Sat_{\mathcal{A}}^+(\Psi)) = \widetilde{Pre}(\gamma(\{a\})) = \gamma(\{a\}) \setminus \{s_0\}$. Thus, the grey concrete initial state s_0 is moved to $\{a, \neg \Psi\}$. All other refinement steps leave the model unchanged. Refine$(\mathcal{A}, \Phi)$ returns the model with components $\mathcal{U}_1, O_1$ as shown below.

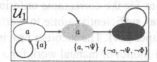
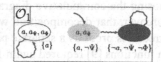

In the following model checking phase, $NewSat(\Psi) = NewSat(\Phi) = NewSat(\neg \Psi) = \emptyset$. $NewSat(\neg \Phi)$ consists of the grey abstract state $\sigma = \{a, \neg \Psi\}$. Therefore, we move $\gamma(\sigma) = \{s_0\}$ to the abstract state $\sigma' = \{a, \neg \Psi, \neg \Phi\}$. We obtain an abstract Φ-model $\mathcal{A}_2$ where the abstract interpretation of the concrete initial state s_0 is $\alpha_2(s_0) = \sigma'$. As σ' contains $\neg \Phi$, the condition $\mathcal{A}_2 \models \neg \Phi$ in the repeat-loop of Algorithm 2 holds (see Def. 3). Hence, Algorithm 2 terminates with the correct answer "no". □

Remark : There is no need for an explicit treatment of the *boolean connectives* $\vee$ and $\wedge$ in the model checking or refinement step. For instance, if $\Psi = \Psi_1 \vee \Psi_2$ is a subformula of Φ then improving the approximations for the sets $Sat_{\mathcal{M}}(\Psi_1)$ automatically yields an improvement for the underapproximation for $Sat_{\mathcal{M}}(\Psi)$. "Moving" a block B from an abstract state σ to the abstract state $\sigma' = \lceil \sigma \cup \{\Psi_1\} \rceil$ has the side effect that B is added to both $Sat_{\mathcal{A}}^-(\Psi_1)$ and $Sat_{\mathcal{A}}^-(\Psi)$. This is due to the axioms, we require for the elements in S_Φ. The corresponding observation holds for the overapproximations $Sat_{\mathcal{A}}^+(\cdot)$. □

Remark: The *atomic propositions* a_Ψ play a crucial role in both the model checking and the refinement procedure. The labelings $L_{\mathcal{U}}$ and L_O cover the information that might got lost due to the transition relations $\rightarrow_\alpha$ and $\leadsto_\alpha$. In the refinement phase, they are necessary to detect when the computation of a least or greatest fixed point is finished. □

Theorem 1. [Partial Correctness] *If Algorithm 2 terminates with the answer "yes" then $\mathcal{M} \models \Phi$. If Algorithm 2 terminates with the answer "no" then $\mathcal{M} \not\models \Phi$.* □

Because of the similarities with stable partitioning algorithms for calculating the (bi-) simulation equivalence classes [37, 7, 32, 24] it is not surprising that our algorithm terminates provided that the (bi-)simulation quotient space of $\mathcal{M}$ is finite.

Theorem 2. [Termination] *If the concrete model $\mathcal{M}$ has a finite simulation or bisimulation quotient then Algorithm 2 terminates.*

4 Summary of Results

A single-issue 5-stage pipelined DLX processor [8] can be formally verified with
EVC in 0.2 seconds on a 336 MHz Sun4. In contrast, SVC [16]—a tool that does not
exploit Positive Equality—does not complete the evaluation of the same formula in
24 hours. Furthermore, the theorem proving approach of completion functions [9]
could be applied to a similar design after 1 month of manual work by an expert user.
Finally, the symbolic simulation tool of Ritter, *et al.* [14] required over 1 hour of
CPU time for verification of that processor. A dual-issue superscalar DLX with one
complete and one arithmetic pipeline can be formally verified with EVC in 0.8 seconds [21]. A comparable design was verified by Burch [5], who needed 30 minutes
of CPU time only after manually identifying 28 case-splitting expressions, and manually decomposing the commutative diagram for the correctness criterion into three
diagrams. Moreover, that decomposition was sufficiently subtle to warrant publication of its correctness proof as a separate paper [24]. The theorem proving approach
of completion functions [9] required again 1 month of manual work for a comparable
dual-issue DLX.

EVC has been used to formally verify processors with exceptions, multicycle functional units, and branch prediction [19]. It can automatically abstract the forwarding
logic of memories that interact with stalling logic in a conservative way that results
in an order of magnitude speedup with BDDs [21]. A comparative study [22] of 28
SAT-checkers, 2 decision diagrams—BDDs [1][6] and BEDs [23]—and 2 ATPG
tools identified the SAT-checker Chaff [11] as the most efficient means for evaluating the Boolean formulas generated by EVC, outperforming the other SAT procedures by orders of magnitude. We also compared the e_{ij} [7] and the small domains
[12] encodings for replacing equality comparisons that are both negated and not
negated in the correctness EUFM formula. We found the e_{ij} encoding to result in 4
times faster SAT checking when verifying complex correct designs and to consistently perform better for buggy versions. Now a 9-wide VLIW processor that imi-
tates the Intel Itanium in many speculative features such as predicated execution,
register remapping, branch prediction, and advanced loads can be formally verified
in 12 minutes of CPU time by using Chaff. That design was previously verified in
31.5 hours with BDDs [20]. It can have up to 42 instructions in flight and is far more
complex than any other processor formally verified in an automatic way previously.
We also found Positive Equality to be the most important factor for our success—
without this property the verification times increase exponentially for very simple
processors [22], even when using Chaff.

A preliminary version of the tools has been released to the Motorola M•Core
Microprocessor Design Center for evaluation.

5 Conclusions and Future Work

EVC is an extremely powerful validity checker for the logic of Equality with Uninterpreted Functions and Memories (EUFM) [4]. Its efficiency is due to exploiting the
property of Positive Equality [2] in order to translate a formula in EUFM to a propo-

sitional formula that can be evaluated with SAT procedures, allowing for gains from their improvements. In the future, we will automate the translation of formally verified high-level microprocessors, defined in our HDL and verified with EVC, to synthesizable gate-level Verilog [17]. TLSim and EVC, as well as the benchmarks used for experiments, are available by ftp (http://www.ece.cmu.edu/~mvelev).

References

[1] R.E. Bryant, "Symbolic Boolean Manipulation with Ordered Binary-Decision Diagrams," ACM Computing Surveys, Vol. 24, No. 3 (September 1992), pp. 293-318.

[2] R.E. Bryant, S. German, and M.N. Velev, "Processor Verification Using Efficient Reductions of the Logic of Uninterpreted Functions to Propositional Logic," ACM Transactions on Computational Logic (TOCL), Vol. 2, No. 1 (January 2001).

[3] R.E. Bryant, and M.N. Velev, "Boolean Satisfiability with Transitivity Constraints,"[2] Computer-Aided Verification (CAV'00), E.A. Emerson and A.P. Sistla, eds., LNCS 1855, Springer-Verlag, July 2000, pp. 86-98.

[4] J.R. Burch, and D.L. Dill, "Automated Verification of Pipelined Microprocessor Control," Computer-Aided Verification (CAV'94), D.L. Dill, ed., LNCS 818, Springer-Verlag, June 1994, pp. 68-80. http://sprout.stanford.edu/papers.html.

[5] J.R. Burch, "Techniques for Verifying Superscalar Microprocessors," 33rd Design Automation Conference (DAC '96), June 1996, pp. 552-557.

[6] CUDD-2.3.0, http://vlsi.colorado.edu/~fabio.

[7] A. Goel, K. Sajid, H. Zhou, A. Aziz, and V. Singhal, "BDD Based Procedures for a Theory of Equality with Uninterpreted Functions," Computer-Aided Verification (CAV '98), A.J. Hu and M.Y. Vardi, eds., LNCS 1427, Springer-Verlag, June 1998, pp. 244-255.

[8] J.L. Hennessy, and D.A. Patterson, Computer Architecture: A Quantitative Approach, 2nd edition, Morgan Kaufmann Publishers, San Francisco, CA, 1996.

[9] R. Hosabettu, "Systematic Verification of Pipelined Microprocessors," Ph.D. thesis, Department of Computer Science, University of Utah, August 2000.

[10] M. Kaufmann, P. Manolios, J.S. Moore, Computer-Aided Reasoning: ACL2 Case Studies, Kluwer Academic Publishers, Boston/Dordrecht/London, 2000.

[11] M.W. Moskewicz, C.F. Madigan, Y. Zhao, L. Zhang, and S. Malik, "Chaff: Engineering an Efficient SAT Solver," 38th Design Automation Conference (DAC'01), June 2001.

[12] A. Pnueli, Y. Rodeh, O. Shtrichman, and M. Siegel, "Deciding Equality Formulas by Small-Domain Instantiations," Computer-Aided Verification (CAV'99), N. Halbwachs and D. Peled, eds., LNCS 1633, Springer-Verlag, June 1999, pp. 455-469.

[13] PVS Specification and Verification System (PVS), http://pvs.csl.sri.com.

[14] G. Ritter, H. Eveking, and H. Hinrichsen, "Formal Verification of Designs with Complex Control by Symbolic Simulation," Correct Hardware Design and Verification Methods (CHARME'99), L. Pierre and T. Kropf, eds., LNCS 1703, Springer-Verlag, September 1999, pp. 234-249.

[15] J. Sawada, "Formal Verification of an Advanced Pipelined Machine," Ph.D. thesis, Department of Computer Science, University of Texas at Austin, December 1999.

[16] Stanford Validity Checker (SVC), http://sprout.stanford.edu.

[17] D.E. Thomas, and P.R. Moorby, The Verilog® Hardware Description Language, 4th edition, Kluwer Academic Publishers, Boston/Dordrecht/London, 1998.

[18] M.N. Velev, and R.E. Bryant, "Superscalar Processor Verification Using Efficient Reductions of the Logic of Equality with Uninterpreted Functions to Propositional Logic," *Correct Hardware Design and Verification Methods (CHARME'99)*, L. Pierre and T. Kropf, *eds.*, LNCS 1703, Springer-Verlag, September 1999, pp. 37-53.
Available from: http://www.ece.cmu.edu/~mvelev

[19] M.N. Velev, and R.E. Bryant, "Formal Verification of Superscalar Microprocessors with Multicycle Functional Units, Exceptions, and Branch Prediction," *37th Design Automation Conference (DAC'00)*, June 2000, pp. 112-117.

[20] M.N. Velev, "Formal Verification of VLIW Microprocessors with Speculative Execution," *Computer-Aided Verification (CAV'00)*, E.A. Emerson and A.P. Sistla, *eds.*, LNCS 1855, Springer-Verlag, July 2000, pp. 296-311.
Available from: http://www.ece.cmu.edu/~mvelev.

[21] M.N. Velev, "Automatic Abstraction of Memories in the Formal Verification of Superscalar Microprocessors," *Tools and Algorithms for the Construction and Analysis of Systems (TACAS'01)*, T. Margaria and W. Yi, *eds.*, LNCS, Springer-Verlag, April 2001, pp. 252-267. Available from: http://www.ece.cmu.edu/~mvelev.

[22] M.N. Velev, and R.E. Bryant, "Effective Use of Boolean Satisfiability Procedures in the Formal Verification of Superscalar and VLIW Microprocessors," *38th Design Automation Conference (DAC'01)*, June 2001. Available from:
http://www.ece.cmu.edu/~mvelev.

[23] P.F. Williams, "Formal Verification Based on Boolean Expression Diagrams," Ph.D. thesis, Department of Information Technology, Technical University of Denmark, Lyngby,   Denmark, August 2000.

[24] P.J. Windley, and J.R. Burch, "Mechanically Checking a Lemma Used in an Automatic Verification Tool," *Formal Methods in Computer-Aided Design (FMCAD'96)*, M. Srivas and A. Camilleri, *eds.*, LNCS 1166, Springer-Verlag, November 1996, pp. 362-376.

AGVI – Automatic Generation, Verification, and Implementation of Security Protocols

Dawn Song, Adrian Perrig, and Doantam Phan

University of California, Berkeley
{dawnsong,perrig}@cs.berkeley.edu
dphan@hkn.eecs.berkeley.edu

Abstract. As new Internet applications emerge, new security protocols and systems need to be designed and implemented. Unfortunately the current protocol design and implementation process is often ad-hoc and error prone. To solve this problem, we have designed and implemented a toolkit *AGVI, Automatic Generation, Verification, and Implementation of Security Protocols*. With AGVI, the protocol designer inputs the system specification (such as cryptographic key setup) and security requirements. AGVI will then automatically find the near-optimal protocols for the specific application, proves the correctness of the protocols and implement the protocols in Java. Our experiments have successfully generated new and even simpler protocols than the ones documented in the literature.

1 Introduction

As the Internet and electronic commerce prospers, new applications emerge rapidly and require that new security protocols and systems are designed and deployed quickly. Unfortunately, numerous examples show that security protocols are difficult to design, to verify the correctness, and particularly hard to implement correctly:

- Different security protocols even with the same security properties vary in many system aspects such as computation overhead, communication overhead and battery power consumption. Therefore it is important to design *optimal* security protocols that suit specific applications. Unfortunately the current process of designing a security protocol is usually ad-hoc and involves little formalism and mechanical assistance. Such a design process is not only slow and error prone but also often miss the optimal protocols for specific applications.
- Experience shows that security protocols are often flawed even when they are designed with care. To guarantee the correctness of security protocols, we need formal and rigorous analysis of the protocols, especially automatic protocol verifiers.
- Software is notoriously flawed. Even if the design of the security protocol is correct, various implementation bugs introduced by programmers could still easily break the security of the system.

G. Berry, H. Comon, and A. Finkel (Eds.): CAV 2001, LNCS 2102, pp. 241–245, 2001.
© Springer-Verlag Berlin Heidelberg 2001

To solve these problems, we designed and implemented the *AGVI* toolkit which stands for Automatic Generation, Verification, and Implementation of Security Protocols. With AGVI, the protocol designer specifies the desired security requirements, such as authentication and secrecy, and system specification, e.g., symmetric or asymmetric encryption/decryption, low bandwidth. A *protocol generator* then generates *candidate* security protocols which satisfy the system requirements using an intelligent exhaustive search in a combinatorial protocol space. Then a *protocol screener* analyzes the candidate protocols, discards the flawed protocols, and outputs the correct protocols that satisfy the desired security properties. In the final step, a *code generator* automatically outputs a Java implementation from the formal specification of the generated security protocols.

Even a simple security protocol can have an enormous protocol space (for example, for a four-round authentication protocol, even after constraining message format and sending order, we estimate that there are at least 10^{12} possible variation protocols that one would need to consider to find an optimal one for the specific application!). Facing this challenge, we have developed powerful reduction techniques for the protocol generator to weed out obviously flawed protocols. Because the protocol generator uses simple criteria to rule out obviously flawed protocols, it is fast and can analyze $10,000$ protocols per second. Protocols that were not found flawed by the protocol generator are then send to the protocol screener which can prove whether the protocol is correct or not. Our protocol screener has the ability to analyze protocol executions with any arbitrary protocol configuration. When it terminates, it either provides a proof that a protocol satisfies its specified property under any arbitrary protocol configuration if it is the case, or it generates a counterexample if the property does not hold. It also exploits many state space reduction techniques to achieve high efficiency. On average, our protocol screener can check 5 to 10 synthesized protocols per second (measured on a 500 MHz Pentium III workstation running Linux).

We have successfully experimented with AGVI in several applications. We have found new protocols for authentication and key distribution protocols using AGVI and some of them are even simpler than the standard protocols documented in the literature such as ISO standards [Int93]. Details about the experiments and techniques in the tool can be found in [PS00a,PS00b].

2   Components in AGVI

2.1   The Protocol Generator

Our protocol generator generates candidate protocols that satisfy the specified system specification and discards obviously flawed protocols at an early stage. Intuitively, the protocol space is infinite. To solve this problem is to use *iterative deepening*, a standard search technique. In each iteration, we set a *cost threshold* of protocols. We then search through the protocol space to generate all the protocols below the given cost threshold. After sorting the protocols, the protocol screener tests them in the order of increasing cost. If one protocol satisfies the desired properties, it is minimal with respect to the cost metric function given by the user and the generation process stops. Otherwise, we increase the cost threshold and generate more protocols.

A simple three-party authentication and key distribution protocol has a protocol space of order 10^{12}. Our protocol generator generates and analyzes 10000 protocols per second, which would take over three years to explore the entire space. We have developed powerful protocol space reduction techniques to prune the search tree at an early stage. With these pruning techniques, it only takes the protocol generator a few hours to scan through the protocol space of order 10^{12}. More details are included in [PS00a,PS00b].

2.2   The Protocol Screener

We use Athena as the protocol screener [Son99,SBP00]. Athena uses an extension of the recently proposed Strand Space Model [THG98] to represent protocol execution. Athena incorporates a new logic that can express security properties including authentication, secrecy and properties related to electronic commerce. An automatic procedure enables Athena to evaluate well-formed formulae in this logic. For a well-formed formula, if the evaluation procedure terminates, it will generate a counterexample if the formula is false, or provide a proof if the formula is true. Even when the procedure does not terminate when we allow any arbitrary configurations of the protocol execution, (for example, any number of initiators and responders), termination could be forced by bounding the number of concurrent protocol runs and the length of messages, as is done in most existing automatic tools.

Athena also exploits several state space reduction techniques. Powered with techniques such as backward search and symbolic representation, Athena naturally avoids the state space explosion problem commonly caused by asynchronous composition and symmetry redundancy. Athena also has the advantage that it can easily incorporate results from theorem proving through unreachability theorems. By using the unreachability theorems, it can prune the state space at an early stage, hence, further reduce the state space explored and increase the likely-hood of termination. These techniques dramatically reduce the state space that needs to be explored.

2.3   The Code Generator

Our goal for the automatic code generator is to prevent implementation weaknesses, and obtain a secure implementation if the initial protocol is secure. The code generator is essentially a translator which translates the formal specification into Java code. Given that the translation rules are correct, the final implemenation can be shown to be correct using proof by construction. In particular, we show that our implementation is secure against some of the most common vulnerabilities:

- **Buffer overruns** account for more than half of all recent security vulnerabilities. Since we use Java as our implementation language, our automatically generated code is immune against this class of attack.

- **False input attacks** result from unchecked input parameters or unchecked conditions or errors. Our automatic implementation ensures that all input parameters are carefully checked to have the right format before used.
- **Type flaws** occur when one message component can be interpreted as another message component of a different form. In the implementation, we use typed messages to prevent type flaws.
- **Replay attacks** and **freshness attacks** are attacks where the attacker can reuse old message components in the attack. Athena already ensures that the protocols are secure against these attacks. To ensure that the implementation is secure, we use cryptographically secure pseudo-random number generators to create secure nonces.

The code generator uses the same protocol description as Athena uses. The generated code provides a simple yet flexible API for the application programmer to interface with. More details about the code generator can be found in [PPS00].

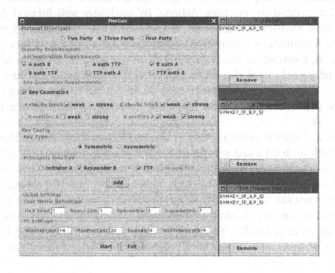

Fig. 1. AGVI GUI.

3   Experiments

We have used AGVI to automatically generate and implement authentication and key distribution protocols involving two parties with or without a trusted third party. In one experiment, we vary the system aspects: one system specication has a low computation overhead but a high communication overhead and another system specication has a low communication overhead and a high computation overhead. The AGVI found different optimal protocols for metric functions used in the two different cases. In another experiment, we vary the security properties required by the system. Key distribution protocols normally have a long list of possile security properties and an application might only require a subset of the list. The AGVI also found different optimal protocols for different security requirements. In both experiments, AGVI found new protocols that are more efficient or as efficient as the protocols documented in the literature. More details can be found in [PS00a,PS00b].

Acknowledgments

We would like to thank Doug Tygar for his encouragement and stimulating discussions.

References

[CJ97]   J. Clark and J. Jacob.   A survey of authentication protocol literature. http://www.cs.york.ac.uk/~jac/papers/drareview.ps.gz, 1997. Version 1.0.

[CJM98]   E.M. Clarke, S. Jha, and W. Marrero. Using state space exploration and a natural deduction style message derivation engine to verify security protocols. In *In Proceedings of the IFIP Working Conference on Programming Concepts and Methods (PROCOMET)*, 1998.

[Int93]   International Standards Organization. *Information Technology - Security techniques — Entity Authentication Mechanisms Part 3: Entity authentication using symmetric techniques*, 1993. ISO/IEC 9798.

[Mea94]   C. Meadows. The NRL protocol analyzer: An overview. In *Proceedings of the Second International Conference on the Practical Applications of Prolog*, 1994.

[Mil95]   J. Millen. The Interrogator model. In *Proceedings of the 1995 IEEE Symposium on Security and Privacy*, pages 251–260, 1995.

[MMS97]   J. C. Mitchell, M. Mitchell, and U. Stern. Automated analysis of cryptographic protocols using murφ. In *Proceedings of the 1997 IEEE Symposium on Security and Privacy*. IEEE Computer Society Press, 1997.

[PPS00]   Adrian Perrig, Doantam Phan, and Dawn Xiaodong Song. ACG–automatic code generation. automatic implementation of a security protocol. Technical Report 00-1120, UC Berkeley, December 2000.

[PS00a]   Adrian Perrig and Dawn Song. A first step towards the automatic generation of security protocols. In *Network and Distributed System Security Symposium*, February 2000.

[PS00b]   Adrian Perrig and Dawn Xiaodong Song. Looking for diamonds in the dessert: Automatic security protocol generation for three-party authentication and key distribution. In *Proc. of IEEE Computer Security Foundations Workshop CSFW 13*, July 2000.

[SBP00]   Dawn Song, Sergey Berezin, and Adrian Perrig. Athena, a new efficient automatic checker for security protocols. *Submitted to Journal of Computer Security*, 2000.

[Son99]   Dawn Song. Athena: An automatic checker for security protocol analysis. In *Proceedings of the 12th Computer Science Foundation Workshop*, 1999.

[THG98]   F.Javier Thayer, Jonathan C. Herzog, and Joshua D. Guttman. Strand spaces: Why is a security protocol correct? In *Proceedings of 1998 IEEE Symposium on Security and Privacy*, 1998.

ICS: Integrated Canonizer and Solver*

Jean-Christophe Filliâtre[1], Sam Owre[2], Harald Rueß[2], and Natarajan Shankar[2]

[1] LRI, URA 410 CNRS Bat 490, Université Paris Sud 91405 Orsay Cedex, France
Jean-Christophe.Filliatre@lri.fr
[2] Computer Science Laboratory SRI International
333 Ravenswood Ave. Menlo Park, CA 94025, USA
{owre,ruess,shankar}@csl.sri.com

Decision procedures are at the core of many industrial-strength verification systems such as ACL2 [KM97], PVS [ORS92], or STeP [MtSg96]. Effective use of decision procedures in these verification systems require the management of large assertional contexts. Many existing decision procedures, however, lack an appropriate API for managing contexts and efficiently switching between contexts, since they are typically used in a *fire-and-forget* environment.

ICS (Integrated Canonizer and Solver) is a decision procedure developed at SRI International. It does not only efficiently decide formulas in a useful combination of theories but it also provides an API that makes it suitable for use in applications with highly dynamic environments such as proof search or symbolic simulation.

The theory decided by ICS is a quantifier-free, first-order theory with uninterpreted function symbols and a rich combination of datatype theories including arithmetic, tuples, arrays, sets, and bit-vectors. This theory is particularly interesting for many applications in the realm of software and hardware verification. Combinations of a multitude of datatypes occur naturally in system specifications and the use of uninterpreted function symbols have proven to be essential for many real-world verifications.

The core of ICS is a congruence closure procedure [RS01] for the theory of equality and disequality with both uninterpreted and interpreted function symbols. This algorithm is based on the concepts of canonization and solving as introduced by Shostak [Sho84]. These basic notions have been extended to include inequalities over linear arithmetic terms and propositional logic. Altogether, the theory supported by ICS is similar to the ones underlying the PVS decision procedures and SVC [BDL96]; it includes:

- Function application $f(t_1, \ldots, t_n)$ for uninterpreted function symbols f of arity n.
- The usual propositional constants true, false and connectives not, &, |, =>, <=>.
- Equality (=) and disequality (/=).
- Rational constants and the arithmetic operators +, *, -; note that the decision procedure is complete only for multiplication restricted to multiplication

---

* This work was supported by SRI International, by NSF Grant CCR-0082560, DARPA/AFRL Contract F33615-00-C-3043, and by NASA Contract NAS1-00079. ICS (TM) is a trademark of SRI International.

G. Berry, H. Comon, and A. Finkel (Eds.): CAV 2001, LNCS 2102, pp. 246–249, 2001.

by constants. Arithmetic predicates include an integer test and the usual inequalities <, <=, >, >=.

- Tuples $(t_1, \ldots, t_n)$ together with the proj[i,n](t) operator for projecting the i-element in an n-tuple.
- Lookup $a[x]$ and update $a[x:=t]$ operations for a functional array a.
- The constant sets (empty, full), set membership (x in s), and set operators, including complement (compl(s)), union (s_1 union s_2), and intersection (s_1 inter s_2).
- Fixed-sized bitvectors including constants, concatenation (b_1 ++ b_2), extraction ($b[i:j]$), bit-wise operations like bit-wise conjunction, and built-in arithmetic relations such as add(b_1, b_2, b). This latter constraint encodes the fact that the sum of the unsigned interpretations of b_1 and b_2 equals the unsigned interpretation of b. Fixed-sized bitvectors are decided using the techniques described in [MR98].

ICS is capable of deciding formulas such as

- x+2 = y => f(a[x:=3][y-2]) = f(y-x+1)
- f(y-1)-1 = y+1 & f(x)+1 = x-1 & x+1 = y => false
- f(f(x)-f(y)) /= f(z) & y <= x & y >= x+z & z >= 0 => false

These formulas contain uninterpreted function symbols such as f and interpreted symbols drawn from the theories of arithmetic and the functional arrays.

Verification conditions are usually proved within the context of a large number of assertions derived from the antecedents of implications, conditional tests, and predicate subtype constraints. These contexts must be changed in an incremental manner when assertions are either added or removed. Through the use of functional data structures, ICS allows contexts to be incrementally enriched in a side-effect-free manner.

ICS is implemented in Ocaml, which offers satisfactory run-time performance, efficient garbage collection, and interfaces well with other languages like C. The implementation of ICS is based on optimization techniques such as hash-consing and efficient data structures like Patricia trees for representing sets and maps efficiently. ICS uses arbitrary precision rational numbers from the GNU multi-precision library (GMP).

There is a well-defined API for manipulating ICS terms, asserting formulas to the current database, switching between databases, and functions for maintaining normal forms and for testing the validity of assertions by means of canonization. This API is packaged as a C library, an Ocaml module, and a CommonLisp interface. The C library API, for example, has been used to connect ICS with PVS [ORS92], and both an interaction and a batch processing capability have been built using this API.

Consider, for example, processing f(y - 1) - 1 = y + 1, f(x) + 1 = x - 1, and x + 1 = y from left-to-right using the interactive mode of ICS.

```
$ ics
ICS interpreter. Copyright (c) 2001 SRI International.
Ctrl-d to exit.

>  assert f(y - 1) - 1 = y + 1.
```

This equation is asserted in its solved form as $y = -2 + f(-1 + y)$. This equation is indeed considered to be in solved form, since y on the right-hand side occurs only in the scope of the uninterpreted f. Terms in the database are partitioned into equivalence classes, and the canonical representative of any term t with respect to this partition is represented by can t; for example:

```
>  can -1 + y.
-3 + f(-1 + y)
```

It can be shown that can t_1 is identical to can t_2 iff the equality $t_1 = t_2$ is derivable in the current context. Now, the second equation is processed

```
>  assert f(x) + 1 = x - 1.
```

by canonizing it to $1 + f(x) = -1 + x$ and solving this equation as $x = 2 + f(x)$. Finally, can $x + 1$ yields $3 + f(x)$ and can y is $-2 + f(-1 + y)$. Thus, the third equation is solved as $f(x) = -5 + f(-1 + y)$. Since $f(x) = f(-1 + y)$, using $x = -1 + y$ and congruence, there is a contradiction $-5 = 0$. Indeed, ICS detects this inconsistency, when given the assertion below.

```
>  assert x + 1 = y.
Inconsistent!
```

The efficiency and scalability of ICS in processing formulas, the richness of its API, and its ability for fast context-switching should make it possible to use it as a black box for discharging verification conditions not only in a theorem proving context but also in applications like static analysis, abstract interpretation, extended type checking, symbolic simulation, model checking, or compiler optimization.

ICS is available free of charge under the PVS license. It will also be included in the upcoming release of PVS 3.0. The complete sources and documentation of ICS are available at

http://www.icansolve.com

References

[BDL96] Clark Barrett, David Dill, and Jeremy Levitt. Validity checking for combinations of theories with equality. In Mandayam Srivas and Albert Camilleri,
editors, *Formal Methods in Computer-Aided Design (FMCAD '96)*, volume
1166 of *Lecture Notes in Computer Science*, pages 187–201, Palo Alto, CA,
November 1996. Springer-Verlag.

[KM97] Matt Kaufmann and J Strother Moore. An industrial strength theorem prover
for a logic based on Common Lisp. *IEEE Transactions on Software Engineering*, 23(4):203–213, April 1997.

[MR98] O. Möller and H. Rueß. Solving bit-vector equations. In G. Gopalakrishnan
and Ph. Windley, editors, *Formal Methods in Computer-Aided Design (FM-
CAD '98)*, volume 1522 of *Lecture Notes in Computer Science*, pages 36–48,
Palo Alto, CA, November 1998. Springer-Verlag.

[MtSg96] Z. Manna and the STeP group. STeP: Deductive-algorithmic verification
of reactive and real-time systems. In R. Alur and T. A. Henzinger, editors,
Computer Aided Verification (CAV 96), volume 1102 of *Lecture Notes in
Computer Science*, pages 415–418, New Brunswick, NJ, July/August 1996.
Springer-Verlag.

[ORS92] S. Owre, J. M. Rushby, and N. Shankar. PVS: A prototype verification system. In Deepak Kapur, editor, *11th International Conference on Automated
Deduction (CADE)*, volume 607 of *Lecture Notes in Artificial Intelligence*,
pages 748–752, Saratoga, NY, June 1992. Springer-Verlag.

[RS01] Harald Rueß and N. Shankar. Deconstructing Shostak. To be presented at
LICS'2001, available from http://www.csl.sri.com/papers/lics01/, 2001.

[Sho84] Robert E. Shostak. Deciding combinations of theories. *Journal of the ACM*,
31(1):1–12, January 1984.

μCRL: A Toolset for Analysing Algebraic Specifications

Stefan Blom[1], Wan Fokkink[1], Jan Friso Groote[2], Izak van Langevelde[1],
Bert Lisser[1], and Jaco van de Pol[1]

[1] CWI, Department of Software Engineering
PO Box 94079, 1090 GB Amsterdam, The Netherlands
{sccblom,wan,izak,bertl,vdpol}@cwi.nl
[2] Eindhoven University of Technology, Department of Computing Science
PO Box 513, 5600 MB Eindhoven, The Netherlands
jfg@win.tue.nl

1 Introduction

μCRL [13] is a language for specifying and verifying distributed systems in an
algebraic fashion. It targets the specification of system behaviour in a process-
algebraic style and of data elements in the form of abstract data types. The
μCRL toolset [21] (see http://www.cwi.nl/~mcrl) supports the analysis and
manipulation of μCRL specifications. A μCRL specification can be automatically
transformed into a *linear process operator* (LPO). All other tools in the μCRL
toolset use LPOs as their starting point. The simulator allows the interactive
simulation of an LPO. There are a number of tools that allow optimisations on
the level of LPOs. The instantiator generates a labelled transition system (LTS)
from an LPO (under the condition that it is finite-state), and the resulting LTS
can be visualised, analysed and minimised.

An overview of the μCRL toolset is presented in Figure 1. This picture is
divided into three layers: μCRL specifications, LPOs and LTSs. The rectangular
boxes denote different ways to represent instances of the corresponding layer (for
example, LPOs can be represented in a binary or a textual form). A solid arrow
denotes a transformation from one instance to another that is supported by the
μCRL toolset; keywords are provided to these arrows to give some information
on which kinds of transformations are involved. Finally, the oval boxes represent
several ways to analyse systems, and dashed arrows show how the different representations of LPOs and LTSs can be analysed. The box named BCG and its
three outgoing dashed arrows actually belong to the CADP toolset (see Section
4). The next three sections are devoted to explaining Figure 1 in more detail.

The μCRL toolset was successfully used to analyse a wide range of protocols
and distributed algorithms. Recently it was used to support the optimised redesign of the Transactions Capabilities Procedures in the SS No. 7 protocol stack
for telephone exchanges [1, 2], to detect a number of mistakes in a real-life protocol over the CAN bus for lifting trucks [10], to analyse a leader election protocol
from the Home Audio/Video interoperability (HAVi) architecture [20], and to
perform scenario-based verifications of the coordination language SPLICE [6].

G. Berry, H. Comon, and A. Finkel (Eds.): CAV 2001, LNCS 2102, pp. 250–254, 2001.
© Springer-Verlag Berlin Heidelberg 2001

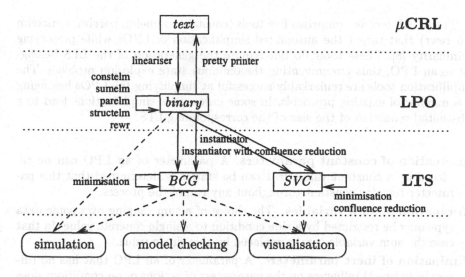

Fig. 1. The Main Components of the μCRL Toolset.

2   μCRL Specifications

The μCRL language is based on the process algebra ACP. It allows one to specify system behaviour in an algebraic style using atomic actions, alternative and sequential composition, parallelism and communication, encapsulation, hiding, renaming and recursive declarations. Furthermore, μCRL supports equationally specified abstract data types. In order to intertwine processes and data, atomic actions and recursion variables carry data parameters. Moreover, an if-then-else construct enables that data elements influence the course of a process, and alternative quantification chooses from a possibly infinite data domain.

3   Linear Process Operators

When investigating systems specified in μCRL, our current standard approach is to transform the μCRL specification under scrutiny to a relatively simple format without parallelism or communication, called an LPO. In essence this is a vector of data parameters together with a list of condition, action and effect triples, describing when an action may happen and what is its effect on the vector of data parameters. It is stored in a binary format or as a plain text file. From an LPO one can generate an LTS, in which the states are parameter vectors and the edges are labelled with parametrised actions.

In [14] it is described how a large class of μCRL processes can be transformed automatically to a bisimilar LPO. The resulting LPO and its data structures are stored as ATerms. The ATerm library [5] stores terms in a very compact way by minimal memory requirements, employing maximal sharing, and using a tailor-made garbage collector. Moreover, the ATerm library uses a file format that is even more compact than the memory format.

The μCRL toolset comprises five tools (constelm, sumelm, parelm, structelm and rewr) that target the automated simplification of LPOs while preserving bisimilarity [8]. These tools do not require the generation of the LTS belonging to an LPO, thus circumventing the ominous state explosion problem. The simplification tools are remarkably successful at simplifying the LPOs belonging to a number of existing protocols. In some cases these simplifications lead to a substantial reduction of the size of the corresponding LTS.

Elimination of constant parameters. A parameter of an LPO can be replaced by a constant value, if it can be statically determined that this parameter remains constant throughout any run of the process.

Elimination of sum variables. The choice of a sum ranging over some data type may be restricted by a side condition to a single concrete value. In that case the sum variable can be replaced by this single value.

Elimination of inert parameters. A parameter of an LPO that has no (direct or indirect) influence on the parameters of actions or on conditions does not influence the LPO's behaviour and can be removed. Whereas the two reduction techniques mentioned above only simplify the description of an LPO, elimination of inert parameters may lead to substantial reduction of the LTS underlying an LPO. If the inert parameter ranges over an infinite domain, the number of states can even reduce from infinite to finite by this operation. This typically happens after hiding part of the system's behaviour.

Elimination of data structures. Sometimes, the operations above cannot be applied to single parameters, but they can be applied to parts of the data structures that these variables range over. For this to take place, such data structures must be partitioned into their constituents.

Rewriting data terms. The data terms occurring in an LPO can be rewritten using the equations of the data types. If a condition is rewritten to false, then the corresponding condition, action and effect triple in the LPO is removed.

Confluence is widely recognised as an important feature of the behaviour of distributed communicating systems. Roughly, a τ-transition from a state in an LTS, representing an internal computation that is externally invisible, is confluent if it commutes with any other transition starting in this same state. In [18] it was shown that confluence can be used in process verification. In [15] several notions of confluence were studied on their practical applicability, and it was shown that on the level of LPOs confluence can be expressed by means of logical formulas. In [4] it is shown that the presence of confluence within an LPO can be exploited at a low cost at the level of the instantiator, i.e., during the generation of the associated LTS. A prototype of this generation algorithm was implemented, and experience learns that this exploitation of confluence within an LPO may lead to the generation of an LTS that is several orders of magnitudes smaller compared to the standard instantiator. The detection of confluence in an LPO is performed using the automated reasoning techniques that are surveyed in Section 5.

4   Labelled Transition Systems

The SVC format [17] offers an extremely compact file format for storing LTSs. This format is open in its specification and implementation, and allows states to be labelled by ATerms. A prototype visualisation tool has been developed for the SVC format, dubbed Drishti. A reduction algorithm based on confluence and minimisation algorithms modulo equivalences such as bisimulation and branching bisimulation have been implemented, collapsing equivalent states.

Alternatively, LTSs belonging to μCRL specifications can be visualised and analysed using the Cæsar/Aldébaran Development Package (CADP) [7]. This toolset originally targets the analysis of LOTOS specifications. Cæsar generates the LTS belonging to a LOTOS specification, and supports simulation. Aldébaran performs equivalence checking and minimisation of LTSs modulo a range of process equivalences. XTL offers facilities for model checking formulas in temporal logics. The CADP toolset comprises the BCG format, which supports compact storage of LTSs. SVC files can be translated to BCG format and vice versa, given a CADP license (as the BCG format is not open source).

In [11] a reduction algorithm for LTSs is presented, based on priorisation of confluent τ-transitions. First the maximal class of confluent τ-transitions is determined, and next outgoing confluent τ-transitions from a state are given priority over all other outgoing transitions from this same state. For LTSs that do not contain an infinite sequence of τ-transitions, this reduction preserves branching bisimulation. An implementation of this algorithm is included in the μCRL toolset. In some cases it reduces the size of an LTS by an exponential factor. Furthermore, the worst-case time complexity of the reduction algorithm from [11] compares favourably with minimisation modulo branching or weak bisimulation equivalence. Hence, the algorithm from [11] can serve as a useful preprocessing step to these minimisation algorithms.

5   Symbolic Reasoning about Infinite-State Systems

For very large finite-state systems, a symbolic analysis on the level of LPOs may result in the generation of much smaller LTSs. For systems with an inherently infinite number of states the use of theorem proving techniques is indispensable.

The original motivation behind the LPO format was that several properties of a system can be uniformly expressed by first-order formulae. Effective proof methods for LPOs have been developed, incorporating the use of invariants [3] and state mappings [16]. Also the confluence property of an LPO can be expressed as a large first-order formula [15]. Using these techniques, large distributed systems were verified in a precise and logical way, often with the help of interactive theorem provers. See [9] for an overview of such case studies.

Since the confluence properties and the correctness criteria associated with state mappings for industrial-scale case studies tend to be rather flat but very large, we are developing a specialised theorem prover based on an extension of BDDs with equality [12]. A prototype tool has been implemented [19], which was used to detect confluence in a leader election protocol and in a Splice specification from [6]. (This information on confluence was exploited using the method of [4]; see Section 3.) This tool can also check invariants and the correctness criteria associated with a state mapping between a specification and its implementation.

References

1. Th. Arts and I.A. van Langevelde. How μCRL supported a smart redesign of a real-world protocol. In *Proc. FMICS'99*, pp. 31–53, 1999.
2. Th. Arts and I.A. van Langevelde. Correct performance of transaction capabilities. In *Proc. ICACSD'2001*. IEEE, 2001.
3. M.A. Bezem and J.F. Groote. Invariants in process algebra with data. In *Proc. 5th Conference on Concurrency Theory*, LNCS 836, pp. 401–416. Springer, 1994.
4. S.C.C. Blom. Partial τ-confluence for efficient state space generation. Technical Report, CWI, 2001.
5. M.G.J. van den Brand, H. de Jong, P. Klint, and P.A. Olivier. Efficient annotated terms. *Software – Practice and Experience*, 30(3):259–291, 2000.
6. P.F.G. Dechering and I.A. van Langevelde. The verification of coordination. In *Proc. COORDINATION'2000*, LNCS 1906, pp. 335–340. Springer, 2000.
7. J.-C. Fernandez, H. Garavel, A. Kerbrat, L. Mounier, R. Mateescu, and M. Sighireanu. CADP – a protocol validation and verification toolbox. In *Proc. 8th Conference on Computer-Aided Verification*, LNCS 1102, pp. 437–440. Springer, 1996.
8. J.F. Groote and B. Lisser. Computer assisted manipulation of algebraic process specifications. Technical Report, CWI, 2001.
9. J.F. Groote, F. Monin, and J.C. van de Pol. Checking verifications of protocols and distributed systems by computer. In *Proc. 9th Conference on Concurrency Theory*, LNCS 1466, pp. 629–655. Springer, 1998.
10. J.F. Groote, J. Pang, and A.G. Wouters. Analysis of a distributed system for lifting trucks. Technical Report, CWI, 2001.
11. J.F. Groote and J.C. van de Pol. State space reduction using partial τ-confluence. In *Proc. MFCS'2000*, LNCS 1893, pp. 383–393. Springer, 2000.
12. J.F. Groote and J.C. van de Pol. Equational binary decision diagrams. In *Proc. LPAR'2000*, LNAI 1955, pp. 161–178. Springer, 2000.
13. J.F. Groote and A. Ponse. The syntax and semantics of μCRL. In *Proc. ACP'94*, Workshops in Computing, pp. 26–62. Springer, 1995.
14. J.F. Groote, A. Ponse, and Y.S. Usenko. Linearization of parallel pCRL. To appear in *Journal of Logic and Algebraic Programming*.
15. J.F. Groote and M.P.A. Sellink. Confluence for process verification. *Theoretical Computer Science*, 170(1/2):47–81, 1996.
16. J.F. Groote and J. Springintveld. Focus points and convergent process operators: a proof strategy for protocol verification. In *Proc. ARTS'95*, 1995.
17. I.A. van Langevelde. A compact file format for labeled transition systems. Technical Report SEN R0102, CWI, 2001.
18. R. Milner. *Communication and Concurrency*. Prentice Hall, 1989.
19. J.C. van de Pol. A prover for the μCRL toolset with applications – version 1. Technical Report SEN R0106, CWI, 2001.
20. Y.S. Usenko. State space generation for the HAVi leader election protocol. To appear in *Science of Computer Programming*.
21. A.G. Wouters. Manual for the μCRL toolset (version 1.11). Technical Report, CWI, 2001.

Truth/SLC — A Parallel Verification Platform for Concurrent Systems

Martin Leucker and Thomas Noll

Lehrstuhl für Informatik II, Aachen University of Technology
Ahornstr. 55, D–52056 Aachen, Germany
{leucker,noll}@informatik.rwth-aachen.de

1 Introduction

Concurrent software and hardware systems play an increasing rôle in today's applications. Due to the large number of states and to the high degree of non–determinism arising from the dynamic behavior of such systems, testing is generally not sufficient to ensure the correctness of their implementation. Formal specification and verification methods are therefore becoming more and more popular, aiming to give rigorous support for the system design and for establishing its correctness properties, respectively (cf. [2] for an overview).

In view of the inherent complexity of formal methods it is desirable to provide the user with tool support. It is even indispensable for the design of safety-critical concurrent systems where an *ad hoc* or conventional software engineering approach is not justifiable. There is one particularly successful automated approach to verification, called model checking, in which one tries to prove that (a model of) a system has certain properties specified in a suitable logic.

During the recent years several prototypes of model–checking tools have been developed, e.g., CWB [13], NCSU–CWB [4], SPIN [5], and the symbolic model checker SMV [9]. Most of these are tailored to a specific setting, choosing, e.g., the CCS process algebra with transition–system semantics as the specification language and offering model checking for the modal μ–calculus.

However, in the theoretical modeling and in the implementation of concurrent systems there exists a wide range of specification formalisms, semantic domains, logics, and model–checking algorithms. Our aim is therefore to offer a modular verification system which can be easily adjusted to different settings. We started out in 1998 with the development of an initial version of our tool, called TRUTH, which is described in Section 2. It was complemented later by rapid prototyping support for specification languages, provided by the SLC specification language compiler generator presented in Section 3. The most recent component of the TRUTH Verification Platform is a dedicated parallel version running on workstation clusters which is intended for high–end verification tasks, and which is briefly described in Section 4.

2 Truth: The Basic Tool

Here we give a short account of the actual TRUTH tool. For a more thorough presentation, the reader is referred to [6] and to [16], where different releases can be downloaded.

G. Berry, H. Comon, and A. Finkel (Eds.): CAV 2001, LNCS 2102, pp. 255–259, 2001.

In its basic version TRUTH supports the specification and verification of concurrent systems described in CCS, a well–known process algebra [12]. To support the understanding of the system's behaviour, the specification can be graphically simulated in an interactive and process–oriented way. Figure 1 shows a screenshot for the simulation of a two–place buffer process B2, composed in parallel of two commicating instances of a unary buffer B1.

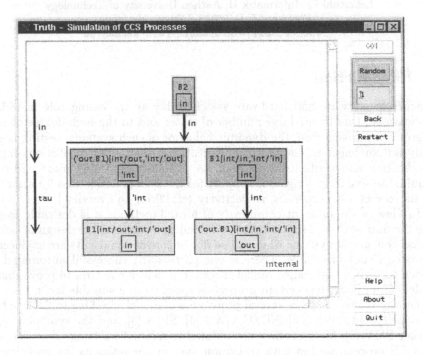

Fig. 1. A Process-Orientted Simulation of a Two-Place Buffer.

From the specification a labeled transition system is built. Its desired properties can be expressed using the μ–calculus, a powerful logic which allows to describe various safety, liveness, and fairness properties. It semantically subsumes the temporal logics CTL (whose operators are implemented as macros in TRUTH), CTL*, and LTL.

TRUTH offers several model checking algorithms, such as the tableau–based model checker proposed in [3]. It has fairly good runtime properties and supports the full μ–calculus. Furthermore, it is a local model checking algorithm, i.e., it has the advantage that in many cases only a part of the transition system has to be built in order to verify or to falsify a formula.

Additionally, a local game–based algorithm has been integrated which can be used to demonstrate the invalidity of a formula by means of an interactive construction of a counterexample [7, 15]. Again, the process visualization component is used to play and visualize this game between the user and the TRUTH tool in order to support debugging of error–prone specifications.

As mentioned in the introduction, we have chosen a modular design that allows easy modifications and extensions of the system. In particular, this feature is exploited by a compiler–generator extension which will be described in the following section. Figure 2 gives an overview of the software architecture.

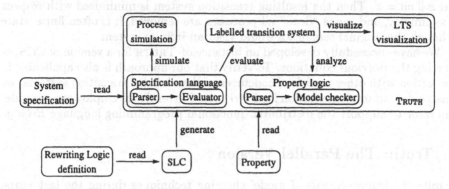

Fig. 2. Structure of TRUTH/SLC.

TRUTH is implemented in Haskell, a general–purpose, fully functional programming language. The choice of a declarative language serves a number of purposes. Changes to the system become easier when using a language which lacks side effects. Moreover many algorithms which are employed in the context of model checking have a very concise functional notation. This makes the implementation easier to understand. Furthermore, in principle it allows to prove the correctness of the implementation which is crucial for a model–checking tool to be used in safety–critical applications. By employing optimization techniques such as state monads for destructive updates we achieve a runtime behaviour which is competitive with other model–checking tools supporting process specifications in CCS.

3 SLC: The Specification Language Compiler Generator

A notable extension of TRUTH is the SLC Specification Language Compiler Generator which provides generic support for different specification formalisms [8]. Given a formal description of a specification language, it automatically generates a corresponding TRUTH frontend (cf. Figure 2).

More specifically, the syntax and semantics of the specification language has to be described in terms of Rewriting Logic, a unified semantic framework for concurrency [11]. From this definition a compiler is derived which is capable of parsing a concrete system specification and of computing the corresponding semantic object, such as a labeled transition system. This compiler is linked together with the TRUTH platform to obtain a model–checking tool which is tailored for the specification language in question.

The description of the specification language formalism consists of three parts. First, the syntax of the language has to be given in terms of a context free grammar (with typing information). The second part is a set of conditional rewrite rules defining the operational semantics.

Finally, the description contains a set of equations between process terms which identify certain states of the respective system, thus reducing the state space. Considering CCS for example, we can define equations like $x \parallel y = y \parallel x$ and $x \parallel nil = x$. Then the resulting transition system is minimized with respect to symmetry, and, since "dead" nil processes are removed, it is often finite–state although the original semantics would yield an infinite system.

We have successfully developed an instance of TRUTH for a version of CCS respecting the previous equations. To verify that our approach is also applicable in connection with other models of concurrency than labeled transition systems, we constructed an implementation for Petri nets. Currently we employ our compiler generator to support the distributed functional programming language *Erlang*.

4   Truth: The Parallel Version

Despite the improvements of model checking techniques during the last years, the so–called *state space explosion* still limits its application. While *partial order reduction* [14] or *symbolic model checking* [10] reduce the state space by orders of magnitude, typical verification tasks still last days on a single workstation or are even (practically) undecidable due to memory restrictions.

On the other hand, cheap yet powerful parallel computers can be constructed by building Networks Of Workstations (*NOWs*). From the outside, a NOW appears as one single parallel computer with high computing power and, even more important, huge amount of memory. This enables parallel programs to utilize the accumulated resources of a NOW to solve large problems.

Hence, it is a fundamental goal to find parallel model checking algorithms which then may be combined with well–known techniques to avoid the state space explosion to gain even more speedup and further reduce memory requirements.

We developed a parallel model checking algorithm for the alternation–free fragment of the μ-calculus. It distributes the underlying transition system and the formula to check over a NOW in parallel and determines, again in parallel, whether the initial state of the transition system satisfies the formula.

Systems with several millions of states could be constructed within half an hour on a NOW consisting of up to 52 processors. We found out that the algorithm scales very well wrt. run–time and memory consumption when enlarging the NOW. Furthermore, the distribution of states on the processors is homogeneous.

While the demand for parallel verification procedures also attracted several other researchers (on overview can be found in [1]), Parallel TRUTH is—to our knowledge—the first parallel model checking tool that allows the validation of safety *and* liveness properties.

A thorough presentation of this algorithm and its runtime properties can be found in [1].

References

1. Benedikt Bollig, Martin Leucker, and Michael Weber. Local parallel model checking for the alternation free μ-calculus. Technical Report AIB-04-2001, RWTH Aachen, March 2001.
2. E. M. Clarke and J. M. Wing. Formal methods: State of the art and future directions. Technical Report CMU-CS-96-178, Carnegie Mellon University (CMU), September 1996.
3. R. Cleaveland. Tableau-based model checking in the propositional mu-calculus. *Acta Informatica*, 27(8):725–748, 1990.
4. R. Cleaveland and S. Sims. The NCSU concurrency workbench. In *Proceedings of the Eighth International Conference on Computer Aided Verification (CAV'96)*, volume 1102 of *Lecture Notes in Computer Science*, pages 394–397, 1996.
5. Jean-Charles Grégoire, Gerard J. Holzmann, and Doron A. Peled, editors. *The Spin Verification System*, volume 32 of *DIMACS series*. American Mathematical Society, 1997. ISBN 0-8218-0680-7, 203p.
6. M. Lange, M. Leucker, T. Noll, and S. Tobies. Truth – a verification platform for concurrent systems. In *Tool Support for System Specification, Development, and Verification*, Advances in Computing Science. Springer-Verlag Wien New York, 1999.
7. M. Leucker. Model checking games for the alternation free mu-calculus and alternating automata. In Harald Ganzinger, David McAllester, and Andrei Voronkov, editors, *Proceedings of the 6th International Conference on Logic for Programming and Automated Reasoning*, volume 1705 of *Lecture Notes in Artificial Intelligence*, pages 77–91. Springer, 1999.
8. Martin Leucker and Thomas Noll. Rewriting logic as a framework for generic verification tools. In *Proceedings of the Third International Workshop on Rewriting Logic and its Applications (WRLA'00)*, volume 36 of *Electronic Notes in Theoretical Computer Science*. Elsevier, 2000.
9. K. L. McMillan. The SMV system, symbolic model checking - an approach. Technical Report CMU-CS-92-131, Carnegie Mellon University, 1992.
10. K. L. McMillan. *Symbolic Model Checking*. Kluwer Academic Publishers, Norwell Massachusetts, 1993.
11. José Meseguer. Rewriting logic as a semantic framework for concurrency: a progress report. In *Seventh International Conference on Concurrency Theory (CONCUR '96)*, volume 1119 of *Lecture Notes in Computer Science*, pages 331–372. Springer Verlag, August 1996.
12. R. Milner. *Communication and Concurrency*. International Series in Computer Science. Prentice Hall, 1989.
13. F. Moller. *The Edinburgh Concurrency Workbench (Version 6.1)*. Department of Computer Science, University of Edinburgh, October 1992.
14. Doron Peled. Ten years of partial order reduction. In *CAV, Computer Aided Verification*, number 1427 in LNCS, pages 17–28, Vancouver, BC, Canada, 1998. Springer.
15. Perdita Stevens and Colin Stirling. Practical model-checking using games. In B. Steffen, editor, *Proceedings of the 4th International Conference on Tools and algorithms for the construction and analysis of systems (TACAS '98)*, volume 1384 of *Lecture Notes in Computer Science*, pages 85–101, New York, NY, USA, 1998. Springer-Verlag Inc.
16. The TRUTH verification tool. http://www-i2.informatik.rwth-aachen.de/Research/MCS/Truth.

The SLAM Toolkit

Thomas Ball and Sriram K. Rajamani

Microsoft Research
http://www.research.microsoft.com/slam/

1 Introduction

The SLAM toolkit checks safety properties of software without the need for user-supplied annotations or abstractions. Given a safety property to check on a C program P, the SLAM process [4] iteratively refines a *boolean program* abstraction of P using three tools:

- C2BP, a predicate abstraction tool that abstracts P into a boolean program $\mathcal{BP}(P, E)$ with respect to a set of predicates E over P [1,2];
- BEBOP, a tool for model checking boolean programs [3], and
- NEWTON, a tool that discovers additional predicates to refine the boolean program, by analyzing the feasibility of paths in the C program.

Property violations are reported by the SLAM toolkit as paths over the program P. Since property checking is undecidable, the SLAM refinement algorithm may not converge. We have applied the SLAM toolkit to automatically check properties of device drivers taken from the Microsoft Driver Development Kit. While checking for various properties, we found that the SLAM process converges to a boolean program that is sufficiently precise to validate/invalidate the property [4].

Several ideas behind the SLAM tools are novel. C2BP is the first automatic predicate abstraction tool to handle a full-scale programming language with procedure calls and pointers, and perform a sound and precise abstraction. BE-BOP is the first model checker to handle procedure calls using an interprocedural dataflow analysis algorithm, augmented with representation tricks from the symbolic model checking community. NEWTON uses a path simulation algorithm in a novel way, to generate predicates for refinement.

2 Overview and Example

We introduce the SLAM refinement algorithm and apply it to a small code example. We have created a low-level specification language called SLIC (Specification Language for Interface Checking) for stating safety properties. Figure 1(a) shows a SLIC specification that states that it is an error to acquire (or release) a spin lock twice in a row. There are two events on which state transitions happen — returns of calls to the functions KeAcquireSpinLock and KeReleaseSpinLock.

We wish to check if a temporal safety property φ specified using SLIC is satisfied by a program P. We have built a tool that automatically instruments

G. Berry, H. Comon, and A. Finkel (Eds.): CAV 2001, LNCS 2102, pp. 260–264, 2001.

<pre>state {
   enum { Unlocked=0, Locked=1 }
      state = Unlocked;
}
KeAcquireSpinLock.return {
   if (state == Locked)
      abort;
   else
      state = Locked;
}
KeReleaseSpinLock.return {
   if (state == Unlocked)
      abort;
   else
      state = Unlocked;
}</pre> | <pre>enum { Unlocked=0, Locked=1 }
   state = Unlocked;

void slic_abort() {
   SLIC_ERROR: ;
}

void KeAcquireSpinLock_return() {
   if (state == Locked)
      slic_abort();
   else
      state = Locked;
}

void KeReleaseSpinLock_return {
   if (state == Unlocked)
      slic_abort();
   else
      state = Unlocked;
}</pre> |
| (a) | (b) |

Fig. 1. (a) A SLIC Specification for Proper Usage of Spin Locks, and (b) Its Compilation into C Code.

the program P with property φ to result in a program P' such that P satisfies φ iff the label SLIC_ERROR is not reachable in P'. In particular, the tool first creates C code from the SLIC specification, as shown in Figure 1(b). The tool then inserts calls to the appropriate SLIC C functions in the program P to result in the instrumented program P'.

Now, we wish to check if the label SLIC_ERROR is reachable in the instrumented program P'. Let i be a metavariable that records the SLAM iteration count. The first iteration ($i = 0$) starts with the set of predicates E_0 that are present in the conditionals of the SLIC specification. Let E_i be some set of predicates over the state of P'. Then iteration i of SLAM is carried out using the following steps:

1. Apply C2BP to construct the boolean program $\mathcal{BP}(P', E_i)$. Program $\mathcal{BP}(P', E_i)$ is guaranteed to *abstract* the program P', as every feasible execution path p of the program P' also is a feasible execution path of $\mathcal{BP}(P', E_i)$.
2. Apply BEBOP to check if there is a path p_i in $\mathcal{BP}(P', E_i)$ that reaches the SLIC_ERROR label. If BEBOP determines that SLIC_ERROR is not reachable, then the property φ is valid in P, and the algorithm terminates.
3. If there is such a path p_i, then we use NEWTON to check if p_i is feasible in P'. There are two outcomes: "yes", the property φ is violated by P and the algorithm terminates with an error path p_i; "no", NEWTON finds a set of predicates F_i that explain the infeasibility of path p_i in P'.
4. Let $E_{i+1} := E_i \cup F_i$, and $i := i + 1$, and proceed to the next iteration.

| ```
void example() {
 do {
  KeAcquireSpinLock();

  nPacketsOld = nPackets;
  req = devExt->WLHV;
  if(req && req->status){
    devExt->WLHV = req->Next;
    KeReleaseSpinLock();

    irp = req->irp;
    if(req->status > 0){
      irp->IoS.Status = SUCCESS;
      irp->IoS.Info = req->Status;
    } else {
      irp->IoS.Status = FAIL;
      irp->IoS.Info = req->Status;
    }
    SmartDevFreeBlock(req);
    IoCompleteRequest(irp);
    nPackets++;
  }
 } while(nPackets!=nPacketsOld);
 KeReleaseSpinLock();

}
``` | ```
   void example() {
    do {
     KeAcquireSpinLock();
A:   KeAcquireSpinLock_return();
     nPacketsOld = nPackets;
     req = devExt->WLHV;
     if(req && req->status){
       devExt->WLHV = req->Next;
       KeReleaseSpinLock();
B:     KeReleaseSpinLock_return();
       irp = req->irp;
       if(req->status > 0){
         irp->IoS.Status = SUCCESS;
         irp->IoS.Info = req->Status;
       } else {
         irp->IoS.Status = FAIL;
         irp->IoS.Info = req->Status;
       }
       SmartDevFreeBlock(req);
       IoCompleteRequest(irp);
       nPackets++;
     }
    } while(nPackets!=nPacketsOld);
    KeReleaseSpinLock();
C:  KeReleaseSpinLock_return();
   }
``` |
| (a) Program P | (b) Program P' |

Fig. 2. (a) A snippet of device driver code P, and (b) program P' resulting from instrumentation of program P due to SLIC specification in Figure 1(a).

Figure 2(a) presents a snippet of (simplified) C code from a PCI device driver. Figure 2(b) shows the instrumented program (with respect to the SLIC specification in Figure 1(a)). Calls to the appropriate SLIC C functions (see Figure 1(b)) have been introduced (at labels A, B, and C).

The question we wish to answer is: is the label SLIC_ERROR reachable in the program P' comprised of the code from Figure 1(b) and Figure 2(b)? The first step of the algorithm is to generate the initial boolean program. A *boolean program* [3] is a C program in which the only type is boolean.

For our example, the inital set of predicates E_0 consists of two *global* predicates $(state = Locked)$ and $(state = Unlocked)$ that appear in the conditionals of the SLIC specification. These two predicates and the program P' are input to the C2BP (C to Boolean Program) tool. The translation of the SLIC C code from Figure 1(b) to the boolean program is shown in Figure 3. The translation of the example procedure is shown in Figure 4(a). Together, these two pieces of code comprise the boolean program $\mathcal{BP}(P', E_0)$ output by C2BP.

```
decl {state==Locked},
   {state==Unlocked} := F,T;

void slic_abort() begin                  void KeReleaseSpinLock_return()
 SLIC_ERROR: skip;                       begin
end                                        if ({state == Unlocked})
                                             slic_abort();
void KeAcquireSpinLock_return()          else
begin                                      {state==Locked},
  if ({state==Locked})                       {state==Unlocked} := F,T;
    slic_abort();                        end
  else
    {state==Locked},
      {state==Unlocked} := T,F;
end
```

Fig. 3. The C code of the SLIC specification from Figure 1(b) compiled by C2BP into a boolean program.

As shown in Figure 3, the translation of the SLIC C code results in the global boolean variables, {state==Locked} and {state==Unlocked}.[1] For every statement s in the C program and predicate $e \in E_0$, the C2BP tool determines the effect of statement s on predicate e and codes that effect in the boolean program. Non-determinism is used to conservatively model the conditions in the C program that cannot be abstracted precisely using the predicates in E_0, as shown in Figure 4(a). Many of the assignment statements in the example procedure are abstracted to the **skip** statement (no-op) in the boolean program. The C2BP tool uses an alias analysis to determine whether or not an assignment statement through a pointer dereference can affect a predicate e.

The second step of our process is to determine whether or not the label SLIC_ERROR is reachable in the boolean program $\mathcal{BP}(P', E_0)$. We use the BEBOP model checker to determine the answer to this query. In this case, the answer is "yes" and BEBOP produces a (shortest) path p_0 leading to SLIC_ERROR (specified by the sequence of labels [A, A, SLIC_ERROR]).

Does p_0 represent a feasible execution path of P'? The NEWTON tool takes a C program and a (potential) error path as an input. It uses verification condition generation to determine if the path is feasible. If the path is feasible, we have found a real error in P'. If the answer is "no" then NEWTON uses a new algorithm to identify a small set of predicates that "explain" why the path is infeasible. In the running example, NEWTON detects that the path p_0 is infeasible, and returns a single predicate ($nPackets = npacketsOld$) as the explanation for the infeasibility.

---

[1] Boolean programs permit a variable identifier to be an arbitrary string enclosed between "{" and "}".

void example()
begin
  do
    skip;
A: KeAcquireSpinLock_return();
    skip;
    if (*) then
      skip;
B: KeReleaseSpinLock_return();
    skip;
    if (*) then
      skip;
    else
      skip;
    fi
    skip;
  fi
  while (*);
  skip;
C: KeReleaseSpinLock_return();
end
	void example()
	begin
	  do
	    skip;
	A: KeAcquireSpinLock_return();
	    b := T;
	    if (*) then
	      skip;
	B: KeReleaseSpinLock_return();
	    skip;
	    if (*) then
	      skip;
	    else
	      skip;
	    fi
	    b := b ? F : *;
	  fi
	  while (!b);
	  skip;
	C: KeReleaseSpinLock_return();
	end

(a) Boolean program $\mathcal{BP}(P', E_0)$	(b) Boolean program $\mathcal{BP}(P', E_1)$

Fig. 4. The two boolean programs created while checking the code from Figure 2(b).

Figure 4(b) shows the boolean program $\mathcal{BP}(P', E_1)$ that C2BP produces on the second iteration of the process. This program has one additional boolean variable (b) that represents the predicate ($nPackets = nPacketsOld$). The assignment statement nPackets = nPacketsOld; makes this condition true, so in the boolean program the assignment b := T; represents this assignment. Using a theorem prover, C2BP determines that if the predicate is true before the statement nPackets++, then it is false afterwards. This is captured by the assignment statement in the boolean program "b := b ? F : *". Applying BEBOP to the new boolean program shows that the label SLIC_ERROR is not reachable.

References

1. T. Ball, R. Majumdar, T. Millstein, and S.K. Rajamani. Automatic predicate abstraction of C programs. In *PLDI 01: Programming Language Design and Implementation*, 2001.
2. T. Ball, A. Podelski, and S.K. Rajamani. Boolean and cartesian abstractions for model checking C programs. In *TACAS 01: Tools and Algorithms for Construction and Analysis of Systems*, LNCS 2031, 2001.
3. T. Ball and S.K. Rajamani. Bebop: A symbolic model checker for Boolean programs. In *SPIN 00: SPIN Workshop*, LNCS 1885, pages 113–130. 2000.
4. T. Ball and S.K. Rajamani. Automatically validating temporal safety properties of interfaces. In *SPIN 01: SPIN Workshop*, LNCS 2057, 2001.

Java Bytecode Verification: An Overview

Xavier Leroy

INRIA Rocquencourt and Trusted Logic S.A.
Domaine de Voluceau, B.P. 105, 78153 Le Chesnay, France
Xavier.Leroy@inria.fr

Abstract. Bytecode verification is a crucial security component for Java applets, on the Web and on embedded devices such as smart cards. This paper describes the main bytecode verification algorithms and surveys the variety of formal methods that have been applied to bytecode verification in order to establish its correctness.

1 Introduction

Web applets have popularized the idea of downloading and executing untrusted compiled code on the personal computer running the Web browser, without user's approval or intervention. Obviously, this raises major security issues: without appropriate security measures, a malicious applet could mount a variety of attacks against the local computer, such as destroying data (e.g. reformatting the disk), modifying sensitive data (e.g. registering a bank transfer via the Quicken home-banking software [4]), divulging personal information over the network, or modifying other programs (Trojan attacks).

To make things worse, the applet model is now being transferred to high-security embedded devices such as smart cards: the Java Card architecture [5] allows for post-issuance downloading of applets on smart cards in sensitive application areas such as payment and mobile telephony. This raises the stake enormously: a security hole that allows a malicious applet to crash Windows is perhaps tolerable, but is certainly not acceptable if it allows the applet to perform non-authorized credit card transactions.

The solution put forward by the Java programming environment is to execute the applets in a so-called "sandbox", which is an insulation layer preventing direct access to the hardware resources and implementing a suitable access control policy [8,32,16]. The security of the sandbox model relies on the following three components:

1. Applets are not compiled down to machine executable code, but rather to bytecode for a virtual machine. The virtual machine manipulates higher-level, more secure abstractions of data than the hardware processor, such as object references instead of memory addresses.
2. Applets are not given direct access to hardware resources such as the serial port, but only to a carefully designed set of API classes and methods that perform suitable access control before performing interactions with the outside world on behalf of the applet.

G. Berry, H. Comon, and A. Finkel (Eds.): CAV 2001, LNCS 2102, pp. 265–285, 2001.

3. Upon downloading, the bytecode of the applet is subject to a static analysis
   called bytecode verification, whose purpose is to make sure that the code
   of the applet is well typed and does not attempt to bypass protections 1
   and 2 above by performing ill-typed operations at run-time, such as forging
   object references from integers, illegal casting of an object reference from
   one class to another, calling directly private methods of the API, jumping
   in the middle of an API method, or jumping to data as if it were code [9,
   36, 15].

Thus, bytecode verification is a crucial security component in the Java "sandbox" model: any bug in the verifier causing an ill-typed applet to be accepted
can potentially enable a security attack. At the same time, bytecode verification
is a complex process involving elaborate program analyses. Consequently, considerable research efforts have been expended to specify the goals of bytecode
verification, formalize bytecode verification algorithms, and prove their correctness.

The purpose of the present paper is to survey briefly this formal work on
bytecode verification. We explain what bytecode verification is, survey the various algorithms that have been proposed, outline the main problems they are
faced with, and give references to formal proofs of correctness. The thesis of this
paper is that bytecode verification can be (and has been) attacked from many
different angles, including dataflow analyses, abstract interpretation, type systems, model checking, and machine-checked proofs; thus, bytecode verification
provides an interesting playground for applying and relating various techniques
in computed-aided verification and formal methods in computing.

The remainder of this paper is organized as follows. Section 2 gives a quick
overview of the Java virtual machine and of bytecode verification. Section 3
presents the basic bytecode verification algorithm based on dataflow analysis.
Sections 4 and 5 concentrate on two delicate verification issues: checking object initialization and dealing with JVM subroutines. Section 6 presents a more
abstract view of bytecode verification as model checking of an abstract interpretation. Some issues specific to low-resources embedded systems are discussed in
section 7, followed by conclusions and perspectives in section 8.

2   Overview of the JVM and of Bytecode Verification

The Java Virtual Machine (JVM) [15] is a conventional stack-based abstract
machine. Most instructions pop their arguments off the stack, and push back
their results on the stack. In addition, a set of registers (also called local variables) is provided; they can be accessed via "load" and "store" instructions that
push the value of a given register on the stack or store the top of the stack in
the given register, respectively. While the architecture does not mandate it, most
Java compilers use registers to store the values of source-level local variables and
method parameters, and the stack to hold temporary results during evaluation
of expressions. Both the stack and the registers are part of the activation record
for a method. Thus, they are preserved across method calls. The entry point for

a method specifies the number of registers and stack slots used by the method, thus allowing an activation record of the right size to be allocated on method entry.

Control is handled by a variety of intra-method branch instructions: unconditional branch ("goto"), conditional branches ("branch if top of stack is 0"), multi-way branches (corresponding to the switch Java construct). Exception handlers can be specified as a table of (pc_1, pc_2, C, h) quadruples, meaning that if an exception of class C or a subclass of C is raised by any instruction between locations pc_1 and pc_2, control is transferred to the instruction at h (the exception handler).

About 200 instructions are supported, including arithmetic operations, comparisons, object creation, field accesses and method invocations. The example in Fig.1 should give the general flavor of JVM bytecode.

Source Java code:

```
static int factorial(int n)
{
    int res;
    for (res = 1; n > 0; n--) res = res * n;
    return res;
}
```

Corresponding JVM bytecode:

```
method static int factorial(int), 2 registers, 2 stack slots
    0:  iconst_1        // push the integer constant 1
    1:  istore_1        // store it in register 1 (the res variable)
    2:  iload_0         // push register 0 (the n parameter)
    3:  ifle 14         // if negative or null, go to PC 14
    6:  iload_1         // push register 1 (res)
    7:  iload_0         // push register 0 (n)
    8:  imul            // multiply the two integers at top of stack
    9:  istore_1        // pop result and store it in register 1
   10:  iinc 0, -1      // decrement register 0 (n) by 1
   11:  goto 2          // go to PC 2
   14:  iload_1         // load register 1 (res)
   15:  ireturn         // return its value to caller
```

Fig. 1. An Example of JVM Bytecode.

An important feature of the JVM is that most instructions are typed. For instance, the iadd instruction (integer addition) requires that the stack initially contains at least two elements, and that these two elements are of type int; it then pushes back a result of type int. Similarly, a getfield $C.f.\tau$ instruction (access the instance field f of type τ declared in class C) requires that the top of the stack contains a reference to an instance of class C or one of its sub-classes (and not, for instance, an integer – this would correspond to an attempt to forge an object reference by an unsafe cast); it then pops it and pushes back a value of type τ (the value of the field f). More generally, proper operation of the JVM is not guaranteed unless the code meets the following conditions:

- Type correctness: the arguments of an instruction are always of the types expected by the instruction.
- No stack overflow or underflow: an instruction never pops an argument off an empty stack, nor pushes a result on a full stack (whose size is equal to the maximal stack size declared for the method).
- Code containment: the program counter must always point within the code for the method, to the beginning of a valid instruction encoding (no falling off the end of the method code; no branches into the middle of an instruction encoding).
- Register initialization: a load from a register must always follow at least one store in this register; in other terms, registers that do not correspond to method parameters are not initialized on method entrance, and it is an error to load from an uninitialized register.
- Object initialization: when an instance of a class C is created, one of the initialization methods for class C (corresponding to the constructors for this class) must be invoked before the class instance can be used.
- Access control: method invocations, field accesses and class references must respect the visibility modifiers (`private`, `protected`, `public`, etc) of the method, field or class.

One way to guarantee these conditions is to check them dynamically, while executing the bytecode. This is called the "defensive JVM approach" in the literature [6]. However, checking these conditions at run-time is expensive and slows down execution significantly. The purpose of bytecode verification is to check these conditions once and for all, by static analysis of the bytecode at loading-time. Bytecode that passes verification can then be executed at full speed, without extra dynamic checks.

3   Basic Verification by Dataflow Analysis

The first JVM bytecode verification algorithm is due to Gosling and Yellin at Sun [9, 36, 15]. Almost all existing bytecode verifiers implement this algorithm. It can be summarized as a dataflow analysis applied to a type-level abstract interpretation of the virtual machine. Some advanced aspects of the algorithm that go beyond standard dataflow analysis are described in sections 4 and 5. In this section, we describe the basic ingredients of this algorithm: the type-level abstract interpreter and the dataflow framework.

3.1   The Type-Level Abstract Interpreter

At the heart of all bytecode verification algorithms described in this paper is an abstract interpreter for the JVM instruction set that executes JVM instructions like a defensive JVM (including type tests, stack underflow and overflow tests, etc), but operates over types instead of values. That is, the abstract interpreter manipulates a stack of types and a register type (an array associating types to register numbers). It simulates the execution of instructions at the level of types. For instance, for the iadd instruction (integer addition), it checks that the stack of types contains at least two elements, and that the top two elements are the type int. It then pops the top two elements and pushes back the type int corresponding to the result of the addition.

$$
\begin{aligned}
&\mathtt{iconst}\ n\ :\ (S,\ R) \to (\mathtt{int}.S,\ R)\ \text{if}\ |S| < M_{stack}\\
&\mathtt{iadd}\ :\ (\mathtt{int}.\mathtt{int}.S,\ R) \to (\mathtt{int}.S,\ R)\\
&\mathtt{iload}\ n\ :\ (S,\ R) \to (\mathtt{int}.S,\ R)\\
&\qquad \text{if}\ 0 \le n < M_{reg}\ \text{and}\ R(n) = \mathtt{int}\ \text{and}\ |S| < M_{stack}\\
&\mathtt{istore}\ n\ :\ (\mathtt{int}.S,\ R) \to (S,\ R\{n \leftarrow \mathtt{int}\})\ \text{if}\ 0 \le n < M_{reg}\\
&\mathtt{aconst\_null}\ :\ (S,\ R) \to (\mathtt{null}.S,\ R)\ \text{if}\ |S| < M_{stack}\\
&\mathtt{aload}\ n\ :\ (S,\ R) \to (R(n).S,\ R)\\
&\qquad \text{if}\ 0 \le n < M_{reg}\ \text{and}\ R(n) <: \mathtt{Object}\ \text{and}\ |S| < M_{stack}\\
&\mathtt{astore}\ n\ :\ (\tau.S,\ R) \to (S,\ R\{n \leftarrow \tau\})\ \text{if}\ 0 \le n < M_{reg}\ \text{and}\ \tau <: \mathtt{Object}\\
&\mathtt{getfield}\ C.f.\tau\ :\ (\mathtt{ref}(D).S,\ R) \to (\tau.S,\ R)\ \text{if}\ D <: C\\
&\mathtt{invokestatic}\ C.m.\sigma\ :\ (\tau'_n \dots \tau'_1.S,\ R) \to (\tau.S,\ R)\\
&\qquad \text{if}\ \sigma = \tau(\tau_1, \dots, \tau_n)\ \text{and}\ \tau'_i <: \tau_i\ \text{for}\ i = 1 \dots n
\end{aligned}
$$

Fig. 2. Selected rules for the type-level abstract interpreter. M_{stack} is the maximal stack size and M_{reg} the maximal number of registers.

Figure 2 defines more formally the abstract interpreter on a number of representative JVM instructions. The abstract interpreter is presented as a transition relation $i : (S, R) \to (S', R')$, where i is the instruction, S and R the stack type and register type before executing the instruction, and S' and R' the stack type and register type after executing the instruction. Errors such as type mismatches on the arguments, stack underflow, or stack overflow, are denoted by the absence of a transition. For instance, there is no transition on iadd from an empty stack.

Notice that method invocations (such as the invokestatic instruction in Fig.2) are not treated by branching to the code of the invoked method, like the concrete JVM does, but simply assume that the effect of the method invocation on the stack is as described by the method signature given in the "invoke" instruction. All bytecode verification algorithms described in this paper proceed method per method, assuming that all other methods are well-typed when verifying the code of a method. A simple coinductive argument shows that if this is the case, the program as a whole (the collection of all methods) is well typed.

The types manipulated by the abstract interpreter are similar to the source-level types of the Java language. They include primitive types (int, long, float, double), object reference types represented by the fully qualified names of the corresponding classes, and array types. The boolean, byte, short and char types of Java are identified with int. Two extra types are introduced: null to represent the type of the null reference, and ⊤ to represent the contents of uninitialized registers, that is, any value. ("Load" instructions explicitly check that the accessed register does not have type ⊤, thus detecting accesses to uninitialized registers.) A subtyping relation between these types, similar to that of the Java language (the "assignment compatibility" relation), is defined as shown in Fig.3.

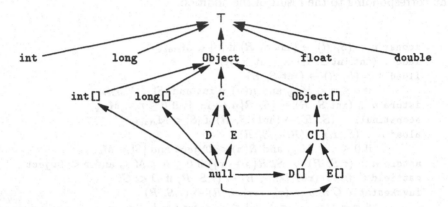

Fig. 3. Type expressions used by the verifier, with their subtyping relation. C, D, E are user-defined classes, with D and E extending C. Not all types are shown.

3.2   The Dataflow Analysis

Verifying a method whose body is a straight-line piece of code (no branches) is easy: we simply iterate the transition function of the abstract interpreter over the instructions, taking the stack type and register type "after" the preceding instruction as the stack type and register type "before" the next instruction. The initial stack and register types reflect the state of the JVM on method entrance: the stack type is empty; the types of the registers $0 \ldots n - 1$ corresponding to the n method parameters are set to the types of the corresponding parameters in the method signature; the other registers $n \ldots M_{reg} - 1$ corresponding to uninitialized local variables are given the type ⊤.

If the abstract interpreter gets "stuck", i.e. cannot make a transition from one of the intermediate states, then verification fails and the code is rejected. Otherwise, verification succeeds, and since the abstract interpreter is a correct approximation of a defensive JVM, we are certain that a defensive JVM will not get stuck either executing the code. Thus, the code is correct and can be executed safely by a regular, non-defensive JVM.

Branches and exception handlers introduce forks and joins in the control flow of the method. Thus, an instruction can have several predecessors, with different stack and register types "after" these predecessor instructions. Sun's bytecode verifier deals with this situation in the manner customary for data flow analysis:

the state (stack type and register type) "before" an instruction is taken to be the least upper bound of the states "after" all predecessors of this instruction. For instance, assume classes C_1 and C_2 extend C, and we analyze a conditional construct that stores a value of type C_1 in register 0 in one arm, and a value of type C_2 in the other arm. (See Fig.4.) When the two arms meet, register 0 is assumed to have type C, which is the least upper bound (the smallest common supertype) of C_1 and C_2.

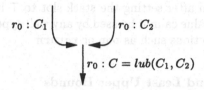

Fig. 4. Handling Joins in the Control Flow.

More precisely, writing $in(i)$ for the state "before" instruction i and $out(i)$ for the state "after" i, the algorithm sets up the following dataflow equations:

$$i : in(i) \rightarrow out(i)$$
$$in(i) = lub\{out(j) \mid j \text{ predecessor of } i\}$$

for every instruction i, plus

$$in(i_0) = (\varepsilon, (P_0, \ldots, P_{n-1}, \top, \ldots, \top))$$

for the start instruction i_0 (the P_k are the types of the method parameters). These equations are then solved by standard fixpoint iteration using Kildall's worklist algorithm [17, section 8.4]: an instruction i is taken from the worklist and its state "after" $out(i)$ is determined from its state "before" $in(i)$ using the abstract interpreter; then, we replace $in(j)$ by $lub(in(j), out(i))$ for each successor j of i, and enter those successors j for which $in(j)$ changed in the worklist. The fixpoint is reached when the worklist is empty, in which case verification succeeds. Verification fails if a state with no transition is encountered, or one of the least upper bounds is undefined.

As a trivial optimization of the algorithm above, the dataflow equations can be set up at the level of extended basic blocks rather than individual instructions. In other terms, it suffices to keep in working memory the states $in(i)$ where i is the first instruction of an extended basic block (i.e. a branch target); the other states can be recomputed on the fly as needed.

The least upper bound of two states is taken pointwise, both on the stack types and the register types. It is undefined if the stack types have different heights, which causes verification to fail. This situation corresponds to a program point where the run-time stack can have different heights depending on the path by which the point is reached; such code must be rejected because it can lead to unbounded stack height, and therefore to stack overflow. (Consider a loop that pushes one more entry on the stack at each iteration.)

The least upper bound of two register types can be $\top$, causing this register to have type $\top$ in the merged state. This corresponds to the situation where a register holds values of incompatible types in two arms of a conditional (e.g. int in one arm and an object reference in the other), and therefore is treated as uninitialized (no further loads from this register) after the merge point. The least upper bound of two stack slots can also be $\top$, in which case Sun's algorithm aborts verification immediately. Alternatively, it is entirely harmless to continue verification after setting the stack slot to $\top$ in the merged state, since the corresponding value cannot be used by any well-typed instruction, but simply discarded by instructions such as pop or return.

3.3 Interfaces and Least Upper Bounds

The dataflow framework presented above requires that the type algebra, ordered by the subtyping relation, constitutes a semi-lattice. That is, every pair of types possesses a smallest common supertype (least upper bound).

Unfortunately, this property does not hold if we take the verifier type algebra to be the Java source-level type algebra (extended with $\top$ and null) and the subtyping relation to be the Java source-level assignment compatibility relation. The problem is that interfaces are types, just like classes, and a class can implement several interfaces. Consider the following classes:

```
interface I { ... }
interface J { ... }
class C1 implements I, J { ... }
class C2 implements I, J { ... }
```

The subtyping relation induced by these declarations is:

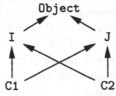

This is obviously not a semi-lattice, since the two types C1 and C2 have two common super-types I and J that are not comparable (neither is subtype of the other).

There are several ways to address this issue. One approach is to manipulate sets of types during verification instead of single types as we described earlier. These sets of types are to be interpreted as conjunctive types, i.e. the set $\{I, J\}$, like the conjunctive type $I \wedge J$, represents values that have both types I and J, and therefore is a suitable least upper bound for the types $\{C1\}$ and $\{C2\}$ in the example above. This is the approach followed by Qian [25] and also by Pusch [24].

Another approach is to complete the class and interface hierarchy of the program into a lattice before performing verification. In the example above, the completion would add a pseudo-interface IandJ extending both I and J, and claim that C1 and C2 implement IandJ rather than I and J. We then obtain the following semi-lattice:

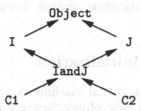

The pseudo-interface IandJ plays the same role as the set type {I, J} in the first approach described above. The difference is that the completion of the class/interface hierarchy is performed once and for all, and verification manipulates only simple types rather than sets of types. This keeps verification simple and fast.

The simplest solution to the interface problem is to be found in Sun's implementation of the JDK bytecode verifier. (This approach is documented nowhere, but can easily be inferred by experimentation.) Namely, bytecode verification ignores interfaces, treating all interface types as the class type Object. Thus, the type algebra used by the verifier contains only proper classes and no interfaces, and subtyping between proper classes is simply the inheritance relation between them. Since Java has single inheritance (a class can implement several interfaces, but inherit from one class only), the subtyping relation is tree-shaped and trivially forms a lattice: the least upper bound of two classes is simply their closest common ancestor in the inheritance tree.

The downside of Sun's approach, compared with the set-based or completion-based approach, is that the verifier cannot guarantee statically that an object reference implements a given interface. In particular, the invokeinterface $I.m$ instruction, which invokes method m of interface I on an object, is not guaranteed to receive at run-time an object that actually implements I: the only guarantee provided by Sun's verifier is that it receives an argument of type Object, that is, any object reference. The invokeinterface $I.m$ instruction must therefore check dynamically that the object actually implements I, and raise an exception if it does not.

3.4   Formalizations and Proofs

Many formalizations and proofs of correctness of Java bytecode verification have been published, and we have reasons to believe that many more have been developed internally, both in academia and industry. With no claims to exhaustiveness, we will mention the works of Cohen [6] and Qian [25] among the first formal specifications of the JVM. Qian's specification is written in ordinary mathematics, while Cohen's uses the specification language of the ACL2 theorem prover. Pusch [24] uses the Isabelle/HOL prover to formalize the dynamic semantics of a fragment of the JVM, the corresponding type-level abstract interpreter used by the verifier, and proves the correctness of the latter with respect to the former: if the abstract interpreter can do a transition $i : (S, R) \to (S', R')$, then for all concrete states (s, r) matching (S, R), the concrete interpreter can do a transition $i : (s, r) \to (s', r')$, and the final concrete state (s', r') matches (S, R). Nipkow [20] formalizes the dataflow analysis framework in Isabelle/HOL and proves its correctness.

4   Verifying Object Initialization

Object creation in the Java virtual machine is a two-step process: first, the instruction new C creates a new object, instance of the class C, with all instance fields filled with default values (0 for numerical fields and null for reference fields); second, one of the initializer methods for class C (methods named C.<init> resulting from the compilation of the constructor methods of C) must be invoked on the newly created object. Initializer methods, just like their source-level counterpart (constructors), are typically used to initialize instance fields to non-default values, although they can also perform nearly arbitrary computations.

The JVM specification requires that this two-step object initialization protocol be respected. That is, the object instance created by the new instruction is considered uninitialized, and none of the regular object operations (i.e. store the object in a data structure, return it as method result, access one of its fields, invoke one of its methods) is allowed on this uninitialized object. Only when one of the initializer methods for its class is invoked on the new object and return normally is the new object considered fully initialized and usable like any other object.

Unlike the register initialization property, this object initialization property is not crucial to ensure type safety at run-time: since the new instruction initializes the instance fields of the new object with correct values for their types, type safety is not broken if the resulting default-initialized object is used right away without having called an initializer method. However, the object initialization property is important to ensure that some invariants between instance fields that is established by the constructor of a class actually hold for all objects of this class.

Static verification of object initialization is made more complex by the fact that initialization methods operate by side-effect: instead of taking an uninitialized object and returning an initialized object, they simply take an uninitialized object, update its fields, and return nothing. Hence, the code generated by Java compilers for the source-level statement x = new C(arg) is generally of the following form:

```
new C               // create uninitialized instance of C
dup                 // duplicate the reference to this instance
code to compute arg
invokespecial C.<init> // call the initializer
astore 3            // store initialized object in x
```

That is, two references to the uninitialized instance of C are held on the stack. The topmost reference is "consumed" by the invocation of C.<init>. When this initializer returns, the second reference is now at the top of the stack and now references a properly initialized object, which is then stored in the register allocated to x. The tricky point is that the initializer method is applied to one object reference on the stack, but it is another object reference contained in the stack (which happens to reference the same object) whose status goes from "uninitialized" to "fully initialized" in the process.

As demonstrated above, static verification of object initialization requires a form of alias analysis (more precisely a must-alias analysis) to determine which object references in the current state are guaranteed to refer to the same uninitialized object that is passed as argument to an initializer method. While any must-alias analysis can be used, Sun's verifier uses a fairly simple analysis, whereas an uninitialized object is identified by the position (program counter value) of the new instruction that created it. More precisely, the type algebra is enriched by the types $\overline{C}_p$ denoting an uninitialized instance of class C created by a new instruction at PC p. An invocation of an initializer method C.<init> checks that the first argument of the method is of type $\overline{C}_p$ for some p, then pops the arguments off the stack type as usual, and finally finds all other occurrences of the type $\overline{C}_p$ in the abstract interpreter state (stack type and register types) and replaces them by C. The following example shows how this works for a nested initialization corresponding to the Java expression new C(new C(null)):

```
 0: new C       // stack type after: C̄₀
 3: dup         //         C̄₀, C̄₀
 4: new C       //         C̄₀, C̄₀, C̄₄
 7: dup         //         C̄₀, C̄₀, C̄₄, C̄₄
 8: aconst_null //         C̄₀, C̄₀, C̄₄, C̄₄, null
 9: invokespecial C.<init>  //  C̄₀, C̄₀, C
12: invokespecial C.<init>  //  C
15: ...
```

In particular, the first invokespecial initializes only the instance created at PC 4, but not the one created at PC 0.

This approach is correct only if at any given time, the machine state contains at most one uninitialized object created at a given PC. Loops containing a new instruction can invalidate this assumption, since several distinct objects created by this new instruction can be "in flight", yet are given the same uninitialized object type (same class, same PC of creation). To avoid this problem, Sun's verifier requires that no uninitialized object type appear in the machine state when a backward branch is taken. Since a control-flow loop must take at least one backward branch, this guarantees that no initialized objects can be carried over from one loop iteration to the next one, thus ensuring the correctness of the "PC of creation" aliasing criterion.

Freund and Mitchell [7] formalize this approach to verifying object initialization. Bertot [2] proves the correctness of this approach using the Coq theorem prover, and extracts a verification algorithm from the proof.

5 Subroutines

Subroutines in the JVM are code fragments that can be called from several points inside the code of a method. To this end, the JVM provides two instructions: jsr branches to a given label in the method code and pushes a return address to the following instruction; ret recovers a return address (from a register) and branches to the corresponding instruction. Subroutines are used to compile certain exception handling constructs, and can also be used as a general code-sharing device. The difference between a subroutine call and a method invocation is that the body of the subroutine executes in the same activation record than its caller, and therefore can access and modify the registers of the caller.

5.1   The Verification Problem with Subroutines

Subroutines complicate significantly bytecode verification by dataflow analysis. First, it is not obvious to determine the successors of a ret instruction, since the return address is a first-class value. As a first approximation, we can say that a ret instruction can branch to any instruction that follows a jsr in the method code. (This approximation is too coarse in practice; we will describe better approximations later.) Second, the subroutine entry point acts as a merge point in the control-flow graph, causing the register types at the points of call to this subroutine to be merged. This can lead to excessive loss of precision in the register types inferred, as the example in Fig.5 shows.

```
                    // register 0 uninitialized here
    0: jsr 100      // call subroutine at 100
    3: ...

   50: iconst_0
   51: istore_0     // register 0 has type "int" here
   52: jsr 100      // call subroutine at 100
   55: iload_0      // load integer from register 0
   56: ireturn      // and return to caller
       ...
                    // subroutine at 100:
  100: astore_1     // store return address in register 1
  101: ...          // execute some code that does not use register 0
  110: ret 1        // return to caller
```

Fig. 5. An Example of Subroutine

The two jsr 100 at 0 and 52 have 100 as successor. At 0, register 0 has type $\top$; at 52, it has type int. Thus, at 100, register 0 has type $\top$ (the least upper bound of $\top$ and int). The subroutine body (between 101 and 110) does not modify register 0, hence its type at 110 is still $\top$. The ret 1 at 110 has 3 and

55 as successors (the two instructions following the two jsr 100). Thus, at 55, register 0 has type T and cannot be used as an integer by instructions 55 and 56. This code is therefore rejected.

This behavior is counter-intuitive. Calling a subroutine that does not use a given register does not modify the run-time value of this register, so one could expect that it does not modify the verification-time type of this register either. Indeed, if the subroutine body was expanded inline at the two jsr sites, bytecode verification would succeed as expected.

The subroutine-based compilation scheme for the try...finally construct produces code very much like the above, with a register being uninitialized at one call site of the subroutine and holding a value preserved by the subroutine at another call site. Hence it is crucial that similar code passes bytecode verification. We will now see two refinements of the dataflow-based verification algorithm that achieve this goal.

5.2 Sun's Solution

We first describe the approach implemented in Sun's JDK verifier. It is described informally in [15, section 4.9.6], and formalized in [29, 25]. This approach implements the intuition that a call to a subroutine should not change the types of registers that are not used in the subroutine body.

First, we need to make precise what a "subroutine body" is: since JVM bytecode is unstructured, subroutines are not syntactically delimited in the code; subroutine entry points are easily detected (as targets of jsr instructions), but it is not immediately apparent which instructions can be reached from a subroutine entry point. Thus, a dataflow analysis is performed, either before or in parallel with the main type analysis. The outcome of this analysis is a consistent labeling of every instruction by the entry point(s) for the subroutine(s) it logically belongs to. From this labeling, we can then determine, for each subroutine entry point ℓ, the return instruction $Ret(\ell)$ for the subroutine, and the set of registers $Used(\ell)$ that are read or written by instructions belonging to that subroutine.

The dataflow equation for subroutine calls is then as follows. Let i be an instruction jsr ℓ, and j be the instruction immediately following i. Let $(S_{jsr}, R_{jsr}) = out(i)$ be the state "after" the jsr, and $(S_{ret}, R_{ret}) = out(Ret(\ell))$ be the state "after" the ret that terminates the subroutine. Then:

$$in(j) = \left(S_{ret}, \{r \mapsto \begin{cases} R_{ret}(r) & \text{if } r \in Used(\ell) \\ R_{jsr}(r) & \text{if } r \notin Used(\ell) \end{cases} \right)$$

In other terms, the state "before" the instruction j following the jsr is identical to the state "after" the ret, except for the types of the registers that are not used by the subroutine, which are taken from the state "after" the jsr.

In the example above, we have $Ret(100) = 110$ and register 0 is not in $Used(100)$. Hence the type of register 0 before instruction 55 (the instruction following the jsr) is equal to the type after instruction 52 (the jsr itself), that is int, instead of T (the type of register 0 after the ret 1 at 110).

While effective in practice, Sun's approach to subroutine verification raises a challenging issue: determining the subroutine structure is difficult. Not only subroutines are not syntactically delimited, but return addresses are stored in general-purpose registers rather than on a subroutine-specific stack, which makes tracking return addresses and matching ret/jsr pairs more difficult. To facilitate the determination of the subroutine structure, the JVM specification states a number of restrictions on correct JVM code, such as "two different subroutines cannot 'merge' their execution to a single ret instruction" [15, section 4.9.6]. These restrictions seem rather ad-hoc and specific to the particular subroutine labeling algorithm that Sun's verifier uses. Moreover, the description of subroutine labeling given in the JVM specification is very informal and incomplete.

Several rational reconstructions of this part of Sun's verifier have been published. The first, due to Abadi and Stata [29], is presented as a non-standard type system, and determines the subroutine structure before checking the types. The second is due to Qian [26] and infers simultaneously the types and the subroutine structure, in a way that is closer to Sun's implementation. The simultaneous determination of types and $Used(\ell)$ sets complicates the dataflow analysis: the transfer function of the analysis is no longer monotonous, and special iteration strategies are required to reach the fixpoint. Finally, O'Callahan [21] and Hagiya and Tozawa [10] also give non-standard type systems for subroutines based on continuation types and context-dependent types, respectively. However, these papers give only type checking rules, but no effective verification (type inference) algorithms.

While these works shed considerable light on the issue, they are carried in the context of a small subset of the JVM that excludes exceptions and object initialization in particular. Delicate interactions between subroutines and object initialization were discovered later by Freund and Mitchell [7], exposing a bug in Sun's verifier. As for exceptions, exception handling complicates significantly the determination of the subroutine structure. Examination of bytecode produced by Java compiler show two possible situations: either an exception handler covers a range of instructions entirely contained in a subroutine, in which case the code of the exception handler should be considered as part of the same subroutine (e.g. it can branch back to the ret instruction that terminates the subroutine); or, an exception handler covers both instructions belonging to a subroutine and non-subroutine instructions, in which case the code of the handler should be considered as outside the subroutine. The problem is that in the second case, we have a branch (via the exception handler) from a subroutine instruction to a non-subroutine instruction, and this branch is not a ret instruction; this situation is not allowed in Abadi and Stata's subroutine labeling system.

5.3   Polyvariant Dataflow Analysis

An alternate solution to the subroutine problem, used in the Java Card off-card verifier [31], relies on a polyvariant dataflow analysis: instructions inside subroutine bodies are analyzed several times, once per call site for the subroutine. The principles of polyvariant flow analyses, also called context-sensitive analyses, are well known [19, section 3.6]: whereas monovariant analyses maintain only one state per program point, a polyvariant analysis allows several states per program point. These states are indexed by *contours* that usually approximate the control-flow path that led to each state.

In the case of bytecode verification, contours are subroutine call stacks: lists of return addresses for the jsr instructions that led to the corresponding state. In the absence of subroutines, all the bytecode for a method is analyzed in the empty contour. Thus, only one state is associated to each instruction and the analysis degenerates into the monovariant dataflow analysis of section 3.2. However, when a jsr ℓ instruction is encountered in the current contour c, it is treated as a branch to the instruction at ℓ in the augmented contour $\ell.c$. Similarly, a ret r instruction is treated as a branch that restricts the current context c by popping one or several return addresses from c (as determined by the type of the register r).

In the example of Fig.5, the two jsr 100 instructions are analyzed in the empty context ε. This causes two "in" states to be associated with the instruction at 100; one has contour $3.\varepsilon$, assigns type $\top$ to register 0, and contains retaddr(3) at the top of the stack[1]; the other state has contour $55.\varepsilon$, assigns type int to register 0, and contains retaddr(55) at the top of the stack. Then, the instructions at 101...110 are analyzed twice, in the two contours $3.\varepsilon$ and $55.\varepsilon$. In the contour $3.\varepsilon$, the ret 1 at 110 is treated as a branch to 3, where register 0 still has type $\top$. In the contour $55.\varepsilon$, the ret 1 is treated as a branch to 55 with register 0 still having type int. By analyzing the subroutine body in a polyvariant way, under two different contours, we avoided merging the types $\top$ and int of register 0 at the subroutine entry point, and thus obtained the desired type propagation behavior for register 0: $\top$ before and after the jsr 100 at 3, but int before and after the jsr 100 at 52.

More formally, the polyvariant dataflow equation for a jsr ℓ instruction at i followed by an instruction at j is

$$in(\ell, j.c) = (\texttt{retaddr}(j).S, T) \text{ where } (S, T) = out(i, c)$$

For a ret r instruction at i, the equation is

$$in(ra, c') = out(i, c)$$

where the type of register r in the state $out(i, c)$ is retaddr(ra) and the context c' is obtained from c by popping return addresses until ra is found, that is, $c = c''.ra.c'$.

Another way to view polyvariant verification is that it is exactly equivalent to performing monovariant verification on an expanded version of the bytecode where every subroutine call has been replaced by a distinct copy of the subroutine body. Instead of actually taking N copies of the subroutine body, we analyze them N times in N different contours. Of course, duplicating subroutine bodies before the monovariant verification is not practical, because it requires prior

---

[1] The type retaddr(i) represents a return address to the instruction at i.

knowledge of the subroutine structure (to determine which instructions are part of which subroutine body), and as shown in section 5.2, the subroutine structure is hard to determine exactly. The beauty of the polyvariant analysis is that it determines the subroutine structure along the way, via the computations on contours performed during the dataflow analysis. Moreover, this determination takes advantage of typing information such as the retaddr(ra) types to determine with certainty the point to which a ret instruction branches in case of early return from nested subroutines.

Another advantage of polyvariant verification is that it has no problem dealing with code that is reachable both from subroutine bodies and from the main program, such as the exception handlers mentioned at the end of section 5.2: rather than deciding whether such exception handlers are part of a subroutine or not, the polyvariant analysis simply analyzes them several times, once in the empty contour and once or several times in subroutine contours.

The downside of polyvariant verification is that it is more computationally expensive than Sun's approach. In particular, if subroutines are nested to depth N, and each subroutine is called k times, the instructions from the innermost subroutine are analyzed k^N times instead of only once in Sun's algorithm. However, typical Java code has low nesting of subroutines: most methods have $N \leq 1$, very few have $N = 2$, and $N > 2$ is unheard of. Hence, the extra cost of polyvariant verification is entirely acceptable in practice.

6   Model Checking of Abstract Interpretations

It is folk lore that dataflow analyses can be viewed as model checking of abstract interpretations [28]. Since a large part of bytecode verification is obviously an abstract interpretation (of a defensive JVM at the type level), it is natural to look at the remaining parts from a model-checking perspective.

Posegga and Vogt [22] were the first to do so. They outline an algorithm that takes the bytecode for a method and generates a temporal logic formula that holds if and only if the bytecode is safe. They then use an off-the-shelf model checker to determine the validity of the formula. While this application uses only a small part of the power and generality of temporal logic and of the model checker, the approach sounds interesting for establishing finer properties of the bytecode that go beyond the basic safety properties of bytecode verification (see section 8).

Unpublished work by Brisset [3] extracts the essence of Posegga and Vogt's approach: the idea of exploring all reachable states of the abstract interpreter. Brisset considers the transition relation obtained by combining the transition relation of the type-level abstract interpreter (Fig.2) with the "successor" relation between instructions. This relation is of the form $(p, S, R) \rightarrow (p', S', R')$, meaning that the abstract interpreter, started at PC p with stack type S and register type R, can abstractly execute the instruction at p and arrive at PC p' with stack type S' and register type R'.

Starting with the initial state $(0, \varepsilon, (P_0, \ldots, P_{n-1}, \mathsf{T}, \ldots, \mathsf{T}))$ corresponding to the method entry, we can then explore all states reachable by repeated applications of the transition function. If we encounter a state where the abstract interpreter is "stuck" (cannot make a transition because some check failed), verification fails and the bytecode is rejected. Otherwise, the correctness of the abstract interpretation guarantees that the concrete, defensive JVM interpreter will never get "stuck" either during the execution of the method code, hence the bytecode is safe.

This algorithm always terminates because the number of distinct states is finite (albeit large), since there is a finite number of distinct types used in the program, and the height of the stack is bounded, and the number of registers is fixed. Brisset formalized and proved the correctness of this approach in the Coq proof assistant, and extracted the ML code of a bytecode verifier from the proof.

This approach is conceptually interesting because it is the ultimate polyvariant analysis: rather than having one stack-register type per control point (as in Sun's verifier), or one such type per control point and per subroutine contour (as in section 5.3), we can have arbitrarily many stack-register types per control point, depending on the number of control-flow paths that lead to this control point. Consider for instance the control-flow joint depicted in Fig.4. While the dataflow-based algorithms verify the instructions following the join point only once under the assumption $r : lub(C_1, C_2) = C$, Brisset's algorithm verifies them twice, once under the assumption $r : C_1$, once under the assumption $r : C_2$.

In other terms, this analysis is polyvariant not only with respect to subroutine calls, but to all conditional or N-way branches as well. This renders the analysis impractical, since it runs in time exponential in the number of such branches in the method. (Consider a control-flow graph with N conditional constructs in sequence, each assigning a different type to registers $r_1 \ldots r_N$; this causes the code following the last conditional to be verified 2^N times under 2^N different register types.)

Of course, the precision of Brisset's algorithm can be degraded by applying widening steps in order to reduce the number of states. Some transitions $(pc, S, R) \rightarrow (pc', S', R')$ can be replaced by $(pc, S, R) \rightarrow (pc', S'', R'')$ where $R' <: R''$ and $S' <: S''$. If the abstract interpreter is still not stuck on any of the reachable states, the bytecode remains safe. The monovariant dataflow analysis of section 3.2 corresponds to keeping only one state per program point by replacing multiple states by their least upper bounds. The polyvariant dataflow analysis of section 5.3 is similar, except that the merging of states into least upper bounds is relaxed for subroutines and controlled via contours.

Another interest of Brisset's approach is that it allows us to reconsider some of the design decisions explained in sections 3.3 and 4. For instance, Brisset's algorithm never computes least upper bounds of types, but simply checks subtyping relations between types. Thus, it can be applied to any subtyping relation, not just relations that form a semi-lattice. Indeed, it can keep track of interface types and verify invokeinterface instructions accurately, without having to deal with sets of types or lattice completion.

7   Bytecode Verification on Small Computers

Java virtual machines run not only in personal computers and workstations, but also in a variety of embedded computers, such as personal digital assistants, mobile phones, and smart cards. Extending the Java model of safe post-issuance code downloading to these devices requires that bytecode verification be performed on the embedded system itself. However, bytecode verification is an expensive process that exceeds the resources (processing power and memory space) of small embedded systems. For instance, a typical Java card (Java-enabled smart card) has 1 or 2 *kilo*-bytes of RAM and an 8-bit microprocessor that is approximately 1000 times slower than a personal computer. Fitting a bytecode verifier into one of these devices requires new verification algorithms, which we discuss now.

7.1   Lightweight Bytecode Verification Using Certificates

Inspired by Necula and Lee's proof-carrying code [18], Rose and Rose [27] propose to split bytecode verification into two phases: the code producer computes the stack and register types at branch targets and transmit these so-called certificates along with the bytecode; the embedded system, then, simply checks that the code is well-typed with respect to the types given in the certificates, rather than inferring these types itself. In other terms, the embedded system no longer solves iteratively the dataflow equations characterizing correct bytecode, but simply checks that the types provided in the code certificates are indeed a solution of these equations.

The benefits of this approach are twofold. First, checking a solution is faster than inferring one, since we avoid the cost of the fixpoint iteration. This speeds up verification to some extent[2]. Second, certificates are only read, but never modified during verification. Hence, they can be stored in persistent rewritable memory (EEPROM or Flash). Smart card-class embedded systems offer relatively large amounts of persistent memory (e.g. 16-32 kilo-bytes). Writing data to such memory is slow (1000-10000 times slower than reading from it), hence it is not possible to store there rapidly-changing data such as the fixpoint computed by a standard verification algorithm. However, Rose and Rose's certificates are written only once, on reception of the bytecode, and only read during verification, so they can fit in the "comfortable" EEPROM memory space.

There are two limitations to this approach. First, it is currently not known how to deal with subroutines in this framework. Indeed, Sun proposed to drop subroutines entirely in order to use Rose and Rose's bytecode verification algorithm in the KVM, one of Sun's embedded variants of the JVM [30]. Second, certificates are relatively large: without compression, about the same size as the code they annotate; with compression, about 20% of the code size. Even if certificates are stored in persistent memory, they can still exceed the available memory space.

---

[2] The speedup is not as important as one might expect, since experiments show that the fixpoint is usually reached after examining every instruction at most twice [13].

7.2 On-Card Verification with Off-Card Code Transformation

The Java Card bytecode verifier described in [13] attacks the memory problem from another angle. Like the standard bytecode verifier, it solves dataflow equations using fixpoint iteration. To reduce memory requirements, however, it has only one global register type that is shared between all control points in the method. In other terms, the solution it infers is such that a given register has the same type throughout the method. For similar reasons, it also requires that the stack be empty at each branch instruction and at each branch target instruction. With these extra restrictions, bytecode verification can be done in space $O(M_{stack} + M_{reg})$, instead of $O(N_{branch} \times (M_{stack} + M_{reg}))$ for Sun's algorithm, where N_{branch} is the number of branch targets. In practice, the memory requirements are small enough that all data structures comfortably fit in RAM on a smart card.

One drawback of this approach is that register initialization can no longer be checked statically, and must be replaced by run-time initialization of registers to safe values (0 or null) on method entrance. Another drawback is that the extra restrictions imposed by the on-card verifier cause perfectly legal bytecode (that passes Sun's verifier) to be rejected. To address the latter issue, we rely on an off-card transformation, performed on the bytecode of the applet, that transforms any legal bytecode (that passes Sun's verifier) into equivalent bytecode that passes the on-card verifier. The off-card transformations include stack normalizations around branches and register reallocation by graph coloring, and increase the size of the code by less than 2% [13].

8 Conclusions and Perspectives

Java bytecode verification is now a well researched technique, although it is still defined only by Sun's reference implementation: all the formal works reviewed in this paper have not yet resulted in a complete formal specification of what it is and what it guarantees.

A largely open question is whether bytecode verification can go beyond basic type safety and initialization properties, and statically establish more advanced properties of applets, such as resource usage (bounding the amount of memory allocated) and reactiveness (bounding the running time of an applet between two interactions with the outside world). Controlling resource usage is especially important for Java Card applets: since Java Card does not guarantee the presence of a garbage collector, applets are supposed to allocate all the objects they need at installation time, then run in constant space.

Other properties of interest include access control and information flow. Currently, the Java security manager performs all access control checks dynamically. Various static analyses and program transformations have been proposed to perform some of these checks statically [35, 23]. As for information flow (an applet does not "leak" confidential information that it can access), this property is essentially impossible to check dynamically; several type systems have been proposed to enforce it statically [34, 33, 11, 1].

Finally, the security of the sandbox model relies not only on bytecode verification, but also on the proper implementation of the API given to the applet. The majority of known applet-based attacks exploit (in a type-safe way) bugs in the API, rather than breaking type safety through bugs in the verifier. Verification of the API is a promising and largely open area of application for formal methods [14, 12].

References

1. M. Abadi, A. Banerjee, N. Heintze, and J. G. Riecke. A core calculus of dependency. In *26th symp. Principles of Progr. Lang*, pages 147–160. ACM Press, 1999.
2. Y. Bertot. A Coq formalization of a type checker for object initialization in the Java virtual machine. Research report 4047, INRIA, 2000. Also published in the proceedings of CAV'01.
3. P. Brisset. Vers un vérifieur de bytecode Java certifié. Seminar given at Ecole Normale Supérieure, Paris, October 2nd 1998.
4. K. Brunnstein. Hostile ActiveX control demonstrated. *RISKS Forum*, 18(82), Feb. 1997.
5. Z. Chen. *Java Card Technology for Smart Cards: Architecture and Programmer's Guide*. The Java Series. Addison-Wesley, 2000.
6. R. Cohen. The defensive Java virtual machine specification. Technical report, Computational Logic Inc., 1997.
7. S. N. Freund and J. C. Mitchell. A type system for object initialization in the Java bytecode language. *ACM Trans. Prog. Lang. Syst.*, 22(5), 2000.
8. L. Gong. *Inside Java 2 platform security: architecture, API design, and implementation*. The Java Series. Addison-Wesley, 1999.
9. J. A. Gosling. Java intermediate bytecodes. In *Proc. ACM SIGPLAN Workshop on Intermediate Representations*, pages 111–118. ACM, 1995.
10. M. Hagiya and A. Tozawa. On a new method for dataflow analysis of Java virtual machine subroutines. In G. Levi, editor, *SAS'98*, volume 1503 of *LNCS*, pages 17–32. Springer-Verlag, 1998.
11. N. Heintze and J. G. Riecke. The SLam calculus: programming with secrecy and integrity. In *25th symp. Principles of Progr. Lang*, pages 365–377. ACM Press, 1998.
12. M. Huisman, B. Jacobs, and J. van den Berg. A case study in class library verification: Java's Vector class. Technical Report CSI-R0007, Computing Science Institute, University of Nijmegen, 2000.
13. X. Leroy. On-card bytecode verification for Java Card. Submitted for publication, available from http://cristal.inria.fr/~xleroy, 2001.
14. X. Leroy and F. Rouaix. *Security properties of typed applets*, volume 1603 of *LNCS*, pages 147–182. Springer-Verlag, 1999.
15. T. Lindholm and F. Yellin. *The Java Virtual Machine Specification*. The Java Series. Addison-Wesley, 1999. Second edition.
16. G. McGraw and E. Felten. *Securing Java*. John Wiley & Sons, 1999.
17. S. S. Muchnick. *Advanced compiler design and implementation*. Morgan Kaufmann, 1997.
18. G. C. Necula. Proof-carrying code. In *POPL'97*, pages 106–119. ACM Press, 1997.
19. F. Nielson, H. R. Nielson, and C. Hankin. *Principles of program analysis*. Springer-Verlag, 1999.

20. T. Nipkow. Verified bytecode verifiers. In *Foundations of Software Science and Computation Structures (FOSSACS'01)*. Springer-Verlag, 2001. To appear.
21. R. O'Callahan. A simple, comprehensive type system for Java bytecode subroutines. In *POPL'99*, pages 70–78. ACM Press, 1999.
22. J. Posegga and H. Vogt. Java bytecode verification using model checking. In *Workshop Fundamental Underpinnings of Java*, 1998.
23. F. Pottier, C. Skalka, and S. Smith. A systematic approach to static access control. In D. Sands, editor, *Proceedings of the 10th European Symposium on Programming (ESOP'01)*, volume 2028 of *LNCS*, pages 30–45. Springer-Verlag, 2001.
24. C. Pusch. Proving the soundness of a Java bytecode verifier specification in Isabelle/HOL. In W. R. Cleaveland, editor, *TACAS'99*, volume 1579 of *LNCS*, pages 89–103. Springer-Verlag, 1999.
25. Z. Qian. A formal specification of Java virtual machine instructions for objects, methods and subroutines. In J. Alves-Foss, editor, *Formal syntax and semantics of Java*, volume 1523 of *LNCS*. Springer-Verlag, 1998.
26. Z. Qian. Standard fixpoint iteration for Java bytecode verification. *ACM Trans. Prog. Lang. Syst.*, 22(4):638–672, 2000.
27. E. Rose and K. Rose. Lightweight bytecode verification. In *Workshop Fundamental Underpinnings of Java*, 1998.
28. D. A. Schmidt. Data flow analysis is model checking of abstract interpretations. In *POPL'98*, pages 38–48. ACM Press, 1998.
29. R. Stata and M. Abadi. A type system for Java bytecode subroutines. *ACM Trans. Prog. Lang. Syst.*, 21(1):90–137, 1999.
30. Sun Microsystems. Java 2 platform micro edition technology for creating mobile devices. White paper, http://java.sun.com/products/cldc/wp/KVMwp.pdf, 2000.
31. Trusted Logic. Off-card bytecode verifier for Java Card. Distributed as part of Sun's Java Card Development Kit, 2001.
32. G. Vigna, editor. *Mobile Agents and Security*, volume 1419 of *Lecture Notes in Computer Science*. Springer-Verlag, 1998.
33. D. Volpano and G. Smith. A type-based approach to program security. In *Proceedings of TAPSOFT'97, Colloquium on Formal Approaches in Software Engineering*, volume 1214 of *LNCS*, pages 607–621. Springer-Verlag, 1997.
34. D. Volpano, G. Smith, and C. Irvine. A sound type system for secure flow analysis. *Journal of Computer Security*, 4(3):1–21, 1996.
35. D. Walker. A type system for expressive security policies. In *27th symp. Principles of Progr. Lang*, pages 254–267. ACM Press, 2000.
36. F. Yellin. Low level security in Java. In *Proceedings of the Fourth International World Wide Web Conference*, pages 369–379. O'Reilly, 1995.

Iterating Transducers*

Dennis Dams[1], Yassine Lakhnech[2], and Martin Steffen[3]

[1] Bell Labs, Lucent Technologies, Murray Hill NJ 07974, USA
On leave from Eindhoven University of Technology, The Netherlands
d.dams@tue.nl
[2] VERIMAG, Centre Equation
2 av. de Vignate, 38610 Gières, France
lakhnech@imag.fr
[3] Institut für angewandte Mathematik und Informatik
Christian-Albrechts-Universität
Preußerstraße 1–9, D-24105 Kiel, Deutschland
ms@informatik.uni-kiel.de

Abstract. Regular languages have proved useful for the symbolic state exploration of infinite state systems. They can be used to represent infinite sets of system configurations; the transitional semantics of the system consequently can be modeled by finite-state transducers. A standard problem encountered when doing symbolic state exploration for infinite state systems is how to explore all states in a finite amount of time. When representing the one-step transition relation of a system by a finite-state transducer $\mathcal{T}$, this problem boils down to finding an appropriate finite-state representation $\mathcal{T}^*$ for its transitive closure.
In this paper we give a partial algorithm to compute a finite-state transducer $\mathcal{T}^*$ for a general class of transducers. The construction builds a quotient of an underlying infinite-state transducer $\mathcal{T}^{<\omega}$, using a novel behavioural equivalence that is based *past* and *future* bisimulations computed on finite approximations of $\mathcal{T}^{<\omega}$. The extrapolation to $\mathcal{T}^{<\omega}$ of these finite bisimulations capitalizes on the structure of the states of $\mathcal{T}^{<\omega}$, which are strings of states of $\mathcal{T}$. We show how this extrapolation may be rephrased as a problem of detecting *confluence* properties of rewrite systems that represent the bisimulations. Thus, we can draw upon techniques that have been developed in the area of rewriting.
A prototype implementation has been successfully applied to various examples.

1 Introduction

Finite-state automata are omnipresent in computer science, providing a powerful tool for representing and reasoning about certain infinite phenomena. They are commonly used to capture dynamic behaviours, in which case an automaton's nodes model the states, and its edges the possible state transitions of a system. More recently, finite-state automata have also been applied to reason about infinite-state systems, in which case a single automaton is used to represent an

---

* This work has been supported by the Esprit-LTR project Vires.

G. Berry, H. Comon, and A. Finkel (Eds.): CAV 2001, LNCS 2102, pp. 286–297, 2001.

infinite set of system states. In regular model-checking [3, 14, 1, 13], regular sets of states of the system to be verified are represented by finite-state automata. For instance, consider a parameterized network of finite-state processes with the states of the processes modeled by the symbols of a finite alphabet. Then for every value of the parameter, i.e., for every fixed size of the network, a global configuration is represented by a word over the alphabet. A set of similar configurations corresponding to different values of the parameter, and hence to different network sizes, can then be modelled by a regular set. Or, in a system with data structures like unbounded message buffers, infinitely many buffer contents may be represented by an automaton. To reason about the dynamic behaviour of such a system, its transition relation is lifted to operate on such symbolically represented sets of states. A natural choice to represent the lifted transition relation are *finite-state transducers*.

Taking finite-state automata and transducers to describe infinite sets of states and their operational evolution is, in general, not sufficient when doing state exploration. To capture all reachable states, one needs to characterize the effect of applying a transducer $\mathcal{T}$ an arbitrary number of times. In other words, one needs to compute the transitive closure of $\mathcal{T}$. In general, this closure is not finite-state anymore. Nonetheless, for length-preserving transducers, partial algorithms have been developed that, if they terminate, produce the closure in the form of a finite-state transducer [3, 13]. These algorithms can be explained in terms of the, in general infinite-state, transducer $\mathcal{T}^{<\omega} = \bigcup_{i \in \omega} \mathcal{T}^i$, the union of all finite compositions of $\mathcal{T}$. Conceptually, they attempt to construct a finite quotient of $\mathcal{T}^{<\omega}$ by identifying states that are equivalent in some way. For example, in [3, 13], the underlying equivalence relation is induced by determinizing on-the-fly and then minimizing $\mathcal{T}^{<\omega}$. General transducers are not determinizable, but that paper considers length-preserving transducers, which are essentially standard automata over pairs of symbols and can be determinized accordingly. The minimal automation is then approximated using a technique called saturation to approximate the minimal automaton.

In this paper, we employ a different quotient construction, resulting in an algorithm whose application is not a-priori limited to length-preserving transducers. It works by computing successively the approximants $\mathcal{T}^{\leq n} = \bigcup_{0 \leq i \leq n} \mathcal{T}^i$ for $n = 0, 1, 2, \ldots$, while attempting to accelerate the arrival at a fixpoint by collapsing states. This quotienting is based on a novel behavioural equivalence defined in terms of *past* and *future bisimulations*. The largest such equivalence, being a relation over the infinite-state transducer $\mathcal{T}^{<\omega}$, may not be effectively computable. To solve this problem, we first identify sufficient conditions on an approximant $\mathcal{T}^{\leq n}$ for its states (which are also states of $\mathcal{T}^{<\omega}$) to be equivalent as states of $\mathcal{T}^{<\omega}$. Then we show that the equivalence of two states of $\mathcal{T}^{\leq n}$ induces the equivalence of infinitely many states of $\mathcal{T}^{<\omega}$.

We illustrate the underlying intuition on a small example in which sets of unbounded natural numbers are represented as automata over the symbols 0 and *succ*. The transitions we consider are given by the function α, defined inductively by $\alpha(0) = even$ and $\alpha(succ(x)) = \neg(\alpha(x))$. It computes the parity *even* or *odd* of a number; $\neg$ is a function that toggles parities. Consider the transition relation $\rightarrow$ that corresponds to a single step in the evaluation of this recursive definition.

Fig. 1(a) gives a transducer, $\mathcal{T}_\alpha$, that represents this transition relation. The slash

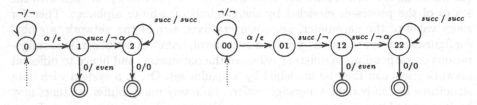

Fig. 1. Left (a): The Transducer $\mathcal{T}_\alpha$. Right (b): Its Product $\mathcal{T}_\alpha^2$.

(/) is used to separate the input symbol from the output symbols. Note that by the self-loop on state 0, the transducer leaves any leading occurrences of the symbol $\neg$ unchanged, and similarly for the trailing occurrences of *succ* before the final 0.

To start approximating $\mathcal{T}_\alpha^{<\omega}$, consider the product transducer $\mathcal{T}_\alpha^2$ shown in Fig. 1(b): It moves the symbol α over one more occurrence of *succ*, while turning it into a $\neg$, as reflected by the edge from state 01 to 12 (ϵ denotes the empty string). In every next product transducer $\mathcal{T}_\alpha^3, \mathcal{T}_\alpha^4, \ldots$, an additional such *succ*/$\neg$-edge will appear. Clearly, the limit transducer $\mathcal{T}_\alpha^{<\omega}$, the union of all approximants, is going to have infinitely many states. On the other hand, the combined effect of the ever-growing sequence of *succ*/$\neg$-edges would be captured by a simple loop if states 01 and 12 were identified. Collapsing $\mathcal{T}_\alpha^{<\omega}$ in this way, we can hope for a finite quotient. To do so, we need to address the following questions: First, how can we justify equating pairs of states like 01 and 12 (they are obviously semantically different in that the realize different transductions), i.e., what is the equivalence notion on $\mathcal{T}_\alpha^{<\omega}$ employed for quotienting, and secondly, how to compute the quotient without prior calculation of the infinite $\mathcal{T}_\alpha^{<\omega}$?

As for the first point, we must require that identifying states in the quotient does not introduce transductions not already present in $\mathcal{T}_\alpha^{<\omega}$. Equating 01 with 12 in the above example, consider the run through the "collapsed" transducer that goes from 00 to 01 (or rather to the new state obtained by collapsing 01 and 12) and then continues from this state as if continuing from 12. Exploiting the equation 01 = 12, this run is introduced by the collapse. Even if the states 01 and 12 are semantically different, as observed above, identifying them does not change the *overall* semantics of $\mathcal{T}_\alpha^{<\omega}$, as there *exists* another state that "glues" together the past of 01 and the future of 12, namely state 1 of $\mathcal{T}_\alpha^1$. Another class of artificial runs are those that go from 00 to 12 and then continue as if continuing from 01. But also in this case, there is a state in $\mathcal{T}_\alpha^{<\omega}$ that glues (this time) the past of 12 to the future of 01, although it has not been constructed when considering $\mathcal{T}_\alpha^{\leq 2}$. This state is 012 and would enter the scene as part of $\mathcal{T}_\alpha^3$, when constructing the next approximant. We formalize these ideas as follows: States q_1 and q_2 may be identified if there exists a past bisimulation P and a future bisimulation F such that the pair (q_1, q_2) is both in the composed relation

$P; F$ and in $F; P$, thus ensuring the existence of both "gluing" states. Indeed, we will require that the bisimulations *swap*, i.e., $F; P=P; F$. So it will be enough to show that (q_1, q_2) is in either one of the composed relations.

The second question is how to know that two states in some approximant $\mathcal{T}_\alpha^{\leq n}$ are equivalent in the above sense, i.e., how do we know that there exists a state somewhere in $\mathcal{T}_\alpha^{<\omega}$ that is past-bisimilar to one and future-bisimilar to the other? For this we exploit the structure of $\mathcal{T}_\alpha^{<\omega}$'s states, namely that they are sequences of states from $\mathcal{T}_\alpha$. It is easily seen that bisimulations are *congruences* under juxtaposition of such sequences. In the example above, this means that we can conclude the existence of an appropriate state without actually having to construct $\mathcal{T}_\alpha^3$. Namely, by looking at $\mathcal{T}^{\leq 2}$ only, we see that 1 and 12 are future bisimilar, whence by congruence also 01 and 012. Similarly, past bisimilarity of 12 and 012 can be inferred by comparing 1 and 01. So we know that 012 is our candidate, without ever having constructed it in any approximant so far. In short, exploiting the congruence property allows to extrapolate the quotienting relation found on a finite $\mathcal{T}_\alpha^{\leq n}$ to the whole $\mathcal{T}_\alpha^{<\omega}$, and thus to obtain a finite quotient of $\mathcal{T}_\alpha^{<\omega}$, without calculating the limit first.

The remainder of the paper is organized as follows. After introducing notation and the relevant preliminary definitions in the next section, Section 3 will formalize the criterion for a sound quotient. An algorithm based on this and profiting from results of rewriting theory forms the topic of Section 4, where we will also report on the results obtained from our prototype implementation. Section 5 concludes and discusses related and future work.

2   Preliminaries

A *transducer* $\mathcal{T} = (Q, Q_i, Q_f, \Sigma, R)$ consists of a set Q of states, sets $Q_i, Q_f \subseteq Q$ of initial resp. final states, a set Σ of symbols, and a set R of rules. A rule has the form $qa \to wq'$ with $q, q' \in Q$, $a \in \Sigma \cup \{\epsilon\}$, and $w \in \Sigma^*$, specifying that when in state q and reading input symbol $a \in \Sigma$ (or reading no input in case $a = \epsilon$), the transducer produces output w and assumes q' as its new state. A finite-state transducer is also called *regular*. The operation of a transducer is captured by the *reduction* relation $\to_R$ on strings consisting of symbols and a state (where ϵ has its usual meaning as neutral element of concatenation), defined as follows: For $t_1, t_2 \in \Sigma^*$, $t_1 qat_2 \to_R t_1 wq't_2$ iff $qa \to wq' \in R$. For this and other arrows we use common notations like $\to^{-1}$ for inverse, $\to^*$ for reflexive-transitive closure, and $\leftrightarrow$ for symmetric closure. $\mathcal{T}$'s *semantics* $[\mathcal{T}] : \Sigma^* \to 2^{(\Sigma^*)}$ is defined as follows: $t_2 \in [\mathcal{T}](t_1)$ iff there exist $q_i \in Q_i$ and $q_f \in Q_f$ such that $q_i t_1 \to_R^* t_2 q_f$. We will use the notation $\to_{\mathcal{T}}$ synonymously for the rewrite relation $\to_R$.

Transducers $\mathcal{T}_1$ and $\mathcal{T}_2$ over the same symbol set can be composed into $\mathcal{T}_2 \circ \mathcal{T}_1$, so that the output of $\mathcal{T}_1$ is input to $\mathcal{T}_2$. This is a standard product construction where the rules R of the composition are defined by

$$\frac{q_j a \to_{R_1} v q'_j \qquad q_i v \to_{R_2}^* w q'_i}{q_{ij} a \to w q'_{ij} \in R}$$

where R_1 and R_2 are the rules of the two constituent transducers, and where we write q_{ij} as short-hand for the tuple (q_i, q_j). Note that multiple steps of T_2 may be needed for q_i to "move through" v (or none, if $v = \epsilon$). This construction captures the semantical composition, i.e., $[T_2] \circ [T_1] = [T_2 \circ T_1]$. The n-fold composition of a transducer T with itself is written as T^n, with T^0 being defined such that it realizes the neutral element wrt. transduction composition, i.e., $[T^0] = Id_{\Sigma^*}$. By the same token, we will use Q^n as the set of states of T^n, when Q is the set of states of T. Finally we will need the *union* of transducers: given two transducers T_1 and T_2 over the same signature, $T_1 \cup T_2$ denotes the transducer over the same signature, given by the union of states, of initial states, of final states, and of rules, respectively, where we assume that the sets of states are disjoint. Union can be easily extended to the union of countably many transducers. Note that finite union preserves finiteness.

To obtain a finite-state transducer out of an a-priori infinite $T^{<\omega}$, we will have to identify "equivalent" states. The notion of equivalence used to this end will be based on *bisimulation* equivalences [18, 16] on states. Besides the standard future bisimulation we need the *past* variant as well.

Definition 1 (Bisimulation). *Let* $T = (Q, Q_i, Q_f, \Sigma, R)$ *be a transducer. An equivalence relation* $F \subseteq Q \times Q$ *is a future bisimulation if for all pairs* (q_1, q_2) *of states,* $q_1 \ F \ q_2$ *implies:*

If $q_1 \in Q_f$, *then* $q_2 \in Q_f$, *and for every* a, w, q_1' *such that* $q_1 a \rightarrow_T w q_1'$, *there exists* q_2' *such that* $q_2 a \rightarrow_T w q_2'$ *and* $q_1' \ F \ q_2'$.

An equivalence relation $P \subseteq Q \times Q$ *is a past bisimulation, if for all pairs* (q_1', q_2') *of states,* $q_1' \ P \ q_2'$ *implies:*

If $q_1' \in Q_i$, *then* $q_2' \in Q_i$, *and for every* a, w, q_1 *such that* $q_1 a \rightarrow_T w q_1'$, *there exists* q_2 *such that* $q_2 a \rightarrow_T w q_2'$ *and* $q_1 \ P \ q_2$.

We call q_1 *and* q_2 *(future) bisimilar, written* $q_1 \sim_f q_2$, *if there exists a future bisimulation* F *with* $q_1 \ F \ q_2$*; and* $q_1 \sim_p q_2$ *denotes two past bisimilar states, defined analogously.*

The bisimulation relations enjoy the expected properties ([16]): For both the future and the past case, the identity relation is a bisimulation, the inverse of a bisimulation is one, as well, and the notion of bisimulation is closed under relational composition. Furthermore, the notions of bisimulation are closed under union, more precisely, given two future bisimulation relations F_1 and F_2, then $(F_1 \cup F_2)^*$ is a future bisimulation, and analogously for the past case. The extra Kleene closure is needed since we require a bisimulation relation to be an equivalence. It is standard to show that future bisimilarity implies semantical equality, i.e., $T_1 \sim_f T_2$ implies $[T_1] = [T_2]$, and that the two relations $\sim_p$ and $\sim_f$ are *congruences* on Q^*, the free monoid over of T's set of states Q. We will exploit this property in Section 4.

The definition of a quotient is fairly standard:

Definition 2 (Quotient). *Let* $T = (Q, Q_i, Q_f, \Sigma, R)$ *be a transducer and* $\cong \subseteq Q \times Q$ *an equivalence relation.* $T_{/\cong}$ *is defined as the transducer* $(Q_{/\cong}, \{[q]_{\cong} \mid q \in$

$Q_i\}, \{[q]_{\cong} \mid q \in Q_f\}, \Sigma, R_{/\cong})$, where $Q_{/\cong}$ is the set of $\cong$-equivalence classes of Q and $[q]_{\cong}$ the $\cong$-equivalence class of q. The rules of $\mathcal{T}_{/\cong}$ are given by $\hat{q}a \to w\hat{q}' \in R_{/\cong}$ iff there exist q, q' such that $\hat{q} = [q]_{\cong}$, $\hat{q}' = [q']_{\cong}$, and $q'a \to wq' \in R$.

3   Sound Quotienting of $\mathcal{T}^{<\omega}$

Next we formalize the equivalence relation used to quotient $\mathcal{T}^{<\omega}$ and show the correctness of the construction. As illustrated on the example of Section 1, the key intuition behind a sound quotient is that, whenever identifying states q_1 and q_2, there must *exist* a state realizing q_1's future and q_2's past, and a state realizing q_1's past and q_2's future. "Having the same future (past)" will be captured by *being future (past) bisimilar*. To ensure the existence of both required states, we will restrict our attention to *swapping* future and past bisimulations:

Definition 3 (Swapping). *Two relations R and S over the same set* swap *(or:* are swapping*), if $R; S = S; R$ (where ; denotes relational composition).*

We are now ready to formulate the section's central result, which allows to collapse the infinite $\mathcal{T}^{<\omega}$ to a (possibly) finite transducer without changing its semantics. Note that the theorem covers collapsing $\mathcal{T}^{<\omega}$ with respect to $\sim_f$ or with respect to $\sim_p$ as special cases, since the identity relation on Q^* is a past as well as a future bisimulation and moreover, as neutral element of relational composition, swaps with every relation. The full proof appears in [5].

Theorem 4. *Let $\mathcal{T}$ be a transducer, and F and P a swapping pair of a future and past bisimulation on $\mathcal{T}^{<\omega}$. Then the quotient $\mathcal{T}^{<\omega}_{/F;P}$ of $\mathcal{T}^{<\omega}$ under $F; P$ is well-defined and preserves the transduction relation, i.e., $[\mathcal{T}^{<\omega}_{/F;P}] = [\mathcal{T}^{<\omega}]$.*

Proof Sketch. With $F; P$ being a congruence, we will write $\equiv_{F;P}$ for that relation in the rest of the proof.

The important direction to show is that $t' \in [\mathcal{T}^{<\omega}_{/\equiv_{F;P}}](t)$ implies $t' \in [\mathcal{T}^{<\omega}](t)$ (the reverse implication is straightforward: Collapsing states never yields fewer transductions). To show this implication requires a characterization of the reductions realized by a quotient: Since for any congruence relation $\cong$, $\mathcal{T}^{<\omega}_{/\cong}$ is given by identifying states of $\mathcal{T}^{<\omega}$ while retaining the reduction relation of $\mathcal{T}^{<\omega}$ (modulo the collapsing of

$$
\begin{array}{ccccc}
t_1 & \xrightarrow[\mathcal{T}^{<\omega}]{} & t_3 & \xrightarrow[\mathcal{T}^{<\omega}\cup\equiv_{F;P}]{*} & t_2 \\
P \Big\| & & P \Big\| & & \Big\| \\
t_1' & \xrightarrow[\mathcal{T}^{<\omega}]{} & t_3'' & \xrightarrow[\mathcal{T}^{<\omega}]{*} & t_2'' \quad \Big\| F;P \\
F \Big\| & & F \Big\| & & \\
t_3' & \xrightarrow[\mathcal{T}^{<\omega}]{*} & t_2'. & &
\end{array}
$$

states), the possible reduction steps of $\mathcal{T}^{<\omega}_{/\cong}$ are either reduction steps from $\mathcal{T}^{<\omega}$ or steps replacing a word by a congruent one, i.e., $[t_1]_{\cong} \to^*_{\mathcal{T}^{<\omega}_{/\cong}} [t_2]_{\cong}$ iff $t_1 (\to_{\mathcal{T}^{<\omega}} \cup \cong)^* t_2$. Using this characterization for the congruence $\equiv_{F;P}$, the above implication can be phrased as (and generalized, for sake of induction, to) the following requirement:

If $t_1(\to_{\mathcal{T}^{<\omega}} \cup \equiv_{F;P})^* t_2$, then there exist words t_1' and t_2' such that $t_1' \to^*_{\mathcal{T}^{<\omega}} t_2'$, and furthermore $t_1 \equiv_{F;P} t_1'$ and $t_2 \equiv_{F;P} t_2'$.

This property is shown by induction on the length of the reduction sequence. Distinguishing in the induction step $t_1 \equiv_{F;P} t_3$ and $t_1 \twoheadrightarrow_{\mathcal{T}^{<\omega}} t_3$, both cases are solved by straightforward induction, where the second one (cf. the above diagram) exploits the assumption that $\equiv_{F;P}$ is swapping.

To see that the result follows from the above implication, use the soundness observation for the unquotiented transducer, that $t' \in [\mathcal{T}^{<\omega}](t)$ iff $t' \in [\mathcal{T}^k](t)$ for some $k \in \omega$, and specialize t_1 resp. t_2 to $q_i \tilde{t}_1$ resp. to $\tilde{t}_2 q_f$, where $\tilde{t}_1, \tilde{t}_2 \in \Sigma^*$, and furthermore $q_i \in Q_i$ and $q_f \in Q_f$. □

4   An On-the-Fly Algorithm for Quotienting $\mathcal{T}^{<\omega}$

To make algorithmic use of the quotienting result, we must be able to effectively compute (and represent) swapping bisimulation relations on $\mathcal{T}^{<\omega}$. In this section, we show how to obtain these by extrapolating from information established on a finite approximant $\mathcal{T}^{\leq n}$, and exploiting the structure of $\mathcal{T}^{<\omega} = \mathcal{T}^0 \cup \mathcal{T}(\mathcal{T}^0) \cup \mathcal{T}(\mathcal{T}(\mathcal{T}^0)) \cup \ldots$. To apply Theorem 4 we must extrapolate two properties: 1) the (future or past) bisimulation requirement, and 2) the property of swapping. In order to do the extrapolation, we will view the relations F and P on $Q^{\leq n}$ as *rewriting systems* on Q^*, indeed a restricted form of ground (i.e., without variables) rewriting systems on strings. We will draw upon various standard notions and results from rewrite theory, briefly recalling them as they occur. A detailed treatment of the field can be found in e.g. [2]. The basic notions can be illustrated on our running example. The fact that states 1 and 12 are future bisimilar is rephrased by assuming two rewrite rules, one saying that 1 may be rewritten into 12, and another saying that 12 may be rewritten into 1. We use $\rightarrow_F$ to denote the *rewrite relation generated by* F, i.e., for $\alpha, \alpha' \in Q^*$, we have $\alpha \rightarrow_F \alpha'$ if $\alpha = \alpha_l \beta \alpha_r$, $\alpha' = \alpha_l \beta' \alpha_r$, and $(\beta, \beta') \in F$ for some $\alpha_l, \alpha_r, \beta, \beta' \in Q^*$; similarly for $\rightarrow_P$. The relations $\leftrightarrow^*_F$ and $\leftrightarrow^*_P$ denote the *congruence closures*[1] of F and P over the monoid Q^* of strings over Q.

We first address question 1) from above. As mentioned in Section 2, the future and past bisimilarity relations are congruences over the monoid Q^*, i.e., if $\alpha \sim_f \alpha'$ and $\beta \sim_f \beta'$, then $\alpha\beta \sim_f \alpha'\beta'$, for all $\alpha, \alpha', \beta, \beta' \in Q^*$, and similarly for $\sim_p$. Based on the congruence property, the following lemma expresses the required extrapolation of bisimulation relations from a finite approximant to $\mathcal{T}^{<\omega}$.

Lemma 5. *Let $\mathcal{T}$ be a finite-state transducer with states Q and, for some $n \geq 0$, let F and $P \subseteq Q^{\leq n} \times Q^{\leq n}$ be future and a past bisimulation on $\mathcal{T}^{\leq n}$. Then the relation $\leftrightarrow^*_F$, resp. $\leftrightarrow^*_P$, is a future, resp. a past, bisimulation on $\mathcal{T}^{<\omega}$.*

After having extended finite bisimulations F and P, question 2) is whether $\leftrightarrow^*_F$ and $\leftrightarrow^*_P$ additionally enjoy the swapping requirement. Now, reducing

---

[1] As F and P are symmetric, taking the symmetric closure has no effect, but we still prefer to write $\leftrightarrow_F$ and $\leftrightarrow_P$ instead of $\rightarrow_F$ and $\rightarrow_P$ in order to stress that they are symmetric.

properties of a many-step rewrite relation to properties of the one-step relation is a standard topic in rewrite theory. First note that swapping of relations is closely related to the notion of *commutation*: R and S commute if $(R^{-1})^*; S^* \subseteq S^*; (R^{-1})^*$ (note the transitive closures). Now for *symmetric* relations, clearly R and S commute iff R^* and S^* swap. The following lemma (see e.g. [2]) reduces commutation to the *commuting-diamond property*: R and S have the commuting-diamond property if $R^{-1}; S \subseteq S; R^{-1}$.

Lemma 6. *Let F and P be two relations on $Q^{\leq n} \times Q^{\leq n}$. If $\leftrightarrow_F$ and $\leftrightarrow_P$ have the commuting-diamond property[2], then they commute.*

To effectively identify cases where the (infinite) relations $\leftrightarrow_F$ and $\leftrightarrow_P$ have the commuting-diamond property, one can restrict attention to the so-called *critical pairs*. Consider rewrite rules (α_F, β_F) and (α_P, β_P) from F and P respectively, such that α_F overlaps with α_P in the following way: either $\gamma_1 \alpha_F = \alpha_P \gamma_2$ with $|\gamma_1| < |\alpha_P|$, or $\alpha_F = \gamma_1 \alpha_P \gamma_2$, for some $\gamma_1, \gamma_2 \in Q^*$. Then the corresponding critical pair is defined as $(\gamma_1 \beta_F, \beta_P \gamma_2)$ in the first case and $(\beta_F, \gamma_1 \beta_P \gamma_2)$ in the second. Now, in order to check whether $\leftrightarrow_F$ and $\leftrightarrow_P$ have the commuting-diamond property, it suffices to check, for every such critical pair (δ_F, δ_P), whether there exists δ such that $\delta_F \; P \; \delta$, and $\delta_P \; F \; \delta$[3]. As the rewrite systems F and P are finite, there are also only finitely many critical pairs to check. Note that this technique offers only a *sufficient* condition for the commuting-diamond property.

Lemma 5 and Lemma 6 together allow now to apply the quotienting Theorem 4 and do the desired extrapolation.

Corollary 7 (Soundness). *Let $\mathcal{T}$ be a transducer with states from Q and, for some n, let $F \subseteq Q^{\leq n} \times Q^{\leq n}$ and $P \subseteq Q^{\leq n} \times Q^{\leq n}$ a future resp. a past bisimulation on $\mathcal{T}^{\leq n}$. If $\leftrightarrow_F$ and $\leftrightarrow_P$ have the commuting-diamond property, then $[\mathcal{T}^{<\omega}] = [\mathcal{T}^{<\omega}_{\leftrightarrow_P^*, \leftrightarrow_F^*}]$.*

To make notation a little less heavy-weight, we will for the rest use $\equiv$ to abbreviate the congruence relation $\leftrightarrow_F^*; \leftrightarrow_P^*$.

Let us illustrate the ideas so far on the transducer from Fig. 1. On the approximant $\mathcal{T}_\alpha^{\leq 2}$ (i.e. the unions of the transducers in parts (a) and (b) of Fig. 1), one pair of a future and a past bisimulation (represented as rewriting systems) is $F = \{(12, 1), (1, 12), (22, 2), (2, 22)\} \cup Id_{\{0,1,\dots,22\}}$ and $P = \{(00, 0), (0, 00), (01, 1), (1, 01)\} \cup Id_{\{0,1,\dots,22\}}$, where Id_S denotes the "identity rewrite system" on S. Indeed, these bisimulations are the largest choices. It can be easily checked that the corresponding rewrite relations $\leftrightarrow_F$ and $\leftrightarrow_P$ have the commuting-diamond property. For example, the overlapping pair consisting of state 1 from the rule $(1, 12)$ of F and state 1 from the rule $(1, 01)$ of P opens a diamond that may be closed again by rewriting both 12 and 01 to 012 (using the same rules). Now, without actually attempting to fully compute the relation

---

[2] In fact, a weaker property suffices, called *strong commutation*: $R^{-1}; S \subseteq (S \cup Id); (R^{-1})^*$.

[3] There is a similar condition in case strong commutation is used.

---

input $\mathcal{T} = (Q, Q_0, \Sigma, R)$
$\mathcal{X} := \mathcal{T}_{id}$;
repeat
$\qquad \mathcal{X} := (\mathcal{T} \circ \mathcal{X}) \cup \mathcal{T}_{id}$;
$\qquad$ determine bisimulations F and P on $\mathcal{X}$ s.t.
$\qquad \Leftrightarrow_F$ and $\Leftrightarrow_P$ swap and each possess the diamond property;
until $\mathcal{X}_{/\equiv} \sim_f (\mathcal{T} \circ \mathcal{X}_{/\equiv}) \cup \mathcal{T}_{id}$

Fig. 3. Calculating $\mathcal{T}^*$

$\equiv$, we can already detect several equivalences between states. Most importantly, the states 1, 01, and 12 belong to the same equivalence class. Furthermore, we have $00 \equiv 0$ and $22 \equiv 2$. Quotienting $\mathcal{T}_\alpha^{\leq 2}$ by this equivalence gives the transducer of Fig. 2, where only the relevant part is shown. It can be checked that the construction stabilizes at this point, so we have arrived at $\mathcal{T}_\alpha^*$. Note that quotienting $\mathcal{T}_\alpha^{<\omega}$ using $\sim_p$ or $\sim_f$ in isolation does not give a finite quotient.

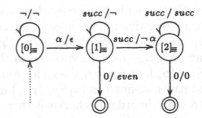

Fig. 2. Transducer $\mathcal{T}_\alpha^*$.

The algorithm based on these ideas is sketched in pseudo-code in Fig. 3. Given a transducer $\mathcal{T} = (Q, Q_0, \Sigma, R)$, the *until*-loop iteratively calculates, in variable $\mathcal{X}$, the approximations $\mathcal{T}^{\leq n}$. On each approximation, bisimulations F and P are computed by a partition refinement algorithm [17,8]. Note that in the termination condition, the approximant transducer $\mathcal{X}$ is quotiented using the whole equivalence $\equiv\ =\ \Leftrightarrow_F^*; \Leftrightarrow_P^*$, and not just by those identifications that happen to be directly detectable on $\mathcal{X}$, as suggested in the example above. The ability to do so relies again on techniques from rewrite theory. First, it can be shown that $\Leftrightarrow_F^*; \Leftrightarrow_P^* = (\Leftrightarrow_F \cup \Leftrightarrow_P)^* = \Leftrightarrow_{F\cup P}^*$. So, the question is when strings are congruent under the rewrite system $F \cup P$. The first answer of rewrite theory is: If this system is *confluent*, i.e., commutes with itself, and *terminating*, i.e., allows no infinite sequences of rewrite steps, then strings are congruent iff they rewrite to the same normal forms. This obviously gives a procedure to determine congruence. Being a special case of commutation, confluence of $F \cup P$ can be checked using Lemma 6, by inspecting critical pairs. In practice, we can avoid duplicating work by the following standard result.

Lemma 8. *If $\Leftrightarrow_F$ and $\Leftrightarrow_P$ commute, then $\Leftrightarrow_F \cup \Leftrightarrow_P$ is confluent if each of $\Leftrightarrow_F$ and $\Leftrightarrow_P$ in separation is confluent.*

So, if commutation of $\Leftrightarrow_F$ and $\Leftrightarrow_P$ has already been checked when determining whether $\Leftrightarrow_F^*$ and $\Leftrightarrow_P^*$ swap, then it suffices to check confluence of the individual relations. In case $\Leftrightarrow_F \cup \Leftrightarrow_P$ turns out to be not confluent, still not all hope is lost. The next, more advanced technique offered by rewrite theory is to try to turn the rewrite system $F \cup P$ into an equivalent rewrite system that is confluent, using so-called Knuth-Bendix *completion* [15]; we refer to [2] for details.

As for checking termination — it is clear that the relations F and P in separation are already non-terminating, as they are reflexive and symmetric. But also in this case, there is the possibility of turning $F \cup P$ into an equivalent system that does terminate. Because of the very simple form of this rewriting system —ground rewriting on strings— it is easy to capture $\leftrightarrow^{*}_{F \cup P}$ by a terminating one: Just order pairs *lexicographically* and remove the "reflexive" part $Id_{Q^{\leq n}}$. In our example, the quotienting relation $\equiv$ can in this way be represented by the four rules $\{(00, 0), (01, 1), (21, 1), (22, 2)\}$, where the right-hand side of each rule is strictly smaller than the corresponding left-hand side in lexicographic order.

A few points concerning the implementation deserve mention. For once, the naive iteration as sketched in the pseudo-code can be optimized in a number of ways, especially by reusing information collected from the lower approximants when treating $T^{\leq n+1}$. For instance, in case one knows already that $(00, 0)$ are past bisimilar after investigating the first two levels, as in our example, there is no need to check $(000, 00)$ for past-bisimilarity at the third (if at all it would be needed to construct that level). Another, more tricky point is that the search for bisimulations F and P under the additional requirements of swapping and confluence, adds an element of *non-determinism* to the process. Namely, it may be that bisimulations as they are found do not swap or are not confluent, but that smaller bisimulations would in fact satisfy these requirements. In such a case we would have to *choose* which pairs of states to delete. However, in the examples we tested, the largest bisimulations $\sim_f$ and $\sim_p$, as given by the partition refinement, always worked.

We tested our implementation on various examples, for instance the one of Fig. 1 or the token array example of [13]. In all but one case, the transitive closure was computed in a short time on a standard desktop workstation. In the remaining case, a *ring* configuration of the token array, the computation took too long. We expect that by implementing some additional optimizations (see below), this and other, larger transducers can be successfully handled.

5   Conclusions, Related Work, and Future Work

We presented a partial algorithm for computing the transitive closure of regular word transducers. This algorithm allows to reason about the effect of iterating transduction relations an unbounded number of times. Such relations are used, for instance, in regular model checking where they represent the transition relation of an infinite-state system. Given a transducer T, our algorithm is based on quotienting, w.r.t. the composition of a future and a past bisimulation, the possibly infinite-state transducer $T^{<\omega}$, the union of all finite compositions of T. To be able to develop our algorithm, we presented sufficient conditions that allow to exploit bisimulations discovered on a finite approximant $T^{\leq n}$, and hence, to avoid constructing $T^{<\omega}$. Though our prototype implementation can be improved in several ways, we obtained encouraging results on the examples we have considered.

In order to compute $T^*(S)$ for a given regular set S, our results specialize to automata, allowing to accelerate the computation of $T^{\leq 0}(S)$, $T^{\leq 1}(S)$, $T^{\leq 2}(S)$, ... This problem, where the set of initial configurations is also a parameter of the algorithm, can be solved in more cases than the general case[4].

Closest to our work is [3, 13], which presents an algorithm using standard subset-construction and minimization techniques from automata theory. Sufficient conditions for termination of the algorithm are identified. Roughly speaking, our algorithm and the one from [3, 13] start from opposite extremes. Our algorithm starts from T and tries to compute a finite quotient of $T^{<\omega}$. Their algorithm starts from the initial state of $T^{<\omega}$, which can be represented by the regular language q_0^*, and tries to compute the states of $T^{<\omega}$ performing a forward symbolic reachability analysis (this is the determinization) while relaxing the condition stating when a state has already been visited. This relaxation (called saturation in their work) assumes a fixed set of equivalences between states of $T^{<\omega}$. On the contrary, our algorithm tries to discover such equivalences dynamically, i.e., during execution. Now, an important assumption in their approach is that the set of pairs $(a, w) \in \Sigma \times \Sigma^*$ that occur along the edges of $T^{<\omega}$ is finite and known in advance (or at least a finite super-set must satisfy these conditions). In case T is a "letter-to-letter" transducer, only pairs from $\Sigma \times \Sigma$ may occur in $T^{<\omega}$, and hence, the assumption is satisfied. However, for non-length-preserving transducers the assumption is in general not satisfied.

Besides the improvements mentioned in Section 4 and implementation improvements like using BDDs to represent transducers, we believe that there are variations of our algorithm that are worth studying. One such variation consists in computing at each iteration of the algorithm the composition of T with the quotiented transducer obtained upto that iteration. This would reduce the number of states of the transducers that occur as intermediate results of the algorithm. A similar idea underlies what is called compositional model-checking, e.g. [10]. The difficulty in our context lies in the generalization of the computed bisimulations to $T^{<\omega}$.

We are currently extending our results to the case of tree transducers. Here, in the general case, one is confronted with negative results from tree transducer theory, the main one being that regular tree transducers are not closed under composition. To avoid this problem, we restrict ourselves to linear tree transducers. A preliminary account, which also provides the full proofs for the word case, can be found in [5].

Acknowledgements

We like to thank the anonymous referees for their careful work and their valuable and insightful comments and suggestions.

---

[4] This suggestion was made both by Kedar Namjoshi and an anonynous referee.

References

1. P. A. Abdulla, A. Bouajjani, and B. Jonsson. On-the-fly analysis of systems with unbounded lossy Fifo-channels. In Hu and Vardi [12], pages 305–318.
2. F. Baader and T. Nipkow. *Term Rewriting and All That.* Cambridge University Press, 1998.
3. A. Bouajjani, B. Jonsson, M. Nilsson, and T. Touili. Regular model checking. In Emerson and Sistla [7], pages 135–145.
4. E. M. Clarke and R. P. Kurshan, editors. *Computer Aided Verification 1990*, volume 531 of *Lecture Notes in Computer Science*. Springer-Verlag, 1991.
5. D. Dams, Y. Lakhnech, and M. Steffen. Iterating transducers. Technical Report TR-ST-01-03, Lehrstuhl für Software-Technologie, Institut für Informatik und praktische Mathematik, Christian-Albrechts-Universität Kiel, Jan. 2001. A preliminary version is available on-line at http://radon.ics.ele.tue.nl/~vires/public/results.htm (reports section).
6. P. Deussen, editor. *Fifth GI Conference on Theoretical Computer Science*, volume 104 of *Lecture Notes in Computer Science*. Springer-Verlag, 1981.
7. E. A. Emerson and A. P. Sistla, editors. *CAV '00, Proceedings of the 12th International Conference on Computer-Aided Verification, Chicago IL*, volume 1855 of *Lecture Notes in Computer Science*. Springer-Verlag, 2000.
8. J. Fernandez. An implementation of an efficient algorithm for bisimulation equivalence. *Science of Computer Programming*, 13:219–236, 1989.
9. S. Graf and M. Schwartzbach, editors. *Proceedings of the Sixth International Conference on Tools and Algorithms for the Construction and Analysis of Systems (TACAS 2000)*, volume 1785 of *Lecture Notes in Computer Science*. Springer-Verlag, 2000.
10. S. Graf and B. Steffen. Compositional minimization of finite state systems. In Clarke and Kurshan [4].
11. O. Grumberg, editor. *CAV '97, Proceedings of the 9th International Conference on Computer-Aided Verification, Haifa. Israel*, volume 1254 of *Lecture Notes in Computer Science*. Springer, June 1997.
12. A. J. Hu and M. Y. Vardi, editors. *Computer-Aided Verification, CAV '98, 10th International Conference, Vancouver, BC, Canada, Proceedings*, volume 1427 of *Lecture Notes in Computer Science*. Springer-Verlag, 1998.
13. B. Jonsson and M. Nilsson. Transitive closures for regular relations for verifying infinite-state systems. In Graf and Schwartzbach [9].
14. Y. Kesten, O. Maler, M. Marcus, A. Pnueli, and E. Shahar. Symbolic model checking with rich assertional languages. In Grumberg [11].
15. D. E. Knuth and P. B. Bendix. Simple word problems in universal algebra. In J. Leech, editor, *Computational Problems in Abstract Algebra*, pages 263–297. Pergamon Press, 1970.
16. R. Milner. *Communication and Concurrency*. Prentice Hall, 1989.
17. R. Paige and R. E. Tarjan. Three partition refinement algorithms. *SIAM Journal on Computing*, 16(6):973–989, 1987.
18. D. Park. Concurrency and automata on infinite sequences. In Deussen [6], pages 167–183.

Attacking Symbolic State Explosion

Giorgio Delzanno[1]*, Jean-François Raskin[2]**, and Laurent Van Begin[2]***

[1] Dipartimento di Informatica e Scienze dell'Informazione
Università di Genova, via Dodecaneso 35, 16146 Genova, Italy
giorgio@disi.unige.it
[2] Département d'Informatique, Université Libre de Bruxelles
Blvd Du Triomphe, 1050 Bruxelles, Belgium
{jraskin,lvbegin}@ulb.ac.be

Abstract. We propose a new symbolic model checking algorithm for parameterized concurrent systems modeled as (Lossy) Petri Nets, and (Lossy) Vector Addition Systems, based on the following ingredients: a *rich assertional language* based on the *graph-based* symbolic representation of upward-closed sets introduced in [DR00], the combination of the *backward reachability algorithm* of [ACJT96] lifted to the symbolic setting with a *new heuristic rule* based on *structural properties* of Petri Nets. We evaluate the method on several Petri Nets and parameterized systems taken from the literature [ABC+95,EM00,Fin93,MC99], and we compare the results with other finite and infinite-state verification tools.

1 Introduction

The theory of well-structured systems [ACJT96,FS01] gives us decision procedures to verify safety properties of *parameterized* systems modeled as Petri Nets [ACJT96,FS01], Lossy Vector Addition Systems [BM99], and Broadcast Protocols [EFM99]. The decision procedures are based on *backward reachability* algorithms like the one proposed in [ACJT96], whose termination (for Petri Nets and their extensions) is guaranteed by Dickson's lemma. It is important to recall that forward approaches like Karp-Miller's coverability tree are not robust when applied to extensions of Petri Nets like Broadcast protocols [EFM99].

Differently from the finite-state case, in parameterized verification *symbolic* representations are ineluctable in order to make the approach *effective*: we *need* to finitely represent infinite collections of states. In the backward approach of [ACJT96,FS01] we need to represent infinite, *upward-closed* sets of *markings*, when we restrict our attention to Petri Nets. Two examples of symbolic representations for *upward-closed sets* of marking are collections of minimal points

---

* This work was partially done when the author was visiting the University of Brussels supported by a grant "Crédit d'ouverture internationale" of the same university.
** This author was partially supported by a "Crédit aux chercheurs" granted by the Belgian National Fund for Scientific Research.
* * * This author was supported by a Walloon Region grant "First Europe".

G. Berry, H. Comon, and A. Finkel (Eds.): CAV 2001, LNCS 2102, pp. 298–310, 2001.
© Springer-Verlag Berlin Heidelberg 2001

[ACJT96], and *linear arithmetic constraints* [DEP99]. The complexity of the algorithm of [ACJT96] is non-elementary. For this reason, naive implementations of the backward approach suffer from the *symbolic state explosion* problem: the number of minimal points or the size of the constraints become unmanageable after few iterations. Symbolic state explosion is the counterpart of the state explosion problem we known from finite-state verification.

In our previous work [DR00] we proposed a new *rich assertional language*, in the terminology of [KMM+97], for representing compactly upward-closed sets of markings. Our data structure, we will call here *Covering Sharing Trees* (CSTs), are *directed graphs* in which we store the minimal points of an upward-closed set as a collection of tuples, and for which we allow the maximal sharing of prefixes and suffixes. To obtain efficient operations, it is crucial to avoid enumerating the paths of a CST. Working on the graph structure of CSTs, we defined all operations needed for lifting the backward reachability algorithm of [ACJT96] to the symbolic level. In the preliminary results given in [DR00], we managed to prove properties of Petri Nets (of small size) that could not be managed from other infinite-state model checkers (working backwards) like HyTech [HHW97].

Following our line of research, the *conceptual contribution* of this paper is a *new* heuristic rule for attacking symbolic state explosion based on the combination of CSTs and well known techniques for the static analysis of Petri Nets. More precisely, the heuristic rule is based on *structural properties* [STC98] of Petri Nets, i.e., on a *fully automatic* static analysis, whose results can be used during the backward reachability algorithm to significantly cut the search space. As the other techniques presented in [DR00], our structural heuristic works in polynomial time on the graph structure of CSTs. When combined with our CSTs-symbolic representation, the heuristic rule allow us to scale up the dimension of the case-studies of one order of magnitude.

As *practical contribution*, we describe a set of benchmarks we obtained with an optimized implementation of the CST-library, integrated with the above mentioned structural heuristic. We have applied the resulting model checking algorithm to a large set of examples of parameterized verification problems that can be solved using decision procedures for coverability of Petri Nets (e.g. mutual exclusion for the parametric models like the Mesh and Multipoll examples of [ABC+95,MC99], and semi-liveness for the PNCSA protocol of [Fin93]). We have also applied our method to verify safety properties of *finite-state* systems (e.g. some of the above mentioned examples for fixed values of the parameter). For these examples, we have compared our results with the results obtained with the specialized tool GreatSPN [CFGR95] for computing the reachability set of Petri Nets. As foreseen by Bultan in [Bul00], in most of the cases proving a parameterized property turns out to be more efficient than proving its finite-state instances.

Before entering in more details, in Section 2 we will briefly recall the main ideas behind the connection between parameterized systems, Petri Nets, backward reachability, and in Section 3 the basics of CSTs. The new heuristic rule is presented in Section 4. The new symbolic algorithm is presented in Section 5;

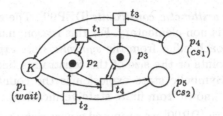

Fig. 1. An example of Petri Net with parametric initial marking $\langle K, 1, 1, 0, 0 \rangle$, $K \geq 1$.

its practical evaluation is presented in Section 6. We finish the paper discussing related works and drawing some conclusions.

2 Petri Nets and Verification of Safety Properties

Following [GS92], asynchronous concurrent systems (possibly with internal states modeled via Boolean variables [BCR01]) can be naturally represented as Petri Nets in which places and transitions are used to model *local states*, *internal actions* and communication via *rendez-vous*. At this level of abstraction, processes can be viewed as undistinguishable black *tokens*. A *marking* $m = \langle m_1, \ldots, m_n \rangle$, a mapping from places to *non-negative* integers, can be viewed as an abstraction of a *global system state* in which we only keep track of the number of processes in every state. The number of processes in the system is determined by the *initial marking* m_0. The *backward reachability* approach for verification of safety properties of Petri Nets is based on the following notions, taken from [ACJT96,FS01]. Given $m = \langle m_1, \ldots, m_n \rangle$ and $m' = \langle m'_1, \ldots, m'_n \rangle$, we say that $m \preccurlyeq m'$ (m' is *subsumed* by m) if and only if $m_i \leq m'_i$ for $i : 1, \ldots, n$. A set of markings U is upward-closed if for any $m \in U$ and any m' such that $m \preccurlyeq m'$, we have that $m' \in U$. Any upward-closed sets in $\mathbb{N}^m$ can be finitely represented by its *finite set* of *minimal points*, we will call $gen(U)$.

The relation $\preccurlyeq$ is a *well-quasi ordering*. This property ensures the termination of backward reachability, whenever the starting point of the exploration is an upward-closed set of markings. As an example, consider the Petri Net of Fig. 1, a monitor for a parameterized system with two mutually exclusive critical sections (cs_1 and cs_2). Initially, all K processes are in p_1. To enter cs_1, a process tests for the presence of processes in cs_2 using p_2, and locks cs_1 using p_3 (transition t_1), and vice versa. Processes leave the critical section using transitions t_3 and t_4. Note that the set U of violations to mutual exclusion is the *upward-closed* set generated by the *minimal violations* $\langle 0, 0, 0, 2, 0 \rangle$, $\langle 0, 0, 0, 0, 2 \rangle$, and $\langle 0, 0, 0, 1, 1 \rangle$ (*at least* 2 tokens in $p_4 + p_5$). To prove that the protocol guarantees *mutual exclusion* for *any* value of K, it is enough to show that no admissible initial marking is in the set of *predecessor* markings $\mathsf{Pre}^*(U)$ of U (Pre is the operator that returns the set of markings that reach some marking in U by *firing* a transition). To compute $\mathsf{Pre}^*(U)$, we iterate the application of the predecessor operator Pre until we reach a fixpoint. During the computation, every newly generated mark-

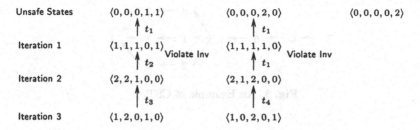

Fig. 2. Backward Reachability Graph.

ing is stored only if it is *not subsumed* by an already visited one. The backward reachability graph of our example is given in Fig. 2 (ignore the annotations for the moment). In Fig. 2 we have omitted all redundant markings (about 30). As mentioned in the introduction, the symbolic backward approach based on the enumeration of minimal points of sets of markings suffers from the symbolic state explosion problem. More sophisticated data structures are necessary to make the approach feasible in practice.

3 The Assertional Language: Covering Sharing Trees

In [DR00], we studied the mathematical foundations of Covering Sharing Trees (CSTs), a new data structure to symbolically manipulate upward-closed sets. CSTs are based on the Sharing Trees of [ZL94]. A k-sharing tree $\mathbf{S}$ is a rooted acyclic graph with nodes partitioned in k-*layers* (apart from the special *root* and *end* nodes) $N = \{root\} \cup N_1 \cup \ldots \cup N_k \cup \{end\}$, successor relation $succ : N \rightsquigarrow 2^N$, and labeling function $val : N \rightsquigarrow \mathbb{Z} \cup \{\top, \bot\}$, such that: (1) all nodes of layer i have successors in the layer $i+1$; (2) a node cannot have two successors with the same label; (3) two nodes with the same label in the same layer do not have the same set of successors. The *flat denotation* of a sharing tree is defined as follows

$$elem(\mathbf{S}) = \{\langle val(n_1), \ldots, val(n_k)\rangle \mid \langle \top, n_1, \ldots, n_k, \bot\rangle \text{ is a path of } \mathbf{S}\}.$$

Conditions (2) and (3) ensure the maximal sharing of prefixes and suffixes among the tuples of the flat denotation of a sharing tree. The *size* of a sharing tree is the number of *nodes* and *edges*. The number of tuples in $elem(\mathbf{S})$ can be exponentially larger than the size of $\mathbf{S}$. As shown in [ZL94], given a set of tuples $\mathcal{A}$ of size k, there exists a unique (modulo isomorphisms of graphs) sharing tree such that $elem(\mathbf{S}_\mathcal{A}) = \mathcal{A}$. A CST is a sharing tree obtained by lifting the denotation of a sharing tree from the flat one of [ZL94] to the following *rich* one

$$cones(\mathbf{S}) = \{m \mid n \preccurlyeq m, \ n \in elem(\mathbf{S})\}.$$

Given an upward closed set of markings U, we define the CST $\mathbf{S}_U$ as the k-sharing tree such that $elem(\mathbf{S}_U) = gen(U)$. Thus, $\mathbf{S}_U$ can be used to *compactly* represent $gen(U)$, and to *finitely* represent U. In the best case the size of $\mathbf{S}_U$ is

$$
\top \;\to\; 0 \;\to\; 0 \;\to\; 0 \;\Big\langle\;
\begin{array}{c}
0 \to 2 \\
1 \to 1 \\
2 \to 0
\end{array}
\;\Big\rangle\; \to\; \bot
$$

Fig. 3. An Example of CST.

logarithmic in the size of $gen(U)$. A CST $\mathbf{S}_U$ can also be viewed as a compact representation of the formula: $\bigvee_{m\in elem(\mathbf{S}_U)} (x_1 \geq m_1 \wedge \ldots \wedge x_n \geq m_n)$. As an example, the CST $\mathbf{S}$ that symbolically represents the set of violations of our example is given in Fig. 3. Let us note that any $\mathbf{S}'$, such that $gen(U) \subseteq elem(\mathbf{S}')$ and such that all additional elements are *redundant* (i.e., are subsumed by elements in $gen(U)$) can still be used to represent U. We will call such a CST *redundant*. In the following we will show that it is often more efficient to work with redundant CSTs. In [DR00], we have defined the operations needed to implement a CST-based backward reachability procedure. The operations work on the graph structure of CSTs. In the following we will use $Union_{CST}(\mathbf{S}, \mathbf{T})$ to indicate the CST whose denotation is $cones(\mathbf{S}) \cup cones(\mathbf{T})$, and $\mathsf{Pre}_{CST}(\mathbf{S}, t)$ to indicate the CST whose denotation is $cones(\mathsf{Pre}(cones(\mathbf{S}), t))$ for some transition t. Checking subsumption between CSTs, namely whether $cones(\mathbf{S}) \subseteq cones(\mathbf{T})$ holds, the complexity of this test is CO-NP hard (event if the two CSTs are not redundant). In [DR00], we have defined a set of *polynomial time* sufficient conditions (with different precision) to check subsumption for CSTs, based on *simulation relations* between *nodes* of the corresponding sharing trees. Formally, a node n in the i-th layer of $\mathbf{S}$ is forward-simulated by node m in the i-th layer of $\mathbf{T}$ if and only if $val(n) \geq val(m)$ and for every successor node n' of n there exists a successor m' of m that forward-simulates n'. If the the root node of $\mathbf{S}$ is forward simulated by the root node of $\mathbf{T}$ than $\mathbf{S}$ is subsumed $\mathbf{T}$. Similar definitions and properties can be given for backward and mixed forward-backward simulations. The operations Pre_{CST} and $Union_{CST}$ do not guarantee to generate CSTs that contain *only* the minimal points. However, removing all redundancies is CO-NP hard. As shown in [DR00], simulation relations helped us again to obtain polynomial algorithms to partially eliminate redundancies. (As a technical remark, we point out that these techniques allow us to remove tuples of a given CST that are subsumed either by tuples of *another* CST or by tuples of the *same* CST.) Unfortunately, CST and simulation-based heuristics are not enough to mitigate symbolic state explosion. New heuristics for pruning backward search seem necessary in order to handle large examples.

4   Structural Heuristic

In the backward reachability approach, every place of a Petri Net is initially considered as *unbounded* (in fact, unsafe states are expressed via constraints like $x_1 \geq c_1$, etc.). In many practical cases however, some places are bounded for *any value* of the parameters in the initial configuration. The *Structural Theory* of Petri Nets [STC98] can help us to distinguish between bounded and unbounded places. Let N be a Petri Net with n places, m transitions, and *token flow matrix* $\mathbf{C}$ ($\mathbf{C}$ describes how tokens are moved in the net by the transitions; rows corresponds to places, and columns to transitions). Furthermore, let $\cdot$ denote the vector product $a^T \cdot b = a_1 b_1 + \dots a_n b_n$, where a^T indicates the transpose of vector a. *Place invariants* [STC98] are one of the possible informations we can compute via a static analysis of N. A place invariant (also called P-semiflow) is a vector $p = \langle p_1, \dots, p_n \rangle$ (non-negative) solution of the equation

$$x^T \cdot \mathbf{C} = 0, \; x \geq 0,$$

where x is a vector of variables of dimension n. Given an initial marking m_0, and a place invariant p, the set $\mathcal{O}(m_0, p) = \{m \mid p^T \cdot m = p^T \cdot m_0\}$ over-approximates the reachability set of the Petri Net. This property follows from the definition of place invariant, and from the state equation $m = m_0 + \mathbf{C} \cdot \sigma$ that characterizes a generic marking m reachable from m_0 via the sequence of transitions represented by the firing vector σ (see [STC98]). As a consequence, the equation

$$p^T \cdot x = p^T \cdot m_0$$

for some place invariant p gives us a *structural invariant* we can use to analyze the net. Let us consider our running example. The three following equations are invariants of the net in Fig. 1 with the parametric initial marking $\langle K, 1, 1, 0, 0 \rangle$: (i) $x_2 + x_5 = 1$, (ii) $x_3 + x_4 = 1$, (iii) $x_1 + x_4 + x_5 = K$. Unfortunately, the invariants are not sufficient to prove our mutual exclusion property $x_4 + x_5 \leq 1$. Still the invariants contain information that we can exploit during the backward search. A possible way to use the structural analysis would be to make what is usually called *program specialization*, i.e., we can replace the subnet involving places linked by structural invariants (e.g. p_2, p_5 for $x_2 + x_5 = 1$) with a control part (a finite-state automata). This way however, the net resulting from the specialization may become of unmanageable size. As an alternative, we propose to use the structural invariants directly as heuristics for efficient backward reachability.

4.1   Pruning the Backward Search Space

Let U be an upward-closed set of markings denoting *unsafe states*, and let $U' = U \cap \mathcal{O}(m_0, p)$ for some place invariant p. We first note that if $U' = \emptyset$, then we can immediately infer that the net is *safe*. However, as in our example, invariants might not be sufficient to directly verify the property. We will use them to prune the backward search as follows. Let us consider again our running example and the backward reachability graph of fig. 2. After the first iteration, two generators $\langle 1, 1, 1, 0, 1 \rangle$ and $\langle 1, 1, 1, 1, 0 \rangle$ that are not subsumed by previous elements are computed. The first generator defines a set of markings that has no intersection with the set of markings defined by the invariant $x_2 + x_5 = 1$, while the second generator defines a set of markings that have no intersection

$$\top \xrightarrow[1]{\ (0,1)\ } \xrightarrow[1]{\ (0,1)\ } \xrightarrow[1]{\ (1,0)\ } \begin{array}{c}(1,1)\\ \cdots\end{array}$$

Fig. 4. The CST S denoting $Pre_{CST}(\mathbf{S})$, where S is given in Fig. 3.

with the set of markings defined by the invariant $x_3 + x_4 = 1$. As a consequence, we deduce that no markings defined by those two generators can be reached from an instance of the parametrized initial marking (recall that the markings satisfying the invariant over-approximate the set of reachable markings.) As a consequence, we can stop the backward search after the first iteration instead of having to consider 3 iterations as in the naive search. Let us now examine how we can incorporate this idea in our CST-based backward search. Since U' is not upward-closed, it cannot be used as the starting point of our symbolic backward search. The following theorem however gives us indications on how to proceed.

Theorem 1. *Given a Petri Net N with initial marking m_0, a place invariant p, and an upward-closed set of markings U represented by a CST $\mathbf{S}$, suppose $cone(m) \cap \mathcal{O}(m_0, p) = \emptyset$ for some $m \in elem(\mathbf{S})$. Furthermore, let $\mathbf{S}'$ be the CST such that $elem(\mathbf{S}') = elem(\mathbf{S}) \setminus \{m\}$, and m_0' be any instance of m_0. Then,*

$$m_0' \in \text{Pre}^*(cones(\mathbf{S})) \ \textit{iff} \ m_0' \in \text{Pre}^*(cones(\mathbf{S}')).$$

The theorem shows that during the computation of $\text{Pre}^*(U)$ we can prune the search space by *safely* removing *all* elements $m \in elem(\mathbf{S}_U)$ (redundant or not) such that $cone(m)$ has empty intersection with the set of markings defined by a structural invariant. We call such elements *useless*. To prune the space efficiently, we must avoid the explicit enumeration of all elements stored in a CST. In fact, the number of those elements is potentially exponential in the size of the CST. Instead of trying to remove all the useless elements for a give invariant p, we use an *heuristic* rule that works directly on the graph structure of the CST and does not enumerate its paths. To describe the heuristic rule, we need the following definitions. Let $\mathbf{S}$ be a CST , and let $e = (\mathbf{v}, \mathbf{w})$ be an edge of $\mathbf{S}$ connecting nodes of two adjacent layers. We define $elem_e(\mathbf{S})$ as the set of tuples from $elem(\mathbf{S})$ denoted by paths of $\mathbf{S}$ passing through e. Formally, $m = \langle val(v_1), \ldots, val(v_n) \rangle \in elem_e(\mathbf{S})$ iff there exists a path $\langle \top, v_1, \ldots, \mathbf{v}, \mathbf{w}, \ldots, v_n, \bot \rangle$ in $\mathbf{S}$ such that $e = (\mathbf{v}, \mathbf{w})$. Consider now a *structural invariant*, say $\mathcal{I}$, having the form $p^T \cdot x = p^T \cdot m_0$, where p is a place invariant (hence, $p \succcurlyeq 0$) and, such that $p^T \cdot m_0$ is an integer, i.e., $p^T \cdot m_0$ does not contain occurrences of the parameters (e.g. we keep $x_2 + x_5 = 1$ and $x_3 + x_4 = 1$, and discharge $x_1 + x_4 + x_5 = K$). Our heuristic rule works by removing an edge e of $\mathbf{S}$, whenever we can prove that the elements in $elem_e(\mathbf{S})$ denote cones that do not intersect with the structural invariant $\mathcal{I}$. To check this condition on the edge e connecting a node of layer i and a node of layer $i + 1$, we first compute the two values $min_{\prec}(e)$ and $min_{\succ}(e)$

defined as follows: $min_{\prec}(e)$ is the minimal value of *prefixes* $\langle m_1, \ldots, m_i \rangle$ of tuples in $elem_e(\mathbf{S})$ evaluated on the function $\boldsymbol{x} \rightsquigarrow \boldsymbol{p}^T \cdot \boldsymbol{x}$; symmetrically, $min_{\succ}(e)$ is computed for *suffixes* $\langle m_{i+1}, \ldots, m_n \rangle$. Specifically, we define

$$min_{\prec}(e) = min \{ \boldsymbol{p}^T \cdot \langle m_1, \ldots, m_i, 0, \ldots, 0 \rangle \mid \langle m_1, \ldots, m_n \rangle \in elem_e(\mathbf{S}) \},$$
$$min_{\succ}(e) = min \{ \boldsymbol{p}^T \cdot \langle 0, \ldots, 0, m_{i+1}, \ldots, m_n \rangle \mid \langle m_1, \ldots, m_n \rangle \in elem_e(\mathbf{S}) \}.$$

The following two properties characterize our heuristic rule.

Theorem 2. *Given the initial marking* $\boldsymbol{m_0}$, *the CST* $\mathbf{S}$, *the structural property* $\boldsymbol{p}^T \cdot \boldsymbol{x} = \boldsymbol{p}^T \cdot \boldsymbol{m_0}$, *and the edge* e *of* $\mathbf{S}$, *if* $min_{\prec}(e) + min_{\succ}(e) > \boldsymbol{p}^T \cdot \boldsymbol{m_0}$, *then* $cone(m) \cap \mathcal{O}(\boldsymbol{m_0}, \boldsymbol{p}) = \emptyset$ *for any* $m \in elem_e(\mathbf{S})$

Theorem 3. *Given a CST* $\mathbf{S}$, *an edge* e, *and the invariant* $\boldsymbol{p}^T \cdot \boldsymbol{x} = \boldsymbol{p}^T \cdot \boldsymbol{m_0}$ *such that* $\boldsymbol{p}^T \cdot \boldsymbol{m_0} \in \mathbb{Z}$, *there exists a polynomial time algorithm that computes the values* $min_{\prec}(e)$ *and* $min_{\succ}(e)$.

Based on the previous property, we can devise a procedure to heuristically cut the CSTs produced during the backward search. As an example of application of the structural heuristic, consider the CST of fig. 4. The CST $\mathbf{S}$ contains the elements obtained at iteration 1, the pairs of values on the arcs are the values $min_{\prec}(e)$ and $min_{\succ}(e)$ for the place invariant $x_2 + x_5 = 1$, the dashed edges can be removed and thus the useless element $\langle 1, 1, 1, 0, 1 \rangle$ is removed from the CST. Note that if we use the invariant $x_3 + x_4 = 1$ then the last element can also be eliminated. The heuristic rule simply traverses a CST layer by layer, removing all edges that satisfy the hypothesis of Theorem 2. To complete the scenario, we need to compute automatically the structural invariants. This can be done using specialized libraries to compute place invariants like the one available with GreatSPN [CFGR95].

5   Symbolic Backward Reachability

The three main problems we had to solve to obtain an efficient CST-based backward reachability algorithms were: (1) avoid to generate too many redundant elements during the fixpoint computation; (2) use an efficient fixpoint test using sufficient conditions for CST-subsumption; (3) remove useless elements (elements that cannot be reached from the given initial state). As a practical solution to those problems, we propose the algorithm of Fig. 5. The algorithm uses simulation-based heuristics to remove redundancies and for testing subsumption between CSTs, in combination with the heuristic rule proposed in the previous section. Let us give some more detail on the algorithm of Fig. 5. The variable $\mathbf{S}$ stores the current *frontier* of the breadth-first performed by the algorithm. The variable $\mathbf{T}$ stores the set of visited generators. Before entering the main loop, we need to test subsumption between $\mathbf{S}$ and $\mathbf{T}$. For this purpose, the following heuristic seems to work well in practice. We first compute the forward and backward simulation relations between the nodes of $\mathbf{S}$ and the nodes of $\mathbf{T}$. If the root of $\mathbf{S}$ is forward simulated by the root of $\mathbf{T}$ or if the end node of $\mathbf{S}$ is backward

Proc $\text{Pre}^*_{CST}(\mathbf{S}_U : CST)$
    $\mathbf{S} := \mathbf{S}_U;\ \ \mathbf{T} := empty_{CST};$
    while $not(Subsumes_{CST}(\mathbf{T}, \mathbf{S}))$ **do**
        $\mathbf{T} := Union_{CST}(\mathbf{T}, \mathbf{S});\ \ \mathbf{R} := empty_{CST};$
        for each $transition\ t$ **do**
            $\mathbf{N} := \text{Pre}_{CST}(\mathbf{S}, t);$
            $structural\_reduction_{CST}(\mathbf{N});$
            $remove\_redundancies_{CST}(\mathbf{N}, \mathbf{R}, \mathbf{T});$
            $minimize_{CST}(\mathbf{N});$
            $\mathbf{R} := Union_{CST}(\mathbf{N}, \mathbf{R});$
        $\mathbf{S} := \mathbf{R};$
    return $\mathbf{T};$

Fig. 5. The CST-Based Symbolic Model Checking Algorithm.

simulated by the end node of $\mathbf{T}$, then we know that all the generators of $\mathbf{S}$ are subsumed by some generators of $\mathbf{T}$ (see [DR00]), thus the fixpoint is reached. If the test fails, we perform a depth-first, top-down visit of the CST $\mathbf{S}$ in order to compare its tuples with those of $\mathbf{T}$. During the depth-first visit, we use however the information previously computed via the forward simulation as follows. Each time we reach a node n that is forward simulated by a node of $\mathbf{T}$, we stop the exploration: all the elements in the subtree rooted at n will be subsumed by elements of $\mathbf{T}$. In the main loop, we compute the new frontier $\mathbf{N}$ transition by transition via the symbolic operator $\text{Pre}_{CST}(\mathbf{S}, t)$. In order to keep the size of $\mathbf{N}$ small, after computing $\text{Pre}_{CST}(\mathbf{S}, t)$, we first apply the new heuristic rule (via the function $structural\_reduction_{CST}$), and then we apply simulation-based heuristics to remove redundancies. The function $remove\_redundancies_{CST}(\mathbf{N}, \mathbf{R}, \mathbf{T})$ uses simulation relations between nodes of $\mathbf{N}$ and nodes of $\mathbf{R}$ (the CST collecting the generators created via all transitions) and $\mathbf{T}$; the function $minimize_{CST}(\mathbf{N})$ uses simulation relations of nodes of $\mathbf{N}$. We discuss the practical evaluation of the resulting algorithm in the following section.

6 Experimental Results

Based on a new optimized implementation of the CST-library presented in [DR00], and using the library for computing *minimal* place invariants (a system of generators for the positive solutions of $x^T \cdot \mathbf{C} = 0$) coming with GreatSPN [CFGR95], we have implemented the algorithm of Fig. 5 and tested on several types of verification problems expressible in terms of *coverability* of markings for Petri Nets. The parameters taken into considerations in our evaluation are listed in Fig. 6.

Parameterized Problems. More precisely, we have considered *mutual exclusion* properties for the parameterized, concurrent and production systems like the Multipoll of [MC99], the Mesh 2x2 of [ABC+95] (Fig. 130, p. 256), its extension to the 3x2 case, the CSM of [ABC+95] (Fig. 76, p. 154), and for an extension

Size of the Petri Net
  P=Number of places;
  T = Number of transitions.
Verification problem (VP) (only the type of property)
  ME=Mutual exclusion property;
  C=Covering for a random marking;
  SL=Semi-liveness.
Use of heuristics
  I=Invariant-based reductions (structural heuristic rule);
  S=Simulation-based reductions.
Statistics: execution
  EX=Execution time (in seconds) on an AMD Athlon 900 Mhz;
  NI=N. of iterations before termination (with *=before stopping the execution).
Quality of analysis
  R=An initial state has been reached.
Statistics: use of memory
  MaxE(N)=N. of *elements* (*nodes*) of the biggest CST associated to S of Fig. 5;
  NE(N)=Number of *elements* (*nodes*) of the CST for the fixpoint;
Ratio of memory saving (using CSTs)
  RM=MAX-N/(MAX-E × P) in pct.;
  RN=NN/(NE × P) in pct.

Fig. 6. Parameters of the Experimental Evaluation.

of the Readers-Writers example given in [Rei86] in which we use several buffers with 45 slots. Furthermore, we have considered *semi-liveness* and *coverability* problems for the PNCSA communication protocol analyzed in [BF99,Fin93]. The experimental results are listed in Fig. 7. We performed every example either enabling or disabling the structural heuristic rule and the reductions based on simulation relations. As shown in Fig. 7, the heuristics turned out to be fundamental to ensure termination in reasonable time for most of the examples. To compare our results with other infinite-state systems, we ran some of the parameterized examples like CSM and Mesh using the efficient model checker based on polyhedra (i.e. constraint solver over the reals) HyTech [HHW97]. In the experiments on the largest examples (using backward analysis) HyTech was still computing after more than *one day.*

Finite-state Problems. After having fixed the value of the parameter K in the initial marking, we have also tested some case-studies using the specialized Petri Net tool GreatSPN [CFGR95]. GreatSPN uses efficient encodings of markings and simplification rules that reduce the input net to produce the *reachability set* of *bounded* Petri Nets. We performed our experiments on a Pentium 133Mhz measuring the value of K from which GreatSPN is *not able* to compute the entire reachability graph: $K = 3$ for the Mesh 2x2; $K = 9$ for Multipoll, and $K = 115$ for CSM. In contrast, as shown in Fig. 7, we managed to verify mutual exclusion properties for any value of K (assuming $K \geq 1$ in the initial marking) with the following execution times: 1.26s for Mesh 2x2; 1.05s and 324s for Multipoll; and

0.04s for CSM. As already noticed by Bultan in other case-studies [Bul00], lifting a verification problem from the *finite-state* to the *parameterized* case can make its solution easier! Also note that the use of invariants makes the backward analysis sensible to the initial marking. This effect is clear looking at the execution times obtained using different values for K for the Mesh2x2 in Fig. 7 (e.g., we found more useful invariants for $K = 1$ than for $K \geq 1$).

Finally, we have also considered safety properties for *non-parametric examples* (i.e., where it makes no sense to put parameters in the initial marking) like the classical Peterson's and Lamport's mutual exclusion algorithms [MC99,EM00]. As a result, we managed to prove safety properties for all these examples with negligible execution times.

7   Related Works and Conclusions

In this paper we have presented new heuristic rule, based on the structural theory of Petri Nets, to be used in the backward approach of [ACJT96,FS01]. Efficient algorithms allow us to apply the heuristic rule avoiding the enumeration of the minimal points of upward-closed sets generated in the computation of Pre*. This way, we manage to mitigate the symbolic state explosion in practical examples we did not manage to handle with previous *backward* technology. With the set of benchmarks of Fig. 7, we hope it will be possible to establish connections with other recent attempts of attacking symbolic state explosion [AN00,BLP+99]. The combination of structural and enumerative techniques has been studied before in the context of *forward reachability*, where invariants are used as heuristic for efficient encodings of markings [CFGR95,PCP99]. Structural properties are also used to statically compute over-approximations of the reachability set of a Petri Net [EM00,STC98]. We are not aware of previous attempts of combining structural heuristics and backward reachability.

References

[ABC+95]   M. Ajmone Marsan, G. Balbo, G. Conte, S. Donatelli, and G. Franceschinis. *Modelling with Generalized Stochastic Petri Nets.* Series in Parallel Computing. John Wiley & Sons, 1995.

[AN00]   P. A. Abdulla and A. Nylén. Better is Better than Well: On Efficient Verification of Infinite-State Systems. In *Proc. LICS 2000*, pages 132-140, 2000.

[ACJT96]   P. A. Abdulla, K. Ceräns, B. Jonsson and Y.-K. Tsay. General Decidability Theorems for Infinite-State Systems. In *Proc. LICS '96*, pages 313–321, 1996.

[BCR01]   T. Ball, S. Chaki, S. K. Rajamani. Parameterized Verification of Multi-threaded Software Libraries. MSR Technical Report 2000-116. In *Proc. TACAS 2001*, LNCS 2031, pages 158-173, 2001.

[BLP+99]   G. Behrmann, K. G. Larsen, J. Pearson, C. Weise, and W. Yi. Efficient Timed Reachability Analysis Using Clock Difference Diagrams. In *Proc. CAV '99*, LNCS 1633, pages 341–353, 1999.

[BF99]   B. Bérard and L. Fribourg. Reachability analysis of (timed) Petri nets using
            real arithmeti In *Proc. CONCUR '99*, LNCS 1664, pages 178-193, 1999.
[BM99]   A. Bouajjani, and R. Mayr. Model Checking Lossy Vector Addition Sys-
            tems. In *Proc. STACS '99*, LNCS 1563, pages 323-333, 1999.
[Bul00]   T. Bultan. BDD vs. Constraint-Based Model Checking: An Experimental
            Evaluation for Asynchronous Concurrent Systems. In *Proc. TACAS 2000*,
            LNCS 1785, pages 441-455, 2000.
[BGP97]   T. Bultan, R. Gerber, and W. Pugh. Symbolic Model Checking of Infinite-
            state Systems using Presburger Arithmetics. In *Proc. CAV '97*, LNCS 1254,
            pages 400–411, 1997.
[CFGR95]   G. Chiola, G. Franceschinis, R. Gaeta, and M. Ribaudo. GreatSPN 1.7:
            Graphical Editor and Analyzer for Timed and Stochastic Petri Nets. *Per-
            formance Evaluation*, 24(1-2), pages 47-68, 1995.
[Del00]   G. Delzanno. Automatic Verification of Parameterized Cache Coherence
            Protocols. In *Proc. CAV 2000*, LNCS 1855, pages 53–68, 1996.
[DEP99]   G. Delzanno, J. Esparza, and A. Podelski. Constraint-based Analysis of
            Broadcast Protocols. In *Proc. CSL '99*, LNCS 1683, pag. 50–66, 1999.
[DR00]   G. Delzanno, and J. F. Raskin. Symbolic Representation of Upward-closed
            Sets. In *Proc. TACAS 2000*, LNCS 1785, pages 426-440, 2000.
[EN98]   E. A. Emerson and K. S. Namjoshi. On Model Checking for Non-
            deterministic Infinite-state Systems. In *Proc. LICS '98*, pages 70–80, 1998.
[EFM99]   J. Esparza, A. Finkel, and R. Mayr. On the Verification of Broadcast
            Protocols. In *Proc. LICS '99*, pages 352–359, 1999.
[EM00]   J. Esparza and S. Melzer. Verification of safety properties using integer pro-
            gramming: Beyond the state equation. Formal Methods in System Design,
            16:159-189, 2000.
[Fin93]   A. Finkel. The minimal coverability graph for Petri nets. In In *Advances
            in Petri Nets '93*, LNCS 674, pages 210-243. Springer, 1993.
[FS01]   A. Finkel and P. Schnoebelen. Well-structured transition systems every-
            where! *Theoretical Computer Science*, 256(1-2):63-92, 2001.
[GS92]   S. M. German, A. P. Sistla. Reasoning about Systems with Many Processes.
            JACM 39(3): 675–735 (1992)
[HHW97]   T. A. Henzinger, P.-H. Ho, and H. Wong-Toi. HyTech: a Model Checker
            for Hybrid Systems. In *Proc. CAV '97*, LNCS 1254, pages 460–463, 1997.
[KMM⁺97]   Y. Kesten, O. Maler, M. Marcus, A. Pnueli, E. Shahar. Symbolic Model
            Checking with Rich Assertional Languages. In *Proc. CAV '97*, LNCS 1254,
            pages 424–435, 1997.
[MC99]   A. Miner, and G. Ciardo. Efficient Reachability Set Generation and Storage
            using Decision Diagrams. In *Proc. of ICATPN '99*, pages 6-25, 1999.
[PCP99]   E. Pastor, J. Cortadella, M. A. Peña. Structural Methods to Improve the
            Symbolic Analysis of Petri Nets. In *Proc. ICATPN '99*, LNCS 1639, pages
            26-45. Springer, 1999.
[Rei86]   W. Reisig. Petri Nets. An introduction. EATCS Monographs on Theoretical
            Computer Science, Springer 1986.
[STC98]   M. Silva, E. Teruel, and J. M. Colom. Linear Algebraic and Linear Pro-
            gramming Techniques for Analysis of Place/Transition Net Systems. In
            W. Reisig and G. Rozenberg, editors. Lectures on Petri Nets I: Basic Mod-
            els. *Advances in Petri Nets*, LNCS 1491, pages 308-309. Springer, 1998.
[ZL94]   D. Zampuniéris, and B. Le Charlier. Efficient Handling of Large Sets of
            Tuples with Sharing Trees. In *Proceedings of the Data Compressions Con-
            ference (DCC'95)*, 1995.

CST-Based Symbolic Backward Reachability: Practical Evaluation

Case-study	P	T	VP	I	S	EX(sec)	NI	R	MAX-E	MAX-N	RM	NE	NN	RN
Ex-Fig. $1_{K \geq 1}$	5	4	ME	✓	✓	0.00	1		1	7	140	1	7	140
Ex-Fig. $1_{K \geq 1}$	5	4	ME		✓	0.02	4		4	17	85	9	29	64.4
Ex-Fig. $1_{K \geq 1}$	5	4	ME			0.01	4		7	22	62.9	15	32	42.7
Ex-Fig. $1_{K \geq 1}$	5	4	ME	✓		0.00	1		1	7	140	1	7	140
$CSM_{K \geq 1}$	14	13	ME	✓	✓	0.08	9		15	73	35	70	68	7
$CSM_{K \geq 1}$	14	13	ME		✓	0.19	11		29	115	28	152	109	5
$CSM_{K \geq 1}$	14	13	ME			39.25	11		33737	7342	1	25220	4680	1
$CSM_{K=2}$	14	13	ME	✓	✓	0.08	9		15	73	35	70	68	7
$CSM_{K=75}$	14	13	ME	✓	✓	0.08	9		15	73	35	70	68	7
$CSM_{K=115}$	14	13	ME	✓	✓	0.08	9		15	73	35	70	68	7
Multip.$_{K \geq 1}$	18	21	ME		✓	2.98	18		881	435	3	5641	196	0.2
Multip.$_{K \geq 1}$	18	21	ME			>20000	18*		8544367	60922	0.04	–	–	–
Multip.$_{K \geq 1}$	18	21	ME		✓	117.21	21		9416	2404	1	77015	652	0.04
Multip.$_{K=1}$	18	21	ME	✓	✓	1.96	18		649	341	2.9	4361	140	0.2
Multip.$_{K=4}$	18	21	ME	✓	✓	3.06	18		881	435	2.7	5641	196	0.2
Multip.$_{K=9}$	18	21	ME	✓	✓	3.06	18		881	435	2.7	5641	196	0.2
Mesh2x2$_{K \geq 1}$	32	32	ME	✓	✓	1.11	15		54	340	20	429	277	2
Mesh2x2$_{K \geq 1}$	32	32	ME		✓	1.14	15		54	340	20	429	294	2
Mesh2x2$_{K \geq 1}$	32	32	ME	✓	✓	7.37	20		272	921	11	2138	935	1
Mesh2x2$_{K \geq 1}$	32	32	ME		✓	9.34	20		342	951	9	2418	1157	1
Mesh2x2$_{K \geq 1}$	32	32	ME		✓	16.65	16		282	1367	15	2130	1741	2
Mesh2x2$_{K \geq 1}$	32	32	ME	✓		>20000	14*		433665	105607	1	–	–	–
Mesh2x2$_{K=1}$	32	32	ME	✓	✓	0.69	13		30	272	28	211	326	5
Mesh2x2$_{K=2}$	32	32	ME	✓	✓	1.11	15		51	353	22	407	294	2
Mesh2x2$_{K=3}$	32	32	ME	✓	✓	1.11	15		54	340	20	429	277	2
Mesh3x2$_{K \geq 1}$	52	54	ME	✓	✓	11.18	21		335	1192	7	2441	1074	1
Mesh3x2$_{K \geq 1}$	52	54	ME		✓	12.06	21		343	1198	7	2447	1076	5
Mesh3x2$_{K=1}$	52	54	ME	✓	✓	8.4	21		153	1183	15	1159	1643	3
R/W$_{K \geq 1}$	24	22	ME	✓	✓	3215.34	122		12590	5911	2	29119	1936	0.3
R/W$_{K \geq 1}$	24	22	ME		✓	>20000	16*		160197	30941	1	–	–	–
R/W$_{K \geq 1}$	24	22	ME			>20000	9*		1239466	73724	0.2	–	–	–
R/W$_{K \geq 1}$	24	22	ME	✓		>20000	13*		1672064	122510	0.3	–	–	–
PNCSA	31	36	SL	✓	✓	0.98	10	✓	55	418	24	117	594	16
PNCSA	31	36	SL		✓	6.98	10	✓	268	1590	19	356	1744	16
PNCSA	31	36	C	✓	✓	52.6	33	✓	590	1604	9	604	751	4
PNCSA	31	36	C		✓	25871.28	33	✓	12495	8174	2	19435	10886	2
Peterson	14	12	ME	✓	✓	0.01	2		2	28	100	3	28	67
Peterson	14	12	ME		✓	0.18	9		36	118	23	181	169	7
Peterson	14	12	ME			23.12	9		15732	7212	0.3	12125	4331	2
Peterson	14	12	ME	✓		0.01	2		2	28	100	3	28	67
Lamport	11	9	ME	✓	✓	0.01	1		1	13	118	1	13	118
Lamport	11	9	ME		✓	0.08	10		16	66	37	57	80	13
Lamport	11	9	ME			1.09	10		4100	1864	4.1	4260	1396	2.9

Fig. 7. The experimental results have been obtained using an AMD Athlon 900 Mhz. The parameters of the evaluation are described in Fig. 6.

A Unifying Model Checking Approach for Safety Properties of Parameterized Systems

Monika Maidl

LFCS, University of Edinburgh
The Kings's Buildings, Edinburgh EH9 3JZ

Abstract. We present a model checking algorithm for safety properties that is applicable to parameterized systems and hence provides a unifying approach of model checking for parameterized systems. By analysing the conditions under which the proposed algorithm terminates, we obtain a characterisation of a subclass for which this problem is decidable. The known decidable subclasses, token rings and broadcast systems, fall in our subclass, while the main novel feature is that (unnested) quantification over index variables is allowed, which means that global guards can be expressed.

1 Introduction

We present a model checking algorithm for safety properties that is applicable to parameterized systems. A parameterized system is a family of systems, one for each instantiation of the parameter, where an instantiation by n is the composition of n copies of the system, and the verification problem consists in checking whether all instantiations fulfil a given property. Model checking for parameterized systems has been shown to be undecidable in general Suz88, so the problem can only be approached for subclasses or by semi-algorithmic methods. Solutions based on different technical frameworks have been proposed. Since our model checking algorithm is applicable to parameterized systems in general, it provides a unifying method for different subclasses.

By exploring under which restrictions the algorithm terminates, we obtain a characterisation of a class of parameterized systems for which model checking of safety properties is decidable. It turns out that the restrictions concern almost exclusively the way the copies communicate with each other: The admissible forms of communication are the very restricted synchronisation of token rings (no information exchanged between neighbours except "I have/have not the token") and the anonymous synchronisation of broadcast protocols. Another form of communication, using values of variables in neighbouring copies in guards or assignments like in the Dining Philosophers example, has to be restricted. We can however allow communication by global variables and by global guards, (expressed by universal quantification over index variables, which run over the instantiated copies). The latter is used e.g. in the Bakery algorithm, and in cache coherence protocols with a global condition considered in Del00, and extends the known subclasses of decidable systems.

G. Berry, H. Comon, and A. Finkel (Eds.): CAV 2001, LNCS 2102, pp. 311–323, 2001.

As specification logic, we consider a linear time logic built over state predicates that can contain index variables. We restrict ourselves to safety properties; liveness properties of broadcast protocols were shown to be undecidable in EFM99, so decidability of model-checking certainly does not extend to liveness properties for the whole class we characterise.

Related Work. Model checking for parameterized systems has been addressed by many researchers. One line of research is concerned with restrictions that, when imposed on parameterized systems, make model checking decidable for safety properties or even full temporal logic. The systems considered there are either token rings, like in EN95, or broadcast protocols, which were introduced in EN98 and also considered in EFM99; GS92 deals with a restricted form of broadcast protocols. Both types are subsumed by our subclass.

The approach for broadcast systems in EN98 and EFM99 falls under the paradigm of using well-ordered sets for the verification of infinite-state systems ACJT96. All sets that are considered are sets that are upward closed with respect to a well order. This means that all guards of transitions have to describe upward closed sets, which excludes certain global conditions, e.g. the one used in the cache coherence protocol that Delzanno considered in Del00.

Regular model checking, advocated by e.g. KMM$^+$97 and BW98, is based on representing sets of states by regular languages. Termination is obtained by applying some form of acceleration in order to compute the transitive closure of the transition relation BJNT00. Emphasis lies not on detecting decidable classes but providing general, not necessarily exact methods to handle a large class of systems. In this context, handling global guards was considered in ABJN00; our method provably terminates on the examples considered there. The main difference is that is our work is not based on acceleration techniques.

The specification language we use is rather general: The properties considered by EN95 had restricted number of quantified variables, and the properties for broadcast protocols considered in EN98; EFM99 can only express upward closed properties about numbers of processes being in a certain control state.

Overview. First we explain the types of parameterized systems we consider. The third section contains our model checking algorithm for ordinary systems, while in the fourth section it is adapted to parameterized systems, and the conditions under which the algorithm terminates are given. Missing proofs and details can be found in the full version at http://www.dcs.ed.ac.uk/~monika.

2   Framework

As program notation we use concurrent state-based guarded-command systems; a system is hence of form $(V, C_1, \ldots, C_n, I)$, where V is a set of variables, C_i are components and I is a predicate describing the initial states. A component consists of a set of transitions, where guards and assignments are built over boolean or enumerative variables or integer terms. More precisely, the terms occurring on the right-hand side of assignments are terms of Presburger arithmetic, enumerative constants or formulas of Presburger arithmetic[1], depending on the sort of the left-hand side of the assignment, and guards are formulas of *Presburger arithmetic*. The restriction to Presburger arithmetic, i.e. to multiplication only with constants, guarantees decidability. A step is defined by choosing some component and one of its transitions with a guard that is satisfied in the current state, and performing all assignments of this transition simultaneously. As an example of the program notation, consider Table 1, the well-known Bakery algorithm, in a version for 2 components.

Table 1. Program Text for the 2-Component Bakery Algorithm.

V: $c_1, c_2 : \{T, W, C\}$, $n_1, n_2 : NAT$
I: $c_1 = T \wedge c_2 = T \wedge n_1 = 0 \wedge n_2 = 0$

Component 1:	Component 2:
$c_1 = T \longrightarrow \left\langle \begin{array}{l} c_1 := W \\ n_1 := max(n_1, n_2) + 1 \end{array} \right\rangle$	$c_2 = T \longrightarrow \left\langle \begin{array}{l} c_2 := W \\ n_2 := max(n_1, n_2) + 1 \end{array} \right\rangle$
$c_1 = W \wedge$ $(n_2 = 0 \vee n_1 < n_2) \longrightarrow \langle c_1 := C \rangle$	$c_2 = W \wedge$ $(n_1 = 0 \vee n_2 < n_1) \longrightarrow \langle c_2 := C \rangle$
$c_1 = C \longrightarrow \left\langle \begin{array}{l} c_1 := T \\ n_1 := 0 \end{array} \right\rangle$	$c_2 = C \longrightarrow \left\langle \begin{array}{l} c_2 := T \\ n_2 := 0 \end{array} \right\rangle$

2.1 Parameterized Systems

Before describing our notion of parameterized systems, we first have to define their state language.

Definition 1 (Index Predicates). *Index terms are of form $j + k$ or k, where j is an index variable and k is an integer constant.*
Index predicates *are defined as follows:*

- *Basic index predicates are the formulas of Presburger arithmetic without quantification[2], where variables can (but need not) be indexed by index terms.*
- *We say that the index term $j + k$ occurs in the index predicate p if there is some variable y occurring in p in form $y[j + k]$.*
- *If p is a basic index predicate and $j_1, \ldots, j_n$ are index variables s.t. all index terms occurring in p that contain some j_i have constant 0, then*
  $$\forall j_1 \ldots \forall j_n (a \rightarrow p) \text{ and } \exists j_1 \cdots \exists j_n (a \wedge p)$$
  are index predicates, where a is a conjunction of expressions of form $j_i \neq k$ or $j_i \neq j + k$ for an index variable j.
- *Index predicates are closed under boolean operations.*

---

[1] For simplicity, we consider boolean variables and equations between enumerative variables also to be formulas of Presburger arithmetic.

[2] Since the system variables are intended to have finite domain, quantification over integer variables would not add expressive power.

The restriction to unnested quantification is used in the proof of Theorem 1, while the restriction that a quantified variable j can only occur in index terms without constants is necessary for termination of the model checking algorithm, more precisely to guarantee that no new index terms are generated by instantiating quantifiers.

Models of index predicates with respect to n consist of a valuation v for the occurring index variables in $\{0, \ldots, n-1\}$ and of a valuation s for the system variables, where for every indexed system variable y, s defines values for $y[0], \ldots, y[n-1]$. We write $s, v \models_n p$ if s and v form a model for p with respect to n.

A **parameterized system** $S = (V, C[i], I)$ differs from an ordinary system in that the transitions of $C[i]$ are parameterized by the index variable i.[3] Accordingly, some variables of V are indexed, while the others act as global variables. The guards of an *parameterizable component* $C[i]$, are index predicates, but we do not allowed quantification over index variables on the right-hand side of assignments. This guarantees that the predicates generated during model checking remain in the class of indexed predicates. The only index variable appearing freely in transitions of $C[i]$ is i, and on the left-hand side of an assignment we only allow i as index term, without constant, which means that a copy can only modify its own variables. This not necessary but simplifies the computation of weakest preconditions. The initial predicate I is a closed index predicate. A parameterized version of the Bakery algorithm, shown in Table 2, should illustrate the notion of parameterized system.

Table 2. Parameterized Bakery Algorithm.

$V :\ c[i] : \{T, W, C\},\ n[i] : \text{INT}$

$I :\ \forall i\,(n[i] = 0 \wedge c[i] = T)$

$c[i] = T \longrightarrow \left\langle \begin{array}{l} c[i] := W \\ n[i] := (max_j n[j]) + 1 \end{array} \right\rangle$

$c[i] = W \wedge \forall j (j \neq i \rightarrow n[i] < n[j] \vee n[j] = 0) \longrightarrow \left\langle\, c[i] := C \,\right\rangle$

$c[i] = C \longrightarrow \left\langle \begin{array}{l} c[i] := T \\ n[i] := 0 \end{array} \right\rangle$

For a natural number n, the **instantiation** $S[n]$ **of a parameterized system** S is $(V[n], C[0], \ldots, C[n-1], I[n])$, where $V[n]$ is the set of ordinary variables of V together with, for every indexable variable y in V, $y[0], \ldots, y[n-1]$, and where for a natural number h, $C[h]$ is obtained by replacing i by h in all indexed expressions. All expressions are intended to be *modulo* n. This can be done on

---

[3] The proposed approach is applicable to systems composed of different parameterizable components and of ordinary components. For simplicity of the presentation, this generalization is omitted.

the syntactic level by replacing all terms and predicates X by X mod n as follows: For a variable y and an index term $i + k$, $y[i + k]$ mod n is $y[(i + k)$ mod $n]$; this is extended in the usual way to terms and basic predicates. For quantified predicates, we define $\forall j\, (a \rightarrow p)$ mod n to be $\bigwedge_{0 \leq h < n} (a$ mod $n \rightarrow p[j := h]$ mod $n)$ and $\exists j\, (a \wedge p)$ mod n to be $\bigvee_{0 \leq h < n} (a$ mod $n \wedge p[j := h]$ mod $n)$.

The interpretation of $(i + k)$ mod n under a given valuation v is the natural one. Note that the instantiation of a parameterized system is an ordinary system since i is the only free index variable occurring in $C[i]$.

The following **decidability result** is crucial for the model checking procedure we present. For any index predicate p and any n, satisfiability of p mod n is decidable since the domains of the free index variables can be restricted to $\{0, \ldots, n - 1\}$. Decidability holds since it suffices to check satisfiability for some large enough n, more precisely for n so that all of the index terms and all of the existentially quantified variables can be interpreted with different values. This argument does not hold for nested quantification, since if variable j is existentially quantified in the scope of a universal quantification over i, then for every value for i the possibility of a new value for j has to be considered, but this new value for j must be taken into consideration as value for i, which results in a cycle.

Theorem 1. *Satisfiability of index predicates is decidable.*

In a **specification logic** for parameterized systems, it is desirable to be able to quantify over index variables. For example, the property of mutual exclusion in the Bakery example can be formulated as: $\forall i_1 \forall i_2\, (i_1 \neq i_2 \rightarrow G\,(c[i_1] \neq C \vee c[j_2] \neq C))$. More generally, we consider formulas of the form: $\forall j_1 \cdots \forall j_n\, (a \rightarrow \phi)$, where ϕ is an LTL formula with index predicates as state formulas, where $j_1, \ldots, j_n$ are the free index variables occurring in ϕ and where a is a conjunction of inequalities $j_i \neq [i+]k$ for some index variable i. In Mai01 we specified a fragment of LTL for which it is possible to allow universal quantification over index variables anywhere in the formula.

Now we can formally state the **model-checking problem for parameterized systems**:

$$S \models \forall j_1 \cdots \forall j_m\, (a \rightarrow \phi) \quad \text{if f. a. } n,\ S[n], s \models_n (\forall j_1 \cdots \forall j_m\, (\rightarrow \phi)\ \text{mod } n.$$

2.2 Types of Parameterized Systems

The characterisation we give of parameterized systems for which model checking is decidable concerns mainly the communication between different copies. A possible way of communication is to read the value of a variable of a different copy. This is the case if on the right-hand side of an assignment or in a guard, an expression $y[i + k]$ occurs, where k is not zero, and hence the transition depends of the value of the variable y in the k-th neighbour. An example for this type of communication is the following, a transition from the Dining Philosophers algorithm.

$$c[i] = h \wedge pr[i] \wedge \neg pr[i-1] \wedge \ c[i-1] \neq e \wedge c[i+1] \neq e \longrightarrow \left\langle \begin{array}{l} c[i] := e \\ pr[i] := \text{false} \end{array} \right\rangle$$

While this general form of communication has to be restricted severely (see Definition 4), other forms of communication, namely that of token rings and broadcast systems are unproblematic.

Both token rings and broadcast systems have a *control-state*, i.e. there is a special variable c of enumerative sort $\mathcal{D}_{control}$ such that the guard of every transition is of form $c[i] = d \wedge p$ for some index predicate p, and contains an assignment $c[i] := d'$.

A **token ring** (EN98) is a control-state component $C[i]$ for which some transitions are marked by *send* and some by *rec*. In all transitions of $C[i]$, only i occurs as index term, so a copy can only read the value of its own variables or that of global variables. With the execution of a *rec* transition, the copy acquires the token, while with a *send* transition, the token is passed to the right neighbour. We require that *send* and *rec* transitions alternate along every path through $C[i]$. Token rings are not executed in a completely asynchronous fashion as the general parameterized systems we consider here: To execute *send* or *rec* transitions, neighbouring copies have to synchronise: For any instantiation with n and some $0 \leq h < n$, a transition in $C[h]$ marked by *rec* can only be executed in parallel with a *send* transition in $C[h-1]$ (or $C[n-1]$ if $h = 0$ resp.), and vice versa. By $\mathcal{D}_{token}$ we denote the set of control states in a token ring in which the copy "has the token", i.e. which are reachable by a sequence transitions such that the last marked transition was a *rec*-transition.

Table 3. Illinois Protocol.

$V : \ c[i] : \{invalid, exclusive, dirty, shared\}$

$I : \ \forall i \, (c[i] = invalid)$

$(read!!), (write!!), (rep!!) \ c[i] = invalid \longrightarrow \left\langle c[i] = invalid \right\rangle$

$(read??) \ c[i] = invalid \longrightarrow \left\langle \begin{array}{l} p \longrightarrow c[i] := shared \\ \neg p \longrightarrow c[i] := exclusive \end{array} \right\rangle$

$\vdots$

p abbreviates the global guard: $\exists j \, (j \neq i \wedge c[j] \neq invalid)$

A **broadcast component** (EN98) is again a control-state component $C[i]$, and communication between copies is only possible in form of synchronisation. But the copy to synchronise with is not determined but can be any other copy that can execute a matching transition. Moreover, a broadcast synchronisation is possible: In such a synchronisation step, all copies execute a transition. More formally, let $\Sigma = \Sigma_{rv} \cup \Sigma_{bc}$ be an *action alphabet*, where Σ_{rv} and Σ_{bc} are disjoint finite sets. The transitions can be marked by $a!$ or $a?$ for $a \in \Sigma_{rv}$, or by $a!!$ or

a?? for $a \in \Sigma_{bc}$. The semantics of broadcast systems is as follows: A transition marked by a? in some component can only be executed simultaneously with a transition marked by a! in some other component and vice versa. The broadcast actions a!! can only be executed simultaneously with an action marked by a?? in all other components, and an action marked by a?? can only be executed in such a situation.

The cache coherence protocol used as example in Del00 can be modelled as broadcast protocol as partly shown in Table 3, and provides an example of a broadcast protocol with global guards.

3 Model Checking by Tree Construction

Model checking of safety linear temporal logic formulas can be restricted to model checking of formulas of form $EF\,p$ for some state predicate p by using an automaton that accepts the bad prefixes for a safety linear temporal logic formula (KV99). The fixed point approach for verifying that S satisfies $EF\,q$ uses the fact that the set of states satisfying $EF\,q$ is the least fixed point of the functional: $F(X) = \{s \mid s \models q\} \cup \neg wp.S.\neg X$.[4] We carry out the fixpoint computation on predicates, i.e. we compute a state predicate which characterises the least fixed point of F, starting with the empty predicate false. The necessary ingredients needed to do this are:

- Decidability of implication and satisfiability for state predicates. The former is needed to decide whether a fixed point has been reached, and the latter for deciding whether an initial state satisfies an expression.
- For a given state predicate p, a state predicate representing the *weakest precondition* [5] of the set of states satisfying p must be computable.

For a program S and a given state predicate p, a predicate $wp.S.p$ that represents $wp.S.\{s \mid s \models p\}$ is easy to define: Let $Tr(C)$ be the set of all transitions of component C, where a transition is of form $g \longrightarrow < v_0 := t_0, \ldots, v_k := t_k >$, then $wp.S.p = \bigwedge_{C \text{ comp. of } S} = \bigwedge_{C \text{ comp. of } S} \bigwedge_{g \longrightarrow < v_0 \doteq t_0, \ldots, v_k \doteq t_k > \in Tr(C)} (g \to p[v_0 := t_0, \ldots, v_k := t_k])$, where $[v_0 := t_0, \ldots, v_k := t_k]$ denotes simultaneous substitution.

The specific feature of our algorithm is that the fixed point computation is represented in form of a tree over $\mathbb{N}$, i.e. as set of finite sequences over $\mathbb{N}$ that is closed under prefix-formation: The root is denoted by ϵ, and e. g. 00 is the first successor of the first successor of the root. Note that the algorithm works directly on the program notation.

Definition 2 (Proof Tree Construction). *Let q be a predicate of the form $\bigwedge_i p_i$ for literals p_i. The proof tree $\mathcal{T}(EF\,q, S)$ is a tree over $\mathbb{N}$ with labelling $l : \mathcal{T}(EF\,q, S) \longrightarrow \{\bigwedge_i p_i \mid p_i$ literals $\}$ such that*

---

[4] The set $\neg wp.S.\neg X$ consists of all states that have at least on successor in X.

[5] For a system S and a set of states X, the weakest precondition $wp.S.X$ is the set of states s of S so that all successors of s lie in X.

- $l(\epsilon) = q$ and
- $\bigvee_j l(xj) \Leftrightarrow \neg wp.S.\neg l(x).$[6]

A node $x \in \mathcal{T}(EF\,q, S)$ is a leaf if one of the following conditions holds:

(i) $l(x)$ is not satisfiable (unsuccessful leaf);

(ii) $I \wedge l(x)$ is satisfiable (where I is the initial predicate of the system), i.e. there is an initial state of S satisfying $l(x)$ (successful leaf);

(iii) there is a node $y \in \mathcal{T}(EF\,q, S)$ such that $|x| > |y|$ and $l(x) \Rightarrow l(y)$ (unsuccessful leaf).

The tree $\mathcal{T}(EF\,q, S)$ is successful if it has a successful leaf. The following theorem states the correctness of the algorithm.

Theorem 2. (a) $S \models AG\,(\neg q)$ if and only if $\mathcal{T}(EF\,q, S)$ is not successful.
(b) If all sorts of variables of S are finite, then the construction of $\mathcal{T}(EF\,q, S)$ terminates.

To illustrate the tree construction, the first steps of the proof tree construction for the 2-component Bakery algorithm are shown in Figure 1. For the root, $\neg wp.S.\neg(c_1 = C \wedge c_2 = C)$ is $(c_1 = W \wedge (n_1 < n_2 \vee n_2 = 0) \wedge c_2 = C) \vee (c_1 = C \wedge (n_2 < n_1 \vee n_1 = 0) \wedge c_2 = W)$, and by transforming this into disjunctive normal form, the four successors of the root node are obtained.

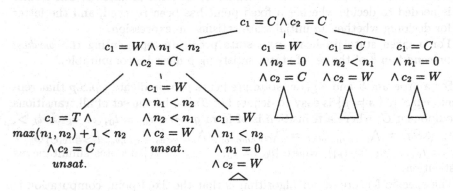

Fig. 1. Proof Tree for the 2-Component Bakery Algorithm.

An advantage of using a tree structure to represent the least fixed point is that the predicates labelling the nodes are relatively small and automatically only elements of the frontier set are considered for the next iteration step. This distinguishes the approach from other approaches to use Presburger arithmetic for representing sets of states during the fixed point iteration BGP97 and makes it easier to check the Conditions (i), (ii) and (iii). Producing counterexamples is easy since the paths in the tree form potential refutation sequences.

---

[6] It is irrelevant for the correctness which representation in disjunctive normal form is chosen.

4   Model Checking for Parameterized Systems

4.1   Adaption of the Tree Construction to Parameterized Systems

The first of the requirements on page 317 for the proof tree construction is guaranteed by Lemma 1. It remains to explain the computation of $\neg wp.S.\neg p$ for a parameterized system S. For an ordinary parameterized system S and a given instantiation with n, and for an index predicate p without free index variables, $wp.S[n].p$ can be define as on page 317. This easily generalizes to token rings or a broadcast systems: All possibilities of synchronisation have to be considered.

For the computation of $wp.C[t].p$, where $C[i]$ is the component of S, t is an index term, and p is an index predicate, it has to be clear which indexed variables are modified by a transition of $C[t]$. So if p contains other index terms t', either $t \neq t'$ or $t = t'$ has to be assumed to be able to compute $wp.C[t].p$. The obvious solution is to consider all possibilities of dividing the index terms in p in those that are equal to t and those that are not equal to t, and to compute $wp.C[t].p$ for each of those possibilities. To make this precise, we need some notation. Let $t_1, \ldots, t_n$ be the free index terms occurring in p. For an ordinary parameterized system, we define

- $G(p) \stackrel{\text{def}}{=} \{Equ(t_{i_1}, \ldots, t_{i_k}) \mid \{i_1, \ldots, i_k\} \subseteq \{1, \ldots, n\}\}$, where
- $Equ(t_{i_1}, \ldots, t_{i_k}) \stackrel{\text{def}}{=} t_{i_1} = t_{i_2} \wedge \cdots \wedge t_{i_1} = t_{i_k} \wedge \bigwedge_{r \in \{1, \ldots, n\} \setminus \{i_1, \ldots, i_k\}} t_{i_1} \neq t_r$, [7]
- $Equ(\emptyset) = \bigwedge_{1 \leq r \leq n} i^* \neq t_r$, where i^* is a new index variable.

For an element $g \in G(p)$, let $rep(g)$ be t_{j_1} or i^* respectively. For token rings, in addition sets of index terms that equal $rep(g)+1$ or $rep(g)-1$ have to be selected, and for broadcast systems, a set of index terms standing for the component that is chosen for synchronisation has to be chosen.

For $g \in G(p)$, by $p\langle g \rangle$ we denote the result of replacing all index terms that are by g equal to $rep(g)$ by $rep(g)$ throughout p, and by replacing quantified subexpressions as follows: $(\forall j (a \rightarrow p))\langle g \rangle = (a \rightarrow p)[j := rep(g)]\langle g \rangle \wedge \forall j ((a \wedge j \neq rep(g) \rightarrow p)\langle g \rangle)$, and the definition for existential quantification is accordingly, using disjunction.

By $wp^{simp}.C[t].p$ we denote the result of computing the weakest precondition of p (e.g. by the formula given on page 317) by considering variables with index terms syntactically different from t to be not modifiable by $C[t]$. The following lemma states that $wp.S[n].p$ can be represented by computing wp^{simp} for all elements of $G(p)$. Note that $p[\{j := v(j) \mid j$ free index variable in $p\}]$ mod n does not contain free index variables and can hence be considered as ordinary predicate over the system variables of $S[n]$.

Lemma 1. *For all n, states s and valuations v with respect to n:*
For all valuations w of the index variables introduced in $G(p)$,

$$s, v + w \models_n (\bigwedge_{g \in G(p)} g \rightarrow wp^{simp}.C[rep(g)].p\rangle g) \bmod n$$

$$\iff s, v \models_n wp.S[n].(p[\{j := v(j) \mid j \text{ free index variable in } p\}] \bmod n).$$

---
[7] Note that $i + k = i + k'$ can be satisfiable in some instantiation for even if $k \neq k'$.

Lemma 1 implies that for parameterized systems, a proof tree can be constructed generically for all instantiations $S[n]$ by computing

$$\neg wp.S.\neg q = \bigvee_{g \in G(q)} (g \wedge \neg wp^{simp}.C[rep(g)].\neg q\langle g \rangle).$$

The key property is the following: There is some n and s, v with respect to n, and a valuation w for the new index variables in $G(q)$ such that $s, v+w \models_n \neg wp.S.\neg q$, iff there is a successor s' of s in $S[n]$ such that $s', v \models_n \neg q$.

So we can now define the adaption of the proof tree construction for parameterized systems. Note that there is only one additional termination conditions, which only applies to token rings.

Definition 3 (Proof Tree Construction for Parameterized Systems).
Let p be an index predicate. $\mathcal{B}^{para}(EF\,p, S)$ is a tree over $\mathbb{N}$ with labelling $\bigwedge_i p_i$, where p_i is either a quantifier-free index predicate which is a literal, or a quantified index predicate.

- $l(\epsilon) = p$ and
- $\bigvee_j l(xj) = \neg wp.S.\neg l(x)$.

A node $x \in \mathcal{B}^{para}(EF\,p, S)$ is a leaf if one of the following holds:

(i) *$l(x)$ is not satisfiable (unsuccessful leaf);*
(ii) *$I \wedge l(x)$ is satisfiable (successful leaf);*
(iii) *there is a node $y \in \mathcal{B}^{para}(EF\,q, S)$ such that $|x| > |y|$ and $\exists\,l\,(x) \Rightarrow \exists\,l\,(y)$, where $\exists_-$ denotes existential quantification over all free index variables (unsuccessful leaf).*
(iv) *For a token ring component $C[i]$: Let $i + k_1, \ldots, i + k_r$ be all index terms containing i that occur in p (note that in $C[i]$, only i occurs as index term) and let k_1 and k_r be maximal resp. minimal among $\{k_1 \ldots, k_r\}$. Then all labels containing $i + k_r - 2$ as index term, are leaves (unsuccessful leaf). Furthermore, all labels that have more than one token are leaves, i.e. those containing literals of form $c[t] = d$ and $c[t'] = d'$ for $d, d' \in D_{token}$ and for two index terms t and t' such that $t \neq t'$, where c is the control-state variable of $C[i]$ (unsuccessful leaf).*

Note that the existential quantification in Condition (iii) can be applied since I is a closed index predicate. The reason why Condition (iv) is correct is that due to the restricted communication, if a label contains an expression $P[i + k_r - k]$ that contains $i + k_r - k$ as index term for some $k > 2$, then there also is a node that does not differ in the expressions that contain $i + k_1, \ldots, i + k_r$ as index terms and besides that only contains $P[i + k_r - 2]$. It follows that if the former node is satisfiable, then already the latter is satisfiable, under the additional requirement that for token rings, the initial state is uniform in all indices execpt 0. Furthermore, due to the synchronisation, labels that contain index terms $i + k_1 + k$ for some $k > 1$ necessarily contain several tokens.

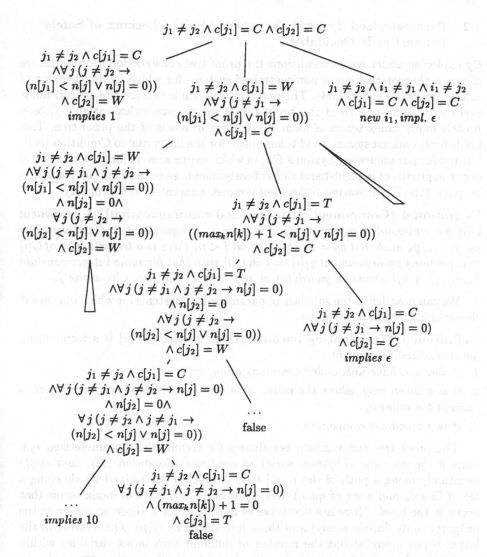

$$j_1 \neq j_2 \wedge c[j_1] = C \wedge c[j_2] = C$$

$j_1 \neq j_2 \wedge c[j_1] = C$
$\wedge \forall j \, (j \neq j_2 \rightarrow$
$(n[j_1] < n[j] \vee n[j] = 0))$
$\wedge c[j_2] = W$
implies 1

$j_1 \neq j_2 \wedge c[j_1] = W$
$\wedge \forall j \, (j \neq j_1 \rightarrow$
$(n[j_1] < n[j] \vee n[j] = 0))$
$\wedge c[j_2] = C$

$j_1 \neq j_2 \wedge i_1 \neq j_1 \wedge i_1 \neq j_2$
$\wedge c[j_1] = C \wedge c[j_2] = C$
new i_1, *impl.* ϵ

$j_1 \neq j_2 \wedge c[j_1] = W$
$\wedge \forall j \, (j \neq j_1 \wedge j \neq j_2 \rightarrow$
$(n[j_1] < n[j] \vee n[j] = 0))$
$\wedge n[j_2] = 0 \wedge$
$\forall j \, (j \neq j_2 \rightarrow$
$(n[j_2] < n[j] \vee n[j] = 0))$
$\wedge c[j_2] = W$

$j_1 \neq j_2 \wedge c[j_1] = T$
$\wedge \forall j \, (j \neq j_1 \rightarrow$
$((max_k n[k]) + 1 < n[j] \vee n[j] = 0))$
$\wedge c[j_2] = C$

$j_1 \neq j_2 \wedge c[j_1] = T$
$\wedge \forall j \, (j \neq j_1 \wedge j \neq j_2 \rightarrow n[j] = 0)$
$\wedge n[j_2] = 0$
$\wedge \forall j \, (j \neq j_2 \rightarrow$
$(n[j_2] < n[j] \vee n[j] = 0))$
$\wedge c[j_2] = W$

$j_1 \neq j_2 \wedge c[j_1] = C$
$\wedge \forall j \, (j \neq j_1 \rightarrow n[j] = 0)$
$\wedge c[j_2] = C$
implies ϵ

$j_1 \neq j_2 \wedge c[j_1] = C$
$\wedge \forall j \, (j \neq j_1 \wedge j \neq j_2 \rightarrow n[j] = 0)$
$\wedge n[j_2] = 0 \wedge$
$\forall j \, (j \neq j_2 \wedge j \neq j_1 \rightarrow$
$(n[j_2] < n[j] \vee n[j] = 0))$
$\wedge c[j_2] = W$

. . .
false

$j_1 \neq j_2 \wedge c[j_1] = C$
$\wedge \forall j \, (j \neq j_1 \wedge j \neq j_2 \rightarrow n[j] = 0)$
$\wedge (max_k n[k]) + 1 = 0$
$\wedge c[j_2] = T$
false

. . .
implies 10

Fig. 2. Proof Tree for the Parameterized Bakery Algorithm.

Figure 2 gives an example for the proof tree construction for a parameterized system. The first successor of the root represents the condition that has to hold if $C[j_2]$ takes a step, the second condition is the case that $C[j_1]$ takes a step, and the third successor is the dual of the weakest precondition for the case that $C[i_1]$, where i_1 is a new variable, takes a step. Since this is obviously only necessary if there are global variables (which could be modified by $C[i_1]$), this step is omitted in the rest of the tree. Only parts of the tree are displayed, while the full tree has 31 nodes. The full paper also discusses the proof tree construction for the Illinois protocol.

4.2   Parameterized Systems for which Model Checking of Safety Properties Is Decidable

By exploring under which conditions the proof tree construction terminates, we obtain a characterisation of parameterized systems for which model checking of safety properties is decidable. The main observation is that Condition (iii) holds eventually along a path of the proof tree if for a given index variable j, only *finitely many* index terms of form $j + k$ occur in labels of the proof tree. This holds for broadcast systems and token rings (for the latter due to Condition (iv)), but not for parameterized systems $C[i]$ in which expressions of form $i+k$ for $k \neq 0$ occur in guards of in right-hand sides of assignments as in the example transition on page 316. The following restriction however guarantees this property.

Definition 4 (Component with bounded communication). *A component* $C[i]$ *has* unbounded communication *if there is a sequence of indexed variables* $y_0, y_1, \ldots, y_n$ *such that* $y_0 = y_n$, *and for all* $j < n$, *there is a transition tr of* $C[i]$ *that contains an assignment* $y_j[i] := t$ *in* $C[i]$ *such that for some integer constant* k_j, $y_{j+1}[i + k_j]$ *occurs in guard(tr) or in t, and* $k_j \neq 0$ *for at least one* j.

We can now define the subclass of parameterized systems for which our model checking algorithm terminates:

Definition 5 (Terminating parameterized system). $C[i]$ *is a* terminating parameterized component *if*

1. *it does not have unbounded communication, or*

2. *it is a token ring, where the initial predicate must be uniform for all indices except the index* 0,

3. *it is a broadcast component.*

The proof tree construction terminates for terminating parameterized systems if the domains of system variables are finite: Condition (iii) must apply eventually along a path of the proof tree: A label is determined by choosing a set of literals and a set of quantified expressions, and a set of index terms that occur in the label. There are two types of index variables, those occurring in the property (only finitely many) and those introduced by $G(p)$. The number of the latter is not bounded but the number of different such index variables within one label is bounded by the maximal iteration depth of quantifiers occurring in the property or in some guard plus 1. As argued above, the number of different index variables also bounds the number of different index terms. So up to equivalence after existentially quantifying over index variables (which is used in Condition (iii)), there are only finitely many possibilities for labels.

We can summarise the properties of the extended proof tree construction in the following theorem. By using an automaton representing bad prefixes for ψ, this extends to formulas $\forall j_1 \ldots \forall j_m (a \rightarrow \psi)$ with ψ an LTL safety-formula.

Theorem 3. *(a)* $S \models \forall j_1 \ldots \forall j_m (a \rightarrow AG(\neg p))$ *iff* $\mathcal{B}^{para}(EF\,p, S)$ *is not successful.*

(b) If all system variables of S *have finite domains, then the construction of* $\mathcal{B}^{para}(EF\,p, S)$ *terminates.*

References

[ABJN00] Abdulla, P. A., Bouajjani, A., Jonsson, B. and Nilsson, M. *Handling global conditions in parameterized system verification.* In: *Proc. 12th Intl. Conf. on Computer Aided Verification.* 2000, LNCS 1855.

[ACJT96] Abdulla, P., Cerans, K., Jonsson, B. and Tsay, Y.-K. *General decidability theorems for infinite-state systems.* In: *Proc. 11th Symp. Logic in Computer Science.* 1996.

[BGP97] Bultan, T., Gerber, R. and Pugh, W. *Symbolic model checking of infinite state systems using Presburger arithmetic.* In: *Proc. 9th Intl. Conf. on Computer Aided Verification.* 1997, LNCS 1254.

[BJNT00] Bouajjani, A., Jonsson, B., Nilsson, M. and Touili, T. *Regular model checking.* In: *Proc. 12th Intl. Conf. on Computer Aided Verification.* 2000, LNCS 1855.

[BW98] Boigelot, B. and Wolper, P. *Verifying systems with infinite but regular state space.* In: *Proc. 10th Intl. Conf. on Computer Aided Verification.* 1998.

[Del00] Delzanno, G. *Automatic verification of parameterized cache coherence protocols.* In: *12th Intl. Conf. on Computer Aided Verification.* 2000, LNCS 1855.

[EFM99] Esparza, J., Finkel, A. and Mayr, R. *On the verification of broadcast protocols.* In: *Proc. 14th Symp. Logic in Computer Science.* 1999.

[EN95] Emerson, E. A. and Namjoshi, K. S. *Reasoning about rings.* In: *Proc. 22th ACM Conf. on Principles of Programming Languages.* 1995.

[EN98] Emerson, E. A. and Namjoshi, K. S. *On model checking for nondeterministic infinite-state systems.* In: *Proc. 13th Symp. Logic in Computer Science.* 1998.

[GS92] German, S. M. and Sistla, A. P. *Reasoning about systems with many processes.* J. ACM, 39(3): 675–735, July 1992.

[KMM+97] Kesten, Y., Maler, O., Marcus, M., Pnueli, A. and Shahar, E. *Symbolic model checking with rich assertional languages.* In: *Proc. 9th Intl. Conf. on Computer Aided Verification.* 1997, LNCS 1254.

[KV99] Kupferman, O. and Vardi, M. Y. *Model checking of safety properties.* In: *Proc. 11th Intl. Conf. on Computer Aided Verification.* 1999, LNCS 1633.

[Mai01] Maidl, M. *Temporal logic extended by universal quantifiers*, 2001. Presented at AVIS 01 Workshop in Berlin.

[Suz88] Suzuki, I. *Proving properties of a ring of finite state machines.* Information Processing Letters, 28: 213–214, 1988.

A BDD-Based Model Checker
for Recursive Programs

Javier Esparza and Stefan Schwoon

Technische Universität München
Arcisstr. 21, 80290 München, Germany
{esparza,schwoon}@in.tum.de

Abstract. We present a model-checker for boolean programs with (possibly recursive) procedures and the temporal logic LTL. The checker is guaranteed to terminate even for (usually faulty) programs in which the depth of the recursion is not bounded. The algorithm uses automata to finitely represent possibly infinite sets of stack contents and BDDs to compactly represent finite sets of values of boolean variables. We illustrate the checker on some examples and compare it with the Bebop tool of Ball and Rajamani.

1 Introduction

Boolean programs are C programs in which all variables and parameters (call-by value) have boolean type, and which may contain procedures with recursion. In a series of papers, Ball and Rajamani have convincingly argued that they are a good starting point for investigating model checking of software [1, 2].

Ball and Rajamani have also developed Bebop, a tool for reachability analysis in boolean programs. As part of the SLAM toolkit, Bebop has been successfully used to validate critical safety properties of device drivers [2]. Bebop can determine if a point of a boolean program can be reached along some execution path. Using an automata-theoretic approach it is easy to extend Bebop to a tool for safety properties. However, it cannot deal with liveness or fairness properties requiring to examine the infinite executions of the program. In particular, it cannot be used to prove termination.

In this paper we overcome this limitation by presenting a model-checker for boolean programs and arbitrary LTL-properties. The input to the model checker are symbolic pushdown systems (SPDS), a compact representation of the pushdown systems studied in [4]. A translation of boolean programs into this model is straightforward. The checker is based on the efficient algorithms for model checking ordinary pushdown systems (PDS) of [4]. While SPDSs have the same expressive power as PDSs, they can be exponentially more compact. (Essentially, the translation works by expanding the set of control states with all the possible values of the boolean variables.) Therefore, translating SPDSs into PDSs and then applying the algorithms of [4] is very inefficient. We follow a different path: We provide symbolic versions of the algorithms of [4] working on SPDSs, and use BDDs to succintly encode sets of (tuples of) values of the boolean variables.

G. Berry, H. Comon, and A. Finkel (Eds.): CAV 2001, LNCS 2102, pp. 324–336, 2001.

This paper (and its full version [5]) contribute symbolic versions of the algorithms of [4], tuned to minimise the number of required BDD variables; an efficient implementation including three heuristic improvements; some experimental results on different versions of Quicksort; and, finally, a performance comparison with Bebop using an example of [1].

The paper is structured as follows. PDSs and SPDSs are introduced in Section 2. The symbolic versions of the algorithms of [4] are presented in Section 4 and their complexity is analysed. In particular, we analyse the complexity in terms of the number of global and local variables. In Section 5 we discuss the improvements in the checker and present our results on verifying Quicksort; in particular we analyse the impact of the improvements. Section 6 contains the comparison with Bebop, and Section 7 contains conclusions.

2 Basic Definitions

In this section we briefly introduce the notions of pushdown systems and linear time logic, and establish our notations for them.

2.1 Pushdown Systems

We mostly follow the notation of [4]. A *pushdown system* is a four-tuple $\mathcal{P} = (P, \Gamma, c_0, \Delta)$ where P is a finite set of *control locations*, Γ is a finite *stack alphabet*, and $\Delta \subseteq (P \times \Gamma) \times (P \times \Gamma^*)$ is a finite set of *transition rules*. If $((q, \gamma), (q', w)) \in \Delta$ then we write $\langle q, \gamma \rangle \hookrightarrow \langle q', w \rangle$. A *configuration* of $\mathcal{P}$ is a pair $\langle p, w \rangle$ where $p \in P$ is a control location and $w \in \Gamma^*$ is a *stack content*. c_0 is called the *initial configuration* of $\mathcal{P}$. The set of all configurations is denoted by $\mathcal{C}$.

If $\langle q, \gamma \rangle \hookrightarrow \langle q', w \rangle$, then for every $v \in \Gamma^*$ the configuration $\langle q, \gamma v \rangle$ is an *immediate predecessor* of $\langle q', wv \rangle$, and $\langle q', wv \rangle$ an *immediate successor* of $\langle q, \gamma v \rangle$. The *reachability relation* $\Rightarrow$ is the reflexive and transitive closure of the immediate successor relation. A *run* of $\mathcal{P}$ is a sequence of configurations such that for each two consecutive configurations $c_i c_{i+1}$, c_{i+1} is an immediate successor of c_i.

The predecessor function $pre: 2^{\mathcal{C}} \to 2^{\mathcal{C}}$ of $\mathcal{P}$ is defined as follows: c belongs to $pre(C)$ if some immediate successor of c belongs to C. The reflexive and transitive closure of pre is denoted by pre^*. We define $post(C)$ and $post^*$ similarly.

In the next section, when we model boolean programs as pushdown systems, we will see that it is natural to consider a product form for P and G. More precisely, it is convenient to introduce sets P_0 and G such that $P = P_0 \times G$, and sets Γ_0 and L such that $G = \Gamma_0 \times L$. G and L are called sets of global and local values, since they are, loosely speaking, the possible valuations of the global and local variables of the program, respectively. So, for the rest of the paper, we assume

$$P = P_0 \times G \quad \text{and} \quad G = \Gamma_0 \times L \,.$$

A symbolic pushdown system is a pushdown system in which sets of transition rules are represented by symbolic transition rules. Formally, a *symbolic pushdown system* is a tuple $\mathcal{P}_S = (P, \Gamma, c_0, \Delta_S)$, where Δ_S is a set of *symbolic transition rules* of the form $\langle p, \gamma \rangle \xrightarrow{R} \langle p', \gamma_1 \ldots \gamma_n \rangle$, and $R \subseteq (G \times L) \times (G \times L^n)$ is a relation. A symbolic pushdown system corresponds to a normal pushdown system $(P_0 \times G, \Gamma_0 \times L, c_0, \Delta)$ in the sense that a symbolic rule $\langle p, \gamma \rangle \xrightarrow{R} \langle p', \gamma_1 \ldots \gamma_n \rangle$ denotes a set of transition rules as follows:

if $(g, l, g', l_1, \ldots, l_n) \in R$, then $\langle (p, g), (\gamma, l) \rangle \hookrightarrow \langle (p', g'), (\gamma_1, l_1) \ldots (\gamma_n, l_n) \rangle \in \Delta$

In practice, R should have an efficient symbolic representation. In our applications we have $G = \{0, 1\}^n$ and $L = \{0, 1\}^m$ for some n and m, and so R can be represented by a BDD.

Given a pushdown system $\mathcal{P} = (P, \Gamma, c_0, \Delta)$, we use $\mathcal{P}$-*automata* to represent regular sets of configurations of $\mathcal{P}$. A $\mathcal{P}$-automaton uses Γ as alphabet, and P as set of initial states. Formally, a $\mathcal{P}$-automaton is a tuple $\mathcal{A} = (\Gamma, Q, \delta, P, F)$ where Q is a finite set of states, $\delta \subseteq Q \times \Gamma \times Q$ is a set of *transitions*, P is the set of *initial states* and $F \subseteq Q$ is the set of *final states*. An automaton *accepts* or *recognises* a configuration $\langle p, w \rangle$ if $p \xrightarrow{w} q$ for some $p \in P$, $q \in F$. The set of configurations recognised by an automaton $\mathcal{A}$ is denoted by $Conf(\mathcal{A})$. A set of configurations of $\mathcal{P}$ is *regular* if it is recognized by some automaton.

A *symbolic $\mathcal{P}_S$-automaton* is a tuple $\mathcal{A}_S = (\Gamma_0, Q, \delta_S, P_0, F)$, where the *symbolic transition relation* is a function $\delta_S \colon (Q \times \Gamma_0 \times Q) \to (G \times L \times G)$. The relation δ_S should be seen as the symbolic representation of the transition relation δ: $\delta_S(q, \gamma, q')$ is the set of all (g, l, g') such that $((q, g), (\gamma, l), (q', g')) \in \delta$. If $R \subseteq (G \times L \times G)$, we denote by $q \xrightarrow[R]{\gamma} q'$ the set of transitions $((q, g), (\gamma, l), (q', g'))$ such that $(g, l, g') \in R$. In the sequel, $\mathcal{P}$-*automata* and *symbolic $\mathcal{P}_S$-automata* are just called automata and symbolic automata, respectively.

2.2 The Model-Checking Problem for LTL

We briefly recall the results of [3] and [4]. Given a formula φ of LTL, the model-checking problem consists of deciding if c_0 violates φ, that is whether there is some run starting at c_0 that violates φ. The problem is solved in [4] using the automata-theoretic approach. First, a Büchi pushdown system is constructed as the product of the original pushdown system and a Büchi automaton $\mathcal{B}$ for the negation of φ. This new pushdown system has a set of final control states. We define a new reachability relation $\Longrightarrow$ with respect to this set; we write $c \xRightarrow{r} c'$ if c' can be reached from c while visiting some final control state along the way. Now, define the *head* of a transition rule $\langle p, \gamma \rangle \hookrightarrow \langle p', w \rangle$ as the configuration $\langle p, \gamma \rangle$. A head $\langle p, \gamma \rangle$ is *repeating* if there exists $v \in \Gamma^*$ such that $\langle p, \gamma \rangle \xRightarrow{r} \langle p, \gamma v \rangle$ holds. We denote the set of repeating heads by Rh. It is shown in [4] that the model-checking problem reduces to either checking whether $c_0 \in pre^*(Rh\,\Gamma^*)$, or, equivalently, checking whether $post^*(\{c_0\}) \cap Rh\,\Gamma^* \neq \emptyset$. Furthermore, it is shown that the problem can be solved in $\mathcal{O}(|P|^2\,|\Delta|\,|\mathcal{B}|^3)$ time and $\mathcal{O}(|P|\,|\Delta|\,|\mathcal{B}|^2)$ space.

3 Modelling Programs as Symbolic Pushdown Systems

Pushdown systems find a natural application in the analysis of sequential programs with procedures (written in C or Java, for instance). We allow arbitrary

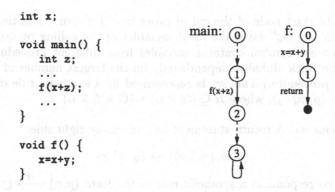

Fig. 1. An Example Program (left) and the Associated Flowgraph (right).

recursion, even mutual procedure calls, between procedures; however, we require that the data types used in the program be finite. In the following, we present informally how to derive a symbolic pushdown system from such a program.

In a first step, we represent the program by a system of *flow graphs*, one for each procedure. The nodes of a flow graph correspond to control points in the procedure, and its edges are annotated with statements, e.g. assignments or calls to other procedures. Non-deterministic control flow is allowed and might for instance result from abstraction. Figure 1 shows a small C program and the corresponding flow graphs. The procedure main ends in an infinite loop to ensure that all executions are infinite. In the example, a finitary fragment of the type integer has to be chosen.

Given such a system of flow graphs, we derive a pushdown system and a corresponding symbolic pushdown system. For simplicity, we assume that all procedures have the same local variables. The sets G and L contain all the possible valuations of the global and local variables, respectively. E.g., if the program contains three boolean global variables and each procedure has two boolean local variables, then we have $G = \{0,1\}^3$ and $L = \{0,1\}^2$. P_0 contains one single element p, while Γ is the set of nodes of the flow graphs.

Program statements are translated to pushdown rules of three types.

Assignments. An assignment labelling a flow-graph edge from node n_1 to node n_2 is represented by a set of rules of the form

$$\langle glob, (n_1, loc) \rangle \hookrightarrow \langle glob', (n_2, loc') \rangle.$$

where $glob$ and $glob'$ (loc and loc') are the values of the global (local) variables before and after the assigment. This set is represented by a symbolic rule of the form $\langle p, n_1 \rangle \xrightarrow{R} \langle p, n_2 \rangle$, where $R \subseteq (G \times L) \times (G \times L)$.

Procedure Calls. A procedure call labelling a flow-graph edge from node n_1 to node n_2 is translated into a set of rules with a right-hand side of length two according to the following scheme:

$$\langle glob, (n_1, loc) \rangle \hookrightarrow \langle glob', (m_0, loc') (n_2, loc'') \rangle$$

Here m_0 is the start node of the called procedure; loc' denotes initial values of its local variables; loc'' saves the local variables of the calling procedure. (Notice that no stack symbol contains variables from different procedures; hence the size of the stack alphabet depends only on the largest number of local variables in any procedure.) This set is represented by a symbolic rule of the form $\langle p, n_1 \rangle \stackrel{R}{\hookrightarrow} \langle p, m_0 n_2 \rangle$, where $R \subseteq (G \times L) \times (G \times L \times L)$.

Return Statements. A return statement has an empty right side:

$$\langle glob, (n, loc) \rangle \hookrightarrow \langle glob', \varepsilon \rangle$$

These rules correspond to a symbolic rule of the form $\langle p, n \rangle \stackrel{R}{\hookrightarrow} \langle p, \varepsilon \rangle$, where $R \subseteq (G \times L) \times G$. Procedures which return values can be simulated by introducing an additional global variable and assigning the return value to it.

Notice that the size of the symbolic pushdown system may be exponentially smaller than the size of the pushdown system. This is the fact we exploit in order to make model-checking practically usable, at least for programs with few variables. Notice also that in the symbolic pushdown system we have $|P_0| = 1$ and Γ_0 is the set of nodes of the flow graphs.

Since a symbolic pushdown system is just a compact representation of an ordinary pushdown system, we continue to use the theory presented in [4]. In this paper we provide modified versions of the model-checking algorithms that take advantage of a more compact representation. In our experiments, we consider programs with boolean variables only and use BDDs to represent them. Integer variables with values from a finite range are simulated using multiple boolean variables.

4   Algorithms

According to Section 2 we can solve the model-checking problem by giving algorithms for the following three tasks:

- to compute the set $pre^*(C)$ for a regular set of configurations C (which will be applied to $C = Rh\,\Gamma^*$)
- to compute the set $post^*(C)$ for a regular set of configurations C (which will be applied to $C = \{c_0\}$)
- to compute the set of repeating heads Rh

In [4] efficient implementations for these three problems were proposed for ordinary pushdown systems. In this section, we sketch how the algorithms may be lifted to the case of symbolic pushdown systems. More detailed presentations are given in the full version of the paper [5]. We fix a symbolic pushdown system $\mathcal{P} = (P_0 \times G, \Gamma_0 \times L, c_0, \Delta_S)$ for the rest of the section.

4.1   Computing Predecessors

Given a regular set C of configurations of $\mathcal{P}$, we want to compute $pre^*(C)$. Let $\mathcal{A}$ be a $\mathcal{P}$-automaton that accepts C. We modify $\mathcal{A}$ to an automaton that accepts $pre^*(C)$. The modification procedure adds only new transitions to $\mathcal{A}$, but no new states are created. Without loss of generality, we assume that $\mathcal{A}$ has no transitions ending in an initial state.

In ordinary pushdown systems, new transitions are added according to the following *saturation rule*:

$$\boxed{\begin{array}{l} \text{If } \langle p, \gamma \rangle \hookrightarrow \langle p', \gamma_1 \ldots \gamma_n \rangle \text{ and } p' \xrightarrow{\gamma_1} q_1 \xrightarrow{\gamma_2} \cdots \xrightarrow{\gamma_n} q \\ \text{in the current automaton, add a transition } (p, \gamma, q). \end{array}}$$

The correctness of the procedure was proved in [3]. For the symbolic case, the corresponding rule becomes:

$$\boxed{\begin{array}{l} \text{If } \langle p, \gamma \rangle \xrightarrow{R} \langle p', \gamma_1 \gamma_2 \ldots \gamma_n \rangle \text{ and } p' \xrightarrow[R_1]{\gamma_1} q_1 \xrightarrow[R_2]{\gamma_2} \cdots \xrightarrow[R_n]{\gamma_n} q \text{ in the} \\ \text{current automaton, replace } p \xrightarrow[R']{\gamma} q \text{ by } p \xrightarrow[R'']{\gamma} q \text{ where} \\ R'' = R' \cup \{ (g, l, g_n) \mid (g, l, g_0, l_1, \ldots, l_n) \in R \\ \qquad \wedge \exists g_1, \ldots, g_{n-1} \colon \forall 1 \leq i \leq n \colon (g_{i-1}, l_i, g_i) \in R_i \}. \end{array}}$$

The computation of R'' can be carried out using standard BDD operations. A detailed, efficient implementation of the procedure can be found in [5].

4.2   Computing the Repeating Heads

For ordinary pushdown systems [4] we construct a directed graph whose nodes are the heads of the transition rules (and so elements of $P \times \Gamma$). There is an edge from (p, γ) to (p', γ') iff there is a rule $\langle p, \gamma \rangle \hookrightarrow \langle p'', v_1 \gamma' v_2 \rangle$ where $\langle p'', v_1 \rangle \Rightarrow \langle p', \varepsilon \rangle$ holds. The edge has label 1 iff either p is an accepting Büchi state, or $\langle p'', v_1 \rangle \xrightarrow{r} \langle p', \varepsilon \rangle$. The edges are computed using pre^*. A head (p, γ) is repeating iff it belongs to a strongly connected component (SCC) containing a 1-labelled edge. The SCCs are computed in linear time using Tarjan's algorithm [9].

For symbolic pushdown systems we represent the graph compactly as a symbolic graph SG. The nodes of SG are elements of $P_0 \times \Gamma_0$, and its edges are annotated with a relation $R \subseteq (G \times L)^2$ (plus a boolean, which is easy to handle and is omitted in the following discussion for clarity). An edge $(p_0, \gamma_0) \xrightarrow{R} (p'_0, \gamma'_0)$ stands for the set of edges $(p_0, g, \gamma_0, l) \rightarrow (p'_0, g', \gamma'_0, l')$ such that $(g, l, g', l') \in R$. Unfortunately, when R is symbolically represented Tarjan's algorithm cannot be applied. A straightforward approach is to "saturate" SG instead according to the following two rules:

- If $(p_0, \gamma_0) \xrightarrow{R} (p''_0, \gamma''_0) \xrightarrow{R'} (p'_0, \gamma'_0)$, then add $(p_0, \gamma_0) \xrightarrow{R''} (p'_0, \gamma'_0)$, where $R'' := \{((g, l), (g', l')) \mid \exists (g'', l'') \colon ((g, l), (g'', l'')) \in R \wedge ((g'', l''), (g', l')) \in R'\}$.
- If $(p_0, \gamma_0) \xrightarrow{R} (p'_0, \gamma'_0)$ and $(p_0, \gamma_0) \xrightarrow{R'} (p'_0, \gamma'_0)$, then replace these two arcs by $(p_0, \gamma_0) \xrightarrow{R \cup R'} (p'_0, \gamma'_0)$

The saturation procedure terminates when a fixpoint is reached. It is easy to see that this algorithm has complexity $\mathcal{O}(n \cdot m)$ where n and m are the number of nodes and edges of G. Using this method, the model-checking problem for symbolic systems has a worse asymptotic complexity than for normal systems.

In practice, this disadvantage can be made up for, mainly due to the more succinct representation. Moreover, the straightforward approach can be replaced with more refined strategies that work better in practice (see the discussion in Section 5).

4.3   Computing Successors

Given an automaton $\mathcal{A}$ accepting the set C, we modify it to an automaton accepting $post^*(C)$. Again we assume that $\mathcal{A}$ has no transitions leading to initial states, and moreover, that $|w| \leq 2$ holds for all rules $\langle p, \gamma \rangle \xrightarrow{R} \langle p', w \rangle$. This is not an essential restriction, as all systems can be transformed into one of this form with only a linear increase in size.

In the ordinary case, we allow ε-moves in the automaton. We write $\overset{\gamma}{\Longrightarrow}$ for the relation $(\xrightarrow{\varepsilon})^* \xrightarrow{\gamma} (\xrightarrow{\varepsilon})^*$. The algorithm works in two steps [4]:

- If $\langle p, \gamma \rangle \hookrightarrow \langle p', \gamma'\gamma'' \rangle \in \Delta$, add a state (p', γ') and a transition $(p', \gamma', (p', \gamma'))$.
- Add new transitions to $\mathcal{A}$ according to the following saturation rules:

> If $\langle p, \gamma \rangle \hookrightarrow \langle p', \epsilon \rangle \in \Delta$ and $p \overset{\gamma}{\Longrightarrow} q$ in the current automaton,
> add a transition (p', ϵ, q).
>
> If $\langle p, \gamma \rangle \hookrightarrow \langle p', \gamma' \rangle \in \Delta$ and $p \overset{\gamma}{\Longrightarrow} q$ in the current automaton,
> add a transition (p', γ', q).
>
> If $r = \langle p, \gamma \rangle \hookrightarrow \langle p', \gamma'\gamma'' \rangle \in \Delta$ and $p \overset{\gamma}{\Longrightarrow} q$ in the current automaton,
> add a transition $((p, \gamma), \gamma'', q)$.

For the symbolic case, the corresponding first step looks like this: For each symbolic rule $\langle p, \gamma \rangle \xrightarrow{R} \langle p', y'y'' \rangle$ we add a new state (p', γ'). We must adjust the symbolic transition relation slightly for these new states; e.g. when q and q' are such states, then $\delta_S(q, \gamma, q')$ is a subset of $(G \times L) \times L \times (G \times L)$. Moreover, for each such rule we add a transition $t = (p', y', (p', y'))$ s.t. $\delta_S(t) = \{ (g', l', (g', l')) \mid \exists (g, l, g', l', l'') \in R \}$. Concerning ε-transitions, $\delta_S(q, \varepsilon, q')$ is a subset of $G \times G$. In the second step, we proceed as follows:

> If $\langle p, \gamma \rangle \xrightarrow{R} \langle p', \varepsilon \rangle \in \Delta_S$ and $p \overset{\gamma}{\underset{R'}{\Longrightarrow}} q$ in the current automaton,
> add to $\delta_S(p', \varepsilon, q)$ the set $\{ (g', g'') \mid \exists (g, l, g') \in R, (g, l, g'') \in R' \}$.
>
> If $\langle p, \gamma \rangle \xrightarrow{R} \langle p', \gamma' \rangle \in \Delta_S$ and $p \overset{\gamma}{\underset{R'}{\Longrightarrow}} q$ in the current automaton,
> add to $\delta_S(p', \gamma', q)$ the set $\{ (g', l', g'') \mid \exists (g, l, g', l') \in R, (g, l, g'') \in R' \}$.
>
> If $\langle p, \gamma \rangle \xrightarrow{R} \langle p', \gamma'\gamma'' \rangle \in \Delta_S$ and $p \overset{\gamma}{\underset{R'}{\Longrightarrow}} q$, add to $\delta_S((p', \gamma'), \gamma'', q)$
> the set $\{ ((g', l'), l'', g'') \mid \exists (g, l, g', l', l'') \in R, (g, l, g'') \in R' \}$.

In [5] we present an efficient implementation of these rules.

4.4 Complexity Analysis

Let $\mathcal{P} = (P, \Gamma, c_0, \Delta)$ be an ordinary pushdown system, and let $\mathcal{B}$ be a Büchi automaton corresponding to the negation of an LTL formula φ. Then, according to [4], the model-checking problem for $\mathcal{P}$ and $\mathcal{B}$ can be solved in $\mathcal{O}(|P|^2 \cdot |\Delta| \cdot |\mathcal{B}|^3)$ time and $\mathcal{O}(|P| \cdot |\Delta| \cdot |\mathcal{B}|^2)$ space.

Consider a pushdown system representing a sequential program with procedures. Let n be the size of a program's control flow, i.e. the number of statements. Let m_1 be the number of global (boolean) variables, and let m_2 be the maximum number of local (boolean) variables in any procedure. Assuming that the programs use deterministic assignments to variables, each statement translates to $2^{m_1+m_2}$ different pushdown rules. Since the number of control locations is 2^{m_1}, we would get an $\mathcal{O}(n \cdot 2^{3m_1+m_2} \cdot |\mathcal{B}|^3)$ time and $\mathcal{O}(n \cdot 2^{2m_1+m_2} \cdot |\mathcal{B}|^2)$ space algorithm by translating the program to an ordinary pushdown system.

When we use symbolic system, the complexity gets worse. The graph SG has $\mathcal{O}(|\Delta|)$ nodes and $\mathcal{O}(|P| \cdot |\Delta|)$ edges. So our symbolic algorithm for computing the SCCs has complexity $\mathcal{O}(|P| \cdot |\Delta|^2)$. We therefore get $\mathcal{O}(n^2 \cdot 2^{3m_1+2m_2} \cdot |\mathcal{B}|^3)$ time in the symbolic case. (The space complexity remains the same.) However, as mentioned before, the more compact representation in the symbolic case compensates for this disadvantage in the examples we tried.

5 Efficient Implementation

We have implemented the algorithms of Section 4 in a model-checking tool. Three refinements with respect to the abstract description of the algorithms are essential for efficiency.

Procedure for the Model-Checking Problem. As mentioned in section 2.2, the model-checking problem reduces to (a) checking whether $c_0 \in pre^*(Rh\,\Gamma^*)$, or (b) checking whether $post^*(\{c_0\}) \cap Rh\,\Gamma^* \neq \emptyset$. In order to compute (b) symbolically, we first compute the reachable configurations (i.e., $post^*(\{c_0\})$). Then, in each symbolic rule $\langle p, \gamma \rangle \overset{R}{\hookrightarrow} \langle p', \gamma_1 \ldots \gamma_n \rangle$ we replace R by a new relation R_{reach} defined as follows: $(g, l, g', l_1, \ldots l_n) \in R_{reach}$ if $(g, l, g', l_1, \ldots l_n) \in R$ and some configuration $\langle (p, g), (\gamma, l)w \rangle$ is reachable from c_0. This dramatically reduces the efforts needed for some computations if the number of reachable variable valuations is much smaller than the number of possible valuations. In this case, much of the work in (a) would be spent on finding cycles among unreachable valuations.

Efficient Computation of the Repeating Heads. As mentioned in section 4.2, the computation of the repeating heads reduces to determining the SCCs of a graph symbolically represented as a labelled graph SG. The nodes of SG are elements of $P_0 \times \Gamma_0$, and its edges are annotated with a relation $R \subseteq (G \times L)^2$ (and a boolean). In our implementation, we first compute the components "roughly", i.e., ignoring the Rs in the edges, using Tarjan's algorithm. Then we refine the search (including the Rs) within the components. For this problem a number of different approaches could be tried. The algorithm of Section 4.2 corresponds to computing the transitive closure of the edges. The transitive closure can be computed using a stepwise computation or iterative squaring (see also [7]); the stepwise method seems to work better in general. Xie and Beerel [10] suggest a more sophisticated approach for searching the components in a symbolic setting. Moreover, these possibilities can be combined with a preprocessing of the edge relation. The preprocessing looks for BDD variables that can change their values from only 0 to 1 (or vice versa), but not in the other direction and removes such edges for such variables, effectively limiting the length of the paths in the graph.

Variable Ordering. It is well known that the performance of BDD-based algorithms is very sensitive to the variable ordering. When checking the Quicksort example (see below) we found that a useful variable ordering was to place the inputs (i.e. the array of data to be sorted) at the end and the 'control variables' (i.e. indices into the array) at the beginning. Our intuition for this is that every instruction changes at most two elements of the array, and that such changes can be described with small BDDs. So we need one such BDD for each of the (relatively few) possible valuations of the control variables. If the input data was placed at the beginning, the BDDs would first branch into the (relatively many) possible valuations of the input data. While it is difficult to make a general assessment of variable orderings, there is hope that this ordering would also be useful in other examples where the same division between inputs and control variables can be made. Since the inputs are stored in global variables, this criterion corresponds to placing the local variables before the global variables.

In the rest of the section we give an idea of the performance of the algorithm by applying it to some versions of Quicksort. Then we show the impact of the three improvements listed above by presenting the running times when one of the improvements is switched off. All computations were carried out on an Ultrasparc 60 with 1.5 GB memory. Operations on BDDs were implemented using the CUDD package [8].

5.1   Quicksort

We intend to sort the global array a in ascending order; a call to the quicksort function in figure 2 should sort the fragment of the array starting at index left and ending at index right. The program is parametrised by two variables: n, the number of bits used to represent the integer variables, and m, the number of array entries. We are interested in two properties: first, all executions of the program should terminate, and secondly, all of them should sort the array correctly.

Termination. For this property we can abstract from the actual array contents and just regard the local variables. The program in figure 2 is faulty; it is not guaranteed to terminate (finding the fault is left as an exercise to the reader). A corrected version (containing one more integer variable) is easy to obtain from the counterexample provided by our checker. Figure 2 lists some experimental results. For each n, we list the number of resulting local variables in terms of booleans. Since the array contents are abstracted away here, there are no global variables, and m does not play a rôle.

```
void quicksort (int left,int right)
{
  int lo,hi,piv;

  if (left >= right) return;
  piv = a[right]; lo = left; hi = right;
  while (lo <= hi) {
    if (a[hi] > piv) {
      hi--;
    } else {
      swap a[lo],a[hi];
      lo++;
    }
  }
  quicksort(left,hi);
  quicksort(lo,right);
}
```

n	locals	time	memory
	faulty version		
3	12	0.14 s	4.6 M
4	16	0.39 s	5.3 M
5	20	1.37 s	7.2 M
6	24	6.86 s	10.5 M
7	28	53 s	12.3 M
8	32	592 s	14.6 M
9	36	> 3600 s	–
	corrected version		
3	15	0.22 s	4.8 M
4	20	0.67 s	6.1 M
5	25	3.63 s	9.4 M
6	30	48.67 s	14.7 M
7	35	1238 s	15.1 M
8	40	> 3600 s	–

Fig. 2. Left: Faulty Version of Quicksort. Right: Results for Termination Check.

n	m	globals	locals	normal		randomised	
				time	memory	time	memory
3	4	12	18	1 s	7.2 M	1 s	8.0 M
3	5	15	18	4 s	14.5 M	8 s	15.2 M
3	6	18	18	38 s	22.3 M	82 s	29.9 M
4	4	16	24	3 s	12.1 M	6 s	12.3 M
4	5	20	24	24 s	18.7 M	48 s	25.1 M
4	6	24	24	193 s	77.4 M	531 s	134 M
4	7	28	24	1742 s	414 M	>3600 s	–

Fig. 3. Results for Correctness of Sorting.

Correctness of the Sorting. In this case we also need to model the array contents as global variables. Figure 3 lists the results for the corrected version of the algorithm in figure 2, as well as for a variant in which the pivot element is chosen randomly.

Impact of the Improvements. Figure 4 shows the impact of the three improvements in the task of checking the correctness of Quicksort. We consider the non-randomised version with $n = 3$, and $m = 4$. The line NONE contains the reference values when all improvements are present. The lines VORD and PROC give the time and space consumption when the improvements concerning variable ordering and procedure for solving the model-checking problem are "switched off", respectively. More precisely, in the VORD line we use a BDD ordering corresponding to the order *left, right, lo, hi, piv* (i.e. all BDD variables used for representing *left* before and after a program step come before those for repre-

	time	memory
NONE	1.02 s	7.2 M
VORD	49 s	6.8 M
PROC	624 s	60.6 M

	with preprocessing	w/o preprocessing
closure	0.40 s	213 s
method of [10]	35 s	14 s

Fig. 4. Impact of the Improvements.

senting *right* etc.) plus automatic reordering. In the PROC line we compute $pre^*(Rh\,\Gamma^*)$ instead of $post^*(\{c_0\}) \cap Rh\,\Gamma^*$.

In the right part of the figure we show results for different methods of computing the repeating heads. In all cases we first computed the 'rough' components based on control flow information. We tried the transitive closure approach and the method of [10], both with and without the preprocessing described earlier. The times are for the computation of the heads only. In these experiments, the preprocessing combined with a transitive closure computation worked best, followed by the method of [10] *without* preprocessing; interestingly, using [10] combined with preprocessing led to worse results.

In this example, the times achieved by the model checker would not be possible without the symbolic representation of the variables. The translation into a normal pushdown system would create thousands or even millions of rules, and in a test we made just creating these took far longer than the model-checking with the symbolic approach.

6   Comparison with Bebop

In [1], Ball and Rajamani used the following example (see figure 5) to test their reachability checker Bebop. The example consists of one main function and n functions called level$_i$, $1 \leq i \leq n$, for some $n > 0$. There is one global variable g. Function main calls level$_1$ twice. Every function level$_i$ checks g; if it is true, it increments a 3-bit counter to 7, otherwise it calls level$_{i+1}$ twice. Before returning, level$_i$ negates g. The checker is asked to find out if the labelled statement in main is reachable, i.e. if g can end with a value of false. Since g is not initialised, the checker has to consider both possibilities.

Despite the example's simplicity, some its features are worth pointing out. There is no recursion in the program, and so its state space is finite. However, typical finite-state approaches would flatten the procedure call hierarchy, blowing up the program to an exponential size. Moreover, the program has exponentially many states, yet we can solve the reachability question in time linear in n. Finally, there are $\mathcal{O}(n)$ different variables in the program; however, only two of them are in scope at any given time. For this reason, we can keep the stack alphabet very small, exploiting the locality inherent in the program's structure.

Running times for different values of n are listed in table 5. In [1] a running time of four and a half minutes using the CUDD package and one and a half minutes with the CMU package is reported for $n = 800$, but unfortunately

```
bool g;                  void leveli() {
                           int (0..7) i;
void main() {            if (g) {
  level1();                 i = 0;
  level1();                 while (i < 7) i++;
  if (!g) {              } else if (i < n) {
    reach: skip;             leveli+1();
  }                         leveli+1();
}                         }
                          g = !g;
                        }
```

n	time
200	0.50 s
400	0.94 s
600	1.46 s
800	1.99 s
1000	2.41 s
2000	4.85 s
5000	13.63 s

Fig. 5. Left: The Example Program. Right: Experimental Results.

the paper does not say on which machine. More significant is the comparison of space consumption. We have a peak number of 155 live BDD nodes, *independent of n*. On the contrary, Bebop's space consumption for BDDs increases linearly, reaching more than 200,000 live BDD nodes for $n = 800$. The reason of this difference is that our BDDs require 4 variables (one for the global variable g and three for the 3-bit counter in scope), while Bebop's BDDs require 2401 variables (one variable for g and 2400 for the 800 3-bit counters). Since [1] does not describe the model checking algorithm in detail, we cannot say if this difference in the number of BDD variables is inherent to the algorithms or due to a suboptimal implementation.

7   Conclusions

We have presented a model-checker to verify arbitrary LTL-properties of boolean programs with (possibly recursive) procedures. To the best of our knowledge this is the first checker able to deal with liveness properties. The Bebop model checker by Ball and Rajamani, the closest to ours, can also deal with recursive boolean programs, but it can only check safety properties [1].

Our checker works on a model called symbolic pushdown systems (SPDSs). While this model is definitely more abstract than Bebop's input language, a translation of the former into the latter is simple (see Section 3).

Moreover, having SPDSs as input allows us to make use of the efficient automata-based algorithms described in [4], which leads to some efficiency advantages. In particular, the maximal number of variables in our BDDs depends only on the maximal number of local variables of the procedures, and not on the recursion depth of the program.

Another interesting feature of the reachability algorithms of our checker is that they can be used to compute the set of reachable configurations of the program, i.e. we obtain a complete description of all the reachable pairs of the form (control point, stack content). This makes them applicable to some security problems of Java programs which require precisely this feature [6]. Even more generally, we can compute the set of reachable configurations from any regular set of initial configurations.

Acknowledgements

Many thanks to Ahmed Bouajjani for helpful discussions on how to obtain symbolic versions of the algorithms of [4], and to one anonymous referee for interesting comments and suggestions.

References

1. T. Ball and S. K. Rajamani. Bebop: A symbolic model checker for boolean programs. In *SPIN 00: SPIN Workshop*, LNCS 1885, pages 113–130, 2000.
2. T. Ball and S. K. Rajamani. Automatically validating temporal safety properties of interfaces. Technical report, 2001.
3. A. Bouajjani, J. Esparza, and O. Maler. Reachability analysis of pushdown automata: Application to model-checking. In *Proceedings of CONCUR '97*, LNCS 1243, pages 135–150, 1997.
4. J. Esparza, D. Hansel, P. Rossmanith, and S. Schwoon. Efficient algorithms for model checking pushdown systems. In *Proceedings of CAV '00*, LNCS 1855, 2000.
5. J. Esparza and S. Schwoon. A BDD-based Model Checker for Recursive Programs. Technical report, Institut für Informatik, Technische Universität München, 2001. Available at http://www7.in.tum.de/gruppen/theorie/publications/.
6. T. Jensen, D. L. Métayer, and T. Thorn. Verification of control flow based security properties. In *Proceedings of 1999 IEEE Symposium on Security and Privacy*, IEEE Press, 1999.
7. J.R. Burch, E.M. Clarke, D.E. Long, K.L. MacMillan, and D.L. Dill. Symbolic model checking for sequential circuit verification. *IEEE Transactions on Computer-Aided Design of Integrated Circuits and Systems*, 13(4):401–424, 1994.
8. F. Somenzi. Colorado University Decision Diagram Package. Technical report, University of Colorado, Boulder, 1998.
9. R. E. Tarjan. Depth first search and linear graph algorithms. In *SICOMP 1*, pages 146–160, 1972.
10. A. Xie and P. A. Beerel. Implicit enumeration of strongly connected components. In *Proceedings of ICCAD*, pages 37–40, San Jose, CA, 1999.

Model Checking the World Wide Web*

Luca de Alfaro

Department of Electrical Engineering and Computer Sciences
University of California at Berkeley, Berkeley, CA 94720-1770, USA
dealfaro@eecs.berkeley.edu

Abstract. Web design is an inherently error-prone process. To help with the detection of errors in the structure and connectivity of Web pages, we propose to
apply model-checking techniques to the analysis of the World Wide Web. Model
checking the Web is different in many respects from ordinary model checking of
system models, since the Kripke structure of the Web is not known in advance, but
can only be explored in a gradual fashion. In particular, the model-checking algorithms cannot be phrased in ordinary μ-calculus, since some operations, such as
the computation of sets of predecessor Web pages and the computations of greatest fixpoints, are not possible on the Web. We introduce *constructive μ-calculus*,
a fixpoint calculus similar to μ-calculus, but whose formulas can be effectively
evaluated over the Web; and we show that its expressive power is very close
to that of ordinary μ-calculus. Constructive μ-calculus can be used not only for
phrasing Web model-checking algorithms, but also for the analysis of systems
having a large, irregular state space that can be only gradually explored, such
as software systems. On the basis of these ideas, we have implemented the Web
model checker MCWEB, and we describe some of the issues that arose in its implementation, as well as the type of errors that it was able to find.

1 Introduction

The design of a Web site is an inherently error-prone process. A Web site must be
correctly designed both at a local and at a global level. Good design at the local level
implies that the pages contain well-formed HTML code, have the intended visual appearance, and have no broken links. Several tools are available for checking such local
properties, either on single pages, or more commonly by crawling over an entire Web
site: see for example [7, 20, 12, 13, 9, 14, 6, 11, 5, 19, 21, 8]. Good design at the global
level requires that the Web site satisfies properties concerning its connectivity and cost
of traversal, as well as properties that depend on the path followed to reach the pages,
rather than on the pages only. Examples of such global properties are that every page
of a Web site is reachable from all other pages, and that all paths from the main page
to pages with confidential information must go through an access control page. Current
Web verification tools focus essentially on local properties. On the other hand, model
checking has proved to be an effective technique for the specification and verification
of global properties of the large graphs that correspond to the state-space and transition
relation of systems [4, 17]. Hence, it is natural to ask whether model checking can be

---

* This research was supported in part by the AFOSR MURI grant F49620-00-1-0327 and the
NSF Theory grant CCR-9988172.

G. Berry, H. Comon, and A. Finkel (Eds.): CAV 2001, LNCS 2102, pp. 337–349, 2001.

applied to the analysis of global properties of Web sites. This paper answers this question affirmatively, by showing how model-checking techniques can be adapted to the analysis of the Web, and by illustrating which types of errors are amenable to discovery with such techniques. In particular, we show that model-checking techniques can be used for the analysis of the following three classes of properties:

- *Connectivity properties.* Connectivity properties refer to the graph structure of a Web site.
- *Frame properties.* Since each link loads only a portion of a frame-based page, the content of a frame-based page depends on the path followed by the browser in a site: hence, frame properties are essentially path properties.
- *Cost properties.* Cost properties refer to the number of links or bytes, that must be followed or downloaded while browsing a Web site. An example consists in the computation of the all-pair longest path in a Web site.

Model-checking methods can be broadly classified in *enumerative* methods and *symbolic* methods. Enumerative methods operate on *states* as the basic entities [4, 17], and represent sets of states and transition relations in terms of the individual states. Symbolic methods operate directly on symbolic representations of sets of states [3, 2].

Our approach to the model checking of the Web is enumerative, in that we represent sets of Web pages as collections of single pages. However, we argue that it is convenient to phrase our model-checking algorithms as symbolic algorithms, based on the manipulation of sets of Web pages. In fact, a set-based approach lends itself better to parallelization: given a set S of Web pages, the computation of the set $Post(S)$ of Web pages that can be reached from S by following one link can proceed largely in parallel, by following simultaneously all links originating from pages in S. Since the page fetch time on the Web is typically dominated by response time, rather than transfer time, such a parallel approach is significantly more efficient than a sequential one. Nevertheless, the model checking of the Web differs in several respects from usual symbolic model checking. In particular, some of the basic operations performed by standard model-checking methods cannot be performed on the Web:

1. Given a predicate P defining a property of Web pages, we cannot construct the set S_P consisting of all the Web pages that satisfy P.
2. Given a set S of Web pages, we cannot construct the set $Pre(S)$ of pages that can reach some page of S by following one link.[1]
3. The set V of all Web pages is not known in advance. Likewise, given a set $U \subseteq V$ of Web pages, we cannot construct its complement $V \setminus U$.

These limitations imply in particular that we cannot phrase our model-checking algorithms in standard μ-calculus [15, 10]. In fact, limitation 3 implies that we cannot evaluate expressions that involve the greatest fixpoint operator ν: in $\nu x.\phi(x)$, we cannot set $x_0 = V$ in order to compute the limit $\lim_{k \to \infty} x_k$ of $x_{k+1} = \phi(x_k)$, for $k \geq 0$. Limitation 1 implies that we must introduce restrictions in the use of predicates, and Limitation 2 prevents us from using the standard predecessor operator *Pre*.

---

[1] Search engines such as Google do in fact provide such a service, but the answer they provide is only approximate.

We introduce *constructive μ-calculus*, a fixpoint calculus similar to equational μ-calculus [1], but containing only expressions and constructs that can be effectively evaluated within the above limitations. Constructive μ-calculus differs from standard equational μ-calculus in the following respects:

- The greatest fixpoint operator ν is replaced by the operator ν_x, where x is a set of states that must be already known, and that acts as the "universe set" in which the largest fixpoint is computed.
- The predecessor operator Pre is replaced by its guarded version $GPre(U, W)$, defined by $GPre(U, W) = U \cap Pre(W)$. Since the pages in U are already known when $GPre(U, W)$ is evaluated, all links from U to W are also known, ensuring that $GPre(U, W)$ can be computed.
- Predicates cannot be used to generate sets of states, but only to select from existing sets the states that satisfy given propositional formulas.

We show that these restrictions are enough to ensure that the expressions of constructive μ-calculus are effectively computable, and we provide a precise characterization of the expressive power of constructive μ-calculus. In particular, we show that in spite of the above differences, the expressive power of constructive μ-calculus is essentially the same as the one of ordinary μ-calculus. We phrase our Web model-checking algorithms in constructive μ-calculus.

We argue that the limitations 1–3 are not peculiar to the Web, but are shared by a large class of systems that have a large or infinite state space without regular structure, among which software programs. In the analysis of complex programs, we often have no way of constructing in advance the set of all states, and we may not know what are the predecessors of a given set of states unless we have already encountered those states in the course of the model checking. Constructive μ-calculus is well-suited for phrasing model-checking algorithms that operate on-the-fly over irregular graphs that can be explored only gradually.

In order to experiment with Web model checking, we have implemented the model checker MCWEB, which enables the analysis of connectivity, frame, and cost properties of Web sites. We report our experience in using MCWEB, and we summarize the most common classes of errors that we were able to find using it.

2 The Graph Structure of the Web

As a first step in the application of model-checking techniques to the Web consists in fixing a graph structure of the Web. The simplest choice consists in disregarding the frame structure of the Web, and in modeling the Web as a graph of pages, with links due to both a (anchor) and frame (sub-frame) tags as edges. We call this the *flat* model of the Web. The flat model suffices for many purposes, among which broken link detection and HTML consistency analysis, and indeed many current tools for Web analysis rely on the flat model. Nevertheless, some reachability properties cannot easily be checked on the flat model. For example, the property that the home page of a site is reachable from all pages of the site is often not true in the flat model of a frame-based site, since the link to the home page may be in a separate frame (and thus, a separate graph node) than the main content of the page. For this reason, our graph model of the Web takes into account the frame structure of the pages, unlike the flat model.

2.1   URLpages and Webnodes

An *URL* a is a string that uniquely specifies a document on the Web; it is composed of a protocol field (such as HTTP), a domain name, and a document locator on the domain. In this paper, we restrict our attention to URLs that refer to the HTTP protocol. Given an URL a, we can fetch the corresponding document $s = GetUrl(a)$; we call s the *URLpage* corresponding to the URL a. The URLpage $s = \langle g_s, h_s, F_s, A_s \rangle$ consists in the URL g_s from which the document is retrieved, the textual content h_s, a set of *frame tags* F_s, and a set of *anchor tags* A_s. The URL g_s may be different from s due to automatic redirection, as effected by the HTTP protocol. Since images are loaded automatically by most current browsers, we consider them to be an integral part of h_s, even though they are specified by separate anchors. A *frame tag* $\langle b, \ell \rangle$ consists of the URL b to be loaded into the subframe, and of a name ℓ used to label the subframe. An *anchor tag* $\langle b, \ell \rangle$ consists of the URL b specifying the link destination, and of a *target name* ℓ, which specifies in which subframe the new URL should be loaded [16, 18] (if no target is specified, we take ℓ to be the empty string ε). While this is only a partial subset of the tags and attributes that occur in HTML documents, it will suffice for our purpose of defining the graph structure of the Web.

The nodes of our graph model of the Web, called the *webgraph*, consist in *webnodes*. A webnode w is a tree with URLpages as nodes; the edges of the tree are labeled by frame names. We write $s \in w$ to denote that an URLpage s is a node in the tree w. If $s \in w$ and $F_s = \{\langle a_1, \ell_1 \rangle, \ldots, \langle a_n, \ell_n \rangle\}$, then the URLpage s has n URL-pages $t_1, \ldots, t_n$ as children in w; for $1 \leq i \leq n$, the edge from s to t_i is labeled with ℓ_i. Given an URLpage t, the webnode $w = WebNode(t)$ is obtained by "load-ing" recursively all the subframes of t. Precisely, w consists in a tree with root t, where each URLpage $s \in w$ has as descendants the set $\{GetUrl(a) \mid \langle a, \ell \rangle \in F_t\}$ of URLpages corresponding to subframes of t. For brevity, given an URL a we define $GetWeb(a) = WebNode(GetUrl(a))$.

The edges of the webgraph correspond to page links; the precise definition takes into account the way in which pages are loaded into subframes. Given a webnode w, and an URLpage $s \in w$, we denote by $subtree(w, s)$ the subtree of w with root in s. Given a webnode w, an URLpage $s \in w$, and a link $\langle a, \ell \rangle \in A_s$, we denote by $target(w, s, \ell)$ the subtree of w that will be replaced by the webnode $GetWeb(a)$ when the link $\langle a, \ell \rangle$ is followed, defined according to the HTML standard [16, 18]. Pre-cisely, if $\ell = \_blank$ or $\ell = \_top$, we have $target(w, s, \ell) = w$; if $\ell = \_self$ or $\ell = \varepsilon$ then $target(w, s, \ell) = subtree(w, s)$, if $\ell = \_parent$ then $target(w, s, \ell) = subtree(w, t)$, where t is the parent of s in the tree w. Finally, if ℓ is any other string, then $target(w, s, \ell) = subtree(w, t)$, where t is the unique URLpage such that the link in w from the parent of t to t is labeled ℓ; if there is no such link, or if the link is not unique, then we treat the link as a "broken link", and we take as its destination a spe-cial error webnode. Given a webnode w, a subtree u of w, and another webnode v, we denote by $w[v/u]$ the result of replacing u by v in w. Given a webnode w and an URL-page $s \in w$, the destination of a non-broken link $\langle a, \ell \rangle \in A_s$ consists in the webnode $dest(w, s, \langle a, \ell \rangle) = w[GetWeb(a)/target(w, s, \ell)]$.

Example 1 . In Figure 1, we depict a webnode $w = WebNode(s_0)$, and two webnodes u, v reachable from w by following links. We have $F_{s_0} = \{\langle a_1, \ell_1 \rangle, \langle a_2, \ell_2 \rangle\}$; the chil-dren of s_0 in w are s_1, s_2: by convention, we denote $GetUrl(a_i) = s_i$ for all $i \geq 0$.

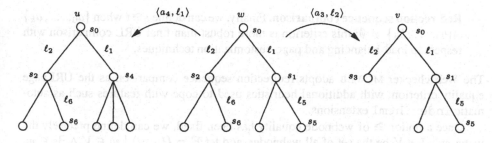

Fig. 1. A primary webnode $w = WebNode(s_0)$, and two secondary webnodes u, v.

Only some of the edge labels and URLpages are indicated, to avoid clutter. URLpage s_1 contains the anchor tag $\langle a_3, \ell_2 \rangle$; taking this link leads to webnode v. URLpage s_2 contains the anchor tag $\langle a_4, \ell_1 \rangle$; taking this link leads to webnode u. URLpage s_5 contains the anchor tag $\langle a_7, \ell_6 \rangle$. Note that the link corresponding to the anchor tag $\langle a_7, \ell_6 \rangle$ is broken in v, since there is no label ℓ_6 in v; the link is not broken in w, and it is not present in u. This illustrates how links can become broken in secondary pages.

2.2 The Webgraph

In order to fix the structure of the webgraph, we need to establish a criterion for webnode equality. Two webnodes w and u are equal, written $w \cong u$, if their trees of URLpages are equal: hence, webnode equality is defined in terms of URLpage equality. There are several possible definitions for URLpage equality; to understand the issue, we need to explain in more detail how URLpages are fetched from the Web. Given an URL a_0, we can issue an HTTP request for a_0. The result can either be the URLpage $GetUrl(a_0)$, or a redirection URL a_1. In the latter case, we can issue a page request for a_1, obtaining either $GetUrl(a_1)$, or a redirection URL a_2. The process continues until either an error occurs, or until we reach a $k \geq 0$ such that a request for a_k returns an URLpage s; we set then $GetUrl(a_0) = \cdots = GetUrl(a_k) = s$. Consider two sequences $a_0, \ldots, a_k$, $GetUrl(a_0)$ and $b_0, \ldots, b_n$, $GetUrl(b_0)$ of redirections and final pages, and let $s = GetUrl(a_0)$ and $t = GetUrl(b_0)$; note that we have $g_s = a_k$, and $g_t = b_n$. We can define whether s is equal to t, written $s \cong t$, in several ways.

- **Textual comparison.** We can define $s \cong t$ when $h_s = h_t$, i.e., when the texts of the two URLpages s and t are identical. According to this definition, however, different domains containing two textually identical pages (for instance, two empty pages) would share a webnode in the webgraph, leading to unexpected results when reachability analysis is performed. In addition, textual comparison is sensitive to minor differences in the pages retrieved, such as visitation counter updates.
- **Final URL comparison.** Another possibility consists in defining $s \cong t$ when $a_k = b_n$, or equivalently when $g_s = g_t$. Occasionally, however, a request to an URL a is redirected to any of a large number of URLs $c_1, \ldots, c_m$, in order either to distribute the load between machines, or to provide slightly different content in terms of advertising. Final URL comparison would consider $GetUrl(c_1) \neq \cdots \neq GetUrl(c_m)$, in spite of the fact that those pages are essentially the same page.

– **Redirection sequence comparison.** Finally, we can define $s \cong t$ when $\{a_0, \ldots, a_k\}$ $\cap \{b_0, \ldots, b_n\} \neq \emptyset$; this criterion is more robust than final URL comparison with respect to load-balancing and page-customization techniques.

The Web checker MCWEB adopts redirection sequence comparison as the URLpage equality criterion, with additional heuristics used to cope with features such as automatic index.html extensions.

Once a notion $\cong$ of webnode equality has been fixed, we can define precisely the webgraph. Let V be the set of all webnodes, and let $E = \{(w, u) \mid w \in V \land \exists s \in w.$ $\exists \langle a, \ell \rangle \in A_s.u = dest(w, s, \langle a, \ell \rangle)\}$ be the set of all edges between webnodes. The *webgraph* $(V/\cong, E/\cong)$ is the quotient of (V, E) with respect to the equality notion $\cong$. We note that this definition is not completely precise, as it depends on the function *GetUrl*, that given an URL returns the corresponding URL. This definition also does not capture the fact that the true connectivity Web is time-varying. Nevertheless, this definition formalizes the structure of the Web to a sufficient degree for the development of our model-checking algorithms.

We say that a webnode $w \in V$ is *primary* if there is an URL a such that $w = GetWeb(a)$, and that w is *secondary* otherwise. Primary webnodes correspond to Web pages that can be obtained by loading an URL with a browser. Secondary webnodes cannot be loaded directly; they are reached by traversing links and updating the frame structure starting from primary webnodes. Most current tools for Web analysis only consider primary webnodes. Yet, many errors arise only in secondary webnodes, as illustrated by Example 1. Our experience with MCWEB indicates that the difficulty of examining all secondary webnodes is a common cause of errors on the Web.

3 Model Checking the Web

As remarked in the introduction, the ordinary μ-calculus is not suited for the model checking of the Web, since it includes several operations that are not effectively computable on the Web. We introduce constructive μ-calculus, a fixpoint calculus similar to μ-calculus, but containing only expressions that can be effectively computed.

3.1 Constructive μ-Calculus

Syntax. Constructive μ-calculus $(C\mu C)$ is derived from the equational μ-calculus of [1]. A $C\mu C$ formula $\langle (B_1, \ldots, B_n), x_m \rangle$ consists of $n > 0$ *blocks* $B_1, \ldots, B_n$, and of an *output variable* x_m, with $m \in \{1, \ldots, n\}$. Each block B_i, for $1 \leq i \leq n$, has the form $\lambda_i.x_i = e_i$, where x_i is a variable, e_i a *set expression*, and λ_i is a quantifier tag equal to either μx_i, or to $\nu x_i \subseteq x_j$ for some $j > i$. Hence, the quantifier tag of the outermost block B_n must be μx_n. Each set expression e_i is defined according to the following grammar:

$$\Phi ::= x \mid \Phi \cup \Phi \mid \Phi \cap \Phi \mid \Phi \setminus \Phi \mid \Phi \cap \Theta \mid a$$
$$\mid Post(\Phi) \mid \widetilde{GPost}(\Phi, \Phi) \mid GPre(\Phi, \Phi) \mid \widetilde{GPre}(\Phi, \Phi)$$

where a is a constant, x is one of $x_1, \ldots, x_n$, and Θ is a *predicate expression*. Predicate expressions are defined by the grammar

$$\Theta ::= \Theta \vee \Theta \mid \neg\Theta \mid P,$$

where P is a predicate belonging to some basic set of predicates $\mathcal{P}$. The use of the set difference operator in set expressions is subject to the following restriction. For $i,j \in \{1, \ldots, n\}$, we say that the block B_i depends directly on block B_j, written $B_i \succ B_j$, if x_j appears in e_i, and we let $\overset{*}{\succ}$ be the reflexive transitive closure of $\succ$. For $i, j \in \{1, \ldots, n\}$, we say that that the variable x_j occurs with negative polarity in e_i if it occurs within an odd number of right-hand sides of the set-difference operator $\backslash$. Then, we require that for all $i, j \in \{1, \ldots, n\}$, the variable x_j occurs with negative polarity in e_i only when $B_i \overset{*}{\not\succ} B_j$. We say that a $C\mu C$ formula is *negation-free* if it does not contain occurrences of the set difference operator $\backslash$. We denote by $C\mu C^+$ the negation-free fragment of $C\mu C$.

Syntax of Ordinary Equational μ-Calculus. In order to compare the expressive power of constructive and ordinary μ-calculus, we define also the semantics of the equational μ-calculus of [1], denoted by μC. The formulas of μC have the same structure of those of $C\mu C$, except that the quantifier tag λ_i can be equal to either μx_i, or to νx_i. The syntax of set expressions is given by the grammar

$$\Phi ::= x \mid \Phi \cup \Phi \mid \Phi \cap \Phi \mid \Theta \mid \neg\Theta \mid a \mid Post(\Phi) \mid \widetilde{Post}(\Phi) \mid Pre(\Phi) \mid \widetilde{Pre}(\Phi)$$

Semantics. For conciseness, we define the semantics of a calculus that is a superset of both $C\mu C$ and μC; the semantics of $C\mu C$ and μC are obtained by considering the appropriate fragments of this calculus. The semantics is defined with respect to a *Kripke structure* $\mathcal{K} = (V, E, \mathcal{C}, f^c, \mathcal{P}, f^p)$, where (V, E) is a graph, $\mathcal{C}$ is a set of constants, $f^c : \mathcal{C} \mapsto V$ is the interpretation of the constants, $\mathcal{P}$ is a set of predicates, and $f^p : \mathcal{P} \mapsto 2^V$ is the interpretation of the predicates. In the model checking of the Web, we take V, E as in the webgraph, $\mathcal{C}$ to be the set of valid URLs, f^c to be *GetWeb*, $\mathcal{P}$ to be a set of effectively checkable predicates defined on webnodes, and $f^p(P) = \{w \in W \mid w \models P\}$ for all $P \in \mathcal{P}$. Given such a Kripke structure, all the operators in set and predicate expressions have their standard meanings, except for the predecessor and successor operators. The semantics of the predecessor and successor operators is defined, for all $U, W \subseteq V$, by

$$Pre(W) = \{u \in V \mid \exists v \in W.(u, v) \in E\} \qquad GPre(U, W) = U \cap Pre(W)$$

$$\widetilde{Pre}(W) = \{u \in V \mid \forall v.((u, v) \in E \to v \in W)\} \qquad \widetilde{GPre}(U, W) = U \cap \widetilde{Pre}(W)$$

$$Post(W) = \{u \in V \mid \exists v \in W.(v, u) \in E\}$$

$$\widetilde{Post}(W) = \{u \in V \mid \forall v.((v, u) \in E \to v \in W)\} \qquad \widetilde{GPost}(U, W) = U \cap \widetilde{Post}(W)$$

The intuition is that in $C\mu C$ we can compute the set of predecessors of a given set W of webnodes only relative to another set U of webnodes; similarly for the other constructive operators. The operational semantics of constructive μ-calculus, given by Algorithm 1 below, will ensure that all the webnodes in U have already been explored when $GPre(U, W)$ is computed (resp. $\widetilde{GPre}(U, W)$, $\widetilde{GPost}(U, W)$), thus ensuring that all the links from U to W are known.

The definition of semantics follows the lines of [1]. Consider a Kripke structure $\mathcal{K}$ and a formula $\langle\langle B_1, \ldots, B_n \rangle, x_m \rangle$ of $C\mu C$, where each block B_i, $1 \leq i \leq n$, has the form $\lambda_i.x_i = e_i$, for λ_i equal to either μx_i or $\nu x_i \subseteq x_j$. Let $\Gamma = (\{x_1, \ldots, x_n\} \mapsto 2^V)$ be the set of valuations of the variables in the formula. Given $\gamma \in \Gamma$ and $1 \leq i \leq n$, we indicate with $\gamma \circ (x_i = U)$ the valuation that coincides with γ, except that it associates value $U \subseteq V$ to x_i. Given a valuation γ and a set expression e_i, for $1 \leq i \leq n$, we denote by $[\![e_i \mid \mathcal{K}, \gamma]\!] \subseteq V$ the value of e_i in the Kripke structure $\mathcal{K}$ under valuation γ. Given $\gamma \in \Gamma$ we define recursively, for $i = 0$ to n, the valuation $Eval_{\mathcal{K}}^i(\langle B_1, \ldots, B_i \rangle \mid \gamma) \in \Gamma$. The definition relies on two auxiliary functions $f_{\mathcal{K},\gamma}^i, g_{\mathcal{K},\gamma}^i : \Gamma \mapsto \Gamma$, defined as follows:

$$g_{\mathcal{K},\gamma}^i(\delta) = Eval_{\mathcal{K}}^{i-1}(\langle B_1, \ldots, B_{i-1} \rangle \mid \delta) \circ (x_{i+1} = \gamma(x_{i+1})) \circ \cdots \circ (x_n = \gamma(x_n))$$

$$f_{\mathcal{K},\gamma}^i(\delta) = g_{\mathcal{K},\gamma}^i(\delta) \circ (x_i = [\![e_i \mid \mathcal{K}, g_{\mathcal{K},\gamma}^i(\delta)]\!]) \qquad \text{if } \lambda_i \text{ is } \mu x_i \text{ or } \nu x_i$$

$$f_{\mathcal{K},\gamma}^i(\delta) = g_{\mathcal{K},\gamma}^i(\delta) \circ (x_i = \gamma(x_j) \cap [\![e_i \mid \mathcal{K}, g_{\mathcal{K},\gamma}^i(\delta)]\!]) \qquad \text{if } \lambda_i \text{ is } \nu x_i \subseteq x_j$$

We then define $Eval_{\mathcal{K}}^i(\langle B_1, \ldots, B_i \rangle \mid \gamma) = \lambda\delta.(\delta = f_{\mathcal{K},\gamma}^i(\delta))$, where $\lambda = \mu$ if λ_i is μx_i, and $\lambda = \nu$ if λ_i is $\nu x_i \subseteq x_j$. The restrictions on the use of negation, together with the Tarski-Knaster theorem [22], ensure that the fixpoints exist. It can be readily verified that $Eval_{\mathcal{K}}^n(\langle B_1, \ldots, B_n \rangle \mid \gamma)$ does not depend on γ. The meaning of the complete formula is the valuation of the output variable: we define $[\![\langle\langle B_1, \ldots, B_n \rangle, x_m \rangle]\!]_{\mathcal{K}} = Eval_{\mathcal{K}}^n(\langle B_1, \ldots, B_n \rangle \mid \gamma)(x_m)$, for an arbitrary $\gamma \in \Gamma$.

3.2   Expressivity

In order to study the relationship between the expressive power of $C\mu C$ and μC, we consider fixed infinite and countable sets $\mathcal{P}$ and $\mathcal{C}$ of predicates and constants, so that the syntax of the formulas is fixed. Given a class $\mathcal{U}$ of Kripke structures, let $\mathcal{V} = \bigcup \{V \mid (V, E, \mathcal{C}, f^c, \mathcal{P}, f^p) \in \mathcal{U}\}$ be the set of all states. A formula ϕ of fixpoint calculus defines a function $[\![\phi]\!] : \mathcal{U} \mapsto 2^{\mathcal{V}}$ by $[\![\phi]\!](\mathcal{K}) = [\![\phi]\!]_{\mathcal{K}}$. Given $\mathcal{U}$ and two fixpoint calculi C and C', we say that C is *as expressive* as C' over $\mathcal{U}$, written $C \sqsupseteq_{\mathcal{U}} C'$, if for every formula ϕ' of C' there is a formula ϕ of C such that $[\![\phi]\!]$ and $[\![\phi']\!]$ are the same function. We say that C and C' are *equally expressive* over $\mathcal{U}$, written $C \equiv_{\mathcal{U}} C'$, if both $C \sqsupseteq_{\mathcal{U}} C'$ and $C \sqsubseteq_{\mathcal{U}} C'$ hold, and we say that C is *strictly more expressive* than C' over $\mathcal{U}$, written $C \sqsupset C'$, if $C \sqsupseteq_{\mathcal{U}} C'$ holds but $C \sqsubseteq_{\mathcal{U}} C'$ does not. Let $\mathcal{K}_{fin}$ and $\mathcal{K}_{cnt}$ be the classes of Kripke structures with finite and countable state space, respectively. The following theorem relates the expressive power of μC and $C\mu C^+$.

Theorem 1. $\mu C \sqsupset_{\mathcal{K}_{fin}} C\mu C^+$, and $\mu C \sqsupset_{\mathcal{K}_{cnt}} C\mu C^+$.

The difference in expressive power is essentially due to the inability of $C\mu C$ of considering portions of the Kripke structure that are unreachable from named constants.

This is confirmed by the following result. We say that a class $\mathcal{U}$ of Kripke structures is *finitely rooted* if there is a finite set of constants $\{a_1, \ldots, a_n\}$ such that for all $(V, E, \mathcal{C}, f^c, \mathcal{P}, f^p) \in \mathcal{U}$, we have that every state of V is reachable in (V, E) from $f^c(a_1) \cup \cdots \cup f^c(a_n)$ in a finite number of steps.

Theorem 2 . *For all classes $\mathcal{U}$ of finitely-rooted Kripke structures, we have $\mu C \equiv_{\mathcal{U}} C\mu C^+$.*

Proof. There is a straightforward translation of $C\mu C^+$ into μC. The translation from μC to $C\mu C^+$ is as follows. Consider a μC expression $\langle B_1, \ldots, B_n, x_m \rangle$, where for $1 \leq i \leq n$ the block B_i has the form $\lambda x_i . x_i = e_i$, for $\lambda \in \{\mu, \nu\}$. An equivalent $C\mu C$ expression is $\langle B_1', \ldots, B_n', B_{n+1}', x_m \rangle$, where the block B_{n+1}' is $\mu y . y = GetWeb(a_1) \cup \cdots \cup GetWeb(a_n) \cup Post(y)$, and for $1 \leq i \leq n$, the block B_i' is obtained from B_i by replacing νx_i with $\nu x_i \subseteq y$ and $Pre(\Phi)$ with $GPre(y, \Phi)$, $\widetilde{Pre}(\Phi)$ with $\widetilde{GPre}(y, \Phi)$, and $\widetilde{Post}(\Phi)$ with $\widetilde{GPost}(y, \Phi)$. $\blacksquare$

The converse is also true, under some general conditions. We say that a Kripke structure is *non-trivial* if it contains at least one predicate symbol.

Theorem 3 . *Consider a class $\mathcal{U}$ of non-trivial Kripke structures. If $\mu C \equiv_{\mathcal{U}} C\mu C^+$, then all the structures in $\mathcal{U}$ are finitely rooted.*

The following result follows from the presence of the set-difference operator $\backslash$ in the definition of $C\mu C$, and can be proved similarly to Theorem 2.

Theorem 4 . *On finitely-rooted Kripke structures, the fixpoint calculus $C\mu C$ is closed under complementation.*

The difference in expressive power between $C\mu C$ and μC on finitely-rooted structures is due to the fact that μC is not closed under complementation. Let μC^D be the calculus obtaining by adding to μC the operator *DGetWeb*, applicable only to constants, with semantics defined by $DGetWeb(a) = \{w \in V \mid w \neq f^c(a)\}$. The calculus μC^D is then closed under complementation, leading to the following theorem.

Theorem 5 . *The following assertions hold.*

1. $\mu C^D \sqsupseteq_{\mathcal{K}_{fin}} C\mu C$, and $\mu C^D \sqsupseteq_{\mathcal{K}_{cnt}} C\mu C$.
2. *For all classes $\mathcal{U}$ of finitely-rooted Kripke structures, we have $\mu C^D \equiv_{\mathcal{U}} C\mu C$.*

3.3 Evaluation of Constructive μ-Calculus Formulas

While μC and $C\mu C$ have similar expressive power, the calculus $C\mu C$ guarantees that, whenever the interpretations of the variables at the fixpoint consists in finite sets, then the fixpoint itself can be computed in finite time. An algorithm for doing so is given below.

Algorithm 1. **Input:** a Kripke structure $\mathcal{K} = (V, E, \mathcal{C}, f^c, \mathcal{P}, f^p)$, and a $C\mu C$ formula $\phi = \langle\langle B_1, \ldots, B_n\rangle, x_m\rangle$, where each block B_i, $1 \le i \le n$, has the form $\lambda_i.x_i = e_i$.
Output: $[\phi]_\mathcal{K}$.
Procedure: Let $\Gamma = \{x_1, \ldots, x_n\} \mapsto 2^V$. Given a valuation $\gamma \in \Gamma$, we define recursively, for $i = 0$ to n, the valuation $Compute(\langle B_1, \ldots, B_i\rangle \mid \gamma) \in \Gamma$. For $i = 0$, we let $Compute(\langle\rangle \mid \gamma) = \gamma$. For $i > 0$, the definition is as follows.

   Init: If λ_i is μx_i, then let $\gamma'_0 = \gamma \circ (x_i = \emptyset)$; if λ_i is $\nu x_i \subseteq x_j$, then let
   $\gamma'_0 = \gamma \circ (x_i = \gamma(x_j))$.
   Update: For $k \ge 0$, let $\gamma''_k = Compute(\langle B_1, \ldots, B_{i-1}\rangle \mid \gamma'_k)$,
   $W_k = [e_i \mid \mathcal{K}, \gamma''_k]$, and $\gamma'_{k+1} = \gamma''_k \circ (x_i = W_k)$.
   Define: $Compute(\langle B_1, \ldots, B_i\rangle \mid \gamma) = \lim_{k \to \infty} \gamma'_k$.

Return: $Compute(\langle B_1, \ldots, B_n\rangle \mid \gamma)(x_m)$, where γ is arbitrary.

The following theorem states that the fixpoints of $C\mu C$, if finite, can be effectively computed. We say that an operation can be *effectively computed* if it involves only finitely many states of the Kripke structure.

Theorem 6. *Consider a $C\mu C$ formula $\langle\langle B_1, \ldots, B_n\rangle, x_m\rangle$, and assume that for a variable interpretation γ, we have $|Eval^n_\mathcal{K}(\langle B_1, \ldots, B_n\rangle \mid \gamma)(x_i)| < \infty$ for all $1 \le i \le n$. Then, Algorithm 1 consists of effectively computable steps, and it terminates returning $[\langle\langle B_1, \ldots, B_n\rangle, x_m\rangle]_\mathcal{K}$.*

The result is a consequence of the fact that, if all variables have finite extension at the fixpoint, then only a finite portion of the Kripke structure is explored. Note that the result is independent from the cardinality of V. In contrast, it is well known that when V is infinite, the formulas of μC cannot be evaluated iteratively, even when the fixpoints are finite.

3.4   Predicates for Web Analysis

After some experimentation, we have chosen to include in the Web model checker MCWEB the following families of predicates, for all strings α, domains Δ, and $k > 0$:

- predicate $contains_{\alpha_1, \alpha_2, \ldots, \alpha_k}$ holds for a webnode w if there is an URLpage $s \in w$ such that h_s contains all the strings $\alpha_1, \ldots, \alpha_k$.
- predicate in_domain_Δ holds for a webnode w if there is an URLpage $s \in w$ such that g_s contains the substring Δ;
- predicate $all\_in\_domain_\Delta$ holds for a webnode w if all URLpages $s \in w$ are such that g_s contains the substring Δ;
- predicate $http\_error_k$ holds for a webnode w if the HTTP error k occurred while loading some URLpage in w;
- predicate $frames\_error$ is a catch-all predicate, that holds for a webnode w if the frame structure at w contains errors. Among the errors currently checked are: duplicated frame names (a name ℓ that occurs in more than one frame tag), frame trees deeper than a fixed threshold, and non-existent link targets (anchors tags $\langle a, \ell\rangle$ such that ℓ does not appear in any frame tag).

3.5 A Semi-decision Procedure for Non-emptiness

Consider a $C\mu C^+$ formula $\phi = \langle\langle B_1, \ldots, B_n\rangle, x_m\rangle$, where each block B_i has the form $\lambda_i.x_i = e_i$, for $1 \leq i \leq n$. During the evaluation of ϕ according to Algorithm 1, we call *checkpoints* the stages where all the variables x_i with quantifier tag equal to $\nu x_i \subseteq x_j$ for some $j > i$ have reached a fixpoint (even if some variables with μ-tag have not). Then, if the interpretation of the output variable x_m at some checkpoint is non-empty, we know that also $[\![\phi]\!]_{\mathcal{K}} \neq \emptyset$. To make this observation precise, we consider a $C\mu C^+$ formula $\phi = \langle\langle B_1, \ldots, B_n\rangle, x_m\rangle$, and we let $\{i \in \{1, \ldots, n\} \mid \lambda_i \text{ is } \mu x_i\} = \{i_1, \ldots, i_j\}$ be the set of indices of the μ-blocks in ϕ; we denote by $\sharp\mu(\phi) = j$ the number of such indices. Given $k_1, k_2, \ldots, k_j \geq 0$, we compute $[\![\phi]\!]_{\mathcal{K}}^{k_1, \ldots, k_j}$ by following Algorithm 1, except that for $1 \leq l \leq j$ we take $Compute(\langle B_1, \ldots, B_{i_l}\rangle \mid \gamma)_{i_1, \ldots, i_l} = \gamma'_{k_l}$. Hence, $[\![\phi]\!]_{\mathcal{K}}^{k_1, \ldots, k_j}$ is computed by performing $k_1, k_2, \ldots, k_j$ iterations of the μ-blocks, rather than waiting until the fixpoint is reached.

Theorem 7 . *For all $C\mu C^+$ formulas ϕ and Kripke structures $\mathcal{K}$, if $[\![\phi]\!]_{\mathcal{K}}^{k_1, \ldots, k_{\sharp\mu(\phi)}} \neq \emptyset$ for some $k_1, \ldots, k_{\sharp\mu(\phi)} \geq 0$, then $[\![\phi]\!]_{\mathcal{K}} \neq \emptyset$.*

Given a $C\mu C^+$ formula ϕ and a (possibly infinite) finitely-branching Kripke structure $\mathcal{K}$, this theorem provides a semi-decision procedure for $[\![\phi]\!]_{\mathcal{K}} \neq \emptyset$: it suffices to enumerate the lists of non-negative integers $\langle k_1, \ldots, k_{\sharp\mu(\phi)}\rangle$, checking for each list whether $[\![\phi]\!]_{\mathcal{K}}^{k_1, \ldots, k_{\sharp\mu(\phi)}} \neq \emptyset$. As an example, consider the formula

$$\phi = \langle\langle \nu y \subseteq x.y = \widetilde{Pre}(y), \mu x.x = \text{in\_domain}_\Delta \cap (Post(x) \cup a)\rangle, y\rangle,$$

where Δ is a domain name, and a is an URL in that domain. If $\mathcal{K}$ is the webgraph, then $[\![\phi]\!]_{\mathcal{K}}$ is the set of webnodes in domain Δ that are reachable from the URL a, and that have no link sequence leading outside Δ. The variable x keeps track of the portion of Δ that is reachable from a. If the domain Δ contains infinitely many webnodes (as can be the case in sites with dynamically generated pages), then the evaluation of $[\![\phi]\!]_{\mathcal{K}}$ does not terminate. On the other hand, we can obtain a semi-decision procedure for $[\![\phi]\!]_{\mathcal{K}} \neq \emptyset$ by evaluating $[\![\phi]\!]_{\mathcal{K}}^k$ for $k = 0, 1, 2, \ldots$, and by checking for non-emptiness for each value of k. This provides a semi-decision procedure for detecting pages in a Web site that cannot reach the rest of the Web.

4 Web Model Checking in Practice

In order to experiment with Web model checking, we have implemented the model checker MCWEB. The checker MCWEB is written in Python; its input consists in constructive μ-calculus formulas, augmented with the capability of post-processing the output in order to perform quantitative analysis of Web properties.

In some domains, such as hardware, the cost of errors that go undetected until the production stage is very large, and consequently a large effort is done in order to detect them early. Formal verification methods such as model checking are usually called to help in finding error that cannot be found with other methods. Consequently, finding errors with formal methods is a difficult task. In Web model checking, the situation is very different. Due to the lower cost of undetected errors on the Web, many collections of Web pages are checked cursorily, if at all, and in our experience errors are abundant, and come in great variety. The sites where we found the highest density of errors were medium-sized sites: small sites often have a simple structure that limits the number of errors; large commercial sites are usually produced with the help of automated tools, that help in avoiding structural errors. Nevertheless, errors were found even in large sites such as amazon.com.

In the course of the experimentation with MCWEB, we have identified some categories of errors and properties that are commonly of interest.

- **Broken links.** Detecting broken links is an ability that MCWEB shares with many other tools. MCWEB implicitly checks for broken links whenever the *Post* operator is applied to a set of webnodes.
- **Duplicated frame names.** MCWEB checks automatically for ill-formed frame structures using the predicate frames_error described earlier. For example, to check that no webnode with ill-formed frame structure is present in the site Δ with home page a, it suffices to evaluate the formula $\langle\langle\mu x.x = a \cup (Post(x) \cap \text{in\_domain}_\Delta), \mu y.y = x \cap \text{frames\_error}\rangle, y\rangle$.
- **Non-hierarchical frame content.** If an URLpage t of webnode w is not in the same domain as the root URLpage s of w, then the content and the links in t are typically not under the control of the author of s. Moreover, if s can be reached from t, then this usually leads to a webnode containing two instances of the same URLpage s. We can check that all webnodes in domain Δ are composed only of URLpages in Δ by evaluating the formula $\langle\langle\mu x.x = a \cup (Post(x) \cap \text{in\_domain}_\Delta), \mu y.y = x \cap \neg\text{all\_in\_domain}_\Delta\rangle, y\rangle$, where a is the home page of Δ.
- **Reachability.** Suppose that A is a set of webnodes containing publicly available information, B is a set of webnodes with private content, and C is a set of access control webnodes, We can check that all paths from A to B in domain Δ contain a webnode in C by checking the emptiness of the formula $\langle\langle\mu y.y = (x \cap A) \cup (Post(y) \cap \text{in\_domain}_\Delta \cap \neg C), \mu x.x = a \cup (Post(x) \cap \text{in\_domain}_\Delta), \mu z.z = y \cap B\rangle, z\rangle$, where we assume that A, B, C are definable in terms of predicate contains, and a is the home page of Δ.
- **Repeated reachability.** To compute which pages of a Web site Δ cannot reach the home page a without leaving Δ, we can evaluate the formula $\langle\langle\mu z.z = a \cup Pre(x, z), \mu x.x = a \cup (Post(x) \cap \text{in\_domain}_\Delta), \mu y.y = x \setminus z\rangle, y\rangle$.
- **Longest paths.** MCWEB also contains an extension that enables the computation of the longest and shortest paths in a set of webnodes, where the "length" of a path consists in the number of bytes, or the number of links, that must be downloaded in order to follow it. For example, to find the all-pair longest path between webnodes of a domain Δ, MCWEB post-processes the output of the formula $\langle\langle\mu x.x = a \cup (Post(x) \cap \text{in\_domain}_\Delta)\rangle, x\rangle$. The computation of the all-pair longest path can provide information about the bottlenecks in the navigation of a site.

Acknowledgments

I would like to thank Tom and Monika Henzinger, Jan Jannink, and Freddy Mang for many helpful discussions and suggestions.

References

1. G. Bhat and R. Cleaveland. Efficient model checking via the equational μ-calculus. In *Proc. 11th IEEE Symp. Logic in Comp. Sci.*, pages 304–312, 1996.
2. J.R. Burch, E.M. Clarke, K.L. McMillan, D.L. Dill, and L.J. Hwang. Symbolic model checking: 10^{20} states and beyond. In *Proc. 5th IEEE Symp. Logic in Comp. Sci.*, pages 428–439. IEEE Computer Society Press, 1990.
3. J.R. Burch, K.L. McMillan, E.M. Clarkes, and D.L. Dill. Sequential circuit verification using symbolic model checking. In *Proc. of the 27th ACM/IEEE Design Automation Conference*, pages 46–51, Orlando, FL, USA, June 1990.
4. E.M. Clarke and E.A. Emerson. Design and synthesis of synchronization skeletons using branching time temporal logic. In *Proc. Workshop on Logic of Programs*, volume 131 of *Lect. Notes in Comp. Sci.*, pages 52–71. Springer-Verlag, 1981.
5. Electronic Software Publishing Co. Linkscan. http://www.elsop.com/linkscan/.
6. Watchfire Co. Linkbot. http://www.watchfire.com/products/linkbot.htm.
7. R.T. Fielding. Maintaiing distributed hypertext infostructures: Welcome to MOMspider's web. In *Proceedings of First Intl. Conference on the World-Wide Web (WWW 94)*, 1994.
8. Voget Selbach Enterprises GmbH. Link tester. http://vse-online.com/link-tester/.
9. Tilman Hausherr. Link sleuth. http://home.snafu.de/tilman/xenulink.html.
10. T.A. Henzinger, O. Kupferman, and S. Qadeer. From *pre*historic to *post*modern symbolic model checking. In A.J. Hu and M.Y. Vardi, editors, *CAV 98: Computer-aided Verification*, Lecture Notes in Computer Science 1427, pages 195–206. Springer-Verlag, 1998.
11. Biggbyte Software Inc. Infolink. http://www.biggbyte.com/infolink/index.html.
12. Link Alarm Inc. Link alarm. http://www.linkalarm.com/.
13. NetMechanic Inc. Html toolbox. http://www.netmechanic.com/.
14. InContext. Web analyzer 2.0. http://www.incontext.com/WAinfo.html.
15. D. Kozen. Results on the propositional μ-calculus. *Theoretical Computer Science*, 27(3):333–354, 1983.
16. C. Musciano and B. Kennedy. *HTML: The Definitive Guide*. O'Reilly & Associates, Inc., 1998. Third Edition.
17. J.P. Queille and J. Sifakis. Specification and verification of concurrent systems in Cesar. In *Proc. 5th International Symposium on Programming*, volume 137 of *Lect. Notes in Comp. Sci.*, pages 337–351. Springer-Verlag, 1981.
18. D. Raggett, A. Le Hors, and I. Jacobs. HTML 4.01 specification, 1999. W3C Recommendation 24 December 1999.
19. Internet Software Services. Theseus. http://www.matterform.com/theseus/.
20. IXActa Visual Software. Ixsite web analyzer. http://ixacta.com/products/ixsite/.
21. DACPro Computer Solutions. Webtester. http://awsd.com/scripts/webtester/.
22. A. Tarski. A lattice-theoretical fixpoint theorem and its applications. *Pacific Journal of Mathematics*, 25(2):285–309, 1955.

Distributed Symbolic Model Checking for μ-Calculus

Orna Grumberg[1], Tamir Heyman[1,2], and Assaf Schuster[1]

[1] Computer Science Department, Technion, Haifa, Israel
[2] IBM Haifa Research Laboratories, Haifa, Israel

Abstract. In this paper we propose a distributed symbolic algorithm for model checking of propositional μ–calculus formulas. μ-calculus is a powerful formalism and many problems like (fair) CTL and LTL model checking can be solved using the μ–calculus model checking. Previous works on distributed symbolic model checking were restricted to reachability analysis and safety properties. This work thus significantly extends the scope of properties that can be verified for very large designs.

The algorithm distributively evaluates subformulas. It results in sets of states which are evenly distributed among the processes. We show that this algorithm is scalable, and thus can be implemented on huge distributed clusters of computing nodes. In this way, the memory modules of the computing nodes collaborate to create a very large store, thus enables the checking of much larger designs. We formally prove the correctness of the parallel algorithm. We complement the distribution of the state sets by showing how to distribute the transition relation.

1 Introduction

In the early 1980's, model checking procedures have been suggested [5, 15, 12], which could handle systems with few thousands states. In the early 1990's, symbolic model checking methods have been introduced. These methods, based on Binary Decision Diagrams (BDDs) [2], could verify systems with 10^{20} states and more [4]. This progress has made model checking applicable to industrial designs of medium size. Significant efforts have been made since to fight the *state explosion problem*. But the need in verifying larger systems grows faster than the capacity of any newly developed method.

Recently, a new promising method for increasing the memory capacity was introduced. The method uses the collective pool of memory modules in a network of processes. In [10], distributed symbolic reachability analysis has been performed, for finding the set of all states reachable from the initial states. In [1], a distributed symbolic on-the-fly algorithm has been applied in order to model check properties written as regular expression. Experimental results show that distributed methods can achieve an average memory scale-up of 300 on 500 processes. Consequently, they find errors that were not found by sequential tools.

This paper extends the scope of properties that can be verified for large designs, by presenting a distributed symbolic model checking for the μ-calculus. The *μ-calculus* is a powerful formalism for expressing properties of transition systems using fixpoint operators. Many verification procedures can be solved by translating them into μ–calculus model checking[4]. Such problems include (fair) CTL model checking, LTL model checking, bisimulation equivalence and language containment of ω-regular automata.

G. Berry, H. Comon, and A. Finkel (Eds.): CAV 2001, LNCS 2102, pp. 350–362, 2001.

Many algorithms for μ-calculus model checking have been suggested [9, 16, 18, 7, 13]. In this work we parallelize a simple sequential algorithm, as presented in [6]. The algorithm works bottom-up through the formula, evaluating each subformula based on the evaluation of its own subformulas. A formula is interpreted as the set of states in which it is true. Thus, for each μ-calculus operation, the algorithm receives a set (or sets) of states and returns a new set of states.

The distributed algorithm follows the same lines as the sequential one, except that each process runs its own copy of the algorithm and each set of states is stored distributively among the processes. Every process *owns* a slice of the set, so that the disjunction of all slices contains the whole set. An operation is now performed on a set (or sets) of slices and returns a set of slices. At no point in the distributed algorithm a whole set is stored by a single process.

Distributed computation might be subtle for some operations. For instance, in order to evaluate a formula of the form $\neg g$, the set of states satisfying g should be complemented. It is impossible to carry this operation locally by each process. Rather, each process sends the other processes the states they own, which are not in g to the best of its knowledge. If none of the processes "knows" that a state is in g, then it is (distributively) decided to be in $\neg g$.

While performing an operation, a process may obtain states that are not owned by it. For instance, when evaluating the formula $\mathbf{EX}f$, a process will find the set of all predecessor of states in its slice for f. However, some of these predecessors may belong to the slice of another process. Therefore, the procedure exch is executed (in parallel) by all processes, and each process sends its non-owned states to their respective owner.

Keeping the memory requirements low is done through frequent calls to a memory balancing procedure. It ensures that each set is partitioned evenly among the processes. This ensures that the memory requirements, commonly proportional to the size of the manipulated set, are evenly distributed among the processes. However, this also requires different slicing functions for different sets. As a result, we may need to apply an operation to two sets that are sliced according to different partitions. In the case of *conjunction*, for instance, first the two sets should be re-sliced according to the same partition. Only then the processes apply conjunction to their individual slices.

Distributing the sets of states is only one facet of the problem. The transition relation also strongly influences the memory peaks that appear during the computation of pre-image (**EX**) operations. The pre-image operation has one of the highest memory requirements in model checking. Even when its final result is of tractable size, its intermediate results might explode the memory. We propose a scalable distributed method for the pre-image computation, including partitioning of the transition relation.

2   Preliminaries

2.1   The Propositional μ–Calculus

Below we define the propositional μ–calculus [11]. We will not distinguish between a set of states and the boolean function that characterizes this set. By abuse of notation we will apply both set operations and boolean operations on sets and boolean functions. Let AP be a set of atomic propositions and let $VAR = \{Q, Q_1, Q_2, \ldots\}$ be a set of relational variables. The μ–calculus formulas are defined as follows: if $p \in AP$, then p

is a formula; a relational variable $Q \in VAR$ is a formula; if f and g are formulas, then $\neg f, f \wedge g, f \vee g$, **EX** f are formulas; if $Q \in VAR$ and f is a formula, then $\mu Q.f$ and $\nu Q.f$ are formulas. μ–calculus consists of the set of *closed* formulas, in which every relational variable Q is within the scope of μQ or νQ.

Formulas of the μ–calculus are interpreted with respect to a *transition system* $M = (St, R, L)$ where St is a nonempty and finite set of states; $R \subseteq St \times St$ is the transition relation, and $L : St \rightarrow 2^{AP}$ is the labelling function that maps each state to the set of atomic propositions true in that state.

In order to define the semantics of μ–calculus formulas, we use an *environment* $e : VAR \rightarrow 2^{St}$, which associates with each relational variable a set of states from M.

Given a transition system M and an environment e, the semantics of a formula f, denoted $[[f]]_M e$, is the set of states in which f is true. We denote by $e[Q \leftarrow W]$ a new environment that is the same as e except that $e[Q \leftarrow W](Q) = W$. The set $[[f]]_M e$ is defined recursively as follows (where M is omitted when clear from the context).

- $[[p]]e = \{ s \mid p \in L(s) \}$ • $[[g_1 \wedge g_2]]e = [[g_1]]e \cap [[g_2]]e$
- $[[Q]]e = e(Q)$ • $[[g_1 \vee g_2]]e = [[g_1]]e \cup [[g_2]]e$
- $[[\neg g]]e = St \setminus [[g]]e$ • $[[\textbf{EX}g]]e = \{ s \mid \exists t \, [(s,t) \in R \text{ and } t \in [[g]]e] \}$
- $[[\mu Q.g]]e$ and $[[\nu Q.g]]e$ are the least and greatest fixpoints, respectively, of the predicate transformer $\tau : 2^{St} \rightarrow 2^{St}$ defined by: $\tau(W) = [[g]]e[Q \leftarrow W]$

Tarski [17] showed that least and greatest fixpoints always exist if τ is monotone. If τ is also continuous, then the least and greatest fixpoints of τ can be computed by $\cup_i \tau^i(False)$ and $\cap_i \tau^i(True)$, respectively. In [6] it is shown that if M is finite then any monotone τ is also continuous.

In this paper we consider only monotone formulas. Since we consider only finite transition systems, they are also continuous. The function fixpt on the right-hand-side of Figure 1 describes an algorithm for computing the least or greatest fixpoint, depending on the initialization of Q_{val}. If the parameter I is $False$ then the least fixpoint is computed. Otherwise, if $I = True$, then the greatest fixpoint is computed.

Given a transition system M, an environment e, and a formula f of the μ–calculus, the *model checking* algorithm for μ–calculus finds the set of states in M that satisfy f. Figure 1 presents a sequential recursive algorithm for evaluating μ–calculus formulas. For closed μ–calculus formulas, the initial environment is irrelevant. The necessary environments are constructed during recursive applications of the ev function.

2.2   Elements of Distributed Symbolic Model Checking

Our distributed algorithm involves several basic elements that were developed in [10]. For completeness, we briefly mention these elements in this subsection.

intermediate results, are represented by BDDs. the algorithm execution, the sets of states obtained are partitioned among the processes. A set of *window functions* is used to define the partitioning, determining the slice that is stored (we say: *owned*) by each process.

Definition 1. *[Complete Set of Window Functions] A window function is a boolean function that characterizes a subset of the state space. A set of window functions*

```
1 function ev(f,e)                              1 function fixpt(Q,g,e,I)
2  case                                         2  Q_val = I
3    f = p:     res = {s | p ∈ L(s)}            3  repeat
4    f = Q:     res = e(Q)                      4    Q_old = Q_val
5    f = ¬g:    res = ¬ev(g,e)                  5    Q_val =ev(g,e[Q ← Q_old])
6    f = g₁∨g₂: res =ev(g₁,e)∨ev(g₂,e)          6  until (Q_val = Q_old)
7    f = g₁∧g₂: res =ev(g₁,e)∧ev(g₂,e)          7  return Q_val
8    f =EXg:    res = {s | ∃t[sRt ∧ t ∈ev(g,e)]} 8 end function
9    f = μQ.g:  res =fixpt(Q,g,e,False)
10   f = νQ.g:  res =fixpt(Q,g,e,True)
11  endcase
12  return(res)
13 end function
```

Fig. 1. Pseudo–code for Sequential μ-Calculus Model Checking.

$W_1, \ldots, W_k$ *is complete if and only if for every* $1 \leq i, j \leq k$, $i \neq j$, $W_i \wedge W_j = 0$ *and* $\bigvee_{i=1}^{k} W_i = 1$.

Unless otherwise stated, we assume that all sets of window functions are complete.

We use the *slicing algorithm*, as described in [10] to get a set of window functions. The objective of this algorithm is to distribute a given set evenly among the nodes. Its input is a set of states, and its output is a set of window functions. These functions slices the input set into subsets that are approximately of the same size.

Maintaining balanced memory requirement by the processes is done by means of a *memory balance* algorithm, as described in [10]. When this algorithm is applied at an already sliced set of states, a new partitioning is computed, one that will balance the size of the subsets. The new partitioning is computed by pairing large slice of the set with small one and re-slicing their union. This algorithm defines a new set of window functions that will be used to produce further intermediate results.

During the memory balance algorithm, as well as during other parts of the distributed model checking algorithm, BDDs are shipped between the processes. The communication uses a compact and universal BDD representation, as described in [10]. Different variable order is allowed in the different processes.

3 Distributed Model Checking for μ-Calculus

The general idea of the distributed algorithm is as follows. The algorithm consists of two phases. The initial phase starts as the sequential algorithm, described in Section 2.1. It terminates when the memory requirement reaches a given threshold. At this point, the distributed phase begins. In order to distribute the work among the processes, the state space is partitioned into several parts, using a slicing procedure. Throughout the distributed phase, each process *owns* one part of the state space for every set of states associated with a certain subformula. When computation of a subformula produces states owned by other processes, these states are sent out to the respective processes. A memory balancing mechanism is used to repartition imbalance sets of states which are produced during the computation. Distributed termination algorithm is used to announce global termination. In the rest of this section, we describe elements used by this algorithm.

3.1 Switching from Initial to Distributed Computation

When the initial phase terminates, several subformulas have already been evaluated and the sets of states associated with them are stored. In order to start the distributed phase, we slice the sets of states found so far and distribute the slices among the processes.

Each set of states is represented by a BDD and its size is measured by the number of BDD nodes. All sets are managed by the same BDD manager, where parts of the BDDs that are used by several sets are shared and stored only once. Thus, when partitioning the sets, there are two factors involved: the required storage space for the sets, and the space needed to manipulate them. In order to keep the first factor small, it is best to partition the sets so that the space used by the BDD manager for all sets in each process is small. To keep the second factor small, observe that the memory used in performing an operation is proportional to the size of the set it is applied to, thus the part of each set in each process should be small.

In model checking, the most acute peaks in memory requirement usually occur while operations are performed. Thus, it is more important to reduce the second factor. Indeed, rather than minimizing the total size of each process, our algorithm slices each set in a way that reduces the size of its parts. It is important to note that as a result the slicing criterion may differ for different sets.

We use a slicing algorithm[10] described generally in Section 2.2. In order to slice all the sets that where already evaluated at the point of phase switching, slicing is applied to each one of them.

While the slicing algorithm works it updates two tables: $InitEval$ and $InitSet$. $InitEval$ keeps track of which sets have been evaluated by the initial phase of the algorithm. $InitEval(f)$ is $True$ if and only if f has been evaluated by the initial algorithm. Each process id has the table $InitSet$ that for each formula f, holds the subset of the set of states satisfying f and owned by this process. Formally, for each process id, $InitSet(f) = f \wedge W_{id}$. The distributed phase will start by sending the tables $InitEval$ and $InitSet$ and the list of slices W_i to all the processes.

3.2 The Distributed Phase

The distributed version of the model checking algorithm for the μ–calculus is given in Figure 2. While the sequential algorithm finds the set of states in a given model that satisfy a formula of the μ–calculus logic, in the distributed algorithm each process finds the part of this set that the process owns. Intuitively, the distributed algorithm works as follows: given a set of slices W_i, a formula f, and an environment e, the process id finds the set of states $\mathbf{ev}(f, e) \wedge W_{id}$.

In fact, a weaker property is required in order to guarantee the correctness of the algorithm. We only need to know that when evaluating a formula f, every state satisfying f is collected by at least one of the processes. For efficiency, however, we require in addition that every state is collected by exactly one process.

Given a formula f the algorithm first checks if the initial phase has already evaluated it by checking if $InitEval(f) = True$. If so, it uses the result stored in $InitSet(f)$. Otherwise, it evaluates the formula recursively. Each recursive application associates a set of states with some subformula.

Preserving the work load is an inherent problem in distributed computation. If the memory requirement in one of the processes is significantly larger than the others, then the effectiveness of the distributed system is destroyed. To avoid this situation, whenever a new set of states is created a memory balance procedure is invoked to keep a balanced memory requirement by the new set. The memory balance procedure changes the slices W_i and updates the parts of the new set in each of the processes accordingly.

Each process in the distributed algorithm evaluates each subformula f as follow (see Figure 2):

A propositional formula $p \in AP$: evaluated by collecting all the states s that satisfy two conditions: p is in the labelling $L(s)$ of s and in addition s is owned by this process.

A relational variable Q: evaluated using the local environment of the process. Since only closed μ–calculus formulas are evaluated, the environment must have a value for Q (computed in a previous step).

A subformula of the form $\neg g$: evaluated by first evaluating g, and then using the special function exchnot. Given a set of states S and a partition $S_1, \ldots, S_k$ of S, each process i runs the procedure exchnot on S_i. The process reports all other processes of the states that do not belong to S "as far as it knows". Since each state in S belongs to some process, if none of the processes knows that s is in S, then s is in $\neg S$.

Since each process holds only the states of $\neg S$ that it owns, the processes actually send each other only states that owned by the receiver. This reduces communication.

A subformula of the form $g_1 \vee g_2$: evaluated by first evaluating g_1 and g_2, possibly with different slicing functions. This means that a process can hold a part of g_1 with respect to one slicing and a part of g_2 with respect to another slicing. Nevertheless, since each state of g_1 and of g_2 belongs to one of the processes, each state of $g_1 \vee g_2$ now belongs to one of the processes. Applying the function exch results in a correct distribution of the states among the processes, according to the current slicing.

A subformula of the form $g_1 \wedge g_2$ can be translated using De Morgan's laws to $\neg(\neg g_1 \vee \neg g_2)$. However, evaluating the translated formula requires four communication phases (via exch and exchnot). Instead, such a formula is evaluated by first evaluating g_1 and g_2. As in the previous case, they might be evaluated with respect to different window functions. Here, however, the slicing of the two formulas should agree before a conjunction can be applied. This is achieved by applying exch twice, thus the overall communication is reduced to only two rounds.

A subformula of the form EXg: evaluated by first evaluating g and then computing the pre-image using the transition relation R. Since every state of g belongs to one of the processes, every state of the pre-image also belongs to one. In fact, a state may be computed by more than one process if it is obtained as a pre-image of two parts. Applying exch completes the evaluation correctly.

Subformulas of the form $\mu Q.g$ and $\nu Q.g$ (the least fixpoint and greatest fixpoint, respectively): evaluated using a special function fixpt that iterates until a fixpoint is found. The computations for the formulas differ only in the initialization which is $False$ for $\mu Q.g$ and the current window functions for $\nu Q.g$.

```
1 function pev(f, e)
2   case
3     InitEval(f):      return (InitSet(f))
4     f = p:            res = {s | p ∈ L(s)} ∧ W_id
5     f = Q:            return (e(Q))
6     f = ¬g:           res = exchnot(pev(g,e))
7     f = g₁ ∨ g₂:      res = exch(pev(g₁,e)∨pev(g₂,e))
8     f = g₁ ∧ g₂:      res₁ = pev(g₁,e)  res₂ = pev(g₂,e)
9                       res = exch(res₁)∧exch(res₂)
10    f = EXg:          res = exch({s | ∃t[sRt ∧ t ∈pev(g,e)]})
11    f = µQ.g:         res = fixpt(Q,g,e,False)
12    f = νQ.g:         res = fixpt(Q,g,e,W_id)
13  endcase
14  ldBlnc(res)  /* balances W; updates res accordingly */
15  return(res)
16 end function

1 function fixpt(Q,g,e,init)
2   Q_val = init
3   repeat
4     Q_old = Q_val
5     Q_val = pev(g,e[Q ← Q_old])
6   until (parterm(exch(Q_val)=exch(Q_old)))
7   return Q_val
8 end function

1 function exch(S)                         1 function exchnot(S)
2   res = S ∧ W_id                         2   res = (¬S) ∧ W_id
3   for each process i ≠ id                3   for each process i ≠ id
4     sendto(i, S ∧ W_i)                   4     sendto(i, (¬S) ∧ W_i)
5   for each process i ≠ id                5   for each process i ≠ id
6     res = res∨ receivefrom(i)            6     res = res∧ receivefrom(i)
7   return res                             7   return res
8 end function                             8 end function
```

Fig. 2. Pseudo–code for a Process *id* in the Distributed Model Checking

3.3   Sources of Scalability

The efficiency of a parallelization approach is determined by the ratio between computation complexity, normalized by computation speed, and communication complexity, normalized by communication bandwidth. In our parallel model checking algorithm, this ratio (excluding normalization, which is dependent on the underlying platform) can be estimated by observing that peak memory requirement for a single μ-calculus operation of a symbolic computation is a lower bound on the computation complexity of this operation. On average, in the distributed setup, the size of BDD structures that are sent (received) by a process is a fraction of its BDD manager size at the end of the operation (after memory balance). Thus, roughly speaking, for a single operation computation, peak memory utilization bounds from below the computation complexity, whereas the size of the BDD manager represents the communication complexity. General wisdom holds that the ratio between peak and manager sizes reaches 2 or 3 orders of magnitudes, which, for current computing platforms is sufficient to keep the processor and communication subsystems equally busy. Indeed, our experiments with previous parallel symbolic computations in a distributed setup consisting of a slow network confirmed the efficiency of this approach [10, 1].

Scalability of a parallel system is the ability to include more processes in order to handle larger inputs of higher complexity. Linear scalability is used to describe a parallel system that does not loose performance while scaling up. Recall that the volume of communication performed by a single process in our algorithm during a single operation, may be represented on average by a fraction of its BDD manager size at the end of the operation. Also, the corresponding peak memory that is used by the process during that operation is bounded by the size of its memory module (otherwise the operation overflows). By the above mentioned ratio between the sizes of the peak and the BDD manager, the manager size (in between operations) is also bounded. Thus, using our effective slicing procedure, the local BDD manager size does not increase when the system is scaled up globally in order to check larger models using more processes. Thus, the ratio between computation and communication for each process does not vary substantially when the system scales up, implying almost linear scalability of our distributed model checking algorithm.

Finally, we note that a higher ratio of peak to BDD manager sizes, which may result from a larger transition system in larger models, will enhance the scalability of our parallel approach. Since the size of memory module limits the peak size, a higher ratio implies smaller BDD manager, which, in turn, implies lower communication volumes. Thus, when the checked models grow, the method may exhibit super-linear scalability.

4   Correctness

In this section we prove the correctness of the distributed algorithm, assuming the sequential algorithm is correct. The sequential algorithm evaluates a formula by computing the set of states satisfying this formula. In the distributed algorithm every such set is partitioned among the processes. The union over all the partitions for a given subformula is called the *global set*. In the proof we show that, for every μ-calculus formula, the set of states computed by the sequential algorithm is identical to the global set computed by the distributed algorithm. Note that, the global set is never actually computed and is introduced only for the sake of the correctness proof. In the proof that follows we need the following definition.

Definition 2. *[Well Partitioned Environment] An environment e is well partitioned by parts $e_1, \ldots, e_k$ if and only if, for every $Q \in VAR$, $e(Q) = \bigvee_{i=1}^{k} e_i(Q)$.*

The procedures exch are applied by all processes with a set of non-disjoint subsets S_i that cover a set res. Given a set of window functions, the procedures exchange non-owned parts so that at termination each process has all the states from res it owns. The set of window functions do not change.

Let f be a μ-calculus formula, e_{id} be the environment in process id. $\mathrm{pev}_{id}(f, e_{id})$ denotes the set of states returned by procedure pev, when run by process id on f and e_{id}.

Theorem 1 defines the relationship between the outputs of the sequential and the distributed algorithms.

Theorem 1 (Correctness). *Let f be a μ–calculus formula, e be a well partitioned environment by $e_1, \ldots e_k$, e' be the environment when $\mathrm{ev}(f, e)$ terminates and for all $i = 1, \ldots, k$, e_i' be the environment when $\mathrm{pev}_i(f, e_i)$ terminates. Then, e' is well partitioned by $e_1', \ldots e_k'$ and $\mathrm{ev}(f, e) = \bigvee_{i=1}^{k} \mathrm{pev}_i(f, e_i)$.*

Proof: We prove the theorem by induction on the structure of f. In all but the last two cases of the induction step the environments are not changed and therefore e' is well partitioned by $e_1', \ldots e_k'$. Due to lack of space we only consider several of the more interesting cases.

Base: $f = p$ for $p \in AP$ – Immediate.

Induction:

$\underline{f = Q}$, where $Q \in VAR$ is a relational variable: $\bigvee_{i=1}^{k} \mathrm{pev}_i(Q, e_i) = \bigvee_{i=1}^{k} e_i(Q)$. Since e is well partitioned, $e(Q) = \bigvee_{i=1}^{k} e_i(Q)$, which is equal to $\mathrm{ev}(f, e)$.

$\underline{f = \neg g}$: $\mathrm{pev}_{id}(\neg g, e_{id})$ first applies $\mathrm{pev}_{id}(g, e_{id})$ which results with S_{id}. It then runs the procedure $\mathtt{exchnot}(S_{id})$ that returns the result res_{id}.

$$res_{id} = ((\neg S_{id}) \wedge W_{id}) \wedge \bigwedge_{j \neq id} ((\neg S_j) \wedge W_{id}) = \bigwedge_{j=1}^{k} ((\neg S_j) \wedge W_{id}).$$

When $\mathtt{exchnot}$ terminates in all processes, the global set computed by all processes is (recall that $\bigvee_{i=1}^{k} W_i = 1$):

$$\bigvee_{i=1}^{k} \left(\bigwedge_{j=1}^{k} ((\neg S_j) \wedge W_i) \right) = \bigwedge_{j=1}^{k} (\neg S_j) \wedge \bigvee_{i=1}^{k} W_i = \bigwedge_{j=1}^{k} (\neg S_j) = \neg \bigvee_{j=1}^{k} S_j.$$

Since $S_i = \mathrm{pev}_i(g, e_i)$, $\neg \bigvee_{j=1}^{k} S_j = \neg \bigvee_{j=1}^{k} \mathrm{pev}_j(g, e_j)$, which by the induction hypothesis is identical to $\neg\, \mathrm{ev}(g, e)$. This, in turn, is identical to $\mathrm{ev}(\neg g, e)$. Applying $\mathtt{ldBlnc}$ at the end of $\mathtt{pev}$, repartitions the subsets between the processes, however, their disjunction remains the same. Thus, $\mathrm{ev}(\neg g, e) = \bigvee_{i=1}^{k} \mathrm{pev}_i(\neg g, e_i)$.

$\underline{f = g_1 \vee g_2}$: $\mathrm{pev}_{id}(f, e_{id})$ first computes $\mathrm{pev}_{id}(g_1, e_{id}) \vee \mathrm{pev}_{id}(g_2, e_{id})$. At the end of this computation, the global set is:

$$\bigvee_{i=1}^{k} (\mathrm{pev}_i(g_1, e_i) \vee \mathrm{pev}_i(g_2, e_i)) = \bigvee_{i=1}^{k} \mathrm{pev}_i(g_1, e_i) \vee \bigvee_{i=1}^{k} \mathrm{pev}_i(g_2, e_i).$$

By the induction hypothesis, this is identical to $\mathrm{ev}(g_1, e) \vee \mathrm{ev}(g_2, e)$ which is identical to $\mathrm{ev}(g_1 \vee g_2, e)$. Applying the procedures $\mathtt{exch}$ and $\mathtt{ldBlnc}$ change the partition of the sets among the processes, but not the global set.

$\underline{f = \mu Q.g}$, a least fixpoint formula: As in previous cases, we would like to prove that $\bigvee_{i=1}^{k} \mathrm{pev}_i(\mu Q.g, e_i) = \mathrm{ev}(\mu Q.g, e)$. Since $\mathtt{ldBlnc}$ does not change the correctness of this claim, we only need to prove that $\bigvee_{i=1}^{k} \mathtt{fixpt}_i(Q, g, e_i, False)) = \mathtt{fixpt}(Q, g, e, False))$. In addition, we need to show that the environment remains well partitioned when the computation terminates. The following lemma proves stronger requirements. The lemma uses the following property of procedure $\mathtt{parterm}$.

Property 1. Procedure `parterm` is invoked by each of the processes with a boolean parameter. If all parameters are *True*, then `parterm` returns *True* to all processes. Otherwise, it returns *False* to all processes.

Lemma 1. *Let Q^j, be the value of Q_{val} in iteration j of the sequential fixpoint algorithm. Similarly, let Q_{id}^j be the value of Q_{val} in iteration j of the distributed fixpoint algorithm in process id. Q^0 is the initialization of the sequential algorithm; Q_{id}^0 is the initialization of the distributed algorithm. Then,* • *In every iteration, e is well partitioned by $e_1, \ldots, e_k$.* • *For every j: $Q^j = \bigvee_{i=1}^{k} Q_i^j$.* • *If the sequential* `fixpt` *algorithm terminates after i_0 iterations then so does the distributed fixpoint algorithm.*

Proof: We prove the lemma by induction on the number j of iterations in the loop of the sequential function `fixpt`.
Base: $j = 0$:
• At iteration 0, e is well partitioned based on the induction hypothesis of Theorem 1.
• In case $f = \mu Q.g$, the initialization of the sequential algorithm, as well as the distributed algorithm is *False*. Hence, $Q^0 = Q_{id}^0 = False$ which implies $Q^0 = \bigvee_{i=1}^{k} Q_i^0$.
• Both algorithms perform at least one iteration, so they do not terminate at iteration 0.
Induction: Assume Lemma 1 holds for iteration j. We prove it for iteration $j + 1$.
• Let $e', e_1', \ldots, e_k'$ be the environments at the end of iteration $j + 1$, and assume that e is well partitioned by $e_1, \ldots, e_k$ at the end of iteration j. The only changes to the environments in iteration $j + 1$ may occur in line 5 of the distributed and sequential algorithms. In the sequential algorithm e may be changed in two ways: $e(Q)$ is assigned a new value Q^j, or a recursive call to ev may change e. Similarly, in the distributed algorithm two changes may occur: $e_{id}(Q)$ is assigned a new value Q_{id}^j, or a recursive call to pev$_{id}$ may change e_{id}.

By the induction hypothesis of Lemma 1 we know that $Q^j = \bigvee_{i=1}^{k} Q_i^j$, hence $e[Q \leftarrow Q^j](Q) = \bigvee_{i=1}^{k} e_i[Q \leftarrow Q_i^j](Q)$. Since no other change has been made to the environments, and since e is well partitioned, we conclude that $e[Q \leftarrow Q^j]$ is well partitioned by $e_1[Q \leftarrow Q_1^j], \ldots, e_k[Q \leftarrow Q_k^j]$.

In iteration $j + 1$, ev in now invoked with an environment that is well partitioned by the environments pev$_{id}$ is invoked with. The induction hypothesis of Theorem 1 therefore guarantees that e' is well partitioned by $e_1', \ldots, e_k'$.
• $Q^{j+1} = \text{ev}(g, e[Q \leftarrow Q^j])$ (line 5 of the sequential algorithm) and $Q_{id}^{j+1} = \text{pev}_{id}(g, e[Q \leftarrow Q_{id}^j])$ (line 5 of the distributed algorithm).

By the first bullet above, $e[Q \leftarrow Q^j]$ is well partitioned. Thus, the induction hypothesis of Theorem 1 is applicable and implies that $\text{ev}(g, e[Q \leftarrow Q^j]) = \bigvee_{i=1}^{k} \text{pev}_i(g, e[Q \leftarrow Q_i^j])$. Hence, $Q^{j+1} = \bigvee_{i=1}^{k} Q_i^{j+1}$.
• The sequential `fixpt` procedure terminates at iteration $j + 1$ if $Q^j = Q^{j+1}$. We prove that this holds if and only if for every process id, $\text{exch}(Q_{id}^j) = \text{exch}(Q_{id}^{j+1})$ and therefore `parterm` returns *True* to all processes.

Let $W_1, \ldots, W_k$ be the current window functions. By the second bullet above, $Q^j = \bigvee_{i=1}^{k} Q_i^j$ and $Q^{j+1} = \bigvee_{i=1}^{k} Q_i^{j+1}$.

$$\forall id[\text{exch}(Q_{id}^j) = \text{exch}(Q_{id}^{j+1})] \;\Leftrightarrow\; \forall id[\bigvee_{i=1}^{k} Q_i^j \wedge W_{id} = \bigvee_{i=1}^{k} Q_i^{j+1} \wedge W_{id}] \;\Leftrightarrow$$

$$\forall id[Q^j \wedge W_{id} = Q^{j+1} \wedge W_{id}] \iff Q^j = Q^{j+1}.$$

The last equality is implied by the previous one since the window functions are complete. This complete the proof of the lemma and also the proof of the theorem. Q.E.D.

The above theorem can be extended to state that when all procedures $\mathrm{pev}_{id}(f, e_{id})$ terminate, the subsets owned by each of the processes are disjoint. This is important in order to avoid duplication of work. However, it is not necessary for the correctness of the model checking algorithm.

5   Scalable Distributed Pre-image Computation

The main goal of our distributed algorithm is to reduce the memory requirement. In symbolic model checking, pre-image is one of the operations with the highest memory requirement. Given a set of states S, pre-image computes $pred(S)$ (also denoted by EX S in μ-calculus), which is the set of all predecessors of states in S. The pre-image operation can be described by the formula $pred(S) = \exists s'[R(s, s') \wedge S(s')]$. It is easy to see that the memory requirement of this operation grows with the sizes of the transition relation R and the set S. Furthermore, intermediate results sometimes exceed the memory capacity even when $pred(S)$ can be held in memory.

Our distributed algorithm reduces memory requirements by slicing each of the computed sets of states. This takes care of the S parameter of pre-image, but not of R. In order to make our method scalable for very large models, we need to reduce the size of the transition relation as well.

The transition relation consists of pairs of states. We distinguish between the source states and the target states by refer to the latter as St'. Thus, $R \subseteq St \times St'$.

A reduction of the second parameter of R, St', can be achieved by applying the well-known restriction operator [8]: Prior to any application of pre-image, a process that owns a slice S_i of S reduces its copy of R by restricting St' to S_i. This reduction is *dynamic* since pre-image operations are applied to different sets during model checking.

We further reduce R by adding a *static* slicing of St according to (possibly different) window functions $U_1, \ldots, U_m$. The slicing algorithm of Section 2.2 can be used to produce $U_1, \ldots, U_m$, so that R is partitioned to m slices of similar size. Each slice R_j is a subset of $(St \cap U_j) \times St'$. Since R does not change during the computation, $U_1, \ldots, U_m$ do not change as well.

Having k window functions $W_1, \ldots, W_k$ for S and m window functions $U_1, \ldots, U_m$ for R, we use k groups of m processes each. All processes in the same group have the same W_i, and hence own the same $S_i = S \cap W_i$. However, each process in the group has a different U_j. Process (i, j) with W_i and U_j computes pre-image of S_i by $pred_j(S_i) = \exists s'[R_j(s, s') \wedge S_i(s')]$. Since $U_1, \ldots, U_m$ is a complete set of window functions, $\bigvee_{j=1}^{m} pred_j(S_i) = pred(S_i)$. Thus, the group with window function W_i computes the same set as process i in the algorithm of Section 3.

Once the computation is completed, procedure exch is applied to exchange non-owned states (according to W_i). Procedure ldBlnc is used to update the W_i window functions in order to balance the memory load. Both procedures are defined as before. However, when ldBlnc changes the window functions, all members in each of the groups should agree on the new window function.

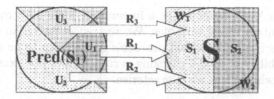

The Figure above demonstrates a pre-image computation using sliced transition relation with $k = 2$ and $m = 3$. Given a set S sliced into S_1, S_2 according to W_1, W_2 respectively, the pre-image of S_1 is computed by three processes. Each process uses a different slice of the transition relation, R_1, R_2 and R_3, according to U_1, U_2 and U_3.

The method suggested in this section applies slicing to the full transition relation in case it can be held in memory, but is too large to enable a successful completion of the pre-image operation. However, often the transition relation is given *partitioned*, i.e., given as a set of small relations N_l, each defining the value of variable v_l in the next states. The size of the partitioned transition relation is usually small, therefore can be constructed by one process and then be sliced using the algorithm suggested in [14]. In this case the model checking is done directly with the partitioned transition relation [3].

5.1 Distributed Construction of the Sliced Full Transition Relation

The full transition relation R is a conjunction of all N_l. Here we consider cases where either R or its construction cannot fit into the memory of a single process.

Our goal is to construct slices R_j of R, with none of the processes ever holding R. Each process starts constructing by gradually conjuncting partitions N_l, until a threshold is reached. The current (partial) transition relation is then partitioned among the processes, using the slicing algorithm. Each process continues to conjunct the partitions that have not been handled yet, until all partitions are conjuncted. During conjunction, further slicing or balancing are applied so that the final slices will be balanced.

Acknowledgement

We would like to thank Ken McMillan for his time and patient and for his help in choosing a notation for the μ–calculus model checking algorithm.

References

1. S. Ben-David, T. Heyman, O. Grumberg, and A. Schuster. Scalable Distributed On-the-Fly Symbolic Model Checking. In *Third International Conference on Formal methods in Computer-Aided Design (FMCAD'00)*, Austin, Texas, November 2000.
2. R. E. Bryant. Graph-based Algorithms for Boolean Function Manipulation. *IEEE Transactions on Computers*, C-35(8):677–691, 1986.
3. J. R. Burch, E. M. Clarke, and D. E. Long. Symbolic Model Checking with Partitioned Transition Relations. In A. Halaas and P. B. Denyer, editors, *Proceedings of the 1991 International Conference on Very Large Scale Integration*, August 1991.
4. J. R. Burch, E. M. Clarke, K. L. McMillan, D. L. Dill, and L. J. Hwang. Symbolic Model Checking: 10^{20} States and Beyond. *Information and Computation*, 98(2):142–170, 1992.

As specification logic, we consider a linear time logic built over state predicates that can contain index variables. We restrict ourselves to safety properties; liveness properties of broadcast protocols were shown to be undecidable in EFM99, so decidability of model-checking certainly does not extend to liveness properties for the whole class we characterise.

Related Work. Model checking for parameterized systems has been addressed by many researchers. One line of research is concerned with restrictions that, when imposed on parameterized systems, make model checking decidable for safety properties or even full temporal logic. The systems considered there are either token rings, like in EN95, or broadcast protocols, which were introduced in EN98 and also considered in EFM99; GS92 deals with a restricted form of broadcast protocols. Both types are subsumed by our subclass.

The approach for broadcast systems in EN98 and EFM99 falls under the paradigm of using well-ordered sets for the verification of infinite-state systems ACJT96. All sets that are considered are sets that are upward closed with respect to a well order. This means that all guards of transitions have to describe upward closed sets, which excludes certain global conditions, e.g. the one used in the cache coherence protocol that Delzanno considered in Del00.

Regular model checking, advocated by e.g. KMM+97 and BW98, is based on representing sets of states by regular languages. Termination is obtained by applying some form of acceleration in order to compute the transitive closure of the transition relation BJNT00. Emphasis lies not on detecting decidable classes but providing general, not necessarily exact methods to handle a large class of systems. In this context, handling global guards was considered in ABJN00; our method provably terminates on the examples considered there. The main difference is that is our work is not based on acceleration techniques.

The specification language we use is rather general: The properties considered by EN95 had restricted number of quantified variables, and the properties for broadcast protocols considered in EN98; EFM99 can only express upward closed properties about numbers of processes being in a certain control state.

Overview. First we explain the types of parameterized systems we consider. The third section contains our model checking algorithm for ordinary systems, while in the fourth section it is adapted to parameterized systems, and the conditions under which the algorithm terminates are given. Missing proofs and details can be found in the full version at http://www.dcs.ed.ac.uk/~monika.

2 Framework

As program notation we use concurrent state-based guarded-command systems; a system is hence of form $(V, C_1, \ldots, C_n, I)$, where V is a set of variables, C_i are components and I is a predicate describing the initial states. A component consists of a set of transitions, where guards and assignments are built over boolean or enumerative variables or integer terms. More precisely, the terms occurring on

The Temporal Logic Sugar

Ilan Beer[1], Shoham Ben-David[1], Cindy Eisner[1], Dana Fisman[1,2],
Anna Gringauze[1], and Yoav Rodeh[1,2]

[1] IBM Haifa Research Laboratory
[2] Weizmann Institute of Science, Rehovot, Israel
danaf@il.ibm.com

1 Introduction

Since the introduction of temporal logic for the specification of computer programs [5], usability has been an issue, because a difficult-to-use formalism is a barrier to the wide adoption of formal methods. Our solution is Sugar, the temporal logic used by the RuleBase formal verification tool [2]. Sugar adds the power of regular expressions to CTL [4], as well as an extensive set of operators which provide *syntactic sugar*. That is, while these operators do not add expressive power, they allow properties to be expressed more succinctly than in the basic language. Experience shows that Sugar allows hardware engineers to easily and intuitively specify their designs. The full language is used for model checking, and a significant portion can be model checked on-the-fly [3]. The automatic generation of simulation checkers from the same portion of Sugar is described in [1]. While previous papers have described various features of the language, this paper presents the first complete description of Sugar.

2 The Basic Language

We use boolean expressions to describe states in the model, and Sugar Extended Regular Expressions to describe sequences of states, and define them as follows:

Definition 1. (Boolean Expression).

1. *Every atomic proposition is a boolean expression.*
2. *If b, b_1, and b_2 are boolean expressions, then so are $\neg b$ and $b_1 \wedge b_2$.*

Definition 2. (Sugar Extended Regular Expressions (SEREs)).

1. *Every boolean expression is a SERE.*
2. *If r, r_1, and r_2 are SEREs, then so are the following: i) r_1, r_2 ii) $r_1 \sim r_2$ iii) $r_1 || r_2$ iv) $r_1 \&\& r_2$ v) $r[*]$*

A comma denotes concatenation, $\sim$ denotes overlapping concatenation, where the last state of r_1 coincides with the first state of r_2, $||$ denotes disjunction, $\&\&$ denotes conjunction, and $[*]$ is used to specify 0 or more repetitions.

There are two ways to use SEREs in Sugar formulas. The first is to link two SEREs in order to form Sugar formulas of the linear fragment, as defined in Definition 3 below. A second way is to link a single SERE with a general Sugar formula, as defined in Definition 4 below.

M. Kerckhove (Ed.): Scale-Space 2001, LNCS 2106, pp. 363–367, 2001.
© Springer-Verlag Berlin Heidelberg 2001

Definition 3. (Sugar Formulas of the Linear Fragment[1]).   *If r_1 and r_2 are SEREs, then $\{r_1\} \mapsto \{r_2\}!$ and $\{r_1\} \mapsto \{r_2\}$ are Sugar formulas of the linear fragment.*

The $\{r_1\} \mapsto \{r_2\}!$ and $\{r_1\} \mapsto \{r_2\}$ constructs are known as *strong suffix implication* and *weak suffix implication*, respectively. Strong suffix implications are liveness formulas, indicating that every sequence of states on which r_1 holds must be followed by a sequence of states on which r_2 holds. Weak suffix implications are safety formulas, indicating that every sequence of states on which r_1 holds may not be followed by a sequence of states which contradicts r_2. For instance, the Sugar formula $\{[*], p, q\} \mapsto \{s[*], t\}!$ requires that every sequence of two states such that p is valid in the first and q is valid in the second, must be followed by a sequence of states in which s is valid for some number of states, and then t is valid in the final state of the sequence. The weak form of this formula does not require that the second sequence "reach its end": a sequence matching $\{p, q\}$ must be followed either by a sequence in which s holds forever, or by a sequence in which s holds for some number of states, and then t holds.

Definition 4. (Sugar Formulas).

1. *Every boolean expression is a Sugar formula.*
2. *Every Sugar formula of the linear fragment is a Sugar formula.*
3. *If f, f_1, and f_2 are Sugar formulas and r is a SERE, then the following are Sugar formulas: i) $\neg f$ ii) $f_1 \wedge f_2$ iii) EXf iv) $E[f_1 U f_2]$ v) EGf vi) $\{r\}(f)$*

The operators $\neg$, $\wedge$, EX, EU, and EG have the usual meaning. The construct $\{r\}(f)$ (*suffix implication*) holds for a state s if, for all finite sequences starting from s on which r holds, formula f holds on the final state in the sequence r.

3   Syntactic Sugar

Because the basic language can be verbose, Sugar adds syntactic sugar: additional operators which allow many properties to be expressed succinctly in an intuitive manner. We will now illustrate the advantages of the syntactic sugar with a few examples[2].

The *next_event* **Operators.** These operators are a conceptual extension of the AX operator. While AX refers to the next state, *next_event* refers to the next state in which a boolean expression is valid. For instance, the following:

$$AG(hi\_pri\_req \to next\_event\_f(gnt)[1..2](dst = hi\_pri)) \qquad (1)$$

---

[1] Note that Sugar formulas of the linear fragment are not closed under the boolean operators. The result of a boolean operation on two Sugar formulas of the linear fragment is a general Sugar formula as described in Definition 4.

[2] The abbreviations presented here and in Appendix B are given as an explanatory semantics and do not imply the actual implementation.

expresses the requirement that whenever hi_pri_req is asserted, one of the next two assertions of signal gnt must have dst equal to hi_pri.

The $next\_event$ operator, and its variant $next\_event\_f(b)[1..2](f)$ are defined in terms of the weak until (AW) operator as follows: $A[f_1\ W\ f_2]$ is equivalent to $\neg E[\neg f_2\ U\ \neg f_1 \wedge \neg f_2]$, $next\_event(b)(f)$ is equivalent to $A[\neg b\ W\ b \wedge f]$, and $next\_event(b)[1..2](f)$ is equivalent to $next\_event(b)(f \vee AX next\_event(b)(f))$. Thus, Formula 1 can be expressed in CTL with the addition of the AW operator as follows:

$$AG(hi\_pri\_req \rightarrow A[\neg gnt\ W\ ((gnt \wedge dst = hi\_pri)\vee$$
$$(gnt \wedge AX A[\neg gnt\ W\ (gnt \wedge dst = hi\_pri)])])]) \qquad (2)$$

The *within* Operators. The *within* operators ease the expression of requirements such as the following: "every transaction must complete, and within every transaction, a full data transfer must occur", which is expressible in Sugar as:

$$AG\ within!(tr\_strt, tr\_end)\{\textbf{true}[*], dat\_strt, \textbf{true}[*], dat\_end\} \qquad (3)$$

$within!(r_1, b)\{r_2\}$ is equivalent to $\{r_1\} \mapsto \{r_2\ \&\&\ \{\neg b[*]\}, \neg b[*], b\}!$. Thus, Formula 3 can be expressed (albeit somewhat cryptically) in CTL as follows:

$$AG(tr\_strt \rightarrow A[\neg dat\_strt \wedge \neg tr\_end\ U$$
$$dat\_strt \wedge A[\neg tr\_end\ U\ dat\_end \wedge A[\neg tr\_end\ U\ tr\_end]]]) \qquad (4)$$

Counters. Counters are used to describe sequences of events that would otherwise be tedious to specify. For example, i consecutive occurrences of sequence r can be expressed as $r[i]$, and i non-consecutive occurrences of boolean expression b can be expressed as $b[= i]$. Formally, $r[0]$ is equivalent to $\textbf{false}[*]$, while $r[i]$ is equivalent to i concatenations of r, and $b[= i]$ is equivalent to $\{\neg b[*], b\}[i], \neg b[*]$. The utility of the $b[= i]$ construct is illustrated in the following Sugar formula:

$$AG(\{go, \{get[= 8]\}\&\&\{kill[= 0]\}\} \mapsto \{\textbf{true}, \{put[= 8]\}\&\&\{end[= 0]\}\}) \qquad (5)$$

which expresses the requirement that a sequence beginning with the assertion of signal go, and containing eight not necessarily consecutive assertions of signal get, during which signal $kill$ is not asserted, must be followed by a sequence containing eight assertions of signal put before signal end can be asserted. The equivalent CTL formula is both non-intuitive and tedious. The CTL formula expressing the same requirement but for sequences of only two gets and puts illustrates this point:

$$AG\neg(go \wedge EX\ E[\neg get \wedge \neg kill\ U\ get \wedge \neg kill \wedge EX\ E[\neg get \wedge \neg kill\ U\ get \wedge \neg kill$$
$$\wedge E[\neg put\ U\ end] \vee E[\neg put \wedge \neg end\ U\ (put \wedge \neg end \wedge EX E[\neg put\ U\ end])]]]) \qquad (6)$$

Formulas 1, 3 and 5 can also be expressed in LTL [6]. However, the equivalent LTL formulas are not any less daunting to code or decipher than the CTL versions, while the Sugar version expresses the requirements succinctly, in a manner accessible to the non-logician.

References

1. Y. Abarbanel and I. Beer et al. FoCs - automatic generation of simulation checkers from formal specifications. In *CAV '00*, LNCS 1855. Springer-Verlag, 2000.
2. I. Beer, S. Ben-David, C. Eisner, and A. Landver. RuleBase: an industry-oriented formal verification tool. In *DAC '96*, pages 655–660, June 1996.
3. I. Beer, S. Ben-David, and A. Landver. On-the-fly model checking of RCTL formulas. In *CAV '98*, LNCS 1427, pages 184–194. Springer-Verlag, 1998.
4. E. Clarke and E. Emerson. Design and synthesis of synchronization skeletons using branching time temporal logic. In *Proc. Workshop on Logics of Programs*, LNCS 131, pages 52–71. Springer-Verlag, 1981.
5. A. Pnueli. The temporal logic of programs. In *Proc. 18th Annual IEEE Symposium on Foundations of Computer Science*, pages 46–57, 1977.
6. A. Pnueli. A temporal logic of concurrent programs. *Theoretical Computer Science*, 13:45–60, 1981.

A   Formal Semantics

The semantics of a Sugar formula are defined with respect to a model M. A model is a quintuple (S, S_0, R, P, L), where S is a finite set of states, $S_0 \subseteq S$ is a set of initial states, $R \subseteq S \times S$ is the transition relation, P is a non-empty set of atomic propositions, and L is the valuation, a function $L : S \longrightarrow 2^P$, mapping each state with a set of atomic propositions true in that state. R is total with respect to its first argument. A computation path π of a model M is an infinite sequence of states $\pi = (\pi_0, \pi_1, \pi_2, \cdots)$ such that $R(\pi_i, \pi_{i+1})$ for every i. We will denote by $\pi^{i,j}$ a finite sequence of states starting from π_i and ending in π_j.

The semantics of SEREs are defined over the alphabet 2^P. Thus, a letter is a subset of the set of atomic propositions P. We will denote a letter from 2^P by ℓ and a finite word over 2^P by w. The concatenation of w_1 and w_2 is denoted by $w_1 w_2$. The empty word is denoted by ϵ, so that $w\epsilon = \epsilon w = w$. The notation $w \in \mathcal{L}(r)$, where r is a SERE, means that w is in the language of r. The semantics of SEREs are defined as follows:

1. $w \in \mathcal{L}(p) \iff$ there exists an ℓ s.t. $w = \ell$ and $p \in \ell$
2. $w \in \mathcal{L}(\neg b) \iff w \notin \mathcal{L}(b)$
3. $w \in \mathcal{L}(b_1 \wedge b_2) \iff w \in \mathcal{L}(b_1)$ and $w \in \mathcal{L}(b_2)$
4. $w \in \mathcal{L}(r_1, r_2) \iff$ there exist w_1 and w_2 s.t. $w = w_1 w_2$ and $w_1 \in \mathcal{L}(r_1)$ and $w_2 \in \mathcal{L}(r_2)$
5. $w \in \mathcal{L}(r_1 \sim r_2) \iff$ there exist w_1, w_2, and ℓ s.t. $w = w_1 \ell w_2$ and $w_1 \ell \in \mathcal{L}(r_1)$ and $\ell w_2 \in \mathcal{L}(r_2)$
6. $w \in \mathcal{L}(r_1 || r_2) \iff w \in \mathcal{L}(r_1)$ or $w \in \mathcal{L}(r_2)$
7. $w \in \mathcal{L}(r_1 \&\& r_2) \iff w \in \mathcal{L}(r_1)$ and $w \in \mathcal{L}(r_2)$
8. $w \in \mathcal{L}(r[*]) \iff$ either $w = \epsilon$ or there exist $w_1, w_2, \ldots, w_j$ s.t. $w = w_1 w_2 \ldots w_j$ and, for all i, $1 \leq i \leq j$, $w_i \in \mathcal{L}(r)$

Recall that every state $s \in S$ in a model $M = (S, S_0, R, P, L)$ is associated with a set of atomic propositions by the valuation L. We define $\hat{L}$, an extension of the valuation function L as follows: $\hat{L}(\pi_i, \pi_{i+1}, \ldots \pi_j) = L(\pi_i) L(\pi_{i+1}) \ldots L(\pi_j)$. Thus we have a mapping from states in M to letters of 2^P, and from finite sequences of states in M to words over 2^P.

We now turn to the semantics of Sugar formulas. The notation $M, s \models f$ means that formula f holds in state s of model M. The notation $M \models f$ is equivalent to $\forall s \in S_0$ $M, s \models f$, in other words, f is valid for all initial states of M. We use p, p_1 and p_2 to denote atomic propositions, b, b_1 and b_2 to denote boolean expressions, r, r_1 and r_2 to denote SEREs, and f, f_1 and f_2 to denote Sugar formulas. The semantics of a Sugar formula are defined as follows:

1. $M, s \models p \iff p \in L(s)$
2. $M, s \models \neg f \iff M, s \not\models f$
3. $M, s \models f_1 \wedge f_2 \iff M, s \models f_1$ and $M, s \models f_2$

4. $M, s \models r_1 \mapsto r_2! \iff$ for all paths π s.t. $\pi_0 = s$, for all j s.t. $\hat{L}(\pi^{0,j}) \in \mathcal{L}(r_1)$, there exists a k s.t. $\hat{L}(\pi^{j,k}) \in \mathcal{L}(r_2)$

5. $M, s \models r_1 \mapsto r_2 \iff$ for all paths π s.t. $\pi_0 = s$, for all j s.t. $\hat{L}(\pi^{0,j}) \in \mathcal{L}(r_1)$, either there exists a k s.t. $\hat{L}(\pi^{j,k}) \in \mathcal{L}(r_2)$, or for all k, there exists a word w (not necessarily a computation path in M) s.t. $\hat{L}(\pi^{j,k}) w \in \mathcal{L}(r_2)$

6. $M, s \models EX\ f \Longleftrightarrow$ for some path π s.t. $\pi_0 = s$, $M, \pi_1 \models f$
7. $M, s \models E[f_1 U f_2] \Longleftrightarrow$ for some path π s.t. $\pi_0 = s$, there exists k s.t. $M, \pi_k \models f_2$ and for all j s.t. $j < k$, $M, \pi_j \models f_1$
8. $M, s \models EG\ f \Longleftrightarrow$ for some path π s.t. $\pi_0 = s$, for all $j \geq 0$, $M, \pi_j \models f$
9. $M, s \models \{r\}(f) \Longleftrightarrow$ for all paths π s.t. $\pi_0 = s$, for all j s.t. $\hat{L}(\pi^{0,j}) \in \mathcal{L}(r)$, $M, \pi_j \models f$

B   The Full Syntactic Sugar

Additional boolean operators
1. $b_1 \vee b_2 = \neg(\neg b_1 \wedge \neg b_2)$ 2. $b_1 \to b_2 = \neg b_1 \vee b_2$
2. $b_1 \to b_2 = \neg b_1 \vee b_2$ 4. $b_1 \oplus b_2 = (b_1 \wedge \neg b_2) \vee (\neg b_1 \wedge b_2)$

Additional SERE operators (where i, j, and k are integer constants s.t. $i \geq 0$, $j \geq i$, $k > 0$)
1. $r[+] = r, r[*]$ 2. $r[i] = \begin{cases} \textbf{false}[*] & \text{if } i = 0 \\ \overbrace{r, r, \ldots, r}^{i\ times} & \text{otherwise} \end{cases}$ 3. $r[i..j] = r[i]\|r[i+1]\|\ldots\|r[j]$

4. $r[i..] = r[i], r[*]$ 5. $r[..i] = r[0]\|r[1]\|r[2]\|\ldots\|r[i]$ 6. $[+] = \textbf{true}[+]$
7. $[*] = \textbf{true}[*]$ 8. $[i] = \textbf{true}[i]$ 9. $[i..j] = \textbf{true}[i..j]$
10. $[i..] = \textbf{true}[i..]$ 11. $[..i] = \textbf{true}[..i]$ 12. $b[= i] = \{\neg b[*], b\}[i], \neg b[*]$
13. $b[> i] = b[= i+1], [*]$ 14. $b[< k] = b[= 0]\|b[= 1]\|\ldots\|b[= (k-1)]$
15. $b[\geq i] = b[> i]\|b[= i]$ 16. $b[\leq i] = b[< i]\|b[= i]$ 17. $b[> i, < j] = b[> i] \&\& b[< j]$
18. $b[\geq i, < j] = b[\geq i] \&\& b[< j]$ 19. $b[> i, \leq j] = b[> i] \&\& b[\leq j]$ 20. $b[\geq i, \leq j] = b[\geq i] \&\& b[\leq j]$

Additional linear operators
1. $always\{r\} = \{\textbf{true}[*]\} \mapsto \{r\}$ 2. $never\{r\} = \{\textbf{true}[*], r\} \mapsto \{\textbf{false}\}$
3. $eventually!\{r\} = \{\textbf{true}\} \mapsto \{\textbf{true}[*], r\}!$ 4. $within!(r_1, b)\{r_2\} = \{r_1\} \mapsto \{r_2 \&\& b[= 0], \neg b[*], b\}!$
5. $within(r_1, b)\{r_2\} = \{r_1\} \mapsto \{r_2 \&\& b[= 0]\}$
6. $within!_{-}(r_1, b)\{r_2\} = \{r_1\} \mapsto \{\{r_2 \&\& b[= 0], \neg b[*], b\}\|\{r_2 \&\& \{\neg b[*], b\}\}\}!$
7. $within_{-}(r_1, b)\{r_2\} = \{r_1\} \mapsto \{r_2 \&\& \{\neg b[*], \textbf{true}\}\}$ 8.$whilenot!(b)\{r\} = within!(\textbf{true}, b)\{r\}$
9. $whilenot(b)\{r\} = within(\textbf{true}, b)\{r\}$ 10. $whilenot!_{-}(b)\{r\} = within!_{-}(\textbf{true}, b)\{r\}$
11. $whilenot_{-}(b)\{r\} = within_{-}(\textbf{true}, b)\{r\}$ 12. $\{r_1\} \mapsto \{r_2\}! = \{r_1\} \mapsto \{\textbf{true}, r_2\}!$
13. $\{r_1\} \mapsto \{r_2\} = \{r_1\} \mapsto \{\textbf{true}, r_2\}$

Additional branching operators (where i and j are integers s.t. $i > 0$ and $j \geq i$)
1. $EF\ f = E[\textbf{true} U f]$ 2. $AXf = \neg EX \neg f$ 3. $AGf = \neg E[\textbf{true} U \neg f]$
4. $A[f_1\ U\ f_2] = \neg(E[\neg f_2\ U\ \neg f_1 \wedge \neg f_2] \vee EG \neg f_2)$
5. $AFf = A[\textbf{true}\ U\ f]$ 6. $E[f_1\ W\ f_2] = E[f_1\ U\ f_2] \vee EG f_1$7. $A[f_1\ W\ f_2] = \neg E[\neg f_2\ U \neg f_1 \wedge \neg f_2]$

8. $AX[i]f = \overbrace{AXAX\ldots AX}^{i\ times} f$ 9. $ABG[i..j]f = AX[i]f \wedge AX[i+1]f \wedge \ldots \wedge AX[j]f$

10. $ABF[i..j]f = \overbrace{AX[i](f \vee AX(f \vee AX(\ldots f \vee AX(f)\ldots)))}^{j-i\ times}$
11. $f_1\ until!\ f_2 = A[f_1\ U\ f_2]$ 12. $f_1\ until\ f_2 = A[f_1\ W\ f_2]$
13. $f_1\ until!_{-}\ f_2 = A[f_1\ U\ f_1 \wedge f_2]$ 14. $f_1\ until_{-}\ f_2 = A[f_1\ W\ f_1 \wedge f_2]$
15. $f_1\ before!\ f_2 = A[\neg f_2\ U\ f_1]$ 16. $f_1\ before\ f_2 = A[\neg f_2\ W\ f_1]$
17. $f_1\ before!_{-}\ f_2 = A[\neg f_2\ U\ f_1 \wedge \neg f_2]$ 18. $f_1\ before_{-}\ f_2 = A[\neg f_2\ W\ f_1 \wedge \neg f_2]$
19. $next\_event!(b)(f) = A[\neg b\ U\ b \wedge f]$ 20. $next\_event(b)(f) = A[\neg b\ W\ b \wedge f]$
21. $next\_event!(b)[i](f) = next\_event!(b)$
$$\overbrace{(AX next\_event!(b)(AX next\_event!(b)\ldots(AX next\_event!(b)(f)\ldots)))}^{i-1\ times}$$
22. $next\_event(b)[i](f) = next\_event(b)$
$$\overbrace{(AX next\_event(b)(AX next\_event(b)\ldots(AX next\_event(b)(f)\ldots)))}^{i-1\ times}$$
23. $next\_event!(b)[i..j](f) = next\_event!(b)[i](f) \wedge \ldots \wedge next\_event!(b)[j](f)$
24. $next\_event(b)[i..j](f) = next\_event(b)[i](f) \wedge \ldots \wedge next\_event(b)[j](f)$
25. $next\_event\_f!(b)[i..j](f) = next\_event!(b)[i]$
$$\overbrace{(f \vee AX next\_event!(b)(f \vee AX next\_event!(b)\ldots(f \vee AX next\_event!(b)(f)\ldots)))}^{j-i\ times}$$
26. $next\_event\_f(b)[i..j](f) = next\_event(b)[i]$
$$\overbrace{(f \vee AX next\_event(b)(f \vee AX next\_event(b)\ldots(f \vee AX next\_event(b)(f)\ldots)))}^{j-i\ times}$$

TREX: A Tool for Reachability Analysis of Complex Systems

Aurore Annichini[1], Ahmed Bouajjani[2], and Mihaela Sighireanu[2]

[1] VERIMAG, Centre Equation, 2 av. de Vignate, 38610 Gières, France
[2] LIAFA, University of Paris 7, 2 place Jussieu, 75251 Paris Cedex 5, France

1 Introduction

Finite-state model-checkers such as SMV [13] and SPIN [11] do not allow to deal with important aspects that appear in modelling and analysing complex systems, e.g., communication protocols. Among these aspects: real-time constraints, manipulation of unbounded data structures like counters, communication through unbounded channels, parametric reasoning, etc.

The tool we propose, called TREX, allows to analyse automatically automata-based models equipped with variables of different kinds of *infinite*-domain data structures and with *parameters* (i.e., uninstantiated constants). These models are, at the present time, parametric (continuous-time) timed automata, extended with integer counters and communicating through unbounded lossy FIFO queues.

The techniques used in TREX are based on *symbolic reachability analysis*. Symbolic representation structures are used to represent infinite sets of configurations, and forward/backward exploration procedures are used to generate a symbolic reachability graph. The termination is not guaranteed, but efficient *extrapolation techniques* are used to help it. These techniques are based on computing the (exact) effect of the iteration of control loops detected dynamically during the search.

The kernel algorithm used in TREX is generic and can be used for any kind of data structures for which it is possible to provide a symbolic representation structure, a symbolic successor/predecessor function, and an extrapolation procedure. In the current version, TREX provides packages for symbolic representation of configurations of lossy FIFO channels and parametric timed automata and clock automata.

TREX allows to check on-the-fly safety properties, as well as to generate the set of reachable configurations and a finite symbolic graph. The set of reachable configurations can be used as an invariant of the system. For instance, if the analysed infinite-state model M is already an abstraction of a more concrete one M', the set of reachable configurations of M can be used to construct an invariant of M' which may help in its analysis. On the other hand, the generated finite symbolic graph is a finite abstraction of the analysed model, which can be used for (conservative) finite-state model checking.

G. Berry, H. Comon, and A. Finkel (Eds.): CAV 2001, LNCS 2102, pp. 368–372, 2001.

TREX is connected to the IF [5] environment which allows: (1) the use of high-level specification languages such as SDL, (2) the interaction with abstraction tools and invariant checkers such as INVEST [3], (3) the use of finite-state model checkers such as CADP [8] and SPIN to verify properties on the finite symbolic graph.

TREX has been used to analyse several nontrivial protocols in their parametric versions, such as the Bounded Retransmission Protocol (BRP) [6]. This particular example requires the full power of TREX since it is a parametric heterogeneous model involving clocks, counters, and lossy channels. Moreover, the constraints manipulated in this model are nonlinear (contain products between variables). As far as we know, TREX is the only existing tool which allows to deal fully automatically with such a complex model. Indeed, tools like HYTECH [10] and LPMC [12] deal with timed/hybrid automata and linear constraints, while LASH [15] deals with counter automata.

2 Architecture

Figure 1 shows the overall environment and architecture of TREX.

In addition to the description of the model in IF, the user of TREX can specify the initial constraints (invariants) on parameters, the initial symbolic configuration for the beginning of reachability analysis, and/or the safety property to be checked on-the-fly, expressed by an observer written in IF.

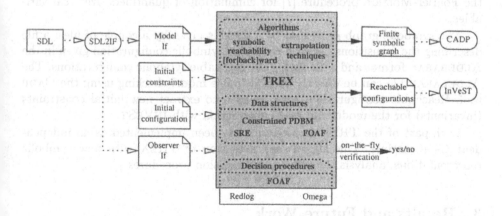

Fig. 1. Overview of the TREX's Architecture and Environment.

From the analysis of the input model, TREX instantiates *automatically* the generic reachability algorithm with the representation structures needed by the infinite data domains used.

Two such representations are actually provided in TREX. The first one is well suited for representing the contents of unbounded lossy FIFO-channels. We implemented a package for manipulating a class of regular expressions, *simple regular expressions* (SREs) [1], which is exactly the class of downward closed regular languages. This representation is interesting because the operations manipulating SREs during the symbolic analysis (the inclusion test, the effect of a transition, and the arbitrary number of executions of a control loop) are polynomial.

The second representation deals with sets of configurations of parametric timed automata and counter automata. We implemented a package for manipulating Constrained PDBMs (*Parametric Difference Bound Matrices*) [2]. The use of Constrained PDBMs allows to deal in a uniform way with counter/clock automata, parametric/non-parametric models, and systems generating linear or nonlinear arithmetical constraints. The package provides compact representation of PDBMs and efficient methods for operations used during symbolic analysis (e.g., emptiness check, intersection, and inclusion test). A special effort has been devoted to develop efficient representation of terms and formulas used in Constrained PDBMs, and simplification techniques on these objects. For this, we implemented a package, called FOAF (*First-Order Arithmetical Formulas*), which also gives the kind (linear or non-linear) of terms and formulas. This analysis is needed in order to apply the right decision procedure for the satisfiability of formulas.

The external decision procedures used actually by TREX are those offered by OMEGA [14] for formulas over integers and by the REDLOG package of REDUCE [9] for formulas over reals. Moreover, we implemented in the FOAF package the Fourier-Motzkin procedure [7] for elimination of quantifiers over real variables.

The symbolic graph generated by TREX is given by a couple of files: a file describing the transitions between reachable symbolic configuration given in the ALDEBARAN format and a file listing the reachable symbolic configurations. The ALDEBARAN file can be directly used for finite model-checking using the CADP tool. Reachable configurations may be used to extract new initial constraints (invariants) for the model and to do abstraction with INVEST.

Each part of the TREX architecture has been implemented as an independent C++ module. This allows easy extension of TREX with new symbolic representations, analysis algorithms, and decision procedures.

3   Results and Future Work

TREX has been applied in a number of infinite state and/or parameterized protocols like: lift controller, Backery algorithm, BRP protocol, FDDI protocol, Fischer's protocol, alternating bit protocol (ABP), etc.

Table 1 gives the performances obtained by applying TREX on these examples. We consider two versions of TREX, depending on the package used for the decision procedure on reals: the first (*Standard*) uses the FOAF package and the second uses REDLOG.

The columns *"version"* specify the number of different kinds of variables used by each example: p for parameters, c for clocks, n for counters, $f(m)$ for lossy FIFO-channels with m messages, b for booleans, and $e(v)$ for enumerations with v values. The column *"# reach. conf."* specifies the number of reachable symbolic configurations generated during symbolic analysis.

Table 1. Performance Statistics on a Sun Ultra 10 (Space in Mbytes, Time in seconds).

Case study	version						Standard		with REDLOG		# reach.
	p	c	n	$f(m)$	b	$e(v)$	space	time	space	time	config.
Lift 10	-	-	3	-	-	-	6.5	7.52	6.5	7.52	8
Lift N	1	-	3	-	-	-	6.5	8.05	6.5	8.05	9
Backery	-	-	2	-	-	-	6.6	5.68	6.6	5.68	33
Fischer	2	2	-	-	-	1(3)	7	0.65	7	0.61	25
	2	3	-	-	-	1(4)	9.2	159.04	8.2	105.82	261
	2	4	-	-	-	1(5)	140	124 920	140	70 316	3 633
ABP	-	-	-	2(4)	-	-	6.9	0.05	6.9	0.05	8
FDDI	4	5	-	-	2	-	20	1 603.50	21	4 445	731
BRP	-	-	-	2(4)	-	-	6.8	0.30	6.8	0.30	36
	2	-	2	2(7)	4	-	16.4	195.93	16.4	195.93	173
	4	2	1	2(6)	2	-	89	5 518.57	85	5 563	106

The most complex example for which TREX has been applied is the BRP protocol. It is a timed file transfer protocol used by Philips. The three versions verified correspond to: (1) abstraction of clocks and counters—only lossy FIFO-channels are considered, (2) abstraction of clocks—counters and channels are used, (3) full version with channels, counters for the number of retransmissions, and clocks for timeouts. For the last version, TREX generates automatically the (non-linear) constraint needed to satisfy the timing response property of the protocol. The constraint relates three parameters of the protocol: the timeouts for the sender and for the receiver, and the number of retransmissions.

In future work, we plan to implement other data structures for the representation of configurations over counters and clocks, as well as to extend the input model to infinite nets of identical processes [4]. The version 1.0 of TREX is available at http://www-verimag.imag.fr/~annichin/trex/.

References

1. P.A. Abdulla, A. Bouajjani, and B. Jonsson. On-the-fly analysis of systems with unbounded, lossy, FIFO channels. In *Proceedings of the 10th CAV*, volume 1427 of *LNCS*, pages 305–317. Springer Verlag, 1998.
2. A. Annichini, E. Asarin, and A. Bouajjani. Symbolic techniques for parametric reasoning about counter and clock systems. In E.A. Emerson and A.P. Sistla, editors, *Proceedings of the 12th CAV*, volume 1855 of *LNCS*, pages 419–434. Springer Verlag, July 2000.

3. S. Bensalem, Y. Lakhnech, and S. Owre. InVeSt: A tool for the verification of invariants. In *Proceedings of the 10th CAV*, volume 1427 of *LNCS*. Springer Verlag, 1998.

4. A. Bouajjani, B. Jonsson, M. Nilsson, and T. Touili. Regular model checking. In E.A. Emerson and A.P. Sistla, editors, *Proceedings of the 12th CAV*, volume 1855 of *LNCS*, pages 403–418, July 2000.

5. M. Bozga, J.-C. Fernandez, L. Girvu, S. Graf, J.-P. Krimm, and L. Mounier. If: A validation environment for times asynchronous systems. In E.A. Emerson and A.P. Sistla, editors, *Proceedings of the 12th CAV*, volume 1855 of *LNCS*, pages 543–547. Springer Verlag, July 2000.

6. P.R. D'Argenio, J.-P. Katoen, T.C. Ruys, and J. Tretmans. The bounded retransmission protocol must be on time! In *Proceedings of 3rd Conference on Tools and Algorithms for the Construction and Analysis of Systems*, volume 1217 of *LNCS*, pages 416–432. Springer Verlag, 1997.

7. B.C. Eaves and U.G. Rothblum. Dines-fourier-motzkin quantifier elimination and an application of corresponding transfer principles over ordered fields. *Mathematical Programming*, 53:307–321, 1992.

8. J.-C. Fernandez, H. Garavel, A. Kerbrat, R. Mateescu, L. Mounier, and M. Sighireanu. Cadp (cæsar/aldebaran development package): A protocol validation and verification toolbox. In R. Alur and T.A. Henzinger, editors, *Proceedings of the 8th CAV*, volume 1102 of *LNCS*, pages 437–440. Springer Verlag, August 1996.

9. A.C. Hearn. *REDUCE — User's and Contributed Packages Manual*. Codemist Ltd., February 1999. version 3.7.

10. T.A. Henzinger, P.-H. Ho, and H. Wong-Toi. Hytech: A model checker for hybrid systems. *Software Tools for Technology Transfer*, 1(1):110–122, 1997.

11. G.J. Holzmann. *Design and Validation of Computer Protocols*. Software Series. Prentice Hall, 1991.

12. R.F. Lutje Spelberg, W.J. Toetenel, and M. Ammerlaan. Partion refinement in real-time model checking. In A.P. Ravn and H. Rischel, editors, *Proceedings of 5th FTRTFT*, volume 1486 of *LNCS*, pages 143–157. Springer Verlag, 1998.

13. K.L. McMillan. *The SMV system*. Cadence Berkeley Labs, 1999.

14. Omega Team. *The Omega Library*, November 1996. version 1.1.0.

15. P. Wolper and B. Boigelot. On the construction of automata from linear arithmetic constraints. In S. Graf and M. Schwartzbach, editors, *Proceedings of the 6th Conference on Tools and Algorithms for the Construction and Analysis of Systems*, volume 1785 of *LNCS*. Springer Verlag, 2000.

BOOSTER: Speeding Up
RTL Property Checking of Digital Designs
by Word-Level Abstraction

Peer Johannsen

Siemens AG, Corporate Technology, Design Automation, CT–SE–4
81730 Munich, Germany
peer.johannsen@mchp.siemens.de

Abstract. In this paper we present a tool which operates as a pre- and postprocessor for RTL property checking and simplifies word-level specifications before verification, thus speeding up property checking runtimes and allowing larger design sizes to be verified. The basic idea is to scale down design sizes by exploiting word-level information. BOOSTER implements a new technique which computes a one-to-one RTL abstraction of a digital design in which the widths of word-level signals are reduced with respect to a property, i.e. the property holds for the abstract RTL if and only if it holds for the original RTL. The property checking task is completely carried out on the scaled-down version of the design. If the property fails then the tool computes counterexamples for the original RTL from counterexamples found on the reduced model.

1 High-Level Property Checking of Digital Designs

Today's digital circuit designs frequently contain up to several million transistors and designs need to be checked to ensure that manufactured chips operate correctly. Formal methods for verification are becoming increasingly attractive since they confirm design behavior without exhaustively simulating a design. Over the past years, bounded model checking and property checking have increased in significance in electronic design automation [1, 9]. Promising approaches to enhance capabilities of hardware verification tools are decision procedures which make use of high-level design information [2–5, 11], and automated abstraction techniques, e.g. using uninterpreted functions and small domain instantiations [6, 10].

We consider a property checking flow in which design specifications are given as VHDL or Verilog source code. Properties are specified in a linear time logic used in Symbolic Trajectory Evaluation and describe the intended behavior of the design within a finite bounded interval of time. As a first step, design and property are synthesized into a flattened RTL netlist, including word-level signals, word-level gates, arithmetic units, comparators, multiplexors and memory elements. Each word-level signal x has a fixed width $n \in \mathbb{N}_+$ and takes bitvectors of respective length as values. A property checker, which reads RTL netlists as input, translates such representation of design and property into an internal

G. Berry, H. Comon, and A. Finkel (Eds.): CAV 2001, LNCS 2102, pp. 373–377, 2001.
© Springer-Verlag Berlin Heidelberg 2001

bit-level representation (i.e. an instance of propositional SAT) and uses SAT, BDD and ATPG methods to either prove that the property holds for the given design or to compute a counterexample. A counterexample is an indication that a circuit does not function in the way intended by the designer and is given in terms of assignments of values to the circuit inputs, such that a violation of the desired behavior, which is described by the property, can be observed.

BOOSTER (Boolean String Length Reduction) implements a new word-level abstraction technique developed in [7], which is embedded within the flow. In a preprocessing step prior to the property checker (see fig.), the tool takes the RTL netlist and computes a scaled down RTL model of the design in which each word-level signal x is replaced by a corresponding shrunken signal of width $m_x \leq n$, where n is the original width of x, while guaranteeing that the property holds for the reduced RTL if and only if it holds for the original RTL. Design and abstract model differ from each other only as far as signal widths are concerned. The reduced RTL is given to the property checker instead of the original RTL. Depending on the degree of reduction, the internal bit-level representation computed from the reduced RTL contains significantly less variables than the one computed when using the non-reduced RTL. If the property does not hold, the counterexample returned by the property checker is taken, which is a counterexample relating to the signals of the reduced RTL. A corresponding counterexample for the original RTL is computed, using information about the applied reduction, gathered during the preprocess.

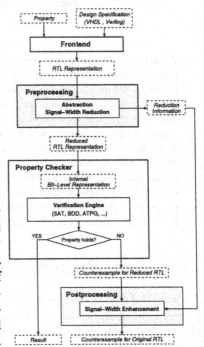

2   Scaling Down RTL Designs by Signal Width Reduction

BOOSTER reads an RTL representation of a design and a property and generates a system E of equations over a theory of fixed-size bitvectors based on [7], which is an extension of the core theory of bitvectors presented in [5]. Our theory features high-level operators like bitwise Boolean operations, arithmetics (cf. [2]) and if-then-else, and allows complete RTL designs to be modeled. E is satisfiable if and only if the property does not hold for the RTL. Word-level signals in the RTL correspond to bitvector variables in E, thus the information, which bits belong to the same signal, is kept. A satisfying solution of E yields a counterexample for the RTL. For each bitvector variable occurring in E the smallest possible number of bits is computed, such that a second system E' of bitvector equations, which differs from E solely in the manner that variable widths are shrunken to these computed numbers, is satisfiable if and only if E is satisfiable. E' is generated using these minimum signal widths and then retranslated into a netlist, which is output by the tool and represents a scaled down version of the original RTL.

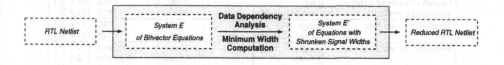

The process of scaling down signal widths is separated into two subsequent phases. The high-level operators occurring in the equations of E impose structural and functional dependencies on the bitvector variables. Thereby, variables typically have non-uniform data dependencies, i.e. different dependencies exist for different chunks of a signal. Our method analyzes such dependencies and, for each variable, determines contiguous parts in which all bits are treated uniformly in the exact same manner with respect to data dependencies. Such decomposition of a variable into a sequence of chunks is called a granularity. For each such chunk of a signal, the necessary minimum width is computed, as required by dynamical data dependencies. According to these computed minimum chunk widths, the reduced width for the corresponding shrunken signal is reassembled (see [7, 8] for further details on the reduction).

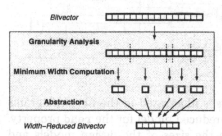

3   Experimental Results

BooStER is implemented in C++ and was tested in several case studies at the EDA department of Siemens Corp. in Munich and at Infineon Techn. in San Jose. Test cases were run on a PII 450 Mhz Linux PC with 128 MB. The tool operated as a preprocessor to the property checker used at Siemens and Infineon. All runtimes on reduced models were compared to those achieved on the original designs without preprocessing. As an example, we here consider the management unit of an ATM switching element. The design consists of 3.000 lines of Verilog code, the netlist synthesis has approx. 24.000 gates and 35.000 RAM cells. The RTL incorporates 16 FIFO queue buffers and complex control logic. Data packages are fed on 33 input channels to the management unit, stored in the FIFOs and upon request are output on one of 17 output channels, while the cell sequence has to be preserved and no package must be dropped from the management unit.

	Property	Original design	Shrunken model
Computation times for pre- and postprocessing	nop		2.96 secs
	read		6.53 secs
	write		3.24 secs
FIFO sizes on RTL	nop	160 cells × 10 bit	160 cells × 2 bit
	read / write	160 cells × 10 bit	160 cells × 3 bit
Overall number of bits in all signals in cone of influence of property	nop	20925	5034 (24.0 %)
	read	31452	10592 (33.6 %)
	write	14622	5163 (35.3 %)
Overall number of gates in synthesized netlist	nop	23801	5661 (27.9 %)
	read / write	23801	7929 (33.3 %)
Number of state bits	nop	1658	362 (21.8 %)
	read / write	1658	524 (31.6 %)
Property checker runtimes	nop	23:33 min	37.96 secs (2.7 %)
	read	42:23 min	3:27 min (8.1 %)
	write_fail	2:08 min	25.66 secs (19.5 %)
	write_hold	27:08 min	1:08 min (4.2 %)

Three different properties (nop, read, write) had to be verified, which specified the intended behavior within a range of 4 timesteps (nop, write) and 6 timesteps (read). Results and CPU times are are shown above. As can be seen, in all cases

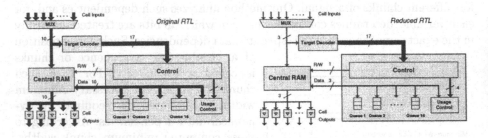

the data path signals could be scaled. This is illustrated in the block diagrams above, showing the original design and the reduced model for the read property. We encountered a significant reduction in the sizes of the design models and a tremendous drop in the runtimes of the property checker. It turned out that the write property did not hold due to a design bug in the Verilog code. A counterexample for the reduced model was found (write_fail) from which the tool computed a counterexample for the original design, whereupon the bug was fixed and the property was again checked on the corrected design (write_hold).

4 Conclusions

Reducing runtimes and the amount of memory needed in computations is one requirement in order to match today's sizes of real world designs in hardware verification. We have presented a tool that efficiently simplifies word-level circuit specifications for RTL property checking by scaling down the widths of input, output and internal signals. A linear reduction from n bits down to m bits, $m < n$, causes an exponential reduction of the induced state space of the signal from 2^n to 2^m, while reduced state space sizes coincide with increased verification performance. Our method provides a one-to-one RTL abstraction, which interprets all RTL operators and which strictly separates the pre- and postprocessing of design and counterexample, and the property checking process itself. Thus, the proposed method is independent of the concrete realization of the property checker and can be combined with a variety of existing techniques which take RTL netlists as input. Due to providing a one-to-one abstraction, postprocessing of counterexamples is straightforward, false-negatives cannot occur. Moreover, if preprocessing yields that no reduction is possible for a given design and a property, then abstract model and original design are identical, so the verification task itself is not impaired by using the proposed abstraction, and in all case studies pre- and postprocessing runtimes were negligible. Test cases showed that the tool cooperated particularly well with a SAT and BDD based property checking multi-engine, because the complexity of those techniques often depends on the number of bits occurring in a design. Furthermore, experiments revealed that the proposed abstraction seems to be well qualified for hardware verification of memories, FIFOs, queues, stacks, bridges and interface protocols.

References

1. A. Biere, A. Cimatti, E.M. Clarke, M. Fujita, Y. Zhu. Symbolic Model Checking Using SAT Procedures instead of BDDs. *DAC'99*, pages 317–320. 1999.
2. C.W. Barrett, D.L. Dill, J.R. Levitt. A Decision Procedure for Bit-Vector Arithmetic. *DAC'98*, pages 522–527. 1998.
3. N. Bjørner, M.C. Pichora. Deciding Fixed and Non-fixed Size Bit-vectors. *TACAS'98*, pages 376–392. 1998.
4. C.Y. Huang, K.T. Cheng. Assertion checking by combined word-level ATPG and modular arithmetic constraint-solving techniques. *DAC'00*, pages 118–123. 2000.
5. D. Cyrluk, M.O. Möller, H. Ruess. An Efficient Decision Procedure for the Theory of Fixed-Sized Bit-Vectors. *CAV'97*, pages 60–71. 1997.
6. R. Hojati, A.J. Isles, D. Kirkpatrick, R.K. Brayton. Verification Using Uninterpreted Functions and Finite Instantiations. *FMCAD'96*, pages 218–232. 1996.
7. P. Johannsen. Scaling Down Design Sizes in Hardware Verification. *Ph.D. Dissertation at the Christian-Albrechts-University of Kiel*, to appear in 2001.
8. P. Johannsen. Computing One-to-One Minimum-Width Abstractions of Digital Designs for RTL Property Checking. *Intern. Report, Siemens AG, CT-SE-4*, submitted to ICCAD'01.
9. J.P. Marques da Silva, K.A. Sakallah. Boolean satisfiability in electronic design automation. *DAC'00*, pages 675–680. 2000.
10. A. Pnueli, Y. Rodeh, O. Shtrichman, M. Siegel. Deciding Equality Formulas by Small Domains Instantiations. *CAV'99*, pages 455–469. 1999.
11. Z. Zeng, P. Kalla, M. Ciesielski. LPSAT: A Unified Approach to RTL Satisfiability. *DATE'01*. 2001.

SDLcheck: A Model Checking Tool

Vladimir Levin and Hüsnü Yenigün

Bell Laboratories, Lucent Technologies, Murray Hill, NJ 07974
{levin,husnu}@research.bell-labs.com

Introduction

SDLcheck is a verification tool developed to support model checking for asynchronous (concurrent) programs written in SDL [1,2]. Given an SDL program and a specification of a desired behavior of the program, SDLcheck generates a verification model that consists of two ω-automata, P and T: P models the program and T the specification. Then, the automaton language containment, $L(P) \subset L(T)$, is tested by model checking with Cospan [3].

The majority of model checking tools designed for asynchronous program verification make use of interleaving systems as a model platform. In contrast, SDLcheck translates asynchronous SDL programs into synchronous ω-automata. Concurrent execution (interleaving) of SDL processes is modeled using a simple technique described below in the paper. The reason for this choice is in order to efficiently combine partial order reduction, which is known to be useful for asynchronous programs, with BDD-based symbolic verification, which is known to be useful for large synchronous models. For this, SDLcheck implements the algorithm described in [4] that realizes partial order reduction through modifying a program model P prior to model checking. Although model checking tools for SDL and other programming and design languages are being intensively developed in research, in a practical sense, they mostly remain prototypes lacking optimizations necessary to cope with large programs. There are several advanced model checking tools that mainly relate to hardware verification, where synchronous ω-automata, on one hand, naturally match synthesizable hardware designs and, on the other hand, support symbolic verification. For software verification, combining IF [5] and SPIN [6], as reported in [7], supports complementary sets of model checking optimizations. This combination nonetheless lacks symbolic verification, as do all other SDL verification tools of which we are aware.

SDLcheck is also capable of supporting software/hardware co-design verification. This is realized through Cospan, which is also used as the model checker in hardware verification, namely, in the commercial tool FormalCheck[TM] . [1] Through the synchronous ω-automaton model platform, SDLcheck combined with Cospan supports both software specific and hardware specific model checking optimizations.

SDL Subset and Co-design Extensions

SDLcheck accepts the SDL'96 standard [1,2] including ASN.1 related features, however, without axiomatic data definitions, services and OO features. It also requires the SDL program model to be finite state — so no unbounded recursion.

---

[1] licensed by Lucent Technologies to Cadence Design Systems.

G. Berry, H. Comon, and A. Finkel (Eds.): CAV 2001, LNCS 2102, pp. 378–381, 2001.

To support co-verification, SDLcheck implements extensions to SDL (suggested in [8]) that allow description of a software process interfacing to a hardware module. The hardware part of a co-design is expressed in a hardware description language, Verilog or VHDL. On the software side written in SDL, SDLcheck supports read/write access to a hardware variable (wire or port) through the declaration of an associated *interface* variable. The interface variable is either sourced from, or feeds the hardware variable. SDLcheck also supports a none input action. It does not read the process buffer and only triggers a transition from the current state of the process when the enabling condition which guards this action evaluates to true. A none input action matches well the concept of a hardware transition triggered by an event, such as clock rising (or falling) or signal reset. Being associated with an interface variable value, a hardware event, say, value 1 on wire $A.B.y$, may be tested in the enabling condition and trigger a transition in the corresponding software process. Once triggered, this transition executes like a hardware transition: synchronously (simultaneously) with all enabled transitions of the co-design hardware part. Other (*software*) transitions of software processes execute asynchronously according to usual SDL rules.

Verification Technology and the Tool Architecture
SDLcheck performs three steps:

1. The compiler sdl2sr translates both an SDL program and a behavior specification into S/R, the input language of Cospan. The specification is expressed using macro notations $always(x)$, $eventually(x)$, etc. that reflect linear temporal logic operators and useful combinations of those, with arguments being SDL boolean expressions over the program variables. The specification language is similar to that used in FormalCheck[TM]. In a co-design case, S/R code generated by sdl2sr is mechanically concatenated with S/R code produced by the FormalCheck[TM] compiler for hardware modules.
2. Cospan performs model checking on this S/R code, with any valid combination of its options, including symbolic verification and localization reduction. If it detects that the program model fails to satisfy the specification, it produces an error track demonstrating one of the failure scenarios.
3. The tool T2sdl extracts from the error track pieces related to the SDL program and prints those with back referencing S/R names to SDL sources. In a co-design case, the remaining pieces are back referenced to the HDL.

Translation into S/R ω-Automata
In S/R, an ω-automaton that models an SDL program is described as a synchronous product of primitive ω-automata, each being represented by a distinct state variable whose transitions are defined by a single if-then-else constructor:
asgn $x - > a_1 ? g_1 \mid a_2 ? g_2 \mid \ldots \mid a_{n-1} ? g_{n-1} \mid a_n$
where the omitted guard of the default alternative a_n is $true$ and the complete guard for alternative a_i, $1 < i \leq n$, is $\neg g_1 \wedge \ldots \neg g_{i-1} \wedge g_i$.

After flattening complicated data (structures, arrays, etc.), each variable of an SDL program is translated into a separate state variable.

The sequentiality of process actions is implemented by designating one state variable per process to encode the process control flow graph, say, variable C_Q

for process Q. It works like a program counter: it is assigned to labels of a process' input states and statements, assuming that all statements have been labeled. Transitions between values of C_Q mimic the control flow in the process Q. The variable C_Q is then used in transition guards of other variables owned by the process, including its local and shared variables, and buffer. Since, the buffer queue is updated by both the owner process and a sender process, a buffer transition guard may also test whether the sender process program counter points to the corresponding output action.

In S/R, non-determinism may be captured and controlled using *selection* variables [3] that are assigned to sets of values rather than to distinct values. Selection variables do not contribute to the state space. The concurrency (interleaving) of actions executed by different SDL processes is implemented by designating a special selection variable, say, S, which is non-deterministically assigned to any one of the SDL program processes:

asgn $S := \{Q_1, \ldots Q_k\}$.

Then, each normal transition of the program counter C_Q is guarded by the condition $S = Q$. If the condition evaluates to $false$, the program counter C_Q self-loops at its current point. For example, let the SDL process Q consist of only one statement which is a two branch decision (i.e. if-then-else) and variable x be assigned, respectively, to y_1 and y_2 in its branches. Then, S/R code for this process will have these two assignments:

asgn $C_Q - >$
  L_{then} ? $(S = Q) \wedge (C_Q = L_{start}) \wedge d_{if} \mid L_{else}$? $(S = Q) \wedge (C_Q = L_{start}) \wedge \neg d_{if} \mid$
  L_{stop} ? $(S = Q) \wedge (C_Q = L_{then} \vee C_Q = L_{else}) \wedge true \mid C_Q$
asgn $x - > y_1$? $(S = Q) \wedge (C_Q = L_{then}) \mid y_2$? $(S = Q) \wedge (C_Q = L_{else}) \mid x$

where d_{if} is the decision condition and $L_{start}, L_{then}, L_{else}, L_{stop}$ are labels of nodes in the process control flow graph. Thus, the variable S models the interleaving of the processes $Q_1, \ldots Q_k$ and C_Q the control flow in the process Q. Note the regular structure of the C_Q alternatives: in each alternative guard, its rightmost conjunction factor expresses the condition under which the process control flow (whenever allowed to move by $(S = Q)$) moves from its current point, which is captured by the middle conjunction factor, to its next point, which is the alternative's value.

Optimizations

On the top of this method, SDLcheck implements partial order reduction, which optimizes model checking by selecting only one of all possible interleavings between independent actions provided that others have the same verification effect on the behavior specification. This optimization is implemented by modifying the original ω-automaton model of an SDL program to restrict its transition relation. For this, SDLcheck imposes a control over the selection variable S. Namely, if an action of process Q may be selected to execute with ignoring other possible interleavings, it is marked by the SDLcheck compiler as *ample*. In the optimized model, the selection variable S is forced to be assigned to process Q, if the current action of this process is ample. If there are several such processes, only one of them is chosen: this is a deterministic though arbitrary choice, made in advance by compiler. Only when no ample actions are enabled, S remains non-deterministically assigned by the model to any one of the program processes $\{Q_1, \ldots Q_k\}$. This technique may significantly reduce the original non-determinism in the state space exploration. The objective is to have more ample actions. As explained in [4], non-ample actions appear, in particular, because of the neccesisty to break global cycles in the state space exploration by allowing the complete non-determinism at least at one point in each global cycle. To statically deal with this problem, we might mark one action as non-ample in every local loop in each process control flow graph. However, SDLcheck performs better. It statically analyzes control flow loops that belong to different processes but semantically compensate each other: for example, a loop with output of signal z is compensated by a loop (in a different process) with an input action for the same signal z. As shown in [4], to break a global cycle that executes along compensated control flow loops, it is sufficient to have a non-ample action in only one of those loops. It is how SDLcheck implements partial order reduction. As an option, SDLcheck strengthens this optimization more by forcing to execute simultaneously "by a parallel leap" (instead of sequentially) all current actions that have been marked ample.

Applications

[9] reports on verification of a robot control system developed in an UML-like graphical notation. The verification has been supported by translating the robot control system into an internal representation of SDL used by SDLcheck and then applying SDLcheck and Cospan for model checking. SDLcheck is also applied for debugging an SDL description of the H.248 gateway control protocol issued by ITU–T in 2000.

References

1. *ITU–T Recommendation Z.100 (03/93) — Specification and Description Language (SDL)* , Geneva, 1993.
2. *ITU–T Recommendation Z.100 (10/96) — Specification and Description Language (SDL)* , Addendum 1, Geneva, 1996.
3. R. P. Kurshan, *Computer-Aided Verification of Coordinating Processes: The Automata-Theoretic Approach*, Princeton University Press, 1994.
4. R. P. Kurshan, V. Levin, M. Minea, D. Peled, and H. Yenigün. Static Partial Order Reduction, *Proc. of 4th International Conference Tools and Algorithms for the Construction and Analysis of Systems, LNCS* no. 1384, pp. 345-357, 1998.
5. M. Bozga, J. C. Fernandez, L. Ghirvu, S. Graf, J. P. Krimm, L. Mounier, J. Sifakis, IF: An Intermediate Representation for SDL and its Applications. *Proc. of the SDL Forum*, Montreal, Canada, 1999.
6. G. J. Holzmann, The Model Checker Spin, *IEEE Trans. on Software Engineering* Vol. 23, No. 5, 1997.
7. D. Bosnacki, D. Damm, L. Holenderski, N. Sidorova, Model checking SDL with Spin, *Proc. of the Tools and Algorithms for the Construction and Analysis of Systems*, Berlin, Germany, 2000.
8. Levin, V., E. Bounimova, O. Başbuğoğlu, and K. İnan, A Verifiable Software/Hardware Co-design Using SDL and COSPAN, *Proceedings of the COST 247 International Workshop on Applied Formal Methods In System Design*. Maribor, Slovenia, pp. 6–16, 1996.
9. N. Sharygina, R. P. Kurshan, J. C. Browne, A Formal Object-oriented Analysis for Software Reliability, To appear at FASE 2001.

EASN: Integrating ASN.1 and Model Checking

Vivek K. Shanbhag[1], K. Gopinath*[1], Markku Turunen[2],
Ari Ahtiainen[2], and Matti Luukkainen[3]

[1] CSA Dept, Indian Institute of Science, Bangalore, India
{vivek,gopi}@csa.iisc.ernet.in
[2] Nokia Research Center, Helsinki, Finland
{markku.turunen,ari.ahtiainen}@nokia.com
[3] Department of Computer Science, University of Helsinki, Finland
Matti.Luukkainen@cs.Helsinki.fi

Abstract. Telecommunication protocol standards have in the past and typically still use both an English description of the protocol and an ASN.1[5] specification of the data-model. ASN.1 (Abstract Syntax Notation One) is an ITU/ISO data definition language which has been developed to describe abstractly the values protocol data units can assume; this is of considerable interest for model checking as ASN.1 can be used to constrain/construct the state space of the protocol accurately. However, with current practice, any change to the English description cannot easily be checked for consistency while protocols are being developed. In this work, we have developed a SPIN-based tool called EASN (Enhanced ASN.1) where the behavior can be formally specified through a language based upon Promela for control structures but with data models from ASN.1. We use the X/Open standard on ASN.1/C++ translation so that our tool can be realised with pluggable components. We have used EASN to validate a simplified RLC in the W-CDMA (3G GSM) stack. In this short paper[1], we discuss the EASN language, the tool, and an example usage.

1 Introduction

Next generation protocols for mobile devices have become very complex and it is becoming increasingly difficult for standards bodies to be sure of the correctness of protocols during the standardization process. This has become an impediment in defining new standards. What one needs is a way of specifying an evolving protocol and have some confidence that, at a certain level of abstraction, the protocol is consistent inspite of modifications.

Why ASN.1? There are languages like Promela that can be used, but their data structuring capabilities do not match those of ASN.1, for instance, that is

---

* Supported by funding from Nokia Research Center, under SID project 99033.
[1] See [2] for a full paper discussing the implementation & some performance indicators.

G. Berry, H. Comon, and A. Finkel (Eds.): CAV 2001, LNCS 2102, pp. 382–386, 2001.

widely used in telecommunication protocol specification. It will help the standardization process if a model checker could be augmented with ASN.1 data modeling capabilities to check correctness of interim versions of a protocol before establishing a standard.

ASN.1 separates data modeling into abstract and transfer syntax. The abstract syntax only specifies the universe of abstract values that can be assumed by variables in the model without any concern for how they are mapped to a particular machine, compiler, OS, etc. Hence from the point of view of model checking, an abstract syntax constrains the state space as much as possible IF there is a mechanism by which a system state vector can be encoded with exactly only the possible values of its constituent substates. The latter is a chief feature of the state compaction infrastructure that has been developed for the EASN system described here. ASN.1 has a subtyping feature with a well developed notation for expressing constraints. Note that data here actually means the control data in the protocols and hence our concerns are different from those approaches that exploit symmetry, etc. We derive our EASN tool by marrying ASN.1 with the well known model checker SPIN.

Why SPIN? SPIN[1] is an effective model checking tool for asynchronous systems, especially designed for communication protocols. Nondeterminism and guarded commands in Promela (input language of SPIN) makes it convenient to express behavior of communicating protocol entities. SPIN has many capabilities for validation of safety and liveness properties[4]. Algorithms that effect substantial space and time savings, like bit-state hashing, on-the-fly[3] model-checking and partial-order reduction have been incorporated into SPIN.

SPIN has a **simulator** that randomly checks only a portion of the state space and also a (generated) **validator** that can attempt to exhaustively check the state space of the system or can use techniques like bit-state hashing to check a substantial portion of the state space with a fairly high level of assurance. Our EASN system also has these components.

EASN Language. ASN.1 can only be used to define the datatypes and constant values in an application. Promela, however, is a complete language with a set of basic data types and typedef construct to help users compose datatypes, and control constructs that are used to define the behavior of protocol entities.

The EASN Language *replaces* all the datatyping capabilities of Promela with ASN.1. Hence, none of the data types of Promela are retained in EASN, except the *chan* construct. As ASN.1 has richer and more expressive datatypes compared to Promela, EASN needs to overload the semantics of many of the operators of Promela, so as to support a natural set of operations on data. In addition, we have also augmented the set of operators as necessary. In brief,

EASN = Promela - {mtype, typedef, bit, byte, bool, short, int} + ASN.1
+ overloaded semantics for existing operators + few new operators.

2   EASN, the Verification Tool

Encoding State Efficiently: SPIN represents state quite efficiently but, for reasons of alignment, allows padding and other extraneous matter in the state vector. Since our system uses ASN.1 data modules, we require that all variables be as constrained as possible in the space of values that they can take through the use of subtyping. For instance, if there are only two variables, that are constrained between (say) 5..7 and 3..7, there are only 15 possibilities, and can be represented in only 4 bits instead of either 2+3 (5 bits) or worse 3+3 (6 bits)[2].

Our state compaction infrastructure views the state space of the system as a multi-dimensional array (with one dimension for every component of the state), and consequently, every state of the system, as a point in this multi-dimensional space. We use column-major linearisation.

SPIN does various kinds of state compaction, and in EASN, we have a comparable mechanism for most of them that perform atleast as well in space. But some are unnecessary in EASN. Geldenhuys and Villiers[8] also attempt state compression in SPIN along similar lines as ours but by adding a simple construct to Promela but with restrictions. For example, different orders of process activation along different execution paths are forbidden in their approach as much of the state component placement is done statically. The ranges of their variables must start at zero. We do not have such restrictions.

The EASN Tool: SPIN is open source[7]. We intend EASN to be open source too. NRC has an ASN.1 parser that we could use but we did not want to compromise others from using EASN as open source. We, therefore, have used the X/Open ASN.1/C++ translator std[6] to architect the tool so as to enable other users besides us and NRC to realise it by plugging in any compliant ASN.1/C++ translator into the system. A block diagram of the EASN system is given in the accompanying figure.

An EASN system specification (for simulation/verification) consists of two *compilation units*. One containing all the ASN.1 modules (the dEASN spec.) that is parsed by the ASN.1/C++ translator to generate C++ source, and the other containing the *behavioral* specification of the protocol entities (the cEASN spec.) that is parsed by the EASN parser (a modified Promela parser, derived from SPIN). It is the variable declarations in the cEASN spec that ties it to the dEASN spec as their types are defined in the ASN.1 modules. The EASN parser *imports* all the relevant information regarding a type, from the generated C++ source, by querying its meta-data interface.

The Parser and Simulator: The executable that can parse and simulate a given cEASN spec. is fetched from linking the C++ generated by the translator (corresponding to the associated dEASN spec.) along with all the (appropriately modified) SPIN modules. This executable is the EASN tool. The EASN simulator requires to access data values and modify them through permitted operations.

---

[2] Experienced ASN.1 users may note that such an encoding is even better than the often very compact PER encoding.

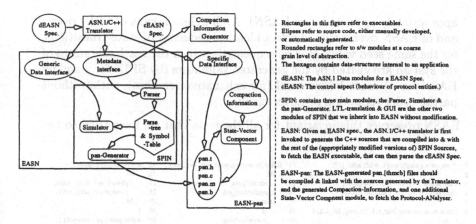

However, since the simulator engine has no knowledge of the specific ASN.1 types that might be used in different EASN specifications, these data operations must be carried out using the *ASN.1/C++ Generic Data Interface* that supports operations on objects conforming to the *ASN.1 data-model*.

The Generated Validator: SPIN generates C code that is compiled to obtain the validator. EASN, however, generates C++ code that has to be linked with the code generated by the ASN.1/C++ translator, the code generated by the *Compaction information generator* and the compaction infrastructure to obtain the validator.

The *compaction information* is a set of C++ functions that export all information about value-constraints expressed in the original ASN.1 spec, through the C++ interface as required by the generic *compaction infrastructure* module. Through these two additional components of our framework, we implement incrementally the computation of the linearised representation of the state of the system that needs to be stored into the hash-table, and also the hash-value of the bucket in the table.

RLC/ABP Examples: We have used EASN to validate a simplified RLC in the W-CDMA (3G GSM) stack. It uses less memory but more time than SPIN. Further details of the performance of EASN have been submitted to the FMICS workshop. Due to its length, we present a much simpler ABP protocol in figure 2. Note that the state vector for EASN is half the size of SPIN's.

Correctness of Implementation *vis-a-vis* **SPIN:** In crafting EASN from SPIN, we identified the following invariant that could be a necessary and sufficient condition to convince oneself that our implementation is sane:

> Given a Promela spec. *s* and a cEASN spec. *e*, derived from *s* by changing its variable types to equivalent ASN.1 types (defined in an ASN.1 module

appropriately imported into EASN): A. Simulation runs of SPIN over s and of EASN over e should select identical sequence of state-transitions, for the same seed value; B. The sequence in which the reachable states of the system are visited by the generated validators (by SPIN for s and by EASN for e) must be identical (for exhaustive searches), with/without partial-order reduction or never-claims.

EASN preserves this invariant for all the tests that we have tried so far.

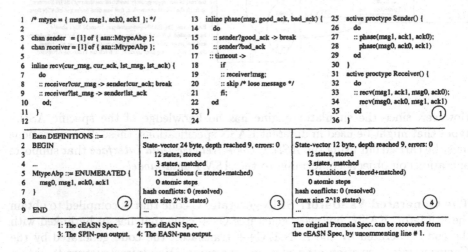

```
1  /* mtype = { msg0, msg1, ack0, ack1 }; */          13 inline phase(msg, good_ack, bad_ack) {        25 active proctype Sender() {
2                                                      14   do                                          26   do
3  chan sender   = [1] of { asn::MtypeAbp };          15   :: sender?good_ack -> break                 27   :: phase(msg1, ack1, ack0);
4  chan receiver = [1] of { asn::MtypeAbp };          16   :: sender?bad_ack                           28      phase(msg0, ack0, ack1)
5                                                      17   :: timeout ->                               29   od
6  inline recv(cur_msg, cur_ack, lst_msg, lst_ack) {  18     if                                        30 }
7    do                                                19     :: receiver!msg;                          31 active proctype Receiver() {
8    :: receiver?cur_msg -> sender!cur_ack; break      20     :: skip /* lose message */                32   do
9    :: receiver?lst_msg -> sender!lst_ack             21     fi;                                       33   :: recv(msg1, ack1, msg0, ack0);
10   od;                                               22   od                                          34      recv(msg0, ack0, msg1, ack1)
11 }                                                   23 }                                             35   od
12                                                     24                                               36 }
```

①

	3: SPIN-pan output	4: EASN-pan output
1 Easn DEFINITIONS ::=	...	...
2 BEGIN	State-vector 24 byte, depth reached 9, errors: 0	State-vector 12 byte, depth reached 9, errors: 0
3	12 states, stored	12 states, stored
4 ...	3 states, matched	3 states, matched
5 MtypeAbp ::= ENUMERATED {	15 transitions (= stored+matched)	15 transitions (= stored+matched)
6 msg0, msg1, ack0, ack1	0 atomic steps	0 atomic steps
7 }	hash conflicts: 0 (resolved)	hash conflicts: 0 (resolved)
8 ②	(max size 2^18 states) ③	(max size 2^18 states) ④
9 END	...	...

1: The cEASN Spec.   2: The dEASN Spec.
3: The SPIN-pan output.   4: The EASN-pan output.

The original Promela Spec. can be recovered from the cEASN Spec, by uncommenting line # 1.

Fig. 1. ABP in SPIN and EASN.

References

[1] Holzmann, Gerald J., Doron Peled, "The state of SPIN", CAV '96.

[2] Shanbhag, Vivek K., K. Gopinath, "A Spin based model checker for telecommunication protocols", May 2001, 8th Intl SPIN Workshop on Model Checking of Software.

[3] G. Gerth, D. Peled, M. Y. Vardi, P. Wolper, "Simple On-the-fly Automatic Verification of Linear Temporal Logic", PSTV94.

[4] Holzmann, G.J., Design and Validation of Computer Protocols, Prentice Hall, 1992.

[5] Information Technology - Abstract Syntax Notation One (ASN.1): Specification of Basic Notation, ITU-T Rec. X.680 (1994); Information Object Specification, ITU-T Rec. X.681 (1994); Constraint Specification, ITU-T Rec. X.682 (1994); Parametrization of ASN.1 specifications, ITU-T Rec. X.683 (1994).

[6] ASN.1/C++ Application Programming Interface, Part 1: Base Classes & Specific Interface, NMF 040-1; Part 2: Generic Interface, NMF 040-2, Issue 1.0, Feb. 1998

[7] Holzmann, G.J., SPIN Sources, Version 3.4.6, 29th March. 2001.

[8] J.Geldenhuys, PJA de Villiers, 'Runtime Efficient State Compaction in SPIN,' 5th Intl SPIN Workshop on Theoretical Aspects of Model Checking, ed. D. Dams, M. Massnik.

RTDT: A Front-End for Efficient Model Checking of Synchronous Timing Diagrams

Nina Amla[1], E. Allen Emerson[1], Robert P. Kurshan[2], and Kedar Namjoshi[2]

[1] Department of Computer Sciences, University of Texas at Austin[***]
{namla,emerson}@cs.utexas.edu
[2] Bell Laboratories, Lucent Technologies
{k,kedar}@research.bell-labs.com

1 Introduction

Model checking [6, 13] is an automated procedure for determining whether a finite state program satisfies a temporal property. Model checking tools, due to the complex nature of the specification methods, are used most effectively by verification experts. In order to make these tools more accessible to non-expert users, who may not be familiar with these formal notations, we need to make model checkers easier to use. Visually intuitive specification methods may provide an alternative way to specify temporal behavior.

One such visual notation that is already widely used in industrial practice to specify the timing behavior of hardware systems is timing diagrams. *Synchronous Regular Timing Diagrams* (SRTDs) [1] are a class of timing diagrams that correspond to regular languages. SRTDs are a very effective formal specification notation since (1) they have a simple syntax and semantics that corresponds to common usage, and (2) there are efficient linear-time model checking algorithms [1] for SRTDs.

Compositional reasoning ameliorates the state explosion problem by reducing reasoning about the entire system to reasoning about individual components. One flavor of compositional reasoning is assume-guarantee reasoning where each component guarantees certain properties based on assumptions about other components. There are several difficulties in applying assume-guarantee reasoning: firstly, decomposing the specification is essential, and secondly, auxiliary assertions are often necessary. These tasks require a non-trivial amount of manual effort. The decompositional nature of SRTDs, however, makes it possible to do assume-guarantee style compositional reasoning [2] in an efficient and fully automated manner.

The Regular Timing Diagram Translator (RTDT) tool provides a user-friendly graphical editor, that is used to create and edit SRTDs, plus a translator that implements the compositional and non-compositional model checking algorithms. RTDT forms a formal and efficient timing diagram interface to the model checker *COSPAN* [10].

[***] Supported in part by NSF 980-4736 and TARP 003658-0650-1999.

G. Berry, H. Comon, and A. Finkel (Eds.): CAV 2001, LNCS 2102, pp. 387–390, 2001.

2   Synchronous Regular Timing Diagrams

An SRTD is specified by describing a number of waveforms over a number of clock cycles. The clock is depicted as a special waveform that is defined over $\{0,1\}$ where the value toggles at consecutive points. In SRTDs, any change in the signal value must occur at either the rising edge or falling edge of the clock waveform.

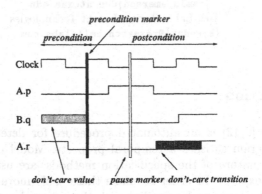

Fig. 1. Annotated Synchronous Regular Timing Diagram.

A waveform at any point may be either 0 (low), 1 (high), or one of two *don't cares*. The *don't care value* specifies that the value at that point is unimportant and can be either 0 or 1. The *don't care transition* specifies that the value of the signal changes exactly once and remains stable for the remainder of the specified interval. A *pause* specifies that all the signals, except the clock, remain unchanged for an arbitrary but finite period of time until a definite change in value of at least one waveform indicates the end of the pause.

The waveforms are partitioned into an initial *precondition* part and the following *postcondition* part. In [1] it is shown that we can construct regular expressions for the precondition T_{pre} and the postcondition T_{post} of an SRTD T. An infinite computation σ *satisfies* an SRTD T (written $\sigma \models T$) if and only if any finite sub-computation that satisfies T_{pre} is immediately followed by a sub-computation that satisfies T_{post}.

3   The RTDT Tool

The main features of the RTDT tool are described below.

– RTDT has a user friendly editor for graphically creating and editing SRTDs.
– Non-compositional verification - The translation algorithm generates an ω-*NFA* for the complement of the SRTD. This ω-*NFA* can be used as the property in the automata theoretic approach to model checking, resulting in a model checking procedure that is linear both in the size of the system and the SRTD specification (see [1] for details).

- Assume-guarantee reasoning - An SRTD can be partitioned into bundles of waveforms called *fragments* such that each fragment contains all the waveforms controlled by an implementation module. The translation algorithm, with a minor modification, is used to generate an ω-*NFA* for each such fragment. There is also an algorithm to automatically generate auxiliary processes from an SRTD such that the parallel composition of these processes generates the language of the SRTD (see [2] for details). These algorithms can be used, in a fully automated way, with an assume-guarantee proof rule [2], that is sound and complete for both safety and liveness properties. The model checking process is very efficient, linear in the size of the system and the diagram.
- The user can execute *COSPAN* from within RTDT. When a verification check fails, RTDT displays the resulting error trace as an SRTD and allows the option of editing this diagram.

4 Case Studies

RTDT has been used with *COSPAN* to verify timing diagram properties of a number of interesting examples, such as a memory access controller and Lucent's PCI Interface Core. RTDT was used to automatically generate the ω-*NFA* for complement of the SRTD property and the auxiliary processes. *COSPAN* was used to discharge the proof obligations in the assume-guarantee proof rule.

The verification checks were done compositionally and non-compositionally. We observed significant reductions in BDD size, space and time required. In the memory access controller example, we saw a savings of 21% to 69% in BDD size. For the PCI Interface Core, we formulated the SRTD properties from the actual diagrams found in the PCI Local Bus specification [12]. The PCI interface core yielded more dramatic results; we observed a reduction in BDD size of 41% up to 84%. Some non-compositional verification checks failed to complete due to a shortage of memory but all the compositional checks completed successfully.

5 Conclusions and Related Work

Various researchers have investigated the use of timing diagrams in formal verification. *SACRES* [4, 5] is a verification environment for embedded systems that allows users to graphically specify properties as Symbolic Timing Diagrams (STDs) [7]. The monolithic translation algorithms for STDs may be exponential. In later work (cf. [11]), a compositional verification methodology is used to verify STD properties. This work uses timing diagrams as a convenient notation for expressing temporal properties, while the assume-guarantee reasoning is left to the verifier. Fisler [8] provides a procedure to decide regular language containment of non-regular timing diagrams, but the model checking algorithms have a high complexity (PSPACE). They [9] have implemented a monolithic translation algorithm that compiles a regular subset of these diagrams into ω-automata. Unlike our work, however, they do not address temporal ambiguity.

Another approach [3] uses Presburger formulas to determine whether the delays and guarantees of an implementation satisfy constraints specified as a timing diagram. The algorithm for verifying Presburger formulas is multi-exponential.

We have outlined the key features of the tool RTDT, which is based on a visual specification formalism called Synchronous Regular Timing Diagrams (SRTDs) [1]. RTDT consists of an editor that allows a user to graphically create and edit an SRTD. The tool implements an efficient model checking algorithm that is linear in both the size of the system and the SRTD specification. RTDT also implements a sound and complete assume-guarantee proof rule [2] that can be applied to SRTDs in a fully automated way. RTDT will be integrated into an upcoming release of the industrial verification tool *FormalCheck*.

Acknowledgments

The authors thank Rebecca Paul for enhancements made to the editor.

References

1. N. Amla, E.A. Emerson, R.P. Kurshan, and K.S. Namjoshi. Model checking synchronous timing diagrams. In *FMCAD*, volume 1954 of *LNCS*, 2000.
2. N. Amla, E.A. Emerson, K. Namjoshi, and R. Trefler. Assume-guarantee based compositional reasoning for synchronous timing diagrams. In *TACAS*, volume 2031 of *LNCS*, 2001.
3. T. Amon, G. Borriello, T. Hu, and J. Liu. Symbolic Timing Verification of Timing Diagrams Using Presburger Formulas. In *DAC*, 1997.
4. A. Benveniste. Safety Critical Embedded Systems Design: the SACRES approach. Technical report, INRIA, May 1998. URL: http://www.tni.fr/sacres/index.html.
5. U. Brockmeyer and G. Wittich. Tamagotchis need not die-Verification of STATE-MATE Designs. In *TACAS*. Springer-Verlag, March 1998.
6. E. M. Clarke and E. A. Emerson. Design and Synthesis of Synchronization Skeletons using Branching Time Temporal Logic. In *Workshop on Logics of Programs*, volume 131. Springer Verlag, 1981.
7. W. Damm, B. Josko, and Rainer Schlör. Specification and Verification of VHDL-based System-level Hardware Designs. In Egon Borger, editor, *Specification and Validation Methods*. Oxford University Press, 1994.
8. K. Fisler. Containment of Regular Languages in Non-Regular Timing Diagrams Languages is Decidable. In *CAV*. Springer Verlag, 1997.
9. K. Fisler. On Tableau Constructions for Timing Diagrams. In *NASA Langley Workshop on Formal Methods*, 2000.
10. R.H. Hardin, Z. Har'el, and R.P. Kurshan. COSPAN. In *CAV*, volume 1102 of *LNCS*, 1996.
11. J. Helbig, R. Schlor, W. Damm, G. Dohmen, and P. Kelb. VHDL/S - integrating statecharts, timing diagrams, and VHDL. *Microprocessing and Microprogramming*, 38, 1993.
12. PCI Special Interest Group. PCI Local Bus Specification Rev 2.1. Technical report, December 1998.
13. J.P. Queille and J. Sifakis. Specification and Verification of Concurrent Systems in CESAR. In *Proc. of the 5th International Symposium on Programming*, volume 137 of *LNCS*, 1982.

TAXYS: A Tool for the Development and Verification of Real-Time Embedded Systems*

Etienne Closse[1], Michel Poize[1], Jacques Pulou[1], Joseph Sifakis[2],
Patrick Venter[1], Daniel Weil[1], and Sergio Yovine[2]

[1] France Telecom R&D, 28 chemin du Vieux Chêne, 38243 Meylan cedex, France
firstname.lastname@rd.francetelecom.fr
[2] UMR VERIMAG, 2 rue Vignate, 38610 Gières, France
firstname.lastname@imag.fr

The correct behavior of real-time applications depends not only on the correctness of the results of computations but also on the times at which these results are produced. As a matter of fact, violations of real-time constraints in embedded systems are the most difficult errors to detect, because they are extremely sensitive both to the patterns of external events stimulating the system and to the timing behavior of the system itself. Clearly, the development of real-time systems requires rigorous methods and tools to reduce development costs and "time-to-market" while guaranteeing the quality of the produced code (in particular, respect of the temporal constraints).

The above requirements motivated the development of the TAXYS tool, dedicated to the design and validation of real-time telecommunications software. One of the major goal of the TAXYS tool is to produce a formal model that captures the temporal behavior of the whole application which is composed of the embedded computer and its external environment. For this purpose we use the formal model of timed automata [2]. The choice of this model allows the use of results, algorithms and tools available. Here, we use the KRONOS model checker [4] for model analysis.

From the source code of the application, an ESTEREL program annotated with temporal constraints, the TAXYS tool produces on one hand a sequential executable code and on the other hand a timed model of the application. This model is again composed with a timed model of the external environment in order to obtain a global model which is statically analyzed to validate timing constraints. This validation should notably shorten design time by limiting tedious test and simulation sessions.

1 TAXYS

The objective of the TAXYS project is to propose a framework for *developing real-time embedded code and verifying its correct behavior with respect to quantitative timing constraints*.

---

* This work is supported by the RNRT project TAXYS and the ITEA-DESS project

G. Berry, H. Comon, and A. Finkel (Eds.): CAV 2001, LNCS 2102, pp. 391–395, 2001.
© Springer-Verlag Berlin Heidelberg 2001

We use ESTEREL [3] as development language of the application. This language provides powerful constructs for management of parallelism and exceptions. It has rigorously defined semantics. ESTEREL programs run in a single thread on a single processor with a non-preemptive interrupt routine and can refer to external data and routines written in C for complex (numerical) computations. Thus, the application is decomposed into a control part, written in ESTEREL and a functional part written in C, and it is compiled with the ESTEREL compiler SAXO-RT [5].

The use of synchronous languages for the development of real-time reactive applications relies on a "synchrony assumption" meaning that the application reacts infinitely fast with respect to its environment. This assumption, very convenient in practice, must be validated for a given implementation on a target machine. In practice, validating the synchrony assumption amounts to show that the environment does not take too much lead over the application. This requires the use of a "realistic" synchrony assumption strongly depending on the application, on the speed of the machine and on its interactions with the environment. To interface the real-time system with its environment, we use an external event-handler $\mathcal{H}$, generated by SAXO-RT from an ad-hoc specification [1], and which precisely takes into account the way external events are captured by the interrupt mechanisms and sent to the application.

The behavior of such systems can be modelled by the composition of 3 systems represented as automata : the application automaton $\mathcal{A}$, the external event handler $\mathcal{H}$, which abstracts the behavior of the interrupt routine and buffers external events before they are taken into account by the next synchronous reaction, and the environment model $\mathcal{E}$ which specifies the scenarios in which the application must run [1].

The environment of a real-time embedded system can exhibit different behaviors that must be captured by some non-deterministic model. As ESTEREL programs are deterministic, we add a non-deterministic instruction *npause* to the ESTEREL language. The environment can thus be written in the same language as the application. The timing constraints are specified directly by pragmas in the ESTEREL code of $\mathcal{A}$ and $\mathcal{E}$.

TAXYS design flow is shown in Fig. 1. SAXO-RT generates three C-modules which compute $\mathcal{A}$, $\mathcal{H}$ and $\mathcal{E}$ transition functions : the model of the application contains the *embedded code itself*. KRONOS [4] explores the system states space by composing on-the-fly $\mathcal{A}$, $\mathcal{H}$ and $\mathcal{E}$. Thus, no intermediate state explosion occurs before composition and only reachable states are computed. If any timing constraint is violated, a trace leading to this error is generated. This trace is then re-executed step by step on the SAXO-RT graphical debugger to provide to the user more precise diagnostics.

2   Timing Analysis

We make the following assumption on the temporal behavior of the application: execution time is spent in the functional part to compute C-functions which

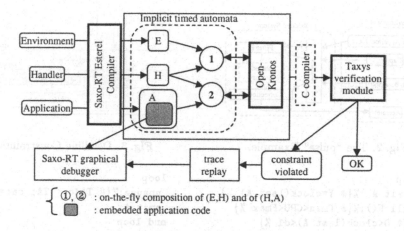

Fig. 1. TAXYS Design Flow.

have been previously instrumented by profiling. The ESTEREL code is annotated with this information. This hypothesis is true for many reactive applications if the embedded code has been compiled efficiently [5]. We then specify two kinds of real-time constraints : *throughput* and *deadline* constraints. A throughput constraint is a global constraint and expresses the fact that the system reacts fast enough for a given environment model. The violation of a throughput constraint corresponds to an overflow of $\mathcal{H}$. A deadline constraint is "local" and expresses for example, a maximum delay between a given input and a given output of the system.

This approach is illustrated by the toy example "pulse" on Fig. 2, which is composed of two parallel tasks. The first, triggered by input A, calls filter F. The second, triggered by B, computes some correction G on an actuator using result of function F. F (resp. G) consumes between $Fmin$ (resp. $Gmin$) and $Fmax$ (resp. $Gmax$) CPU time. The buffer size of the external event handler $\mathcal{H}$ is 1.

The *throughput constraint* is specified by the environment model written in timed ESTEREL (Fig. 5). It is composed of two independent periodic tasks, the first one strictly periodic with a period T_A and the second one with a period T_B jittered by an interval $[0, \varepsilon]$, for some constant ε.

There are two *deadlines constraints* on function F and G (Fig. 3) : ($\mathcal{D}_1$) F must terminate $d1$ time units after arrival of event A and ($\mathcal{D}_2$) G must compute value of actuator with data not older than $d2$ time units i.e., G terminates at most $d2$ time units after the arrival of the last event A which was consumed by function F. The annotated application code is given on Fig. 4 : $\mathcal{D}_1$ is specified by the pragma $0 < clock(lastA) < d1$, and $\mathcal{D}_2$ by the two pragmas $Y = clock(lastA)$ (which starts a new clock each time F is executed), and $0 < Y < d2$.

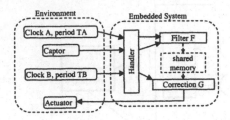

Fig. 2. The "pulse" Example.

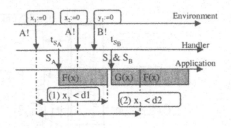

Fig. 3. Deadline Constraints.

```
loop
  await A ;%{# Y=clock(last A) %}
  call F();%{# Fmin<CPU<Fmax %}
  %{# 0<clock(last A)<d1 %}
end loop
||
  loop
  await B ;
  call G();%{# Gmin<CPU<Gmax %}
  %{# 0<Y <d2 %}
end loop
```

Fig. 4. Application Code.

```
loop
  npause;%{# TA<ca< TA; ca:=0}
  emit A;
end loop
||
  loop
  npause;%{# TB<cb<TB+ε;cb:=0}
  emit B;
end loop
```

Fig. 5. Environment Code.

3   Experimental Results

We used TAXYS for verifying the ESTEREL code for the communication mode of a GSM terminal developed by Alcatel (815 ESTEREL lines and 48000 C lines). We found 4 scenarios leading to deadline violations caused by a wrong scheduling between two C-functions [1].

We present here results obtained on a digital phone prototype carrying simultaneously voice and data produced by a graphic tablet, implemented on a 32 MIPS Digital Signal Processor. Audio data are processed at 8kHz and their processing consumes 3900 CPU cycles over the 4000 CPU cycles available every $125\mu s$. Graphic tablet data are compressed by a vectorization algorithm which consumes sporadically between 15000 and 20000 CPU cycles. 6 experiments were carried out with the *same* ESTEREL code for the application but with different environment models and handler buffer sizes. $ISDN_1$ and $ISDN_2$ with an environment model composed of two strictly periodic and independent tasks (the first carrying audio data at 8kHz and the second the graphic tablet data at 100Hz). $ISDN_3$ and $ISDN_4$ with the second task being aperiodic and emitting bursts at rates varying in a non-deterministic manner between 25 and 100Hz. $ISDN_5$ and $ISDN_6$ with a third additional periodic task modelling switching between several audio modes. In all cases, the application $\mathcal{A}$ consists of 3000 C lines and 258 ESTEREL lines, and the environment $\mathcal{E}$ of 120 ESTEREL lines.

Results presented in table 3 show that a buffer size of at least 6 is necessary for absorbing the sporadic task. We observe that the number of symbolic states explored by KRONOS increases exponentially with the "degree" of non-determinism of the environment. Therefore, to cope with state explosion due to environment non-determinism, it is necessary to find appropriate environment model approximations preserving the verified properties.

Table 1. TAXYS Experimental Results.

Name	Buff. size	Symb. states	Verif. time	Diagnostic
$ISDN_1$	5	2 200	1.27 s	buffer overflow
$ISDN_2$	6	10 849	5 s	OK
$ISDN_3$	5	15 894	6.29 s	buffer overflow
$ISDN_4$	6	633 472	10 mn 47 s	OK
$ISDN_5$	5	22 695	13.6 s	buffer overflow
$ISDN_6$	6	$> 10^7$	?	aborted

4   Conclusion

We have presented an original approach for specifying, designing and validating real-time embedded systems. This approach is implemented in an entirely automated tool applicable to industrial size examples. Specifications are written in a user friendly and compositional formalism which does not require from the user any knowledge about timed automata or temporal logic. Its limitations are mainly those of model-checking techniques. Any advance in these techniques can be taken into account, transparently for the user. Furthermore, because the embedded code is effectively executed during validation, the validation is trustworthy and is therefore particularly suited to safety critical applications.

References

1. V. Bertin, M. Poize, J. Pulou, J. Sifakis, *Towards Validated Real-Time Software*, 12th Euromicro Conference on Real-Time Systems, Stockholm, Sweden, June 2000
2. R. Alur, D. Dill, *A theory of timed automata*, Theoretical Computer Science, 126:183–235, 1994. Elsevier.
3. G. Berry, G. Gonthier, *The* ESTEREL *Synchronous Programming Language : Design, Semantics, Implementation*, Science of Computer Programming, vol. 19-2, pp. 87-152, 1992.
4. C. Daws, A. Olivero, S. Tripakis and S. Yovine. The tool KRONOS. In Hybrid Systems III, Verification and Control, Lecture Notes in Computer Science 1066, Springer-Verlag, 1996.
5. D. Weil, V. Bertin, E. Closse, M. Poize, P. Venier, J. Pulou, *Efficient Compilation of* ESTEREL *for Real-Time Embedded Systems*, Proceeding of CASES'2000, pp. 2-8, San Jose, November 2000.

Microarchitecture Verification by Compositional Model Checking

Ranjit Jhala[1]* and Kenneth L. McMillan[2]

[1] University of California at Berkeley
[2] Cadence Berkeley Labs

Abstract. Compositional model checking is used to verify a processor microarchitecture containing most of the features of a modern microprocessor, including branch prediction, speculative execution, out-of-order execution and a load-store buffer supporting re-ordering and load forwarding. We observe that the proof methodology scales well, in that the incremental proof cost of each feature is low. The proof is also quite concise with respect to proofs of similar microarchitecture models using other methods.

1 Introduction

Compositional model checking methods reduce the proof of a complex system, through decomposition and abstraction, to a set of lemmas that can be verified by a model checker. It has been shown that the proof of systems with unbounded or infinite state can be reduced to tractable model checking problems on finite state abstractions. For example, an instruction processing unit using Tomasulo's algorithm [Tom67] was proved using the method [McM00] for unbounded resources. The proof was substantially simpler than that of a similar model using a general purpose theorem prover [AP99]. The safety proof involved just three simple lemmas verified by a model checker. The relative simplicity of the proof using compositional model checking owed principally to the lack of user generated inductive invariants and the lesser need for manual proof guidance. Nonetheless, the important question of the *scalability* of the method remains open. That is, does the manual proof effort increase in reasonable proportion to the size and complexity of a system?

We approach this question by considering the verification of a complete processor microarchitecture, containing most of the important features of a modern microprocessor. These include branch prediction, speculative execution, out-of-order execution (with in-order retirement and clean exceptions) and a load-store buffer supporting re-ordering and load forwarding. The question is whether the complexity of the proof increases by some reasonable increment with each new

* Supported by SRC contract 99-TJ-683.003, AFOSR MURI grant F49620-00-1-0327, NSF Theory grant CCR-9988172

G. Berry, H. Comon, and A. Finkel (Eds.): CAV 2001, LNCS 2102, pp. 396–410, 2001.

architectural feature, or whether it increases intractably, making proofs of complex systems impractical. We find that the incremental proof cost of each architectural feature is small (just a few additional lemmas) and that the interaction of these features, though complex, does not make the proof expand intractably.

The microarchitecture model that we verify is similar in its feature set to models that have been verified using theorem proving methods [HGS00,SH98]. We compare our proof to the proofs obtained by these methods, with emphasis on the use of inductive invariants and its effect on proof complexity.

Section 2 provides a brief overview of the proof method. Then section 3 describes the microarchitecture model that we verified, and its specification. In section 4 we discuss the proof, and consider the question of scalability. Section 5 compares the proof with proofs obtained previously for similar microarchitectures. In section 6 we conclude with some remarks on the strengths and weaknesses of the method, and how the weaknesses might be addressed.

2   Background

To verify the microarchitecture, we use the SMV proof assistant [McM00]. This tool supports the reduction of correctness conditions for unbounded or infinite-state systems to lemmas that can be verified by model checking. The general approach is to divide the intended computation into "units of work" that use only finite resources in the implementation, such as instructions in a processor, or packets in a packet router. Correctness of a given unit of work is then reduced to a finite state problem using a built-in collection of abstract interpretations. In effect, we disregard those components of the system state not involved in the given unit of work. Because specifications can be temporal, we avoid the need to write and verify an inductive invariant of the system. Instead, we exploit the model checker's ability to compute the reachable states (strongest invariant) of the abstract models. This greatly simplifies the proofs.

The Proof Methodology. A system is specified with respect to a reference model. For a processor, this is an "instruction set architecture" (ISA) model that executes one instruction at a time in program order. The correctness condition is a temporal property relating executions of the implementation to executions of the reference model. We decompose correctness into "units of work" by specifying *refinement relations*. These are temporal properties specifying the data values at internal points in the implementation in terms of the reference model. For example, in a processor we may specify the operands read from the register file and the results computed by the ALU. To make such specifications possible, we may add auxiliary state variables that record the correct data values as they are computed by the reference model. A definitional mechanism in the proof assistant allows us to add auxiliary variables in a sound manner.

Mutually Inductive Temporal Proofs. The refinement relations are then proved by mutual induction over time. Each refinement relation is a temporal property of the form $G\phi$, meaning that ϕ is true at all times t. To prove that ϕ is true at time t, we may assume by induction that the other refinement relations hold for all times less than t. This is useful in a methodology based on model checking, because the notion that q up to time $t - 1$ implies p at time t can be expressed in temporal logic as $\neg(q\ \mathcal{U} \neg p)$. Hence, this proposition can be checked by a model checker.[1] This mutually inductive approach is important to the proof decomposition. It allows us to assume, for example, when proving correctness of an instruction's source operand, that the results of all earlier instructions have been correct. Note that this is quite different from the method of proof by invariant, in which we show that some state property at time $t - 1$ implies itself at t. Here the properties are temporal, and the inductive hypotheses are assumed for all times less than t, and not just at $t - 1$. This is important, since it allows us to avoid writing auxiliary invariants.

Temporal Case Splitting. Next we specialize the properties we wish to prove, so that they depend on only a finite part of the overall state. For example, suppose there is a state variable v, which is read and written by processes $p_1 \ldots p_n$. We wish to prove a property $G\phi$ of v. We add an auxiliary state variable w which points to the most recent writer of variable v. Now, suppose we can prove for *all* process indices i that $G((w = i) \Rightarrow \phi)$. That is, ϕ holds whenever the most recent writer is p_i. Then $G\phi$ must hold, since at all times w must have some value. We call this "splitting cases" on the variable w, since it generates a parameterized property with one instance for each value of w. For a given value of i, we may now be able to abstract away all processes except p_i, since the case $w = i$ depends directly only on process p_i.

Abstract Interpretation. Finally, we wish to reduce the verification of each parameterized property to a set of tractable model checking problems. The difficulty is that there may be variables in the model with large or unbounded ranges (such as memory addresses) and arrays with a large or unbounded number of elements (such as memory arrays). We solve this problem by using abstract interpretation to reduce each data type to a small number of abstract values. For example, suppose we have a property with a parameter i ranging over memory addresses. We reduce the type A of memory addresses to a set containing two values: the parameter value i, and a symbol $A \setminus i$ representing all values other than i. In the abstract interpretation, accessing an array at location i will produce the value of that location, whereas accessing the array at $A \setminus i$ produces $\bot$, a symbol representing an unknown value.

In effect, for each time the user "splits cases" on a variable of a given type, there is one value in the abstract type and one element in each abstracted array indexed by that type. If there are two parameters i and j of type A, the proof assistant may split the problem into two cases: one where $i = j$ and one where $i \neq j$. Alternatively, it may consider separately the cases $i < j$, $i = j$ and $i > j$, if information about the order of these values is important to the property.

The abstractions used by the proof assistant are sound, in the sense that validity of a formula in the abstract interpretation implies validity in the concrete model for all valuations of the parameters. Of course, the abstraction may be too

---

[1] In some cases we can also assume that another refinement relation holds for all times *less than or equal* to t, provided we do not do this in a circular way.

coarse to verify the given property (*i.e.*, the truth value in the abstract model may be ⊥) even though the property is true. Note, however that the user does not need to verify the correctness of the abstraction, since this is drawn from a fixed set built into the proof assistant.

The proof process proceeds as followings. First, the user specifies refinement relations (and other lemmas, as necessary), which are proved by mutual temporal induction. These properties are parameterized by "splitting cases" on appropriate variables, so that any particular case depends on only a finite part of the system state. Finally, the proof assistant abstracts the model relative to the parameter values, reducing the types with large or unbounded ranges to small finite sets. The resulting proof obligations are discharged by a model checker.

We now consider how this methodology can be applied to processor microarchitectures with features such as speculative execution, out-of-order execution and load-store buffers.

3 The Processor Model

The processor microarchitecture that we model has out-of-order, speculative execution using a variant of Tomasulo's algorithm with a reorder buffer. It implements branch prediction and precise exceptions, and has an out-of-order load-store buffer with load forwarding. For simplicity, we separate program and data memories. The model is generic, in that many functions, such as the ALU (arithmetic-logic unit) and the instruction decoder have been replaced by uninterpreted function symbols. A specific ISA may be implemented by defining these functions appropriately. Our proof, however, is independent of these functions.

3.1 The Specification

The microarchitecture is specified with respect to a reference model, which executes one instruction per step in program order. The ISA consists of the following instruction classes. A *load* (LD) takes two register operands, source address and destination. It reads data memory at the source address, and loads the value into the destination register. A *store* (ST) takes two register operands, the source and the destination address. It stores the source value at the destination address in data memory. An *ALU* operation (ALU) takes two register operands and a destination register. This generic instruction models all the instructions using the ALU by a single uninterpreted function. Although we do not explicitly model immediate operands, these can be folded into the generic ALU function. A *branch* (BC) performs a test on its two register operands. If true, it sets the program counter to the branch target value. Both the test and the branch target computation are modeled by uninterpreted functions. A *jump* (JMP) sets the program counter to the address in the source register. This is to implement non-local jumps such as returns from exception handlers. Finally, an *output* operation (OUT) sends its register operand to the processor's output port. The LD, ST and ALU operations can cause an exception to be raised, in which case control is transferred to the exception handler address. Asynchronous interrupts are not modeled.

3.2 The Implementation Model

The microarchitecture is depicted in figure 1. It is out-of-order, in that instructions are executed when their operands are available, not necessarily in program order. Instruction execution begins by fetching the instruction from program

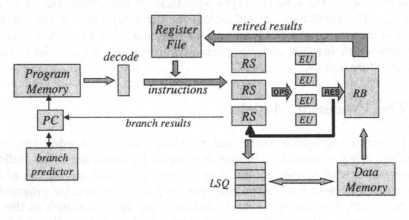

Fig. 1. Microarchitecture.

memory at the program counter address (PC). The instruction is then decoded to determine the operation type, the operand registers, the branch target, *etc.* The program counter is updated by incrementing its current value. Since the increment depends on the instruction width, we model incrementation by an uninterpreted function. In case of a conditional branch, however, the branch predictor guesses the value of the branch condition. Thus we continue fetching instructions even though the actual branch condition is not yet known, at the risk of having to cancel the ensuing instructions if the guess is incorrect. If the predicted branch condition is true, the PC is loaded from the branch target. Since branch predictions do not affect correctness, the branch predictor is modeled as a non-deterministic choice, though this can be replaced by any desired function.

The instruction then reads its source operands from the register file, and is loaded into the next available *reservation station* (RS) to await execution. A source register may contain an actual data value, or it may contain a *tag*, pointing to the RS that will produce the data value when it completes. In the case of a tag, the RS must wait until the corresponding data value returns on the result bus (RES). When both operand values are available, the instruction may be *issued* to an execution unit. When the result of the operation is computed, it returns on the result bus, with its tag, and may be forwarded to any instructions holding that tag. The result is stored in the *reorder buffer* (RB) until the instruction *retires*. At retirement, the result is written to the register file. Instructions are retired in program order, so that the state of the register file is always consistent. This allows clean recovery from exceptions or mispredicted branches.

When a branch instruction retires, we compare the computed value of the branch condition to the predicted value. If these are not the same, subsequent instructions may have been fetched from an incorrect program counter. Thus, they must be *flushed*. When this happens, the program counter is set to the alternative that was *not* chosen at fetch time.

Load and store operations are recorded in a *load-store buffer* (LSQ) in program order. In our model, this buffer is unbounded, however it could be refined by any fixed size buffer. Loads and stores are not necessarily executed in program order. A load operation may execute after it has issued (*i.e.*, its operands have been obtained) and after all earlier stores *to the same address* have executed. Alternatively, a load instruction may execute by *forwarding* the data value from the most recent store to that address, even if that store has not yet executed. A store instruction can execute after it has issued, and after all previous loads *and* stores to the same address have executed.[2]

The above conditions avoid the classic hazard conditions (RAW, WAR and WAW), guaranteeing correct operation even when operations occur out of program order. In addition, we must ensure that a store cannot execute until the instruction has actually retired, since the store cannot be undone if the instruction were to be flushed. When a store instruction retires, it is marked *committed* in the load-store buffer, and cannot subsequently be flushed. The choice of which available operation to execute is non-deterministic, though this could be replaced by any desired scheduling policy.

4 Verification

Our correctness criterion is that the sequence of output values produced by the reference model and the microarchitecture model should be the same, for corresponding initial states. The reference model chooses non-deterministically at each time whether to take a step. By witnessing this choice, we align the reference model's operation temporally with that of the implementation.

The two most interesting aspects of the proof deal with speculative execution and with partially ordered operations, such as register reads/writes or memory loads/stores. We introduce proof decompositions to handle these situations, using compositional model checking.[3]

---

[2] Note this implies that the actual address operands of all earlier stores (and loads) must be known before a load (store) can execute.

[3] Proof and prover may be found at http://www-cad.eecs.berkeley.edu/~kenmcmil.

4.1   Specifying Refinement Relations

Our basic approach is to decompose the proof into "units of work", in this case instructions. We prove correctness of a single instruction, relative to the reference model, given that all earlier instructions execute correctly. To reduce the verification complexity, we may further decompose the instruction into smaller steps, such as operand read, result computation, memory load, *etc.* We then write refinement relations, specifying the data values at various points in the implementation, in terms of the reference model.

Of course, to specify data items in the implementation, we must determine their correct values. This is done by defining *auxiliary variables* that record the correct data values as computed by the reference model. For example, when an instruction is fetched, the reference model executes it atomically, computing the correct operand and result values. The instruction is then stored in an RS. We record the correct operands and result for that RS. For example, here is the SMV code that does this:

```
if(¬stallout ∧ iopin in {ALU,LD,ST,BC}){
    next(aux[st_choice].opra) := opra;
    next(aux[st_choice].oprb) := oprb;
    next(aux[st_choice].res) := res;}
```

Here, *st_choice* is the index of the reservation station, and *opra*, *oprb* and *res* are values from the reference model. We now specify that, when the reservation station holds an operand value, it is equal to the stored correct value in the *aux* structure (and similarly for result values).

To do this, we must take into account speculative execution. That is, if an instruction occurs after an exception or a mispredicted branch, we say it is *shadowed*. A shadowed instruction does not correspond to any instruction executed by the reference model. Thus we cannot specify its correct operand and result values. In fact, these values are spurious, and must never affect the register file or memory. To write refinement relations, we must know whether an instruction in the implementation is shadowed. Fortunately, this is easy to determine. We set an auxiliary state bit *shadow* when the predicted branch condition differs from the correct branch condition, or when an exception occurs. The *shadow* bit is cleared when a flush occurs. Here is the SMV description:

```
init(shadow) := 0;
next(shadow) := ¬flush ∧ (shadow ∨
    ¬stallarch ∧ ( exn_raised ∨ (opin = BC ∧ taken ≠ itaken)));
```

Here, *taken* is the correct branch condition (from the reference model) and *itaken* is the predicted branch condition. Now, any instruction fetched while *shadow* is true is marked shadowed, by setting the auxiliary bit *aux[st_choice].shadow*. While *shadow* is set, we stall the reference model, since no valid instructions are being executed. Now we write the refinement relation for operands. We specify that if a *non-shadowed* RS holds an operand value, it must be the correct value. Here is the specification for the *a* operand:

forall(*k* **in** *TAG*) **layer** *lemma1* :
    if(*st*[*k*].*valid* ∧ *st*[*k*].*opra.valid* ∧ ¬*aux*[*k*].*shadow*)
      st[*k*].*opra.val* := *aux*[*k*].*opra*;

This specifies the *a* operand value for RS *k*, when it is *valid* (holding and instruction), and when the *a* operand is valid, and when it is not shadowed. Otherwise the value is unspecified. We can write a similar specification for the result value, and for other data values in the machine as necessary.

4.2 Verifying Operand Correctness

Now we must verify the above lemma. To verify data, we split cases on the possible sources of the data. Here, an operand value we read is generated by the most recent instruction to write the source register. We can identify this instruction's RS by recording the tag of the most recent RS to write each register. We then assume, by induction, that results computed at earlier times are correct. We need one additional fact, however: that the most recent writer in execution order is in fact the most recent writer in program order. If this is the case, then we must read the same value read by the reference model.

One way to establish this is to split cases on both the most recent writer in the implementation *and* the most recent writer in program order. Since the implementation retires instructions in program order, these two must be the same, hence correct values are always read. However, there is a complexity problem: the abstraction in this case will involve three distinct tag values, and hence the states of three distinct RS's. In practice, we found the time and space required to verify this model prohibitive. Instead, we used an intermediate lemma to simplify the problem. We observed that a register value is only read when no writes to the register pending, in which case its value is up-to-date with respect to the reference model. Thus, we specified the register contents as follows:

forall (*i* **in** *REG*) **layer** *uptodateReg* :
    if (¬*ir*[*i*].*resvd*) *ir*[*i*].*val* := *r*[*i*];

That is, if no write is pending to register *ir*[*i*], its value matches reference model register *r*[*i*]. This is verified using the case split described above, which is given to SMV as follows:

subcase *uptodateReg*[*i*][*k*][*c*] **of** *ir*[*j*].*val*//*uptodateReg*
    for *auxLastIssuedRS*[*j*]=*i* ∧ *auxLastWriterRS*[*j*]=*k* ∧ *r*[*j*]=*c*;

That is, we let *i* be the last writer to register *j* in program order, *k* the last writer in the implementation, and *c* the correct data value. In this case there are only two distinguished tag values, *i* and *k*, so the abstraction contains only two RS's.

In fact, the first attempt to check this property produced a counterexample in which some abstracted instruction causes a flush, cancelling the instruction that should write register *j*. The abstract model allows this because the states of RS's other than *i* and *k* are unknown. To deal with this, we introduce a *non-interference* lemma, stating that no unshadowed instruction is flushed:

forall(i **in** TAG**)** *lemma5*$[i]$: **assert G**
    ($flush \Rightarrow shadow \wedge (complete\_st \neq i \Rightarrow \neg(st[i].valid \wedge \neg aux[i].shadow)))$;

Here, *complete_st* is the tag of the RS causing the flush. We prove this by splitting cases on the flushing instruction. This eliminates the above counterexample to the up-to-date register property, leaving another counterexample in which a shadowed instruction writes register j and corrupts its value. This calls for another lemma stating that no shadowed instruction retires:

lemma6 : **assert G** (*retiring* $\Rightarrow \neg aux[complete\_st].shadow$);

This can be proved by splitting cases on the currently retiring instruction and the instruction that set the *shadow* bit (*e.g.* a mispredicted branch). That is, the latter must retire and cause a flush before the shadowed instruction can retire. With this additional lemma, the up-to-date register property is verified. Now operand correctness is easily proved by splitting cases on the source register and the operand's tag, which indicates the data source when forwarding from the result bus:

subcase *lemma1*$[i][j][c]$ **of** $st[k].opra.val//lemma1$
    for $st[k].opra.tag = i \wedge aux[k].srca = j \wedge aux[k].opra = c$;

The specification for results returning from execution units can be verified using operand correctness. This requires a non-interference lemma stating that unexpected results are never returned.

4.3 Verifying Memory Data Correctness

We also specify the the results returning from the data memory, as follows:

lemma4 : **assert G** ($\neg mqaux[mq\_head].shadow \wedge mem\_ld \wedge mem\_enable$
    $\wedge load\_from\_mem \Rightarrow mem\_rd\_data = mqaux[mq\_head].data$);

Here, *mq_head* points to the currently executing operation in the load-store queue. That is, if the current operation is an unshadowed load, then the data from memory are the correct data stored in the auxiliary array *mqaux*. We break this into two cases – when data are read from memory and when data are forwarded from the load-store queue. Here we consider only the former case, although the latter is similar.

This property is similar to the one specifying values read from the register file. Here, we must prove that, for any load, the most recently executed store to the same address (call it S_E) is also the most recent in program order (call it S_P). As before, we use auxiliary variables to identify S_E and S_P in the queue. Splitting cases on these two stores and the current load, we should be able to prove that S_E and S_P are the same, hence read data are correct.

Unfortunately, the abstract model with two stores and one load is too large to model check. We cannot solve this problem as before by writing an "up-to-date" lemma for the memory, since we may read the memory when it is not up-to-date.

Instead, we split cases only on the current load L and on S_E. This produces a counterexample in which $S_E < S_P < L$ in program order. That is, at the time L occurs, S_E has executed but S_P has not. This cannot really happen, because the unexecuted store S_P would block load L. However, since S_P is abstracted, this information is lost. To avoid splitting cases on S_P, we simply state as a lemma that $S_P \leq S_E$. In SMV, we say:

$$lemma4a : \textbf{assert G } (\neg mqaux[mq\_head].shadow \wedge mem\_ld \wedge mem\_enable$$
$$\wedge\ load\_from\_mem \Rightarrow (imtag[mem\_addr] \geq mqaux[mq\_head].lastWrite));$$

Here $imtag[mem\_addr]$ is S_E, while $mqaux[mq\_head].lastWrite$ is S_P. This can be proved using another lemma, stating that stores always occur in program order. All three properties can be proved using just two memory queue elements. We reduce the problem further by writing a refinement relation for the data in the load-store queue. This allows us to abstract out the RS's when proving memory properties. This required a lemma stating that unshadowed queue elements are never flushed, which follows directly from the fact that unshadowed RS's are never flushed. The resulting abstract models can be handled easily by the model checker. At the cost of additional lemmas, we have reduced an intractable problem to a tractable one.

4.4   Remaining Steps

For the program counter (PC), we write a refinement relation stating that, when the *shadow* bit is not set, the implementation PC equals the reference model PC:

$$\textbf{layer } opok : \textbf{if}(\neg shadow)\ ipc := pc;$$

Since the PC can be loaded from an RS (in case of a flush) or from a register (for a JMP), we split cases on the most recent reservation station to and on the source register of the previous instruction. We also use the two lemmas about speculation. Further refinement relations specify the decoded instruction and branch target. This isolates the uninterpreted functions computing these values.

Finally, we must prove our overall correctness criterion, correctness of outputs. The OUT instruction reads a register and sends its value to the output port. Thus, the up-to-date register property suffices to prove output correctness. Overall, the proof[4] consists of the following elements: (1) refinement maps for the program counter, instruction decoder, register file, RS's and load-store queue, (2) two non-interference lemmas for speculative execution, two for the result bus, and four for the load-store queue (3) case splitting instructions for the above and hints for adjusting the abstractions, and (4) auxiliary variable declarations. All told, this information comprises less than 18K bytes, somewhat *less* than the size of the microarchitecture model and its specification.

---

[4] By "proof", we mean all the input used to guide a mechanical prover, and not a proof in the mathematical sense.

Table 1. Proof Size *vs.* Feature Set.

Model	Proof size
A (baseline)	5700 bytes
B = A + out-of-order	7000 bytes
C = B + speculation	13K bytes
D = C + load-store buffer	18K bytes

To summarize, our strategy is to reduce the verification problem "units of work", in this case instructions. Since each instruction uses only finite resources, we can verify its correctness using a finite abstraction of the system. We identify the resources used by the instruction (*e.g.* RS's, registers, *etc.*), by introducing auxiliary variables. Once we "split cases" on these resources, the pointer types and arrays are automatically reduced, yielding a finite abstract model.

The novel aspects of this proof are in the treatment of speculation, and of read/write hazards. We handled speculation by introducing an auxiliary *shadow* bit for each instruction in the machine. We then show two key facts about the system: that unshadowed instructions are never canceled, and that shadowed instructions never retire. To handle read/write hazards, we use an abstraction strong enough to prove that the most recent writes to an address in execution and program order are the same.

Finally, to address the question of scalability, we consider four designs of increasing complexity: design A is a simple in-order processor, design B adds Tomasulo's algorithm for out-of-order execution, design C adds speculative execution and design D adds a load-store buffer. Table 1 shows the textual size of the proofs we obtained for these four designs. Adding Tomasulo's algorithm is the simplest step, involving only a few additional case splits and two non-interference lemmas. Adding speculation and the load-store buffer is more complex, because of the register and memory ordering properties we must prove. Nonetheless, we find that the complexity of the interactions between these features does not make the proof intractable. Rather, the proof increment associated with adding a feature remains moderate, at least for this example.

5   Comparison with Other Approaches

We now compare our proof with proofs of similar microarchitecture models using other methods. We consider proofs by Sawada and Hunt [SH98], Velev and Bryant [VB00] and Hosabettu *et al.* [HGS00]. All of these proofs are variations in some form on the method of Burch and Dill [BD94], in which an abstraction function is constructed by "flushing" the implementation, *i.e.*, inserting null operations until all pending instructions are completed. This yields a "clean" state which can be compared to the reference model state. One then proves a *commutative diagram*, that is, that taking one implementation step and then applying the abstraction function yields the same state as applying the abstraction function followed by zero or more reference model steps. This can be done in an almost fully automated way for simple pipelines, and has the advantage that the abstraction function is mechanically constructed.

However, the method has two distinct disadvantages. First, for complex architectures, the abstraction function is generally not strong enough to be inductively invariant. It must be manually strengthened with information about reachability of control states. In our method, no such information is required. Second, the the abstraction function depends on the entire machine state, including all the instructions that are currently in the machine. For complex architectures, it becomes intractable to deal with it automatically. In our method, we reason about only one or two instructions. Thus, the proof obligations are local, and can be handled by model checking. By contrast, most recent work using abstraction functions manually decomposes the flushing function into smaller, more tractable parts. Thus the Burch and Dill method's advantage of full automation is lost. To see this, we consider the extant proofs in more detail. A comparison of textual sizes of models and proofs is given in table 2.

Sawada and Hunt. The work of Sawada and Hunt [SH98] is perhaps the first formal proof a "modern" microprocessor architecture. Their processor model uses Tomasulo's algorithm, branch prediction, precise exceptions and a load store buffer with forwarding. The model is qualitatively similar to ours, with a few differences. They model asynchronous interrupts, while we do not. They use a fixed set of execution units (one per instruction type) while we do not. Thus, they associate RS's statically with execution units, while we choose the execution unit at issue time, to maximize use of the execution units. Also, their load-store buffer holds two loads and one store, while we model an arbitrary number of entries.

The model is defined by a collection of Common LISP functions in the theorem prover ACL2 [KM96]. We report in table 2 the approximate textual size of the functions describing the processor architecture, excluding theorems and generic functions not related to processor modeling. This is roughly three times the textual size of our model in the SMV language. In our estimation, this difference is largely accounted for by the greater conciseness of the SMV language as a hardware description language. However, some details present in the Sawada and Hunt model, such as an explicit instruction decoding function, are not present in our model, since we model them generically using uninterpreted functions. Defining these functions explicitly would increase the description size, but would not affect the proof.

Sawada and Hunt use an intermediate abstraction called a MAETT, a table tracking of the status of all instructions being executed in the machine. They then relate the MAETT to the implementation and the reference model using invariants, which are proved by induction. We do not use an intermediate abstraction, although our auxiliary variables do contain information similar to that in the MAETT. The chief difficulty reported by Sawada and Hunt is that the invariant must be strengthened by auxiliary invariants of the implementation state. No such invariants occur in our proof (although we do need a few lemmas concerning which events may occur in certain states). This leads to a stark difference in the textual size of the proofs: their proof (for the FM9801 processor) is roughly 1909K bytes, of which nearly a megabyte is the inductive invariant. Our proof is less that 20K bytes, smaller than the model description itself. This difference of two orders of magnitude is more than enough to account for differences in models, the succinctness of representation, whitespace, *etc.* By another measure, the Sawada and Hunt proof has roughly 4000 lemmas, whereas ours has approximately 18 (depending on how one counts).

Velev and Bryant. The approach of Velev and Bryant [VB00] is closely based on the Burch-Dill technique. They focus on efficiently checking the commutativity condition for complex microarchitectures by reducing the problem to checking equivalence of two terms in a logic with equality, and uninterpreted function symbols. Under certain conditions, their decision algorithm is able to check equivalence of the massive formulas obtained from flushing complex models. Some manual work is required, however, to put the problem in a form suitable for the tool. They handle architectures with deep and multiple pipelines, multiple-issue, multi-cycle execution units, exceptions and branch prediction, for fixed finite models (note, we treat models with unbounded resources). Notably, they do not treat out-of-order execution, or load-store buffers. We conjecture that this is due to the complexity of the flushing functions, and the need for complex auxiliary invariants in these cases.

Hosabettu et al. Hosabettu *et al.* have published a series of papers on microprocessor verification, based on the "completion functions" approach. The microarchitecture they model in [HGS00] is similar to ours in that it has out-of-order execution, branch prediction, precise exceptions and it buffers stores (but not loads, which are atomic). Stores are executed in program order, while in our model they can be out-of-order. Also, they model a processor status word, while we do not.

Hosabettu *et al.* prove a commutative diagram, but decompose the abstraction function into *completion functions* for each instruction in the machine. A completion function specifies the future effect of an unfinished instruction on the observable state. They define completion functions for each instruction type, in terms of the present status of the instruction in the machine, and also whether that instruction will *squash* subsequent instructions, ensuring they do not affect the program state. The abstraction function is the composition of the completion functions. A commutative diagram is proved using PVS [ORSvH95] for the decomposed abstraction function.

This approach has the advantage of avoiding applying a decision procedure to the entire flushing function. However, proofs of the commutativity obligations require auxiliary invariants that characterize the reachable states of the model. To reason about the composite abstraction function, one must enumerate manually the various instructions in a particular state, the exact transitions they

Table 2. Textual sizes of the Models and Proofs.

Technique Used	Proof Assistant	Size of Machine Spec	Size of Proof
Sawada & Hunt [SH98]	ACL2	˜60K bytes	1909K bytes
Hosabettu et al. [HGS00]	PVS	˜70K bytes	˜2300K bytes
Compositional Model Checking	SMV	20K bytes	18K bytes

might make, the position of the "squashing" instruction, and so on. While decomposing the abstraction function makes reasoning about each case simpler, considerable manual effort is still required in stating invariants and guiding the prover.

The authors report that the proof took much less time than that of Sawada and Hunt. However, the textual size is comparable. The proof uses approximately 300K bytes of PVS specifications, and 2000K bytes of proof script (manual prover guidance). The latter, while generated manually, contains considerable redundancy. Thus its large size may not accurately reflect the effort needed to create it. We conjecture the large proof size results from the need for auxiliary invariants, and the theorem prover's greater need for manual guidance *vis-à-vis* model checkers.

6   Conclusion

We have shown that compositional model checking methods can verify a processor microarchitecture with most of the architectural features of a modern microprocessor. We introduced proof strategies to handle speculative execution (using shadow bits) and to handle read/write hazards (case splitting on the most recent writes in program and execution order). The proof methodology scales well in that the incremental proof cost associated with each processor feature is low. Moreover, the proof is concise relative to proofs using other methods (and is smaller than the model description itself). Although proof size is not necessarily an indication of the human effort required, we consider the difference of two orders of magnitude to reflect a qualitative difference in proof complexity. We ascribe this difference to several factors.

First, as reported both by Sawada and Hunt and by Hosabettu et al., one of the most time consuming aspects of their methods is specifying auxiliary invariants. We exploit the model checker's ability to compute reachable states to avoid writing such invariants. Second, by stating refinement relations as temporal properties we can decompose the proof into "units of work", such as instructions, that are temporally and spatially distributed but use finite resources. This avoids reasoning about the entire state of the machine, and allows us to use small, finite-state abstractions. Finally, we exploit the fact that model checkers require less manual guidance than theorem provers do.

Nonetheless, there remains much room for improvement. For example, some lemmas in our proof could be eliminated if the model checker were able to handle three instructions in the abstraction instead of two. We have found that the

410   Ranjit Jhala and Kenneth L. McMillan

symbolic model checker can handle abstract models with only about half the number of state bits that can be handled with concrete models. The reason for this is unclear, though it may be that the abstract state spaces are less sparse, or that there is greater nondeterminism in the transition relation. This does not affect the scalability of the proof methodology, but the "constant factor" would be improved if the model checker could handle larger abstract models.

To handle asynchronous interrupts, it would be useful to implement "prophecy variables", so that the witness function that stalls the reference model could depend on the future of the implementation. Also, to implement a specific instruction set architecture, we must substitute concrete functions for the uninterpreted functions in our model. Support for this is currently lacking in the prover, though it would be straightforward to implement.

On the whole, although proofs of this sort are considerably more laborious than model checking finite state machines, we feel that the methodology scales well, and that additional processor features, such as a first-level cache, an address translation unit, or multiple-issue could be handled in a straightforward manner, with the addition of a few lemmas for each feature.

References

[AP99]   T. Arons and A. Pnueli. Verifying tomasulo's algorithm by refinement. In *12th Int. Conf. on VLSI Design (VLSI'99)*, pages 306–9. IEEE Comput. Soc., June 1999.

[BD94]   J. R. Burch and D. L. Dill. Automated verification of pipelined microprocessor control. In D. L. Dill, editor, *Computer-Aided Verification (CAV94)*, LNCS 818, pages 68–80. Springer-Verlag, 1994.

[HGS00]   R. Hosabettu, G. Gopalakrishnan, and M. Srivas. Verifying advanced microarchitectures that support speculation and exceptions. In E. A. Emerson and A. P. Sistla, editors, *Computer-Aided Verification (CAV2000)*, LNCS 1855, pages 521–37. Springer-Verlag, 2000.

[KM96]   M. Kaufmann and J. S. Moore. ACL2: An industrial strength version of Nqthm. In *Conf. on Computer Assurance (COMPASS-96)*, pages 23–34. IEEE Comp. Soc. Press, 1996.

[McM00]   K. L. McMillan. A methodology for hardware verification using compositional model checking. *Sci. of Comp. Prog.*, 37(1–3):279–309, May 2000.

[ORSvH95] S. Owre, J. Rushby, N. Shankar, and F. von Henke. Formal verification for fault tolerant architectures: Prolegomena to the design of PVS. *IEEE Trans. on Software Eng.*, 21(2):17–125, Feb 1995.

[SH98]   J. Sawada and W. D. Hunt. Processor verification with precise exceptions and speculative execution. In A. J. Hu and M. Y. Vardi, editors, *Computer-Aided Verification (CAV98)*, LNCS 1427, pages 135–146. Springer, 1998.

[Tom67]   R. M. Tomasulo. An efficient algorithm for exploiting multiple arithmetic units. *IBM J. of Research and Development*, 11(1):25–33, Jan. 1967.

[VB00]   M. Velev and R. E. Bryant. Formal verification of superscalar microprocessors with multicycle functional units, exceptions and branch prediction. In *37th Design Automation Conference (DAC 2000)*. IEEE, June 2000.

Rewriting for Symbolic Execution of State Machine Models

J. Strother Moore*

Department of Computer Sciences, University of Texas at Austin
Taylor Hall 2.124, Austin, Texas 78712
moore@cs.utexas.edu   Telephone: 512 471 9568
http://www.cs.utexas.edu/users/moore

Abstract. We describe an algorithm for simplifying a class of symbolic expressions that arises in the symbolic execution of formal state machine models. These expressions are compositions of state access and change functions and if-then-else expressions, laced together with local variable bindings (e.g., lambda applications). The algorithm may be used in a stand-alone way, but is designed to be part of a larger system employing a mix of other strategies. The algorithm generalizes to a rewriting algorithm that can be characterized as outside-in or lazy, with respect both to variable instantiation and equality replacement. The algorithm exploits memoization or caching.

Keywords: Hardware modeling, verification, microprocessor simulation, theorem proving, pipelined machine.

1 Relevance to Processor Modeling

A common application of such mechanized theorem provers as ACL2 [13], HOL [8] and PVS [17] is the modeling and analysis of microprocessors and other state machines [3, 6, 11, 12, 14–16, 18, 9].

The ACL2 theorem prover [13, 12] is particularly suited to processor modeling because it supports an efficient functional programming language based on Common Lisp [19]. Hence, operational models formalized in ACL2 can be executed as processor simulators. This is not a speculative assertion. Rockwell Collins has constructed microarchitectural executable formal models of some of its custom microprocessors in ACL2 [20]. The models have been integrated into a standard execution environment, replacing preexisting simulators written in more common programming languages such as C. The ACL2 models run at roughly the same speed as the original models. (How this is possible will become clear below). Reasoning about state machines requires symbolic simplification of terms representing states. Straightforward simplification algorithms can cause unnecessary exponential blowups in the size of the expression. This paper presents an algorithm for avoiding many of those explosions.

---

* This work was supported in part by Advanced Technology Center, Rockwell Collins, Inc., Cedar Rapids, Iowa.

G. Berry, H. Comon, and A. Finkel (Eds.): CAV 2001, LNCS 2102, pp. 411–422, 2001.
© Springer-Verlag Berlin Heidelberg 2001

412   J. Strother Moore

2   The Problem

We present an algorithm for simplifying expressions that arise from the symbolic manipulation of formally described state machines. We use ACL2 term notation (i.e., Lisp notation). But the algorithm is of general interest in any formal setting where (a) terms are used to represent states, (b) "access" and "change" functions are provided, and (c) variable binding is present (e.g., Lisp let expressions, lambda applications, or, more generally, the application of defined functions). Our algorithm also deals with if-then-else constructs.

For example, a state, s, might have three components, named a, b, and c. We write (a s) to access the a component of s and (update-a x s) to create a new state like s but with x as its a component.

Of special interest are nests of updates. A simple example is shown below.

```
(let ((s (update-a (new-a x s) s)))          ; [*1]
  (let ((s (update-b (new-b x s) s)))
    (let ((s (update-c (new-c x s) s)))
      s)))
```

Each successive let changes the assignment of the variable s. So the s in the new-b expression refers to the state obtained by updating the a slot of the "original" (free) s.

Logically speaking, (let ((v_1 a_1) ... (v_n a_n)) b) is equal to the instance of b obtained by simultaneously replacing all free occurrences of each v_i by the corresponding a_i. It is often read "let v_1 be a_1, ..., and v_n be a_n in b," or perhaps more suggestively as "b, where v_1 is a_1, ..., and v_n is a_n."

In ACL2, let expressions are syntactic sugar for certain lambda applications. Roughly speaking, (let ((v_1 a_1) ... (v_n a_n)) b) is just ((lambda (v_1 ... v_n) b) a_1 ... a_n). We say "roughly speaking" because in ACL2 when we translate lets into lambda applications we make sure that every free variable of b is captured by the formal variables of the lambda (by adding extra formals and the corresponding actuals, as needed).

Replacing the lets in an expression by the corresponding lambda applications and performing beta reduction (i.e., expanding the lambdas away) may yield an exponentially larger term, because of variable duplication. This happens in [*1].

We use let nests to describe state transformations as sequences of assignments to the components of the state. Formal models so expressed can be executed efficiently. The variable symbol s in [*1] is used in a "single-threaded" [5] way so that during execution on concrete data the original state may be destructively modified to create the new one. This efficiency is crucial to the use of the model as a simulator.

Now imagine defining a series of functions, e.g., phase1, phase2, ..., in terms of expressions like [*1] and using them as the "updaters" in some let expression that produces a state. Realistic models involve many layers of definitions, culminating in some top-level state transition expression, e.g., (machine x s).

We will present an algorithm for simplifying such expressions as (b (machine x s)) with less computation than may at first appear necessary. One could do this by expanding away the lets, beta reducing all the lambdas and expanding all the (non-recursively) defined function applications, and then applying the obvious accessor/update rewrite rules, possibly in a "lazy" or outside-in way. However, the reader is urged to dismiss the thought that complete beta reduction (or the equivalent expansion of all non-recursively defined function definitions) is practical. Consider a C simulator for a system of interest and count the number of assignment statements: that is about the number of let bindings in the executable formal version of that model. Researchers at Rockwell Collins report [private communication]

> The typical complexity of high-level language models of these machine architectures has a depth around 300 assignment statements. That is, the execution of the simulator for one microcycle can involve the execution of about 300 state updates, which means that the translated-into-ACL2 model is a nest of state updates about 300 levels deep. Each "level" of the update nest typically contains at least two instances of state: the state being updated and a value being inserted typically expressed as a function of the state being updated.

If state is used twice at every level, the full beta reduction of such a term would contain on the order of 2^{300} occurrences of the updaters. From such considerations we conclude that it is impractical to contemplate full beta reduction of such models. We thus focus on simplification in the presence of such bindings.

3 Some Tests

Before presenting our algorithm we will present a simple test suite for it and show some performance data to motivate the rest of the paper. The simple test here is available at
http://www.cs.utexas.edu/users/moore/publications/nu-rewriter.

In our simple test suite, we first declare a state object s, with two fields, a and b, accessed by functions of those names and updated by update-a and update-b. We next declare three uninterpreted function symbols, v0, v1 and v2. Then we define phase1 to do six successive updates on s, changing the a field to contain a new value computed conditionally as a function of the current a field using the three uninterpreted functions.

```
(defun phase1 (s)
  (let ((s (update-a
             (if (v0 1 (a s)) (v1 1 (a s)) (v2 1 (a s)))
             s)))
  (let ((s (update-a
             (if (v0 2 (a s)) (v1 2 (a s)) (v2 2 (a s)))
             s)))
  ...
  s...)))
```

Our first example, named b-phase1, is the theorem that phase1 does not change the contents of the b field: (equal (b (phase1 s)) (b s)).

The second theorem, b-phase1-phase1, just composes phase1 with itself, (equal (b (phase1 (phase1 s))) (b s)), and could be proved trivially from b-phase1 except that we prevent such a proof by disabling b-phase1.

The third theorem, a-phase1, describes the value of the a field after phase1.

We then complicate the test by defining two more phases. Phase0 copies the a field into the b field. Phase2 copies the b field into the a field. We define machine to do phase0, then two phase1 steps, and then phase2.

The fourth theorem, a-machine, shows that machine does not change the a field, (equal (a (machine s)) (a s)). The fifth, b-machine, shows that the final b field is the initial a field, (equal (b (machine s)) (a s)).

Each theorem can be proved by rewriting alone. We prove each with ACL2 Version 2.6 (the first to include our algorithm) in each of two configurations. In "standard ACL2," the algorithm is disabled; in "ν-ACL2," the algorithm is enabled. All of the tests were conducted running under Allegro Common Lisp on a 731 MHz dual-processor Pentium III. Time is measured in seconds. The results are shown in Figure 1.

Theorem	standard ACL2	ν-ACL2
b-phase1	0.48	0.01
b-phase1-phase1	128.76	0.01
a-phase1	0.41	0.04
a-machine	139.39	0.02
b-machine	143.91	0.02

Fig. 1. Seconds to Prove Theorems on 731 MHz Pentium III

Note the growth in standard ACL2's times from b-phase1 to b-phase1--phase1. Comparing the old rewriter's performance with that of the new one on industrial data is essentially impossible because the old rewriter exhausts resources before completing interesting problems of the kind handled routinely by the improved system. (Adding one more phase1 step to b-phase1-phase1 causes standard ACL2 to exhaust memory after six hours of computation; ν-ACL2 does "b-phase1^3" in 0.11, b-phase1^4 in 6.46, and b-phase1^5 in 412 seconds.)

The terms arising in typical machine models are not as regular as those in this test suite. Our algorithm does not distinguish "control" from "data," require the identification of "phases," or limit itself to single-threaded states. In addition, typical industrial machine states have hundreds of components. Some of those components are atomic (e.g., contain booleans, integers, etc.) others may themselves be structured as records or arrays. ACL2 supports states containing arrays and the simplification algorithm we have implemented does also. But in this paper we confine our attention to "flat" states.

4 Terminology

We now prepare to describe our algorithm precisely, starting with the terminology and conventions we use. In ACL2, `let` expressions are just syntactic sugar for `lambda` applications. `Lambda` expressions are handled just like other function applications. Each `lambda` expression has a list of *formal variables* and a term for a *body*. All free variables in the body are among the formals. Functions may only be applied to the correct number of actuals. The function application $(f\ a_1\ \ldots\ a_n)$ is equal to its beta reduction, the result of instantiating the body of f with the substitution replacing v_i by a_i. We use the verbs "to open" or "to expand" to describe the replacement of a function application by its beta reduction. If f is a `lambda` expression or f is a function symbol and that symbol is not used as a function symbol in the body of f, we say f is *non-recursive*. Henceforth, we do not talk formally about `let`s but about non-recursive function applications.

In ACL2 the state accessor and updater functions are logically defined in terms of a "universal" accessor `nth` and a "universal" updater, `update-nth`, where (`nth i s`) extracts the ith element of the list `s` and (`update-nth i v s`) constructs a list like `s` but whose i^{th} element is `v`. Thus, a term like (`b (update-c x s)`) expands to (`nth 1 (update-nth 2 x s)`). Our algorithm is fundamentally concerned with applying the theorem

Theorem. nth-update-nth:
```
(equal (nth i (update-nth j v s))
       (if (equal (nfix i) (nfix j)) v (nth i s)))
```

as a rewrite rule (left-to-right). The function `nfix` is the identity on natural numbers and otherwise is 0. Its use in the theorem above is a reflection of the absence of syntactic typing in the language. The theorem says that the ith component of the state produced by updating the jth component of `s` with `v` is either `v` or the ith component of `s`, depending on whether i and j are equal. The definitions of user-level state access/update functions (e.g., `b` and `update-c`) are treated as ordinary function definitions like `phase1` above.

We call expressions like [*1] "nth/update expressions" or *ν-expressions* (for "nu" or "nth/update"). This loosely defined class of expressions includes state accessor/updater functions defined in terms of `nth` and `update-nth`, their array counterparts, if-then-else expressions, and variable binding constructs such as `let` or function or `lambda` application.

5 Binding Stacks, Facets, and Reconciliation

ACL2's standard rewriter is inside-out. To rewrite $(f\ a_1\ \ldots\ a_n)$ it first rewrites the a_i to standardize them. Thus, the opportunity to apply `nth-update-nth` to (`b (phase1 x s)`) occurs only after (`phase1 x s`) is expanded to an `update-nth` expression. This may exponentially increase the size of the term.

Instead of rewriting a_2 in (`nth` a_1 a_2) we wish to "look ahead" to see whether we can "see" a_2 as an `update-nth` expression, expanding non-recursive functions as necessary. For example [*1] can be seen as an update-c expression, which can, in turn, be seen as an update-nth expression. These expressions must be understood in an appropriate variable binding environment. Note that the update-c expression in [*1] buried in the expression and would be the late in the process of ordinary rewriting. By nth-update-nth, if the indices in the nth and update-nth expressions are the same, the answer is (new-c x s), under appropriate bindings for x and s; if the indices are unequal, the answer is (nth a_1 s), under appropriate bindings. Clearly, if we can decide the equality of the indices then work can be saved. (Often, in this setting, the indices are constants.) The challenge is to keep the bindings straight.

Many applications require descending through hundreds of lambda expressions. We want to "be" inside the deepest lambda without creating the instance. We therefore introduce the idea of seeing a term in the context of a substitution and we represent the substitution as a stack of function call frames. This is just a generalized version of a nest of lambda applications. We call this object a "facet" and define it below.

A *binding stack* is a stack of frames. Each frame contains a list of n variables and a list of n terms. The free variables occurring in the terms of a frame (other than the deepest frame) are among the variables of the frame immediately below.

We represent stacks as lists, where the first element of the list is the top frame. Here is a stack containing two frames,

```
(((a b)    . ((afn u w) (bfn u v)))        ; frame 1
 ((u w v) . ((ufn s) (wfn s) (vfn s)))))  ; frame 2
```

Call this stack σ. In the top frame of σ, frame 1, a is associated with (afn u w) and b with (bfn u v). We say (afn u w) is the term *corresponding* to a in that frame. The representation of frames this way, rather than as association lists, makes them faster and cheaper to create.

A stack *represents* the substitution created by pairing each variable in the top frame with the result of instantiating its corresponding term with the substitution represented by the rest of the stack. Thus, the stack σ represents the substitution that replaces a by (afn (ufn s) (wfn s)) and b by (bfn (ufn s) (vfn s)).

A *facet* is a pair consisting of a term t and stack σ, written $< t, \sigma >$, and represents the instance of t under the substitution represented by σ. Hence, if σ is the example stack above, the facet $<$(h a b),$\sigma >$ represents (h (afn (ufn s) (wfn s)) (bfn (ufn s) (vfn s))).

When we refer to a facet as though it were a term, we mean to refer to its term component. An *empty facet* is one whose stack is the empty list, ().

The function symbol of a non-variable, non-constant facet is the same as the function symbol of the term it represents. This allows us seldom to create the substitutions represented by stacks or the terms represented by facets. Instead, we "chase" the variable bindings when we need them. Facets are similar to the records and binding environments of the structure sharing representation of clauses [4]. Another way to think of a facet is that it is a nest of lambda applications turned inside out and flattened. Given a nest of lambda applications, the term of the corresponding facet is the body of the innermost **lambda** expression and the stack of the facet is the list of paired formals and actuals, starting with that for the innermost **lambda** application and proceeding outwards. Facets have two computationally convenient properties. First, if the term of a facet is an application of a defined non-recursive function, then we can represent the expansion of that function by a facet easily derived from the first. Second, if the term of a facet mentions a variable symbol then we can easily find out how that variable symbol is replaced by the substitution and we can represent the actual expression by another facet easily derived from the first. **Lambda** expressions are nested the "wrong way" to make these operations efficient.

We define finite chains of facets related by a generalized notion of expansion. Let ϕ be the non-empty facet $< t, \sigma >$. Then its *expansion*, ϕ', is defined as follows. If t is a variable symbol that is not a member of the variables in the top frame of σ or t is a constant, ϕ' is $< t, () >$. If t is a variable symbol that is a member of the variables in the top frame of σ, ϕ' is $< t', \sigma' >$, where t' is the term corresponding to t in the top frame and σ' is the result of removing the top frame from σ. If t is the application of a defined non-recursive function, f, with formals v and body b, to actual expressions a, ϕ' is $< b, ((v . a) . \sigma) >$, i.e., the facet whose term is the body of f and whose stack is obtained from σ by pushing a new frame containing the formals and actuals. In all other cases no expansion is possible.

All the facets in an expansion chain represent equal terms. We call them "facets" because they are different ways of looking at a term.

The *preferred* facet of a facet ϕ is the last facet in its expansion chain. Note that since **update-nth** is a recursive function, if ϕ can be seen as an instance of an **update-nth** term by sufficient expansions of non-recursive functions, then the preferred facet of ϕ will have an **update-nth** term as its term component.

Given a facet we can economically create a term equal to the one it represents, using **lambda** abstraction. The **lambda** *abstraction* of the facet $< b, () >$ is the term b. The **lambda** *abstraction* of $< b, ((v.a) . \sigma >$ is the **lambda** abstraction of $<((\text{lambda } v \ b) \ a), \sigma >$. Note the bindings of the abstraction occur in the opposite order. The size of the **lambda** abstraction of a facet is linear in the size of the facet.

An important optimization of **lambda** abstraction is to eliminate unnecessary bound variables. If the body of a **lambda** does not use a variable symbol that is listed in the formals, it and the corresponding actual can be eliminated. Another optimization is that variables bound to constants can be eliminated.

Because we will manipulate facets in lieu of the terms they represent, we will also have occasion to form new facets by putting together several others.

For example, let ϕ_i, $1 \leq i \leq n$, be n facets, each of the form $< t_i, \sigma_i >$. Each ϕ_i represents a term r_i. Think of the ϕ_i as having been generated by applying our algorithm to the arguments of a call of some function f. We wish to represent the term $(f \ r_1 \ldots r_n)$ as a facet. We call this the *reconciliation* of $(f \ \phi_1 \ldots \phi_n)$. Note that $(f \ \phi_1 \ldots \phi_n)$ is neither a term nor a facet. It fails to be a term because it contains facets. It fails to be a facet because there is no single, outermost stack.

The reconciliation of $(f\ \phi_1\ \ldots\ \phi_n)$ is computed as follows. We first find the greatest common ancestor stack, σ, of the σ_i. Let ρ_i be the top part of σ_i, down to the common ancestor σ. Thus, σ_i is the concatenation of ρ_i and σ. Let t'_i be the lambda abstraction of the facet $< t_i, \rho_i >$. Then $<(f\ t'_1\ \ldots\ t'_n), \sigma >$ is the reconciliation of $(f\ \phi_1\ \ldots\ \phi_n)$ and is a facet that represents a term equal to $(f\ r_1\ \ldots\ r_n)$.

Reconciliation has two important optimizations. The first is that preferred constant facets, i.e., facets whose terms are constant expressions, have empty stacks. If these empty stacks participate in the greatest common ancestor computation, the ancestor stack is always $()$, meaning the reconciled subexpressions share no subterms. But constants denote themselves in any stack. So we ignore constant facets when determining the ancestor. The second optimization of reconciliation exploits an empirical observation. Frequently all the non-constant facets in a reconciliation have the same stack. In that case, that stack is the ancestor. This case arises so frequently (in 98% of the cases over a test involving roughly 100,000 reconciliations) that it is worthwhile to code for it.

6   Our Algorithm

We now describe an algorithm for simplifying a term by applying nth-update-- nth and expanding functions. We call the rewriter the "ν-rewriter." The algorithm operates on facets. To use it on terms we apply it to the empty facet containing the term and then we lambda abstract the resulting facet.

The ν-Rewrite Algorithm

1. We wish to ν-rewrite the facet ϕ. Let ϕ' be the preferred facet of ϕ. If ϕ' is a variable or constant facet or the term of ϕ' does not begin with nth, we return ϕ'.

2. Otherwise, ϕ' is $<(\text{nth}\ i\ t), \sigma >$. Let $\hat{i}$ be the facet obtained by ν-rewriting $< i, \sigma >$. Let $\hat{t}$ be the preferred facet of $< t, \sigma >$. If $\hat{t}$ is a variable or constant, we reconcile and return $(\text{nth}\ \hat{i}\ \hat{t})$.

3. At this point, we know $\hat{t}$ is a function application. Since $\hat{t}$ is a preferred facet, its term is not a lambda application. Let f be the function symbol of $\hat{t}$. Our code considers five cases on f: it is if, update-nth, update-nth-array, nth, or some other symbol.

   3.1 If f is if, then $\hat{t}$ is of the form $<(\text{if}\ a\ b\ c), \rho >$. Let ϕ_1 be the result of reconciling and ν-rewriting $(\text{nth}\ \hat{i}\ < b, \rho >)$ and let ϕ_2 be the result of reconciling and ν-rewriting $(\text{nth}\ \hat{i}\ < c, \rho >)$.

      3.1.1. If ϕ_1 and ϕ_2 are the same facet, return ϕ_1.

      3.1.2. If no applications of nth-update-nth were made in producing ϕ_1 or ϕ_2, then return the reconciliation of $(\text{nth}\ \hat{i}\ \hat{t})$.

3.1.3. Otherwise, let ϕ_0 be the result of ν-rewriting $< a, \rho >$.

3.1.3.1. If ϕ_0 is a constant facet, return ϕ_2 or ϕ_1 according to whether the constant is nil (i.e., the test of the if can be decided).

3.1.3.2. Otherwise, return the reconciliation of (if ϕ_0 ϕ_1 ϕ_2).

3.2. If f is update-nth, $\hat{t}$ is of the form $<$(update-nth j v s)$, \rho >$. Let $\hat{j}$ be the result of ν-rewriting the facet $< j, \rho >$.

3.2.1. If $\hat{i}$ and $\hat{j}$ represent equal naturals, we return the result of ν-rewriting the facet $< v, \rho >$.

3.2.2. If $\hat{i}$ and $\hat{j}$ represent unequal naturals, we return the result of ν-rewriting the reconciliation of (nth $\hat{i}$ $< s, \rho >$).

3.2.3. Otherwise, we return the reconciliation of (if (equal (nfix $\hat{i}$) (nfix $\hat{j}$)) $< v, \rho >$ (nth $\hat{i}$ $< s, \rho >$)).

3.3 and 3.4. If f is either update-nth-array or another nth, then (assuming the original term was derived from a state access/update nest) we are dealing with an array or some other structured component. To keep this paper brief, we do not discuss that case here, but it is analogous to what we have described.

3.5. If f is some other symbol, then we return the reconciliation of (nth $\hat{i}$ $\hat{t}$).

7 Discussion

The algorithm focuses entirely on terms of the form (nth i t). The main case split is on the form of t.

In paragraph 3.1 we consider the case that t can be seen as an if-then-else expression. We might be ν-rewriting a term like (nth i (if a b c)), but more often we are ν-rewriting a term like (nth i (phase a s)), where phase is defined to be a nest of lets with an if expression as the body.

Observe that in attacking (nth i (if a b c)) we first "distribute" the if, moving the nth onto b and c. After rewriting these two subgoals we ask whether the resulting facets are equal. If so, we can avoid rewriting a by virtue of (if x y y) = y. Of course, we might have chosen to rewrite a first and determined that it is equal to nil, say, thereby avoiding the need to rewrite b. But the ν-rewriter has relatively little support for deciding propositions (since it is context free and does not use the ACL2 type system or other decision procedures).

To see why the "(if x y y)" heuristic so often wins, consider the origins of the problem. Here b and c are state transformations, the modeled machine is branching on a, and we are interested in determining the ith component of the new state. But most state transformations on the machines we have seen leave most state components unchanged. Thus, in many cases neither b nor c change the value of the ith component and our heuristic makes the superior choice.

In paragraph 3.1.2 we basically abandon the rewriting of (nth i (if a b c)) if no nth-update-nth rule was applied while rewriting (nth i b) or (nth i c). We prefer to keep the if inside the nth to avoid case splitting. To implement the test, the ν-rewriter returns a flag that indicates whether it used any rules. It is insufficient to test whether the rewritten facets are equal to their unrewritten versions since quite often b and c will have been replaced by their preferred facets (i.e., we may have opened function applications).

Paragraph 3.2 is the case for which the algorithm was invented. It applies the nth-update-nth theorem.

Paragraphs 3.3 and 3.4 deal with arrays in our setting and are not discussed here.

We have optimized the algorithm in several ways. The most important is to use caching or memoization to avoid recomputing the ν-rewrite of a previously seen facet. In our implementation, we use a hash table with 64K entries, each of which is a ring containing (at most) the five most recently seen facets that hashed to that location and the results of the corresponding ν-rewrites. Even though we hit on a hash entry only approximately 6% of the time, we find that the savings is significant and, indeed, makes the difference between being practical or impractical on industrial-scale problems.

Recall the tests in Section 3. Consider the theorem there called b-phase1--phase1. Implementing the algorithm without caching gives rise to 10,236 calls of the ν-rewriter. With caching, that theorem generates 124 calls. Of those 124 calls, 18 hit in the cache, giving a cache hit rate of 14%. Each hit, however, saves the algorithm from re-exploring a potentially large subtree.

In practical applications, the cache is of supreme importance. For example, in a theorem taken from the proprietary Rockwell test suite, the cached version of the ν-rewriter was called 216,524 times. The cache hit rate was 6.2%. But without the cache the algorithm would require about 3×10^{26} calls.[1]

Because of our desire to cache the results, we have made the ν-rewriter completely "context-free." That is, it does not take any arguments that encode the hypotheses governing the current term, since to do so would mean that we would have to cache that contextual information and probably have to probe the cache to look for prior calls in weaker contexts rather than identical contexts.

For a discussion of several elaborations of the algorithm, how it is used in ACL2's rewriter, and some proposed improvements, see
http://www.cs.utexas.edu/users/moore/publications/nu-rewriter.

8   Related Work

A term representation similar to our facets is provided by the "term module" of Hickey and Nogin's modular theorem proving architecture [10]. Their notion of "delayed substitution" is motivated by the same considerations that led us to

---

[1] The number is 338,664,298,746,582,325,860,641,409. This is too large compute by the brute force method of eliminating the cache and counting calls. It was computed by using the cache to remember how much work was done for each entry.

introduce facets. Their framework is more general than ours; in particular, they provide utilities for fast tactic-based theorem proving. However, their approach to delayed substitution is, essentially, to use `lambda` applications to represent terms and to implement the operations of destructuring such terms without doing the substitution implied by beta reduction. Our facet data structure is more efficient for the operations we support. This is important when dealing with very deep `lambda` nests.

Our notion of reconciliation, which is designed to generate a facet from a term-like structure containing facets, has no counterpart in their system because their "facets" are already terms. We can afford reconciliation because, as noted, about 98% of the time the facets to be reconciled all have the same stack.

The architecture of [10] does not provide caching, which we have found is crucial to good performance on large problems.

Facets are suggestive but independent of "explicit substitution" logics [7, 1, 2]. Our view of facets is that they merely provide an efficient data structure for implementing certain simplification strategies in conventional logics. The idea of "nameless" substitutions might be usefully incorporated in future work.

9 Conclusion

Our algorithm is being tested under fire in industrial applications. We are still "tuning" our integration of the algorithm, focusing on tactics for using it and certain low-level implementation details. Of particular interest are the management of the cache and the associated hashing function used to cache Lisp s-expressions. The algorithm sometimes generates unnecessarily large intermediate expressions as suggested by the `b-phase1`[i] series mentioned in Section 3. We are working on preventing these explosions

Nonetheless, the ν-rewriter has been extremely effective in the full-scale industrial application for which it was developed for Rockwell Collins. It has been used in the proofs of hundreds of theorems that were previously well beyond the capability of ACL2 to simplify. We take this as a good sign but still regard this as a work in progress.

Acknowledgments

I thank Dave Greve and Matt Wilding of the Advanced Technology Center of Rockwell Collins for their inspiration and support of this idea. I also thank Mark Bickford, Matt Kaufmann, Pete Manolios, and Matt Wilding for their contributions to this paper.

References

1. M. Abadi, L. Cardelli, P.-L. Curien, and J.-J. Lévy. Explicit substitutions. *Journal of Functional Programming*, 1(4):375–416, 1991.
2. M. Ayala-Ricon and Cesar Munoz. Explicit subsitutions and all that. Technical Report TR-2000-45, ICASE, NASA Langley Research Center, Hampton, Virginia, November 2000.
   http://www.icase.edu/Dienst/UI/2.0/Describe/ncstrl.icase/TR-2000-45.
3. W.R. Bevier, W.A. Hunt, J.S. Moore, and W.D. Young. Special issue on system verification. *Journal of Automated Reasoning*, 5(4):409–530, 1989.
4. R.S. Boyer and J.S. Moore. The sharing of structure in theorem-proving programs. In *Machine Intelligence 7*, pages 101–116. Edinburgh University Press, 1972.
5. R. S. Boyer and J.S. Moore. Single-threaded objects in ACL2. *(submitted for publication)*, 1999.
6. Bishop Brock and Warren A. Hunt, Jr. Formally specifying and mechanically verifying programs for the Motorola complex arithmetic processor DSP. In *1997 IEEE International Conference on Computer Design*, pages 31–36. IEEE Computer Society, October 1997.
7. N.G. de Bruijn. A namefree lambda calculus with facilities for internal definition of expressions and segments. Technical Report TH-Report 78-WSK-03, Department of Mathematics, Technological University Eindhoven, Netherlands, 1978.
8. M. Gordon and T. Melham. *Introduction to HOL: A Theorem Proving Environment for Higher Order Logic*. Cambridge University Press, 1993.
9. J. Grundy. Verified optimizations for the intel ia-64 architecture. In *TPHOLs 2000, LNCS 1869*, pages 215–232. Springer-Verlag, 2000.
10. J. Hickey and A. Nogin. Fast tactic-based theorem proving. In *TPHOLs 2000, LNCS 1869*, pages 252–267. Springer-Verlag, 2000.
11. W.A. Hunt and B. Brock. A formal HDL and its use in the FM9001 verification. *Proceedings of the Royal Society*, April 1992.
12. M. Kaufmann, P. Manolios, and J.S. Moore, editors. *Computer-Aided Reasoning: ACL2 Case Studies*. Kluwer Academic Press, 2000.
13. M. Kaufmann, P. Manolios, and J.S. Moore. *Computer-Aided Reasoning: An Approach*. Kluwer Academic Press, 2000.
14. P. Manolios. Correctness of pipelined machines. In *Formal Methods in Computer-Aided Design, FMCAD 2000*, pages 161–178. Springer-Verlag LNCS 1954, 2000.
15. S.P. Miller and M. Srivas. Formal verification of the AAMP5 microprocessor: A case study in the industrial use of formal methods. In *Proceedings of WIFT '95: Workshop on Industrial-Strength Formal Specification Techniques*, pages 2–16. IEEECS, April 1995.
16. J.S. Moore. *Piton: A Mechanically Verified Assembly-Level Language*. Automated Reasoning Series, Kluwer Academic Publishers, 1996.
17. S. Owre, J. Rushby, and N. Shankar. PVS: A prototype verification system. In D. Kapur, editor, *11th International Conference on Automated Deduction (CADE)*, pages 748–752. Lecture Notes in Artificial Intelligence, Vol 607, Springer-Verlag, June 1992.
18. J. Sawada and W. Hunt. Processor verification with precise exceptions and speculative execution. In *Computed Aided Verification, CAV '98*, pages 135–146. Springer-Verlag LNCS 1427, 1998.
19. G. L. Steele, Jr. *Common Lisp The Language, Second Edition*. Digital Press, 30 North Avenue, Burlington, MA 01803, 1990.
20. Matthew Wilding, David Greve, and David Hardin. Efficient simulation of formal processor models. *Formal Methods in System Design*, to appear. Draft TR available as http://pobox.com/users/hokie/docs/efm.ps.

Using Timestamping and History Variables to Verify Sequential Consistency*

Tamarah Arons

The John von Neumann Minerva Center for Verification of Reactive Systems
Weizmann Institute of Science, Rehovot, Israel
tamarah@wisdom.weizmann.ac.il

Abstract. In this paper we propose a methodology for verifying the sequential consistency of caching algorithms. The scheme combines timestamping and an auxiliary history table to construct a serial execution 'matching' any given execution of the algorithm. We believe that this approach is applicable to an interesting class of sequentially consistent algorithms in which the buffering of cache updates allows stale values to be read from cache. We illustrate this methodology by verifying the high level specifications of the lazy caching and ring algorithms.

In shared memory multiprocessor systems a *memory consistency model* specifies how memory operations will appear to execute to the programmer. The closer the memory consistency model forces the shared memory to behave as a *serial memory system* – a system in which all operations are performed atomically directly on memory with no buffering or caching (Figure 1(a)) – the easier it is for the programmer to write correct code for the system. However, the stricter the memory model the more hardware and compiler optimizations are disallowed. *Sequential consistency* is an intuitive memory model, in which, "the result of any execution is the same as if the [memory] operations of all the processors were executed in some sequential order, and the operations of each individual processor appear in this sequence in the order specified by the program"[24]. Sequential consistency is a relatively restrictive model when compared with the more relaxed memory models (such as partial or total store ordering, or release consistency) which are supported by some commercially available architectures (e.g. PowerPC, SPARC, Digital Alpha)[1].

Many sequentially consistent models implement *coherence*, an even stricter consistency model. Whereas an execution is sequentially consistent if all of the processors' local views can be interleaved to form a single serial behavior, regardless of the relative ordering of events at different processors, coherence requires that the events, as ordered *globally*, be a trace of serial memory [2].

To prove sequential consistency of a proposed memory implementation M it suffices to construct, for every σ_M, an execution of M, a matching serial execution σ_S such that all operations in σ_S read and write the same values as in σ_M. However, the creation of such a "witness" serial execution may require that a

---

* Research supported in part by a grant from the German-Israel bi-national GIF foundation and a gift from Intel.

G. Berry, H. Comon, and A. Finkel (Eds.): CAV 2001, LNCS 2102, pp. 423–435, 2001.

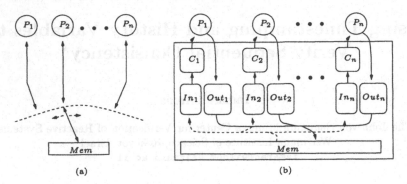

Fig. 1. Architecture of (a) a serial memory and (b) the lazy caching algorithm.

potentially unbounded number of operations be re-ordered. In fact, the problem of verifying sequential consistency is known to be undecidable [3]. Thus, unlike coherence which can often be verified quite easily, sequential consistency does not comfortably fit the pattern of standard refinement techniques (trace inclusion, bisimulation, testing preorder). The non-coherent lazy caching algorithm was therefore proposed by Rob Gerth as an example on which different refinement methods can be tried [15], and in 1999 a special edition of *Distributed Computing* was devoted to this project [13].

In this paper we present a proof methodology which involves *timestamping* the cache reads and shared memory updates of an execution and placing them in a *history table*. Intuitively, every processor P_i has a cache C_i which contains a subset of the values in the shared memory at some time $t_i \leq t_G$, where t_G is the global system time. All writes to memory occurring in the interval $(t_i, t_G]$ have not yet been applied to C_i. The *local time* t_i is precisely the time at which the global memory had contents consistent with C_i. We timestamp instructions with the local time (and other information, in order to create a total ordering between instructions executing at the same local time) and place them in a *history table* ordered by timestamp. The information in the history table contains sufficient information for a matching serial execution to be built, and the algorithm to be proved sequentially consistent.

We believe that this methodology is suitable for the verification of the sequential consistency of many non-coherent memory models, as demonstrated by our applying this proof method, using the PVS [27] theorem prover, to two examples, *lazy caching* [2, 15] and a *ring* algorithm [6][1]. While this methodology is theoretically applicable to coherent snoopy protocols, we believe that it is more complicated than is required for such algorithms. Current work considers increasing the automation of deductive proofs, and we hope later to consider the application of the methodology to other classes of caching algorithms.

The paper is structured as follows: In Section 1 we describe the lazy caching algorithm. In Section 2 we explain how timestamping and the history table are

---

[1] The PVS files are available at [4].

Event	Enabling conditions	Action
$R_i(a,d)$	Instruction pc_i is "READ a" $\wedge C_i(a).valid \wedge C_i(a).data = d$ $\wedge$ no *starred* entries in In_i $\wedge Out_i = \{\}$	$pc_i := pc_i + 1$
$W_i(a,d)$	Instruction pc_i is "WRITE a, d"	$Out_i := push(Out_i, (a,d)) \wedge pc_i := pc_i + 1$
$MW_i(a,d)$	$head(Out_i) = (a,d)$	$Mem[a] := d \wedge Out_i := tail(Out_i)$ $\wedge \forall_{k \neq i} In_k := push(In_k, (a,d))$ $\wedge In_i := push(In_i, (a,d,*))$
$MR_i(a)$	$C_i(a).valid = false$	$In_i := push(In_i, (a, Mem[a]))$
$CU_i(a,d)$	$head(In_i) = (a,d) \vee$ $head(In_i) = (a,d,*)$	$In_i := tail(In_i) \wedge C_i(a).data := d$ $\wedge C_i(a).valid := true$
$CI_i(a)$	$C_i(a).valid = true$	$C_i(a).valid := false$
I_i (idle)		

Fig. 2. Lazy Caching Transitions.

used to derive a serial execution. In Section 3 we define the ring algorithm and describe how it fitted into our methodology. Section 4 discusses related works and in Section 5 we summarize our conclusions.

1 Lazy Caching

The "lazy cache algorithm"[2] is a sequentially consistent protocol in which cache updates can be postponed, and writes are buffered, allowing processors to access stale cache data.

As illustrated in Figure 1(b), the system consists of n processors, $P_1, \ldots, P_n$ with each P_i owning a cache C_i, and FIFO *in-* and *out-queues* In_i and Out_i, respectively. We have further associated with each processor an unbounded *instruction list*, containing instruction of the form "READ a" and "WRITE a, d". Instructions in the instruction list are executed sequentially, with a program counter, pc_i, pointing to the next instruction.

A processor P_i initiates a write event W_i by placing a record recording the instruction address and new value at the tail of Out_i. When this record reaches the top of Out_i it can be popped off and the memory write MW_i occurs. That is, the shared memory is updated, and a new record recording the address and value is placed in the *in-queue* In_j of all processors P_j. The copy placed in In_i is *starred*. When the entry at the head of In_i is popped off a cache update CU_i occurs, and C_i is updated with the value recorded in the In_i entry.

A read event R_i can be performed if the address a requested is in the cache, Out_i is empty and In_i does not contain any starred entries. The value read is that in the cache. We note that this value may differ from that in the memory if a write to a is buffered in In_i. Locations (which are not currently in cache) can be brought into the cache by placing the memory value in the *in* queue in a memory read (MR_i) action, and can be summarily evicted by cache invalidation (CI).

426   Tamarah Arons

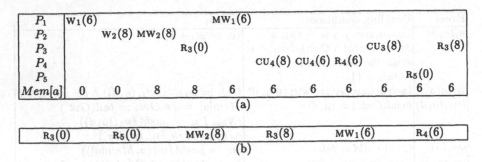

P_1	$\text{W}_1(6)$				$\text{MW}_1(6)$					
P_2		$\text{W}_2(8)$ $\text{MW}_2(8)$								
P_3			$\text{R}_3(0)$					$\text{CU}_3(8)$		$\text{R}_3(8)$
P_4						$\text{CU}_4(8)$ $\text{CU}_4(6)$ $\text{R}_4(6)$				
P_5									$\text{R}_5(0)$	
$Mem[a]$	0	0	8	8	6	6	6	6	6	6	6

(a)

$\text{R}_3(0)$	$\text{R}_5(0)$	$\text{MW}_2(8)$	$\text{R}_3(8)$	$\text{MW}_1(6)$	$\text{R}_4(6)$

(b)

Fig. 3. (a) A partial execution of the lazy caching algorithm. All transitions refer to address a. Time increases from left to right. (b) A matching serial execution, where "read" and "write" instructions correspond to R and MW events.

In our interleaving model at any step a processor can either initiate a read or write (if one is enabled), pop an entry off its *in*- or *out*-queue if they are non-empty, initiate a cache update, invalidate a cache entry, or idle (I). The system is parameterized by the number of processors and there is no restriction on the maximum size of the queues, the address space, or the set of memory values. Our model, summarized in Figure 2, very closely resembles that of Gerth [15]. The reader is referred to this paper, or our PVS source files [4], for more information.

An Example Execution Fragment. In Figure 3(a) we consider a very small execution sequence which illustrates the non-coherent nature of the lazy caching algorithm. We assume that address a has initial value 0. Process P_1 initiates a write of 6 to a, placing the tuple $(a, 6)$ on its *out*-queue. Process P_2 then initiates a write of 8 to a. Process P_2 pops $(a, 8)$ off Out_2, in a memory write MW_2 action, pushing the (address, data) tuple onto the *in*-queues of all processors. Sometime thereafter action MW_1 also occurs. Process P_3 reads the value of 0 for a, updates its cache with 8, and then reads 8 as the value of a, while the write of 6 is buffered. Process P_4 updates its cache with both values before reading reading a as 6; process P_5 reads a as 0.

We note that the memory is updated in the opposite order to which the writes were initiated, and thus a has the final value of 6. Furthermore, processors P_3 and P_5 read stale values for a *after* P_4 has read the new value.

2   Creating a Serial Execution

To prove an algorithm sequentially consistent we show that each of its executions has an equivalent *serial* execution. In the serial execution all operations are executed directly on memory, in some sequential order, and the operations of each individual processor are in program order, where "read" and "write" instructions correspond to R and MW events. It is shown that reads in the two executions return the same value, and the final memory values are identical. Figure 3(b) gives the serial execution corresponding to the lazy caching execution of Figure 3(a).

2.1 Logical Time

Each processor has a view of memory which is consistent with the values memory had at some time in the past: It sees the memory as it was before it was modified by the last x writes, these being the writes which are buffered in the in-queue.

The *global time* t_G is determined by an auxiliary global clock, and is initially zero. Every time a memory write occurs the global time is incremented by one.

Each processor has an auxiliary local clock which counts the number of writes which have been applied to its cache. This clock gives its *local time*. It is updated each time a process performs a cache update which was initiated by a memory write. These cache updates are termed *countable*. (In order to distinguish countable cache updates from those initiated by memory reads, we add an auxiliary processor id field to in-queue records. An entry is the result of a memory read exactly if the processor id in the record is that of the processor and the record is not starred.) The processor has a view of memory consistent with the values that memory held when the global time was the current local time of the processor.

Every read (R) or memory write (MW) event in the system is given a unique *timestamp* when it occurs. The timestamp is a tuple (t, r, id), where t is the local time at which the event occurs, r is the numbers of reads which this processor has performed since the last counted cached update, and id is the identifier of the processor that initiated the read/write. On a read $R_i(a, d)$ we add to the history table H an entry $R_i(a, d)$, its timestamp $(t_i, r_i + 1, i)$ and the current program counter, pc_i of P_i. The local read counter, r_i, is incremented by 1. On a memory write $MW_j(a, d)$ we add to the history table H an entry $MW_j(a, d)$, its timestamp $(t_G + 1, 0, j)$ and pc_j and we set $t_G := t_G + 1$. On a counted cache update CU_k we set $t_k := t_k + 1, r_k := 0$.

The timestamps induce a strict order on memory events:
$$(t_1, r_1, id_1) \prec (t_2, r_2, id_2) \Leftrightarrow t_1 < t_2 \vee t_1 = t_2 \wedge (r_1 < r_2 \vee r_1 = r_2 \wedge id_1 < id_2)$$

Time 0 is the time given to all reads of the initial, unmodified memory. For every $t_i > 0$ the "smallest" timestamp with time t_i will always be a memory write (MW), as the *reads* field of a timestamp is zero exactly when it represents a memory write operation. Since the local clocks are incremented every time that a cache update is performed, there is only one memory write at time t_i and all other operations timestamped with $t = t_i$ are reads. As they are all reads from the same memory, with no intervening writes, they will return the same value irrespective of the ordering between them. However, it is desirable that the program order of each processor be maintained, and this is done by the *reads* field of the timestamp. The id field of the timestamp is used to order operations at the same local time by different processors. The relative ordering of these operations is unimportant, and ours in one of a number of possibilities.

These counters and timestamps are variants of Lamport clocks [23]. However, in our system each processor updates its clock independently, without reading the timestamps on incoming messages.

(a)

Instruction	Action	Timestamp (t,r,id)	P_1 t a r	P_2 t a r	P_3 t a r	P_4 t a r	P_5 t a r	Global Time	Memory a
			0 0 0	0 0 0	0 0 0	0 0 0	0 0 0	0	0
$P_1 : a := 6$	$W_1(a,6)$		0 0 0	0 0 0	0 0 0	0 0 0	0 0 0	0	0
$P_2 : a := 8$	$W_2(a,8)$		0 0 0	0 0 0	0 0 0	0 0 0	0 0 0	0	0
	$MW_2(a,8)$	$(1,0,2)$	0 0 0	0 0 0	0 0 0	0 0 0	0 0 0	1	8
$P_3 : $ read a	$R_3(a,0)$	$(0,1,3)$	0 0 0	0 0 0	0 0 1	0 0 0	0 0 0	1	8
	$MW_1(a,6)$	$(2,0,1)$	0 0 0	0 0 0	0 0 1	0 0 0	0 0 0	2	6
	$CU_4(a,8)$		0 0 0	0 0 0	0 0 1	1 8 0	0 0 0	2	6
	$CU_4(a,6)$		0 0 0	0 0 0	0 0 1	2 6 0	0 0 0	2	6
$P_4 : $ read a	$R_4(a,6)$	$(2,1,4)$	0 0 0	0 0 0	0 0 1	2 6 1	0 0 0	2	6
	$CU_3(a,8)$		0 0 0	0 0 0	1 8 0	2 6 1	0 0 0	2	6
$P_5 : $ read a	$R_5(a,0)$	$(0,1,5)$	0 0 0	0 0 0	1 8 0	2 6 1	0 0 1	2	6
$P_3 : $ read a	$R_3(a,8)$	$(1,1,3)$	0 0 0	0 0 0	1 8 1	2 6 1	0 0 1	2	6

(b)

Index	Timestamp	Operation	pc
1	$(0,1,3)$	$R_3(a,0)$	1
2	$(0,1,5)$	$R_5(a,0)$	1
3	$(1,0,2)$	$MW_2(a,8)$	1
4	$(1,1,3)$	$R_3(a,8)$	2
5	$(2,0,1)$	$MW_1(a,6)$	1
6	$(2,1,4)$	$R_4(a,6)$	1

(c)

Instruction	$Mem[a]$
$P_3 : $ read a	0
$P_5 : $ read a	0
$P_2 : a := 8$	8
$P_3 : $ read a	8
$P_1 : a := 6$	6
$P_4 : $ read a	6

Fig. 4. An execution of the lazy caching algorithm with history table and matching serial execution. (a) Building the history table. (b) The history table ordered by timestamp. (c) A serial execution.

2.2   Extracting a Serial Execution from the History Table

The history table is an ordered list of entries sorted in non-decreasing order of timestamp. Since memory writes always have a greater timestamp than any other elements in the table at the time they occur they are appended to its end. Reads, however, may be inserted in the middle of the history table. The function $size(H)$ returns the number of entries in H. For every $x \leq size(H)$, $H[x]$ refers to the x'th entry of H.

In Figure 4(a) we revisit the example of Section 1, showing how the history table would be constructed. For each processor the table records its local time t, the value it stores for a, and r, the number of reads it has performed since the last countable cache update. The timestamp column indicates the timestamp of the entry which is added to the history table at the step in which it is added. Time progresses from top to bottom in the table.

A serial execution can be derived from the history table such that the i'th entry in the history table corresponds to the i'th operation in the serial execution. It is proved that in this serial execution every processor issues its instructions in the same order as in the original execution, all reads return the same values as in the lazy caching execution, and the final memory values are the same as in the original execution.

Type	Definition
TIME	$\mathbb{N}$
PROC_ID	$1 \ldots n$; for $n > 1$ a system parameter
ADDRESS	$\mathbb{N}$
VALUE	$\Re$
PC_RANGE	$\mathbb{N}^+$
MEMORY	ADDRESS $\mapsto$ VALUE

Basic types

Field	Type
t	TIME
r	$\mathbb{N}$
id	PROC_ID
operation	{R, MW}
address	ADDRESS
data	VALUE
pc	PC_RANGE

Entries of the history table, H

Field	Type
memory	MEMORY
id	PROC_ID
pc	PC_RANGE

Entries of $memHist$

Field	Type
cache	ADDRESS $\mapsto$ [$valid$: BOOLEAN, $data$: VALUE]
pc	PC_RANGE
inQueue, outQueue	QUEUE
t	TIME
$readCounter$	$\mathbb{N}$
$readValues$	PC_RANGE $\mapsto$ VALUE

Processors of the lazy caching system

Field	Type
address	ADDRESS
star	BOOLEAN
data	VALUE
t	TIME
pc	PC_RANGE
id	PROC_ID

Queue entries

Fig. 5. Some of the data structures. Auxiliary variables in the processor and queue structures are italicized.

In Figure 4(b) we present the history table built in the example of Figure 4(a), with entries ordered by timestamp. The table illustrates all the fields in the history table. Figure 4(c) illustrates the serial execution which is derived.

2.3   The Proof

The auxiliary *history* (H) list and *memHist* array and *readValues* arrays are intrinsic to the presented proof. Each processor has a *readValues* array which maps instruction indices to values. Every time a read operation occurs the value read is stored in the relevant entry of the *readValues* array. This array is later used to insure that the lazy caching and serial executions return identical values for every read. The *memHist* array is a history of memory contents, where *memHist*[t] is a copy of the shared memory at global time t. In addition, *memHist* also stores for every time t the processor id and program counter for the instruction that updated memory from *memHist*[$t - 1$] to *memHist*[t]. We also found it useful to add auxiliary fields to the *in-* and *out-*queue entries: in addition to the address, value and "*" fields, we added auxiliary fields recording the processor id and program counter of the related instruction, and the global time at which the related event occurs. We note that this time field is *not* used to update the processors local clocks, or any other variables. Some of the data structures are detailed in Figure 5.

In order to construct the serial execution we prove a one to one relationship between executed operations and history table entries. The bulk of the proof effort involved manually defining properties of the lazy caching algorithm and then proving their invariance in the PVS[27] system. We list some of the invariants used in the proof.

For every two entries $H[x]$ and $H[y]$ of history table H with timestamps (t_x, r_x, id_x) and (t_y, r_y, id_y) respectively, and $x, y \leq size(H)$:

- If $x \neq y$ then $(t_x, r_x, id_x) \neq (t_y, r_y, id_y)$. (Distinct entries have distinct timestamps).
- $x < y$ iff $(t_x, r_x, id_x) \prec (t_y, r_y, id_y)$. ($H$ is ordered by timestamp).
- Entry $H[x]$ corresponds to a memory write operation iff $r_x = 0$.
- If $t_x = t_y$ and $r_x = 0$ then $r_y \neq 0$. (At most one memory write at any global time).
- For all $0 < t \leq t_G$ there is an index $z \leq size(H)$ such that $H[z]$ is timestamped $(t, 0, id)$ for some id. (Every time period greater than zero is initiated by a memory write).
- For all $0 < r < r_x$, there is an entry $H[z]$, $z < x$ timestamped (t_x, r, id_x) in H. (Reads are counted sequentially, with no gaps in the counting).
- The time t_x is not greater than the global time t_G and if t_x is greater than the local time t_{id_x} then there is an entry in In_{id_x} corresponding to $H[x]$.
- The contents of $memHist$ for the current global time equal the current memory. That is, $memHist[t_G] = Mem$.
- For every address a and processor P_i with cache C_i and local time t_i, $C_i(a).valid \to C_i(a).data = memHist[t_i](a)$. The values of locations in the cache match the $memHist$ values for the processor's local time.
- For every occupied entry $In_i[k]$ of In_i, $t_i \leq In_i[k].t \leq t_G$ and if $t_i = In_i[k].t$ then $In_i[k]$ records a non-countable cache update. Intuitively, for every t such that $t_i < t \leq t_G$ there is an In_i-entry which will be used to update t_i.
- The program counter $H[x].pc$ is less than pc_{id_x}.
- For every value pc less than the program counter pc_i of P_i either there is an entry $H[z]$, $z \leq size(H)$ with timestamp (t_z, r_z, i) such that $H[z].pc = pc$, or there is an entry of Out_i corresponding to this instruction.
- The value $P_{id_x}.readValues[H[x].pc] = memHist[t_x](a)$ where a is the address in the pc'th instruction of P_{id_x}. (The values in the $readValues$ array match the $memHist$ values for the time of the transition.)

The serial execution is inductively built in a list S where $S[x].mem$ and $S[x].procs$ give the global memory and processor states in the serial system after x execution steps. Intuitively, the x'th entry of S corresponds to the x'th entry of H, for all $x \leq size(H)$. That is, in the serial execution transitions occur in the order in which they appear in the history table.

We now define predicate α which describes the relationship between the lazy caching data structures L and S. For clarity we prefix data structures in the lazy caching algorithm with L where confusion could arise.

1. The first entry, $S[0]$, fulfills the initial conditions of the serial system.
2. For every $0 \leq x < size[H]$, $\rho_{serial}(S[x], S[x+1])$. That is, there is a transition in the serial system from $S[x]$ to $S[x+1]$.
3. For every $0 \leq x \leq size[H]$, $S[x].mem = L.memHist[H[x].t]$. That is, the global memory at the x'th entry in S matches the memory recorded in $L.memHist$ for time $H[x].t$.

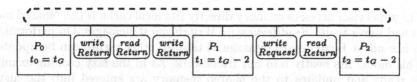

Fig. 6. An Example Configuration in the Ring Algorithm.

4. For every processor P_i and program index p, if the p'th instruction of P_i is a read instruction then $S[size[H]].readValues[i,p] = L.readValues[i,p]$. That is, every read in the two systems returns the same value.
5. The program counter of processor P_i at the end of the sequential execution, $S[size(H)].pc_i$, is equal to $L.pc_i$ if $L.Out_i$ is empty, and the (auxiliary) program counter field in the top $L.Out_i$ entry, otherwise.

We prove inductively that for every reachable lazy caching state L there is an S such that $\alpha(L, S)$: We first prove that predicate α holds for the initial states of the two systems, and then that if $\alpha(L, S)$ holds, then for any L' such that $\rho_{lazy}(L, L')$ is a lazy caching transition, we can build an S' such that $\alpha(L', S')$.

From parts (1) and (2) of α S records a legal serial execution. Given that $L.memHist[t_G]$ is proved to equal $L.Mem$, the currently lazy caching memory, from (3) we can deduce that the memory values in the two systems agree. From (4) we prove that both systems return the same value for every read.

We complete the proof by showing that the lazy caching system can always progress meaningfully.

3 The Ring Algorithm

In order to test the applicability of our methodology we applied it also to a model based on Collier's ring algorithm [6]:

Processors $P_0, \ldots, P_{n-1}$ are connected in a ring, with P_i sending messages only to its successor, $P_{i+1 \bmod n}$. The channels between every two successive processors are FIFO queues of messages. Processor P_0 is designated the *supervisor*. If processor $P_i, i \neq 0$ wants to perform a write of value v to address a it sends to its successor a *WriteRequest(a, v)* message and enters a *waiting* state. This write request is passed around the ring until it reaches the supervisor. The supervisor updates memory with this address and value, and then sends a *WriteReturn(a, v)* message. On receiving a *WriteReturn* message all processors update their caches, and then pass it on to their successor. Process P_i also releases itself from its *waiting* state and can proceed. When the write return reaches the supervisor, it is removed from the system.

A processor can execute a read instruction if the address is in its cache. Otherwise it sends a *ReadRequest*, which the supervisor answers with a *ReadReturn*. After thus bringing the address into the cache, the read can be executed.

The supervisor accesses memory directly (its local cache *is* the "shared memory") and never issues *ReadRequest* or *WriteRequest* messages. On performing a write it sends a *WriteReturn* message so that all other caches can be updated.

This model fits neatly into our framework. As in the lazy caching example, cache reads and updates to the shared memory are entered into the history table when they occur. (In this algorithm the memory update occurs when a *WriteReturn* in initiated by the supervisor.) The supervisor increments its local clock when it sends a *WriteReturn*, and all other processors increment their local clocks on receiving the *WriteReturn*. The local time of the supervisor is the global system time. The local time t_i of P_i is the global time minus the number of *writeReturns* on channels between P_0 and P_i. An example configuration is given in Figure 6.

4 Related Works

Various methodologies, ranging from CSP [5,9], to abstraction [16] and model checking [19] have been used to verify lazy caching. The primary difficulty in verifying lazy caching seems to be that at the time that a memory is updated by a write in the lazy caching system, it is not known how many reads reading the stale value will still occur. That is, nondeterministic choices in the abstract (serial) system occur earlier than in the concrete (lazy caching) system. One solution is to input the computation of the concrete system into a transducer, which queues segments of the concrete computation until they can be matched with an abstract execution [21]. Similarly, [19] propose a finite state observer that observes and re-orders the memory operations, while [22] use an auxiliary queue to record writes which have updated memory but have not yet updated the cache. Step-wise refinement, in which the lazy caching system is transformed in a number of steps to a serial system, is used in [5] and [22]. Composition [20] and abstraction [16] are two other methodologies proposed, while in [9] decomposition is coupled with the use of CSP to prove trace inclusion.

The paper introducing lazy caching [2] presents a semantic proof that it is sequentially consistent. A *WriteCounter* is used to assign a sequence numbers to updates of the shared memory. Reads are assigned numbers according to the last write which the processor has popped off its *in*-queue. An auxiliary *Hist* variable is used, with semantics similar to that of our *memHist* variable.

Of the above mentioned verification efforts only [19] has been mechanized at all. The model-checking verification in [19] is of a restricted system in which there is no *out*-queue and the *in*-queue is of size at most one. Given the problems of state explosion, it is unclear how a more detailed system could be verified. It is claimed that the type of abstractions that are used in [16] could be computed algorithmically, thus partially mechanizing this proof.

Timestamping, using variants of logical Lamport clocks [23], has been used to verify various memory consistency models [7, 8]. The algorithms are verified at a lower level than we have considered, including message passing protocols. Timestamping is used to divide logical time into *coherence epochs*, intervals of logical time in which a node has read-only or read-write access to a block of data.

Thus, it is possible for one epoch to contain multiple, or no, stores. Furthermore the same write can be given different timestamps when it is used to update different caches. In contrast, in our timestamping each memory update is identified with an epoch and has a unique timestamp. This underscores a difference in our approaches to memory consistency – whether block control or memory contents are the primary concern. The difference in emphasis is appropriate given the different levels (high level versus message passing) at which verification occurs, and the different algorithms considered. The proofs presented are entirely manual.

Theorem proving has been used by Park and Dill [11,12] and Stoy et al [28] to verify cache coherence protocols at the message passing level. Park and Dill *aggregate* the steps of each transaction in the implementation into a single atomic transition in the specification. A *commit* point is identified, for each transition, and the aggregation function intuitively is a function completing committed instructions. This methodology has been used to effectively verify a detailed model of the complex FLASH protocol. However, it is unclear how it could be used in our examples, where instructions may commit out of order (a read instruction may return an older value than a previous read, by another processor, for the same address). In [28] a PVS [27] implementation of Lamport's TLA [25] is used. Queues are *drained* to empty them of messages, and an abstraction function used to show refinement between two protocols.

A lot of research has been done on using model checking to verify cache coherence protocols. However, due to the difficulties of verifying large systems many of these methodologies are restricted. E.g., the 'test model-checking' of [17] in incomplete, the work by Delzanno, Pong and Dubois [10, 14] based on FSMs is only appropriate to coherent algorithms. Lazic [26] shows that data independence theorems can be used to make model checking of cache protocols more tractable.

Our construction of a serial execution is reminiscent of work by Glusman and Katz [18]. They allow independent operations to be re-ordered to create a *convenient computation*. Our "convenient" serial execution is not only a re-ordering of the events, but also a change in the nature of the occurring events.

There are more points of similarity between our work and those mentioned above. The auxiliary variables in [22,19] perform some of the functions of our history table. While timestamping has been used previously in verifying cache consistency protocols [8], the similarities between this work and ours are in the terminology more than the semantics. Our timestamping is closer in meaning to the *WriteCounter* variable in [2]. Their *Hist* variable is also similar to our *memHist* variable. However, the proof in [2] is 'on a semantical level and not grounded in a refinement methodology'[15]. By creating a full timestamping scheme, and using a history table, we have developed a formal verification framework which allows mechanical verification, and can easily be applied to different verification problems.

The centrality of the history table, and the method in which it is coupled with timestamping is new, and provides a relatively simple proof which is amenable to *mechanical verification*. We believe that mechanical verification provides a higher degree of confidence than pen and paper proofs, and testifies to a relatively simple and natural methodology.

5   Conclusion

In this paper we present a refinement methodology for the verification of sequential consistency. Given that the general problem is known to be undecidable, our proof method cannot be complete. However, we believe that there is a class of 'difficult', non-coherent algorithms, to which this methodology is suited, as illustrated by the successful verification of the lazy caching and ring algorithms.

We take cache reads and shared memory updates to be the important events to be recorded, and show that a correct ordering of these events allow the construction of a matching serial execution. While the idea of using timestamps (or, more generally, Lamport clocks) to order events is far from new, the timestamping that we have devised is particularly well suited to sequential consistency. It allows us to give a relative order (timestamp) to an "important event", when it occurs, relative to all past and possible *future* such events in the system. The history table provides a means of dynamically ordering these events, so that a serial execution can be extracted.

The methodology is sound – when it is applied a corresponding serial execution can be built. Since all steps are mechanically verified in the PVS theorem prover, this gives a very solid proof of sequential consistency.

The major drawback of this methodology is the large amount of human effort required (several person-weeks), devoted primarily to deriving the invaraint properties and directing the theorem prover. We are currently researching techniques to increase the automation of the proofs, and hope later to consider the extension of our methodology to other classes of algorithms.

Acknowledgements

Prof. Amir Pnueli, my supervisor, provided invaluable criticsims and suggestions; Jürgen Niehaus suggested the ring algorithm.

References

1. S. V. Adve and K. Gharachorloo. Shared memory consistency models: A tutorial. Technical Report 9512, Rice University, 1995.
2. Y. Afek, G. Brown, and M. Merrit. Lazy caching. *ACM Transactions on Programming Languages and Systems*, 15(1):182–205, 1993.
3. R. Alur, K. L. McMillan, and D. Peled. Model checking of correctness conditions for concurrent objects. In *MICS'96*:219–228, 1996.
4. T. Arons. Homepage. http://www.wisdom.weizmann.ac.il/~tamarah/caching/.
5. E. Brinksma. Cache consistency by design. *Dist. Comp.*, 12:61–74, 1999.
6. W. W. Collier. *Reasoning about Parallel Architectures*. Prentice Hall, 1992.
7. A. E. Condon, M. D. Hill, M. Plakal, and D. J. Sorin. Lamport clocks: Reasoning about shared-memory correctness. Technical Report CS-TR-1367, University of Wisconsin, Madison, 1998.
8. A. E. Condon, M. D. Hill, M. Plakal, and D. J. Sorin. Lamport clocks: Verifying a directory cache-coherence protocol. In *Proc. 10th ACM Symp. Parallel Algorithms and Architectures (SPAA)*, 1998.

9. J. Davies and G. Lowe. Using CSP to verify sequential consistency. *Dist. Comp.*, 12:91–103, 1999.
10. G. Delzanno. Automatic verification of parametrized cache coherence protocols. *CAV'00*:53–68, 2000.
11. D. L. Dill and S. Park. Verification of FLASH cache coherence protocol by aggregation of distributed transactions. In *SPAA '96*:288–296, 1996.
12. D. L. Dill and S. Park. Verification of cache coherence protocols by aggregation of distributed transactions. In *Theory of Computing Systems*. 1998.
13. *Distributed Computing*, Volume 12 Number 2/3, 1999.
14. M. Dubois and F. Pong. Verification techniques for cache coherence protocols. *ACM Computing Surveys*, 29(1):82–126, 1997.
15. R. Gerth. Sequential consistency and the lazy caching algorithm. *Dist. Comp.*, 12:57–59, 1999.
16. S. Graf. Characterization of a sequentially consistent memory and verification of a cache memory by abstraction. *Dist. Comp.*, 12:75–90, 1999.
17. R. Ghughal, G. Gopalakrishnan, A. Mokkedem, and R. Nalumasu. The 'test model-checking' approach to the verification of formal memory models of multiprocessors. *CAV'98*:464–376, 1998.
18. M. Glusman and S. Katz. Mechanizing proofs of computation equivalence. *CAV'99*:354–367, 1999.
19. T. Henzinger, S. Qadeer, and S. K. Rajamani. Verifying sequential consistency on shared-memory multiprocessor systems. *CAV'99*:301–315, 1999.
20. W. Janssen, M. Poel, and J. Zwiers. The compositional approach to sequential consistency and lazy caching. *Dist. Comp.*, 12:105–127, 1999.
21. R. Jonsson, A. Pnueli, and C. Rump. Proving refinement using transduction. *Dist. Comp.*, 12:129–149, 1999.
22. P. Ladkin, L. Lamport, B. Olivier, and D. Roegel. Lazy caching in TLA. *Dist. Comp.*, 12:151–174, 1999.
23. L. Lamport. Time, clocks and the ordering of events. *Communications of the ACM*, 21(7):558–565, 1978.
24. L. Lamport. How to make a multiprocessor computer that correctly executes multiprocess programs. *IEEE Transactions on Computers*, C-82(9):690–691, 1979.
25. L. Lamport. The temporal logic of actions. *ACM Trans. Prog. Lang. Sys.*, 16(3):872–923, May 1994.
26. R. S. Lazic. *A Sematic Study of Data Independed with Appliations to Model Checking*. PhD thesis, Oxford University Computing Laboratory, 1999.
27. S. Owre, J. M. Rushby, N. Shankar, and M. K. Srivas. A tutorial on using PVS for hardware verification. *TPCD'94*:258–279, 1994.
28. J. Stoy, X. Shen, and Arvind. Proofs of correctness of cache-coherence protocols. In *Formal Methods Europe, FME'01*, Springer-Verlag, 2001.

Benefits of Bounded Model Checking
at an Industrial Setting

Fady Copty[1], Limor Fix[1], Ranan Fraer[1], Enrico Giunchiglia[2],
Gila Kamhi[1], Armando Tacchella[2], and Moshe Y. Vardi[*][3]

[1] Formal Property Verification, Intel Corporation, Haifa, Israel
[2] DIST, University of Genova, Genova, Italy
[3] Dept. of Computer Science, Rice University, Houston, USA

Abstract. The usefulness of Bounded Model Checking (BMC) based on propositional satisfiability (SAT) methods for bug hunting has already been proven in several recent work. In this paper, we present two industrial strength systems performing BMC for both verification and falsification. The first is *Thunder,* which performs BMC on top of a new satisfiability solver, *SIMO.* The second is *Forecast,* which performs BMC on top of a BDD package. SIMO is based on the Davis Logemann Loveland procedure (DLL) and features the most recent search methods. It enjoys *static* and *dynamic* branching heuristics, advanced *back-jumping* and *learning* techniques. SIMO also includes new heuristics that are specially tuned for the BMC problem domain. With Thunder we have achieved impressive capacity and productivity for BMC. Real designs, taken from Intel's Pentium⊙4, with over 1000 model variables were validated using the default tool settings and without manual tuning. In Forecast, we present several alternatives for adapting BDD-based model checking for BMC. We have conducted comparison of Thunder and Forecast on a large set of real and complex designs and on almost all of them Thunder has demonstrated clear win over Forecast in two important aspects: capacity and productivity.

1 Introduction

The success of formal verification is no longer measured in its ability to verify interesting design behaviors; it is measured in its contribution to the correctness of the design in comparison to the contribution of other validation methods, i.e., simulation. Therefore, technologies and methodologies that enhance the productivity of formal verification are of special interest. Our research identifies Bounded Model Checking (BMC) based on propositional satisfiability (SAT) to be such a technology.

BMC based on SAT methods [bcrz99, bccz99, sht00] has recently been introduced as a complementary technique to BDD-based Symbolic Model Checking. The basic idea is to search for a counterexample in executions whose length is bounded by some integer k. Given this bound, the model checking problem can be efficiently reduced to a SAT problem, and can therefore be solved by SAT methods rather than BDDs.

---

*Work partially supported by NSF grants CCR-9700061 and CCR-9988322, BSF grant 9800096, and a grant from the Intel Corporation.

G. Berry, H. Comon, and A. Finkel (Eds.) : CAV 2001, LNCS 2102, pp. 436-453, 2001.

In this paper, we report our detailed evaluation of SAT-based BMC at an industrial setting. Our initial interest in BMC and SAT technology has been due to the several recent papers [bcrz99, bccz99, sht00] that have compared BDD-based model checking to SAT-based model checking and have concluded that many of the (BDD-based model checking) hard problems can easily be solved by SAT-based model checkers. The test cases used in the comparisons reported in [sht00] were drawn from the internal benchmark of a state-of-the-art BDD based symbolic model checker, RuleBase [bee96a, bee97a]. Therefore, in [sht00], no definite conclusions could be derived on the capacity benefit of the SAT technology, since all the verification cases were in the capacity ballpark of RuleBase. Although Biere et al. report in [bcrz99] that their SAT-based BMC consistently outperformed the BDD-based symbolic model checker, SMV, the results that they convey are on verification test cases made up of hundreds of sequential elements and inputs well in the capacity range of BDD-based symbolic model checkers.

Furthermore, prior comparisons [sht00] leave open the question whether the difference in performance and capacity is due to the underlying technology--BDD versus SAT, or is due to the difference between bounded and unbounded model checking. Moreover, both in [bcrz99, sht00] no extensive expert configuration and tuning have been done in the extraction of the performance numbers for BDD-based model checkers in their comparison with tuned SAT-based bounded model checkers.

In order to understand the clear benefit of bounded model checking and SAT technology at a formal-verification setting, we undertook the task of developing industrial strength BMC using both BDD and SAT algorithms and have thus provided the means for a fair comparison. On one hand, we have optimized Intel's unbounded BDD-based model checker, Forecast, for bounded model checking. On the other hand, we have developed a state-of-the-art SAT-based bounded model checker, Thunder.

Since our interest in SAT technology was in addressing the productivity problem of the current formal verification techniques, we have evaluated the benefits of BDD-based and SAT-based bounded model checking with respect to productivity. We have built a performance benchmark made up of a large number of hard real-life falsification test cases chosen from the unbounded Forecast's internal benchmark base. For each problem, we have built a falsification version that results in a counterexample of minimal length k, and a verification version of length k-1. In this manner, we have evaluated the power of SAT based bounded model checking for both verification and falsification.

In order to understand the benefits of SAT technology with respect to productivity, we tuned both Thunder and Forecast for the domain of bounded model checking and came up with a default best configuration for both engines. Since it is very hard to measure the tuning effort, we have compared tuned and default Forecast versus default Thunder. Surprisingly the default and best setting for Thunder was the same for all the test cases in the benchmark. Although Thunder significantly outperformed untuned Forecast; its performance was very similar to tuned Forecast for almost all the cases except for a few cases that could not be verified by any setting of Thunder. The performance benchmark therefore showed a clear productivity gain achieved by Thunder in the drastic reduction of user ingenuity and tuning effort in running the tools.

The capacity benchmark that we extracted by eliminating the pruning directives on all the test cases of the performance benchmark demonstrated that Thunder with no pruning effort could verify most of the test cases. These benchmarks, corresponding to circuits with thousands of sequential elements and inputs, are far beyond the capacity of Forecast and of any other BDD-based symbolic model checker. Therefore, the conclusion from the capacity benchmark was that Thunder has impressive capacity (can verify designs with over thousands of inputs and sequential elements) and potentially increases the productivity of the verification engineer by reducing the pruning effort significantly.

Thunder reads in RTL models, e.g., written in Verilog or VHDL, and in addition a set of assumptions and assertions expressed in our new temporal specification language, ForSpec [arm01]. Thunder is compatible with a wide-range of recently developed, state-of-the-art SAT solvers (e.g., GRASP, SATO, Prover). We report the benchmark results of Thunder based on a new SAT solver SIMO, developed at the University of Genova. SIMO is based on the Davis-Logemann-Loveland procedure (DLL) [dll62]. Similar to other state-of-the-art DLL-based algorithms, SIMO's strength is based on: (1) advanced procedures for *choosing* the next variable on which to split the search and (2) advanced *backtracking* mechanisms. SIMO features various forms of backtracking. In particular, besides the standard backtrack to the last choice point, SIMO implements a *Conflict-directed BackJumping schema, CBJ*, and *CBJ-with-Learning* [dec90a, pro93a, bs97a]. *CBJ-with-Learning* algorithm was chosen to be the best setting following intensive benchmarking with real-life test cases. In the context of heuristics to choose the splitting variable, we evaluated a wide range of known dynamic heuristics, both greedy (e.g., MOMS) and Boolean Constraint Propagation (BCP) [fre95a] based (e.g., Unit), and introduced a new dynamic heuristics, *UniRel2*, that proves to be the best for the Intel bounded-model checking benchmark. Unirel2 is a domain specific heuristics, since it gives preference to model variables, and also takes into account the simplification imposed on the auxiliary variables. Previous evaluation [sht00] of dynamic splitting heuristics reported static heuristics to be a clear winner over dynamic heuristics. Our results are not compatible with [sht00] in the sense that for our benchmark the dynamic splitting heuristics, Unirel2, worked much better than the available static heuristics in SIMO. Since we have not evaluated Unirel2 versus the original static heuristics introduced in [sht00], our conclusion is that dynamic splitting heuristics tuned for the domain of bounded model checking as is Unirel2 can be very robust for industrial size designs. Our intensive evaluation clearly pinpointed *Unirel2* and *CBJ-with-Learning* as the winning setting of Thunder for Intel's benchmark.

Our BDD-based model checker, Forecast, is built on top of a powerful BDD package, and contains most of the recently published state-of-the-art algorithms for symbolic model checking. In addition to the *unbounded* model checking algorithms in Forecast we developed *bounded* ones in order to give BDD based BMC a fair chance in the comparisons against Thunder. We tried to get an automatic (not requiring additional human tuning) default setting for Forecast as we have done for Thunder. We were not able to get a default setting that is good for all the test cases and an automatic static BDD variable ordering that beats the best humanly tuned variable order. Therefore, we compare both best default setting and tuned setting for Forecast with default setting of Thunder. The comparison reveals the productivity boost gained by Thunder, since the default setting of Thunder clearly outperforms the default setting of Forecast and is very competitive with the tuned Forecast setting.

As a summary, the unique contribution of this work is in the adaptation of unbounded BDD-based model checking to bounded model checking, optimizations of SAT based methods (mainly dynamic splitting heuristics) for bounded model checking and a thorough and fair evaluation of bounded model checking on SAT versus BDD based model checking making use of a rich set of real-life complex verification and falsification test cases.

The paper is organized as follows. In Section 2, we give an overview on Thunder and present experimental results that demonstrate the best SIMO and CNF generator configuration for Thunder. Section 3 describes our effort to achieve best results for BMC on BDD. In Section 4 we present experimental results comparing Thunder with Forecast. Section 5 describes our conclusion and future research directions.

2 Thunder: Bounded Model Checker on SAT

Thunder, our bounded checker on SAT technology, resembles the work of Bierre et al. [bccz99] in the reduction of the symbolic model checking problem to a bounded model checking problem and consequently to the problem of propositional satisfiability. Thunder, which makes use of a powerful DLL-based engine, SIMO, as its default SAT engine, is also compatible with other state-of-the-art SAT engines such as GRASP, SATO, Prover Plug-In™ [PPI, sta89]. We report in this paper our experience of Thunder with SIMO since our contribution is mainly in the tuning of DLL-based algorithms in the context of bounded-model checking.

2.1   Transforming the Bounded Model Checking Problem to Formulas

The basic idea in SAT based bounded model checking is to consider only paths of bounded length k and to construct a propositional formula that is satisfiable iff there is a counterexample of length k. BMC is concerned with finding counterexamples of limited length k, and thus it targets falsification and partial verification rather than full verification.

In order to fully verify a property one needs to look for longer and longer counterexamples by incrementing the bound k, until reaching the diameter of the finite state machine [bccz99]. However, the diameter might be very large in some examples, and there is no easy way to compute it in advance. This issue is addressed in [sss00] which incorporates induction in BMC that allows the algorithm to be used both for verification and falsification.

Assume that we have a finite state machine M with initial states I and transition relation TR, where both I and TR are encoded symbolically as Boolean formulas. Assume also, that we want to check if an invariance property P holds for all states reachable in a bounded number of steps. It is sufficient to focus only on invariance properties since the safety specifications expressed in our temporal language, ForSpec, are compiled into such invariance properties.

Our experience shows that the performance and capacity of Thunder is very dependent on the way we generate the propositional formulae describing the counterexample. Similarly to CMU's implementation of BMC, Thunder provides different settings that we describe below. We also provide experimental results that compare the various settings.

The propositional formula describing a path from s_0 to s_k requires s_0 to be an initial state and also that there is a transition from s_i to s_{i+1} for $0 \le i < k$:

$$Path(s_0,...,s_k) = I(s_0) \wedge TR(s_0, s_1) \wedge ... TR(s_{k-1}, s_k)$$

Thunder implements three different checks for a counterexample (similar to what is provided in CMU's BMC tool). The first one, referred to as *bound k*, looks for a violation of P in all the cycles from 0 to k:

$$Path(s_0,...,s_k) \wedge (\neg P(s_0) \vee ... \vee \neg P(s_k))$$

The second check, referred to as *exact k*, looks for a violation of P exactly in the last cycle k:

$$Path(s_0,...,s_k) \wedge \neg P(s_k)$$

Finally, the third check, referred to as *exact-assume k*, looks for a violation of P at cycle k and assumes P to be true in all the cycles from 0 to k-1:

$$Path(s_0,...,s_k) \wedge P(s_0) \wedge ... \wedge P(s_{k-1}) \wedge \neg P(s_k)$$

As expected, using *exact* or *exact-assume* is significantly faster than *bound*, but then they solve an easier problem. For the sake of a fair comparison with BDD model checking, all the results in this section are obtained with *bound*. We will return in section 5 to the *exact* and *exact-assume* checks, since they are the only ones who can cope with the capacity challenging examples presented there.

We also implemented the Bounded Cone of Influence (BCOI) optimization proposed in [bcrz99]. This optimization rarely negatively affects so we use it as a default, such that all the results below are obtained in the presence of BCOI. Our experiments used a DLL-based SAT solver, SIMO [tac00], described in the next section.

2.2   DLL Based Satisfiability Engine - SIMO

As many other modern SAT solvers, SIMO [tac00] is based on the well-known Davis-Logemann-Loveland (DLL) algorithm [dll62]. DLL assumes the propositional formula to be in Conjunctive Normal Form (CNF) and it employs a backtracking search. At each node of the search tree, DLL assigns a Boolean value to one of the variables that are not resolved yet. The search continues in the corresponding sub-tree after propagating the effects of the newly assigned variable, using Boolean Constraint Propagation (BCP) [fre95a]. BCP is based on iterative application of the unit clause rule. The procedure backtracks once a clause is found to be unsatisfiable, until either a satisfying assignment is found or the search tree is fully explored. The last case implies that the formula is unsatisfiable.

SIMO's strength is based on: (1) advanced *backtracking* mechanisms (2) advanced procedures for *choosing* the next variable on which to split the search. Besides the standard backtracking to the last choice point, SIMO implements also *Conflict-directed Back-Jumping* (CBJ) and *CBJ-with-Learning* [dec90a, pro93a, bs97a]. In Section 3.2.1, we explain at a high-level the *CBJ-with-Learning* algorithm which was chosen to be the best setting following intensive benchmarking with real-life test cases.

In the context of heuristics to choose the splitting variable, we compare several dynamic heuristics and introduce a new dynamic heuristics, *UniRel2*, that proves to be the best for the Intel bounded-model checking benchmark. Section 3.2.2 explains at a high level the heuristics that have been compared and the experimental results that justify our decision.

2.2.1 CBJ-with-Learning

Since the basic DLL algorithm relies on simple chronological backtracking, and most heuristics are targeted to select the literal that satisfies the largest number of clauses, it is not infrequent for DLL implementations to get stuck in possibly large sub-trees whose leaves are all dead-ends. This phenomenon occurs when some selection performed way up in the search tree is responsible for the constraints to be violated. The solution, borrowed from constraint network solving [dec92], is to jump back over the selections that were not at the root of the conflict, whenever one is found. The corresponding technique is widely known as *Conflict-directed Back-Jumping* (CBJ) [pro93]. It has been reported from the authors of RELSAT [bs97], GRASP [ss96] and SATO [zha97] that CBJ proved a very effective technique to deal with real-world instances.

It turns out that in all these solvers, CBJ is tightly coupled with another technique, called *Learning*. CBJ can be very effective in "shaking" the solver from a sub-tree whose leafs are all dead ends, but since the cause of the conflict is discarded as soon as it gets mended, the solver may get repeatedly stuck in such local minima. To escape this pattern, some sort of global knowledge is needed: the causes of the conflicts may be stored to avoid repeating the same mistake over and over again. This process is usually called no-good or recursive learning. Our BMC experience with SIMO agrees with previous work [bs97] that reports that CBJ with relevance learning is essential for good performance in the domain of SAT.

2.2.2 Splitting Heuristics

The splitting heuristic needs to decide which variable to assign next from the set S of variables that were not assigned yet. Since the conversion to CNF [pg86] introduces many additional variables (one for each non-atomic sub-formula of the original formula) we restrict the set S to the variables of the original formula, also called *relevant* variables. As pointed out in [sht00], this optimization is very useful and our results confirm this conclusion.

SIMO features a static splitting heuristic that relies on a user-supplied order to choose each splitting variable among relevant variables. Additionally, SIMO has a wide range of dynamic splitting heuristics that showed to be very effective in our experience with bounded model checking.

SIMO's dynamic splitting heuristics fall broadly into two categories: BCP heuristics, and greedy heuristics. BCP heuristics choose the splitting variable by tentatively assigning truth-values to (some of) the unassigned variables and then performing BCP. In this way the exact amount of simplification produced by each possible assignment can be calculated. Moreover, BCP heuristics can detect *failed literals*, i.e., literals that once assigned produce a contradiction after a single sweep of BCP. *Greedy* heuristics choose the splitting variable by *estimating* the amount of simplification caused by an assignment. Relying on an estimate rather than an exact calculation makes greedy heuristics faster than BCP heuristics, but also less precise and incapable of detecting failed literals. In this regard, greedy heuristics can be seen as an approximation to the BCP ones. Both types of heuristics branch on the variable that produces- or is estimated to produce- the maximum simplification in the formula. We used heuristics from both categories in our experiments with SIMO.

Among the greedy heuristics, we have used *Moms* and *Morel* heuristics. For each open variable *p*, *Moms* computes the number of binary clauses in which *p* occurs, and uses this quantity as the expected amount of simplification when assigning *p*. *Morel* works in the same way as *Moms*, but its choice is restricted to relevant variables only.

From the class of BCP heuristics, we have used three BCP heuristics, called *Unit*, *Unirel*, and *Unirel2*. For each open variable *p*, *Unit* tentatively assigns both *p* and $\neg p$: for both choices, BCP is performed and the number of unit-propagated variables is collected. If the heuristic yields a contradiction by assigning *p* (resp. $\neg p$) then it immediately assigns $\neg p$ (resp. *p*): if also $\neg p$ (resp. *p*) fails, then *Unit* halts and backtracks, otherwise it goes on in trying to select a variable. If all variables are assigned during this process or all the clauses are satisfied, *Unit* reports that a satisfying assignment was found. *Unirel* works in the same way as *Unit*, except it considers only relevant variables when collecting the number of unit-propagated variables. *Unirel2*, on the other hand, tentatively assigns only relevant variables, but it collects the number of all the unit-propagated variables.

We compared the performance of *Moms, Morel, Unit, Unirel, Unirel2*, and *Static* heuristics in SIMO making use of a benchmark of 26 real-life test cases. The benchmark is evenly distributed between falsification and verification test cases. Unirel2 heuristics provides a clear performance and capacity boost over the other heuristics. We chose to report only timings of the dynamic heuristics, since SIMO does not include all the known static heuristics. The current static heuristics in SIMO performed much worse than the dynamic heuristics for our benchmark. However, in order to derive any accountable conclusions on the effectiveness of dynamic heuristics versus static heuristics, SIMO needs to be enriched with the latest static heuristics for bounded model checking [sht00].

For all the runs reported in Figure 1, we use 3-hour time-out limit. As can be seen, Moms heuristics is significantly inferior to Unit and Unirel2 (except for circuit12). On the other hand, Unirel2 provides a clear performance boost over Unit heuristics.

In the analysis of the results, let us concentrate on three representative heuristics from each category: Moms, Unit and Unirel2. Moms is the basic and most popular greedy heuristics. Unit is the simplest of the BCP-based heuristics, and Unirel2 is the overall fastest of the 6 (Static, Moms, Morel, Unit, Unirel, Unirel2) that we have tried. Our results indicate clearly that BCP heuristics perform better than greedy heuristics for this domain of problems. BCP heuristics take into account the structure of the CNF formula which closely reflects the structure of the original formula (before the CNF conversion). Indeed, in the CNF formula there are (possibly long) chains of implications. With BCP heuristics, a literal occurring at the top of a chain is preferred to a literal occurring in the middle of the same chain. This is not guaranteed to be the case with greedy heuristics, where only the number of occurrences counts. Moreover, both Unit and Unirel2 feature the failed literal detection mechanism that

Moms heuristics is missing. This mechanism allows Unit and Unirel2 to perform more simplifications at each node.

Unirel2 considers only the relevant variables (i.e., the model variables) whereas Unit heuristics considers all the variables as a candidate for splitting. Although the greedy nature of Unit heuristics makes it more accurate, in most cases the time spent to choose a variable will be much more in Unit than Unirel2 (since the number of all the variables can be significantly larger than the number of relevant variables). Therefore, to give up a bit on quality provides better overall performance for Unirel2.

3 Forecast – A BDD-Based Symbolic Model Checker

Several recent papers [bcrz99, bccz99, bccfz99, sht00] compare traditional BDD - based model checking with SAT-based model checking, showing that in many cases SAT technology dramatically outperforms BDD technology. Such comparisons (except [bccz99]), however, neglect one crucial aspect that distinguishes the two approaches. Traditional BDD-based model checking searches for counterexamples of *unbounded* length. In contrast, SAT-based model checking searches for counterexamples of a predetermined *bounded* length. Thus, prior comparison leaves open the question whether the difference in performance is due to the underlying technology--BDD vs. SAT, or is due to the difference between bounded and unbounded model checking. To answer this question, we undertook the task to first adapt a BDD-based model checker to bounded model checking and then compare its performance to a SAT-based model checker.

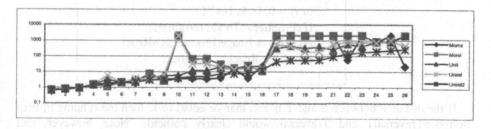

Fig. 1. Comparison of Thunder run-time with the dynamic heuristics Moms, Morel, Unit, Unirel and Unirel2   for a benchmark of 26 test cases on a logarithmic scale. In the reported runs, time-out has been set to 3 hours. The x axis indicates the test case where the y axis indicates the Thunder run-time. We can clearly see that Moms and Unit heuristics times out for 6 and 1 out of 26 test cases, respectively.

3.1   Adapting Forecast for Bounded Model Checking

Forecast is a BDD-based model checker developed and deployed in Intel, using an in-house BDD package. Forecast can run in two modes. In the standard mode, Forecast applies either forward or backward breadth-first-search *traversal* from a source set S to a target set T with respect to a transition relation TR, when *Image* refers to a pre-image or post-image operation:

```
Traversal(S,T,R)
Reach=Frontier=S
while (Frontier ≠ ∅) {
    if (Frontier ∩T≠ ∅) terminate;
    Frontier := Image(Frontier,R) - Reach
    Reach := Reach ∪ Frontier
}
```

A difficulty often faced by standard traversal is the excessive growth of the Frontier or the Reach set ("state explosion"). To address the former problem, Forecast can apply a *prioritized-traversal* algorithm, see [fkzvf00]. In prioritized traversal mode, we split the Frontier into two balanced parts when its BDD size reaches some predetermined threshold. Thus, instead of maintaining one frontier, the algorithm maintains several frontiers, organized in a priority queue. A given traversal step consists of choosing one frontier set and applying the image operator to that set. Thus, prioritized traversal can be viewed as a mixed bread-first/depth-first search.

How can we adapt standard traversal and prioritized traversal to bounded model checking? The first change is to bound the length of the traversal.

```
BoundedTraversal1(S,T,R,k)
I :=0
Reach=Frontier=S
For (I = 0; I< k; I++) {
    If (Frontier ∩T≠ ∅) terminate;
    Frontier := Image(Frontier,R)-Reach
    Reach := Reach ∪ Frontier;
}
```

If the distance between S and T is less than or equal to k, then the running time of BoundedTraversal1 and Traversal would clearly coincide. Note, however, that termination is not an issue in bounded traversal. Thus, from a termination point of view, there is no need to maintain Reach.

```
BoundedTraversal(S,T,R,k)
Frontier=S
For (I = 0; I< k; I++) {
    If (Frontier ∩T≠ ∅) terminate;
    Frontier := Image(Frontier,R);
}
```

However, besides guaranteeing termination, *Reach* was used in the classic algorithm to cut down on the size of *Frontier*. Thus, one would expect BoundedTraversal to run into huge Frontiers, resulting in weak performance. This is where prioritized traversal comes to the rescue. As before, we split the Frontier whenever its BDD gets larger than some threshold, maintaining a set of frontiers in a priority queue. With each frontier we maintain its distance from the source set S. We choose frontiers and apply the image operator, making sure that the bound is never exceeded. This results in a prioritized version of BoundedTraversal.

So far we have treated S and T in a symmetrical fashion. In practice, however, the initial states are defined in terms of many state variables, while the error state is defined in terms of a small number of state variables, called the *error variables*. Cone-of-influence (COI) reduction algorithms take advantage of that by eliminating state variables that cannot have any effect on the error variables. In the context of BMC, one can be more aggressive and eliminate variables that cannot have an effect on the error variables in a bounded number of clock cycles. This optimization called Bounded Cone-of-Influence (BCOI) was introduced in [bcrz99].

Forecast has a "lazy"mode [yt00] that effectively applies a BCOI reduction. This mode is effective only in backward traversal – for each pre-image, one identifies the relevant variables appearing in the frontier and builds a smaller TR based on those relevant variables. Naturally, this reduction is more effective when the Frontier has a small number of state variables, e.g., when the Frontier is close to the set of error states. We have adapted the "lazy model checking" mode of Forecast to BMC (i.e., we search for a counter-example for k pre-image steps).

3.2   Default Configuration for Forecast

Since we built the benchmark of bounded model checking from internal Intel's benchmark base[†] of Forecast, every test case had the best setting for unbounded Forecast meaning

- The right pruning directives to reduce the size of the model
- The best initial order that the FV expert user could get
- The best (CPU time-wise) configuration that the FV expert user could get

The time spent by the FV expert to get to the best initial order and tool configuration could not be derived from the   benchmark. Furthermore, the configuration in the benchmark base was for unbounded Forecast. In order to make a fair comparison with Thunder, in search for a best default setting, we experimented with three recent state-of-the-art algorithms of Forecast described in Section 3.1 : bounded prioritized-traversal, unbounded prioritized traversal [fkzvf00], and bounded lazy model checking. For all the runs a partitioned transition relation was used.

We present results achieved by Forecast under two different configurations.
- *Automatic* : the initial variable order is automatically computed by a static variable ordering algorithm
- *Semi-automatic* : the initial order is taken from the order that was calculated by previous runs of Forecast with dynamic reordering[‡]

[†] All the properties verified were safety properties.
[‡] This evaluation is similar to RB2 configuration in [sht00a]; however, in our case the order gets refined by the dynamic reordering output of more than one run of the model checker.

Both of the configurations were run with dynamic reordering with the threshold of 500K BDD nodes (meaning dynamic reordering will be turned on when the total number of BDD nodes allocated exceeds 500K).

TestCase	Bound	Forecast Lazy (secs)	Forecast Prioritized (secs)	Forecast Prioritized Unbounded (secs)
Circuit 1	5	27.3	1340	114.1
Circuit 2	7	1.1	0.56	2.1
Circuit 3	7	2.1	15.00	106.1
Circuit 4	11	9.1	2233.00	6189.0
Circuit 5	11	TIMEOUT	107800.00	4196.2
Circuit 6	10	TIMEOUT	TIMEOUT	2354.1
Circuit 7	20	4187.2	TIMEOUT	2795.1
Circuit 8	28	TIMEOUT	TIMEOUT	TIMEOUT
Circuit 9	28	TIMEOUT	TIMEOUT	TIMEOUT
Circuit 10	8	TIMEOUT	TIMEOUT	2487.1
Circuit 11	8	TIMEOUT	TIMEOUT	2940.5
Circuit 12	10	TIMEOUT	TIMEOUT	5524.1
Circuit 13	37	TIMEOUT	TIMEOUT	TIMEOUT

Table 1. Automatic Setting Comparisons. Forecast performance comparisons for different configurations with automatically generated initial order. A time-out limit of 3 hours has been set.

Table 1 and Table 2 summarizes the time spent by Forecast in verifying these test cases when a time limit of 3 hours has been set. All experiments were run on HP J6000 work station with 2 Gigabyte memory. Table 1 reports Forecast runs when the initial order is automatically generated by the tool and Table 2 reports the results when Forecast is given a semi-manual order (i.e. the enhanced order is obtained by running Forecast with dynamic ordering several times).

The bottom line of Table 2 is the criticality of "a good initial order" for good performance of a BDD-based model checking. Without a good order, Forecast is far from being competitive. Although unbounded prioritized traversal does not outperform the other two algorithms for the test cases that all three complete, we selected it to be the winner configuration for the automatic default setting, since it times out much less than the other two (only three times). Although the success of unbounded prioritized traversal versus the bounded version is intriguing, we believe it to be due to the better suitability of the initial variable orders to the unbounded prioritized traversal.

Table 2 dilutes the effect of bad initial order; however still no winner configuration for all or most of the test cases can be chosen indicating the difficulty to set an always winning setting for BDD-based model checkers. Lazy model checking in Table 2 for the test cases that it can complete beats the other two. On the other hand, it cannot complete 6 verification cases in the time set. No clear winner could be found between the bounded and unbounded versions of Prioritized Traversal. Although performance of prioritized traversal is worse than lazy model checking for all the test cases where lazy model checking completes, it times out less (4 times).

As can be seen no good (overall winning) default setting could be selected for Forecast based on the results of Table 1 and Table 2. We have selected the unbounded prioritized traversal as the default setting, since it is a clear winner for Table 1 and not performing worse than the others for Table 2; moreover, the setting in Table 1 is more fair for comparison with default setting of Thunder, since the initial order selection time is included in the overall Thunder run time.   Table 2 numbers do not include the time spent in the generation of the initial order time (i.e, the runs of symbolic model checking to generate good orders). However, note that although unbounded prioritized traversal is not guaranteed to find the counter-example of the minimal length, for all the falsification test cases that we have tried a counter-example of length k or less was reported.

TestCase	Bound	Forecast Lazy (secs)	Forecast PrioritizedBounded (secs)	Forecast Prioritized UnBounded (secs)
Circuit 1	5	7.4	21.0	21.8
Circuit 2	7	1.6	1.8	1.9
Circuit 3	7	2.3	5.2	5.6
Circuit 4	11	6.7	89.9	241
Circuit 5	11	6432.5	64.2	80.4
Circuit 6	10	TIMEOUT	44.6	36.8
Circuit 7	20	134.3	7250.2	TIMEOUT
Circuit 8	28	TIMEOUT	1421.1	1287.5
Circuit 9	28	TIMEOUT	TIMEOUT	1040.3
Circuit 10	8	147.4	693.1	694.6
Circuit 11	8	143.9	260.6	261.0
Circuit 12	10	2379.2	4657.0	1041.5
Circuit 13	37	TIMEOUT	TIMEOUT	4188.0
Circuit 14	41	TIMEOUT	1864.36	TIMEOUT
Circuit 15	12	423.1	TIMEOUT	TIMEOUT
Circuit 16	40	16.1	783.0	TIMEOUT
Circuit 17	40	TIMEOUT	TIMEOUT	33.1

Table 2. Semi-automatic Setting Comparions. Forecast performance comparisons for different configurations with semi-automatic generated good initial order.

4 Comparison of Thunder and Forecast

We evaluated bounded Thunder versus bounded Forecast with respect to performance and capacity. For each of these, we studied the aspect of productivity.

Our performance benchmark consists of 15 real-life falsification test cases. All the 15 test cases were from the unbounded Forecast benchmark base (meaning all the test cases could be falsified at special settings of Forecast). Since unbounded version of Forecast finds counterexamples of minimal length, we knew beforehand the minimal length k for the counterexamples that can be generated for each test case. Therefore, we could generate for each test case a bounded k-1 verification version. Furthermore, we added to our benchmark two hard verification cases where we requested both Forecast and Thunder to verify that no counter-example exists. In this manner, we evaluated the power of bounded Thunder versus the power of bounded Forecast for both verification and falsification test cases.

We built the capacity benchmark (made up of 11 test cases) by eliminating the pruning directives of some of the test cases in the performance benchmark and we added brand-new test cases clearly surpassing the capacity limits of Forecast and other state-of-the-art model checkers (i.e., verification test case with over 2000 sequential elements and inputs).

4.1   Analysis of Performance Benchmark Results

Table 3 compares the performance of default Thunder setting with default and tuned settings of Forecast. The default setting of Forecast (prioritized traversal + dynamic reordering + partitioned transition relation + automatic initial ordering) is far from being competitive. For tuned Forecast results, we report the configuration that has worked best. All the tuned configurations, except the ones explicitly reported do not activate dynamic reordering. As can be seen they include variations of transition relation (*tr part (partitioned)*, *tr mono (monolithic)*), variations of priorities (*min size, max states, BFS, DFS*) for prioritized search and variations of configurations for lazy model checking.

The comparison of default settings of Thunder and Forecast reveals that Forecast's default performance and capacity is far below Thunder's. On the other hand, the comparison results reveal that Thunder at default setting provides compatible performance to tuned Forecast results. For 6 benchmarks out of 17, Thunder default settings beat tuned Forecast setting's results by 2 to 3X (See in Table 3 the comparison on Circuit 3, 5, 8, 9, 10, and 11). For Circuit 13, Thunder default performance wins over Forecast tuned performance by 9X. Nevertheless, tuned Forecast results are 2 to 3 X better for Circuit 7 and Circuit 12. Thus, there is no clear winner with respect to performance when default Thunder and tuned Forecast's performance is compared. The only conclusion is that Thunder gives a significant productivity boost. In short, unlike Forecast Thunder does not require high tuning effort to perform well.

Through the performance benchmark, we also tested the capacity of Thunder versus Forecast. Three test cases that could be easily verified by tuned Forecast setting could not be verified by any heuristics of Thunder (Circuit 14 (bound 40, 41), Circuit 16 (bound 40), Circuit 17 (bound 60)). Although Thunder could not solve (except for Circuit 16) the bounded model checking problem for these test cases, it could solve a variation of the problem (exact, exact-assume described in Section 2.1). As seen in Figure 2, although *exact* and *exact-assume* modes are significantly faster than the *bound mode*, the problem solved is simpler. By exact-assume, we are verifying the existence of a counterexample of exactly length k. Clearly, the solution of k exact-assume verification cases where the existence of a counter-example of length 1 to length k are verified will be equivalent to verifying *bound k* problem. Although too time consuming, the fact that Thunder could solve the exact-assume problem for most of the hard test cases for the bound version, indicates that the solution of these problems is in the capacity range of Thunder.

4.2   Analysis of Capacity Benchmark Results

We generated the capacity benchmark by eliminating the pruning directives set to get the model checking cases through. The size of the test cases in the capacity benchmark containing thousands of sequential elements and inputs is clearly far beyond the capacity of Forecast and any other state-of-the art BDD-based symbolic model checker. Therefore, no results are reported for Forecast. Thunder has successfully verified a wide range of the test cases in the capacity benchmark indicating a clear win over Forecast for un-pruned test cases. The fact that Thunder could verify these test cases without the extensive pruning effort required for BDD-based model checker is also a clear indication of productivity gain achieved by Thunder.

In Table 4, we report the CPU time of the overall run of Thunder for 11 test cases. The test cases, circuit 1, 3 and 4, are the same test cases that have been used for the performance evaluation. For this benchmark, the pruning directives set by the user to get the verification fit the capacity of BDD-based model checking have been eliminated.   We report the number of latches and inputs before and after the application of automatic pruning operation (cone-of-influence reduction with respect to property). As can be seen, using Thunder, test cases with over 9000 latches and inputs could be verified without requiring any additional manual pruning effort. In Table 4, the bounded model checking problem fed into Thunder SAT engine represents a verification case (i.e., Ncircuit8) of total 6832 inputs and sequential elements representing 121786 SAT variables and 358334 clauses. These results, although in the domain of bounded model checking, are a clear indication of the promise in this technology to establish model checking as a robust and popular technique at industrial validation environments.

Fig. 2. Performance comparison results of bound and exact-assume modes of Thunder for the same k. The x axis represents the test cases when the y axis represents Thunder run-time in seconds.

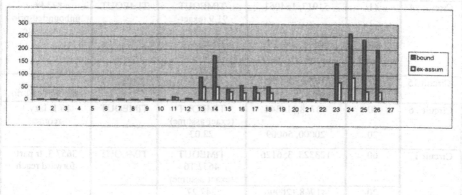

TestCase	Bound	Variables, Clauses in Thunder	Thunder Default (secs)	Bounded Forecast Default (secs)	Bounded Forecast Tuned(secs), Configuration
Circuit 1	5	5055, 14690	2.43	114	2.80, lazy
	4	3987, 11559	1.59		
Circuit 2	7	2000, 5727	0.81	2	0.56, lazy
	6	1688, 4820	0.64		
Circuit 3	7	3419, 8977	2.01	106	1.29, lazy
	6	2908, 7623	1.17		
Circuit 4	11	6740, 18884	1.91	6189	1.04, lazy
	10	6085, 17030	1.53		
Circuit 5	11	10258, 29515	10.12	4196	35.14, unbounded-prio, tr part
	10	9303, 26746	8.78		
Circuit 6	10	8829, 25587	5.51	2354	8.34, unbounded-prio, tr part
	9	7918, 22927	4.85		
Circuit 7	20	28769, 85033	236.29	2795	76.88, unbounded-prio: minimum size
	19	27316, 80732	140.65		
Circuit 8	28	38836, 116803	45.66	TIMEOUT	141.00, unbounded-prio: BFS, tr mono
	27	37427, 112558	52.85		
Circuit 9	28	37451, 112465	39.96	TIMEOUT	85.50, unbounded-prio : max states
	27	36092, 108377	50.65		
Circuit 10	8	8734, 25631	5.01	2487	13.90, lazy
	7	7517, 22031	5.79		
Circuit 11	8	8734, 25631	5.01	2940	13.89, lazy
	7	7517, 22031	5.76		
Circuit 12	10	8331, 24497	378.05	5524	159.20, unbounded-prio, tr part
	9	7429, 21826	139.47		
Circuit 13	37	60779, 169824	195.15	TIMEOUT	1586.00, unbounded-prio
	36	59118, 165175	217.75		
Circuit 14	41	51917, 154061	TIMEOUT 91.9 (exact-assume)	TIMEOUT	833.96, unbounded-prio maxstates
	40	50616, 150220	TIMEOUT 83.88(exact-assume)		
Circuit 15	12	9894, 29138	1070.65	TIMEOUT	17.31, unbounded-prio
	11		4209.1		
Circuit 16	40	40718,114344	TIMEOUT (exact-assume)	TIMEOUT	16.1, lazy + reorder
	20	20000, 56009	22.03		
Circuit 17	60	123323, 356126	TIMEOUT 4652.76 (exact-assume)	TIMEOUT	3657.3, tr part, forward reach
	20	41968,120996	247.27		

Table 3. Performance comparison results of default Thunder versus default and tuned Forecast. For Forecast, no timing for bound k-1 is reported (clearly it is less than the time reported for bound k).

Unpruned Test Cases	Bound	Num. Latches + Inputs before Automatic Pruning	Num. Latches + Inputs after Automatic Pruning	Variables, Clauses	Thunder time (secs)
Circuit 1	5	12011	152	6831, 19759	6.1
	4	12011	152	5403, 15591	5.1
Circuit 3	7	7054	0.81	24487, 65332	96.1
	6	7054	0.64	200552, 54774	16.37
Circuit 4	11	6586	2.01	119248, 353400	78.61
	10	6586	1.17	107838, 319404	68.2
Ncircuit 6	5	9704	1.91	21351, 61499	29.39
Ncircuit 7	5	17262	1.53	TIMEOUT	TIMEOUT
Ncircuit 8	6	6832	10.12	121786, 358334	576.24
Ncircuit 9	11	3321	8.78	35752, 105268	73.32
Ncircuit 10	6	1457	5.51	50578, 149668	267.91

Table 4. Results from the Capacity Benchmark.

5 Conclusions

In this paper, we have reported our effort to develop industrial strength BMC and the impressive productivity gain achieved by using SAT-based BMC (Thunder) versus BDD-based BMC (Forecast). This gain is achieved by drastic reduction in the required user ingenuity and tuning effort in running the tools. Our work agrees with previous work [bccz99, bcrz99, sht00] in the observation that SAT-based BMC can outperform BDD-based BMC. We show that this statement holds mainly in comparison of SAT-based BMC with untuned BDD-based BMC supporting our conclusion on productivity boost of SAT. Moreover, the evaluation of SAT-based BMC on verification test cases of over thousands of inputs and sequential elements reveals its outstanding capacity to verify designs far beyond the capacity ballpark of the state-of-the-art BDD-based model checkers.

The tuning effort that we have invested to get best default setting for SAT-based BMC introduces a new dynamic heuristics, *Unirel2*, which is a winner for Intel's bounded model checking benchmark supporting the statement made on the productivity gain achieved by Thunder over Forecast.

Acknowledgements

We would like to thank Roy Armoni for his contribution to the development of the infrastructure of Thunder.

References

[abe00] P. A. Abdulla, P. Bjesse, and N. E'en. Symbolic reachability analisys based on SAT solvers. In Proc. of the 6th International Conference of Tools and Algorithms for Construction and Analisys of Systems (TACAS 2000), volume 1785 of LNCS, pages 411-425, Berlin, 2000. Springer.

[arm01] R.Armoni, L.Fix, R.Gerth, B.Ginsburg, T.Kanza, S.Mador-Haim, E.Singerman, A.Tiemeyer, M.Y.Vardi. ForSpec: A Formal Temporal Specification Language, Submitted to ICCAD'01

[bee96a] I.Beer, S.Ben-David, C.Eisner, A.Landver. "RuleBase: An industry-oriented formal verification tool". In Proc. Design Automation Conference 1996 (DAC'96).

[bee97a] I.Beer, C.Eisner, D. Geist, L.Gluhovsky, T.Heyman, A.Landver, P.Paanah, Y.Rodeh, G.Ronin, Y.Wolfsthal. "RuleBase: Model Checking at IBM", Proceedings of CAV'97.

[bcm92] J.R. Burch, E.M. Clarke, and K.L. McMillan. Symbolic model checking: 1020 states and beyond.Information and Computation, 98:142-170, 1992.

[bcrz99] Armin Biere, Edmund Clarke, Richard Raimi, and Yunshan Zhu. "Verifying Safety Properties of a PowerPC Microprocessor Using Symbolic Model Checking without BDDs". Proc. of Computer Aided Verification, 1999 (CAV'99).

[bccz99] A. Biere, A Cimatti, E. M. Clarke, and Y. Zhu. "Symbolic model checking without BDDs". TACAS'99

[bccfz99] A. Biere, A. Cimatti, E. Clarke, M.Fujita, and Y. Zhu. Symbolic model checking using SAT procedures instead of BDDs. In Proc. of the 36th Conference on Design Automation (DAC '99), pages 317-320. ACM Press, 1999.

[bry92] R. E. Bryant. Symbolic Boolean manipulation with ordered binary-decision diagrams. ACM Computing Surveys, 24(3):293-318, September 1992.

[bs97] R. J. Bayardo, Jr. and R. C. Schrag, "Using CSP Look-Back Techniques to Solve Real-World SAT Instances", pages 203-208, Proc. AAAI, 1997.

[dll62] M. Davis and G. Logemann and D. Loveland, "A machine program for theorem proving", Journal of the ACM, vol. 5, 1962.

[dec90a] R. Dechter, "Enhancement Schemes for Constraint Processing: Backjumping, Learning, and Cutset Decomposition", Artificial Intelligence, pages 273-312, vol. 41, n.3, 1990.

[fkzvf00a] R.Fraer, G.Kamhi, B.Ziv, M.Vardi, L.Fix, "Efficient Reachability Computation Both for Verification and Falsification", Proceedings of International Conference on Computer-Aided Design, (CAV'00).

[fre95a] J.W. Freeman, "Improvements to propositional satisfiability search algorithms", PhD Thesis. University of Pennsylvania, 1995.

[mcm93] K.L. McMillan. Symbolic Model Checking: an Approach to the State Explosion Problem. Kluwer Academic Publishers, 1993.

[pg86] D.A. Plaisted and S. Greenbaum, "A Structure-preserving Clause Form Translation", Journal of Symbolic Computation, vol.2, pages=293-304, 1986.

[PPI] *Prover 4.0 Application Programming Reference Manual*, Prover Technology AB, 2000. PPI-01-ARM-1.

[pro93a] P. Prosser, "Hybrid algorithms for the constraint satisfaction problem", Computational Intelligence, vol. 9, n. 3, pages 268-299, 1993.

[sht00] O. Shtrichman, "Tuning SAT checkers for Bounded Model-Checking" Proc. of Computer Aided Verification, 2000 (CAV'00).

[sss00] M. Sheeran, S. Singh and G. Staalmarck, "Checking safety properties using induction and a SAT solver" Proceedings of Formal Methods in Computer Aided Design 2000 (FMCAD00)

[ss96] J.P. Marques Silva and Karem A. Sakallah. GRASP - a new search algorithm for satisfiability.Technical report, University of Michigan, April 1996.

[ss98] M. Sheeran and G. Stalmarck. A tutorial on Stalmarck's proof procedure for propositional logic. In Proc. of the 2nd International Conference on Formal Methods in Computer Aided Design (FMCAD '98), volume 1522 of LNCS, pages 82-99, Berlin, 1998. Springer.

[sta89] G. Stalmarck. System for Determining Propositional Logic Theorems by Applying Values and Rules to Triplets that are Generated From Boolean Formula. Swedish Patent No. 467076 (approved 1992), US Patent No. 5276897 (1994), European Patent No. 0403454 (1995), 1989.

[tac00] A. Tacchella. "SAT Based decision procedures for knowledge representation and Formal Verification". PhD Thesis. University of Genova. 2000.

[wbcg00] P. F. Williams, A. Biere, E. M. Clarke, and A. Gupta. Combining Decision Diagrams and SAT Procedures for Efficient Symbolic Model Checking. In Proc. of the 12th International Conference on Computer Aided Verification (CAV 2000), volume 1855 of LNCS, pages 124-138, Berlin, 2000. Springer.

[yt00] J.Yang, A.Tiemeyer." Lazy Symbolic Model Checking". DAC'00.

[zha97] H. Zhang. SATO: An efficient propositional prover. In William McCune, editor, Proceedings of the 14th International Conference on Automated deduction, volume 1249 of LNAI, pages 272-275, Berlin, July13-17 1997. Springer.

Finding Bugs in an Alpha Microprocessor Using Satisfiability Solvers

Per Bjesse[1], Tim Leonard[2], and Abdel Mokkedem[2]

[1] Chalmers University of Technology, Sweden
bjesse@cs.chalmers.se
[2] Compaq Computer Corporation, USA
{tim.leonard,abdel.mokkedem}@compaq.com

Abstract. We describe the techniques we have used to search for bugs in the memory subsystem of a next-generation Alpha microprocessor. Our approach is based on two model checking methods that use satisfiability (SAT) solvers rather than binary decision diagrams (BDDs).

We show that the first method, bounded model checking, can reduce the verification runtime from days to minutes on real, deep, microprocessor bugs when compared to a state-of-the-art BDD-based model checker. We also present experimental results showing that the second method, a version of symbolic trajectory evaluation that uses SAT-solvers instead of BDDs, can find as deep bugs, with even shorter runtimes. The tradeoff is that we have to spend more time writing specifications.

Finally, we present our experiences with the two SAT-solvers that we have used, and give guidelines for applying a combination of bounded model checking and symbolic trajectory evaluation to industrial strength verification.

The bugs we have found are significantly more complex than those previously found with methods based on SAT-solvers.

1 Introduction

Getting microprocessors right is a hard problem, with harsh punishments for failure. With current design methods, hundreds to thousands of bugs must be found and removed during the design of a new processor, and there are heavy economic incentives to get most of them out before first silicon.

Current designs are so complex that simulation-based methods are no longer adequate. Most companies in the industry, including at least AMD, Compaq, HP, IBM, Intel, Motorola, and Sun, have therefore investigated formal verification. Their choices of methods, tools, and application areas have varied, as has their level of success.

One of the areas we have concentrated on at Compaq is property verification for our microprocessor designs. Among other things, we have investigated the use of symbolic model checking [9] to find *Register Transfer Level* (RTL) bugs in a next-generation Alpha processor. Our goal in this work has been to find bugs, rather than to prove their absence, since there are many bugs to find in a design under development.

G. Berry, H. Comon, and A. Finkel (Eds.): CAV 2001, LNCS 2102, pp. 454–464, 2001.
© Springer-Verlag Berlin Heidelberg 2001

Our initial experiments with symbolic model checking convinced us that the capacity limits of many model checkers prevent us from finding bugs cost effectively. The best model checker we could find, an experimental version of Cadence SMV [10], needs several hours to days to check simple properties of heavily reduced components. As a consequence, we have also looked at model checking using satisfiability (SAT) solvers [3, 2, 16]. These methods have shown real promise, especially for finding bugs, when compared to BDD-based model checkers like SMV.

In this paper, we describe how we have applied two SAT-based verification techniques to find real bugs in the memory subsystem of the Alpha chip. The first technique, bounded model checking (BMC) [3], has previously been applied to industrial verification, but not for finding bugs of length anywhere near what we will describe. The second of these techniques, symbolic trajectory evaluation (STE) [12], has previously not been used together with SAT-solvers at all.

We compare the performance of SAT-based bounded model checking to state-of-the-art BDD-based model checking, and present results showing the usefulness of SAT-based STE. Our experiences are very positive: the use of SAT-based methods has reduced the time for finding certain bugs from days to a few minutes. We also compare the performance, when finding bugs in real designs, of the two SAT-solvers we have used: GRASP [15], and Prover Technology's PROVER [14] proof engine. Finally, we present guidelines for applying a combination of BMC and SAT-based STE to microprocessor bug finding.

Related Work. *Bounded model checking* [3] (BMC) was invented by Biere and coworkers as a method for using SAT-solvers to do model checking. BMC has previously been applied to bug finding for Power PC chips [4]. To our knowledge, BMC is the only SAT-based model checking method that has been used in realistic microprocessor verification.

In the Power PC verification, the authors did not model the environment of the designs under analysis. BMC quickly found short counterexamples to the properties being verified, but they were false failures due to illegal input sequences. BMC did well at this compared to BDD-based model checking, but the results said little about whether BMC could find real bugs, which are generally much deeper. We, on the other hand, present the results of searching for, and finding, real, deep bugs. One of our important contributions is therefore that we demonstrate that BMC together with cutting edge SAT-solvers has the capacity to find realistic bugs in industrial designs.

Symbolic trajectory evaluation (STE) is a model checking method invented by Seger and Bryant [12] that consists of an interesting mix of abstract interpretation and symbolic evaluation. STE is in industrial use, primarily for data path and memory verification, at companies including Intel [1] and Motorola. Up to now, STE has always been implemented using BDDs; the use of SAT-solvers to do STE has not been reported previously in the literature. Moreover, we apply symbolic trajectory evaluation to verification at the synchronous gate level—a fairly high level of abstraction for STE, which has previously been used predominantly at the transistor level.

There are other ways of doing SAT-based model checking than the ones that we discuss in this paper. We refer readers interested in these alternative approaches to [2, 16, 7, 13, 5].

The paper is organised as follows. In Sections 3 and 4, we give brief introductions to BMC and STE. We then describe the component that we have focused on, the merge buffer, and the process we have used to analyse it. After that, we go on to describe the actual use of the verification tools and the results. Finally, we give guidelines for using a combination of BMC and STE for heavy-duty industrial verification.

2   Preliminaries

In this paper, we will search for counterexamples to properties of synchronous gate-level hardware. Such circuits can be viewed as finite transition systems, where the states are value assignments to a vector $s = (s.0, \ldots, s.n)$ of boolean variables called the system's *state variables* [6]. The transition system for a given circuit can be represented as two propositional logic formulas [2]:

$Init(s)$	Initial states formula
$Trans(s, s')$	Transition relation formula

The first formula, $Init$, is a formula that characterises the initial states by evaluating to true exactly for the assignments to the state variables that are initial states. The second formula, $Trans$, evaluates to true for s and s' precisely when there is a transition from the state assigned to s to the state assigned to s'.

Our analyses take as inputs the formulas $Init$ and $Trans$ together with a description of a property to check. Such a property might for example be "a store instruction to an IO address is never discarded." The aim of the analyses is then to generate a trace, if one exists, where an IO store is thrown away.

In the case of BMC, we will specifically focus on detecting failures of *safety properties*. Informally, safety properties are properties of the form "in every reachable state of the system, the property P holds."

3   Bounded Model Checking

Bounded model checking tries to find bugs in a system by constructing a formula that is satisfiable precisely if there exists a length N or shorter trace violating a property given by the user. The BMC procedure feeds this formula to an external SAT-solver, and uses the returned assignment (if any) to extract a *failure trace*.

The bound N is given by the user, and will affect both the size of the generated formulas, and the length of the failure trace that can be detected. A negative answer from the SAT-solver for a given N does not mean that the whole system is safe, only that there are no failure traces of length N or shorter. BMC is thus used to find bugs, rather than to prove their absence.

We assume that the safety property we are interested in has been encoded as a propositional logic formula $Prop(s)$ that will evaluate to true exactly for the states fulfilling the property. Given the bound N, and the formulas $Init(s)$, $Trans(s, s')$, and $Prop(s)$, the BMC procedure constructs the following formula, which characterises failure traces of length N or shorter:

$$Init(s_1) \wedge$$
$$Trans(s_1, s_2) \wedge \ldots \wedge Trans(s_{N-1}, s_N) \wedge$$
$$(\neg Prop(s_1) \vee \ldots \vee \neg Prop(s_N))$$

If the SAT-solver returns an assignment to the state variables in $s_1 \ldots s_N$ that makes this formula true, then there exists an initial state s_1 in the system, from which we can reach another state s_k ($k \in \{1 \ldots N\}$) where the property fails. The BMC procedure can thus extract a failure trace from the assignment.

4 Symbolic Trajectory Evaluation

A symbolic trajectory evaluator takes $Trans(s, s')$ as input together with a so called *trajectory assertion* of the form $Ant \Rightarrow Cons$. The antecedent and consequent of the trajectory assertion, Ant and $Cons$, are lists of equal length, in each of which the ith entry says something about the system's state variables at time i. Informally, a trajectory assertion will be true with respect to a system if a trace of the system that agrees with the antecedent necessarily must agree with the consequent. The objective of symbolic trajectory evaluation is to generate a failure trace for the system that satisfies the antecedent, and violates the consequent.

As an example, assume that we have constructed a circuit whose state variables $s.a$ and $s.b$ should contain the **or** and the **and**, respectively, of the current and previous value of the state variable $s.i$. The following trajectory assertion specifies this property:

$$[\text{node } s.i \text{ is } x, \text{node } s.i \text{ is } y]$$
$$\Rightarrow$$
$$[\langle \cdot \rangle, \text{node } s.a \text{ is } x \vee y \text{ and node } s.b \text{ is } x \wedge y]$$

Here $\langle \cdot \rangle$ means "no requirements on the state variables", so the assertion can be read, "if we have a trace of the system where $s.i$ contains the value x at some time t, and $s.i$ contains the value y at time $t + 1$, then at time $t + 1$ $s.a$ and $s.b$ contains the logical **or** and the logical **and** of x and y, respectively."

In order to generate a failure trace, the trajectory evaluator first computes a boolean expression ok over the user-introduced variables x and y. This expression has the property that it evaluates to true for the assignments to x and y for which the antecedent guarantees the consequent (and no others). A key element of symbolic trajectory evaluation is that ok is constructed by symbolic reasoning in a four-valued logic. In addition to the two standard values $True$ and $False$, the four-valued logic contains the values X (unknown), and $\top$ (overspecified).

The value X is used to model unknown contents of state variables, and the value $\top$ is used to model the contents of state variables that are required to contain two different values at the same time.

When *ok* has been computed, the evaluator uses an external SAT-solver to check whether there exists an assignment to x and y that makes *ok* evaluate to false. If there exists such an assignment, there is a trace of the circuit that is consistent with the antecedent but violates the consequent. The trajectory evaluator then instantiates x and y with the falsifying values, and constructs a failure trace that is given back to the user.

5   The Merge Buffer

Alpha processors, like most state-of-the-art microprocessors, have a very hierarchical structure. A processor is divided into a handful of so called *boxes*, each responsible for dealing with a particular aspect of instruction execution. For example, the IBox handles instruction fetch, and the MBox executes memory-reference instructions. Each box is further divided into a handful of parts that we will call subboxes.

The subbox that is the focus of our attention in this paper is the *merge buffer*, an important component of the MBox for a next-generation Alpha chip. We chose the merge buffer as it is one of the most complex subboxes in the processor. Our hope is that if we can cost-effectively find bugs in this component, then we can use the same methods on most other subboxes.

The function of the merge buffer is to receive requests to write into memory, and to reduce the traffic on the memory bus by merging stores to the same physical address. In order to do the merging correctly, the merge buffer communicates with four other subboxes: (1) the *store queue*, where store instructions are saved until they are written out of the merge buffer; (2) the *load queue*, where load instructions are stored until they have received results from memory; (3) the *CBox*, which deals with the cache coherence protocol; and (4) the *backend tag module*.

The merge buffer is essentially a large buffer with a very complex policy for reading in entries, merging stores, and writing out stores to the memory. It has about 14 400 latches, 400 primary inputs, and 15 pipeline stages. The pipeline has complex feedback that prevents us from retiming away latches.

6   Analysis Cycle

In Figure 1 we show the analysis cycle that we have used to locate bugs in the merge buffer.

We start off with the original RTL description of the circuit. As the full-size merge buffer contains more than ten thousand latches—too much state to be feasible to verify using standard model checking technology—we need to reduce the size of the model. The idea is to remove portions of the state in the circuit in ways that do not alter the circuit behaviour with respect to the properties of interest. The most important reductions are *symmetry reductions* [8], which we

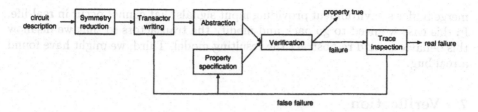

Fig. 1. Our Verification Flow.

use to reduce the number of buffer entries, address bits per entry, data bytes per entry, and bits per data byte.

We do not mind if some of our reductions do not preserve all possible properties of the circuit, as long as we can find problems in the reduced circuit that also are present in the full size circuit. The reason for this is that we are interested in finding bugs, as opposed to proving correctness. We are thus permitted to do ad-hoc reductions that are formally incorrect, but that preserve most of the interesting behaviour of the circuit.

After the reductions, the merge buffer has about 40 primary inputs. When the merge buffer is in use, these inputs will be connected to the four subboxes with which the merge buffer communicates. If we leave them unrestricted, the verification will be done under the assumption that any inputs can occur at any time. However, in order to function correctly, the merge buffer relies on assumptions about the behaviour of its environment. We therefore have to restrict the input to the merge buffer by adding *transactor* state machines that provide a verification environment that rules out input behaviours that could not arise in real use.

We then abstract the resulting circuit in two ways. First, we use an RTL compiler to optimise the circuit by performing transformations like constant propagation and common subexpression elimination. The reduced merge buffer now has about 1800 latches and 10 free primary inputs. We then do a final abstraction step that removes redundant latches, and replaces groups of transparent latches with standard flip-flops (a single transparent latch can not be modelled synchronously, but we can often model clusters of transparent latches). The final model has about 600 state nodes in the cone of most properties.

The end result of the reductions and abstractions is the model that we give to the verification tools. However, before we can do that, we need to write down the property of interest in a format that the tool we want to use accepts. Given the model and the property, the verification tool then either produces a failure trace, or tells us that the property is true (which has little meaning as we have performed ad-hoc reductions).

A lot of design knowledge is needed to decipher a failure trace; a property can fail for more than one reason. First of all, we might have made a specification mistake that causes the tool to diagnose an intended behaviour of the system as a failure. In this case we need to modify the property. Second, the trace might be a trace that the real system could not exhibit, because it has arisen due to the merge buffer's environment providing input signals that cannot occur in real-life. In this case we need to go back and modify the transactors so that we disallow this behaviour, and re-abstract the resulting model. Third, we might have found a real bug.

7   Verification

In this section, we describe our experiences of applying BDD-based symbolic model checking, BMC, and STE to the merge buffer. The areas of the merge buffer that we target have previously been well explored with simulation-based verification.

7.1   BDD-Based Symbolic Model Checking

SMV was the first BDD-based tool that we evaluated that showed some promise for checking non-trivial merge buffer properties. (We have evaluated several.) However, most of the interesting merge-buffer properties contain about 600 latches in the cone of influence, and BDD-based model checking of state machines containing more than a couple of hundred latches is highly non-trivial. In order to find bugs using SMV, we therefore have to decrease the size of the cone by setting a subset of the 10 free primary inputs to specific values during the run. These values restrict the part of the state space that we explore using the model checker.

In order to get better performance out of SMV, we have ported it to the 64-bit Alpha architecture. This allows us the benefits of performing the model checking runs on a high performance server with 8 GB of main memory. To further improve SMVs capacity, we have also augmented the standard variable reordering heuristics with two special purpose tactics.

In spite of the improvements to SMV, each property still takes several hours to explore on the server. We have found many bugs this way, but it is slow.

7.2   Bounded Model Checking

The first alternative to BDD-based model checking that we have investigated is bounded model checking, as implemented in the SAT-based model checking workbench FIXIT [2].

One of the SAT-solvers that we wanted to use together with FIXIT, PROVER [14], was not available for the Alpha architecture when this work was done. We have therefore done all of our BMC runs on a 32-bit PC. The performance of the BMC analysis is still remarkable. Even though we are not using a high-performance processor with many gigabytes of memory, we can find failures in a fraction of the time needed by SMV. In Table 1 we compare the runtimes of BMC, running on a 450 MHz 32-bit PC, to SMV, running on a 700 MHz 64-bit Alpha.

The first column of BMC runtimes is obtained using CAPTAIN PROVE, a command-line tool from Prover Technology. CAPTAIN PROVE uses PROVER's

Table 1. Comparison between Bounded Model Checking and SMV.

Failure length	SMV sec	CAPTAIN PROVE BMC sec	GRASP BMC sec
25	62 280	85	25
26	32 940	19	19
34	11 290	586	272
38	18 600	39	101
53	54 360	1 995	[>10000 s]
56	44 640	2 337	[>10000 s]
76	27 130	619	6 150
144	44 550	10 820	[>10000 s]

application programming interface [11] to search for models using *strategies*. A simple such strategy, which we will refer to as the *timed strategy*, looks as follows:

```
sat 1 time 3600.
back level 5 [ sat 1 time 30. ].
```

The timed strategy first does a preprocessing step called *1-saturation* [14] for 3600 seconds. This analysis tries to find information restricting the search space we have to traverse for a model. The 1-saturation is then followed by the actual search, *backtracking*. At every fifth level of the search tree, the SAT-solver is instructed to do 30 seconds of additional 1-saturation.

The use of strategies allows us to control the search for assignments. We use different choices of strategies for different bounds N. When N is less than 40, we use the default strategy of 1-saturation without a time limit followed by normal backtracking. For N larger than 40, we use the timed strategy with different values for the initial 1-saturation. For example, for length 60 traces we normally need 1000 seconds of initial saturation, whereas for traces over 100 cycles long we use 10 000 or 20 000 seconds of initial saturation.

As can be seen from Table 1, BMC using CAPTAIN PROVE detects the failures significantly faster than SMV. In some cases it reduces the runtime for finding a bug from a day to a couple of minutes. The lengths of failures that are detected range from 25 cycles up to well over a hundred cycles.

The second column of BMC runtimes is obtained using GRASP [15], a high-capacity public domain SAT-solver. As can be seen in the table, CAPTAIN PROVE and GRASP both work well for short failures. For longer failures, CAPTAIN PROVE outperforms GRASP. (Please note that the reason for the [>10000 s] table entries is that GRASP automatically terminates after 10 000 seconds; we have not cut it off.)

7.3 SAT-Based Symbolic Trajectory Evaluation

The second alternative to BDD-based model checking that we have investigated is a SAT-based version of symbolic trajectory evaluation that we have implemented in FIXIT.

The advantage of using STE instead of BMC is that we are not forced to give symbolic values to each time-instance of a state variable. Instead we can choose to give concrete values to some state variables, or leave them to contain X. This potentially permits us to do much deeper exploration of the state-space than we can do using BMC, while preserving the short run times.

However, in order to take full advantage of this increased flexibility, we have to spend more time coming up with a good specification that judiciously gives concrete and symbolic values to the right variables.

For example, if we do not give concrete or symbolic values to some of the state variables, they are initialised to contain the unknown value X. This value often propagates, since it may be impossible to draw conclusions about the outputs of a gate with an unknown input. We might also have forgotten to assign a value to a primary input at an important time. When a property fails because of such underspecification, we have to make the specification more detailed by introducing symbolic or concrete values. A given STE specification will thus often have to go through several iterations of revision.

Table 2. Runtimes for detecting failures using symbolic trajectory evaluation.

Failure length	CAPTAIN PROVE sec	GRASP sec
77	7.7	33.3
77	7.7	34.2
112	10.8	51.9
123	11.7	51.9

In Table 2, we present the runtimes needed to find four bugs in the merge buffer using STE. The times to do the actual detections are short, but we had to spend a lot of time developing the specifications. Luckily, the turnaround time for discovering that an assertion is underspecified is a few seconds at most, which means that the specification work is very interactive.

The table shows a clear difference between the performance of STE using GRASP and CAPTAIN PROVE. However, the actual runtimes are very low in both cases. For the purpose of using SAT-based STE to locate bugs in the merge buffer, we can clearly make do with a public domain SAT solver.

8   A Proposal for a Methodology

From the previous section, it is clear that BDD-based model checking, BMC, and STE have very different characteristics. Based on the experiences we have had while locating design errors in the merge buffer, we have the following suggestion for a methodology:

– Start the analysis of a new subbox with bounded model checking.

- Initially test a new property with a small bound, so that the check only takes a few seconds. This will catch low-hanging fruit, and alert us to simple problems with inputs that are not properly constrained.
- Remove false counterexamples by modifying the transactors or the property, as appropriate.
- Start looking for long failures of the property. Choose a small set of bounds, ranging from medium long up to very challenging, and check each of them using the timed CAPTAIN PROVE strategy. Use longer and longer saturation times.
- Use STE to quickly check that the problem is fixed whenever the designers have corrected a bug found using BMC. Also abstract the failure trace by making some of the inputs or control signals symbolic. This allows quick checking for failures that are similar to the original failure.
- When the BMC checks start taking more than half an hour or so, start working in parallel on using STE to find the bug.
- If neither BMC nor STE seems to find any failures, try SMV or move on to another property.

9   Conclusions

In this paper, we have presented the techniques that we have used to find bugs in a crucial component of a microprocessor in design. Our approach is based on bounded model checking and a SAT-based version of symbolic trajectory evaluation that we have developed.

Our experimental results demonstrate that it is possible for BMC to out-perform state-of-the-art BDD-based symbolic model checking by two orders of magnitude, even when we look for bugs in deeply pipelined industrial components. None of the bugs described here has been a false counterexample. As a result, their complexity in terms of the length of minimum failure traces has been significantly larger than previously have been found using SAT-based techniques.

We have had less time to evaluate the use of SAT-based STE, but it seems clear that it is a very attractive bug-finding method. We have used STE to find bugs as deep as the ones we have been able to find using BMC, with negligible runtimes. However, this does not come for free; we have decreased the tool's runtime by spending more time developing specifications.

We have also presented a comparison of the performance of CAPTAIN PROVE and GRASP for BMC and STE, and suggested a methodology for SAT-based industrial bug finding.

We believe that the approach we have presented here can be cost effective, and that the techniques we have used will become vital instruments in the standard verification toolbox. During the two months when the work that is presented in this paper was done, we improved the SAT-based framework FIXIT significantly and removed many bottlenecks that we had not encountered on academic examples. The dramatic decrease in runtimes that we achieved in this short time makes us believe that there is a large potential for further improvement.

Acknowledgements

Many thanks to Gunnar Andersson, Luis Baptista, Arne Borälv, and João Marques Silva, who gave advice on running the SAT-solvers. We would also like to thank Gabriel Bischoff, John Matthews and Mary Sheeran for their useful comments on earlier drafts of this paper. Finally, Per Bjesse thanks Compaq's Alpha Development group for hosting him during the autumn of 2000.

References

1. M. Aagaard, R.B. Jones, T.F. Melham, J.W. O'Leary, and C.-J. H. Seger. A methodology for large-scale hardware verification. In *Formal Methods in Computer Aided Design*, November 2000.
2. P. A. Abdulla, P. Bjesse, and N. Eén. Symbolic reachability analysis based on SAT-solvers. In *Proc. TACAS '00, 9th Int. Conf. on Tools and Algorithms for the Construction and Analysis of Systems*, 2000.
3. A. Biere, A. Cimatti, E.M. Clarke, and Y. Zhu. Symbolic model checking without BDDs. In *Proc. TACAS '99, 8th Int. Conf. on Tools and Algorithms for the Construction and Analysis of Systems*, 1999.
4. A. Biere, E.M. Clarke, R. Raimi, and Y. Zhu. Verifying safety properties of a PowerPC[tm] microprocessor using symbolic model checking without BDDs. In *Proc. 11th Int. Conf. on Computer Aided Verification*, 1999.
5. P. Bjesse and K. Claessen. SAT-based verification without state space traversal. In *Formal Methods in Computer Aided Design*, November 2000.
6. E.M. Clarke, O. Grumberg, and D. Peled. *Model Checking*. MIT Press, December 1999.
7. A. Gupta, Z. Yang, and P. Ashar. SAT-based image computation with application in reachability analysis for verification. In *Formal Methods in Computer Aided Design*, November 2000.
8. C.N. Ip and D. Dill. Better verification through symmetry. *Formal Methods in System Design*, 9(1/2):41–75, August 1996.
9. K.L. McMillan. *Symbolic Model Checking*. Kluwer Academic Publishers, 1993.
10. K.L. McMillan. The SMV language. Technical report, Cadence Berkeley Labs, 1999.
11. Prover Technology AB. *Prover 4.0 Application Programming Reference Manual*, 2000. PPI-01-ARM-1.
12. C.-J. H. Seger and R.E. Bryant. Formal verification by symbolic evaluation of partially ordered trajectories. *Formal Methods in System Design*, 6(2):147–190, March 1995.
13. M. Sheeran, S. Singh, and G. Stålmarck. Checking safety properties using induction and a SAT-solver. In *Formal Methods in Computer Aided Design*, November 2000.
14. M. Sheeran and G. Stålmarck. A tutorial on Stålmarck's proof procedure for propositional logic. *Formal Methods in System Design*, 16(1):23–58, January 2000.
15. J.P.M. Silva. *Search algorithms for satisfiability problems in combinational switching circuits*. PhD thesis, EECS Department, University of Michigan, May 1995.
16. P.F. Williams, A. Biere, E.M. Clarke, and A. Gupta. Combining decision diagrams and SAT procedures for efficient symbolic model checking. In *Proc. 12th Int. Conf. on Computer Aided Verification*, 2000.

Towards Efficient Verification of
Arithmetic Algorithms over Galois Fields $GF(2^m)$

Sumio Morioka, Yasunao Katayama, and Toshiyuki Yamane

IBM Tokyo Research Laboratory
1623-14 Shimotsuruma, Yamato-shi, Kanagawa-ken 242-8502, Japan
e02716@jp.ibm.com
Tel: +81-46-215-5736   Fax: +81-46-273-7413

Abstract. The Galois field $GF(2^m)$ is an important number system that is widely used in applications such as error correction codes (ECC), and complicated combinations of arithmetic operations are performed in those applications. However, few practical formal methods for algorithm verification at the word-level have ever been developed. We have defined a logic system, GF_{2^m}-arithmetic, that can treat non-linear and non-convex constraints, for describing specifications and implementations of arithmetic algorithms over $GF(2^m)$. We have investigated various decision techniques for the GF_{2^m}-arithmetic and its subclasses, and have performed an automatic correctness proof of a $(n, n-4)$ Reed-Solomon ECC decoding algorithm. Because the correctness criterion is in an efficient subclass of the GF_{2^m}-arithmetic (2^p-field-size independent), the proof is completed in significantly reduced time, less than one second for any $m \geq 3$ and $n \geq 5$, by using a combination of polynomial division and variable elimination over $GF(2^m)$, without using any costly techniques such as factoring or a decision over $GF(2)$ that can easily increase the verification time to more than a day.

1   Introduction

Due to the exponential growth of scale and speed of networks and computer systems, the importance and use of error correction codes (ECC) and crypto systems have been increasing rapidly. In the majority of these algorithms, the Galois field $GF(2^m)$ [1], or finite field, is used as a number system.

Because complicated combinations of arithmetic operations are performed in these algorithms, the necessity of applying formal verification to the entire algorithms at the word level (i.e., checking if the entire combination of operators is correct or not) is very high. The domain space of their inputs can be extremely wide, and therefore, ensuring the correctness of the entire algorithm is almost impossible by any testing-based method.

However, little research has ever been reported on the verification of arithmetic algorithms over Galois fields, although much research has been done for the other number systems such as integers (Presburger arithmetic etc.) [2,3], rational numbers [4], floating point numbers [5] and so on. A decision diagram for Galois fields, based on the decomposition of multiple-valued functions, has been proposed recently [6], but

G. Berry, H. Comon, and A. Finkel (Eds.): CAV 2001, LNCS 2102, pp. 465–477, 2001.
© Springer-Verlag Berlin Heidelberg 2001

treating practical fields such as $GF(2^8)$, $GF(2^{16})$, $GF(2^{32})$ and larger and/or algorithms (formulas) having many operators is still difficult.

In this paper, we investigate how to efficiently prove the correctness of practical algorithms over Galois fields. For describing algorithm specifications and implementations at the word level, we have defined a logic system, GF_{2^m}-arithmetic, that is a subclass of first-order logic and which can describe non-linear and non-convex constraints. This logic can treat the bit level descriptions, too.

We have performed a correctness proof of a key part of a practical $(n, n-4)$ Reed-Solomon ECC decoding algorithm [7,8,9], over $GF(2^8)$ $(m=8)$ or larger. We have examined various decision techniques for the GF_{2^m}-arithmetic or its subclasses. Our first experimental result showed that even a small portion of the entire proof required too much CPU time (more than a day), if proof methods over $GF(2)$ such as decision diagrams (DDs) [10,11] were used. By using a special decision procedure based on a combination of polynomial division and variable elimination over $GF(2^m)$, without using any costly techniques such as factoring [1] and proof methods over $GF(2)$, the CPU time for the proof was significantly reduced to less than one second (Pentium III 800MHz), for any $m \geq 3$ and $n \geq 5$. One of the reasons why we could shorten the proof time significantly is that the correctness criterion for the RS-ECC verification is an efficient subclass of the GF_{2^m}-arithmetic: 2^p-field-size independent.

This paper is organized as follows. In Section 2, we will define a logic system, GF_{2^m}-arithmetic. In Section 3, we will investigate various decision techniques for the GF_{2^m}-arithmetic or its subclasses. In Section 4, we will show how we achieved a short verification time for a practical RS decoding algorithm.

2   A Logic System for Describing Specifications and Implementations of Arithmetic Algorithms over Galois Fields

2.1   The Language and Interpretation of GF_{2^m}-Arithmetic

We have defined a GF_{2^m}-arithmetic that is a subclass of the first-order logic. In any instance (sentence) of the GF_{2^m}-arithmetic, only arithmetic operators over Galois fields $GF(2^m)$ $(+,-,\times,\div)$, equality $(=)$ and logical operators $(\wedge, \vee, \neg)$ can be used as functions or predicates. Please note that m is a given constant value and is not a variable. Symbols used in expressions in the GF_{2^m}-sentence are
$\wedge, \vee, \neg, \forall, \exists, =, +, \times, \div, \alpha, 1, 0, x, y, z, ..., P, Q, R, ..., (,), "$.

Definition of the language is as follows:
1. GF_{2^m} variable and GF_{2^m} constant: $x, y, z, ...$ are GF_{2^m} variables. Unlike integers, every constant value in $GF(2^m)$ has two representations [1]. The first one is the exponentiation representation where an element of $GF(2^m)$ is represented as one of $\{0, 1, \alpha^i\}$. Here, α is a generator element of a given field and i is an integer constant $(1 \leq i \leq 2^m - 2)$. The second one is the vector representation where an element of $GF(2^m)$ is represented as a vector "$c_{m-1}, c_{m-2}, ..., c_0$" over $GF(2)$.
2. Term: Only variables, constants, $T_1 + T_2$, $T_1 - T_2$, $T_1 \times T_2$, and $T_1 \div T_2$ are terms, if T_1 and T_2 are terms.
3. Atom: An expression of the form $T_1 = T_2$ is an atom, where T_1 and T_2 are terms.

4. GF_2 variable and GF_2 constant: 1 and 0 are GF_2 constants (they are also elements of GF_{2^m} constants). $P, Q, R, \ldots$ are GF_2 variables.

5. Formula: Only atoms, GF_2 variables, GF_2 constants, $F_1 \wedge F_2$, $F_1 \vee F_2$, $\neg F_1$, $\forall x F_1$ and $\exists x F_1$ are *formulas*, where F_1 and F_2 are formulas and x is a GF_{2^m} or GF_2 variable.

6. Sentence: A formula which has no free variable is a *sentence*. GF_{2^m}-arithmetic is the set of all sentences.

The interpretation of operators is defined once the field size m, irreducible polynomial and basis (polynomial basis, normal basis, etc. [1]) are fixed. The domain of GF_{2^m} variables is the entire field and the domain of GF_2 variables is $\{1,0\}$. All of the above functions and predicates have their natural interpretations. In the following, we will use various standard abbreviations for simplicity: xy denotes $x \times y$, t^p denotes $\prod_{i=1}^{p} t$, $F_1 \Rightarrow F_2$ denotes $\neg F_1 \vee F_2$, $F_1 \Leftrightarrow F_2$ denotes $(F_1 \wedge F_2) \vee (\neg F_1 \wedge \neg F_2)$, *if F_1 then F_2 else F_3* denotes $(F_1 \Rightarrow F_2) \wedge (\neg F_1 \Rightarrow F_3)$, and so on.

Examples: $\exists x \forall y (x^3 = x^2 y + x \Rightarrow \exists z (x + y = z))$ is a sentence. Neither $\exists x \exists y (x^y = 0)$ (a variable is used as the power for exponentiation) nor $\exists x (x = y)$ (y is a free variable) is a sentence.

2.2   Various Useful Subclasses of the GF_{2^m}-Arithmetic

In most of the actual verification applications, as will be described in Section 4, only limited sentences in the following subclasses of the GF_{2^m}-arithmetic appear. The relationships of the subclasses are shown in Fig.1.

A. Basis Independent Sentences.
These are sentences whose truth is independent of the representation basis. If a sentence contains no vector-constant (constant value in vector representation), then the sentence is basis independent. Usually, if a sentence contains multiplication by a vector-constant, it is basis dependent.

B. Irreducible Polynomial Independent Sentences.
These are sentences whose truth is independent of the irreducible polynomial. Usually, if a sentence contains addition by a constant value in an exponentiation representation, it is irreducible polynomial dependent.

Regarding A and B above, the following interesting theorem holds.

Theorem 1: If a sentence of the GF_{2^m}-arithmetic contains no GF_{2^m}-constant other than 0 or 1, then the sentence is basis and irreducible polynomial independent.   □

(Proof) For any fields A and B whose sizes are the same, there is an isomorphism function δ from the elements in A to the elements in B where $\delta(x + y) = \delta(x) + \delta(y)$, $\delta(xy) = \delta(x)\delta(y)$, $\delta(1) = 1$ and $\delta(0) = 0$. Consider a sentence S over the field A. Then, for any atom $term(x, y, z, \ldots) = 0$ in S, a relation $term(x, y, z, \ldots) = 0$ $\Leftrightarrow$ $term(\delta(x), \delta(y), \delta(z), \ldots) = 0$ holds, if S contains no GF_{2^m}-constant other than 0 and 1. Therefore, the truth of S is the same over the field B, by substituting $\delta(x), \delta(y), \delta(z), \ldots$ into $x, y, z, \ldots$.   □

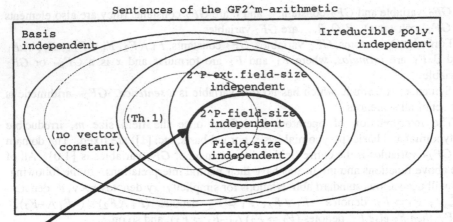

Fig. 1. Relationships of subclasses A-E of the GF_{2^m}-Arithmetic

C. 2^p-Extension-Field-Size Independent Sentences.

A sentence is 2^p-extension-field-size independent, if there exists a constant $p \geq 1$ such that the truth of the sentence is the same over any extension fields of $GF(2^p)$, including $GF(2^p)$. For example, a sentence $\exists x(x^{16} = x \wedge x^4 \neq x)$ is 2^4-extension-field-size independent. This sentence is true over $GF(2^4)$, $GF(2^{2\times4})$, $GF(2^{3\times4})$ and so on. Clearly, any 2^p-extension-field-size independent sentence is both basis and irreducible polynomial independent.

D. 2^p-Field-Size Independent Sentences.

This subclass is important because the correctness criteria for most of the arithmetic algorithms defined over Galois Fields are in this subclass.

A sentence is 2^p-field-size independent, if there exists a constant $p \geq 1$ such that the truth of the sentence is the same over all of $GF(2^i)$ ($i \geq p$). For example, a sentence $\forall x \forall y(y = 1 \Rightarrow x^2 = xy)$ is 2^2-field-size independent. This sentence is false over $GF(2^2)$, $GF(2^3)$, $GF(2^4)$ and so on.

E. Field-Size Independent Sentences.

A 2^1-field-size independent sentence is field-size independent. For example, a sentence $\forall x \forall y(y = x \Rightarrow x^2 = xy)$ is field-size independent.

F. $\exists$-only (or $\forall$-only) Prenex Normal Form Sentences.

One of the most important subclasses of the GF_{2^m}-arithmetic is the prenex normal form sentences where all of quantifiers are $\forall$. Any $\forall$-only prenex normal form sentence can be transformed into $\exists$-only sentences, by using the relation $\forall x p(x) \Leftrightarrow \neg \exists x \neg p(x)$.

3 Deciding the Truth Value of a Sentence of the GF_{2^m}-Arithmetic

3.1 Decidability of the GF_{2^m}-Arithmetic and the Problem of Deciding the Truth Value

Unlike integers or rational numbers, the truth value of any sentences S of the GF_{2^m} -arithmetic are decidable, even if S contains multiplications. This is because the domain of all the variables is finite. The truth of S can be determined by substituting all possible 2^m values into each variable in S. Clearly, the upper bound of computational complexity of this direct substitution method is $O(2^{m v_1} \cdot 2^{v_2})$, where v_1 is the number of GF_{2^m} variables and v_2 is the number of GF_2 variables (please note that the lower bound is not yet known). Therefore, the development of some decision heuristics are necessary.

However, in considering heuristics, we have found that interpreting both addition and multiplication at the same abstraction level can be a difficult problem. The reason is that interpreting multiplication over $GF(2^m)$ can be performed efficiently at the $GF(2^m)$-level, which corresponds to the word level, using the exponential representation by adding the values of the exponents of the elements as natural numbers. On the other hand, interpreting addition over $GF(2^m)$ can be performed efficiently at the $GF(2)$-level, which corresponds to the bit level, using the vector representation by adding corresponding vector elements over $GF(2)$ in parallel. If a sentence contains both addition and multiplication, converting the representation is necessary for evaluating the sentence, but conversion from the vector representation to the exponential representation is a discrete logarithm problem. The *Zech logarithm* is a known method to reduce the size of the addition-table, but only the reduction from $m2^{2m}$ to $m2^m$ is possible.

3.2 Basic Structure of Decision Procedures for the GF_{2^m}-Arithmetic

Following the discussions in Section 3.1, the basic structure of the decision procedure for the GF_{2^m}-arithmetic is as follows:

Step 1 (Decision over $GF(2^m)$): Simplify a given sentence using the well-known mathematical theorems of operators over $GF(2^m)$ (Table 1). Standard techniques of theorem proving (term rewriting, case analysis, etc.) and standard expression transformation rules over propositional logic and first-order logic can be used, too. How to apply those techniques and rules is highly application specific, and an example will be discussed in Section 3.3. In many cases, the truth can not be completely determined in this **Step 1** and if so, go to **Step 2**.

If a given sentence is basis or irreducible polynomial dependent, the truth of the sentence cannot be determined using only the rules in Table 1, because all of the rules in Table 1 are both basis and irreducible polynomial independent transformations. More concretely, sentences that contain constant values other than 0 and 1 usually require **Step 2**.

Step 2 (Decision over $GF(2)$): Apply the techniques in Section 3.4, or substitute all possible values into each variable and evaluate the truth of the sentence. When substitution is performed and m is large, avoiding conversion from vector

Table 1. Mathematical Theorems over $GF(2^m)$
(Basis and irreducible polynomials independent rules).

Field size independent rules			Field size dependent rule
$A + B = B + A$	$A \times B = B \times A$	$A \times (B + C) = (A \times B) + (A \times C)$	$A^{2^m} = A$
$A + (B + C) = (A + B) + C$	$A \times (B \times C) = (A \times B) \times C$	$A^2 + B^2 + \cdots = (A + B + \cdots)^2$	
$A + 0 = A$	$A \times 1 = A$	if $B \neq 0, A \div B = C \Leftrightarrow A = B \times C$	
$A + A = 0$	$A \times 0 = 0$	$A - B = A + B$	

representation to exponential representation by using the following steps will be good, even though each step may sometimes increase the size of the sentence rapidly:
- **Step 2a**: Transform all of the atoms in the sentence into sum-of-product form.
- **Step 2b**: Evaluate all multiplications over $GF(2^m)$ using the exponential representation.
- **Step 2c**: Convert all of the elements in the sentence from exponential representation to vector representation.
- **Step 2d**: Evaluate all addition over $GF(2)$ using the vector representation.

3.3   A Step 1 Implementation for ECC Algorithm Verification

In **Step 1** in Section 3.2, the efficiency of deciding the truth value is very dependent on how a given sentence is evaluated. In the following, we show an example implementation of **Step 1** as it will be used in Section 4.3.3. This example is suitable for word-level verification of an Reed-Solomon ECC, and is constructed so that **Step 2** is unnecessary when a complete (correct) ECC algorithm implementation is given.

As will be shown in Section 4.2, in general, the correctness criteria of a key part of ECC algorithms have the following characteristics:
- Described as $\forall$-only prenex normal sentences, because the correctness criteria mean that output of the algorithm is correct for *any* input value.
- Often transformed into the form $\exists or \forall (term = variable \land formula)$ or $\exists or \forall (term \neq variable \land formula)$.
- Basis and irreducible polynomial independent because the correctness criteria satisfy Theorem 1 in Section 2.2. Therefore, **Step 2** may be unnecessary.
- 2^p-field-size-independent (actual value of p is different for different ECC codes). Therefore, no field-size dependent rule from Table 1 may be required.

Based on the above characteristics, we have implemented **Step 1** as follows:
Step 1a (Preparation): Transform the given sentence S into prenex normal form (usually unnecessary because the given sentence should already be in prenex formal form). Eliminate all $\neg$ by using De Morgan's Law and transform all of the atoms into the form $term = (\neq)0$, where *term* is in the sum-of-product form. Eliminate all division and unnecessary terms by using rules such as $T_1 = T_2 \div T_3 \Leftrightarrow T_1 \times T_3 = T_2$ (when $T_3 \neq 0$) and $T + T = 0$.

Step 1b (Eliminate Variables): Try to transform all of the atoms into the form $term\ T = variable\ V$, where no V appears in T. If any atom is in the form $(T_1^2 + T_2^2 + \cdots + T_k^2) = 0$, replace it by $T_1 + T_2 + \cdots + T_k = 0$. If the form of the entire sentence S becomes $\exists or \forall (T = V \wedge formula)$, eliminate the variable V by substituting T into all occurrences of V in the sentence. After that, again transform all of the atoms into the form $term = (\neq)0$ and then, the truth value of any atom that contains no variable can be determined.

Step 1c (Factoring and Construct Zero/Non-zero Set): Try factoring the left side of all atoms $term \neq 0$ (this factoring can be sometimes omitted, as shown in Section 4.3.3) [1]. If the entire sentence is of the form $\exists or \forall \{T_1 T_2 \cdots T_k \neq 0 \wedge formula\}$, construct a set of non-zero terms $\Phi = \{T_1, T_2, ..., T_k, ...\}$ (otherwise, $\Phi = \phi$). Similarly, if the sentence is of the form $\exists or \forall \{U = 0 \wedge formula\}$, construct a set of zero terms $\Psi = \{U, ...\}$.

Step 1d (Division by Polynomials in Zero/Non-zero Set): If the non-zero set Φ is not empty, test if the left side term of each atom can be factored by an element in Φ. If a term is factored by an element T_i, then replace the term by the quotient and append a new atom $T_i \neq 0$ to the entire sentence, connected by $\wedge$. In the same manner, test by the zero-set Ψ and if a term is factored by an element in Ψ, replace the term by 0.

Step 1e (Transform Expression to Make a New Zero/Non-zero Set): Iterate **Steps 1b-1d** until no change occurs. If the truth value of the entire sentence has been determined, terminate the procedure. Otherwise, apply the techniques (i) and (ii) below. If the form of the entire sentence becomes $\exists or \forall (term = variable \wedge formula)$ or $\exists or \forall (term \neq variable \wedge formula)$ as a result, then return to **Step 1b**. If not, go to **Step 2** in Section 3.2.

(i) If S is a $\forall$-only (or $\exists$-only) prenex normal form sentence $\forall x \forall y \forall z \cdots f(x, y, z, ...)$, make a corresponding new $\exists$-only (or $\forall$-only) sentence $\exists x \exists y \exists z \cdots \neg f(x, y, z, ...)$.

(ii) Case analysis by variable: select the innermost quantified variable V (or any variable, when the sentence is $\forall$-only or $\exists$-only prenex normal form) and partition the entire proof into a case $V = 0$ and another case $V \neq 0$.

3.4 General Verification-Cost Reduction Techniques for Step 2

3.4.1. Field Change for Basis or Irreducible Polynomial Independent Sentences.
If a sentence is basis or irreducible polynomial independent, we can select an appropriate basis or irreducible polynomial at the verification stage, even if a different field is actually used for the algorithm implementation. The cost of evaluating sentences can be reduced by changing the basis or irreducible polynomial, because the cost of a multiplication can be reduced from $O(m^3)$ to $2m^2 - 1$ or fewer operations over $GF(2)$ [12].

3.4.2. Field Change for 2^p-(Extension)-Field-Size Independent Sentences.
If a sentence is 2^p-extension-field-size, 2^p-field-size or field-size independent, we can select a small field at the verification stage, for significant reduction of the variable domain space.

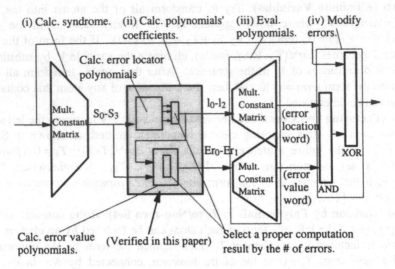

Fig. 2. Block Diagram of the One Shot Reed-Solomon Decoding Algorithm

3.4.3. Use of DDs for ∃-only (or ∀-only) Prenex Normal Form Sentences.
For ∃-only (or ∀-only) prenex normal form sentences S over $GF(2^m)$, the truth value
can be determined as follows: (i) extract the entire S into an equivalent sentence T
over $GF(2)$, by replacing all of the variables and operators by their bit-level
implementations, (ii) transform T into a canonical form U over $GF(2)$ and (iii) check
if U is a constant 0 (or 1). This is the same method used in model checking over
Boolean variables [13] and is usually much faster than the direct substitution method.

4   Verification Example of a Reed-Solomon Decoding Algorithm

4.1   An Ultrafast Reed-Solomon Decoding Algorithm

The systematic (n, k) Reed-Solomon codes (RS codes), where n is the code word
length and k is the information word (or message word) length, have a maximum
error-correcting capability of $[(n - k)/2]$ symbols. They are used in many areas, such
as communication, storage, and fault-tolerant memory systems [7].

In [8,9], an ultrafast decoding algorithm for RS codes (one shot RS algorithm) was
described. This one shot RS algorithm can exceed more than a Gbps of throughput
when implemented in hardware.   It is designed for combinational circuit
implementation and does not use any iterative execution (loops).

We have selected this algorithm for our verification example, because applying
formal verification is highly desired. The algorithm contains many operators and
many mistakes could happen during algorithm implementation. In addition, avoiding
loops is preferable for applying a formal verification procedure, although almost the
same correctness criterion and decision procedure can be applied to other RS
algorithms by adding some proof mechanisms that can handle loops [14].

Table 2. Correctness Criterion for $(n, n-4)$ RS Code (when # of errors = 2).

```
On a given field (given field size m, irreducible poly and basis),
∀s0∀e0∀e1∀s1∀a0··· (for any value of variables)
(    -- input constraints (mathematical def. of syndrome s0-s3)
        s0 = e0 + e1 and s1 = e0*a0 + e1*a1
    and s2 = e0*a0^2 + e1*a1^2 and s3 = e0*a0^3 + e1*a1^3
    and e0 /= 0 and e1 /= 0  -- error values are not 0
    and a0 /= 0 and a1 /= 0  -- error locations are not 0
    and a0 /= a1             -- error locations are different

    -- algorithm formula (compute 10-12 and er0-er1, from s0-s3)
    and 10e2 = s0*s2 + s1^2 and 11e2 = s0*s3 + s1*s2
    and 12e2 = s1*s3 + s2^2 and 11e1 = s0
    and 12e1 = s1 and 10 = 10e2
    and if 10e2 = 0 -- select an error locator polynomial by # of errors
        then  11 = 11e1 and 12 = 12e1
        else  11 = 11e2 and 12 = 12e2
        endif
    and er0 = ((s1*10e2)/11e2) + s0 and er1 = ((s0*10e2)/11e2)
) imply (
    -- output specification (correct polynomials are obtained)
    er1*a1 + er0 = e1 and er1*a0 + er0 = e0      -- error value poly.
    and 10 /= 0 and 11/10 = a0 + a1 and 12/10 = a0*a1 -- error loc poly.
)
```

As shown in Fig.2, the one shot RS algorithm consists of four major blocks: (i) syndrome calculation, (ii) polynomials coefficients calculation, (iii) polynomial evaluation and (iv) error modification. The major difference between the one shot RS and the others is the computation sequence in the shaded block (ii). The most important and complicated part is also block (ii) and this is our verification target. The other blocks perform simple constant matrix multiplications [9], and checking if those matrices are correct or not is neither a difficult nor critical problem.

4.2   Correctness Criterion of the Reed-Solomon Decoding Algorithm

The verified second block computes, from 4 syndrome values S_0, S_1, S_2 and S_3, the coefficients of the error locator polynomial (l_0, l_1 and l_2) and those of the error polynomial (er_0 and er_1). In the block, multiple error locator polynomials and error value polynomials that correspond to different numbers of errors (from 1 to $[(n-k)/2]$) are computed, and one of them is selected as a result of evaluating the number of errors that actually occurred.

In Table 2, the correctness criterion for the second block for $(n, n-4)$RS code is shown. What we have proved is that, assuming the multipliers and adders are correctly implemented in the $GF(2)$-level (bit-level), the formula in the one shot decoding algorithm computes a correct output, if mathematically appropriate input is given. The criterion shown in Table 2 corresponds to the case when the number of errors is two, and it is necessary to independently prove a different case when the number of errors is one (the mathematical definitions of syndrome values are different between these cases).

The criterion is of the form

$$\forall \{\{input\ constraints \wedge algorithm\ formula\} \Rightarrow output\ specification \}$$

Table 3. Cost For proving Entire Correctness Criterion, over $GF(2^8)$ (Pentium III 800MHz).

Proof Method	CPU time
Approach 1: DD (OBDD or OFDD)	> 1 week
Approach 2: Variable elimination and DD	> 1 day (mostly spent by DD)
Approach 3: Polynomial division and variable elimintion	0.2 second

and this statement has to be true under a given field size m, irreducible polynomial and basis. All of identifiers between operators are GF_{2^m} variables. All of variables are bounded by $\forall$ and the correctness criterion is a $\forall$-only prenex normal form sentence.

The input constraints describe the standard mathematical definition of syndromes using the variables a0, a1 (error locations in the error word), e0 and e1 (error values) [7]. The output specification can be easily extracted from standard descriptions of the RS ECC algorithms. This part means that the obtained error locator polynomial $l_0 x^2 + l_1 x + l_2$ should be equivalent to $l_0(x - a_0)(x - a_1)$ and the obtained error value polynomial $Er(x) = er_1 x + er_0$ should satisfy $Er(a_i) = e_i$ ($i = 0, 1$).

The same criterion can be used for any $n \geq 5, m \geq 3$, irreducible polynomial and basis.

4.3   Experimental Results

4.3.1 Approach 1: Direct Proof by DDs over GF(2).
Because the correctness criterion is a $\forall$-only prenex normal form sentence, we first tried to decide the truth of the entire sentence by DDs (see Section 3.4.3). We examined shared-OBDD [10] and shared-OFDD [11]. We thought that FDD would be efficient, because multiplication over $GF(2^m)$ (Mastrovito multiplier [12]) is usually implemented as a positive polarity Reed-Muller formula (PPRM) over $GF(2)$ [9,15]. However, too much proof time was necessary for those DDs (more than a week, when $m = 8$) because too many variables appeared in the correctness criterion.

4.3.2 Approach 2: Variable Elimination over GF(2^m) and DDs over GF(2).
To reduce the number of variables in the sentence, we tried a decision procedure that performs only **Steps 1a, 1b** and **1e** in Section 3.3. Using this procedure, the correctness criterion was transformed into a $\exists$-only sentence $\exists(term = variable \land formula)$, which should be false, and the variables s0, s1, s2, s3, 10e2, 11e2, 12e2, 11e1, 12e1, er0 and er1 were replaced by terms that consist of e0, e1, a0 and a1. However, because the if-sentence in Table 2 still remains as well as the variables 11 and 12 (in the then/else clause of the if-sentence), it was not yet possible to determine the truth value of the entire sentence.

Therefore, we tried to evaluate the truth of the if-condition part which was rewritten as $e_0 e_1 a_0 + e_0 e_1 a_1 = 0$, by using DDs. More precisely, a simple $\exists$-only sentence
$$\exists e_0 \exists e_1 \exists a_0 \exists a_1 ((e_0, e_1, a_0, a_1 \neq 0 \land a_0 \neq a_1) \Rightarrow e_0 e_1 a_0 + e_0 e_1 a_1 = 0)$$
was evaluated separately. However, too much time was still necessary over $GF(2^8)$ (Tables 3,4). Assuming the sentence is field-size independent, we tried to change the

Table 4. Cost for Evaluating the If-condition Part Using BDD/FDD (P-III 800MHz).

Field size and irreducible polynomial	# of bits	OBDD Max. BDD size	CPU time (sec)	OFDD Max. FDD size	CPU time (sec)
$GF(2^2)$, x^2+x+1	8	62	< 1	40	< 1
$GF(2^3)$, x^3+x+1	12	276	< 1	175	< 1
$GF(2^4)$, x^4+x+1	16	1,145	< 1	871	< 1
$GF(2^5)$, x^5+x^2+1	20	4,820	8	6,784	726
$GF(2^6)$, x^6+x^5+1	24	18,520	359	> 50,000	> 22,000
$GF(2^7)$, x^7+x+1	28	75,096	14,277	N/A	N/A

Table 5. Irreducible polynomial vs. max. BDD Size (over $GF(2^6)$) (P-III 800MHz).

Irreducible polynomial	Max. BDD size	CPU time (sec)
x^6+x^5+1	18,520	359
x^6+x+1	18,673	364
$x^6+x^5+x^3+x^2+1$	20,487	439
$x^6+x^5+x^4+x+1$	20,558	439
$x^6+x^5+x^2+x+1$	20,566	459
$x^6+x^4+x^3+x+1$	20,611	469

Table 6. Variable Ordering vs. max. BDD Size (over $GF(2^5)$, x^5+x^2+1) (P-III 800MHz).

Variable ordering (from BDD top to leaf)	Max. BDD size	CPU time (sec)
a1(4)-a1(0), a0(4)-a0(0), e1(4)-e1(0), e0(4)-e0(0)	4,820	8
a1(0)-a1(4), a0(0)-a0(4), e1(0)-e1(4), e0(0)-e0(4)	4,775	8
e1(4)-e1(0), e0(4)-e0(0), a1(4)-a1(0), a0(4)-a0(0)	3,320	10
e1(4)-e1(0), a1(4)-a1(0), a0(4)-a0(0), e0(4)-e0(0)	12,280	57
a1(4)-a1(0), e1(4)-e1(0), a0(4)-a0(0), e0(4)-e0(0)	41,191	355

field size and proved over smaller fields, which was pretty effective for verification cost reduction (Table 4). However, we do not yet know any efficient formal method to prove if the sentence is $(2^p$-)field-size independent or not. Proof over a smaller field at least increases the probability of algorithm correctness.

We also examined changing the polynomial, because this sentence satisfies Theorem 1 in section 2.2, and it is a basis and irreducible polynomial independent sentence. As shown in Table 5, the proof time was slightly better when trinomials were used, because the fewer number of $GF(2)$ operators are used in a multiplier [12]. We examined various variable orderings of DDs, and found it was better to place variables that appeared in the same atoms close together in the ordering (Table 6).

4.3.3. Approach 3: Polynomial Division and Variable Elimination over GF(2^m).
Because proof methods over $GF(2)$ were still too inefficient, we incorporated **Steps 1c** and **1d** into the decision procedure, in order to perform proof only over $GF(2^m)$. As mentioned in Section 3.3, **Step2** in Section 3.2 could be eliminated because the correctness criterion is basis and irreducible polynomial independent.

In these additional steps, a non-zero set {a0, a1, e0, e1, a0+a1} was created, the if-condition part was divided (factored) by the elements of this set, an atom $1 = 0$ was obtained, and finally the truth of the if-condition part was determined. Then, the variables 11 and 12 were eliminated, and the entire sentence was transformed into $\exists \{(T \neq 0) \wedge \cdots \wedge (T = 0)\}$. After appending T to the non-zero set and dividing the atom $T = 0$ by T, the truth of the entire sentence was determined.

In addition, we have found that the factoring in **Step 1c**, that is considered to be the most costly step, can be omitted from the verification process of general Reed-Solomon decoders, if their input/output specifications are described as functions of e_i and a_i. In a $(n, n - 2t)$ Reed-Solomon code, the mathematical formula that evaluates the number of errors is $\prod_{0 \leq i < t} e_i \prod_{0 \leq i < j < t} (a_i + a_j) = 0$ [7], and this is logically equivalent to checking if the left term is factored by each element in $\{e_0, \dots, e_{t-1}, a_0 + a_1, \dots, a_{t-2} + a_{t-1}\}$. All of these terms already exist in the correctness criterion, and therefore, the factoring stage can be omitted. Although general RS decoding algorithms are implemented as functions of syndrome, the above mathematical formula is obtained from the correctness criteria, after eliminating the syndrome variables that are defined by e_i and a_i.

As a result, the proof time was shortened to 0.2 second (PentiumIII 800 MHz). This verification cost is the same for any $n \geq 5$, $m \geq 3$, irreducible polynomial and basis. The proof was fully mechanized.

5   Conclusion

In this paper we have defined a logic system for verification of arithmetic algorithms over Galois fields $GF(2^m)$, and various proof techniques were investigated. We have carried out a correctness proof of a practical $(n, n - 4)$ Reed-Solomon decoding algorithm in less than one second for any $n \geq 5$ and $m \geq 3$, by using a decision procedure based on a combination of polynomial division and variable elimination over $GF(2^m)$.

One of the reasons why we could shorten the proof time significantly is that the correctness criterion is 2^p-field-size independent. If any one of these conditions were not satisfied, achieving efficient verification would be much more difficult, because a decision over $GF(2)$ would be necessary even if the sentence is written over $GF(2^m)$.

The verification of general (n, k) RS codes that can contain increasing numbers of operations can be done efficiently by using our approach. To the best of the authors' knowledge, our work is the first investigation of verifying a practical arithmetic algorithm over $GF(2^m)$ within a reasonable proof time.

References

1. I.F. Blake, X. Gao, R.C. Mullin, S.A. Vanstone and T. Yaghoobian, *Applications of Finite Fields*, Kluwer Academic Publishers (1993).
2. W. Pugh "A practical algorithm for exact array dependence analysis," *Communications of the ACM*, 35(8), pp. 102-114 (1992).
3. S. Morioka, N. Shibata, T. Higashino and K. Taniguchi, "Techniques to Reduce Computation Time in Decision Procedure for Prenex Normal Form Presburger Sentences

Bounded only by Existential Quantifiers," *Journal of IPSJ*, Vol. 38, No. 12, pp. 2419-2426 (1997).

4. N. Shibata, K. Okano, T. Higashino and K. Taniguchi, "A Decision Algorithm for Prenex Normal form Rational Presburger Sentences based on Combinatorial Geometry," *The 2nd Intl. Conf. on Discrete Mathematics and Theoretical Computer Science and the 5th Australian Theory Symposium (DMTCS'99+CATS'99)*, pp. 344-359 (1999).

5. Y.A. Chen, R.E. Bryant, "Verification of Floating-Point Adders," *The 10th Intl. Conf. on Computer Aided Verification (CAV'98)*, pp. 488-499 (1998).

6. R. Stankovic and R. Drechsler, "Circuit Design from Kronecker Galois Field Decision Diagrams for Multiple-valued Functions," *The Intl. Symp. on Multiple-Valued Logic*, pp. 275-280 (1997).

7. S.B. Wicker and V.K. Bhargava (eds.), *Reed-Solomon Codes and Their Applications*, IEEE Press, 1994.

8. Y. Katayama and S. Morioka, "One shot Reed-Solomon decoder," *33rd Annual Conf. on Information Science and Systems (CISS)*, pp. 700-705 (1999).

9. S. Morioka and Y. Katayama, "Design Methodology for one-shot Reed-Solomon Decoder," *1999 IEEE Intl. Conf. on Computer Design (ICCD'99)*, pp. 60-67 (1999).

10. R.E. Bryant, "Graph-based algorithms for Boolean function manipulations," *IEEE Trans. on Computers*, Vol. C-35, No. 8, pp. 677-691 (1986).

11. U. Kebshull and W. Rosenstiel, "Efficient Graph-Based Computation and Manipulation of Functional Decision Diagrams," *European Design Automation Conf. '93*, pp. 278-282 (1993).

12. A. Halbutogullari and C.K. Koc, "Mastrovito Multiplier for General Irreducible Polynomials," *IEEE Trans. on Computers*, Vol. 45, No.5, pp. 503-518 (2000).

13. J.R. Burch, E.M. Clarke, D.E. Long, K.L. McMilan and D.L. Dill, "Symbolic Model Checking for Sequential Circuit Verification," *IEEE Trans. on Computer-Aided Design of Integrated Circuits and Systems*, Vol. 13, No. 14, pp. 401-423 (1994)

14. J. Kitamichi, S. Morioka, T. Higasino and K. Taniguchi, "Automatic Correctness Proof of Implementation of Synchronous Sequential Circuits Using Algebraic Approach," *Intl. Conf. on Theorem Provers in Circuit Design (TPCD94), LNCS Vol. 901*, pp. 165-184 (1994).

15. T. Sasao, "AND-EXOR expressions and their optimization", in Sasao, editor: *Logic Synthesis and Optimization*, Kluwer Academic Publishers, pp. 287-312 (1993).

Job-Shop Scheduling Using Timed Automata*

Yasmina Abdeddaïm and Oded Maler

VERIMAG, Centre Equation
2, av. de Vignate 38610 Gières, France
{Yasmina.Abdeddaim,Oded.Maler}@imag.fr

Abstract. In this paper we show how the classical job-shop scheduling problem can be modeled as a special class of acyclic timed automata. Finding an optimal schedule corresponds, then, to finding a shortest (in terms of elapsed time) path in the timed automaton. This representation provides new techniques for solving the optimization problem and, more importantly, it allows to model naturally more complex dynamic resource allocation problems which are not captured so easily in traditional models of operation research. We present several algorithms and heuristics for finding the shortest paths in timed automata and test their implementation in the tool Kronos on numerous benchmark examples.

1 Introduction

A significant part of verification consists in checking the *existence* of certain paths in very large transition graphs, given as a product (composition) of simpler graphs. Such paths correspond to bad behaviors of the system under consideration. On the other hand, in many application domains (optimal control, Markov decision processes, scheduling) we are interested in selecting, among the possible behaviors, one that *optimizes* some more sophisticated performance measure (note that in "classical" verification we use a very simple performance measure on behaviors, namely, they are either "good" or "bad"). Both verification and optimization suffer from the state-explosion problem, also known as "the curse of dimensionality", and various methods and heuristics have been developed in order to treat larger and larger problems. The main thrust of this work is to explore the possibility of exporting some of the ideas developed within the verification community, such as symbolic analysis of timed automata, to the domain of optimal scheduling, where most of the effort was directed toward a constrained optimization approach.

The observation underlying this paper is that classical scheduling and resource allocation problems can be modeled very naturally using timed automata whose runs correspond to feasible schedules. In this case, finding a time-optimal schedule amounts to finding the shortest path (in terms of elapsed time) in

---

* This work was partially supported by the European Community Esprit-LTR Project 26270 VHS (Verification of Hybrid systems), and the AFIRST French-Israeli collaboration project 970MAEFUT5 (Hybrid Models of Industrial Plants).

G. Berry, H. Comon, and A. Finkel (Eds.): CAV 2001, LNCS 2102, pp. 478–492, 2001.

the automaton. This problem can be solved by some modifications in verification tools for timed automata. Posing the problem in automata-theoretic terms might open the way to an alternative class of heuristics for intractable scheduling problems, coming from the experience of the verification community in analyzing large systems, and this might lead in the future to better algorithms for certain classes of scheduling problems. Even if they do not contribute to improving the performance, automata-based models have a clear *semantic* advantage over optimization-based models as they can model problems of scheduling under uncertainty (in arrival time and duration of tasks) and suggest solutions in terms of *dynamic* schedulers that observe the evolution of the plant.

Most of this work is devoted to establishing the link between the classical job-shop scheduling problem and timed automata and adapting the reachability algorithm of the tool Kronos to find shortest paths in timed automata. This is not a completely straightforward adaptation of standard graph-searching algorithms due to the density of the transition graph. We explore the performance limits of current timed automata technology, and although they cannot yet cope with the state-of-the-art in optimization, the results are rather encouraging.

The rest of the paper is organized as follows. In section 2 we give a short introduction to the job-shop scheduling problem. In section 3 we recall the definition of timed automata and show how to transform a job-shop specification into an acyclic timed automaton whose runs correspond to feasible schedules. In section 4 we describe several algorithms for solving the shortest-path problem for such timed automata (either exactly or approximately) and report the performance results of their implementation numerous benchmark examples.

2   Job-Shop Scheduling

The Job-shop scheduling problem is a generic resource allocation problem in which common resources ("machines") are required at various time points (and for given durations) by different tasks. The goal is to find a way to allocate the resources such that all the tasks terminate as soon as possible (or "minimal makespan" in the scheduling jargon). We consider throughout the paper a fixed set M of resources. Intuitively, a *step* is a pair (m, d) where $m \in M$ and $d \in \mathbb{N}$, indicating the required utilization of resource m for time duration d. A job specification is a finite sequence

$$J = (m_1, d_1), (m_2, d_2), \ldots, (m_k, d_k) \tag{1}$$

of steps, stating that in order the accomplish job J, one needs to use machine m_1 for d_1 time, then use machine m_2 for d_2 time, etc. The formal definition below tries to optimize the notations for the sequel.

Definition 1 (Job-Shop Specification). *Let M be a finite set of resources (machines). A job specification over a set M of resources is a triple $J = (k, \mu, d)$ where $k \in \mathbb{N}$ is the number of steps in J, $\mu : \{1..k\} \to M$ indicates which resource is used at each step, and $d : \{1..k\} \to \mathbb{N}$ specifies the length of each step. A job-shop specification is a set $\mathcal{J} = \{J^1, \ldots, J^n\}$ of jobs with $J^i = (k^i, \mu^i, d^i)$.*

We make the following assumptions: 1) A job can wait an arbitrary amount of time between two steps. 2) Once a job starts to use a machine, it is not preempted until the step terminates. 3) Each machine is used exactly once by every job.[1]

We denote $\mathbb{R}_+$ by T, abuse $\mathcal{J}$ for $\{1, \ldots, n\}$ and let $K = \{1, \ldots, k\}$.

Definition 2 (Feasible Schedules). *Let* $\mathcal{J} = \{J^1, \ldots, J^n\}$ *be a job-shop specification. A feasible schedule for* $\mathcal{J}$ *is a relation* $S \subseteq \mathcal{J} \times K \times T$ *so that* $(i, j, t) \in S$ *indicates that job* J^i *is busy doing its* j^{th} *step at time* t *and, hence, occupies machine* $\mu^i(j)$. *A feasible schedule should satisfy the following conditions:*

1. *Ordering: if* $(i, j, t) \in S$ *and* $(i, j', t') \in S$ *then* $j < j'$ *implies* $t < t'$ *(steps of the same job are executed in order).*
2. *Covering and Non-Preemption: For every* $i \in \mathcal{J}$ *and* $j \in K$, *the set* $\{t : (i, j, t) \in S\}$ *is a non-empty set of the form* $[r, r + d]$ *for some* $r \in T$ *and* $d \geq d^i(j)$ *(every step is executed continuously until completion).[2]*
3. *Mutual Exclusion: For every* $i, i' \in \mathcal{J}$, $j, j' \in K$ *and* $t \in T$, *if* $(i, j, t) \in S$ *and* $(i', j', t) \in S$ *then* $\mu^i(j) \neq \mu^{i'}(j')$ *(two steps of different jobs which execute at the same time do not use the same machine).*

The *length* $|S|$ of a schedule is the maximal t over all $(i, j, t) \in S$. The *optimal job-shop scheduling problem* is to find a schedule of a minimal length. This problem is known to be NP-hard. From the relational definition of schedules one can derive the following commonly used definitions:

1. The *machine allocation function* $\alpha : M \times T \to \mathcal{J}$ stating which job occupies a machine at any time, defined as $\alpha(m, t) = i$ if $(i, j, t) \in S$ and $\mu^i(j) = m$.
2. The *task progress function* $\beta : \mathcal{J} \times T \to M$ stating what machine is used by a job is at a given time, defined as $\beta(i, t) = m$ if $(i, j, t) \in S$ and $\mu^i(j) = m$.

These functions are partial — a machine or a job might be idle at certain times. **Example 1**: Consider $M = \{m_1, m_2\}$ and two jobs $J^1 = (m_1, 4), (m_2, 5)$ and $J^2 = (m_1, 3)$. Two schedules S_1 and S_2 appear in Figure 1. The length of S_1 is 9 and it is the optimal schedule.

We conclude this section with an observation concerning optimal schedules which will be used later. We say that a schedule S exhibits *laziness* at step j of job i if immediately before starting that step there is an interval in which both the job and the corresponding resource are idle. For example in the schedule S of Figure 2, there is a laziness at $(2, 1)$. In the job-shop setting, where there are no *logical dependencies* among the jobs, such idling is of no use. Note that a waiting period which is not adjacent to the beginning of the step, e.g. step $(3, 1)$ of the same schedule, is not considered as laziness.

Definition 3 (Lazy Schedules). *Let* S *be a schedule, let* i *be a job and* j *a step with* $\mu^i(j) = m$ *which starts at time* t. *We say that* S *exhibits laziness at* (i, j) *if there is a time* $r < t$ *such that for every* $t' \in [r, t)$, $\beta(i, t') = \perp$ *and for every* $i' \neq i$, $\beta(i', t') \neq m$. *A schedule* S *is non-lazy if it exhibits no laziness.*

---

[1] This assumption simplifies the presentation but maintains the inherent complexity.
[2] Note that we allow a job to occupy the machine *after* the step has terminated. This helps in simplifying the timed automata but has no effect on the *optimal* solution.

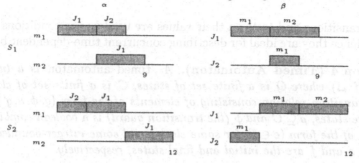

Fig. 1. Two schedule S_1 and S_2 visualized as the machine allocation function α and the task progress function β.

Claim 1 (Non-lazy Optimal Schedules) *Every lazy schedule S can be transformed into a non-lazy schedule $\hat{S}$ with $|\hat{S}| \leq |S|$. Hence every job-shop specification admits an optimal non-lazy schedule.*

Sketch of Proof: The proof is by taking a lazy schedule S and transforming it into a schedule S' were laziness occurs "later". A schedule defines a partial order relation $\prec$ on $\mathcal{J} \times K$ which is generated by the ordering constraints of each job, $(i,j) \prec (i,j+1)$, and by the choices made in the case of conflicts, $(i,j) \prec (i',j')$ if $\mu^i(j) = \mu^{i'}(j')$ and (i,j) precedes (i',j') in S. The laziness elimination procedure picks a lazy step (i,j) which is minimal with respect to $\prec$ and shifts its start time backward to t', to yield a new schedule S', such that $|S'| \leq |S|$. Moreover, the partial order associated with S' is identical to the one induced by S. The laziness at (i,j) is thus eliminated, and this might create new manifestations of laziness at later steps which are eliminated in the subsequent stages of the procedure (see illustration in Figure 2). Let $L(S) \subseteq \mathcal{J} \times K$ be the set of steps that are not preceded by laziness, namely $L(S) = \{(i,j) : \forall (i',j') \preceq (i,j) \text{ there is no laziness in } (i',j')\}$. Clearly the laziness removal procedure increases $L(S)$ and terminates due to finiteness. ◾

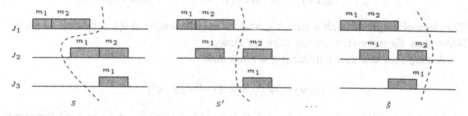

Fig. 2. Removing laziness from a schedule S: first we eliminate laziness at $(2,1)$ and create new ones at $(2,2)$ and $(3,1)$ in S', and those are further removed until a non-lazy schedule $\hat{S}$ is obtained. The dashed line indicates the frontier between $L(S)$ and the rest of the steps.

3   Timed Automata

Timed automata [AD94] are automata augmented with continuous clock variables whose values grow uniformly at every state. Clocks are reset to zero at certain transitions and tests on their values are used as pre-conditions for transitions. Hence they are ideal for describing concurrent time-dependent behaviors.

Definition 4 (Timed Automaton). *A timed automaton is a tuple $\mathcal{A} = (Q, C, s, f, \Delta)$ where Q is a finite set of states, C is a finite set of clocks, and Δ is a transition relation consisting of elements of the form (q, ϕ, ρ, q') where q and q' are states, $\rho \subseteq C$ and ϕ (the transition guard) is a boolean combination of formulae of the form $(c \in I)$ for some clock c and some integer-bounded interval I. States s and f are the initial and final states, respectively.*

A *clock valuation* is a function $\mathbf{v} : C \to \mathbb{R}_+ \cup \{0\}$, or equivalently a $|C|$-dimensional vector over $\mathbb{R}_+$. We denote the set of all clock valuations by $\mathcal{H}$. A configuration of the automaton is hence a pair $(q, \mathbf{v}) \in Q \times \mathcal{H}$ consisting of a discrete state (sometimes called "location") and a clock valuation. Every subset $\rho \subseteq C$ induces a reset function $\mathrm{Reset}_\rho : \mathcal{H} \to \mathcal{H}$ defined for every clock valuation $\mathbf{v}$ and every clock variable $c \in C$ as

$$\mathrm{Reset}_\rho \mathbf{v}(c) = \begin{cases} 0 & \text{if } c \in \rho \\ \mathbf{v}(c) & \text{if } c \notin \rho \end{cases}$$

That is, Reset_ρ resets to zero all the clocks in ρ and leaves the others unchanged. We use $\mathbf{1}$ to denote the unit vector $(1, \ldots, 1)$ and $\mathbf{0}$ for the zero vector.

A *step* of the automaton is one of the following:

- A discrete step: $(q, \mathbf{v}) \xrightarrow{0} (q', \mathbf{v}')$, where there exists $\delta = (q, \phi, \rho, q') \in \Delta$, such that $\mathbf{v}$ satisfies ϕ and $\mathbf{v}' = \mathrm{Reset}_\rho(\mathbf{v})$.
- A time step: $(q, \mathbf{v}) \xrightarrow{t} (q, \mathbf{v} + t\mathbf{1})$, $t \in \mathbb{R}_+$.

A *run* of the automaton starting from $(q_0, \mathbf{v}_0)$ is a finite sequence of steps

$$\xi : \quad (q_0, \mathbf{v}_0) \xrightarrow{t_1} (q_1, \mathbf{v}_1) \xrightarrow{t_2} \cdots \xrightarrow{t_n} (q_n, \mathbf{v}_n).$$

The *logical length* of such a run is n and its *metric length* is $|\xi| = t_1 + t_2 + \cdots + t_n$. Note that discrete transitions take no time.

A *lazy run* is a run containing a fragment

$$(q, \mathbf{v}) \xrightarrow{t} (q, \mathbf{v} + t) \xrightarrow{0} (q', \mathbf{v}')$$

where the transition taken at $(q, \mathbf{v} + t)$ is enabled already at $(q, \mathbf{v} + t')$ for some $t' < t$. In a non-lazy run whenever a transition is taken from a state, it is taken at the earliest possible time. Clearly, from any given configuration there are only finitely many non-lazy continuations and hence for every k there are only finitely many non-lazy runs with k steps.

Next we construct for every job $J = (k, \mu, d)$ a timed automaton with one clock such that for every step j such that $\mu(j) = m$ there will be two states: a state $\overline{m}$ which indicates that the job is waiting to start the step and a state m indicating that the job is executing the step. Upon entering m the clock is reset to zero, and the automaton can leave the state only after time $d(j)$ has elapsed.

Let $\overline{M} = \{\overline{m} : m \in M\}$ and let $\overline{\mu} : K \to \overline{M}$ be an auxiliary function such that $\overline{\mu}(j) = \overline{m}$ whenever $\mu(j) = m$. Note that the clock c is *inactive* at state $\overline{m}$ because it is reset to zero without being tested upon leaving $\overline{m}$.

Definition 5 (Timed Automaton for a Job). *Let $J = (k, \mu, d)$ be job. Its associated timed automaton is $\mathcal{A} = (Q, \{c\}, \Delta, s, f)$ with $Q = P \cup \overline{P} \cup \{f\}$ where $P = \{\mu(1), \ldots \mu(k)\}$, and $\overline{P} = \{\overline{\mu}(1), \ldots, \overline{\mu}(n)\}$. The transition relation Δ consists of the following tuples*

$$(\overline{\mu}(j), true, \{c\}, \mu(j)) \qquad j = 1..k$$
$$(\mu(j), c \geq d(j), \emptyset, \overline{\mu}(j+1)) \; j = 1..k - 1$$
$$(\mu(k), c \geq d(k), \emptyset, f)$$

The initial state is $\overline{\mu}(1)$.

The automata for the two jobs in Example 1 are depicted in Figure 3.

For every automaton $\mathcal{A}$ we define a *ranking function* $g : Q \times \mathbb{R}_+ \to \mathbb{R}_+$ such that $g(q, v)$ is a lower-bound on the time remaining until f is reached from (q, v):

$$g(f, v) = 0$$
$$g(\overline{\mu}(j), v) = \sum_{l=j}^{k} d(l)$$
$$g(\mu(j), v) = g(\overline{\mu}(j), v) - \min\{v, d(j)\}$$

Fig. 3. The automata corresponding to the jobs $J^1 = (m_1, 4), (m_2, 5)$ and $J^2 = (m_1, 3)$.

In order to obtain the timed automaton representing the whole job-shop specification we need to compose the automata for the individual tasks. The composition is rather standard, the only particular feature is the enforcement of mutual exclusion constraints by forbidding global states in which two or more automata are in a state corresponding to the same resource m. An n-tuple $q = (q^1, \ldots, q^n) \in (M \cup \overline{M} \cup \{f\})^n$ is said to be *conflicting* if it contains two components q^a and q^b such that $q^a = q^b = m \in M$.

Definition 6 (Mutual Exclusion Composition). *Let $\mathcal{J} = \{J^1, \ldots, J^n\}$ be a job-shop specification and let $\mathcal{A}^i = (Q^i, C^i, \Delta^i, s^i, f^i)$ be the automaton corresponding to each J^i. Their mutual exclusion composition is the automaton $\mathcal{A} = (Q, C, \Delta, s, f)$ such that Q is the restriction of $Q^1 \times \ldots Q^n$ to non-conflicting states, $C = C^1 \cup \ldots \cup C^n$, $s = (s^1, \ldots, s^n)$, $f = (f^1, \ldots, f^n)$ and the transition relation Δ contains all the tuples of the form*

$$((q^1, \ldots, q^a, \ldots, q^n), \phi, \rho, (q^1, \ldots, p^a, \ldots, q^n))$$

such that $(q^a, \phi, \rho, p^a) \in \Delta^a$ for some a and the global states $(q^1, \ldots, q^a, \ldots, q^n)$ and $(q^1, \ldots, p^a, \ldots, q^n)$ are non-conflicting.

The composition to the two automata of Figure 3 appears in Figure 4.

A run of $\mathcal{A}$ is *complete* if it starts at $(s, 0)$ and the last step is a transition to f. From every complete run ξ one can derive in an obvious way a schedule relation S_ξ such that $(i, j, t) \in S_\xi$ if at time t the ith component of the automaton is at state $\mu(j)$. The length of S_ξ coincides with the metric length of ξ.

Claim 2 (Runs and Schedules) *Let $\mathcal{A}$ be the automaton generated for the job-shop specification $\mathcal{J}$ according to Definitions 1 and 2. Then:*

1. *For every complete run ξ of $\mathcal{A}$, its associated schedule S_ξ is feasible for $\mathcal{J}$.*
2. *For every feasible schedule S for $\mathcal{J}$ there is a run ξ of $\mathcal{A}$ such that $S_\xi = S$. Moreover, if S is non-lazy so is ξ.*

Note that non-laziness of the run does not imply non-laziness of the schedule.

Corollary 1 (Job-Shop Scheduling and Timed Automata). *The optimal job-shop scheduling problem can be reduced to the problem of finding the shortest non-lazy path in a timed automaton.*

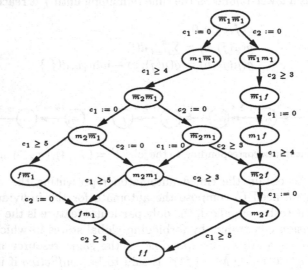

Fig. 4. The global timed automaton for the two jobs.

The two schedules appearing in Figure 1 correspond to the following two runs (we use notation $\perp$ to indicate inactive clocks):

S_1 :
$(\overline{m}_1, \overline{m}_1, \perp, \perp) \xrightarrow{0} (m_1, \overline{m}_1, 0, \perp) \xrightarrow{4} (m_1, \overline{m}_1, 4, \perp) \xrightarrow{0} (\overline{m}_2, \overline{m}_1, \perp, \perp) \xrightarrow{0} (m_2, \overline{m}_1, 0, \perp)$
$\xrightarrow{0} (m_2, m_1, 0, 0) \xrightarrow{3} (m_2, m_1, 3, 3) \xrightarrow{0} (m_2, f, 3, \perp) \xrightarrow{2} (m_2, f, 5, \perp) \xrightarrow{0} (f, f, \perp, \perp)$

S_2 :
$(\overline{m}_1, \overline{m}_1, \perp, \perp) \xrightarrow{0} (\overline{m}_1, m_1, \perp, 0) \xrightarrow{3} (\overline{m}_1, m_1, \perp, 3) \xrightarrow{0} (\overline{m}_1, f, \perp, \perp) \xrightarrow{0} (m_1, f, 0, \perp)$
$\xrightarrow{4} (m_1, f, 4, \perp) \xrightarrow{0} (\overline{m}_2, f, \perp, \perp) \xrightarrow{0} (m_2, f, 0, \perp) \xrightarrow{5} (m_2, f, 5, \perp) \xrightarrow{0} (f, f, \perp, \perp)$

Some words are in order to describe the structure of the job-shop timed automaton. First, it is an *acyclic* automaton and its state-space admits a natural partial-order. It can be partitioned into levels according to the number of discrete transitions from s to the state. All transitions indicate either a component moving from an active to an inactive state (these are guarded by conditions of the form $c_i \geq d$), or a component moving into an active state (these are labeled by resets $c_i := 0$). There are no staying conditions (invariants) and the automaton can stay forever in any given state. Recall that in a timed automaton, the transition graph might be misleading, because two or more transitions entering *the same* discrete state, e.g. transitions to (m_2, f) in Figure 4, might enter it with different clock valuations, and hence lead to different continuations. Consequently, algorithms for verification and quantitative analysis might need to explore all the nodes in the unfolding of the automaton into a tree. Two transitions outgoing from the same state might represent a choice of the scheduler, for example, the two transitions outgoing from the initial state represent the decision to whom to give first the resource m_1. On the other hand some duplication of paths are just artifacts due to interleaving, for example, the two paths outgoing from $(\overline{m}_2, \overline{m}_1)$ to (m_2, m_1) are practically equivalent.

Another useful observation is that from every job-shop specification $\mathcal{J}$ one can construct its reverse problem $\mathcal{J}'$ where the order of every individual job is reversed. Every feasible schedule for $\mathcal{J}'$ can be transformed easily into a feasible schedule for $\mathcal{J}$ having the same length. Doing a forward search on the automaton for $\mathcal{J}'$ is thus equivalent to doing a backward search on the automaton for $\mathcal{J}$.

4   Shortest Paths in Timed Automata

In this section we describe how the symbolic forward reachability algorithm of Kronos is adapted to find a shortest path in a job-shop timed automaton. Although Corollary 1 allows us to use enumerative methods in the case of deterministic job-shop problems, we start with algorithms that do not take advantage of non-laziness, both for the completeness of the presentation and as a preparation for more complex scheduling problems where non-laziness results do not hold. Standard shortest-path algorithms operate on *discrete* graphs with numerical weights assigned to their edges. The transition graphs of timed automata are non-countable and hence not amenable to enumerative algorithms.[3]

We recall some commonly-used definitions concerning timed automata. A *zone* is a subset of $\mathcal{H}$ consisting of points satisfying a conjunction of inequalities of the form $c_i - c_j \geq d$ or $c_i \geq d$. A *symbolic state* is a pair (q, Z) where q is a discrete state and Z is a zone. It denotes the set of configurations $\{(q, \mathbf{z}) : \mathbf{z} \in Z\}$. Symbolic states are closed under the following operations:

- The *time successor* of (q, Z) is the set of configurations which are reachable from (q, Z) by letting time progress:

$$Post^t(q, Z) = \{(q, \mathbf{z} + r\mathbf{1}) : \mathbf{z} \in Z, r \geq 0\}.$$

---

[3] One can, of course, discretize time into unit steps but this will cause an enormous increase in the state-space of the automaton.

We say that (q, Z) is *time-closed* if $(q, Z) = Post^t(q, Z)$.
- The δ-*transition successor* of (q, Z) is the set of configurations reachable from (q, Z) by taking the transition $\delta = (q, \phi, \rho, q') \in \Delta$:

$$Post^\delta(q, Z) = \{(q', \text{Reset}_\rho(z)) : z \in Z \cap \phi\}.$$

- The δ-*successor* of a time-closed symbolic state (q, Z) is the set of configurations reachable by a δ-transition followed by passage of time:

$$Succ^\delta(q, Z) = Post^t(Post^\delta(q, Z)).$$

- The *successors* of (q, Z) is the set of all its δ-successors:

$$Succ(q, Z) = \bigcup_{\delta \in \Delta} (Succ^\delta(q, Z)).$$

To compute all the reachable configurations of the job-shop automaton we use a variant of the standard forward reachability algorithm for timed automata, specialized for acyclic graphs.

Algorithm 1 (Forward Reachability for Acyclic Timed Automata)
Waiting:=$\{Post^t(s, 0)\}$;
while *Waiting* $\neq \emptyset$; **do**
  Pick $(q, Z) \in$ *Waiting*;
  For every $(q', Z') \in Succ(q, Z)$;
    Insert (q', Z') *into Waiting*;
  Remove (q, Z) *from Waiting*
end

This algorithm solves the reachability problem for timed automata — a trivial problem for job-shop automata since all complete runs lead to f. Its adaptation for finding *shortest paths* is rather straightforward. All we do is to use a clock-space $\mathcal{H}'$ which is the clock-space of $\mathcal{A}$ augmented with an additional clock c_{n+1} which is never reset. For any symbolic state (q, Z) reachable in the modified automaton $\mathcal{A}'$, if $(v_1, \ldots, v_n, v_{n+1}) \in Z$ then $(q, (v_1, \ldots, v_n))$ is reachable in $\mathcal{A}$ within any time $t \geq v_{n+1}$. Consequently, the length of the shortest run from the initial state to q via the (qualitative) path which generated (q, Z) is

$$G(q, Z) = \min\{v_{n+1} : (v_1, \ldots, v_n, v_{n+1}) \in Z\}$$

and the length of the optimal schedule is

$$\min\{G(f, Z) : (f, Z) \text{ is reachable in } \mathcal{A}'\}.$$

Hence, running Algorithm 1 on $\mathcal{A}'$ is guaranteed to find the minimal schedule.

The rest of the section is devoted to several improvements of this algorithm, whose naïve implementation will generate a symbolic state for almost every node in the unfolding of the automaton. Experimental results appear in Table 1.

Inclusion Test: This is a common method used in Kronos for reducing the number of symbolic states in verification. It is based on the fact that $Z \subseteq Z'$ implies $Succ^\delta(q, Z) \subseteq Succ^\delta(q, Z')$ for every $\delta \in \Delta$. Hence, whenever a new symbolic state (q, Z) is generated, it is compared with any other (q, Z') in the waiting list: if $Z \subseteq Z'$ then (q, Z) is not inserted and if $Z' \subseteq Z$, (q, Z') is removed from the list. Note that allowing the automaton to stay indefinitely in any state makes the explored zones "upward-closed" with respect to absolute time and increases significantly the effectiveness of the inclusion test.

Domination Test: The inclusion test removes a symbolic state only if *all* its successors are included in those of another symbolic state. Since we are interested only in optimal runs, we can apply stronger reductions that do not preserve all runs, but still preserve the optimal ones. As an example consider an automaton with two paths leading from the initial state to a state q, one by first resetting c_1 and then c_2 and one in the reverse order. The zones reachable via these paths are $Z_1 = c_3 \geq c_1 \geq c_2 \geq 0$ and $Z_2 = c_3 \geq c_2 \geq c_1 \geq 0$, where c_3 is the additional clock which measures absolute time. These zones are incomparable with respect to inclusion, however, for every t they share a "maximal" point (t, t, t) which corresponds to the respective non-lazy runs along each of the paths. Hence it is sufficient to explore only one of the symbolic states (q, Z_1) and (q, Z_2).

Let $(q, (\mathbf{v}, t))$ and $(q, (\mathbf{v}', t'))$ be two reachable configurations in $Q \times \mathcal{H}'$. We say that $(\mathbf{v}, t)$ *dominates* $(\mathbf{v}', t')$ if $t \leq t'$ and $\mathbf{v} \geq \mathbf{v}'$. Intuitively this means that $(q, \mathbf{v})$ was reached not later than $(q, \mathbf{v}')$ and with larger clock values, which implies that steps active at q started earlier along the run to $(q, \mathbf{v})$ and hence can terminate earlier. It can be shown that for every reachable symbolic state (q, Z), Z contains an optimal point $(\mathbf{v}^*, t^*)$ dominating every other point in Z. This point, which is reachable via a non-lazy run, can be computed by letting $t^* = G(q, Z)$ (earliest arrival time) and $\mathbf{v}^* = (v_1^*, \ldots, v_n^*)$ where for every i,

$$v_i^* = \max\{v_i : (v_1, \ldots, v_i, \ldots, v_n, t^*) \in Z\}.$$

We say that Z_1 dominates Z_2 if $(\mathbf{v}_1^*, t_1^*)$ dominates $(\mathbf{v}_2^*, t_2^*)$. We apply the domination test in the same manner as the inclusion test to obtain a further reduction of the number of symbolic states explored.

Best-First Search: The next improvement consists in using a more intelligent search order than breadth-first. To this end we define an evaluation function $E : Q \times \mathcal{H}' \to \mathbb{R}_+$ for estimating the quality of configurations and symbolic states:

$$E((q_1, \ldots, q_n), (v_1, \ldots, v_n, t)) = t + \max\{g^i(q_i, v_i)\}_{i=1}^n$$

where g^i is the previously-defined ranking function associated with each automaton $\mathcal{A}^i$. Note that $\max\{g^i\}$ gives the most optimistic estimation of the *remaining* time, assuming that no job will have to wait. The extension of this function to zones is $E(q, Z) = E(q, (\mathbf{v}^*, t^*))$. It is not hard to see that $E(q, Z)$ gives a lower bound on the length of every complete run which passes through (q, Z).

The modified algorithm now orders the waiting list of symbolic states according to their evaluation (and applies the inclusion and domination tests upon insertion to the list). This algorithm is guaranteed to produce the optimal path

Table 1. The results for n jobs with 4 tasks. Columns #j, #ds and #tree show, respectively, the number of jobs, the number of discrete states in the automaton and the number of different reachable symbolic states (which is close to the number of nodes in the unfolding of the automaton into a tree). The rest of the table shows the performance, in terms of the number of explored symbolic states and time (in seconds), of algorithms employing, progressively, the inclusion test, the domination test, and the best-first search (m.o. indicates memory overflow).

Problem size			Inclusion		Domination		Best-first	
#j	#ds	#tree	#s	time	#s	time	#s	time
2	77	632	212	1	100	1	38	1
3	629	67298	5469	2	1143	1	384	1
4	4929	279146	159994	126	11383	2	1561	1
5	37225	m.o.	m.o.	m.o.	116975	88	2810	1
6	272125	m.o.	m.o.	m.o.	1105981	4791	32423	6

because it stops the exploration only when it is clear that the unexplored states cannot lead to schedules better than those found so far.

Algorithm 2 (Best-First Forward Reachability)
$Waiting:=\{Post^t(s,\mathbf{0})\}$;
$Best:=\infty$
$(q,Z):=$ *first in Waiting*;
while $Best > E(q,Z)$
do
  For every $(q',Z') \in Succ(q,Z)$;
    if $q' = f$ then
      $Best:=\min\{Best,E(q',Z')\}$
    else
      Insert (q',Z') into Waiting;
  Remove (q,Z) from Waiting
  $(q,Z):=$ *first in Waiting*;
end

We have implemented these techniques into Kronos and tested them first on a family of problems consisting of n jobs, $n = 2, \ldots, 6$, each with 4 steps.[4] We also make use of Kronos' capability to handle zones of varying dimensionality, were only active clocks are considered [DY96]. The results, obtained on a Pentium P3, 666 MHz under Linux, with memory restricted to 512MB, are depicted in Table 1. One can see that the number of symbolic states explored by the best-first algorithm is smaller than the number of discrete states in the timed automaton. Nevertheless the combinatorial nature of the problem cannot be avoided.
Points instead of Zones: Following Corollary 1, an optimal run can be found among the non-lazy runs and the search can be restricted to explore only such

---

[4] The problems can be found in www-verimag.imag.fr/~maler/jobshop.

runs. This search can be performed without using zones, but rather using single points in the clock space (which are exactly the dominating points of the reachable zones). This reduces significantly memory usage ($O(n)$ per symbolic state instead of $O(n^2)$) and simplifies the operations.

Sub-optimal Solutions: In order to treat larger problems we abandon optimality and use a heuristic algorithm which can quickly generate sub-optimal solutions. The algorithm is a mixture of breadth-first and best-first search with a fixed number w of explored nodes at any level of the automaton. For every level we take the w best (according to E) symbolic states, generate their successors but explore only the best w among them, and so on. The number w is the main parameter of this technique, and although the number of explored states grows monotonically with w, the quality of the solution does not — sometimes the solution found with a smaller w is better than the one found with a larger w.

In order to test this heuristics we took 10 problems among the most notorious job-shop scheduling problems.[5] Note that these are pathological problems with a large variability in step durations, constructed to demonstrate the hardness of job-shop scheduling. For each of these problems we have applied our algorithms for different choices of w, both forward and backward. In Table 2 we compare our best results on these problems with the results reported in Table 15 of the recent survey [JM99], where the the 18 best-known methods were compared. In order to appreciate the difficulty, we also compare our results with the best results among 3000 randomly-generated solutions for each of the problems.

Table 2. The results for 10 hard problems using the bounded width heuristic. The first three columns give the problem name, no. of jobs and no. of machines (and steps). Our results (time in seconds, the length of the best schedule found and its deviation from the optimum) appear next, followed by the best out of 3000 randomly-generated solutions and by the best known result for each problem.

problem			Kronos			Rand		Opt
name	#j	#m	time	length	deviation	length	deviation	length
FT10	10	10	13	982	5.59 %	1761	89.35 %	930
LA02	10	5	1	655	0.00 %	1059	61.68 %	655
LA19	10	10	12	885	5.11 %	1612	91.45 %	842
LA21	10	15	178	1114	6.50 %	2339	123.61 %	1046
LA24	10	15	186	992	5.98 %	2100	124.00 %	936
LA25	10	15	180	1041	6.55 %	2209	126.10 %	977
LA27	10	20	6	1343	8.74 %	2809	127.45 %	1235
LA29	10	20	193	1295	12.41 %	2713	135.50 %	1152
LA36	15	15	16	1391	9.70 %	2967	133.90 %	1268
LA37	15	15	72	1489	6.59 %	3188	128.20 %	1397

---

[5] The problems are taken from ftp://mscmga.ms.ic.ac.uk/pub/jobshop1.txt.

5   Related Work

This work can be viewed in the context of extending verification methodology in two orthogonal directions: from *verification* to *synthesis* and from *qualitative* to *quantitative* evaluation of behaviors. In verification we check the existence of certain paths in a *given* automaton, while in synthesis we have an automaton in which not all design choices have been made and we can remove transitions (and hence make the necessary choices) so that a property is satisfied. If we add a quantitative dimension (in this case, the duration of the path), verification is transformed to the evaluation of the worst performance measure over all paths, and synthesis into the restriction of the automaton to one or more optimal paths.

The idea of applying synthesis to timed automata was first explored in [WH92]. An algorithm for safety controller synthesis for timed automata, based on operation on zones was first reported in [MPS95] and later in [AMP95], where an example of a simple scheduler was given, and in [AMPS98]. This algorithm is a generalization of the verification algorithm for timed automata [HNSY94,ACD93] used in Kronos [Y97,BDM+98]. In these and other works on treating scheduling problems as synthesis problems for timed automata, such as [AGP99], the emphasis was on yes/no properties, such as the existence of a feasible schedule, in the presence of an uncontrolled adversary.

A transition toward quantitative evaluation criteria was made already in [CY91] where timed automata were used to compute bounds on delays in real-time systems and in [CCM+94] where variants of shortest-path problems were solved on a timed model much weaker than timed automata. To our knowledge, the first quantitative synthesis work on timed automata was [AM99] in which the following problem has been solved: "given a timed automaton with both controlled and uncontrolled transitions, restrict the automaton in a way that from each configuration the worst-case time to reach a target state is minimal". If there is no adversary, this problem corresponds to finding the shortest path. Due to the presence of an adversary, the solution in [AM99] employs backward-computation (dynamic programming), i.e. an iterative computation of a function $h : Q \times \mathcal{H} \to \mathbb{R}_+$ such that $h(q, \mathbf{v})$ indicates the minimal time for reaching the target state from $(q, \mathbf{v})$. The implementation of the forward algorithm used in this paper can be viewed as iterating with a function h such that $h(q, \mathbf{v})$ indicates the minimal time to reach $(q, \mathbf{v})$ from the initial state. The reachable states in the augmented clock-space are nothing but a relational representation of h.

Around the same time, in the framework of the VHS (Verification of Hybrid systems) project, a simplified model of a steel plant was presented as a case-study [BS99]. The model had more features than the job-shop scheduling problem such as upper-bounds on the time between steps, transportation problems, etc. A. Fehnker proposed a timed automaton model of this plant from which feasible schedules could be extracted [F99]. This work inspired us to find a systematic connection between classical scheduling problems and timed automata [M99], upon which this paper is based. Another work in this direction was concerned with another VHS case-study, a cyclic experimental batch plant at Dortmund for which an optimal dynamic scheduler was derived in [NY00].

The idea of using heuristic search is useful not only for shortest-path problems but for verification of timed automata (and verification in general) where some evaluation function can guide the search toward the target goal. These possibilities were investigated recently in [BFH+01a] on several classes of examples, including job-shop scheduling problems, where various search procedures and heuristics were explored and compared.

In [NTY00] it was shown that in order to find shortest paths in a timed automaton, it is sufficient to look at acyclic sequences of symbolic states (a fact that we do not need due to the acyclicity of job-shop automata) and an algorithms based on forward reachability was introduced. A recent generalization of the shortest path problem was investigated by [BFH+01b] and [ATP01]. In this model there is a *different* price for staying in any state and the total cost associated with the run progresses in different slopes along the path. It has been proved that the problem of finding the path with the minimal cost is computable.

6 Conclusions

We have suggested a novel application of timed automata, namely for solving job-shop scheduling problems. We believe that the insight gained from this point of view will contribute both to scheduling and to the study of timed automata. We have demonstrated that the performance of automata-based methods is not inferior to other methods developed within the last three decades. There are still many potential improvements to be explored such as the application of partial-order methods, more symbolic representation of the discrete states, new heuristics, etc. The most interesting challenge is to adapt these techniques for more complex scheduling situation such as those involving uncertainty or logical dependencies among tasks.

Acknowledgment

We are most grateful to Eugene Asarin and Marius Bozga for their help in the theoretical and practical aspects of this work. Thanks also to K. Larsen, S. Engell and anonymous referees for reading previous versions of this paper.

References

[ATP01]   R. Alur, S. La Torre and G.J. Pappas, Optimal Paths in Weighted Timed Automata, *Proc. HSCC'01*, 49-64, LNCS 2034, Springer 2001.

[AGP99]   K. Altisen, G. Goessler, A. Pnueli, J. Sifakis, S. Tripakis and S. Yovine, A Framework for Scheduler Synthesis. *Proc. RTSS'99*, 154-163, IEEE, 1999.

[ACD93]   R. Alur, C. Courcoubetis, and D.L. Dill, Model Checking in Dense Real Time, *Information and Computation* 104, 2-34, 1993.

[AD94]   R. Alur and D.L. Dill, A Theory of Timed Automata, *Theoretical Computer Science* 126, 183-235, 1994.

[AM99]   E. Asarin and O. Maler, As Soon as Possible: Time Optimal Control for Timed Automata, *Proc. HSCC'99*, 19-30, LNCS 1569, Springer, 1999.

[AMP95]   E. Asarin, O. Maler and A. Pnueli, Symbolic Controller Synthesis for Dis-
            crete and Timed Systems, Hybrid Systems II, LNCS 999, Springer, 1995.
[AMPS98]   E. Asarin, O. Maler, A. Pnueli and J. Sifakis, Controller Synthesis for
            Timed Automata, Proc. IFAC Symposium on System Structure and Con-
            trol, 469-474, Elsevier, 1998.
[BFH+01a]   G. Behrmann, A. Fehnker T.S. Hune, K.G. Larsen, P. Pettersson and
            J. Romijn, Efficient Guiding Towards Cost-Optimality in UPPAAL, Proc.
            TACAS 2001, 174-188, LNCS 2031, Springer, 2001.
[BFH+01b]   G. Behrmann, A. Fehnker T.S. Hune, K.G. Larsen, P. Pettersson,
            J. Romijn and F.W. Vaandrager, Minimum-Cost Reachability for Linearly
            Priced Timed Automata, Proc. HSCC'01, 147-161, LNCS 2034, Springer
            2001.
[BS99]   R. Boel and G. Stremersch, VHS case study 5: Modelling and Verification
            of Scheduling for Steel Plant at SIDMAR, Draft, 1999.
[BDM+98]   M. Bozga, C. Daws, O. Maler, A. Olivero, S. Tripakis, and S. Yovine,
            Kronos: a Model-Checking Tool for Real-Time Systems, Proc. CAV'98,
            LNCS 1427, Springer, 1998.
[CCM+94]   S Campos, E. Clarke, W. Marrero, M. Minea and H. Hiraishi, Comput-
            ing Quantitative Characteristics of Finite-state Real-time Systems, Proc.
            RTSS'94, IEEE, 1994.
[CY91]   C. Courcoubetis and M. Yannakakis, Minimum and Maximum Delay Prob-
            lems in Real-time Systems, Proc. CAV'91, LNCS 575, 399-409, Springer,
            1991.
[DY96]   C. Daws and S. Yovine, Reducing the Number of Clock Variables of Timed
            Automata, Proc. RTSS'96, 73-81, IEEE, 1996.
[F99]   A. Fehnker, Scheduling a Steel Plant with Timed Automata, Proc.
            RTCSA'99, 1999.
[HNSY94]   T. Henzinger, X. Nicollin, J. Sifakis, and S. Yovine, Symbolic Model-
            checking for Real-time Systems, Information and Computation 111, 193-
            244, 1994.
[JM99]   A.S. Jain and S. Meeran, Deterministic Job-Shop Scheduling: Past, Present
            and Future, European Journal of Operational Research 113, 390-434, 1999.
[M99]   O. Maler, On the Problem of Task Scheduling, Draft, February 1999.
[MPS95]   O. Maler, A. Pnueli and J. Sifakis. On the Synthesis of Discrete Controllers
            for Timed Systems, Proc. STACS'95, 229-242, LNCS 900, Springer, 1995.
[NTY00]   P. Niebert, S. Tripakis S. Yovine, Minimum-Time Reachability for Timed
            Automata, IEEE Mediteranean Control Conference, 2000.
[NY00]   P. Niebert and S. Yovine, Computing Optimal Operation Schemes for
            Chemical Plants in Multi-batch Mode, Proc. HSCC'2000, 338-351, LNCS
            1790, Springer, 2000.
[WH92]   H. Wong-Toi and G. Hoffmann, The Control of Dense Real-Time Discrete
            Event Systems, Technical report STAN-CS-92-1411, Stanford University,
            1992.
[Y97]   S. Yovine, Kronos: A Verification Tool for Real-time Systems, Int. J. of
            Software Tools for Technology Transfer 1, 1997.

As Cheap as Possible:
Efficient Cost-Optimal Reachability for Priced Timed Automata

Kim Larsen[12], Gerd Behrmann[1], Ed Brinksma[2], Ansgar Fehnker[4],
Thomas Hune[3], Paul Pettersson[5], and Judi Romijn[4]

[1] Basic Research in Computer Science, Aalborg University
[2] Department of Computer Systems, University of Twente
[3] Basic Research in Computer Science, Aarhus University
[4] Computing Science Institute, University of Nijmegen
[5] Department of Information Technology, Uppsala University

Abstract. In this paper we present an algorithm for efficiently computing optimal cost of reaching a goal state in the model of Linearly Priced Timed Automata (LPTA). The central contribution of this paper is a priced extension of so-called zones. This, together with a notion of facets of a zone, allows the entire machinery for symbolic reachability for timed automata in terms of zones to be lifted to cost-optimal reachability using priced zones. We report on experiments with a cost-optimizing extension of UPPAAL on a number of examples.

1 Introduction

Well-known formal verification tools for real-time and hybrid systems, such as UPPAAL [LPY97], Kronos [BDM+98] and HyTech [HHWT97], use symbolic techniques to deal with the infinite state spaces that are caused by the presence of continuous variables in the associated verification models. However, symbolic model checkers still share the "state space explosion problem" with their non-symbolic counterparts as the major obstacle for their application to non-trivial problems. A lot of research, therefore, is devoted to the containment of this problem.

An interesting idea for model checking of reachability properties that has received more attention recently is to "guide" the exploration of the (symbolic) state space such that "promising" sets of states are visited first. In a number of recent publications [Feh99,HLP00,BFH+,NY99,BM00] model checkers have been used to solve a number of non-trivial scheduling problems, reformulated in terms of reachability, viz. as the (im)possibility to reach a state that improves on a given optimality criterion. Such criteria distinguish scheduling algorithms from classical, full state space exploration model checking algorithms. They are used together with, for example, branch-and-bound techniques [AC91] to prune parts of the search tree that are guaranteed not to contain optimal solutions. This observation motivates research into the extension of model checking algorithms

G. Berry, H. Comon, and A. Finkel (Eds.): CAV 2001, LNCS 2102, pp. 493–505, 2001.

with optimality criteria. They provide a basis for the (cost-) guided exploration of state spaces, and improve the potential of model checking techniques for the resolution of scheduling problems. We believe that such extensions can be interesting for real-life applications of both model checking and scheduling.

Based on similar observations an extension of the timed automata model with a notion of *cost*, the *Linearly Priced Timed Automata* (LPTA), was already introduced in [BFH+01]. This model allows for a reachability analysis in terms of accumulated cost of traces, i.e. the sum of the costs of the individual transitions in the trace. Each action transitions has an associated price p determining its cost. Likewise, each location has an associated rate r and the cost of delaying d time units is $d \cdot r$. In [BFH+01], and independently in [ATP], computabitlity of minimal-cost reachability is demonstrated based on a cost-extension of the classical notion of regions.

Although ensuring computability, the region construction is known to be very inefficient. Tools like UPPAAL and Kronos use symbolic states of the form (l, Z), where l is a location of the timed automaton and Z is a *zone*, i.e. a convex set of clock valuations. The central contribution of this paper is the extension of this concept to that of *priced zones*, which are attributed with an (affine) linear function of clock valuations that defines the cost of reaching a valuation in the zone. We show that the entire machinery for symbolic reachability in terms of zones can be lifted to cost-optimal reachability for priced zones. It turns out that some of the operations on priced zones force us to split them into parts with different price attributes, giving rise to a new notion, viz. that of the *facets* of a zone.

The suitability of the LPTA model for scheduling problems was already illustrated in [BFH+], using the more restricted *Uniformly Priced Timed Automata* (UPTA) model, admitting an efficient priced zone implementation via *Difference Bound Matrices* [Dil89]. The model was used to consider traces for the time-optimal scheduling of a steel plant and a number of job shop problems. The greater expressivity of LPTA also supports other measures of cost, like idle time, weighted idle time, mean completion time, earliness, number of tardy jobs, tardiness, etc. We take an aircraft landing problem [BKA00] as the application example for this paper.

The structure of the rest of this paper is as follows. In Section 2 we give an abstract account of symbolic optimal reachability in terms of *priced transition systems*, including a generic algorithm for optimal reachability. In Section 3 we introduce the model of linearly priced timed automata (LPTA) as a special case of the framework of Section 2. We also introduce here our running application example, the aircraft landing problem. Section 4 contains the definition of the central concept of priced zones. The operations that we need on priced zones and facets are provided in Section 5. The implementation of the algorithm, and the results of experimentation with our examples are reported in Section 6. Our conclusions, finally, are presented in Section 7.

2 Symbolic Optimal Reachability

Analysis of infinite state systems require symbolic techniques in order to effectively represent and manipulate sets of states simultaneously (see [FS01],[FS98], [ACJYK96,AJ94,Cer94]). For analysis of cost-optimality, additional information of *costs* associated with individual states needs to be represented. In this section, we describe a *general* framework for symbolic analysis of cost-optimal reachability on the abstract level of priced transition systems.

A *priced transition system* is a structure $\mathcal{T} = (S, s_0, \Sigma, \rightarrow)$, where S is a (infinite) set of states, $s_0 \in S$ is the initial state, Σ is a (finite) set of labels, and, $\rightarrow$ is a partial function from $S \times \Sigma \times S$ into the non-negative reals, $\mathbb{R}_{\geq 0}$, defining the possible transitions of the systems as well as their associated costs. We write $s \xrightarrow{a}_p s'$ whenever $\rightarrow (s, a, s')$ is defined and equals p. Intuitively, $s \xrightarrow{a}_p s'$ indicates that the system in state s has an a-labeled transition to the state s' with the cost of p. We denote by $s \xrightarrow{a} s'$ that $\exists p \in \mathbb{R}_{\geq 0}. s \xrightarrow{a}_p s'$, and, by $s \rightarrow s'$ that $\exists a \in \Sigma. s \xrightarrow{a} s'$. Now, an execution of $\mathcal{T}$ is a sequence $\alpha = s_0 \xrightarrow{a_1}_{p_1} s_1 \xrightarrow{a_2}_{p_2} s_2 \cdots \xrightarrow{a_n}_{p_n} s_n$. The *cost* of α, cost(α), is the sum $\sum_{i \in \{1 \ldots n\}} p_i$. For a given state s, the *minimal cost* of reaching s, mincost(s), is the infimum of the costs of finite executions starting in the initial state s_0 and ending in s. Similar, the minimal cost of reaching a designated set of states $G \subseteq S$, mincost(G), is the infimum of the costs of finite executions ending in a state of G.

To compute minimum-cost reachability, we suggest the use of *priced symbolic states* of the form (A, π), where $A \subseteq S$ is a set of states, and $\pi : A \longrightarrow \mathbb{R}_{\geq 0}$ assigns (non-negative) costs to all states of A. The intention is that, reachability of the priced symbolic state (A, π) should ensure, that any state s of A is reachable with cost arbitrarily close to $\pi(s)$. As we are interested in minimum-cost reachability, π should preferably return as small cost values as possible. This is obtained by the following extension of the *post*-operators to priced symbolic states: for (A, π) a priced symbolic state and $a \in \Sigma$, $Post_a(A, \pi)$ is the priced symbolic state $(post_a(A), \eta)$, where $post_a(A) = \{s' \mid \exists s \in A. s \xrightarrow{a} s'\}$ and η is given by $\eta(s) = \inf\{\pi(s') + p \mid s' \in A \wedge s' \xrightarrow{a}_p s\}$. That is, η essentially gives the cheapest cost for reaching states of B via states in A, assuming that these may be reached with costs according to π. A symbolic execution of a priced transition system $\mathcal{T}$ is a sequence $\beta = (A_0, \pi_0), \ldots, (A_n, \pi_n)$, where for $i < n$, $(A_{i+1}, \pi_{i+1}) = Post_{a_i}(A_i, \pi_i)$ for some $a_i \in \Sigma$, and $A_0 = \{s_0\}$ and $\pi_0(s_0) = 0$. It is not difficult to see, that there is a very close connection between executions and symbolic executions: for any execution α of $\mathcal{T}$ ending in a state s, there is a symbolic execution β of $\mathcal{T}$, that ends in a priced symbolic state (A, π), such that $s \in A$ and $\pi(s) \leq \text{cost}(\alpha)$. Dually, for any symbolic execution β of $\mathcal{T}$ ending in priced symbolic state (A, π), whenever $s \in A$, then mincost(s) $\leq \pi(s)$. From this it follows that the symbolic semantics on priced symbolic states accurately captures minimum-cost reachability in the sense that mincost(G) $= \inf\{\text{mincost}(A \cap G, \pi) : (A, \pi) \text{ is reachable}\}$.

COST := ∞
PASSED := ∅
WAITING := {(({s_0}, π_0)}
while WAITING ≠ ∅ **do**
  select (A, π) from WAITING
  if $A \cap G \neq \emptyset$ **and** $minCost(A \cap G, \pi) <$ COST **then**
    COST := $minCost(A \cap G, \pi)$
  if for all (B, η) in PASSED: $(B, \eta) \not\sqsubseteq (A, \pi)$ **then**
    add (A, π) to PASSED
    add $Post_a(A, \pi)$ to WAITING for all $a \in \Sigma$
return COST

Fig. 1. Abstract Algorithm for the Minimal-Cost Reachability Problem.

Let (A, π) and (B, η) be priced symbolic states. We write $(A, \pi) \sqsubseteq (B, \eta)$ if $B \subseteq A$ and $\pi(s) \leq \eta(s)$ for all $s \in B$, informally expressing, that (A, π) is "as big and cheap" as (B, η). Also, we denote by $minCost(A, \pi)$ the infimum costs in A w.r.t. π, i.e. $\inf\{\pi(s) \mid s \in A\}$. Now using the above notion of priced symbolic state and associated operations, an abstract algorithm for computing the minimum cost of reaching a designated set of goal states G is shown in Fig.1. It uses two data-structures WAITING and PASSED to store priced symbolic states waiting to be examined, and priced symbolic states already explored, respectively. In each iteration, the algorithm proceeds by selecting a priced symbolic state (A, π) from WAITING, checking that none of the previously explored states (B, η) are bigger and cheaper, i.e. $(B, \eta) \not\sqsubseteq (A, \pi)$, and adds it to PASSED and its successors to WAITING. In addition, the algorithm uses the global variable COST, which is initially set to ∞ and updated whenever a goal state is found that can be reached with lower cost than the current value of COST. The algorithm terminates when WAITING is empty, i.e. when no further priced symbolic states are left to be examined. When the algorithm of Fig. 1 terminates, the value of COST equals mincost(G). Furthermore, termination of the algorithm will be guaranteed provided $\sqsubseteq$ is a well-quasi ordering on priced symbolic states.

The above framework may be instantiated by providing concrete syntax for priced transition systems, together with data-structures for priced symbolic states allowing for computation of the *Post*-operations, $minCost$, as well as $\sqsubseteq$ (which should be well-quasi). In the following sections we provide such an instantiation for a priced extension of timed automata.

3   Priced Timed Automata

Linearly priced timed automata (LPTA) [BFH+01,BFH+,ATP] extend the model of timed automata [AD90] with *prices* on all edges and locations. In these models, the cost of taking an edge is the price associated with it, and the price of a location gives the cost-*rate* applied when delaying in that location.

Let $\mathbb{C}$ be a set of clocks. Then $\mathcal{B}(\mathbb{C})$ is the set of formulas that are conjunctions of atomic constraints of the form $x \bowtie n$ and $x - y \bowtie m$ for $x, y \in \mathbb{C}$, $\bowtie \in \{\leq$

$,=,\geq\}$,[1] n a natural number, and m an integer. Elements of $\mathcal{B}(\mathbb{C})$ are called clock constraints or zones over $\mathbb{C}$. $\mathcal{P}(\mathbb{C})$ denotes the power set of $\mathbb{C}$. Clock values are represented as functions from $\mathbb{C}$ to the non-negative reals $\mathbb{R}_{\geq 0}$, called clock valuations. We denote by $\mathbb{R}^{\mathbb{C}}$ the set of clock valuations for $\mathbb{C}$. For $u \in \mathbb{R}^{\mathbb{C}}$ and $g \in \mathcal{B}(\mathbb{C})$, we denote by $u \in g$ that u satisfies all constraints of g.

Definition 1 (Linearly Priced Timed Automata). *A linearly priced timed automaton $\mathcal{A}$ over clocks $\mathbb{C}$ is a tuple (L, l_0, E, I, P), where L is a finite set of locations, l_0 is the initial location, $E \subseteq L \times \mathcal{B}(\mathbb{C}) \times \mathcal{P}(\mathbb{C}) \times L$ is the set of edges, where an edge contains a source, a guard, a set of clocks to be reset, and a target, $I : L \to \mathcal{B}(\mathbb{C})$ assigns invariants to locations, and $P : (L \cup E) \to \mathbb{N}$ assigns prices to both locations and edges. In the case of $(l, g, r, l') \in E$, we write $l \xrightarrow{g,r} l'$.*

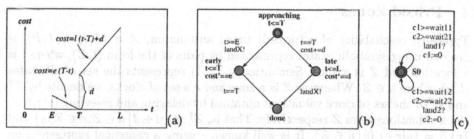

Fig. 2. Figure (a) depicts the cost of landing a plane at time t. Figure (b) shows an LPTA modelling the landing costs. Figure (c) shows an LPTA model of the runway.

The semantics of a linearly priced timed automaton $\mathcal{A} = (L, l_0, E, I, P)$ may now be given as a priced transition system with state-space $L \times \mathbb{R}^{\mathbb{C}}$ with the initial state (l_0, u_0) (where u_0 assigns zero to all clocks in $\mathbb{C}$), and with the finite label-set $\Sigma = E \cup \{\delta\}$. Thus, transitions are labelled either with the symbol δ (indicating some delay) or with an edge e (the one taken). More precisely, the priced transitions are given as follows:

- $(l, u) \xrightarrow{\delta}_p (l, u + d)$ if $\forall 0 \leq e \leq d : u + e \in I(l)$, and $p = d \cdot P(l)$,
- $(l, u) \xrightarrow{e}_p (l', u')$ if $e = (l, g, r, l') \in E$, $u \in g$, $u' = u[r \mapsto 0]$, and $p = P(e)$,

where for $d \in \mathbb{R}_{\geq 0}$, $u + d$ maps each clock x in $\mathbb{C}$ to the value $u(x) + d$, and $u[r \mapsto 0]$ denotes the clock valuation which maps each clock in r to the value 0 and agrees with u over $\mathbb{C} \setminus r$.

Example 1 (Aircraft Landing Problem). As an example of the use of LPTAs we consider the problem of scheduling aircraft landings at an airport, due to [BKA00]. For each aircraft there is a maximum speed and a most fuel efficient speed which determine an earliest and latest time the plane can land. In this

---

[1] For simplicity we do not deal with strict inequalities in this short version.

interval, there is a preferred landing time called target time at which the plane lands with minimal cost. The target time and the interval are shown as T and $[E, L]$ respectively in Fig. 2(a). For each time unit the actual landing time deviates from the target time, the landing cost increases with rate e for early landings and rate l for late landings. In addition there is a fixed cost d associated with late landings. In Fig. 2(b) the cost of landing an aircraft is modeled as an LPTA. The automaton starts in the initial location approaching and lands at the moment one of the two transitions labeled landX![2] are taken. In case the plane lands too early it enters location early in which it delays exactly $T - t$ time units. In case the plane is late the cost is measured in location late (i.e. the delay in location late is 0 if the plane is on target time). After L time units the automaton always ends in location done. Figure 2(c) models a runway ensuring that two consecutive landings takes place with a minimum separation time.   □

4   Priced Zones

Typically, reachability of a (priced) timed automaton, $\mathcal{A} = (L, l_0, E, I, P)$, is decided using symbolic states represented by pairs of the form (l, Z), where l is a location and Z is a zone. Semantically, (l, Z) represents the set of all states (l, u), where $u \in Z$. Whenever Z is a zone and r a set of clocks, we denote by $Z^\uparrow$ and $\{r\}Z$ the set of clock valuations obtained by delaying and resetting (w.r.t. r) clock valuations from Z respectively. That is, $Z^\uparrow = \{u + d \mid u \in Z, d \in \mathbb{R}_{\geq 0}\}$ and $\{r\}Z = \{u[r \mapsto 0] \mid u \in Z\}$. It is well-known – using a canonical representation of zones as *Difference Bounded Matrices* (DBMs) [Dil89] – that in both cases the resulting set is again effectively representable as a zone. Using these operations together with the obvious fact, that zones are closed under conjunction, the *post*-operations may now be effectively realised using the zone-based representation of symbolic states as follows:

- $post_\delta\big((l, Z)\big) = \big(l, (Z \wedge I(l))^\uparrow \wedge I(l)\big)$,
- $post_e\big((l, Z)\big) = \big(l', \{r\}(Z \wedge g)\big)$ whenever $e = (l, g, r, l')$.

Now, the framework given in Section 2 for symbolic computation of minimum-cost reachability calls for an extension of our zone-based representation of symbolic states, which assigns costs to individual states. For this, we introduce the following notion of a *priced* zone, where the *offset*, Δ_Z, of a zone Z is the unique clock valuation of Z satisfying $\forall u \in Z. \forall x \in \mathbb{C}. \Delta_Z(x) \leq u(x)$.

Definition 2 (Priced Zone). *A priced zone $\mathcal{Z}$ is a tuple (Z, c, r), where Z is a zone, $c \in \mathbb{N}$ describes the cost of the offset, Δ_Z, of Z, and $r : \mathbb{C} \to \mathbb{Z}$ assigns a cost-rate $r(x)$ for any clock x. We write $u \in \mathcal{Z}$ whenever $u \in Z$. For any $u \in \mathcal{Z}$ the cost of u in $\mathcal{Z}$, $Cost(u, \mathcal{Z})$, is defined as $c + \sum_{x \in \mathbb{C}} r(x) \cdot (u(x) - \Delta_Z(x))$.*

---

[2] In the example we assume that several automata $A_1, ..., A_n$ can be composed in parallel with a CCS-like parallel composition operator [Mil89] to a network $(A_1, ..., A_n) \backslash Act$, with all actions Act being restricted. We further assume that the cost of delaying in the network is the sum of the cost of delaying in the individual automata.

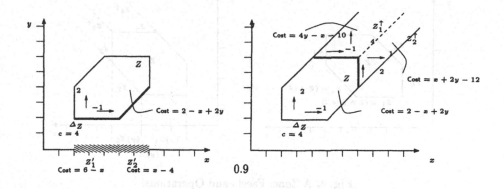

Fig. 3. A Priced Zone and Successor-Sets.

Thus, the cost assignments of a priced zone define a linear plane over the underlying zone and may alternatively be described by a linear expression over the clocks. Figure 3 illustrates the priced zone $\mathcal{Z} = (Z, c, r)$ over the clocks $\{x, y\}$, where Z is given by the six constraints $2 \leq x \leq 7$, $2 \leq y \leq 6$ and $-2 \leq x - y \leq 3$, the cost of the offset $(\Delta_Z = (2, 2)$ is $c = 4$, and the cost-rates are $r(x) = -1$ and $r(y) = 2$. Hence, the cost of the clock valuation $(5.1, 2.3)$ is given by $4 + (-1) \cdot (5.1 - 2) + 2 \cdot (2.3 - 2) = 1.5$. In general the costs assigned by $\mathcal{Z}$ may be described by the linear expression $2 - x + 2y$.

Now, priced symbolic states are represented in the obvious way by pairs $(l, \mathcal{Z})$, where l is a location and $\mathcal{Z}$ a priced zone. More precisely, $(l, \mathcal{Z})$ represents the priced symbolic state (A, π), where $A = \{(l, u) \mid u \in \mathcal{Z}\}$ and $\pi(l, u) = \text{Cost}(u, \mathcal{Z})$.

Unfortunately, priced symbolic states are *not* directly closed under the *Post*-operations. To see this, consider a timed automata $\mathcal{A}$ with two locations l and m and a single edge from l to m with trivial guard (*true*) and resetting the clock y.. The cost-rate of l is 3 and the transition has zero cost. Now, let $\mathcal{Z} = (Z, c, r)$ be the priced zone depicted in Fig. 3 and consider the associated priced symbolic state $(l, \mathcal{Z})$. Assuming that the e-successor set, $\text{Post}_e(l, \mathcal{Z})$, was expressible as a single priced symbolic state $(l', \mathcal{Z}')$, this would obviously require $l' = m$ and $\mathcal{Z}' = (Z', c', r')$ with $Z' = \{y\}Z$. Furthermore, following our framework of Section 2, the cost-assignment of $\mathcal{Z}'$ should be such that $\text{Cost}(u', \mathcal{Z}') = \inf\{\text{Cost}(u, \mathcal{Z}) \mid u \in Z \wedge u[y \mapsto 0] = u'\}$ for all $u' \in Z'$. Since $r(y) > 0$, it is obvious that these infima are obtained along the lower boundary of Z with respect to y (see Fig. 3 left). E.g. $\text{Cost}((2, 0), \mathcal{Z}') = 4$, $\text{Cost}((4, 0), \mathcal{Z}') = 2$, and $\text{Cost}((6, 0), \mathcal{Z}') = 2$. In general $\text{Cost}((x, 0), \mathcal{Z}') = \text{Cost}((x, 2), \mathcal{Z}) = 6 - x$ for $2 \leq x \leq 5$ and $\text{Cost}((x, 0), \mathcal{Z}') = \text{Cost}((x, x - 3), \mathcal{Z}) = x - 4$ for $5 \leq x \leq 7$. However, the disagreement w.r.t. the cost-rate of x (-1 or 1) makes it clear that the desired cost-assignment is *not* linear and hence not obtainable from any *single* priced zone. On the other hand, it is also shows that splitting $Z' = \{y\}Z$ into the sub-zones $Z'_1 = Z' \wedge 2 \leq x \leq 5$ and $Z'_2 = Z' \wedge 5 \leq x \leq 7$, allows the e-successor set $\text{Post}_e(l, \mathcal{Z})$ to be expressed using the union of *two* priced zones (with $r(x) = -1$ in Z'_1 and $r(x) = 1$ in Z'_2).

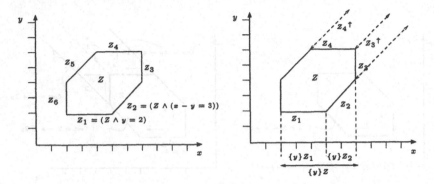

Fig. 4. A Zone: Facets and Operations.

Similarly, priced symbolic states are *not* directly closed w.r.t. $Post_\delta$. To see this, consider again the LPTA $\mathcal{A}$ from above and the priced zone $\mathcal{Z} = (Z, c, r)$ depicted in Fig. 3. Clearly, the set $Post_\delta(l, \mathcal{Z})$ must cover the zone $Z^\uparrow$ (see Fig. 3). It can be seen that, although $Post_\delta(l, \mathcal{Z})$ is not expressible as a *single* priced symbolic state, it may be expressed as a *finite union* by splitting the zone $Z^\uparrow$ into the three sub-zones Z, $Z_1^\uparrow = (Z^\uparrow \backslash Z) \wedge (x - y \leq 1)$, and $Z_2^\uparrow = (Z^\uparrow \backslash Z) \wedge (x - y \geq 1)$.

5   Facets and Operations on Priced Zones

The universal key to expressing successor sets of priced symbolic states as finite unions is provided by the notion of *facets* of a zone Z. Formally, whenever $x \bowtie n$ ($x - y \bowtie m$) is a constraint of Z, the strengthened zone $Z \wedge (x = n)$ ($Z \wedge (x - y = m)$) is a facet of Z. Facets derived from lower bounds on individual clocks, $x \geq n$, are classified as *lower facets*, and we denote by $LF(Z)$ the collection of all lower facets of Z. Similarly, the collection of *upper facets*, $UF(Z)$, of a zone Z is derived from upper bounds of Z. We refer to lower as well as upper facets as *individual clock* facets. Facets derived from lower bounds of the forms $x \geq n$ or $x - y \geq m$ are classified as lower *relative* facets w.r.t. x. The collection of lower relative facets of Z w.r.t. x is denoted $LF_x(Z)$. The collection of upper relative facets of Z w.r.t. x, $UF_x(Z)$, is derived similarly. Figure 4(left) illustrates a zone Z together with its six facets: e.g. $\{Z_1, Z_6\}$ constitutes the lower facets of Z, and $\{Z_1, Z_2\}$ constitutes the lower relative facets of Z w.r.t. y.

The importance of facets comes from the fact that they allow for decompositions of the delay- and reset-operations on zones as follows:

Lemma 1. *Let Z be a zone and y a clock. Then the following holds:*

i) $Z^\uparrow = \bigcup_{F \in LF(Z)} F^\uparrow$ iii) $\{y\}Z = \bigcup_{F \in LF_y(Z)} \{y\}F$

ii) $Z^\uparrow = Z \cup \bigcup_{F \in UF(Z)} F^\uparrow$ iv) $\{y\}Z = \bigcup_{F \in UF_y(Z)} \{y\}F$

Informally (see Fig. 4(right)) *i)* and *ii)* express that any valuation reachable by delay from Z is reachable from one of the lower facets of Z, as well as reachable from one of the upper facets of Z or within Z. *iii)* (and *iv)*) expresses that any valuation in the projection of a zone will be in the projection of the lower (upper) facets of the zone relative to the relevant clock.

As a first step, the delay- and reset-operation may be extended in a straight-forward manner to priced (relative) facets:

Definition 3. *Let $\mathcal{Z} = (F, c, r)$ be a priced zone, where F is a relative facet w.r.t. y in the sense that $y - x = m$ is a constraint of F. Then $\{y\}\mathcal{Z} = (F', c', r')$, where $F' = \{y\}F$, $c' = c$, and $r'(x) = r(y) + r(x)$ and $r'(z) = r(z)$ for $z \neq x$. In case $y = n$ is a constraint of F, $\{y\}\mathcal{Z} = (F', c, r)$ with $F' = \{y\}F$.*[3]

Definition 4. *Let $\mathcal{Z} = (F, c, r)$ be a priced zone, where F is a lower or upper facet in the sense that $y = n$ is a constraint of F. Let $p \in \mathbb{N}$ be a cost-rate. Then $\mathcal{Z}^{\uparrow p} = (F', c', r')$, where $F' = F^{\uparrow}$, $c' = c$, and $r'(y) = p - \sum_{z \neq y} r(z)$ and $r'(z) = r(z)$ for $z \neq y$.*

Conjunction of constraints may be lifted from zones to priced zones simply by taking into account the possible change of the offset. Formally, let $\mathcal{Z} = (Z, c, r)$ be a priced zone and let $g \in \mathcal{B}(\mathbb{C})$. Then $\mathcal{Z} \wedge g$ is the priced zone $\mathcal{Z}' = (Z', c', r')$ with $Z' = Z \wedge g$, $r' = r$, and $c' = \mathsf{Cost}(\Delta_{Z'}, \mathcal{Z})$. For $\mathcal{Z} = (Z, c, r)$ and $n \in \mathbb{N}$ we denote by $\mathcal{Z} + n$ the priced zone $(Z, c + n, r)$.

The constructs of Definitions 3 and 4 essentially provide the *Post*-operations for priced facets. More precisely, it is easy to show that:

$$Post_e(l, \mathcal{Z}_1) = (l', \{y\}(\mathcal{Z}_1 \wedge g) + P(e)) \qquad Post_\delta(l, \mathcal{Z}_2) = (l, (\mathcal{Z}_2 \wedge I(l))^{\uparrow P(l)} \wedge I(l))$$

if $e = (l, g, \{y\}, l')$, $\mathcal{Z}_1$ is a priced relative facet w.r.t. to y and $\mathcal{Z}_2$ is an individual clock facet. Now, the following extension of Lemma 1 to priced symbolic states provides the basis for the effective realisation of *Post*-operations in general:

Theorem 1. *Let $A = (L, l_0, E, I, P)$ be an LPTA. Let $e = (l, g, \{y\}, l') \in E$[4] with $P(e) = q$, $P(l) = p$, $I(l) = J$ and let $\mathcal{Z} = (Z, c, r)$ be a priced zone. Then:*

$$Post_e((l, \mathcal{Z})) = \begin{cases} \{ (l', \{y\}Q + q) \mid Q \in LF_y(\mathcal{Z} \wedge g) \} & \text{if } r(y) \geq 0 \\ \{ (l', \{y\}Q + q) \mid Q \in UF_y(\mathcal{Z} \wedge g) \} & \text{if } r(y) \leq 0 \end{cases}$$

$$Post_\delta((l, \mathcal{Z})) = \begin{cases} \{(l, \mathcal{Z})\} \cup \{ (l, Q^{\uparrow p} \wedge J) \mid Q \in UF(\mathcal{Z} \wedge J) \} & \text{if } p \geq \sum_{x \in \mathbb{C}} r(x) \\ \{ (l, Q^{\uparrow p} \wedge J) \mid Q \in LF(\mathcal{Z} \wedge J) \} & \text{if } p \leq \sum_{x \in \mathbb{C}} r(x) \end{cases}$$

In the definition of $Post_e$ the successor set is described as a union of either lower or upper relative facets w.r.t. to the clock y being reset, depending on the rate of y (as this will determine whether the minimum is obtained at the lower of

---

[3] This "definition" of $\{y\}(\mathcal{Z})$ is somewhat ambigious since it depends on which constraint involving y that is choosen. However, the Cost-function determined will be independent of this choice.

[4] For the case with a general reset-set r, the notion of relative facets may be generalized to sets of clocks.

upper boundary). For similar reason, in the definition of $Post_\delta$, the successor-set is expressed as a union over either lower or upper (individual clock) facets depending on the rate of the location compared to the sum of clock cost-rates.

To complete the instantiation of the framework of Section 2, it remains to indicate how to compute $minCost$ and $\sqsubseteq$ on priced symbolic states. Let $\mathcal{Z} = (Z, c, r)$ and $\mathcal{Z}' = (Z', c', r')$ be priced zones and let $(l, \mathcal{Z})$ and $(l', \mathcal{Z}')$ be corresponding priced symbolic states. Then $minCost(l, \mathcal{Z})$ is obtained by minimizing the linear expression $c + \sum_{x \in C}(r(x) \cdot (x - \Delta_Z(x)))$ under the (linear) constraints expressed by Z. Thus, computing $minCost$ reduces to solving a simple Linear Programming problem. Now let $\mathcal{Z}' \setminus \mathcal{Z}$ be the priced zone (Z^*, c^*, r^*) with $Z^* = Z$, $c^* = c' - \text{Cost}(\Delta_{Z'}, \mathcal{Z})$ and $r^*(x) = r'(x) - r(x)$ for all $x \in C$. It is easy to see that $\text{Cost}(u, \mathcal{Z}' \setminus \mathcal{Z}) = \text{Cost}(u, \mathcal{Z}') - \text{Cost}(u, \mathcal{Z})$ for all $u \in Z'$, and hence that $(l, \mathcal{Z}) \sqsubseteq (l', \mathcal{Z}')$ iff $l = l'$, $Z' \subseteq Z$ and $minCost(\mathcal{Z}' \setminus \mathcal{Z}) \geq 0$) Thus, deciding $\sqsubseteq$ also reduces to a Linear Programming problem.

In exploring LPTAs using the algorithm of Fig. 1, we will only need to consider priced zones $\mathcal{Z}$ with non-negative cost assignments in the sense that $\text{Cost}(u, \mathcal{Z}) \geq 0$ for all $u \in \mathcal{Z}$. Now, application of Higman's Lemma [Hig52] ensures that $\sqsubseteq$ is a well-quasi ordering on priced symbolic states for bounded LPTA. We refer to [BFH+01] for more detailed arguments.

6   Implementation and Experiments

In this section we give further details on a prototype implementation within the tool UPPAAL [LPY97] of priced zones, formally defined in the previous sections, and report on experiments on the aircraft landing problem.

The prototype implements the $Post_e$ (reset), $Post_\delta$ (delay), $minCost$, and $\sqsubseteq$ operations, using extensions of the DBM algorithms outlined in [Rok93]. To minimize the number of facets considered and reduce the size of the LP problems needed to be solved, we make heavy use of the canonical representation of zones in terms a *minimal* set of constraints given in [LLPY97]. For dealing with LP problems, our prototype currently uses a free available implementation of the simplex algorithm.[5] Many of the techniques for pruning and guiding the state space search described in [BFH+] have been used extensively in modelling and verification.

Recall the aircraft landing problem partially described in Example 1. An LPTA model of the costs associated with landing a single aircraft is shown in Fig. 2(b). When landing several planes the schedule has to take into account the separation times between planes to avoid that the turbulence of one plane affecting an other. The separation times depend on the types of the planes that are involved. Large aircrafts for example generate more turbulence than small ones, and successive planes should consequently keep a bigger distance. To model the separation times between two types of planes we introduce an LPTA of the kind shown in Fig. 2(c).

---

[5] lp_solve 3.1a by Michael Berkelaar, ftp://ftp.es.ele.tue.nl/pub/lp_solve.

Table 1. Results for seven instances of the aircraft landing problem. Results were obtained on a PentiumII 333Mhz.

		problem instance	1	2	3	4	5	6	7
runways		number of planes	10	15	20	20	20	30	44
		number of types	2	2	2	2	2	4	2
	1	optimal value	700	1480	820	2520	3100	24442	1550
		explored states	481	2149	920	5693	15069	122	662
		cputime (secs)	4.19	25.30	11.05	87.67	220.22	0.60	4.27
	2	optimal value	90	210	60	640	650	554	0
		explored states	1218	1797	669	28821	47993	9035	92
		cputime (secs)	17.87	39.92	11.02	755.84	1085.08	123.72	1.06
	3	optimal value	0	0	0	130	170	0	
		explored states	24	46	84	207715	189602	62	N/A
		cputime (secs)	0.36	0.70	1.71	14786.19	12461.47	0.68	
	4	optimal value				0	0		
		explored states	N/A	N/A	N/A	65	64	N/A	N/A
		cputime (secs)				1.97	1.53		

Table 1 presents the results of an experiment were the prototype was applied to seven instances of the aircraft landing problem taken from [BKA00][6]. For each instance, which varies in the number of planes and plane types, we compute the cost of the optimal schedule. In cases the cost is non-zero we increase the number of runways until a schedule of cost 0 is found[7]. In all instances, the state space is explored in minimal cost-order, i.e. we select from the waiting list the priced zone $(l, \mathcal{Z})$ with lowest $minCost(l, \mathcal{Z})$. Equal values are distinguished by selecting first the zone which results from the largest number of transitions, and secondly by selecting the zone which involves the plane with the shortest target time. As can be seen from the table, our current prototype implementation is able to deal with all the tested instances. Beasley et al. [BKA00] solves all problem instances with a linear programming based tree search algorithm, in cases that the initial solution – obtained with a heuristic – is not zero. In 7 of the 15 benchmarks (with optimal solution greater than zero) the time-performance of our method is better than theirs. These are the instances 4 to 7 with less than 3 runways. This result also holds if we take into account that our computer is about 50% faster (according to the Dongarra Linpack benchmarks [Don01]). It should be noted, however, that our solution-times are quite incomparable to those of Beasleys. For some instances our approach is up to 25 times slower, while for others it is up to 50 times faster than the approach in [BKA00].

The cost-extended version of UPPAAL has additionally been (and is currently being) applied to other examples, including a cost-extended version of the Bridge Problem [RB98], an optimal broadcast problem and a testing problem.

---

[6] These and other benchmarks are available at ftp://mscmga.ms.ic.ac.uk/pub/.
[7] This is always possible as the cost of landing on target time is 0 and the number of runways can be increased until all planes arrive at target time.

7   Conclusion

In this paper we have considered the minimum-cost reachability problem for LP-TAs. The notions of priced zones, and facets of a zone are central contributions of the paper underlying our extension of the tool UPPAAL. Our initial experimental investigations based on a number of examples are quite encouraging.

Compared with the existing special-purpose, time-optimizing version of UP-PAAL [BFH⁺], the presented general cost-minimizing implementation does only marginally down-grade performance. In particular, the theoretical possibility of uncontrolled splitting of zones does not occur in practice. In addition, the consideration of non-uniform cost seems to significantly reduce the number of symbolic states explored.

The single, most important question, which calls for future research, is how to exploit the simple structure of the LP-problems considered. We may benefit significantly from replacing the currently used LP package with some package more tailored towards small-size problems.

References

[AC91]   D. Applegate and W. Cook. A Computational Study of the Job-Shop Scheduling Problem. *OSRA Journal on Computing 3*, pages 149–156, 1991.

[ACJYK96] P. Abdulla, K. Cerans, B. Jonsson, and T. Yih-Kuen. General decidability theorems for infinite-state systems, 1996.

[AD90]   R. Alur and D. Dill. Automata for Modelling Real-Time Systems. In *Proc. of Int. Colloquium on Algorithms, Languages and Programming*, number 443 in Lecture Notes in Computer Science, pages 322–335, July 1990.

[AJ94]   P. Abdulla and B. Jonsson. Undecidability of verifying programs with unreliable channels. In *Proc. 21st Int. Coll. Automata, Languages, and Programming (ICALP'94)*, volume 820 of *LNCS*, 1994.

[ATP]   R. Alun, S. La Torre, and G. J. Pappas. Optimal paths in weighted timed automata. To appear in HSCC2001.

[BDM⁺98]   M. Bozga, C. Daws, O. Maler, A. Olivero, S. Tripakis, and S. Yovine. Kronos: A Model-Checking Tool for Real-Time Systems. In *Proc. of the 10th Int. Conf. on Computer Aided Verification*, number 1427 in Lecture Notes in Computer Science, pages 546–550. Springer–Verlag, 1998.

[BFH⁺]   G. Behrmann, A. Fehnker, T. Hune, K.G. Larsen, P. Pettersson, and J. Romijn. Efficient guiding towards cost-optimality in UPPAAL. To appear in Proceedings of TACAS'2001.

[BFH⁺01]   G. Behrmann, A. Fehnker, T. Hune, K. G. Larsen, P. Pettersson, J. Romijn, and F. Vaandrager. Minimum-Cost Reachability for Priced Timed Automata. To appear in Proceedings of HSCC2001, 2001.

[BKA00]   J.E. Beasley, M. Krishnamoorthy, and D. Abramson. Scheduling Aircraft Landings-The Static Case. *Transportation Science*, 34(2):180–197, 2000.

[BM00]   Ed Brinksma and Angelika Mader. Verification and optimization of a plc control schedule. In *Proceedings of the 7th SPIN Workshop*, volume 1885 of *Lecture Notes in Computer Science*. Springer Verlag, 2000.

[Cer94]   K. Cerans. Deciding properties of integral relational automata. In *Proceedings of ICALP 94*, volume 820 of *LNCS*, 1994.

[Dil89]   D. Dill. Timing Assumptions and Verification of Finite-State Concurrent Systems. In J. Sifakis, editor, *Proc. of Automatic Verification Methods for Finite State Systems*, number 407 in Lecture Notes in Computer Science, pages 197–212. Springer–Verlag, 1989.

[Don01]   Jack J. Dongarra. Performance of Various Computers Using Standard Linear Equations Software. Technical Report CS-89-85, Computer Science Department, University of Tennessee, 2001. An up-to-date version of this report can be found at http://www.netlib.org/benchmark/performance.ps.

[Feh99]   A. Fehnker. Scheduling a steel plant with timed automata. In *Proceedings of the 6th International Conference on Real-Time Computing Systems and Applications (RTCSA99)*, pages 280–286. IEEE Computer Society, 1999.

[FS98]   A. Finkel and P. Schnoebelen. Fundamental structures in well-structured infinite transition systems. In *Proc. 3rd Latin American Theoretical Informatics Symposium (LATIN'98)*, volume 1380 of *LNCS*, 1998.

[FS01]   A. Finkel and Ph. Schnoebelen. Well structured transition systems everywhere. *Theoretical Computer Science*, 256(1-2):64–92, 2001.

[HHWT97]   T.A. Henzinger, P.-H. Ho, and H. Wong-Toi. HYTECH: A Model Checker for Hybird Systems. In Orna Grumberg, editor, *Proc. of the 9th Int. Conf. on Computer Aided Verification*, number 1254 in Lecture Notes in Computer Science, pages 460–463. Springer–Verlag, 1997.

[Hig52]   G. Higman. Ordering by divisibility in abstract algebras. *Proc. of the London Math. Soc.*, 2:326–336, 1952.

[HLP00]   T. Hune, K.G. Larsen, and P. Pettersson. Guided Synthesis of Control Programs Using UPPAAL. In Ten H. Lai, editor, *Proc. of the IEEE ICDCS International Workshop on Distributed Systems Verification and Validation*, pages E15–E22. IEEE Computer Society Press, April 2000.

[LLPY97]   Fredrik Larsson, Kim G. Larsen, Paul Pettersson, and Wang Yi. Efficient Verification of Real-Time Systems: Compact Data Structures and State-Space Reduction. In *Proc. of the 18th IEEE Real-Time Systems Symposium*, pages 14–24. IEEE Computer Society Press, December 1997.

[LPY97]   K.G. Larsen, P. Pettersson, and W. Yi. UPPAAL in a Nutshell. *Int. Journal on Software Tools for Technology Transfer*, 1(1–2):134–152, October 1997.

[Mil89]   R. Milner. *Communication and Concurrency*. Prentice Hall, Englewood Cliffs, 1989.

[NY99]   P. Niebert and S. Yovine. Computing optimal operation schemes for multi batch operation of chemical plants. VHS deliverable, May 1999. Draft.

[RB98]   T.C. Ruys and E. Brinksma. Experience with Literate Programming in the Modelling and Validation of Systems. In Bernhard Steffen, editor, *Proceedings of the Fourth International Conference on Tools and Algorithms for the Construction and Analysis of Systems (TACAS'98)*, number 1384 in Lecture Notes in Computer Science (LNCS), pages 393–408, Lisbon, Portugal, April 1998. Springer-Verlag, Berlin.

[Rok93]   T.G. Rokicki. *Representing and Modeling Digital Circuits*. PhD thesis, Stanford University, 1993.

Binary Reachability Analysis of Pushdown Timed Automata with Dense Clocks

Zhe Dang

School of Electrical Engineering and Computer Science
Washington State University, Pullman, WA 99164, USA
zdang@eecs.wsu.edu

Abstract. We consider pushdown timed automata (PTAs) that are timed automata (with dense clocks) augmented with a pushdown stack. A configuration of a PTA includes a control state, dense clock values and a stack word. By using the pattern technique, we give a decidable characterization of the binary reachability (i.e., the set of all pairs of configurations such that one can reach the other) of a PTA. Since a timed automaton can be treated as a PTA without the pushdown stack, we can show that the binary reachability of a timed automaton is definable in the additive theory of reals and integers. The results can be used to verify a class of properties containing linear relations over both dense variables and unbounded discrete variables. The properties previously could not be verified using the classic region technique nor expressed by timed temporal logics for timed automata and CTL* for pushdown systems.

1 Introduction

A timed automaton [3] can be considered as a finite automaton augmented with a number of dense (either real or rational) clocks. Due to their ability to model and analyze a wide range of real-time systems, timed automata have been extensively studied in recent years (see [1, 29] for recent surveys). In particular, by using the standard region technique, it has been shown that region reachability for timed automata is decidable [3]. This fundamental result and the technique help researchers, both theoretically and practically, in formulating various timed temporal logics [2, 4–6, 22, 25–27] and developing verification tools [21, 28, 24].

Region reachability is useful but has intrinsic limitations. In many real-world applications [11], we might also want to know whether a timed automaton satisfies a non-region (e.g., Presburger) property. Recently, Comon and Jurski [13] have shown that the binary reachability of a timed automaton is definable in the additive theory of reals, by flattening a timed automaton into a real-valued counter machine without nested cycles [12]. The result immediately paves the way for automatic verification of a class of non-region properties that previously were not possible using the region technique.

In this paper, inspired by Comon and Jurski's result [13], we consider *pushdown timed automata* (PTAs) that are obtained by augmenting timed automata with a pushdown stack. The main result in this paper gives a decidable binary reachability characterization for PTAs such that a class of non-region properties can be verified. A possible way to show this result to look at the flattening technique of Comon and Jurski's to see

G. Berry, H. Comon, and A. Finkel (Eds.): CAV 2001, LNCS 2102, pp. 506–517, 2001.
© Springer-Verlag Berlin Heidelberg 2001

whether the technique can be adapted by adding a pushdown stack. However, this approach has an inherent difficulty: the flattening technique, as pointed out in their paper, destroys the structure of the original timed automaton, and thus, the sequences of stack operations can not be maintained after flattening.

In this paper, we introduce a new technique, called the pattern technique, by separating a dense clock into an integral part and a fractional part. For a pair (v_0, v_1) of two tuples of clock values, we define an ordering, called the pattern of (v_0, v_1), on the fractional parts of v_0 and v_1. An equivalent relation "$\approx$" is defined such that $(v_0, v_1) \approx (v'_0, v'_1)$ iff v_0 and v'_0 (v_1 and v'_1 will also) have the same integral parts, and both (v_0, v_1) and (v'_0, v'_1) have the same pattern. "$\approx$" preserves the binary reachability: v_0 can reach v_1 by a sequence of transitions iff v'_0 can reach v'_1 by the (almost) same sequence of transitions. Therefore, by preserving the (almost) same control structure, a PTA can be transformed into a discrete transition system (called the pattern graph) containing discrete clocks (for the integral parts of the dense clocks) and a finite variable over patterns. The pattern graph can be further reduced to a discrete PTA, whose binary reachability is decidable and can be accepted by a nondeterministic pushdown automaton augmented with reversal-bounded counters (NPCM) [15]. By translating a pattern back to a relation over the fractional parts of the clocks, the decidable binary reachability characterization (namely, $(\mathbf{D} + \mathbf{NPCM})$-definable) for PTAs can be derived. Given this characterization, it can be shown that the particular class of safety properties that contain mixed linear relations over both dense variables (e.g., clock values) and discrete variables (e.g., word counts) can be automatically verified for PTAs. In this extended abstract, all the proofs are omitted. For a complete exposition see [14].

2 Preliminaries

A nondeterministic multicounter machine is a nondeterministic machine with a finite number of states, a one-way input tape, and a finite number of integer counters. Each counter can be incremented by 1, decremented by 1, or stay unchanged. Besides, a counter can be tested against 0. A *reversal-bounded nondeterministic multicounter machine (NCM)* is a nondeterministic multicounter machine in which each counter is reversal-bounded (i.e., it changes mode between nondecreasing and nonincreasing for some bounded number of times). A *reversal-bounded nondeterministic pushdown multicounter machine (NPCM)* is an NCM augmented with a pushdown stack. It is known that the emptiness problem for NPCMs (and hence NCMs) is decidable [23].

Let $\mathbf{N}$ be integers, $\mathbf{D} = \mathbf{Q}$ (rationals) or $\mathbf{R}$ (reals), Γ be an alphabet. We use $\mathbf{N}^+$ and $\mathbf{D}^+$ to denote non-negative values in $\mathbf{N}$ and $\mathbf{D}$, respectively. Each value $v \in \mathbf{D}$ can be uniquely expressed as the sum of $\lceil v \rceil + \lfloor v \rfloor$, where $\lceil v \rceil \in \mathbf{N}$ is the integral part of v, and $0 \leq \lfloor v \rfloor < 1$ is the fractional part of v. Given $m \geq 1$. Let x_i, y_i, and w_i be a dense variable over $\mathbf{D}$, an integer variable over $\mathbf{N}$, and a word variable Γ^*, for each $1 \leq i \leq m$, respectively. We use $\#_a(w_i)$ to denote a *count variable* representing the number of symbol $a \in \Gamma$ in w_i. A *linear term* t is defined as follows: $t ::= n \mid x_i \mid y_i \mid \#_a(w_i) \mid t - t \mid t + t$, where $n \in \mathbf{N}, a \in \Gamma$. A *mixed linear relation* l is defined as follows: $l ::= t > 0 \mid t = 0 \mid t_{discr} \bmod n = 0 \mid \neg l \mid l \wedge l$, where $0 \neq n \in \mathbf{N}$ and t_{discr} is a linear term not containing dense variables. A *dense* *linear relation* is a linear relation that contains dense variables only. A *discrete linear relation* is a linear relation that does not contain dense variables.

A tuple of integers and words can be encoded as a string by concatenating the unary representations of each integer and each of the words, with a separator $\# \notin \Gamma$. The domain of H, a predicate over integer variables and word variables, is the set of tuples of integers and words that satisfy H. H is an *NPCM predicate* (or simply NPCM) if there is an NPCM accepting the domain (encoded as a set of strings, i.e., a language) of H. A $(\mathbf{D} + \mathbf{NPCM})$-*formula* f is defined as follows: $f ::= l_{dense} \wedge H \mid l_{dense} \vee H \mid f \vee f$, where l_{dense} is a dense linear relation and H is an NPCM predicate. Given $p, q, r \geq 0$. A predicate A on tuples in $\mathbf{D}^p \times \mathbf{N}^q \times (\Gamma^*)^r$ is $(\mathbf{D} + \mathbf{NPCM})$-*definable* if there is a $(\mathbf{D} + \mathbf{NPCM})$-formula f with p dense variables, $p + q$ integer variables, and r word variables, such that, for all $x_1, \cdots, x_p \in \mathbf{D}$, $y_1, \cdots, y_q \in \mathbf{N}$, and $w_1, \cdots, w_r \in \Gamma^*$, $(x_1, \cdots, x_p, y_1, \cdots, y_q, w_1, \cdots, w_r) \in A$ iff $f(\lfloor x_1 \rfloor, \cdots, \lfloor x_p \rfloor, \lceil x_1 \rceil, \cdots, \lceil x_p \rceil, y_1, \cdots, y_q, w_1, \cdots, w_r)$ holds.

Lemma 1. *(1). Both $l_{discrete} \wedge H$ and $l_{discrete} \vee H$ are NPCM predicates, if $l_{discrete}$ is a discrete linear relation and H is an NPCM predicate. (2). NPCM predicates are closed under existential quantifications (over integer variables and word variables). (3). If A is $(\mathbf{D} + \mathbf{NPCM})$-definable and l is a mixed linear relation, then both $l \wedge A$ and $l \vee A$ are $(\mathbf{D} + \mathbf{NPCM})$-definable. (4). The emptiness (satisfiability) problem for $(\mathbf{D} + \mathbf{NPCM})$-definable predicates is decidable.*

3   Clock Patterns and Their Changes

A dense clock is simply a dense variable on $\mathbf{D}^+$. Fix a $k > 0$ and consider $k + 1$ clocks $x = x_0, \cdots, x_k$. For technical reasons, x_0 is an auxiliary clock indicating the current time *now*. Denote $K = \{0, \cdots, k\}$ and $K^+ = \{1, \cdots, k\}$. A subset K' of K is abused as a set of clocks; i.e., we say $x_i \in K'$ if $i \in K'$. A *(clock) valuation* v is a function $K \to \mathbf{D}^+$ that assigns a value in $\mathbf{D}^+$ to each clock in K. A *discrete (clock) valuation* u is a function $K \to \mathbf{N}^+$ that assigns a value in $\mathbf{N}^+$ to each clock in K. For each valuation v and $\delta \in \mathbf{D}^+$, $\lceil v \rceil$, $\lfloor v \rfloor$ and $v + \delta$ are valuations satisfying $\lceil v \rceil(i) = \lceil v(i) \rceil$, $\lfloor v \rfloor(i) = \lfloor v(i) \rfloor$ and $(v + \delta)(i) = v(i) + \delta$ for each $i \in K$. The *relative representation* $\hat{v}$ of a valuation v is a valuation satisfying: (1). $\lceil \hat{v} \rceil = \lceil v \rceil$, (2). $\lfloor \hat{v} \rfloor(0) = \lfloor 1 - \lfloor v \rfloor(0) \rfloor$, (3). $\lfloor \hat{v} \rfloor(i) = \lfloor \lfloor v \rfloor(i) + \lfloor \hat{v} \rfloor(0) \rfloor$, for each $i \in K^+$. A valuation v_0 is *initial* if clock x_0 has value 0, i.e., $v_0(0) = 0$.

We distinguish two disjoint sets, $K^0 = \{0^0, \cdots, k^0\}$ and $K^1 = \{0^1, \cdots, k^1\}$, of indices. A *pattern* η is a sequence $p_0, \cdots, p_n$, for some $0 \leq n < 2(k+1)$, of nonempty and disjoint subsets of $K^0 \cup K^1$ such that $0^0 \in p_0$ and $\cup_{0 \leq i \leq n} p_i = K^0 \cup K^1$. p_i is called the *i-position*. A pair of valuations (v_0, v_1) is *initialized* if v_0 is initial. An initialized pair (v_0, v_1) *has pattern* $\eta = p_0, \cdots, p_n$, written $(v_0, v_1) \in \eta$, if, for each $0 \leq m, m' \leq n$, each $b, b' \in \{0, 1\}$, and each $i, i' \in K$, $i^b \in p_m$ and $i'^{b'} \in p_{m'}$ imply that

$$\lfloor \widehat{v_b} \rfloor(i) = \lfloor \widehat{v_{b'}} \rfloor(i') \ (\text{resp. } <) \ \text{iff} \ m = m' \ (\text{resp. } m < m').$$

Φ denotes the set of all the patterns ($|\Phi| \leq 2^{6(k+1)^2}$). The *now-position* of η is p_i, for some i, with $0^1 \in p_i$. A pattern is *regulated* if the now-position of η is p_0. A pattern is *initial* if it is the pattern of (v_0, v_0) for some initial valuation v_0. If η is the pattern of (v_0, v_1), we use $init(\eta)$ to denote the pattern of (v_0, v_0). $init(\eta)$ is unique for each η. A pattern is a *merge-pattern* if the now-position is a singleton set (i.e., 0^1 is the only element). A pattern is a *split-pattern* if it is not a merge-pattern, i.e., the now-position contains more than one element. A valuation v_1 *has pattern* η if η is the pattern of (v_0, v_1) for some v_0. A pattern of v_1 tells the fractional orderings between $\lfloor v_1 \rfloor(i)$ and $\lfloor v_1 \rfloor(j)$ and between $\lfloor v_1 \rfloor(i)$ and 0, for all $i, j \in K^+$. Given two initialized pairs (v_0^1, v_1) and (v_0^2, v_2), we write $(v_0^1, v_1) \approx (v_0^2, v_2)$, if (v_0^1, v_1) and (v_0^2, v_2) have the same pattern, and have the same integral parts (i.e., $\lceil v_0^1 \rceil = \lceil v_0^2 \rceil$, $\lceil v_1 \rceil = \lceil v_2 \rceil$).

Example 1. Let $v_0 = (0_{0^0}, 5.5_{1^0}, 2.3_{2^0})$ and $v_1 = (1.6_{0^1}, 2.9_{1^1}, 3.1_{2^1})$, where subscripts are indices. Note that $\widehat{v_0} = (0_{0^0}, 5.5_{1^0}, 2.3_{2^0})$ and $\widehat{v_1} = (1.4_{0^1}, 2.3_{1^1}, 3.5_{2^1})$. The pattern η of (v_0, v_1) can be drawn by collecting the fractional parts in $\widehat{v_0}$ and $\widehat{v_1}$ from small to large while writing down the indices; i.e., $\{0^0\}, \{2^0, 1^1\}, \{0^1\}, \{1^0, 2^1\}$. η is a merge-pattern. Take $v_2 = v_1 + .1$ and compute $\widehat{v_2} = (1.3_{0^1}, 3.3_{1^1}, 3.5_{2^1})$. Observe that the fractional parts (except for the first component) are the same in $\widehat{v_2}$ and $\widehat{v_1}$. The pattern η' of (v_0, v_2) can be drawn similarly: $\{0^0\}, \{2^0, 1^1, 0^1\}, \{1^0, 2^1\}$, which is the result of merging 0^1 to its previous position in η. η' is a split-pattern. Take $v_3 = v_2 + .05$. We can verify the pattern of (v_0, v_3) is $\{0^0\}, \{0^1\}, \{2^0, 1^1\}, \{1^0, 2^1\}$, which is the result of splitting 0^1 from the now-position of η'. This procedure can go on while incrementing v_3: merge 0^1 to the 0-position $\{0^0\}$, and then split 0^1 from it (by appending $\{0^1\}$ at the end), and so on. Eventually, the pattern will repeat when 0^1 returns to the original position in η (e.g., after a total increment of 1 from v_1). ∎

For each $0 < \delta \in D^+$, $v + \delta$ is the result of a clock progress from v by an amount of δ. Function $next : \Phi \times (N^+)^{k+1} \to \Phi \times (N^+)^{k+1}$ describes how a pattern changes after a clock progress. Given any discrete valuation u and pattern $\eta = p_0, \cdots, p_n$ with the now-position being p_i for some i, $next(\eta, u)$ is defined to be (η', u') such that,

- (the case when η is a merge-pattern) if $i > 0$ and $|p_i| = 1$ (that is, $p_i = \{0^1\}$), then η' is $p_0, \cdots, p_{i-1} \cup \{0^1\}, p_{i+1}, \cdots, p_n$ (that is, η' is the result of merging the now-position to the previous position), and for each $j \in K^+$, if $j^1 \in p_{i-1}$, then $u'(j) = u(j) + 1$ else $u'(j) = u(j)$. Besides, if $i = 1$ (i.e., the now-position is merged to p_0; in this case, η' is a regulated pattern), then $u'(0) = u(0) + 1$ else $u'(0) = u(0)$,
- (the case when η is a split pattern) if $i \geq 0$ and $|p_i| > 1$, then η' is the result of splitting 0^1 from the now-position. That is, if $i > 0$, η' is $p_0, \cdots, p_{i-1}, \{0^1\}, p_i - \{0^1\}, p_{i+1}, \cdots, p_n$. However, if $i = 0$, η' is $p_0 - \{0^1\}, p_1, \cdots, p_n, \{0^1\}$. In either case, $u' = u$.

If $next(\eta, u) = (\eta', u')$, η' is called *the next pattern of* η, written $Next(\eta)$.

According to Example 1, we visualize a pattern η as a circle. Applications of $Next$ can be regarded as moving 0^1 along the circle, by performing merge-operations and split-operations alternatively. After enough number of applications of $Next$, 0^1 will return to the original now-position after moving through the entire circle. That is, for each pattern η, $Next^m(\eta) = \eta$, where $m = 2n$ (resp. $m = 2(n+1)$) if η is a merge-pattern (resp. split-pattern). The sequence $\eta, Next(\eta), \cdots, Next^m(\eta)$ is called a *pattern ring*.

Notice that $next^m(\eta, u) = (\eta, u+1)$ for each u. On a pattern ring, merge-patterns and split-patterns appear alternately.

Beside clock progresses, clock resets are the other form of clock behaviors.

Example 2. Take v_0 and v_1 as in Example 1. Consider $v_1' = (1.6_{0^1}, 0_{1^1}, 3.1_{2^1})$ that is the result of resetting x_1 in v_1. The pattern of (v_0, v_1') is $\{0^0\}, \{2^0\}, \{0^1, 1^1\}, \{1^0, 2^1\}$, which is the result of moving 1^1 (the index of x_1 in v_1) into the now-position $\{0^1\}$ of the pattern η of (v_0, v_1) (see Example 1). ∎

Let $r \subseteq K^+$ be (a set of) *clock resets*. Denote $v \downarrow_r$ to be the result of resetting each clock $x_i \in r$ (i.e., $i \in r$). That is, for each $i \in K$, if $i \in r$, then $(v \downarrow_r)(i) = 0$ else $(v \downarrow_r)(i) = v(i)$. Functions $reset_r : \Phi \times (\mathbf{N}^+)^{k+1} \to \Phi \times (\mathbf{N}^+)^{k+1}$ for $r \subseteq K^+$ describe how a pattern changes after clock resets. Given any discrete valuation u and any pattern $\eta = p_0, \cdots, p_n$ with the now-position being p_i for some i, $reset_r(\eta, u)$ is defined to be (η', u') such that,

- η' is $p_0 - r^1, \cdots, p_{i-1} - r^1, p_i \cup r^1, p_{i+1} - r^1, \cdots, p_n - r^1$, where $r^1 = \{j^1 : j \in r\} \subseteq K^1$. Therefore, η' is the result of bringing every index in r^1 into the now-position. Notice that some of positions $p_m - r^1$ may be empty after moving indices in r^1 out of p_m, for $m \neq i$. In this case, these positions are removed from η' (to guarantee that η' is well defined.),
- for each $j \in K$, if $j \in r$, then $u'(j) = 0$ else $u'(j) = u(j)$.

If $reset_r(\eta, u) = (\eta', u')$, η' is written as $Reset_r(\eta)$.

Given an initialized pair (v_0, v) and $0 < \delta \in \mathbf{D}^+$. Assume the patterns of (v_0, v) and $(v_0, v + \delta)$ are η and η', respectively. We say v *has no pattern change for* δ if, for all $0 \leq \delta' \leq \delta$, $(v_0, v + \delta')$ has the same pattern. We say v *has one pattern change for* δ if $Next(\eta) = \eta'$ (recall $Next(\eta) \neq \eta$) and, for all $0 < \delta' < \delta$, $(v_0, v + \delta')$ has pattern η, or, for all $0 < \delta' < \delta$, $(v_0, v + \delta')$ has pattern η'. We say v *has n pattern changes for* δ with $n \geq 1$, if there are positive $\delta_1, \cdots, \delta_n$ in $\mathbf{D}^+$ with $\Sigma_{1 \leq i \leq n} \delta_i = \delta$ such that $v + \Sigma_{1 \leq i \leq j} \delta_i$ has one pattern change for δ_{j+1}, for each $j = 0, \cdots, n - 1$. The following lemma states that both $next$ and $reset_r$ are "correct".

Lemma 2. *For all patterns η and η', for all $r \subseteq K^+$, and for all discrete valuations u and u', the following (1) and (2) hold:*

(1). (correctness of next) $next(\eta, u) = (\eta', u')$ iff there exist an initialized pair (v_0, v) and $0 < \delta \in \mathbf{D}^+$ such that

(1.1). η is the pattern of (v_0, v) and η' is the pattern of $(v_0, v + \delta)$,

(1.2). $u = \lceil v \rceil$ and $u' = \lceil v + \delta \rceil$,

(1.3). v has one pattern change for δ. In particular, if η is a merge-pattern, then for all $0 \leq \delta' < \delta$, η is the pattern of $(v_0, v + \delta')$. If, however, η is a split-pattern, then for all $0 < \delta' \leq \delta$, η' is the pattern of $(v_0, v + \delta')$,

(2). (correctness of $reset_r$) $reset_r(\eta, u) = (\eta', u')$ iff there exist an initialized pair (v_0, v) such that

(2.1). η is the pattern of (v_0, v) and η' is the pattern of $(v_0, v \downarrow_r)$,

(2.2). $u = \lceil v \rceil$ and $u' = \lceil v \downarrow_r \rceil$.

(3). For any fixed initialized pair (v_0, v) and fixed $0 < \delta \in \mathbf{D}^+$, there is a unique finite number n such that v has n pattern changes for δ. In particular, when $\delta = 1$, the number n is exactly the length of the pattern ring starting from the pattern of (v_0, v).

(4). The number n in (3) can be uniformly bounded for each δ. That is, for any fixed $\delta \in \mathbf{D}^+$, there is a finite number m such that, for any initialized pair (v_0, v), v has at most m pattern changes for δ.

(5). For any fixed initialized pair (v_0, v), the pattern of (v_0, v) is a merge-pattern iff there is a $0 < \delta \in \mathbf{D}^+$ such that v has no pattern change for δ.

4 Clock Constraints and Patterns

An *atomic clock constraint* (over clocks $x_1, \cdots, x_k$, excluding x_0) is a formula in the form of $x_i - x_j \# d$ or $x_i \# d$ where $0 \leq d \in \mathbf{N}^+$ and $\#$ stands for $<, >, \leq, \geq, =$. A *clock constraint* c is a Boolean combination of atomic clock constraints. Denote $\mathcal{C}$ to be the set of all clock constraint (over clocks $x_1, \cdots, x_k$). We say $v \in c$ if clock valuation v (for $x_0, \cdots, x_k$) satisfies clock constraint c.

Any clock constraint c can be written as a Boolean combination $I(c)$ of clock constraints over discrete clocks $\lceil x_1 \rceil, \cdots, \lceil x_k \rceil$ and fractional orderings $\lfloor x_i \rfloor \# \lfloor x_j \rfloor$ and $\lfloor x_i \rfloor \# 0$. Therefore, testing $v \in c$ is equivalent to testing $\lceil v \rceil$ and the fractional orderings on $\lfloor v \rfloor$ satisfying $I(c)$.

Assume v has pattern η. We use c^η to denote the result of replacing fractional orderings in $I(c)$ by the truth values given by η. c^η is a clock constraint (over discrete clocks). The following lemma can be observed.

Lemma 3. *(1). For any initialized pair (v_0, v), any pattern $\eta \in \Phi$, if (v_0, v) has pattern η, then, for any clock constraint $c \in \mathcal{C}$, $v \in c$ iff $\lceil v \rceil \in c^\eta$. (2). For any initialized pair (v_0, v) and any $0 < \delta \in \mathbf{D}^+$, if v has at most one pattern change for δ, then, for any clock constraint $c \in \mathcal{C}$, $\forall 0 \leq \delta' \leq \delta(v + \delta' \in c)$ iff $v \in c$ and $v + \delta \in c$. (3). For any initialized pairs (v_0^1, v_1) and (v_0^2, v_2), if $(v_0^1, v_1) \approx (v_0^2, v_2)$, then, for any $c \in \mathcal{C}$, $v_1 \in c$ iff $v_2 \in c$.*

Consider two initialized pairs (v_0^1, v_1) and (v_0^2, v_2) such that $(v_0^1, v_1) \approx (v_0^2, v_2)$. ¿From Lemma 3(3), any test $c \in \mathcal{C}$ will not tell the difference between v_1 and v_2. Assume v_1 can be reached from a valuation v^1 via a clock progress by an amount of δ_1, i.e., $v^1 + \delta_1 = v_1$. We would like to know whether v_2 can be reached from some valuation v^2 also via a clock progress but probably by a slightly different amount of δ_2 such that (v_0^1, v^1) and (v_0^2, v^2) are still equivalent($\approx$). We also expect that for any test c, if during the progress of v^1, c is consistently satisfied, then so is c for the progress of v^2. The following lemma concludes that these, as well as the parallel case for clock resets, can be done. This result can be used later to show that if v_1 is reached from v_0^1 by a sequence of transitions that repeatedly perform clock progresses and clock resets, then v_2 can be also reached from v_0^2 via a very similar sequence such that no test c can tell the difference on the two sequences.

Lemma 4. *For any initialized pairs (v_0^1, v_1) and (v_0^2, v_2) with $(v_0^1, v_1) \approx (v_0^2, v_2)$,*
(1). for any $0 \leq \delta_1 \in \mathbf{D}^+$, for any clock valuation v^1, if $v^1 + \delta_1 = v_1$, then there exist $0 \leq \delta_2 \in \mathbf{D}^+$ and clock valuation v^2 such that (1.1). $v^2 + \delta_2 = v_2$ and

$(v_0^1, v^1) \approx (v_0^2, v^2)$, *(1.2).* v^1 *is initial iff* v^2 *is initial,* $v^1 = v_0^1$ *iff* $v^2 = v_0^2$, *and for any* $c \in C$, $v^1 \in c$ *(resp.* $v_1 \in c$) *iff* $v^2 \in c$ *(resp.* $v_2 \in c$), *(1.3). for any clock constraint* $c \in C$, $\forall 0 \leq \delta' \leq \delta_1(v^1 + \delta \in c)$ *iff* $\forall 0 \leq \delta' \leq \delta_2(v^2 + \delta \in c)$.

(2). for any $r \subseteq K^+$, *for any clock valuation* v^1, *if* $v^1 \downarrow_r = v_1$, *then there exists a valuation* v^2 *such that (2.1).* $v^2 \downarrow_r = v_2$ *and* $(v_0^1, v^1) \approx (v_0^2, v^2)$, *(2.2). same as (1.2).*

5 Pushdown Timed Automata

A *pushdown timed automaton* (PTA) $\mathcal{A}$ is a tuple $\langle S, \{x_1, \cdots, x_k\}, Inv, R, \Gamma, PD \rangle$, where S is a finite set of *states*, $x_1, \cdots, x_k$ are (dense) clocks. $Inv : S \rightarrow C$ assigns a clock constraint over clocks $x_1, \cdots, x_k$, called an *invariant*, to each state. $R : S \times S \rightarrow C \times 2^{\{x_1, \cdots, x_k\}}$ assigns a clock constraint over clocks $x_1, \cdots, x_k$, called a *reset condition*, and a subset of clocks, called *clock resets*, to a (directed) edge in $S \times S$. Γ is the *stack alphabet*. $PD : S \times S \rightarrow \Gamma \times \Gamma^*$ assigns a pair (a, γ) with $a \in \Gamma$ and $\gamma \in \Gamma^*$, called a *stack operation*, to each edge in $S \times S$. A stack operation (a, γ) replaces the top symbol a of the stack with a string (possibly empty) in Γ^*. A *timed automaton* is a PTA without the pushdown stack.

The semantics of $\mathcal{A}$ is defined as follows. A *configuration* is a triple (s, v, w) of a state s, a clock valuation v on $x_0, \cdots, x_k$ (where x_0 is the auxiliary clock), and a stack word $w \in \Gamma^*$. $(s_1, v_1, w_1) \rightarrow_{\mathcal{A}} (s_2, v_2, w_2)$ denotes a *one-step transition* of $\mathcal{A}$ if one of the following conditions is satisfied:

- *(a progress transition)* $s_1 = s_2$, $w_1 = w_2$, and $\exists 0 < \delta \in \mathbf{D}^+$, $v_2 = v_1 + \delta$ and for all δ' satisfying $0 \leq \delta' \leq \delta$, $v_1 + \delta' \in Inv(s_1)$. That is, a progress transition makes all the clocks synchronously progress by amount $\delta > 0$, during which the invariant is consistently satisfied, while the state and the stack content remain unchanged.
- *(a reset transition)* $v_1 \in Inv(s_1) \wedge c$, $v_1 \downarrow_r = v_2 \in Inv(s_2)$, and $w_1 = aw$, $w_2 = \gamma w$ for some $w \in \Gamma^*$, where $R(s_1, s_2) = (c, r)$ for some clock constraint c and clock resets r, and $PD(s_1, s_2) = (a, \gamma)$ for some stack symbol $a \in \Gamma$ and string $\gamma \in \Gamma^*$. That is, a reset transition, by moving from state s_1 to state s_2, resets every clock in r to 0 and keeps all the other clocks unchanged. The stack content is modified according to the stack operation (a, γ) given on edge (s_1, s_2). Clock values before the transition satisfy the invariant $Inv(s_1)$ and the reset condition c; clock values after the transition satisfy the invariant $Inv(s_2)$.

We write $\rightarrow_{\mathcal{A}}^*$ to be the transitive closure of $\rightarrow_{\mathcal{A}}$. Given two valuations v_0^1 and v_1, two states s_0 and s_1, and two stack words w_0 and w_1, assume the auxiliary clock x_0 starts from 0, i.e., v_0^1 is initial. The following result is surprising. It states that, for **any** initialized pair (v_0^2, v_2) with $(v_0^1, v_1) \approx (v_0^2, v_2)$, $(s_0, v_0^1, w_0) \rightarrow_{\mathcal{A}}^* (s_1, v_1, w_1)$ if and only if $(s_0, v_0^2, w_0) \rightarrow_{\mathcal{A}}^* (s_1, v_2, w_1)$. This result implies that, from the definition of $\approx$, for any fixed s_0, s_1, w_0 and w_1, the pattern of $(\lfloor v_0^1 \rfloor, \lfloor v_1 \rfloor)$ (instead of the actual values of $\lfloor v_0^1 \rfloor$ and $\lfloor v_1 \rfloor$), the integral values $\lceil v_0^1 \rceil$, and the integral values $\lceil v_1 \rceil$ are sufficient to determine whether (s_0, v_0^1, w_0) can reach (s_1, v_1, w_1) in $\mathcal{A}$. The proof is an induction on the length of $(s_0, v_0^1, w_0) \rightarrow_{\mathcal{A}}^* (s_1, v_1, w_1)$ using Lemma 4 and Lemma 3.

Lemma 5. *Let* $\mathcal{A}$ *be a PTA. For any states* s_0 *and* s_1, *any two initial clock valuations* v_0^1 *and* v_0^2, *any two clock valuations* v_1 *and* v_2, *and any two stack words* w_0

and w_1, if $(v_0^1, v_1) \approx (v_0^2, v_2)$, then, $(s_0, v_0^1, w_0) \rightarrow_A^* (s_1, v_1, w_1)$ iff $(s_0, v_0^2, w_0) \rightarrow_A^* (s_1, v_2, w_1)$.

Example 3. It is the time to show an example to convince the reader that Lemma 5 indeed works. Consider a timed automaton A shown in Figure 1. Let $v_0^1 = (0, 4.98, 2.52)$,

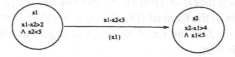

Fig. 1. An Example Timed Automaton A.

$v_3^1 = (5.36, 2.89, 7.88)$. $(s_1, v_0^1) \rightarrow_A^* (s_2, v_3^1)$ is witnessed by: $(s_1, v_0^1) \rightarrow_A$ (progress by 2.47 at s_1) $(s_1, v_1^1) \rightarrow_A$ (reset x_1 and transit to s_2) $(s_2, v_2^1) \rightarrow_A$ (progress by 2.89 at s_2) (s_2, v_3^1). Take a new pair $v_0^2 = (0, 4.89, 2.11)$, $v_3^2 = (5.28, 2.77, 7.39)$. It is easy to check $(v_0^1, v_3^1) \approx (v_0^2, v_3^2)$. ¿From Lemma 5, $(s_1, v_0^2) \rightarrow_A^* (s_2, v_3^2)$. Indeed, this is witnessed by $(s_1, v_0^2) \rightarrow_A$ (progress by 2.51 at s_1) $(s_1, v_1^2) \rightarrow_A$ (reset x_1 and transit to s_2) $(s_2, v_2^2) \rightarrow_A$ (progress by 2.77 at s_2) (s_2, v_3^2). These two witnesses differ slightly (2.47 and 2.89, vs. 2.51 and 2.77). We choose 2.77 and 2.51 by looking at the first witness backwardly. That is, v_2^2 is picked such that $(v_0^2, v_2^2) \approx (v_0^1, v_2^1)$. Then, v_1^2 is picked such that $(v_0^2, v_1^2) \approx (v_0^1, v_1^1)$. The existence of v_2^2 and v_1^2 is guaranteed by Lemma 4. Finally, according to Lemma 4 again, v_1^2 is able to go back to v_0^2. This is because v_1^1 goes back to v_0^1 through a one-step transition and v_0^1 is initial. ∎

Now, we express $\rightarrow_A^*$ in a form that treating the integral parts and the fractional parts of clock values separately. Given a pattern $\eta \in \Phi$, for any discrete valuations u_0 and u_1, and any stack words w_0 and w_1, define $(s_0, u_0, w_0) \rightarrow_{A,\eta}^* (s_1, u_1, w_1)$ to be $\exists v_0 \exists v_1 (v_0(0) = 0 \wedge \lceil v_0 \rceil = u_0 \wedge \lceil v_1 \rceil = u_1 \wedge (v_0, v_1) \in \eta \wedge (s_0, v_0, w_0) \rightarrow_A^* (s_1, v_1, w_1))$.

Lemma 6. *Let A be a PTA. For any states s_0 and s_1, any initialized pair (v_0, v_1), and any stack words w_0 and w_1, $(s_0, v_0, w_0) \rightarrow_A^* (s_1, v_1, w_1)$ iff $\vee_{\eta \in \Phi}(v_0(0) = 0 \wedge (\lfloor v_0 \rfloor, \lfloor v_1 \rfloor) \in \eta \wedge (s_0, \lceil v_0 \rceil, w_0) \rightarrow_{A,\eta}^* (s_1, \lceil v_1 \rceil, w_1))$.*

Once we give a characterization of $\rightarrow_{A,\eta}^*$, Lemma 6 immediately gives a characterization for $\rightarrow_A^*$. A decidable characterization of $\rightarrow_{A,\eta}^*$ is shown in the next section.

6   The Pattern Graph of a Timed Pushdown Automaton

Let $A = \langle S, \{x_1, \cdots, x_k\}, Inv, R, \Gamma, PD \rangle$ be a PTA specified in the previous section. The *pattern graph* G of A is a tuple $\langle S \times \Phi, \{y_0, \cdots, y_k\}, E, \Gamma \rangle$ where S is the states in A, Φ is the set of all patterns. A *node* is an element in $S \times \Phi$. *Discrete clocks* $y_0, \cdots, y_k$ are the integral parts of the clocks $x_0, \cdots, x_k$ in A. E is a finite set of (directed) *edges* that connect pairs of nodes. An edge can be a *progress* edge, a *stay* edge, or a *reset* edge. A progress edge corresponds to progress transitions in A that cause one pattern change.

A stay edge corresponds to progress transitions in $\mathcal{A}$ that cause no pattern change. Since a progress transition can cause no pattern change only from a merge-pattern, a stay edge connects a merge-pattern to itself. A reset edge corresponds to a reset transition in $\mathcal{A}$. Formally, a progress edge $e_{s,\eta,\eta'}$ that connects node (s,η) to node (s,η') is in the form of $\langle (s,\eta), c, (s,\eta') \rangle$ such that $c = Inv(s)$, $\eta' = Next(\eta)$ (thus $\eta \neq \eta'$). A stay edge $e_{s,\eta,\eta}$, with η being a merge-pattern, that connects node (s,η) to itself is in the form of $\langle (s,\eta), c, (s,\eta) \rangle$ such that $c = Inv(s)$. A reset edge $e_{s,s',r,(a,\gamma)}$ that connects node (s,η) to node (s',η') is in the form of $\langle (s,\eta), c, r, a, \gamma, (s',\eta') \rangle$ where $R(s,s') = (c,r)$ and $PD(s,s') = (a,\gamma)$. E is the set of all progress edges, stay edges, and reset edges wrt $\mathcal{A}$. Obviously, E is finite.

A configuration of G is a tuple (s,η,u,w) of state $s \in S$, pattern $\eta \in \Phi$, discrete valuation $u \in (\mathbf{N}^+)^{k+1}$ and stack word $w \in \Gamma^*$. $(s,\eta,u,w) \rightarrow^e (s',\eta',u',w')$ denotes a *one-step transition* through edge e of G if the following conditions are satisfied:

- if e is a progress edge, then e takes the form $\langle (s,\eta), c, (s,\eta') \rangle$ and $s' = s$, $u \in c^\eta$, $u' \in c^{\eta'}$, $next(\eta, u) = (\eta', u')$ and $w = w'$. Here c^η and $c^{\eta'}$ are called the *pre-* and the *post- (progress) tests* on edge e, respectively.
- if e is a stay edge, then e takes the form $\langle (s,\eta), c, (s,\eta) \rangle$ and $s = s'$, $u \in c^\eta$, $u = u'$, $\eta = \eta'$ and $w = w'$. Here c^η is called the *pre-* and the *post- (stay) tests* on edge e.
- if e is a reset edge, then e takes the form $\langle (s,\eta), c, r, a, \gamma, (s',\eta') \rangle$ and $u \in (c \wedge Inv(s))^\eta$, $u' \in Inv(s')^{\eta'}$, $reset_r(\eta, u) = (\eta', u')$ and $w = aw''$, $w' = \gamma w''$ for some $w'' \in \Gamma^*$ (i.e., w changes to w' according to the stack operation). Here $(c \wedge Inv(s))^\eta$ and $Inv(s')^{\eta'}$ are called the *pre-* and the *post- (reset) tests* on edge e, respectively.

We write $(s,\eta,u,w) \rightarrow_G (s',\eta',u',w')$ if $(s,\eta,u,w) \rightarrow^e (s',\eta',u',w')$ for some e. The binary reachability $\rightarrow_G^*$ of G is the transitive closure of $\rightarrow_G$.

The pattern graph G simulates $\mathcal{A}$ in a way that the integral parts of the dense clocks are kept but the fractional parts are abstracted as a pattern. Edges in G indicates how the pattern and the discrete clocks change when a clock progress or a clock reset occur in $\mathcal{A}$. However, a progress transition in $\mathcal{A}$ could cause more than one pattern change. In this case, this big progress transition is treated as a sequence of small progress transitions such that each causes one pattern change (and therefore, each small progress transition in $\mathcal{A}$ can be simulated by a progress edge in G). We first show that the binary reachability $\rightarrow_G^*$ of G is NPCM. Observe that discrete clocks $y_0, \cdots, y_k$ are the integral values of dense clocks $x_0, \cdots, x_k$. Even though the dense clocks progress synchronously, the discrete clocks may not be synchronous (i.e., that one discrete clock is incremented by 1 does not necessarily cause **all** the other discrete clocks incremented by the same amount.). The proof has two parts. In the first part of the proof, a technique is used to translate $y_0, \cdots, y_k$ into another array of discrete clocks that are synchronous. In the second part of the proof, G can be treated as a discrete PTA [15] by replacing $y_0, \cdots, y_k$ with the synchronous discrete clocks. Therefore, Lemma 7 follows by the fact [15] that the binary reachability of discrete PTA is NPCM.

Lemma 7. *For any PTA $\mathcal{A}$, the binary reachability $\rightarrow^*_G$ of the pattern graph G of $\mathcal{A}$ is NPCM. In particular, if $\mathcal{A}$ is a timed automaton, then the binary reachability $\rightarrow^*_G$ is Presburger.*

The following lemma states that G faithfully simulates $\mathcal{A}$ when the fractional parts of dense clocks are abstracted away by a pattern. The if-part of the lemma uses Lemma 2. The only-if-part of the lemma is based upon the argument that a one-step transition of $\mathcal{A}$, when the pattern abstraction is used, can be simulated by a sequence of transitions of G.

Lemma 8. *Let $\mathcal{A}$ be a PTA with pattern graph G. For any $s_0, s_1 \in S$, $\eta \in \Phi$, $w_0, w_1 \in \Gamma^*$, and (u_0, u_1) with $u_0(0) = 0$, $(s_0, u_0, w_0) \rightarrow^*_{\mathcal{A},\eta} (s_1, u_1, w_1)$ iff $(s_0, init(\eta), u_0, w_0) \rightarrow^*_G (s_1, \eta, u_1, w_1)$.*

Now, we conclude this section by claiming that $\rightarrow^*_{\mathcal{A},\eta}$ is NPCM by combining Lemma 7 and Lemma 8.

Lemma 9. *For any PTA $\mathcal{A}$ and any fixed pattern $\eta \in \Phi$, $\rightarrow^*_{\mathcal{A},\eta}$ is NPCM. In particular, if $\mathcal{A}$ is a timed automaton, then $\rightarrow^*_{\mathcal{A},\eta}$ is Presburger.*

7 A Decidable Binary Reachability Characterization and Automatic Verification

Recall that PTA $\mathcal{A}$ actually has clocks $x_1, \cdots, x_k$. x_0 is the auxiliary clock. The *binary reachability* $\leadsto^{*B}_{\mathcal{A}}$ of $\mathcal{A}$ is the set of tuples $\langle s, v_1, \cdots, v_k, w, s', v'_1, \cdots, v'_k, w' \rangle$ such that there exist $v_0 = 0, v'_0 \in D^+$ satisfying $(s, v_0, \cdots, v_k, w) \leadsto^*_{\mathcal{A}} (s', v'_0, \cdots, v'_k, w')$. The main theorem of this paper gives a decidable characterization for the binary reachability as follows. The proof uses Lemma 6 and Lemma 9.

Theorem 1. *The binary reachability $\leadsto^{*B}_{\mathcal{A}}$ of a PTA $\mathcal{A}$ is $(D + NPCM)$-definable. In particular, if $\mathcal{A}$ is a timed automaton, then the binary reachability $\leadsto^{*B}_{\mathcal{A}}$ can be expressed in the additive theory of reals (or rationals) and integers.*

The importance of the above characterization for $\leadsto^{*B}_{\mathcal{A}}$ is that, from Lemma 1, the emptiness of $(D + NPCM)$-definable predicates is decidable. ¿From Theorem 1 and Lemma 1 (3)(4), we have,

Theorem 2. *The emptiness of $l \cap \leadsto^{*B}_{\mathcal{A}}$ with respect to a PTA $\mathcal{A}$ for any mixed linear relation l is decidable.*

The emptiness of $l \cap \leadsto^{*B}_{\mathcal{A}}$ is called a *mixed linear property* of $\mathcal{A}$. Many interesting safety properties (or their negations) for PTAs can be expressed as a mixed linear property. For instance, consider the following property of a PTA $\mathcal{A}$:

"for any two configurations α and β with $\alpha \leadsto^{*B}_{\mathcal{A}} \beta$, if the difference between β_{x_3} (the value of clock x_3 in β) and $\alpha_{x_1} + \alpha_{x_2}$ (the sum of clocks x_1 and x_2 in α) is greater than the difference between $\#_a(\alpha_w)$ (the number of symbol a appearing in the stack word in α) and $\#_b(\beta_w)$ (the number of symbol b appearing in the stack word in β), then $\#_a(\alpha_w) - 2\#_b(\beta_w)$ is greater than 5."

The negation of this property can be expressed in the form required by Theorem 2. Thus, this property can be automatically verified. Notice that this property can not be verified by using results in [8] and (even when clocks are ignored) in [7, 18]. When $\mathcal{A}$ is a timed automaton, by Theorem 1, the binary reachability $\leadsto_{\mathcal{A}}^{*\mathbf{B}}$ can be expressed in the additive theory of reals (or rationals) and integers. Notice that this characterization is essentially equivalent to the one given by Comon and Jurski [13] in which $\leadsto_{\mathcal{A}}^{*\mathbf{B}}$ can be expressed in the additive theory of reals augmented with a predicate telling whether a term is an integer. Because the additive theory of reals and integers is decidable (see [10] for a procedure), we have,

Theorem 3. *The truth value for any closed formula expressible in the (first-order) additive theory of reals (or rationals) augmented with a predicate* $\leadsto_{\mathcal{A}}^{*\mathbf{B}}$ *for a timed automaton $\mathcal{A}$ is decidable. (also shown in [13])*

8   Conclusions

In this paper, we consider PTAs that are timed automata augmented with a pushdown stack. By introducing the concept of a clock pattern and using an automata-theoretic approach, we give a decidable characterization of the binary reachability of a PTA. The results can be used to verify a class of safety properties containing linear relations over both dense variables and unbounded discrete variables.

The results in this paper can be extended to PTAs augmented with reversal-bounded counters. A future research issue is to investigate whether the liveness results in [17] and the approximation techniques in [16] can be extended to dense clocks. Another issue is on the complexity analysis of the decision procedure presented in this paper. However, the complexity for the emptiness problem of NPCMs is still unknown, though it is believed that it can be derived along Gurari and Ibarra [19]. The results in this paper can be used to implement a model-checker for a subset of the real-time specification language ASTRAL [11] as well as for a class of real-time programming language with procedure calls (such as a timed version of Boolean programs [9]).

Acknowledgment

The author would like to thank H. Comon and O. H. Ibarra for discussions on the topic of dense timed pushdown automata during CAV'00 in Chicago, B. Boigelot, P. San Pietro and J. Su for recent discussions on [10], and F. Sheldon for reading an earlier draft of this paper. Thanks also go to anonymous reviewers for many useful suggestions.

References

1. R. Alur, "Timed automata", CAV'99, LNCS 1633, pp. 8-22
2. R. Alur, C. Courcoibetis, and D. Dill, "Model-checking in dense real time," *Information and Computation*, **104** (1993) 2-34
3. R. Alur and D. Dill, "A theory of timed automata," *Theoretical Computer Science*, **126** (1994) 183-236

4. R. Alur, T. Feder, and T. A. Henzinger, *"The benefits of relaxing punctuality," J. ACM*, **43** (1996) 116-146
5. R. Alur, T. A. Henzinger, *"Real-time logics: complexity and expressiveness," Information and Computation*, **104** (1993) 35-77
6. R. Alur, T. A. Henzinger, *"A really temporal logic," J. ACM*, **41** (1994) 181-204
7. A. Bouajjani, J. Esparza, and O. Maler, *"Reachability Analysis of Pushdown Automata: Application to Model-Checking,"*, *CONCUR'97*, LNCS 1243, pp. 135-150
8. A. Bouajjani, R. Echahed, and R. Robbana, *"On the Automatic Verification of Systems with Continuous Variables and Unbounded Discrete Data Structures," Hybrid System II*, LNCS 999, 1995, pp. 64-85
9. T. Ball and S. K. Rajamani, *"Bebop: A Symbolic Model-checker for Boolean Programs," Spin Workshop'00*, LNCS 1885, pp. 113-130.
10. B. Boigelot, S. Rassart and P. Wolper, *"On the expressiveness of real and integer arithmetic automata," ICALP'98*, LNCS 1443, pp. 152-163
11. A. Coen-Porisini, C. Ghezzi and R. Kemmerer, *"Specification of real-time systems using ASTRAL," IEEE Transactions on Software Engineering*, **23** (1997) 572-598
12. H. Comon and Y. Jurski, *"Multiple counters automata, safety analysis and Presburger arithmetic," CAV'98*, LNCS 1427, pp. 268-279.
13. H. Comon and Y. Jurski, *"Timed Automata and the Theory of Real Numbers," CONCUR'99*, LNCS 1664, pp. 242-257
14. Z. Dang, http://www.eecs.wsu.edu/~zdang, the full version of this paper
15. Z. Dang, O. H. Ibarra, T. Bultan, R. A. Kemmerer, and J. Su, *"Binary reachability analysis of discrete pushdown timed automata," CAV'00*, LNCS 1855, pp. 69-84
16. Z. Dang, O. H. Ibarra and R. A. Kemmerer, *"Decidable Approximations on Generalized and Parameterized Discrete Timed Automata," COCOON'01*, LNCS (to appear)
17. Z. Dang, P. San Pietro and R. A. Kemmerer, *"On Presburger Liveness of Discrete Timed Automata," STACS'01*, LNCS 2010, pp. 132-143
18. A. Finkel, B. Willems and P. Wolper, *"A direct symbolic approach to model checking pushdown systems," INFINITY'97*.
19. E. Gurari and O. Ibarra, *"The Complexity of Decision Problems for Finite-Turn Multicounter Machines," J. Computer and System Sciences*, **22** (1981) 220-229
20. T. A. Henzinger, Z. Manna, and A. Pnueli, *"What good are digital clocks?," ICALP'92*, LNCS 623, pp. 545-558
21. T. A. Henzinger and Pei-Hsin Ho, *"HyTech: the Cornell hybrid technology tool," Hybrid Systems II*, LNCS 999, pp. 265-294
22. T. A. Henzinger, X. Nicollin, J. Sifakis, and S. Yovine. *"Symbolic Model Checking for Real-time Systems," Information and Computation*, **111** (1994) 193-244
23. O. H. Ibarra, *"Reversal-bounded multicounter machines and their decision problems," J. ACM*, **25** (1978) 116-133
24. K. G. Larsen, P. Pattersson, and W. Yi, *"UPPAAL in a nutshell," International Journal on Software Tools for Technology Transfer*, **1** (1997): 134-152
25. F. Laroussinie, K. G. Larsen, and C. Weise, *"From timed automata to logic - and back," MFCS'95*, LNCS 969, pp. 529-539
26. J. Raskin and P. Schobben, *"State clock logic: a decidable real-time logic," HART'97*, LNCS 1201, pp. 33-47
27. T. Wilke, *"Specifying timed state sequences in powerful decidable logics and timed automata,"* LNCS 863, pp. 694-715, 1994
28. S. Yovine, *"A verification tool for real-time systems," International Journal on Software Tools for Technology Transfer*, **1** (1997): 123-133
29. S. Yovine, *"Model checking timed automata," Embedded Systems'98*, LNCS 1494, pp. 114-152

Author Index

Lecture Notes in Computer Science

For information about Vols. 1–2025
please contact your bookseller or Springer-Verlag

Vol. 2068: K.R. Dittrich, A. Geppert, M.C. Norrie (Eds.), Advanced Information Systems Engineering. Proceedings, 2001. XII, 484 pages. 2001.

Vol. 2070: L. Monostori, J. Váncza, M. Ali (Eds.), Engineering of Intelligent Systems. Proceedings, 2001. XVIII, 951 pages. 2001. (Subseries LNAI).

Vol. 2071: R. Harper (Ed.), Types in Compilation. Proceedings, 2000. IX, 207 pages. 2001.

Vol. 2072: J. Lindskov Knudsen (Ed.), ECOOP 2001 – Object-Oriented Programming. Proceedings, 2001. XIII, 429 pages. 2001.

Vol. 2073: V.N. Alexandrov, J.J. Dongarra, B.A. Juliano, R.S. Renner, C.J.K. Tan (Eds.), Computational Science – ICCS 2001. Part I. Proceedings, 2001. XXVIII, 1306 pages. 2001.

Vol. 2074: V.N. Alexandrov, J.J. Dongarra, B.A. Juliano, R.S. Renner, C.J.K. Tan (Eds.), Computational Science – ICCS 2001. Part II. Proceedings, 2001. XXVIII, 1076 pages. 2001.

Vol. 2075: J.-M. Colom, M. Koutny (Eds.), Applications and Theory of Petri Nets 2001. Proceedings, 2001. XII, 403 pages. 2001.

Vol. 2076: F. Orejas, P.G. Spirakis, J. van Leeuwen (Eds.), Automata, Languages and Programming. Proceedings, 2001. XIV, 1083 pages. 2001.

Vol. 2077: V. Ambriola (Ed.), Software Process Technology. Proceedings, 2001. VIII, 247 pages. 2001.

Vol. 2078: R. Reed, J. Reed (Eds.), SDL 2001: Meeting UML. Proceedings, 2001. XI, 439 pages. 2001.

Vol. 2080: D.W. Aha, I. Watson (Eds.), Case-Based Reasoning Research and Development. Proceedings, 2001. XII, 758 pages. 2001. (Subseries LNAI).

Vol. 2081: K. Aardal, B. Gerards (Eds.), Integer Programming and Combinatorial Optimization. Proceedings, 2001. XI, 423 pages. 2001.

Vol. 2082: M.F. Insana, R.M. Leahy (Eds.), Information Processing in Medical Imaging. Proceedings, 2001. XVI, 537 pages. 2001.

Vol. 2083: R. Goré, A. Leitsch, T. Nipkow (Eds.), Automated Reasoning. Proceedings, 2001. XV, 708 pages. 2001. (Subseries LNAI).

Vol. 2084: J. Mira, A. Prieto (Eds.), Connectionist Models of Neurons, Learning Processes, and Artificial Intelligence. Proceedings, 2001. Part I. XXVII, 836 pages. 2001.

Vol. 2085: J. Mira, A. Prieto (Eds.), Bio-Inspired Applications of Connectionism. Proceedings, 2001. Part II. XXVII, 848 pages. 2001.

Vol. 2086: M. Luck, V. Mařík, O. Stěpánková, R. Trappl (Eds.), Multi-Agent Systems and Applications. Proceedings, 2001. X, 437 pages. 2001. (Subseries LNAI).

Vol. 2089: A. Amir, G.M. Landau (Eds.), Combinatorial Pattern Matching. Proceedings, 2001. VIII, 273 pages. 2001.

Vol. 2091: J. Bigun, F. Smeraldi (Eds.), Audio- and Video-Based Biometric Person Authentication. Proceedings, 2001. XIII, 374 pages. 2001.

Vol. 2092: L. Wolf, D. Hutchison, R. Steinmetz (Eds.), Quality of Service – IWQoS 2001. Proceedings, 2001. XII, 435 pages. 2001.

Vol. 2093: P. Lorenz (Ed.), Networking – ICN 2001. Proceedings, 2001. Part I. XXV, 843 pages. 2001.

Vol. 2094: P. Lorenz (Ed.), Networking – ICN 2001. Proceedings, 2001. Part II. XXV, 899 pages. 2001.

Vol. 2095: B. Schiele, G. Sagerer (Eds.), Computer Vision Systems. Proceedings, 2001. X, 313 pages. 2001.

Vol. 2096: J. Kittler, F. Roli (Eds.), Multiple Classifier Systems. Proceedings, 2001. XII, 456 pages. 2001.

Vol. 2097: B. Read (Ed.), Advances in Databases. Proceedings, 2001. X, 219 pages. 2001.

Vol. 2098: J. Akiyama, M. Kano, M. Urabe (Eds.), Discrete and Computational Geometry. Proceedings, 2000. XI, 381 pages. 2001.

Vol. 2099: P. de Groote, G. Morrill, C. Retoré (Eds.), Logical Aspects of Computational Linguistics. Proceedings, 2001. VIII, 311 pages. 2001. (Subseries LNAI).

Vol. 2101: S. Quaglini, P. Barahona, S. Andreassen (Eds.), Artificial Intelligence in Medicine. Proceedings, 2001. XIV, 469 pages. 2001. (Subseries LNAI).

Vol. 2102: G. Berry, H. Comon, A. Finkel (Eds.), Computer-Aided Verification. Proceedings, 2001. XIII, 520 pages. 2001.

Vol. 2103: M. Hannebauer, J. Wendler, E. Pagello (Eds.), Balancing Reactivity and Social Deliberation in Multi-Agent Systems. VIII, 237 pages. 2001. (Subseries LNAI).

Vol. 2104: R. Eigenmann, M.J. Voss (Eds.), Open MP Shared Memory Parallel Programming. Proceedings, 2001. X, 185 pages. 2001.

Vol. 2105: W. Kim, T.-W. Ling, Y-J. Lee, S.-S. Park (Eds.), The Human Society and the Internet. Proceedings, 2001. XVI, 470 pages. 2001.

Vol. 2106: M. Kerckhove (Ed.), Scale-Space and Morphology in Computer Vision. Proceedings, 2001. XI, 435 pages. 2001.

Vol. 2109: M. Bauer, P.J. Gymtrasiewicz, J. Vassileva (Eds.), User Modelind 2001. Proceedings, 2001. XIII, 318 pages. 2001. (Subseries LNAI).

Vol. 2110: B. Hertzberger, A. Hoekstra, R. Williams (Eds.), High-Performance Computing and Networking. Proceedings, 2001. XVII, 733 pages. 2001.

Vol. 2111: D. Helmbold, B. Williamson (Eds.), Computational Learning Theory. Proceedings, 2001. IX, 631 pages. 2001. (Subseries LNAI).

Vol. 2118: X.S. Wang, G. Yu, H. Lu (Eds.), Advances in Web-Age Information Management. Proceedings, 2001. XV, 418 pages. 2001.

Vol. 2119: V. Varadharajan, Y. Mu (Eds.), Information Security and Privacy. Proceedings, 2001. XI, 522 pages. 2001.

Vol. 2120: H.S. Delugach, G. Stumme (Eds.), Conceptual Structures: Broadening the Base. Proceedings, 2001. X, 377 pages. 2001. (Subseries LNAI).

Vol. 2121: C.S. Jensen, M. Schneider, B. Seeger, V.J. Tsotras (Eds.), Advances in Spatial and Temporal Databases. Proceedings, 2001. XI, 543 pages. 2001.

Vol. 2123: P. Perner (Ed.), Machine Learning and Data Mining in Pattern Recognition. Proceedings, 2001. XI, 363 pages. 2001. (Subseries LNAI).

Vol. 2126: P. Cousot (Ed.), Static Analysis. Proceedings, 2001. XI, 439 pages. 2001.